# *Sunset*
# Recipe Annual

## 1 9 9 9  E D I T I O N

CELEBRATING
*100*
Y·E·A·R·S
1898 ~ 1998

JAMES CARRIER

Cornmeal Piñon Shortcakes with Berries and Lime Cream (page 192)

By the Editors of Sunset Magazine
and Sunset Books

**Sunset Publishing Corporation**  ■  **Menlo Park, California**

## SUNSET BOOKS

**Vice President, Sales**
Richard A. Smeby

**Editorial Director**
Bob Doyle

**Production Director**
Lory Day

**Art Director**
Vasken Guiragossian

STAFF FOR THIS BOOK
**Managing Editor**
Cornelia Fogle

**Production Coordinator**
Patricia A. Williams

## SUNSET PUBLISHING CORPORATION

**President/Chief Executive Officer**
Stephen J. Seabolt

**VP, Chief Financial Officer**
James E. Mitchell

**VP, Consumer Marketing Director**
Robert I. Gursha

**VP, Manufacturing Director**
Lorinda Reichert

**VP, Editor-in-Chief, Sunset Magazine**
Rosalie Muller Wright

**Managing Editor**
Carol Hoffman

**Senior Editor, Food & Entertaining**
Jerry Anne Di Vecchio

**Designer, Food & Entertaining**
Dennis W. Leong

JAMES CARRIER

*Windy Point Inn Spanish Frittata (page 228)*

# Celebrate our centennial!

This year's edition of the *Recipe Annual* is a special one, celebrating the centennial of *Sunset Magazine*. It not only offers a timely look at the contemporary food scene but also highlights many favorite recipes from past decades (updated and retested for today's cooks). And, of course, you'll find nutritional information for each recipe.

Take a look at our newly remodeled test kitchens, and meet the winners of *Sunset's* Centennial Cook-off contest. You'll find a modern version of the ever-popular adobe oven and up-to-the-minute reports on bread machines and ice cream makers. Special sections feature lightened-up comfort foods in January, low-fat Mexican dishes in July, and our holiday present—a keepsake collection of 101 favorite cookies—in December.

Join us as we salute our rich legacy and look toward our second century.

**Cover:** *Sunset* Centennial Sourdough (page 52). Cover design: Vasken Guiragossian. Photographer: James Carrier.

**Back cover photographer:** James Carrier (3).

First printing November 1998 Copyright © 1998 Sunset Publishing Corporation, Menlo Park, CA 94025. First edition. All rights reserved, including the right of reproduction in whole or in part in any form.

ISBN 0-376-06125-1 (hardcover)
ISBN 0-376-06129-4 (softcover)
ISSN 0896-2170
Printed in the United States

Material in this book originally appeared in the 1998 issues of *Sunset Magazine*. All of the recipes were developed and tested in the *Sunset* test kitchens. If you have comments or suggestions, please let us hear from you. Write us at Sunset Books, Cookbook Editorial, 80 Willow Road, Menlo Park, CA 94025.

# Contents

# A Letter from Sunset

**DEAR READER,**

This year we celebrated our centennial at *Sunset Magazine*.

Turning 100 is no small landmark, in life or in business. In each chapter of the 1999 *Recipe Annual*, which contains all of the 1998 food pages of our centennial year, we rejoice in our rich heritage. We also provide, as usual, a vibrant, contemporary array of recipes for cooking and ideas for entertaining that reflect the cutting-edge character of our territory, the 13 Western states.

For perspective, a little history is in order. *Sunset*, "The Magazine of Western Living," was founded in May 1898 by the Southern Pacific Railroad. The publication was named for its super-train, the *Sunset Limited*. As the railway express raced between New Orleans and Los Angeles, the magazine came aboard to lure Easterners to the West. Clearly, the message got through.

*Sunset* extolled natural wonders from the Grand Canyon to Yosemite to Puget Sound. With no soft-sell, it highlighted the economic opportunities of bountiful lands available for sale (huge tracts were owned by the railroad). This naturally brought up the subject of food—groves of citrus; fields of artichokes; orchards of olives, plums, apricots, pears, and other valued crops. Hotel dining was a frequent topic, sourdough was mentioned now and then, and some festivities involving food were occasionally reported. But not until 1915 were recipes regularly featured. One of our earliest food stories touts the virtues of chayote—a Native American squash that still has an appreciative, though limited audience. Shortly thereafter, directions for cooking artichokes and a recipe for a version of tamale pie appeared, as others have in dozens of issues since. Low-fat tamale pie (page 103) is just a timely interpretation of an old and uniquely Western favorite.

In addition to our 100th birthday, we had much else to celebrate at *Sunset*.

We built the new test kitchens anticipated in last year's *Recipe Annual*; turn to page 206 to see how the project worked out. Within one spacious room there are four complete kitchens, all handsomely detailed and

Behind 100 years of *Sunset* stand 123 years of culinary expertise—that of senior writers Linda Lau Anusasananan (27 years) and Elaine Johnson (on and off, 13 years), 1998 summer intern Jeanne De La Grandiere (from Paris, 1 month), senior food and entertaining editor Jerry Anne Di Vecchio (almost 40 years), senior editor Barbara E. Goldman (6 years), food writer Andrew Baker (3 years), test kitchen services provider Eligio Hernandez (8 years), and test kitchen manager and reader service coordinator Bernadette M. Hart (26 years).

NORMAN A. PLATE

TERRENCE MCCARTHY (2)

equipped with cooktops, ovens, ranges, and other tools that are designed for home—not commercial—use. The area was opened up so film crews can move about more freely as they work in our test kitchens.

To maintain our flow of recipe development and testing through five months of displacement—as the old, well-worn kitchens were gutted—we set up temporary recipe-testing posts throughout our rambling, ranch-style publishing home. We borrowed space from the company's entertainment wing, we claimed some territory in the employee lunch area, and we squeezed our way into the food-styling corner of the photography studio. The magazine marched on, while our new kitchens grew in space, efficiency, and style.

We'd barely settled in when it was time for the Centennial Cook-off contest (page 192). In February, 15 finalists and their guests gathered in our brand-new test kitchens to prepare dishes in five food categories. It was a weekend full of activities, and the contest recipes were judged by notables from the food world: Robert Lawrence Balzer, *Sunset's* original *Chefs of the West* columnist in 1940 (a men-only feature, when men who cooked were rare but politically correct), now an internationally known wine journalist and teacher; Barbara Durbin, food writer at the Portland *Oregonian*; Renée Behnke, owner and executive vice president of Sur La Table kitchenware stores, which offer a highly regarded international catalog; Mark Miller, executive chef and owner of Coyote Cafe in Santa Fe and Las Vegas and partner/executive chef at Red Sage in Washington D.C. and Loongbar in San Francisco; and me.

Then, in April, we gave a weekend-long centennial birthday party with "The Tastes of *Sunset*" at our Menlo Park headquarters. More than 22,000 friends and neighbors, from as near as next door to as far away as Alaska, dropped by to visit the new kitchens, explore our gardens, take cooking lessons from *Sunset* food editors, learn about wines, paint cookies, listen to gardening experts, and just have a good time.

Several major articles in the *Recipe Annual* are retrospectives. They feature enduringly popular recipes, all updated and retested to meet today's standards. The recipes are often interwoven with current developments. For example, the awesome bread machine essay in March (page 48) has up-to-date information on the latest bread machines along with advice on how to hand-craft their loaves, and how to make magnificent sourdough bread (a cultural icon in the West). In May, we produced a

LEFT: Getting serious, *Sunset* Centennial Cook-off finalist Allan Levy (who entered the contest with his wife, Pamela Pierson) prepares artichokes for grilling (see page 195). RIGHT: Contest judges (clockwise from left) Durbin, Balzer, Di Vecchio, Behnke, and Miller sample prize-winning dishes.

special commemorative issue. It included a "Meal of the Century" (page 82), a menu of dishes that have earned their popularity over decades and are grand to serve for dinner any time. In August, we traced the history of barbecuing in *Sunset* (page 168), with outstanding recipes for foods that have become grill standards. We also revisited the adobe oven (page 178) from 1971, a *Sunset* classic for baking and outdoor cooking; the bonus here is updated recipe information with charts for expanded use. In October, the news about the resurgent interest in California olive oils— along with a menu using them from chef Paul Bertolli (page 232)—was yet another of our ongoing reports about the rebirth of an industry that began with the California missions. Winter brought two other significant collections, a cornucopia of all-time favorite Thanksgiving recipes and menus (page 246) and a compendium of Christmas cookies (page 286).

On the food horizon, we reported big changes in chocolate (page 34); trends in Pacific Rim foods (noodle houses, page 74, and a Pacific Rim pantry, page 98); the onset of Brazilian *churrasco* (page 56); the expanding world of fresh chilies (with expert Jean Andrews, page 68); and the proliferation of new foods such as broccolini and baby kiwi fruit (page 190) and Mexican-style cheeses (page 188).

We investigated how Mediterranean-born chefs cooked Mediterranean-style in the West (page 120), and I share how I cook Med-style in Provence each September (page 114).

Continuing interest in quickly prepared recipes and low-fat cooking is served well in a congenial report on real-people comfort foods (page 14), Mexican-inspired mariachi cuisine (page 136), and the regular *Low-Fat Cook* and *Quick Cook* features.

Linda Anusasananan nurtures *Kitchen Cabinet* through its 69th year. This exchange of reader recipes hasn't missed an issue since it first appeared in February 1929. I tend monthly food news and good cooking in *Food Guide*. And Karen MacNeil's *Wine Guide* received a prestigious Maggie award for magazine writing.

Reliable recipes are paramount at *Sunset*. But they don't get that way by chance. Food writers carry the ball all the way from interviewing original sources to developing workable recipes, testing them, and writing the story. Every recipe, at every step, is evaluated for quality by the entire food team. When we agree that it's just right, we call in the retesters.

At "The Tastes of *Sunset*" in *Sunset's* Menlo Park headquarters, Linda Anusasananan demonstrates cooking with chilies (see page 68), while Andrew Baker fields questions from the audience.

Behind the reliability of every *Sunset* recipe stands the careful work of our retest squad. Showing Jerry Di Vecchio and story producer Elaine Johnson a few of the 101 Christmas cookies they tested for the story that begins on page 286 are (in aprons) Barbra Laughlin, Linda Tebben, and Patricia Bainter. On call but not present that day were Dorothy Decker, Donna Jennrich, Odette Morais, Allene Russell, and Jean Strain.

Their job, in our test kitchens, is to stand in your shoes; they follow our recipes exactly, and we watch over their shoulders (it's like being in the kitchen with you). When they run into a problem, we work together to find solutions and improve the language of the recipe. They also catch our mistakes (a typical example might be that the ingredients list includes parsley, but parsley is not mentioned in the directions). Each retester notes how long it takes to make a dish. We average their results (yes, recipes are tested many times). Retesters also check cooking guidelines for doneness by *condition* (e.g. well-browned, tender-crisp); literal timing is a secondary reference, since all appliances work a little differently.

As senior food editor for the magazine, I must be sure that every recipe published meets *Sunset's* standards. But my own palate settles on favorites that catch me on a personal level: the slimmed-down version of that classic "comfort" food, macaroni and cheese (page 18), transports me back to the innocent food-lust of childhood without the guilty aura of impending fat; I love the depth of flavors in the peppered salmon (page 86) from our anniversary-issue "Meal of the Century"; and I remain blissfully loyal to the macadamia-caramel torte (page 90) from the same feature. July's portabella burger (page 133) proves just how meaty a mushroom can be; August's teriyaki "dinosaur bones" (page 172) yields satisfaction so thorough it almost feels prehistoric; and in December, my candidate for the truly consummate oatmeal cookie (page 297) takes an encore bow.

From the huge volume of E-mail we receive, we know many of you are on line. So are we! Visit us at our Web site (www.sunsetmagazine.com). Click on "About *Sunset*" for a virtual tour of our headquarters gardens. Each month's new feature at *Sunset's* site augments stories in the current issue, and includes recipes. The Web site is a way for you to share your comments or submit a recipe, or ask a question or two about previous articles. You can even subscribe or renew your subscription to the magazine. Or nominate your candidates for stories that invite your input.

Cheers, and good cooking!

*Jerry Di Vecchio*
Jerry Di Vecchio
Senior Editor, Food and Entertaining

## TO USE OUR NUTRITIONAL INFORMATION

The most current data from the USDA is used for our recipes: calorie count; fat calories; grams of protein, total and saturated fat, and carbohydrates; and milligrams of sodium and cholesterol.

This analysis is usually given for a single serving, based on the largest number of servings listed. Or it's for a specific amount, such as per tablespoon (for sauces); or by unit, as per cookie.

Optional ingredients are not included, nor are those for which no specific amount is stated (salt added to taste, for example). If an ingredient is listed with an alternative, calculations are based on the first choice listed. Likewise, if a range is given for the amount of an ingredient (such as ½ to 1 cup milk), values are figured on the first, lower amount.

Recipes using broth are calculated on the sodium content of salt-free broth, homemade or canned. If you use canned salted chicken broth, the sodium content will be higher.

Hot Turkey Sandwich with gravy, mashed potatoes, and cranberry sauce—almost like mom used to make (recipe on page 16).

8

# January

# foodguide

BY JERRY ANNE DI VECCHIO

## neat idea

Pairing green spinach pasta with a red sauce, or a red tomato pasta with green pesto, doesn't require much of an aesthetic stretch. But showing off pastas with a greater range of colors takes a more creative choice of sauce. And when it comes to the handsome, multicolored fresh and frozen pastas made (and widely distributed in the West) by Cafferata in Richmond, California, I prefer a transparent approach—especially for the black and gold bumblebee-striped mushroom-filled triangles. ■ *Butter-glaze sauce*. In a 10- to 12-inch frying pan over high heat, boil 1 cup **reduced-sodium chicken broth,** ½ cup **dry white wine,** and ½ teaspoon **dried thyme** until reduced to ¾ cup. Blend 1 teaspoon **cornstarch** with 1 tablespoon **water** and stir into sauce; stir until boiling. Remove from heat, add 2 tablespoons **butter,** and stir until melted. Makes about ¾ cup, enough for 2 to 3 cups cooked pasta (2 servings).

Per serving of sauce: 121 cal., 89% (108 cal.) from fat; 1.2 g protein; 12 g fat (7.2 g sat.); 2.1 g carbo (0 g fiber); 401 mg sodium; 31 mg chol.

JAMES CARRIER (3)

## Segmenting citrus

■ The recipes call for them so casually: perfect, membrane-free citrus segments—from tiny limes to massive grapefruit and pummeloes. And in truth, obtaining them is much easier than it might seem.

1. With a sharp, short-bladed knife, cut away the citrus peel—including the membrane covering the outside of the fruit. (For citrus with a loose peel, like some tangerines, pull off the peel, then cut off the exterior membrane.) Work over a bowl to catch the juices.

2. Cut down between a membrane and the fruit attached to it, to the V-shaped base of the segment. Then tilt the knife up, sliding it under the V of the segment and up against the membrane on the other side to simultaneously cut and lift out the fruit. Repeat for the rest of the segments. Then, with your hand, squeeze the juice from the

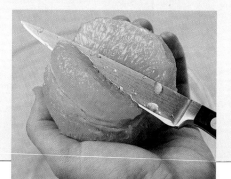

membrane into the bowl.

For a striking contrast of colors and flavors, mix glossy, bittersweet segments of ruby grapefruit, in its winter prime, with dark red, tangy sweetened dried cranberries—recently introduced by several companies, including Ocean Spray and Portland's Craneberries.

*Winter fruit salad.* Mix ½ cup **sweetened dried cranberries** with 3 cups **ruby grapefruit** segments. Add 2 to 3 tablespoons **lime juice,** 1 tablespoon **Asian fish sauce** (*nuoc mam* or *nam pla*), and 1 to 2 teaspoons **sugar** to cut the sharpness. Serves 2.

Per serving: 221 cal., 6.3% (14 cal.) from fat; 3.1 g protein; 1.6 g fat (0.2 g sat.); 52 g carbo (3.7 g fiber); 298 mg sodium; 0 mg chol.

stirring often, until reduced to 2 cups, about 8 minutes.

**3.** Let the apricot chutney cool, then serve. Or pour into a jar, cover airtight, and chill.

Per tablespoon: 45 cal., 12% (5.4 cal.) from fat; 0.6 g protein; 0.6 g fat (0 g sat.); 10 g carbo (0.5 g fiber); 6.1 mg sodium; 0 mg chol.

## Pork Tenderloin with Apricot Chutney

**Prep and cook time:** About 20 minutes

**Notes:** Serve with a curry-seasoned risotto or pilaf and a nippy salad of watercress or Belgian endive. For variation, use boned, skinned, and fat-trimmed chicken thighs (about 1 lb. total) instead of pork; brown the meat (about 6 minutes), then cook with the chutney and water just until the thighs are tender when pierced, 10 to 12 minutes. You may need to add another ¼ cup water or so to keep the sauce from scorching.

**Makes:** 4 servings

- 1 **pork tenderloin** (about 1 lb.), fat-trimmed
- 1 to 2 teaspoons **butter** or margarine
- ⅓ cup **quick apricot chutney** (recipe precedes)
- **Salt** and **pepper**

**1.** If necessary to keep the tenderloin in a compact piece, tie meat at several intervals with cotton string.

**2.** Melt butter in an ovenproof 10- to 12-inch nonstick frying pan over high heat. Add pork tenderloin and turn as needed to brown well on all sides, 5 to 6 minutes total.

**3.** Add apricot chutney and ⅓ cup water to pan and stir to incorporate meat drippings. Baste tenderloin with some of the sauce, and then put it in a 450° oven.

**4.** Roast pork, basting often with sauce, until meat is 150° to 155° in center of thickest part, 12 to 14 minutes. If sauce starts to scorch, stir in water, 2 tablespoons at a time.

**5.** Transfer the tenderloin to a platter. Pour the apricot chutney sauce over pork, or serve the sauce in a small bowl and add to taste. Slice tenderloin and season to taste with salt and pepper.

Per serving: 235 cal., 23% (53 cal.) from fat; 25 g protein; 5.9 g fat (2 g sat.); 21 g carbo (0.9 g fiber); 79 mg sodium; 76 mg chol.

## A TASTE OF THE WEST

# One step at a time

■ When a baby takes its first step, as my wee grandson, Henry, is aiming to do momentarily, a whole new world unfolds. For me, January marks less dramatic, more symbolic changes. Obligations of the old year are settled. The calendar is ready for fresh inscriptions. And finding simpler ways to make interesting dishes freshens up my world.

To me, this means trimming recipe ingredient lists. And often, brevity comes from making use of unexpected, multidimensional elements that on their own complement a variety of foods.

Apricot jam, for instance, can be quickly turned into an excellent chutney. Then the chutney itself can become the essential ingredient of a rich braising sauce for pork tenderloin.

Henry is hankering for a lot of steps. But me—I want fewer.

## Quick Apricot Chutney

**Prep and cook time:** 10 to 15 minutes

**Notes:** This simple, sweet-tart relish lasts as long as a jar of jam, which in my refrigerator can be many moons. Eat the chutney on toast with cream cheese; serve it with meat, poultry, or a curry; or cook with it, as in the pork tenderloin recipe that follows.

**Makes:** 2 cups

- 2 jars (10 oz. each; 1½ cups total) **apricot jam**
- 1 cup **rice vinegar**
- ⅓ cup **mustard seed**
- 1 tablespoon minced **fresh ginger**

**1.** In a 10- to 12-inch frying pan, combine jam, vinegar, mustard seed, and ginger.

**2.** Stirring often, bring mixture to a boil over high heat. Continue boiling,

# gadget

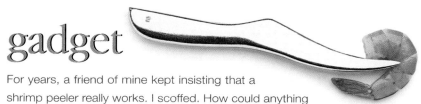

For years, a friend of mine kept insisting that a shrimp peeler really works. I scoffed. How could anything as plain and inexpensive as this curved stick—plastic or metal—be useful? Frustrated by my stubbornness, he finally staged a demonstration. • It was almost too easy. He just slipped the peeler between the shrimp and its shell, pushed the fine tip along the back to gouge out the vein, then slid the peeler around the body. Presto, the shrimp slipped right out. Rinsed and drained, the shrimp were ready to cook almost before I could concede defeat. • You'll find these useful tools at most kitchenware stores and many fish markets for $2 to $6.

## FOOD TRENDS

# An old favorite through new eyes

■ I grew up with crab Louis and loved every bite. Then menus moved on, and this dependable salad fell from grace. But Andrea Hill, chef de cuisine at Accents at the Sutton Place Hotel in Newport Beach, California, is young enough to treat this salad as a discovery—her version is stylish but comforting still with its familiar flavors.

### Crab Louis Accents

*Prep time:* About 20 minutes
*Notes:* To make the salad a little less rich, just add the dressing to taste.
*Makes:* 2 servings

- 1 firm-ripe **avocado** (about ½ lb.)
- ⅓ to ½ pound **shelled cooked Dungeness crab**
  **Louis dressing** (recipe follows)
  **Salt** and **pepper**
- 2 cups **tender salad leaves,** rinsed and crisped
- 2 teaspoons **balsamic vinegar**
- 2 teaspoons **extra-virgin olive oil**
- 4 **Belgian endive** leaves (optional)
- 2 to 4 tablespoons diced **bell pepper** (red, yellow, green, or a combination)
- 1 hard-cooked **large egg,** shelled

1. Cut avocado in half lengthwise, then peel and pit. Turn halves cut side down, then cut each half crosswise into thin slices. With a wide spatula, transfer each avocado half to a dinner plate, keeping slices together. With your fingers, gently pull slices into a loose S that fills the center of the plate.
2. Mix crab gently with Louis dressing. Add salt and pepper to taste.
3. Mix salad leaves with vinegar, oil, and salt and pepper to taste.
4. Lay 2 endive leaves parallel at the tip of each avocado S. Spoon crab mixture beneath the endive and next to the avocado, then mound salad leaves onto base of endive. Scatter plates with the diced bell pepper.
5. Mince egg in a food processor, or rub through a fine strainer. Sprinkle over crab salad.

Per serving without dressing: 303 cal., 65% (198 cal.) from fat; 21 g protein; 22 g fat (3.7 g sat.); 9 g carbo (2.3 g fiber); 254 mg sodium; 181 mg chol.

### Louis Dressing

*Prep time:* 5 to 8 minutes
*Makes:* About 1 cup

- ¼ cup **whipping cream**
- ¼ cup **mayonnaise** (regular or low-fat)
- 2 tablespoons minced **onion**
- 2 to 3 tablespoons **tomato-based chili sauce** (for seafood cocktails)

## QUICK TRICK

# Greening up tomatillos

■ In a beautiful Guadalajara, Mexico, restaurant famous for its game dishes, I was served this brilliant green sauce with venison. Technically, it is salsa, but more subtle and refreshing than the typical red tomato one. Made with canned tomatillos, the sauce can be ready in just minutes. It's also splendid with beef, lamb, salmon, shrimp, and white-flesh fish like halibut and Chilean seabass.

### Green Salsa

*Prep time:* 5 to 10 minutes
*Makes:* About 1¼ cups

- 1 can (12 oz.) **whole tomatillos,** drained
- ¾ cup **fresh cilantro**
- 2 tablespoons chopped **onion**
- 4 to 6 tablespoons **lime juice**
- 1 to 2 tablespoons chopped **fresh jalapeño chilies**
  **Salt**

1. In a food processor or blender, purée tomatillos, cilantro, onion, 4 tablespoons lime juice, and 1 tablespoon chilies until smooth.
2. Taste, then add more lime juice and chilies if desired. Add salt to taste. Serve, or cover and chill up to 3 days.

Per tablespoon: 7.2 cal., 0% (0 cal.) from fat; 0 g protein; 0 g fat (0 g sat.); 1.5 g carbo (0.3 g fiber); 21 mg sodium; 0 mg chol.

- 2 to 3 tablespoons **lemon juice**
  **Cayenne**

1. In a chilled small, deep bowl, beat cream with a mixer on high speed until cream holds soft peaks.
2. Add mayonnaise, onion, chili sauce, lemon juice, and cayenne to taste. Mix gently. If making ahead, cover and chill dressing up to 4 hours. Stir before serving.

Per tablespoon: 40 cal., 88% (35 cal.) from fat; 0.1 g protein; 3.9 g fat (1.1 g sat.); 1.2 g carbo (0 g fiber); 45 mg sodium; 6.2 mg chol. ◆

# The Wine Guide

BY KAREN MACNEIL

## Well grounded in Stags Leap

■ The great wines of the world tell you where in the world they're from. Their aromas and flavors give you the sense that they are intimately and inevitably connected to the ground they were born in. And within that connectedness lies everything that is wonderful about wine: its capacity for personality, its uniqueness, its compellingness.

Aren't most wines, though, bound to the place they come from? Sadly not. Millions of wines are no more revealing of their circumstance than a McDonald's in Tokyo.

This doesn't make a wine bad, exactly. But for me, when a wine is not connected to a place, there's a limit to how profound it can be.

I first began to understand this concept of connectedness when I was in France talking to a man who makes Sancerre (the name of both the wine and the village around which its grapes are grown). All Sancerres, by French law, must be made from Sauvignon Blanc grapes, so I asked the winemaker how he compared his wine with California Sauvignon Blancs. He looked at me completely puzzled. "But I don't make Sauvignon Blanc," he protested. "I make Sancerre."

Place was paramount. As far as he was concerned, Sauvignon Blanc was just the medium through which his special part of the world, Sancerre, could be tasted.

Let's bring this idea home. Every day we see the names of various wine regions—appellations—on bottles: Alexander Valley, Santa Barbara County, Columbia Valley, Napa Valley, and so on. You really can taste these places in the wine, if three things are true.

First, the place has to be small, well defined, and geographically distinct enough to be unique. An area that's big and diverse will yield wines that are all across the board in flavor and style.

Second, for us to truly taste the place, winemakers there must let the wine be itself. If, instead, the wine-

RICK MARIANI

maker uses every razzle-dazzle wine-making technique in the book, the wine will end up tasting more like technology than ground.

Last (though this seems rather cosmically unfair), some places are just plain blessed with more personality than others, and for a wine to be great, it must come from one of these. The Stags Leap wine district is such a spot. Wines from here, like people from Brooklyn, are so marked by the distinctiveness of their place that they can't help being who they are.

Above all, wines with the Stags Leap appellation can't help having texture. Drinking them feels as if someone has just wrapped you up in cashmere pajamas. The wines have such a languorous, sexy aura, they immediately stop you in your tracks. A great one, I swear, could make you stop breathing.

I'm talking about Stags Leap district's Cabernet Sauvignons (some of which are blended with Merlot and Cabernet Franc). Though other grape varieties are grown here and can make very good wine, it's the Cabernets that soar.

Just why Stags Leap Cabs have this soulfully plush, velvety character is only partially known. The region is tucked up against the volcanic Vaca Mountains on the eastern side of the Napa Valley. Towering above it is an outcropping of naked rock that's as hard and ominous as the wines are soft

and seductive. Legend has it that by leaping from one rocky palisade to the next, a stag eluded hunters for years (hence the name Stags Leap).

The soils here provide a small clue to the character of the wines. They are mostly old, gravelly riverbed soils that don't hold water or nutrients very well. The vines, forced to struggle, acquire character (just as people often do through adversity). Then, too, there's the district's quirky microclimate. The east-facing bare rock magnifies the heat during the day, but nearby San Pablo Bay lowers temperatures, sometimes dramatically, by late afternoon. Vines love this seesaw of warmth and coolness; it keeps them in equilibrium.

Beyond texture and structure, however, there's something more elusive (the influence of that stag, perhaps). Unlike many other Cabs, those from the Stags Leap district are rarely green, angular, or herbal. Instead, the best of them are loaded with chocolate, mocha, violet, and blackberry jam flavors.

Last summer, for the first time ever, I made blackberry jam. The warm berries were oozing with ripeness. When the jam was done, I tasted it—Stags Leap Cabernet *déjà vu.* ◆

*quick*
light & *healthy*

The Baca family, page 19

Andrew Hudson, page 19

Alan Lau and grandma, page 22

# Just like Mom made—*almost*

Westerners share their childhood memories of favorite foods.
Our lighter recipes bring the same old-fashioned satisfaction

BY LINDA LAU ANUSASANANAN          FOOD PHOTOGRAPHS BY JAMES CARRIER

■ Remember how Mom's mac 'n' cheese could smooth out a bad day? Chances are, most of her special dishes weren't fancy but took some time to make. They were worth the wait: when you ate them, you felt warm and safe.

The truth is, our comforting food memories don't all run to macaroni and cheese. A broad but informal survey of Westerners, from governors to naturalists, revealed a melting pot—hot turkey sandwiches at Howard Johnson or French toast you're allowed to eat sitting on the couch.

Gourmet ingredients weren't necessarily an advantage. Darrell Corti, a Sacramento grocer and wine merchant whose mother made frittata-and-prosciutto sandwiches on sturdy breads for his school lunches, jokes about his "deprived" childhood. "I loved bologna sandwiches made with Best Foods sandwich spread and soft Won-

der bread. By lunchtime, they were warm, pungent, and greasy. But that was a forbidden treat for me." His solution: swap lunches.

That's just it—it didn't matter to us then if our sandwiches were greasy. Montana humorist and cowboy-poet Gwen Petersen sums it up: "My greatest comfort when I was growing up was we could eat guilt-free."

To bring back that greatest comfort of all, we gathered up the recipes our respondents hankered after and went to work in *Sunset's* test kitchens zapping fat and trimming time. A surprising number of dishes were almost quick, light, and healthy already; shortcut products, leaner ingredients, nonstick pans, and modified techniques transformed the rest into table-ready low-fat realities in 45 minutes or less. Now you can turn back the clock, in more ways than one.

Marc Racicot's family favored crisp, fat-fried chicken and vegetables on Sundays. Oven-frying keeps these choices crisp— and lighter.

## Sunday Fried Chicken

■ "We had a very large family—seven children," says **Marc Racicot**, governor of Montana. "Every Sunday and for picnics we had chicken. Those days it was French-fried." And, he adds, it was always served with French-fried potatoes and broccoli with cauliflower.

***Prep and cook time:*** About 40 minutes

***Makes:*** 4 servings

   4  **chicken breast halves** (about ½ lb. each) or whole legs (thigh and drumstick, about ½ lb. each)

2½  cups **cornflakes**

   1  teaspoon **dried thyme**

  ¾  teaspoon **paprika**

     About ½ teaspoon **salt**

     About ¼ teaspoon **pepper**

   2  **large egg** whites

     **Cooking oil spray**

**1.** Remove and discard skin and excess fat from chicken. Rinse chicken and pat the pieces dry.

**2.** Place cornflakes in a plastic food bag and crush gently with your hands to make very coarse crumbs.

**3.** Add thyme, paprika, ½ teaspoon salt, and ¼ teaspoon pepper to bag; shake to mix.

**4.** In a shallow bowl, beat egg whites with a fork until slightly frothy.

**5.** Coat chicken pieces with egg white, drain briefly, then put in bag with crumb mixture, 1 piece at a time. Turn bag to coat chicken well.

**6.** Arrange chicken pieces slightly apart in a 10- by 15-inch nonstick pan. Lightly mist chicken with cooking oil spray.

**7.** Bake chicken in a 425° oven until meat is no longer pink in thickest part (cut to test), about 25 minutes for breasts, about 30 minutes for legs.

**8.** Add salt and pepper to taste.

Per breast: 228 cal., 7.5% (17 cal.) from fat; 37 g protein; 1.9 g fat (0.5 g sat.); 13 g carbo (0.2 g fiber); 573 mg sodium; 86 mg chol.

Per leg: 221 cal., 20% (45 cal.) from fat; 29 g protein; 5 g fat (1.3 g sat.); 13 g carbo (0.2 g fiber); 588 mg sodium; 104 mg chol.

## Oven Fries

***Prep and cook time:*** About 30 minutes

***Notes:*** Bake the potatoes in the oven with the chicken.

***Makes:*** 4 servings

   2  **russet potatoes** (about ½ lb. each)

   1  tablespoon **butter** or margarine

  ½  teaspoon **paprika**

     About ¼ teaspoon **salt**

     About ⅛ teaspoon **pepper**

**1.** Scrub potatoes and pat dry. Cut each lengthwise into sticks about ½ inch thick.

**2.** In a 10- by 15-inch nonstick pan, melt butter over low heat. Mix in paprika, ¼ teaspoon salt, and ⅛ teaspoon pepper.

**3.** Add potato sticks to pan and turn in seasoned butter to coat, then arrange sticks slightly apart in a single layer.

**4.** Bake potatoes in a 425° oven until browned, turning once, about 25 minutes total.

**5.** Season potatoes with salt and pepper to taste. Serve hot.

Per serving: 118 cal., 24% (28 cal.) from fat; 2.2 g protein; 3.1 g fat (1.8 g sat.); 21 g carbo (1.9 g fiber); 173 mg sodium; 7.8 mg chol.

## Hot Turkey Sandwiches

■ "A real treat was to go to Howard Johnson and eat a hot turkey sandwich with mashed potatoes, gravy, and cranberry sauce. When you're 8 years old and it's not even Thanksgiving, that's ultimate luxury," says **Shirley Kerins**, curator of the Huntington Herb Garden in San Marino, California.

***Prep and cook time:*** About 25 minutes

***Makes:*** 2 servings

At age 8, Shirley Kerins experienced ultimate indulgence with a hot turkey sandwich.

- ¾ pound **Yukon gold potatoes**
- ½ teaspoon **dried thyme**
- ½ pound **boned, skinned turkey breast** slices (about ¼ in. thick)

  **Salt** and **pepper**

  About 3 tablespoons **all-purpose flour**
- 1 teaspoon **salad oil**
- 1¼ cups **chicken broth**
- 2 tablespoons **dry sherry**
- 1 tablespoon **soy sauce**
- 4 teaspoons **cornstarch**

  About 2 tablespoons hot **nonfat milk**
- 2 slices (about 2 oz. total) **white bread**
- 3 to 4 tablespoons **canned cranberry sauce**

**1.** In a 2- to 3-quart pan over high heat, bring 3 cups water to a boil.

**2.** Meanwhile, peel potatoes and cut into 1-inch chunks. Add to boiling water, cover, and simmer over medium heat until potatoes are very tender when pierced, about 15 minutes. Drain potatoes, return to pan, cover, and keep warm.

**3.** As potatoes cook, rub thyme over turkey slices and lightly sprinkle with salt and pepper, then coat with flour, shaking off excess.

**4.** Place a 10- to 12-inch nonstick frying pan over high heat. When pan is hot, add oil and tilt to coat bottom. Add turkey, without crowding, and brown lightly, turning once, 3 to 4 minutes per batch. Meat should be white in center (cut to test). Transfer turkey to a platter as cooked and keep warm.

**5.** Mix broth, sherry, soy sauce, and cornstarch; add to frying pan. Stir over high heat until boiling, about 1 minute. Add salt and pepper to taste.

**6.** Mash potatoes and add enough milk to make them creamy. Add salt and pepper to taste.

**7.** Place a slice of bread on each plate and top each slice with half the turkey. Mound potatoes equally on meat, pour gravy over the sandwich, and accompany with a dollop of the cranberry sauce.

Per serving: 517 cal., 9.7% (50 cal.) from fat; 38 g protein; 5.5 g fat (1.2 g sat.); 73 g carbo (3.8 g fiber); 820 mg sodium; 73 mg chol.

Dana Boussard reminisces about her dad's *kibbeh,* a spicy meat loaf with bulgur.

## Lebanese Meat Loaf

■ "My father is Lebanese. I remember the flat bread that his sister made, and grape leaves, and *kibbeh*—the foods we ate when we gathered as a family. Kibbeh was sort of a steak tartare. My dad ate it raw; no one else would. We flattened it in a pan and baked it like meat loaf," says fiber artist **Dana Boussard** of Arlee, Montana.

*Prep and cook time:* About 35 minutes
*Makes:* 4 servings

- 1 cup **bulgur wheat**
- 2 cups coarsely chopped **onions**
- 1 pound **ground lean** (7% fat or less) **beef** or lamb
- ½ teaspoon **pepper**
- ½ teaspoon **ground cumin**
- ½ teaspoon **ground cinnamon**

  About 1 teaspoon **salt**
- ⅓ cup chopped **parsley**

  **Black peppercorns**
- 1 cup **plain nonfat yogurt**

**1.** Place bulgur in a fine strainer and rinse thoroughly with cool water.

**2.** In a food processor, finely chop the onions. Add beef, ½ cup water, pepper, cumin, cinnamon, and 1 teaspoon salt. Whirl until mixture is a smooth paste.

**3.** Add bulgur and ¼ cup parsley; whirl just to mix.

**4.** Pat meat mixture evenly into a shallow 1- to 1½-quart casserole. Cut through meat mixture to make diamonds 2 to 3 inches wide. Place a peppercorn in the center of each diamond.

**5.** Bake, uncovered, in a 425° oven until meat is no longer pink in center (cut to test), about 25 minutes. Sprinkle with remaining parsley and add salt to taste.

**6.** To serve, cut diamonds apart and accompany with yogurt.

Per serving: 357 cal., 22% (79 cal.) from fat; 32 g protein; 8.8 g fat (3.2 g sat.); 39 g carbo (8 g fiber); 674 mg sodium; 66 mg chol.

## Mom's Best Swiss Steak

■ "I have wonderful, warm memories of cooking with Mom. She made the best Swiss steak ever," says **Alan Tangren,** who is now pastry chef at the legendary Chez Panisse Café & Restaurant in

Berkeley. "She and my grandmother are the reason I'm in the food world."

**Prep and cook time:** About 45 minutes

**Makes:** 4 servings

1 pound **boned beef top sirloin,** ½ inch thick

**Salt** and **pepper**

About ⅓ cup **all-purpose flour**

1 cup thinly sliced **onion**

1 cup thinly sliced **carrots**

1 cup thinly sliced **celery**

½ teaspoon **dried marjoram**

About 2 cups **beef broth**

1 pound **red thin-skinned potatoes** (1½ to 2 in. wide)

**1.** Trim and discard fat from beef. Cut meat into 4 equal pieces, sprinkle lightly with salt and pepper, and coat with flour.

**2.** Pound meat with a ridged mallet until it's ¼ inch thick. Coat with more flour, then shake off excess.

**3.** Place a 12- to 13-inch nonstick frying pan over medium-high heat. When pan is hot, add meat pieces without crowding and brown on each side, about 4 minutes total. Transfer from pan as cooked and keep warm.

**4.** Return all meat and any juices to pan. Add onion, carrots, celery, marjoram, and 2 cups broth. Bring to a boil over high heat, then reduce heat to low, cover, and simmer until meat and vegetables are tender when pierced, 20 to 30 minutes.

**5.** Meanwhile, in a 3- to 4-quart pan over high heat, bring about 1½ quarts water to a boil. Add potatoes, cover, and simmer over medium heat until potatoes are tender when pierced, 20 to 25 minutes. Drain and keep warm.

**6.** With a slotted spoon, transfer meat and vegetables to a platter; keep warm.

**7.** Measure pan juices and, if needed, add water or broth to make 1½ cups; return liquid to frying pan. (If you have too much liquid, boil, uncovered, until reduced to 1½ cups.) Mix 3 tablespoons flour with ¼ cup water and stir into pan. Drain any accumulated juices from platter into pan. Stir sauce over high heat until boiling, then pour over steak and vegetables. Serve with potatoes. Add salt and pepper to taste.

Per serving: 319 cal., 16% (50 cal.) from fat; 31 g protein; 5.5 g fat (1.8 g sat.); 36 g carbo (4.2 g fiber); 147 mg sodium; 69 mg chol.

## Macaroni and Cheese

■ "Even now, I still get a craving for really creamy macaroni and cheese," says *Sunset's* senior food editor, **Jerry Anne Di Vecchio,** after almost four decades of pushing the culinary envelope.

**Prep and cook time:** About 30 minutes

**Makes:** 6 to 8 servings

¾ pound **dried elbow macaroni**

2 slices (2 oz. total) **whole-wheat bread**

1 tablespoon **grated parmesan cheese**

¾ teaspoon **paprika**

1 cup chopped **onion**

¼ cup **all-purpose flour**

2 cans (12 oz. each) **evaporated nonfat milk**

1 cup **vegetable** or chicken **broth**

3 cups (¾ lb.) **shredded reduced-fat** (made with 2% milk) **sharp cheddar cheese**

⅛ teaspoon **ground nutmeg**

**Salt** and **pepper**

**1.** Cook macaroni in about 2 quarts boiling water just until tender to bite, 6 to 8 minutes. Drain.

**2.** Meanwhile, tear bread into ½-inch chunks. In a food processor or blender, combine bread, parmesan cheese, and ¼ teaspoon paprika; whirl until mixture is coarse crumbs.

**3.** In 5- to 6-quart pan over high heat, frequently stir onion and 2 tablespoons water until onion is limp and begins to brown, about 4 minutes. Stir in flour and remaining ½ teaspoon paprika.

**4.** Remove onion mixture from heat and blend in milk and broth until smooth, then stir over high heat until sauce boils, about 5 minutes. Remove from heat again, add cheese, and stir until it melts. Add nutmeg, and salt and pepper to taste.

**5.** Add macaroni to cheese sauce and mix, then pour into a shallow 2- to 2½-quart casserole. Sprinkle with seasoned bread crumbs.

**6.** Bake in a 450° oven until crumbs are browned, 3 to 4 minutes.

Per serving: 415 cal., 22% (90 cal.) from fat; 25 g protein; 10 g fat (6.4 g sat.); 52 g carbo (1.9 g fiber); 532 mg sodium; 34 mg chol.

Macaroni dripping with velvety cheese sauce turns on memories of simpler times for *Sunset's* senior food editor.

## Egg Salad Sandwich

■ "My fondest memory of being a kid was walking to elementary school with my lunch. My mother always packed egg salad sandwiches," says **Andrew Hudson,** who is the press secretary for Mayor Wellington Webb of Denver. Now he goes one better than Mom, making the sandwiches down-right healthy by using alfalfa sprouts, purchased egg substitute, and slices of whole-grain bread.

***Prep and cook time:*** About 10 minutes

***Notes:*** If you use purchased egg substi-tute (½ cup) skip step 1.

***Makes:*** 1 serving

- 1   **large egg**
- 2   **large egg** whites
- 2   tablespoons **nonfat mayonnaise**
- 1   teaspoon **Dijon mustard**
- 1   tablespoon **canned sliced ripe olives,** drained
- 1   tablespoon thinly sliced **green onion,** including green tops
      **Salt** and **pepper**
- 2   slices (about 2 oz. total) **whole-wheat** or 7-grain **bread**
- ½   cup (¾ oz.) **alfalfa sprouts**

1. With a fork, beat egg, egg whites, and 1 tablespoon water to blend.

2. Set a 6- to 8-inch nonstick frying pan over medium heat. When the pan is hot, add the egg mixture. As mixture sets, use a wide spatula to lift up the cooked portion and let liquid flow underneath until the eggs are cooked as you like.

3. Pour cooked eggs into a bowl and break into bite-size pieces with a fork. Let stand to cool slightly.

4. Mix mayonnaise, mustard, olives, and onion. Add mixture to eggs and mix. Add salt and pepper to taste.

5. Spoon egg salad evenly over a bread slice. Top with alfalfa sprouts and the remaining slice of bread.

Per serving: 290 cal., 26% (76 cal.) from fat; 20 g protein; 8.4 g fat (2.2 g sat.); 33 g carbo (4.8 g fiber); 877 mg sodium; 213 mg chol.

A Friday ritual at the Baca family home: stacked enchiladas for dinner.

## Stacked Red Chili Enchiladas

■ "Every Friday night we had stacked cheese enchiladas made with red chili sauce and blue corn tortillas," says **Sam Baca,** who is now community liaison for Corner-stones Commu-nity Part-nerships, a Santa Fe group that helps restore small-town historic churches. "I remember the ex-act taste, but I can't duplicate it. I even have the same pan my mother used to make those enchiladas. Maybe it's the chili—we liked our chili fairly hot. Peo-ple would dry red chilies, grind them, and come around door-to-door with three, four, five kinds in the back of a pickup. To this day, those enchiladas are my favorite food."

***Prep and cook time:*** 25 to 30 minutes

***Makes:*** 1 serving

- 3   **blue** or yellow **corn tortillas** (6 in. wide)
- 1   cup chopped **onion**
- 2   tablespoons **ground New Mexico chilies** (also called chili powder)
- 2   teaspoons **all-purpose flour**
- ¾   cup **vegetable** or chicken **broth**
      **Salt**
- ½   cup **shredded reduced-fat** (made with 2% milk) **cheddar cheese**
      **Nonfat** or low-fat **sour cream** (optional)
- 1   can (8 oz.) **pinto** or black **beans,** heated
- 1   cup shredded **lettuce**
- 2   tablespoons diced **tomato**

1. In a 10- to 12-inch nonstick frying pan over high heat, cook tortillas, in a single layer, until soft and lightly toasted, turning once, about 3 minutes per batch. Set aside as toasted.

2. Reduce heat to medium. Add onion and stir until limp, about 5 minutes; remove from pan.

3. Mix ground chilies and flour in pan and stir over low heat until chilies smell lightly toasted, about 2 minutes.

4. Whisk in broth until smooth. Stir over high heat until sauce boils, about 2 minutes. Add salt to taste.

5. Dip 1 tortilla in chili sauce, coating both sides, then set on a microwave-safe plate. Top tortilla with half the onion and a third of the cheese. Repeat layers, using all tortillas and onion. Pour remaining chili sauce (it thickens as it cools) over this stacked enchilada, then sprinkle with remaining cheese.

*quick*
light&
healthy

**6.** Heat enchilada in a microwave oven at full power (100%) until hot in center, 1½ to 2 minutes.

**7.** Top with sour cream and accompany with beans, lettuce, and tomato.

Per serving: 691 cal., 23% (162 cal.) from fat; 34 g protein; 18 g fat (8.5 g sat.); 102 g carbo (22 g fiber); 1,762 mg sodium; 40 mg chol.

## Cornmeal-crusted Fish with Tartar Sauce

■ "I come from the South. We ate a lot of catfish, hush puppies, coleslaw, and Tabasco sauce," says the author of *Exotic Herbs,* **Carole Saville,** who now resides in Northern California. "The fish wasn't farmed; it was from local waters. Today catfish tastes like the meal they feed it. I like orange roughy, cod, salmon, and halibut these days."

*Prep and cook time:* About 20 minutes

*Makes:* 4 servings

- ½ cup **cornmeal**
- ¼ teaspoon **paprika**
- ¼ teaspoon **white pepper**

  About ¼ teaspoon **salt**
- 1 **large egg** white
- 1 tablespoon **nonfat milk** or water
- 1 pound **skinned, boned fish fillets** (such as catfish, orange roughy, or rockfish), about ½ inch thick

  **Cooking oil spray**
- ¼ cup **nonfat mayonnaise**
- 1 tablespoon **sweet pickle relish**
- 1 tablespoon chopped **onion**
- 1 tablespoon **white wine vinegar**

  **Hot sauce**

**1.** Place a 10- by 15-inch nonstick pan in a 500° oven until pan is hot, about 5 minutes.

**2.** Meanwhile, on a plate mix corn-

meal, paprika, pepper, and ¼ teaspoon salt.

**3.** In a shallow bowl, beat egg white and milk to blend.

**4.** Rinse fish fillets, pat dry, and cut into serving-size pieces.

**5.** Coat fish with egg white mixture, then cornmeal mixture. Set aside in a single layer.

**6.** When pan is hot, mist lightly with cooking oil spray. Quickly arrange fish pieces well apart in pan. Bake until fish is browned on bottom, 3 to 4 minutes. Turn over and continue baking until fish is golden on top and opaque but still moist-looking in thickest part (cut to test), 2 to 3 minutes longer.

**7.** Meanwhile, mix mayonnaise, pickle relish, onion, and vinegar to make tartar sauce.

**8.** With a wide spatula, transfer fish to plates; add salt to taste. Serve with tartar sauce and hot sauce.

Per serving: 233 cal., 33% (77 cal.) from fat; 20 g protein; 8.5 g fat (1.7 g sat.); 17 g carbo (0.9 g fiber); 321 mg sodium; 38 mg chol.

## Spotted Dog

■ "My grandmother would feed everybody who came in the door. We'd start with 10 and end up with 25 for dinner," says **Robert Black Bull,** a Blackfoot artist in Browning, Montana. "We would eat dried meat, potatoes, berry soup, bannock bread, spotted dog. Spotted dog is like a rice pudding with raisins—no dog. Guess someone made it and thought it looked like their spotted dog."

*Prep and cook time:* About 20 minutes
*Makes:* 3 or 4 servings

- 1 cup **precooked dried white rice**

  About 2¼ cups **low-fat** (1%) **milk**
- 1 **cinnamon stick** (3 in. long)
- ¼ cup **sugar**
- ⅛ teaspoon **salt**
- ⅓ cup **raisins**

**1.** In a 1½- to 2-quart nonstick pan, combine rice, 2¼ cups milk, and

Spotted dog pudding reminds Robert Black Bull of his grandmother's hospitality.

cinnamon stick. Bring to a boil over medium-high heat, stirring, 10 to 12 minutes.

**2.** Add sugar, salt, and raisins. Simmer over medium-low heat, stirring often, until most of the milk is absorbed and pudding is creamy, 8 to 10 minutes longer.

**3.** Spoon into bowls and serve warm. Pudding thickens as it stands; if desired, stir in a little more milk.

Per serving: 233 cal., 6% (14 cal.) from fat; 6.7 g protein; 1.6 g fat (0.9 g sat.); 49 g carbo (1 g fiber); 141 mg sodium; 5.5 mg chol.

## Japanese Vegetable Omelet

■ "I remember visiting my grandmother and marveling about how she could always whip something up," says **Janice McCormick,** CFO of Channel Islands Marine Resource Institute in Port Hueneme, California. "This omelet reminds me of her, of close times with my family, of being at home, safe and secure."

***Prep and cook time:*** About 15 minutes

***Notes:*** You can use ¹⁄₂ cup purchased egg substitute for the egg and whites and skip step 2. Nori is dried seaweed; furikake is a seasoning blend of dried fish flakes, sesame seed, and nori. Both are sold in Japanese food stores and well-stocked supermarkets.

***Makes:*** 1 serving

- ¹⁄₂ cup **precooked dried white rice**
- 1 **large egg**
- 2 **large egg** whites
  About ¹⁄₈ teaspoon **salt**
- ¹⁄₂ cup finely shredded **cabbage**
- ¹⁄₄ cup thinly sliced **onion**
  About ¹⁄₈ teaspoon **pepper**
  Finely slivered **nori** or furikake (optional)

**1.** In a 2- to 3-cup microwave-safe bowl, mix rice and ¹⁄₂ cup water. Cover with plastic wrap and cook in a microwave oven on full power (100%) until water

In Lynn Bagley's Italian family, minestrone always started in the garden.

is absorbed, 4 to 5 minutes. Let stand.

**2.** Meanwhile, beat egg, egg whites, and 1 tablespoon water.

**3.** Add ¹⁄₈ teaspoon salt to eggs; blend.

**4.** In a 6- to 8-inch nonstick frying pan, stir cabbage and onion over high heat until onion begins to brown, about 3 minutes. Sprinkle with pepper to taste.

**5.** Reduce heat to medium. Pour egg mixture over cooked vegetables. As eggs set, use a wide spatula to lift cooked portion and let liquid flow underneath.

**6.** When golden on bottom and still moist on top, in about 2 minutes, loosen eggs from pan with spatula, then slide spatula under omelet on one side and flip about ¹⁄₃ of it over the center. Tilt pan to slide unfolded edge of omelet onto a plate, then tip pan to roll remainder of omelet onto that edge.

**7.** Sprinkle with slivered nori. Add salt and pepper to taste. Serve with hot cooked rice.

Per serving: 312 cal., 15% (48 cal.) from fat; 18 g protein; 5.3 g fat (1.6 g sat.); 47 g carbo (2.3 g fiber); 460 mg sodium; 213 mg chol.

## Winter Vegetable Minestrone

■ "Minestrone is comfort food for our Italian family. It's very warming—I literally sweat when I eat it," says **Lynn Bagley,** founder of the Marin County Farmers Market Association in San Rafael, California.

***Prep and cook time:*** About 30 minutes

***Makes:*** 6 to 8 servings

- 1 teaspoon **olive oil**
- 1 cup chopped **onion**

- 2 cloves **garlic,** pressed or minced
- 6 cups **vegetable** or chicken **broth**
- 1 **dried bay leaf**
- ¹⁄₂ pound **banana squash**
- ³⁄₄ pound **Swiss chard**
- 1 can (14¹⁄₂ oz.) **diced tomatoes with Italian seasonings**
- 2 cans (15 oz. each) **cannellini** (white beans), rinsed and drained
  **Salt** and **pepper**
  **Grated parmesan cheese**

**1.** In a 5- to 6-quart pan, combine oil, onion, and garlic. Stir over high heat until onion begins to brown, about 5 minutes.

**2.** Add broth and bay leaf. Bring to a boil over high heat.

**3.** Cut off and discard peel from squash; cut squash into ¹⁄₂-inch cubes and add to pan. Cover and simmer over medium heat until squash is tender when pierced, about 6 minutes.

**4.** Meanwhile, trim off discolored ends of Swiss chard stems. Rinse chard, shake off moisture, stack, and cut in half lengthwise; then cut crosswise into ¹⁄₄-inch-wide strips.

**5.** Add Swiss chard, tomatoes, and beans to squash mixture. Bring to a boil over high heat, stirring often, and boil until chard stems are tender when pierced, 3 to 4 minutes. Ladle into soup bowls.

**6.** Season minestrone with salt, pepper, and cheese to taste.

Per serving: 140 cal., 10% (14 cal.) from fat; 7.8 g protein; 1.6 g fat (0.1 g sat.); 24 g carbo (6 g fiber); 352 mg sodium; 0 mg chol.

## Five-Spice Potatoes

■ "Po-po [Grandma] used to cook potatoes with salt pork, soy sauce, five spice (it had a cinnamon smell), and some kind of green onion. That was my favorite. She would cook it just because I liked it," says **Alan Lau,** Seattle artist, greengrocer, and author of the forthcoming book *Blues and Greens—A Produce Worker's Journal.*

***Prep and cook time:*** About 30 minutes

***Makes:*** 4 servings

- 1½ cups **long-grain white rice**
- ¼ cup **reduced-sodium soy sauce**
- 2 tablespoons minced **fresh ginger**
- 1½ tablespoons **sugar**
- 1 teaspoon **Chinese five spice** (or equal parts ground cinnamon, ground clove, ground ginger, and anise seed)
- 6 ounces **boned lean pork loin,** fat trimmed
- 1 pound **thin-skinned potatoes,** peeled
- ½ cup thinly sliced **green onions,** including green tops
- 1 tablespoon **cornstarch**

**1.** In a 2- to 3-quart pan, combine rice and 2¾ cups water. Bring to a boil over high heat and cook until most of the water is absorbed, 7 to 10 minutes. Turn heat to low, cover, and cook until rice is tender to bite, 10 to 15 minutes longer.

**2.** In 3- to 4-quart pan, bring soy sauce, fresh ginger, sugar, five spice, and 1¾ cups water to a boil over high heat.

**3.** Meanwhile, slice pork into strips about ⅛ inch thick and 2 inches long. Slice potatoes ¼ inch thick.

**4.** When soy mixture is boiling, stir in pork and potatoes. Return to a boil, then cover and simmer over low heat, stirring occasionally, until potatoes are tender when pierced, 15 to 18 minutes. Stir in onions.

**5.** Mix cornstarch with 2 tablespoons water. Add to potato mixture and stir until sauce boils. Ladle into soup bowls and serve with rice.

# side dishes:

■ Coleslaw and cornbread were mentioned often in the same sentence with comfort food; they're obviously favorite side dishes.

## Classic Coleslaw

***Prep and cook time:*** About 5 minutes

***Makes:*** 6 servings

- ⅔ cup **plain nonfat yogurt** or nonfat mayonnaise
- 2 tablespoons **Dijon mustard**
- 2 tablespoons **white wine vinegar**
- 6 cups **coleslaw mix**
- ¼ cup thinly sliced **green onions,** including green tops
  **Salt** and **pepper**

**1.** In a bowl, combine yogurt, mustard, and vinegar.

**2.** Add coleslaw mix and onions, and stir to combine.

**3.** Add salt and pepper to taste.

Per serving: 67 cal., 6.7% (4.5 cal.) from fat; 3.9 g protein; 0.5 g fat (0.1 g sat.); 12 g carbo (0.6 g fiber); 173 mg sodium; 0.5 mg chol.

Per serving: 440 cal., 6.6% (29 cal.) from fat; 17 g protein; 3.2 g fat (0.9 g sat.); 84 g carbo (2.8 g fiber); 636 mg sodium; 25 mg chol.

## Leftover-Lamb Curry

■ "My mother was a very good cook," says **Will Bucklin,** winemaker at King Estate Winery in Eugene, Oregon. "Fortunately, she forced us to eat a lot of foods we didn't want. I was the youngest in the family. A way to get back at my siblings when they teased me was to eat food they hated and pretend I liked it. One of my real favorites, though, was lamb curry. I loved it because it filled the house with smells of garlic, cumin, and curry spices. She made it from meat left over from a roast leg of lamb."

***Prep and cook time:*** About 30 minutes

***Notes:*** Cooked chicken can be substituted for the lamb; increase total broth to 2½ cups.

***Makes:*** 4 servings

- 1½ cups **long-grain white rice**
- 1 pound **cooked lamb,** fat-trimmed

## Buttermilk Cornbread

***Prep and cook time:*** About 25 minutes

***Makes:*** 8 or 9 servings

- 1 cup **all-purpose flour**
- 1 cup **yellow cornmeal**
- ¼ cup **sugar**
- 1 teaspoon **baking soda**
- ¾ teaspoon **salt**
- 1 cup **low-fat buttermilk**
- 2 **large eggs**

**1.** In a bowl, mix flour, cornmeal, sugar, baking soda, and salt.

**2.** With a fork, beat buttermilk and eggs to blend. Add egg mixture to dry ingredients; mix just to moisten. Pour into an 8-inch square or 9-inch-wide round nonstick cake pan.

**3.** Bake in a 400° oven until bread springs back when gently pressed in center, 20 to 22 minutes. Cut into squares or wedges. Serve warm.

Per serving: 162 cal., 14% (22 cal.) from fat; 5.1 g protein; 2.4 g fat (0.9 g sat.); 30 g carbo (1.2 g fiber); 356 mg sodium; 50 mg chol.

- 1 teaspoon **salad oil**
- 1 cup chopped **onion**
- 2 cloves **garlic,** pressed or minced
- 2 tablespoons **curry powder**
- ½ teaspoon **ground cumin**
- 1¾ cups **chicken broth**
- 2 tablespoons **cornstarch**
  **Salt** and **cayenne**
- 1 firm-ripe **banana** (6 oz.), diced
- 1 cup **plain nonfat yogurt**
- ⅔ cup **chutney**
- 1 cup diced **cucumber**
- ½ cup dried **currants**

**1.** In a 2- to 3-quart pan, combine rice and 2¾ cups water. Bring to a boil over high heat and cook until most of the water is absorbed, 7 to 10 minutes. Reduce heat to low, cover, and simmer until rice is tender to bite, 10 to 15 minutes longer.

**2.** Cut the lamb into strips about ¼ inch thick.

**3.** In a 5- to 6-quart pan over medium heat, combine oil, onion, and garlic; stir often until onion begins to brown lightly, 6 to 7 minutes.

**4.** Add curry powder and cumin and stir until spices are fragrant, about 30 seconds.

**5.** Stir in meat. Add 1½ cups broth and bring to a boil over high heat. Mix cornstarch and ¼ cup broth. Stir into pan and stir until boiling resumes. Add salt and cayenne to taste. Spoon curry into a bowl.

**6.** Place condiments—banana, yogurt, chutney, cucumber, and currants—in small bowls. Serve curry with rice and condiments to add to taste.

Per serving: 809 cal., 13% (108 cal.) from fat; 44 g protein; 12 g fat (3.9 g sat.); 128 g carbo (4.1 g fiber); 631 mg sodium; 104 mg chol.

## Mama Locke's Chicken

■ "One of my favorite foods from childhood is still my favorite food today. We call it Mama Locke's chicken. It's fried, and like nothing else I've tasted, because my mother seasoned in her own special way," says the governor of Washington, **Gary Locke,** whose mother came from Hong Kong.
*Prep and cook time:* About 25 minutes
*Makes:* 6 servings

  6  **boned, skinned chicken breast halves** (about 2 lb. total)

  ¼  cup **reduced-sodium soy sauce**

  1  tablespoon **sugar**

  2  cloves **garlic,** pressed or minced

  ½  teaspoon **pepper**

  2  cups **long-grain white rice**

  6  **green onions,** ends trimmed

**1.** Trim and discard fat from chicken. In a plastic food bag, combine chicken, soy sauce, sugar, garlic, and pepper; seal. Let stand 10 to 15 minutes, turning bag occasionally.

**2.** In a 2- to 2½-quart pan, combine rice and 3⅓ cups water. Bring to a boil over high heat and cook until most of the water is absorbed, 7 to 10 minutes. Cover and simmer over low heat, until rice is tender to bite, 10 to 15 minutes longer.

**3.** Set an 11- to 12-inch nonstick frying pan over medium heat. When pan is hot, lift chicken from marinade and place in pan. Cook chicken, turning to brown both sides, until no longer pink in thickest part (cut to test), 6 to 8 minutes total. Lift out chicken and set on a platter; keep warm.

**4.** Pour remaining marinade and ¼ cup water into pan. Stir over high heat until boiling. Pour into a small bowl.

**5.** Serve chicken with rice; garnish with onions. Offer marinade to spoon over rice and chicken.

Per serving: 413 cal., 5.1% (21 cal.) from fat; 40 g protein; 2.3 g fat (0.6 g sat.); 54 g carbo (1 g fiber); 504 mg sodium; 88 mg chol.

## Mother's White Beans

■ "I grew up in Kansas. Mother would make navy beans to go with coleslaw, cornbread, and mashed potatoes—we ate them all on a plate. When I go home, she still makes them for me," says cowboy-poet and wildlife photographer **Mike Logan** of Helena, Montana.
*Prep and cook time:* About 25 minutes
*Makes:* 4 servings

  ¾  cup chopped **onion**

  ⅓  cup chopped **carrot**

  1  clove **garlic,** pressed or minced

  ⅓  cup (2 oz.) coarsely chopped **cooked ham**

  ⅔  cup **chicken** or vegetable **broth**

  2  cans (15 oz. each) **white beans** (small whites or cannellini)

    Chopped **parsley**

**1.** In a 1½- to 2-quart pan, combine onion, carrot, garlic, cooked ham, and broth. Bring to a boil over high heat. Cover and simmer over medium heat until the carrot is soft to bite, about 10 minutes.

**2.** Stir in beans and simmer, covered, over low heat until beans are hot, about 5 minutes. Sprinkle with parsley and serve.

Per serving: 181 cal., 12% (22 cal.) from fat; 16 g protein; 2.4 g fat (0.6 g sat.); 36 g carbo (11 g fiber); 973 mg sodium; 9 mg chol.

## Arabian Meatballs in Broth

■ "I'm Armenian, but I was born in Israel and lived in Iraq," says **Zov Karamardian** of Zov's Bistro in Tustin, California. "When I was growing up, my mother made dumplings with meat inside that she cooked in nice broth. I love that dish (*kouba hamoud*). Every time my mother comes, I make her cook it."
*Prep and cook time:* About 45 minutes
*Makes:* 4 servings

  ½  cup **quick-cooking rice cereal** (½ minute to cook)

  1  cup minced **onion**

  2  tablespoons minced **garlic**

  1½  tablespoons **tomato paste**

  6  cups **beef broth**

  2  tablespoons **long-grain white rice**

Mike Logan still gets a hankering for his mother's white beans.

¾ pound **ground lean** (7% fat or less) **beef**

About ½ teaspoon **salt**

About ¼ teaspoon **pepper**

¼ cup chopped **fresh mint** leaves

2 tablespoons chopped **parsley**

2 tablespoons **lemon juice**

**1.** Mix rice cereal with ⅓ cup cold water; let stand at least 5 minutes.

**2.** Meanwhile, in a 5- to 6-quart nonstick pan, stir half the onion and 1 teaspoon garlic over medium-high heat until limp, about 4 minutes. Stir in tomato paste, broth, and rice. Bring to a boil over high heat, then reduce heat to low, cover, and simmer until rice is tender to bite, 12 to 15 minutes.

**3.** As rice cooks, mix beef with ½ teaspoon salt and ¼ teaspoon pepper.

**4.** Mix half the beef mixture with one-fourth of the rice cereal mixture, remaining onion and garlic, 1 tablespoon mint, and parsley.

**5.** In a food processor, whirl remaining beef mixture and remaining rice cereal mixture until it is a sticky paste.

**6.** Shape each of the meat mixtures into 4 oval pieces. In your palm, flatten 1 piece of the beef paste until it's ¼ inch thick. Lay a coarse-beef oval over the thin piece and fold paste around it, shaping into a 3-inch-long football.

**7.** Repeat to form each meatball, and as shaped, drop into simmering broth.

**8.** Simmer over low heat, covered, turning meatballs once, until no longer pink in center (cut to test), about 10 minutes.

**9.** Add lemon juice, remaining mint, and salt and pepper to taste. Ladle meatball soup into bowls.

Per serving: 290 cal., 20% (57 cal.) from fat; 28 g protein; 6.3 g fat (2.3 g sat.); 29 g carbo (1.2 g fiber); 486 mg sodium; 49 mg chol.

## Creamy Potato Soup

■ "As a kid everything always tasted good to me," says **Al Huffman** of Evergreen, Colorado, who is a rancher and also a Buffalo Bill impersonator. "Everything we ate came off the farm, out of the garden or feed- lot. In the winter we had a lot of potato soup, rich and creamy. Mother sprinkled bacon on top."

*Prep and cook time:* About 30 minutes
*Makes:* 4 servings

3 strips (1½ oz. total) **turkey bacon,** thinly sliced crosswise

1 cup chopped **onion**

1 pound **thin-skinned potatoes,** scrubbed

2 cups **chicken broth**

3 tablespoons **all-purpose flour**

2 cups **low-fat (1%) milk**

¼ cup chopped **parsley**

**Salt** and **pepper**

**1.** In a 5- to 6-quart pan, stir bacon over medium-high heat until lightly browned and crisp, about 10 minutes. Lift from pan with a slotted spoon and drain on paper towels.

**2.** Add onion to pan drippings and stir often until limp, about 3 minutes.

**3.** Meanwhile, cut potatoes into ½-inch cubes.

**4.** Add potatoes and broth to pan. Cover and bring to a boil over high heat. Reduce heat to low and simmer until potatoes are tender when pierced, about 10 minutes, stirring occasionally.

**5.** Blend flour and milk until smooth.

This milk-and-potato soup tastes almost as rich as the one Al Huffman's mom made with cream.

Add to soup and stir over high heat until boiling, about 3 minutes.

**6.** Stir in parsley and ladle soup into bowls. Sprinkle with bacon and season to taste with salt and pepper.

Per serving: 218 cal., 18% (39 cal.) from fat; 10 g protein; 4.3 g fat (1.6 g sat.); 35 g carbo (2.8 g fiber); 269 mg sodium; 14 mg chol.

## Hungarian Goulash

■ "I was the only kid on the block who got Hungarian goulash," says **Catherine Cain,** a naturalist in Divide, Montana. "The name sounded great—like galoshes. My mom is third-generation L.A. Basin. She grew up in Topanga Canyon and played with a lot of children from Eastern Europe there. That's where she got Hungarian goulash from."

*Prep and cook time:* About 30 minutes
*Makes:* 4 servings

¾ pound **boned beef top sirloin,** about 1 inch thick

¼ pound **thin-sliced mushrooms**

1 **onion** (½ lb.), thinly sliced

2 tablespoons **Hungarian** or domestic **paprika**

8 ounces **dried egg noodles**

1 cup **beef broth**

1 tablespoon **cornstarch**

1 cup **nonfat** or low-fat **sour cream**

2 tablespoons chopped **parsley**

**Salt** and **pepper**

1. Trim and discard fat from beef. Cut the meat across the grain into ⅛-inch-thick slices.

2. Place a 12- to 13-inch nonstick frying pan over high heat. When pan is hot, add beef and stir-fry until meat is lightly browned, 2 to 3 minutes. Pour into a bowl.

3. Add mushrooms to pan and stir often until browned, 3 to 4 minutes. Add to beef.

4. Add onion to pan and stir until lightly browned, about 2 minutes. Reduce heat to medium and stir paprika into onion.

5. Meanwhile, cook noodles in about 3 quarts boiling water until barely tender to bite, 4 to 5 minutes. Drain and place on a large platter; keep warm.

6. Mix broth and cornstarch; add to onion mixture and stir just until mixture boils, about 2 minutes.

7. Return beef and mushrooms to pan and stir until hot, about 1½ minutes. Add sour cream and stir just until hot, about 1 minute.

8. Spoon meat mixture over hot noodles. Sprinkle with chopped parsley and season to taste with salt and pepper.

Per serving: 449 cal., 14% (61 cal.) from fat; 33 g protein; 6.8 g fat (1.9 g sat.); 62 g carbo (2.9 g fiber); 134 mg sodium; 112 mg chol.

## Tea Cakes

■ As a child, **Wallace Yvonne McNair,** the administrator and curator of the Black American West Museum & Heritage Center in Denver, often craved this snack—a glass of milk and one or two of the big, soft, jam-dotted cookies that her mother called tea cakes.

**Prep and cook time:** About 25 minutes

**Makes:** 9 cookies

- 1 tablespoon **butter** or margarine, at room temperature
- ¼ cup **sugar**
- ½ teaspoon grated **lemon** peel
- 2 **large egg** whites
- 2 tablespoons **nonfat milk**
- 1 teaspoon **vanilla**
- 1 teaspoon **baking powder**

Cinnamon-scented French toast made Chava Lee feel like a queen.

- 1 cup **all-purpose flour**
- 2¼ teaspoons **raspberry** or strawberry **jam**

1. Beat butter with sugar and lemon peel until well blended.

2. Beat in egg whites, milk, and vanilla.

3. Beat in baking powder.

4. Add flour and stir until batter is evenly moistened.

5. Drop batter in 2-tablespoon portions about 3 inches apart on nonstick baking sheets.

6. Onto the center of each cookie, spoon ¼ teaspoon jam.

7. Bake in a 350° oven until cookies are pale brown on top and golden on bottom, 13 to 15 minutes. Transfer to racks to cool. Serve warm or cool.

Per cookie: 94 cal., 14% (13 cal.) from fat; 2.3 g protein; 1.4 g fat (0.8 g sat.); 18 g carbo (0.4 g fiber); 82 mg sodium; 3.5 mg chol.

## French Toast for a Queen

■ "Sometimes I got to eat French toast on the couch. In our house that was special, since we had a formal dining room and usually dressed for dinner. The toast

Big tea cakes were Wallace Yvonne McNair's favorite childhood snack.

came on a tray, and I was a queen," says **Chava Lee** of the Silverbow Inn and Restaurant in Juneau, Alaska.

**Prep and cook time:** About 25 minutes

**Makes:** 4 servings

- 2 **large eggs**
- 2 **large egg** whites
- ¾ cup **nonfat milk**
- 1 tablespoon **vanilla**
- 2 teaspoons **sugar**
- ½ teaspoon **ground cinnamon**
- ¼ teaspoon **ground nutmeg**
- **Cooking oil spray**
- 8 slices **sweet French** or challah **bread,** about 1 inch thick (8 to 12 oz. total)
- **Powdered sugar**
- **Maple syrup**
- **Orange** wedges

1. In a shallow bowl, whisk to blend eggs, egg whites, milk, vanilla, sugar, cinnamon, and nutmeg.

2. Lightly mist a 10- by 15-inch nonstick pan with cooking oil spray.

3. Soak bread thoroughly on each side, a few pieces at a time, in egg mixture.

4. Place slices slightly apart in a single layer in baking pan.

5. Bake in a 500° oven until toast is golden on bottom, about 5 minutes. With a wide spatula, turn slices over and bake until other side is browned, about 3 to 4 minutes longer. Transfer hot French toast to plates.

6. Sprinkle with powdered sugar, drizzle with maple syrup, and serve with orange wedges, squeezing juice onto toast.

Per serving: 237 cal., 17% (41 cal.) from fat; 11 g protein; 4.6 g fat (1.2 g sat.); 35 g carbo (1.5 g fiber); 428 mg sodium; 107 mg chol. ◆

# Kitchen Cabinet

### READERS' RECIPES TESTED IN SUNSET'S KITCHENS

BY LINDA LAU ANUSASANANAN

### Cranberry Crisp Bars

Jim and Ivy Hermon, Alameda, California

Looking for a nutritious snack for their weekend hikes, Jim and Ivy Hermon came up with this less sweet, adult version of children's cereal-and-marshmallow treats.

*Prep and cook time:* About 30 minutes, plus cooling

*Makes:* 2 dozen bars

- ⅓ cup **sesame seed**
- ⅓ cup **hulled sunflower seed,** chopped
- ⅓ cup chopped **pecans** or walnuts
- ⅓ cup chopped **almonds**
- ⅓ cup **unsweetened shredded dried coconut**
- 3½ cups **crisp toasted rice cereal**
- 1 cup **sweetened dried cranberries,** chopped
- 3 tablespoons **peanut butter**
  About 2 tablespoons **butter** or margarine
- 7 cups (12 oz.) **miniature marshmallows**

**1.** In a 10- to 12-inch frying pan over medium heat, stir sesame seed, sunflower seed, pecans, and almonds until sesame seed is pale gold, about 3 minutes. Add coconut and stir until sesame seed and coconut are golden, about 2 minutes. Stir in cereal and cranberries. Remove from heat.

**2.** Meanwhile, in a 5- to 6-quart pan, combine peanut butter, 2 tablespoons butter, and marshmallows. Stir often over low heat until marshmallows melt and mixture is smooth, about 5 minutes.

**3.** Add cereal mixture and mix quickly to coat evenly. Pour into a buttered 9- by 13-inch pan or dish. Cover with foil and, using pot holders to protect your hands, press firmly to make an even layer. At once, peel off foil.

**4.** Cool or chill until mixture is set. Cut into 24 bars, each about 1½ by 3 inches. Serve, or store airtight at room temperature up to 3 days.

Per bar: 143 cal., 42% (60 cal.) from fat; 2.4 g protein; 6.7 g fat (1.7 g sat.); 20 g carbo (1.1 g fiber); 66 mg sodium; 3 mg chol.

### Winter Squash Pasta

Jeff and Tammy Bourne, Sacramento

Pasta lover Tammy Bourne created this squash pasta sauce as a change from those using tomatoes. Mildly sweet and loaded with vitamins, it just suits the preferences of her toddler. Bourne serves the golden pasta dish with green vegetables.

*Prep and cook time:* About 1 hour

*Makes:* 6 to 8 servings

- 1 **butternut squash** (2 lb.)
- 1 **onion** (6 oz.)
- 2 teaspoons **olive oil**
- ⅓ cup **pine nuts** or slivered almonds
- 1 cup **chicken** or vegetable **broth**
- 1 cup **half-and-half** (light cream)
  **Salt** and **pepper**
- 1 pound **dried linguine**
  Fresh-grated or ground **nutmeg**
  **Grated parmesan cheese**

**1.** Cut squash in half lengthwise. Scoop out and discard seeds. Peel onion and cut in half. Rub cut surfaces of vegetables with oil. Place squash and onion, cut sides down, in a 10- by 15-inch pan.

**2.** Bake in a 350° oven until squash and onion are tender when pressed, 40 to 45 minutes.

**3.** Meanwhile, in a 3- to 4-quart pan over medium heat, stir pine nuts until golden, about 5 minutes. Pour into a bowl.

**4.** Scoop flesh from cooked squash. Purée squash smoothly with onion in a food processor (or in a blender, a

### Crab Pot

Julie Lee, Seattle

Julie Lee grew up in the Puget Sound area, so it's not surprising that she loves crab. For special events, Lee heats the shellfish in broth laced with dry vermouth and garlic, and offers garlic bread to sop it up.

*Prep and cook time:* 10 minutes

*Makes:* 4 servings

- 1 can (14 oz.) **reduced-sodium chicken broth**
- ¾ cup **dry vermouth**
- 2 tablespoons **butter** or margarine (optional)
- 2 tablespoons chopped **parsley**
- 1 tablespoon **soy sauce**
- 1 tablespoon **lemon juice**
- 1 tablespoon minced **garlic**
- 2 **cooked Dungeness crabs** (about 3 lb. total), cleaned and cracked

**1.** In a 6- to 8-quart covered pan over high heat, bring chicken broth, vermouth, butter, parsley, soy sauce, lemon juice, and garlic to a boil.

**2.** Add crab pieces. Cover and simmer over medium-low heat, stirring occasionally, just until crab is hot, about 4 minutes.

**3.** Spoon crab pieces into wide bowls; ladle broth over crab.

Per serving: 145 cal., 9.7% (14 cal.) from fat; 18 g protein; 1.5 g fat (0.2 g sat.); 2 g carbo (0.1 g fiber); 725 mg sodium; 81 mg chol.

portion at a time, using some of the broth to help mix). Add puréed squash mixture to the 3- to 4-quart pan and stir in broth, half-and-half, and salt and pepper to taste.

**5.** Stir over low heat until hot, about 5 minutes; keep warm.

**6.** Meanwhile, cook linguine in 2 to 3 quarts boiling water over high heat just until the pasta is barely tender to bite, 7

Dried cranberries bring a refreshing tang to this cereal-cookie classic.

JAMES CARRIER

Cracked crab, warmed in a flavorful broth, is table-ready in less than 10 minutes.

PHOTO BY JAMES CARRIER AT VINTAGE OAKS, MENLO PARK, CA

**Pepper**

**1.** Cut ribs into serving-size pieces. Place in an 11- by 17-inch roasting pan.

**2.** Mix soy sauce, marmalade, and honey. Pour over ribs; turn to coat.

**3.** Cover pan tightly. Bake in a 350° oven for 1 hour. Turn ribs over, cover, and continue baking until the meat is very tender when pierced, about 30 minutes longer.

**4.** With a slotted spoon, transfer pork ribs to a serving dish. Skim and discard fat from pan juices. Pour pan juices into a bowl and serve to spoon over pork. Add pepper to taste.

Per serving: 426 cal., 38% (162 cal.) from fat; 34 g protein; 18 g fat (6.4 g sat.); 32 g carbo (0 g fiber); 1,250 mg sodium; 112 mg chol.

## Sugar- and Nut-glazed Brie

### Phyllis Kidd, Ojai, California

Because her guests keep asking for the recipe, cooking contest winner Phyllis Kidd has printed copies of this easy appetizer to hand out. The glazed nuts coat the skin of the cheese, winning over the most brie-shy guest.

**Prep and cook time:** About 15 minutes
**Makes:** 6 to 8 appetizer servings

- 2 tablespoons firmly packed **brown sugar**
- 2 tablespoons coarsely chopped **pecans** or almonds
- 1½ teaspoons **brandy**
- 1 firm-ripe **whole brie cheese** (8 oz.)
  **Crackers**
  **Golden Delicious apple** slices

**1.** Stir together the brown sugar, chopped pecans, and brandy.

**2.** Place cheese in a baking dish just slightly larger than the width of the cheese. Bake in a 425° oven just until cheese begins to soften in the center, about 6 minutes.

**3.** Evenly sprinkle sugar mixture over cheese. Bake until sugar melts and cheese is melted in center (cut to test), 3 to 5 minutes longer.

**4.** Scoop hot cheese onto crackers and apple slices to eat.

Per serving: 121 cal., 67% (81 cal.) from fat; 6 g protein; 9 g fat (0.1 g sat.); 3.8 g carbo (0.1 g fiber); 180 mg sodium; 28 mg chol. ◆

to 9 minutes. Drain and pour pasta into a wide bowl.

**7.** Pour squash mixture over pasta. Dust with nutmeg and sprinkle with nuts; add cheese to taste.

Per serving: 345 cal., 23% (79 cal.) from fat; 11 g protein; 8.8 g fat (3 g sat.); 58 g carbo (4.1 g fiber); 34 mg sodium; 12 mg chol.

## Ming Spareribs

### Elaine Boehmer, Seattle

Elaine Boehmer first tried orange marmalade and ground ginger to flavor this pork, but the dry, powdery ginger just floated on top. Now she uses ginger marmalade, and the sauce clings deliciously. Serve the oven-braised ribs with rice to soak up the flavorful juices.

**Prep and cook time:** About 1¾ hours
**Makes:** 6 to 8 servings

- 5 pounds **country-style pork ribs,** fat trimmed
- 1 cup **reduced-sodium soy sauce**
- ⅔ cup **ginger marmalade** or apricot preserves
- ⅓ cup **honey**

Top intense chocolate wedges of Dark Velvet Torte with raspberries and softly whipped cream (recipe on page 36).

JAMES CARRIER

# February

# foodguide

BY JERRY ANNE DI VECCHIO

## cache

Wandering with Neela Paniz through the extensive, unofficial Little India in Artesia, California, opened doors for me to a fascinating cuisine. This Indian-born chef-owner of L.A.'s popular Bombay Cafe knows her stuff. She identified the contents of fragrant bags, mysterious jars, unfamiliar herbs, and more. Neela also introduced me to this stainless steel spice canister, or masala box, compactly filled with small cups of the same metal. Remove just one lid and a collection of spices is instantly accessible. The airtight lid, with or without a window, protects the spices' pungency. This 8-inch-wide model costs about $20. Various styles and sizes are sold in Indian-food and cookware stores. Or order a canister from New World Spices; (800) 347-7795.

RIGHT: RICHARD JUNG    LEFT AND BELOW: JAMES CARRIER

## QUICK TRICK
# Convenience casserole

■ At least three brands of falafel mix—seasoned garbanzo flour—are available at my regular market. And although the mix is made for frying into crisp balls, it has another nifty, neater use. A falafel mix contains some leavening, often other flours, and spices—typically dominated by cumin. Mixed with water, eggs, and a few fresh seasonings, then baked, it becomes a tasty casserole that fills the same role as baked beans or spicy cornbread. I like it with yogurt and grilled lamb or juicy baked lamb shanks.

### Falafel Casserole

***Prep and cook time:*** About 10 minutes to assemble, 30 minutes to bake

***Notes:*** Serve baked falafel with nonfat yogurt mixed with chopped fresh dill or mint.

***Makes:*** 4 servings

- 1 cup (5 oz.) **falafel mix**
- 2 **large eggs**
- ½ teaspoon grated **lemon** peel
- 2 tablespoons **lemon juice**
- ½ cup chopped **parsley**

**1.** In a bowl, use a fork or whisk to blend falafel mix with 1¼ cups water, eggs, lemon peel, lemon juice, and parsley.

**2.** Pour into an oiled, shallow 8-inch-wide casserole; mixture should be about 1 inch deep.

**3.** Bake in a 350° oven until firm in the center when pressed, about 30 minutes.

**4.** Cut or scoop out portions of falafel to serve.

Per serving: 146 cal., 22% (32 cal.) from fat; 14 g protein; 3.6 g fat (0.8 g sat.); 20 g carbo (5.5 g fiber); 620 mg sodium; 106 mg chol.

1 can (7 oz.) **diced green chilies**

½ cup **shredded reduced-fat** (made with 2% milk) **cheddar cheese**

1 firm-ripe **avocado** (½ lb.)

1 tablespoon **lime juice**

**Green tomatillo sauce**

**1.** With a sharp knife, ¾ to 1 inch in from crust rim, cut down to but not through bottom crust. Then cut a circle inside rim of loaf.

**2.** With your fingers, reach down into the cut and pull out center of loaf. Then make the base of the hollow level by pulling out excess bread.

**3.** Brush the interior of the loaf with enough butter to lightly coat. Wrap the crust with foil.

**4.** Bake in a 350° oven until interior is lightly toasted, 7 to 9 minutes.

**5.** Meanwhile, in a food processor or blender, combine yogurt cheese, eggs, ½ cup milk, flour, ground chili, and ¼ teaspoon salt. Whirl until smooth. Stir green chilies into cheese mixture.

**6.** Set hot crust on a baking sheet and pour filling into it. Add remaining ¼ cup milk, stir with a fork, then push enough ½-inch chunks of bread (torn from the center) into the filling to bring it up to the crust rim.

**7.** Return loaf to oven. Bake until center is firmly set when loaf is gently shaken, 40 to 45 minutes. Remove loaf from oven and immediately sprinkle with cheddar cheese.

**8.** Let cool at least 15 minutes. Remove foil. Peel and thinly slice or dice avocado, mix with lime juice, and arrange on chili loaf. Cut loaf and serve with tomatillo sauce and salt to taste.

Per serving: 286 cal., 35% (99 cal.) from fat; 13 g protein; 11 g fat (4 g sat.); 32 g carbo (2.1 g fiber); 694 mg sodium; 83 mg chol.

*Nonfat yogurt cheese.* Line a colander with 2 layers of **cheesecloth** or 1 layer of muslin and set in a larger bowl, elevating the colander at least 1 inch from bottom of bowl. Spoon 1 quart **plain nonfat yogurt** (made without gelatin) into cloth. Seal bowl and colander with plastic wrap. Chill for 2 to 4 days, discarding the liquid whey as it accumulates. Use the cheese or scoop into a container and store airtight up to a week; freeze to store longer. Drain whey before using cheese. Makes about 1½ cups.

Per ½ cup: 106 cal., 0% (0 cal.) from fat; 12 g protein; 0 g fat; 11 g carbo (0 g fiber); 106 mg sodium; 0 mg chol.

## A TASTE OF THE WEST

# The whole loaf

■ There's something dated, hokey— and fun—about filling a hollowed-out loaf with food. My mother used a specially ordered round loaf to hold tiny sandwiches for her tea parties in the '40s. My, how the oohs and aahs of the peplum-waisted ladies in hats with perky veils filled me with pride when she presented this work of art, which I had helped make.

I still get a kick out of serving food in a loaf, but my approach has grown less fussy. One main dish that's quickly assembled and certainly not fussy uses a hollowed-out loaf as the crust for chili quiche. The creamy filling can be reasonably lean if you drain nonfat yogurt for the cheese. Otherwise neufchâtel cheese works fine.

Serve the chili loaf with coleslaw or green salad and toast made from the center you've pulled out of the bread.

## Chili Loaf

*Prep and cook time:* About 10 minutes to assemble, 50 minutes to bake

*Notes:* For additional garnish, use slivered green onions.

*Makes:* 4 to 6 servings

1 **round** or oval **French bread loaf** (1 lb.)

About 1 tablespoon melted **butter** or olive oil

1 cup drained **nonfat yogurt cheese** (directions follow) or 1 package (8 oz.) neufchâtel (light cream) cheese

2 **large eggs**

¾ cup **nonfat milk**

¼ cup **all-purpose flour**

½ teaspoon **ground (mild) California chili** or paprika

About ¼ teaspoon **salt**

LEFT: RICHARD JUNG    BELOW: JAMES CARRIER

## Clam Soup for Tomoko

***Prep and cook time:*** 35 to 40 minutes

***Notes:*** Regular mushrooms, including their stems, can be used in place of the shiitakes; mustard greens can be used instead of mizuna. Season to taste with soy sauce.

***Makes:*** 4 servings

- ¼  pound **fresh shiitake mushrooms**
- 4  cups **chicken broth**
- ½  cup **short-** or medium-**grain white rice**
- 1  **onion** (8 oz.), chopped
- 24  **clams suitable for steaming** (about 2¾ lb. total)
- ¼  pound **mizuna,** coarse stems removed and leaves rinsed

**1.** Rinse and drain shiitakes. Trim off and discard stems. Thinly slice mushroom caps.

**2.** In a 4- to 5-quart pan, combine mushrooms, broth, rice, onion, and 2 cups water. Cover and bring to a boil over high heat. Reduce heat and simmer 10 minutes.

**3.** Meanwhile, scrub clams under cool running water. Discard any that do not close when touched.

**4.** Add clams to pan, turn heat to high, cover, and bring to a boil again. Reduce heat and simmer until clams open, about 10 minutes more.

**5.** Stir in mizuna, then ladle soup into wide bowls.

Per serving: 189 cal., 11% (20 cal.) from fat; 13 g protein; 2.2 g fat (0.8 g sat.); 30 g carbo (1.6 g fiber); 140 mg sodium; 20 mg chol.

## AMONG FRIENDS
# Shopping for soup

■ After I made a sweep of Seattle's Pike Place Market to create dinner for a company of local friends, one guest—Tomoko Matsuno—was intrigued by this shop-and-serve concept. She invited me to stroll through her family's market, the magnificently stocked Uwajimaya, and create an extemporaneous meal with my choices. Although the menu followed no specific ethnic pattern, what emerged as Tomo and I cooked was quite Asian from my perspective, very Western from hers. The refreshing and easy soup from that meal has had many a repeat performance.

## BOOK NOTES
# The spice of life—and death

■ Pirates, plunder, chicanery, murder, genocide, betrayal, fatal scurvy, starvation, hideous torture and subjugation in the name of God, and the puzzle of mapping the earth solved—all for nutmeg. This modest little oval of aromatics will never look the same to me now that I've read Charles Corn's *The Scents of Eden: A Narrative of the Spice Trade* (Kodansha International, New York, 1998; $25).

Corn, a travel writer, tells the gripping, bloodcurdling story of a commerce that brought staggering wealth to some and changed the world for all.

His facts make the piracy fictions of Robert Louis Stevenson look like the children's stories they are. Corn's larger-than-life characters include Ferdinand Magellan and Sir Francis Drake playing themselves without vanity varnish, and supervillains whose names are mercifully forgotten by most.

Corn's writing is particularly vivid because he trod upon the mysterious, illusive islands where nutmeg, cloves, and other coveted spices originated—now quiet, backwater destinations—and followed their turbulent history into dusty archives around the globe.

## PRODUCT
# Tropical cool

■ Step back, strawberry. Move over, orange. Here's the scoop on sorbets—and even ice creams. The tropicals are taking hold. Mango's commonplace. Passion fruit is getting there. Guava, guanabana, mamey, and pitahaya (cactus fruit), along with other fruits we rarely, if ever, encounter fresh, are flavoring sorbets and ice creams in the freezer cases of fancy, natural-food, and Latino supermarkets. What's behind the avalanche? The greater availability of tropical fruit or their frozen pulp, even from the Amazon. Brands we're seeing: Jaguar Gourmet Rainforest from Denver; Sweet Nothings from Junction City, Oregon; Cascadian Farm from Rockport, Washington; Howler Rainforest from San Francisco; and Paradisio Sorbet from Santa Barbara. Even Ben & Jerry's and Häagen-Dazs are part of this tropical blizzard. ◆

# The Wine Guide

BY KAREN MacNEIL

RICK MARIANI

## The cold truth about Anderson Valley

■ The first time I drove to the small coastal town of Mendocino, it was twilight, but I had pancakes on my mind—the ones I intended to eat the next morning at a restaurant called Cafe Beaujolais, which sounded like a wine bar but was famous for its breakfasts.

When the evening light began glistening through the redwoods in luminous shafts, though, and I smelled the ocean in the air, tomorrow's pancakes became irrelevant; I wanted a glass of wine.

I stopped the car in front of an agreeably dilapidated inn. The proprietor poured me a glass of Roederer Estate sparkling wine. It shimmered like the twilight outside.

Though I didn't realize it then, I was in one of Northern California's most beautiful and secluded wine valleys—150 miles north of San Francisco and reachable only by a winding two-lane country road. Sandwiched between two ridges, Anderson Valley is like a pants pocket slanting inward from the Pacific Ocean just below Mendocino.

It's the ocean, in fact, that explains much of the valley's success as a wine region. Day after day, cool breezes roll in off the sea, filling the region with giant puff balls of fog. If the vines here could wear sweaters, they probably would, for it is often quite chilly.

Some grape varieties, however, thrive in cool places: Pinot Noir, Chardonnay, Gewürztraminer, and Riesling, for instance. Plant them someplace hot and they make wine with all the complexity of a Kleenex.

This climate magic holds for sparkling wine too, which, after all, is made mostly from Pinot Noir and Chardonnay. Cool-climate grapes give sparklers the potential for elegance and nuance. Absent the big chill, a sparkling wine becomes a sparkling orangutan.

It's no surprise, then, that the Anderson Valley is home to three of California's best sparkling-wine producers—Roederer Estate, Scharffenberger Cellars, and Navarro Vineyards. In fact, when the French Champagne firm Louis Roederer decided to make a second bubbly, president Jean-Claude Rouzaud

## ANDERSON VALLEY STARS: SPARKLING AND STILL

■ **Navarro Vineyards Brut nonvintage,** $16.50. Gossamer, sheer. Here's utter finesse. (The small amount of sparkling wine Navarro makes is available only from the winery; 800/537-9463.)

■ **Roederer Estate L'Ermitage Brut 1991,** $33. Melts in your mouth. Possibly the most complex, creamy sparkler made in California.

■ **Scharffenberger Brut Rosé nonvintage,** $16.99. A yummy, light explosion of strawberries and pomegranates.

■ **Greenwood Ridge Merlot 1994,** $20. From the warmer hillsides, this Merlot has sleek mocha-berry flavors.

■ **Handley Estate Chardonnay 1995,** $16. A creamy, lemony, every-night wine.

■ **Lazy Creek Gewürztraminer 1996,** $9. Pears, roses, and jasmine with spices.

■ **Navarro Vineyards Gewürztraminer 1996,** $14. An exotic Asian dream: rose petals, gardenias, and litchis.

searched the world for a decade to find just the right cool, Champagne-like climate to nourish the vines. In 1981, Rouzaud discovered the Anderson Valley and promptly bought 580 acres.

Until Roederer and Scharffenberger arrived in the early '80s, the Anderson Valley was a well-kept secret. A handful of tiny, mostly family-run operations sold wine to consumers willing to make the pilgrimage to their back door. In this way, Navarro Vineyards, Lazy Creek Vineyard, Handley Cellars, Greenwood Ridge Vineyards, and several others developed cultlike followings for their Gewürztraminers, Rieslings, Chardonnays, and Pinot Noirs.

The region's 15 wineries still get a lot of their business "from the road." Visiting the Anderson Valley is a great excuse to make the drive to Mendocino. Or maybe going to Mendocino is a great excuse to visit the Anderson Valley. Either way, you'll drink some very good wines. (And even though Cafe Beaujolais is no longer open for breakfast, you still have a shot at those pancakes: the restaurant sells its famous mix to tote home.) ◆

## Navarro knows juice too

*Zowie.* That was my reaction when I tasted Navarro Vineyards 1997 grape juice ($6.50), made from Pinot Noir grapes. Creamy-textured and rich but not too sweet—Welch's this is not!

Tasting such a delicious juice made me wonder: given all the newly reported health benefits of drinking wine, where does grape juice stand?

New research by University of California at Davis wine chemist Andrew Waterhouse shows that wine (particularly red wine) contains more key heart-friendly antioxidants than most fruits, fruit juices, and vegetables. Alas, grape juice has significantly lower levels of antioxidants than red wine—even a little less than white wine, for that matter.

But then, Navarro's juice tastes so good, antioxidants really aren't the point. — *K. M.*

CHOCOLATE POTS DE CRÈME
The essence of melted chocolate
is coolly captured in tiny cups
under clouds of cream.

# For the love of chocolate

## Its secrets are being revealed and extolled

■ "Think of chocolate like wine," suggests Alice Medrich, author, chocolate guru, and founder of the San Francisco Bay Area's Cocolat shops. As with wine, the world of chocolate is one of varietal distinctions, origins, unique blends, and manufacturing methods. But these influences on the character and quality of the confection have long been secrets. Now the nuances are becoming public, and a more aware consumer is bent on obtaining higher-quality chocolate.

Joseph Schmidt, a San Francisco confectioner, uses coffee as a comparison. He notes that chocolate is going through changes similar to those that upgraded coffee in recent years as consumers became aware of varietals, origins, and specialized styles. "People are looking for more intense flavor, more bitterness, less sugar. Dark chocolate is growing."

It's no secret that in the past, European chocolate met a different standard than most American-made confection. European makers and consumers grew aware before we did that it matters what kinds of cocoa beans go into the product, and where they were grown (short of revealing formulas, European chocolate labels often name the types and origins of the cocoa beans). But noted Seattle chocolatier Fran Bigelow observes that Americans' taste for chocolate has gotten more sophisticated with international travel. Our interest has attracted artisans right here to ply their skills in chocolate factories, and they are spilling the beans, so to speak—dispensing more information on labels about their premium chocolates.

And it all starts with the cocoa beans, adds Bigelow. Follow their trek from pod to chocolate on page 37.

Just for the record, chocolate doesn't mean just milk chocolate anymore. Medrich, Schmidt, and Bigelow—and more and more Americans—prefer dark, rich chocolate for eating and cooking. Simple recipes, such as the following, show off a chocolate best. You can use bittersweet or semisweet, the latter of which is usually sweeter, although the FDA definition is the same for both. Keep in mind that chocolate, like butter, absorbs odors and flavors readily, so wrap it well and store in a cool, dry place.

## Chocolate Pots de Crème

***Prep and cook time:*** About 8 minutes, plus 30 to 45 minutes to chill

***Notes:*** If making ahead, cover and chill up to 1 day. For creamiest texture, let desserts stand at room temperature about 30 minutes before eating. Serve topped with small spoonfuls of sweetened, softly whipped cream and more finely chopped chocolate.

***Makes:*** 4 or 5 servings

- 6 ounces **bittersweet** or semisweet **chocolate,** chopped (about 1 cup)
- 1 **large egg**
- ¾ cup **whipping cream**

**1.** In a food processor or blender, whirl chocolate until finely chopped. Pour into a bowl.

**2.** Add the egg to the food processor or blender.

**3.** In a 2-cup glass measure, heat whipping cream in a microwave oven at full power (100%) until cream boils, 1½ to 2 minutes.

**4.** With processor or blender on high speed, add boiling cream to egg. Check temperature of mixture with an instant-read thermometer; if below 160°, pour mixture back into glass measure and reheat in microwave oven at full power just until it reaches 160°, stirring and checking at 15-second intervals.

**5.** Combine hot cream mixture and chopped chocolate in blender or processor; whirl until smooth, about 1 minute.

**6.** Pour chocolate mixture into 4 or 5 ramekins (½-cup size). Chill until softly set, 30 to 45 minutes.

Per serving: 286 cal., 76% (216 cal.) from fat; 4.4 g protein; 24 g fat (14 g sat.); 20 g carbo (0.8 g fiber); 25 mg sodium; 82 mg chol.

BY LINDA LAU ANUSASANANAN • PHOTOGRAPHS BY JAMES CARRIER

DARK VELVET TORTE is intense chocolate that's barely cakelike enough to cut. Wedges beg for raspberries with a sash of softly whipped cream.

## Chocolate Truffle Bites

***Prep and cook time:*** About 6 minutes, plus chilling

***Notes:*** If making ahead, store airtight up to 1 week in the refrigerator or 1 month in the freezer.

***Makes:*** About 32 pieces

- 6 ounces **bittersweet** or semisweet **chocolate,** chopped (about 1 cup)
- 6 tablespoons **whipping cream**
- 2 tablespoons **unsweetened cocoa**

**1.** Combine chocolate and cream in a microwave-safe container. Heat in a microwave oven at 50 percent power, stirring twice, until chocolate is soft, 1½ to 2 minutes total. Remove from oven and stir until mixture is smooth.

**2.** Using plastic wrap, smoothly line the bottom and at least 1 inch up the sides of a 4- by 8-inch loaf pan.

**3.** Pour chocolate mixture into pan. Chill up to 1 hour or freeze up to 30 minutes until firm when pressed.

**4.** Sprinkle cocoa over a sheet of waxed paper on a cutting board. Lift chocolate slab out of pan and turn over onto cocoa; peel off plastic wrap.

**5.** With a knife, immediately cut slab into ¾-inch squares (some chocolates are too brittle to cut neatly; irregular pieces are fine).

**6.** Lift edges of waxed paper and tilt back and forth to completely coat chocolate pieces with cocoa. Lift truffles, shake off excess cocoa, and put truffles on a serving dish.

**7.** Serve cold or at room temperature.

Per piece: 35 cal., 71% (25 cal.) from fat; 0.5 g protein; 2.8 g fat (1.5 g sat.); 3.2 g carbo (0.2 g fiber); 1 mg sodium; 3.1 mg chol.

## Chocolate Sauce

***Prep and cook time:*** About 5 minutes

***Notes:*** Serve warm or cool over anything that goes with chocolate, or use as a dip for strawberries.

***Makes:*** About ¾ cup

- 3 ounces **bittersweet** or semisweet **chocolate,** chopped (about ½ cup)

  About ⅓ cup **whipping cream**

**1.** In a microwave-safe container, combine chocolate and ⅓ cup cream. Heat in a microwave oven at 50 percent power, stirring twice, until chocolate is soft, 1 to 1½ minutes total. Remove from oven and stir until sauce is smooth.

**2.** If sauce is thicker than you like, stir in more cream, a little at a time, to achieve desired consistency. Heat briefly in microwave oven to rewarm.

Per tablespoon: 54 cal., 76% (41 cal.) from fat; 0.6 g protein; 4.5 g fat (2.6 g sat.); 4.1 g carbo (0.2 g fiber); 2.2 mg sodium; 7.3 mg chol.

## Dark Velvet Torte

***Prep and cook time:*** About 35 minutes

***Notes:*** If making ahead, cool cake, cover airtight, and chill up to 1 day. For best texture, let cake stand at room temperature about 1 hour before serving.

***Makes:*** 8 to 10 servings

- 8 ounces **bittersweet** or semisweet **chocolate,** chopped (about 1⅓ cups)
- ½ cup (¼ lb.) **butter,** cut into ½-inch chunks
- 4 **large eggs,** separated
- 2 teaspoons **all-purpose flour**
- ¼ teaspoon **cream of tartar**
- 1 tablespoon **sugar**

  Softly **whipped cream,** sweetened to taste

  **Raspberries,** rinsed and drained

**1.** Place chocolate and butter in a microwave-safe bowl. Heat in a microwave oven at 50 percent power, stirring twice, until chocolate is soft, 3 to 4 minutes total. Remove from oven; stir until mixture is smoothly blended.

**2.** Add egg yolks and flour to chocolate mixture; whisk until smooth.

**3.** In a bowl, combine egg whites and cream of tartar. Beat with a mixer on high speed until whites are foamy. Beat, gradually adding sugar, until whites hold stiff, glossy peaks.

**4.** Add about a fourth of the beaten whites to chocolate mixture; stir to mix. Add remaining whites and gently fold into chocolate mixture until evenly incorporated. Scrape mixture into an 8-inch cake pan with removable rim. Spread batter smooth.

**5.** Bake in a 350° oven until torte puffs slightly and center barely jiggles when pan is gently shaken, 18 to 20 minutes. Cool at least 1 hour in pan on a rack (torte sinks slightly).

**6.** Slide a sharp knife between torte and pan. Remove pan rim.

**7.** Cut torte into wedges and transfer to plates. Spoon whipped cream onto each serving and garnish with berries.

Per serving: 229 cal., 75% (171 cal.) from fat; 4.2 g protein; 19 g fat (11 g sat.); 15 g carbo (0.5 g fiber); 119 mg sodium; 110 mg chol.

# From beans to bars

■ Cocoa trees grow in a tropical belt that undulates across the equator around the world; production areas include Central and South America, the Caribbean, Africa, Southeast Asia, and, for the last decade, Hawaii.

The cocoa (also called cacao) tree, *Theobroma cacao,* has two main varieties, Criollo and Forastero. Criollo cocoa trees, which are finicky, are planted on a limited scale and sparingly produce beans highly valued for their aroma, essential oils, and complexity. Criollos, native to Venezuela, grow in South and Central America, Southeast Asia, and Hawaii.

Forastero cocoa trees, on the other hand, flourish readily and are very fruitful, producing 90 percent of the world's cocoa beans—but the beans are less distinctive than Criollo beans. The top producers are in Africa (Republic of Côte d'Ivoire, Ghana, Nigeria, and Cameroon), Indonesia, Malaysia, Ecuador, and Brazil.

Once extracted from pods that grow on the trees, cocoa beans are put through a natural fermentation process, then sun-dried.

In the hands of the manufacturer, they become chocolate: Roasting deepens their color and flavor. Heavy rollers crush them into a dark, gooey chocolate liquor that's roughly half cocoa solids (which give the chocolate its unique flavors) and half cocoa butter (which makes chocolate melt-in-your-mouth smooth). The liquor is flavored with sugar, vanilla, lecithin (an emulsifier), and other ingredients. Then for hours, or even days, this coarse mass is kneaded until it is an aromatic, thick, silky liquid. This critical step—called conching—determines a chocolate's texture.

Finally, a warm river of molten dark chocolate flows into molds to cool into shiny slabs for eating or cooking.

A few manufacturers, such as Hawaiian Vintage (Hawaii), El Rey (Venezuela), and Valrhona (France), produce chocolate from specific cocoa beans and specific locations (estates or appellations—think wine), and some of the facts are on the label. The majority of chocolate, however, is a blend of varieties, and the formulas are trademarked secrets. But sophistication of processing is becoming an important part of the chocolate scene, especially here in the West. A few manufacturers are customizing chocolate to bring out more complexity in flavors, like John Scharffenberger and Robert Steinberg at Sharffen Berger in South San Francisco.

## A BITTERSWEET TASTING

■ We invited chocolate amateurs and professionals to rate two dozen plain bittersweet and semisweet chocolates in a blind tasting. The professionals were precise about what they liked—rich, balanced overall flavor and a smooth, pleasant meltdown in the mouth. They downgraded chocolates with off-flavors from the beans or flavor defects from processing. The amateurs just went for taste and texture.

Their collective favorites, in alphabetical order:

***Belgian Recipe Gourmet Chocolate.*** Good base chocolate flavor for chips. Nice acidity, along with citrus and honey flavors; smooth.

***Callebaut Bittersweet Chocolate.*** Robust chocolate flavor with vanilla; complex; melts nicely.

***Droste Bittersweet Pastilles.*** Vanilla and slight raspberry or almond flavors; melts nicely.

***Lindt Excellence Swiss Bittersweet Chocolate*** (Criollo beans from Central America). Mild and pleasant, caramel flavor; melts smoothly with just a little graininess.

***Michel Cluizel Chocolat Amer Brut.*** Ends nicely with strong chocolate flavor, bitter edge.

***Valrhona. Equatoriale*** (beans from South America, Africa): basic chocolate flavor with citrus and hints of other fruit, smooth. *Le Noir* (beans from Trinidad): fruity, winy, spice notes. *Le Noir Amer* (beans from Venezuela): clean, sharp chocolate flavor on the acidic side, fruity, winy, smooth but waxy at the start. *Le Noir Gastronomie* (Criollo beans from South America, Forasteros from Africa): good base strength, good vanilla, fruity, winy, smooth; melts nicely. ◆

## Not-so-secret sources

The new premium chocolates are sold with either cooking or snack chocolates in specialty food markets, fancy supermarkets, and natural-food stores. You can also often buy chunks of the huge bitter- and semisweet bars made for commercial confectioners from candymakers. Or you can contact the following for retail sources.

***Dynamic Chocolates*** (800/661-2462) for Belgian Recipe Gourmet Chocolate.

***El Rey Chocolates*** (800/357-3999) for Venezuelan chocolate.

***Hawaiian Vintage Chocolate*** (800/429-6246) for Hawaiian single-estate chocolate.

***Scharffen Berger Chocolate Maker*** (800/930-4528) for hand-crafted chocolate.

# The Quick Cook

MEALS IN 30 MINUTES OR LESS

BY CHRISTINE WEBER HALE

Pasta, Prosciutto, and Pea Soup

Butter Lettuce Salad

Hot Sourdough Baguettes

Sliced Oranges with
Chocolate Ice Cream

## Broth basics

■ Broth. It's the foundation for home-made soups that can be table-ready in minutes. And when dinner is sandwiched between school and sports practice or work and a movie, my secret is a shelf lined with big cans of chicken broth. One is just enough to float ingredients for four to six satisfying main-dish portions. Great soup fixings are often staples lurking in the pantry or disguised as leftovers in the refrigerator. Or I can gather the makings in a quick shop stop. With any of the following soups, all that's needed for a complete menu is salad, bread, and a simple dessert.

## Pasta, Prosciutto, and Pea Soup

**Prep and cook time:** About 30 minutes
**Makes:** About 8 cups; 4 servings

- 1 can (49 oz.) **low-sodium chicken broth**
- ¾ cup **dry white wine**
- 1 cup **dried orzo pasta**
- 3 ounces **thinly sliced prosciutto,** cut into thin slivers
- 1 tablespoon **butter** or margarine
- 1 cup **frozen petite peas**
- 1 cup **fresh basil** leaves, cut into thin slivers
- **Grated parmesan cheese**

**1.** In a covered 5- to 6-quart pan over high heat, bring broth, wine, and pasta to a boil, then simmer until pasta is tender to bite, about 20 minutes total.

**2.** Meanwhile, in an 8- to 10-inch frying pan over medium-high heat, stir prosciutto with butter until crisp, about 5 minutes. Drain on paper towels.

**3.** Stir peas and basil into soup and heat until peas are hot, 1 to 2 minutes.

**4.** Ladle into bowls and add prosciutto. Sprinkle with cheese to taste.

Per serving: 347 cal., 24% (83 cal.) from fat; 19 g protein; 9.2 g fat (3.8 g sat.); 41 g carbo (4.6 g fiber); 654 mg sodium; 31 mg chol.

## FIVE MORE souper RECIPES

Each begins with 1 can (49 oz.) **low-sodium chicken broth** in a 5- to 6-quart pan.

**1.  Mexican Chicken Soup.** To **chicken broth** add 1½ cups **tomato salsa** and ¼ cup **lime juice.** Bring to a boil over high heat. Stir in 2 cups shredded, skinned, **cooked chicken,** 1 cup **frozen corn kernels,** 1 cup **precooked dried white rice,** and ¼ cup minced **fresh cilantro.** Cook until rice is tender to bite, 3 to 5 minutes. Serve in bowls, and add to taste **avocado** wedges, **sour cream,** and juice from **lime** wedges. Makes about

10 cups; 4 to 5 servings.

Per serving: 273 cal., 21% (58 cal.) from fat; 23 g protein; 6.4 g fat (2.1 g sat.); 30 g carbo (1 g fiber); 952 mg sodium; 55 mg chol.

**2. Asian Dumpling Soup.** To **chicken broth** add 3 tablespoons minced **fresh ginger,** 2 cloves minced **garlic,** 2 tablespoons **seasoned rice vinegar,** and 1 tablespoon **soy sauce.** Bring to a boil over high heat. Add 1 pound **frozen potstickers** or won tons and simmer, uncovered, until hot in center (cut to test), 6 to 8 minutes. Add ½ cup sliced **green onion.** Serve in bowls and add **Asian** (toasted) **sesame oil** to taste. Makes about 8 cups; 4 servings.

Per serving: 395 cal., 9.4% (37 cal.) from fat; 16 g protein; 4.1 g fat (1.5 g sat.); 72 g carbo (2.7 g fiber); 1,221 mg sodium; 16 mg chol.

**3. Black Bean Soup.** To **chicken broth** add 2 to 3 cans **black beans** (14 to 15 oz. each), 1 cup chopped **onion,** and 2 cloves minced **garlic.** Bring to a boil over high heat. For a creamy soup, scoop about half the beans into a blender and whirl with some of the broth until puréed. Return to pan, add 2 cups coarsely chopped **cooked beef,**

and heat to simmering. Serve in bowls and add to taste chopped **fresh cilantro**, crumbled **tortilla chips**, and crumbled **cotija cheese**. Makes about 12 cups; 6 servings.

Per serving: 261 cal., 33% (86 cal.) from fat; 23 g protein; 9.6 g fat (3.4 g sat.); 21 g carbo (7.5 g fiber); 546 mg sodium; 42 mg chol.

*4. Minestrone Soup.* To **chicken broth** add 1 can (28 oz.) **pear-shaped tomatoes**, chopped, with juice; about 2 cups chopped **zucchini**; and 1 cup **elbow macaroni**. Bring to boil over high heat, then simmer until pasta is tender to bite, 18 to 20 minutes total. Serve in bowls and add cubed **jack cheese** (8 to 10 oz. total). Season to taste with **prepared pesto** and **grated parmesan cheese**. Makes about 11 cups; 5 to 6 servings.

Per serving: 270 cal., 47% (126 cal.) from fat; 16 g protein; 14 g fat (7.5 g sat.); 22 g carbo (1.7 g fiber); 530 mg sodium; 44 mg chol.

*5. Curried Spinach Soup.* To about 2 cups of the **chicken broth** add 2 packages (10 oz. each) **frozen spinach** and bring to a boil over high heat, breaking spinach apart as it thaws. Whirl mixture in a blender until smooth, a portion at a time, then return to pan and add remaining broth. Season soup to taste with **curry powder** (start with 1 teaspoon) and bring to simmering on high heat, stirring occasionally. Add 2 cups **shelled cooked tiny shrimp**. Serve soup in bowls and add **sour cream** to taste. Makes 9 cups; 4 to 5 servings.

Per serving: 122 cal., 21% (26 cal.) from fat; 19 g protein; 2.9 g fat (1.2 g sat.); 6.6 g carbo (2.5 g fiber); 342 mg sodium; 115 mg chol. ◆

# A table for two

■ **Objective:** An intimate Valentine's Day dinner. **Problem:** Romantic restaurants are jammed, and slaving in the kitchen spoils the mood. **Solution:** Put on a dreamy CD and unpack the groceries. Then, as dinner cooks, sip a little Merlot and bring out the china, crystal, and candles. After chocolate truffles for dessert, let the magic begin.

## Beef Fillet with Merlot Glaze

**Prep and cook time:** About 20 minutes
**Notes:** Pancetta is sold in well-stocked supermarkets and Italian delis. Serve with couscous.
**Makes:** 2 servings

- ½ cup **beef broth**
- ¼ cup **Merlot** or other dry red wine
- 1 tablespoon **seedless raspberry jam**
- ¼ teaspoon **pepper**
- 2 thin slices **pancetta** (2 oz. total)
- 2 **beef fillet steaks** (about 1½ in. thick; ¾ to 1 lb. total)
  **Salt**

**1.** In a 1- to 2-quart pan over high heat, stir broth, Merlot, jam, and pepper until boiling, then boil until reduced to ⅓ cup, about 7 minutes total.

**2.** Meanwhile, unroll pancetta and wrap a slice around the rim of each steak. Broil steaks on a rack in a pan 4 to 6 inches from heat until browned, 6 to 7 minutes. Turn steaks over and broil until tops are browned, 6 to 7 minutes more for rare. Cook longer, if desired.

**3.** Put steaks on warm plates and spoon sauce over them. Add salt to taste.

Per serving: 407 cal., 57% (234 cal.) from fat; 34 g protein; 26 g fat (10 g sat.); 7.4 g carbo (0.2 g fiber); 353 mg sodium; 108 mg chol.

## Spinach in Portabella Mushrooms

**Prep and cook time:** About 20 minutes
**Notes:** Broil mushrooms on the rack beside the steaks.
**Makes:** 2 servings

- 2 **portabella mushrooms** (2 to 3 in. wide), stems trimmed
- 1 tablespoon **balsamic vinegar**
- ½ cup chopped **shallots** (3 oz. total)
- 1 tablespoon **butter** or margarine
- 4 cups **washed spinach leaves**

**1.** Rinse mushrooms. Brush cup side of caps with half the vinegar. Broil, cups up, on rack in a pan 4 to 6 inches from heat until juicy, 6 to 7 minutes.

**2.** Turn mushrooms over, brush them with the remaining vinegar, and broil until browned, 5 to 6 minutes.

**3.** Meanwhile, stir shallots in butter in a 10- to 12-inch frying pan over medium-high heat until limp, 3 to 5 minutes. Add spinach and stir over high heat until leaves wilt, 3 to 4 minutes.

**4.** Place mushrooms, cups up, on plates and fill with spinach.

Per serving: 116 cal., 49% (57 cal.) from fat; 4.5 g protein; 6.3 g fat (3.7 g sat.); 13 g carbo (2.9 g fiber); 112 mg sodium; 16 mg chol. ◆

# Coffee cake

Caffè Borgia, chocolate-flavor coffee with whipped cream and orange peel, inspired this cake. Serve with espresso-flavor whipped cream.

## Caffè Borgia Cake

**Prep and cook time:** About 1¼ hours, plus 1½ hours to cool
**Makes:** 16 servings

- About 1 cup (½ lb.) **butter** or margarine
- 3⅓ cups **sugar**
- ¼ cup **unsweetened cocoa**
- 2 ounces **unsweetened chocolate**, melted
- 2 **large eggs**
- 1 cup **sour cream**
- ½ teaspoon **baking soda**
- 1½ teaspoons **baking powder**
  About 2 cups **all-purpose flour**
- ⅓ cup **orange-flavor liqueur**

**1.** In a bowl, beat 1 cup butter, 1⅓ cups sugar, cocoa, and chocolate with a mixer until fluffy. Add eggs and sour cream. Beat until well mixed.

**2.** Mix together soda, baking powder, and 2 cups flour. Stir into batter, then beat to blend well.

**3.** Butter and flour-dust a 10- to 12-cup tube pan. Scrape batter into pan and spread level. Bake in a 325° oven until cake just begins to pull from pan sides and center springs back when lightly pressed, about 1 hour.

**4.** Meanwhile, in a 1½- to 2-quart pan over high heat, stir 2 cups sugar with 1 cup water until sugar dissolves. Remove syrup from heat and add liqueur.

**5.** Run a knife blade between cake and pan. Let cake cool in pan on a rack for about 10 minutes; invert cake onto rack, then tip cake back into pan. With a thin skewer, pierce cake to pan, making holes an inch apart. Slowly pour syrup over cake. Let cool about 1½ hours.

**6.** Dip cake pan in hot water almost to rim; wipe pan dry. Invert cake onto a plate.

Per serving: 446 cal., 44% (198 cal.) from fat; 4 g protein; 22 g fat (14 g sat.); 59 g carbo (1.4 g fiber); 229 mg sodium; 82 mg chol. ◆

— *Andrew Baker*

# Kitchen Cabinet

## READERS' RECIPES TESTED IN SUNSET'S KITCHENS

### BY LINDA LAU ANUSASANANAN

Onion braised in balsamic vinegar and orange juice seasons salmon.

## Salmon with Balsamic Onion Marmalade

Robin Love, San Francisco

In Modena, Italy, the home of balsamic vinegar, Robin Love bought a small, expensive bottle of a complexly aged balsamic. At home, it disappeared quickly into dishes that it suited well. Hooked on this special sweet flavor, Love hit upon a less costly alternative— everyday balsamic vinegar plus orange juice. It goes nicely with salmon and onion, especially when served with a risotto made with asparagus and no cheese.

*Prep and cook time:* About 1 hour
*Makes:* 2 servings

   1  **red onion** (6 oz.)
   2  teaspoons **olive oil**
  ½  cup **orange juice**
  ¼  cup **balsamic vinegar**
   2  **salmon fillets** (about 6 oz. each), rinsed
     **Salt** and **pepper**

**1.** Peel onion and cut into 8 wedges.

**2.** Pour 1 teaspoon oil into a 2- to 3-quart pan over medium-high heat. When pan is hot, add onion and cook, turning once, to lightly brown, about 5 minutes.

**3.** Add orange juice and vinegar. Bring to a boil over high heat, then reduce heat, cover, and simmer until onion is very tender when pierced, about 45 minutes.

**4.** Shortly before onion is done, pour remaining oil into a nonstick 10- to 12-inch frying pan over medium-high heat. When pan is hot, add salmon. Cook, turning once, until fish is opaque but still moist-looking in thickest part (cut to test), 7 to 9 minutes total.

**5.** Transfer the salmon to plates and serve with onion mixture. Season with salt and pepper to taste.

Per serving: 344 cal., 39% (135 cal.) from fat; 35 g protein; 15 g fat (2.3 g sat.); 15 g carbo (1.3 g fiber); 85 mg sodium; 94 mg chol.

## Chocolate Muffins

Carolyn Larsen, Kennewick, Washington

Carolyn Larsen uses applesauce instead of butter to give these chocolate muffins their moist, tender, cake-like texture. Not only do they taste great, but they're also lower in fat than the flavor suggests.

*Prep and cook time:* About 30 minutes
*Makes:* 12 muffins

 1½  cups **all-purpose flour**
  1  cup **sugar**
  ¾  cup **unsweetened cocoa**
  2  teaspoons **baking powder**
  ½  teaspoon **baking soda**
  ¼  teaspoon **salt**
  1  cup **applesauce**
  1  **large egg**
  ¼  cup **salad oil**
  ¼  teaspoon **almond extract**
  ½  cup **white chocolate chips**

**1.** In a bowl, mix flour with sugar, cocoa, baking powder, baking soda, and salt.

**2.** In another bowl, combine applesauce, egg, oil, and almond extract. Beat to blend, then add flour mixture and stir until evenly moistened.

**3.** Stir in chocolate chips.

**4.** Spoon the chocolate batter into 12 oiled or paper-lined muffin cups (2½ to 2¾ in. wide).

**5.** Bake in a 350° oven until muffins just begin to pull from pan sides and centers spring back when lightly pressed, about 20 minutes.

**6.** Cool muffins in pan about 5 minutes, then turn out onto racks. Serve warm or cool.

Per serving: 257 cal., 33% (84 cal.) from fat; 3.9 g protein; 9.3 g fat (3.6 g sat.); 42 g carbo (2.3 g fiber); 199 mg sodium; 18 mg chol.

## Chili-Lime Broth

Theresa Liu, Alameda, California

Thai food lover Theresa Liu uses this broth as a soup base. She varies it by adding sliced mushrooms, bamboo shoots, or chicken breast. She says, "It's wonderful to have a mug of this when I have a sore throat or when my sinuses are acting up." Buy lime leaves in Thai grocery stores.

**Prep and cook time:** About 25 minutes

**Makes:** 4 to 6 servings

- 6 cups **chicken broth**
- 2 **fresh red** or green **jalapeño chilies** (2 oz. total), stemmed, seeded, and thinly sliced
- ½ cup chopped **fresh cilantro**
- 6 **fresh** or dried **kaffir lime leaves** (optional)
- 5 slices **fresh ginger** (each about the size of a quarter)
- ¼ cup **lime juice**
- ¼ cup thinly sliced **green onions**
- ¼ cup **fresh cilantro** leaves

  **Asian fish sauce** (*nuoc mam* or *nam pla*)

**1.** In a 2- to 3-quart pan, combine broth, chilies, chopped cilantro, lime leaves, and ginger. Bring to a boil over high heat. Cover and simmer over low heat for 15 minutes.

**2.** Pour broth through a fine strainer into a bowl. Add lime juice, onions, cilantro leaves, and fish sauce to taste. Ladle into soup bowls.

Per serving: 37 cal., 38% (14 cal.) from fat; 3.3 g protein; 1.5 g fat (0.8 g sat.); 3.3 g carbo (0.2 g fiber); 108 mg sodium; 3.8 mg chol.

## Miner's Lettuce Salad

Vicki Vermeer, Tuolumne, California

To make salad, Vicki Vermeer gathers miner's lettuce, a succulent tender green that grows abundantly on her 10-acre ranch. This wild native got its name from the gold miners who sought its freshness in their limited diet. Miner's lettuce (*Montia perfoliata*) thrives in moderate climates throughout the West from late winter to early spring. Sometimes it's sold at farmers' markets. As a substitute, use baby spinach leaves.

**Prep and cook time:** About 10 minutes

**Makes:** 4 servings

- ¼ cup **pine nuts** or sesame seed
- 1 tablespoon **olive oil**
- ¼ cup **rice vinegar**
- ¼ cup chopped **fresh basil** leaves or 2 teaspoons dried basil
- 4 cups **miner's lettuce**, including stems and blossoms, rinsed and crisped

  **Salt** and **pepper**

**1.** In a 6- to 8-inch frying pan over low heat, stir nuts in oil until golden, 3 to 4 minutes. Add vinegar. Let cool.

**2.** Pour nut mixture into a wide bowl; add basil and miner's lettuce. Mix and season to taste with salt and pepper.

Per serving: 93 cal., 77% (72 cal.) from fat; 2.4 g protein; 8 g fat (1.1 g sat.); 4.3 g carbo (1.8 g fiber); 6.2 mg sodium; 0 mg chol.

## Mexican Hot Dance Spuds

Nancee Olsen, Tucson

When Nancee Olsen moved from Minnesota to Arizona, she says, "my experiences and taste buds really changed." Mexican foods get the credit.

**Prep and cook time:** About 25 minutes

**Makes:** 4 servings

- 4 **russet potatoes** (8 to 10 oz. each), scrubbed
- 1 pound **ground lean beef** or turkey
- 1 tablespoon **chili powder**
- 1 can (8 oz.) **tomato sauce**
- 1 cup **tomato salsa**
- ¼ pound (1 cup) **shredded cheddar** or jack **cheese** (or ⅛ lb. of each)
- 1 cup chopped **tomato** (optional)
- ½ cup thinly sliced **green onions**, including green tops
- 1 can (4 oz.) **sliced ripe olives**, drained

  **Salt** and **pepper**

**1.** Pierce potatoes with a fork. Cook in a microwave oven on full power (100%), turning over once, until potatoes are tender when pierced, 15 to 20 minutes. Or bake in a conventional oven at 400° until tender when pierced, about 45 to 55 minutes.

**2.** Meanwhile, in a 10- to 12-inch nonstick frying pan over high heat, stir beef until crumbled and lightly browned, about 5 minutes.

**3.** Add chili powder to beef and stir about 1 minute. Add tomato sauce and salsa. Reduce heat and simmer, uncovered, to blend flavors, about 5 minutes.

**4.** Cut the potatoes in half lengthwise. Spoon meat mixture equally onto cut side of each potato half, and top equally with cheese, tomato, onions, and olives. Add salt and pepper to taste.

Per serving: 677 cal., 49% (333 cal.) from fat; 33 g protein; 37 g fat (16 g sat.); 53 g carbo (6.4 g fiber); 1,523 mg sodium; 115 mg chol. ◆

Load microwave-baked potato with Mexican flavors for a fast and filling supper.

Making bread is easier than you think. Machines do the mixing, you craft the loaves—from sourdough to brioche (see page 48).

JAMES CARRIER

# March

# food guide

BY JERRY ANNE DI VECCHIO

Sansho—sometimes called Japanese pepper—isn't a pepper and isn't hot, but it does sparkle on your tongue. The flavor, a subtle blend of lemon and the woods, includes this tickle bonus. Once, in Kyoto, I had a very famous dish of grilled freshwater eel. It was dusted liberally with sansho, the ground dried berries from a species of prickly ash (*Zanthoxylum piperitum*). Sansho's tingling sensation was the surprise that drew me to take bite after bite. This seasoning is also excel-

## tickle me

lent on other fish, especially salmon. And for an everyday appetizer with a kick, I love the zing a generous application of sansho gives salted popcorn—our ubiquitous national snack. You'll find sansho in well-stocked supermarkets as well as Japanese and other Asian markets.

---

BACK TO BASICS

## The perfect poached egg

■ With the help of a few food scientists, we discovered how to perfectly poach an egg more than 30 years ago. The technique bears repeating.

First, gently immerse each *egg in the shell* in boiling water for 8 seconds, adding no more than one layer of eggs to the pan and removing them in the same sequence in which they were added. The heat cooks the thin layer of white just inside the shell, separating it from the thick white around the yolk. Don't worry if the shells crack. You can poach the eggs at once, or chill them up to two days. Best of all, when you poach these eggs side by side, they don't stick together.

*To poach,* fill a pan with enough water to cover an *egg out of the shell* by at least 1 inch. A 12-inch frying pan holds as many as 10 large eggs. Set pan over high heat just until one or two bubbles break the surface of the water. Then reduce heat so bubbles that form on pan bottom only pop to the surface occasionally. An active boil toughens and breaks up the eggs.

Crack eggshells, one at a time, holding each shell close to the water surface as you break it open and letting the egg slide gently into the water (stretching also tears up an egg).

Cook until eggs are as done as you like, poking gently with a spoon tip to check firmness. Soft but safely heated yolks take 4 to 5 minutes. As the eggs are cooked, lift them from the water with a slotted spoon. Serve, or if making ahead, immerse in ice water, cover, and chill up to two days.

*To reheat,* immerse eggs in water that's just hot to touch (but not hot enough to cook them further) until they feel warm, 5 to 10 minutes. Lift out with a slotted spoon (or your hand), drain, and serve.

What makes a perfect poached egg more than perfect? Serve it on crisp, shredded potato pancakes with sautéed onions.

JAMES CARRIER (4)

## Short Rib Supper

***Prep and cook time:*** About 30 minutes to assemble, 3¼ hours to bake

***Notes:*** Horseradish loses its pungency as it bakes on the meat. Have the ribs sawed to size at the meat market.

***Makes:*** 4 servings

- 1 pound **carrots**
- 1 pound **thin-skinned potatoes**
- 1 **onion** (½ lb.)
- 1 **turnip** (about ½ lb.)
- 4 pounds **lean beef short ribs,** fat trimmed, cut into 3- to 4-inch pieces
- 1 cup fat-skimmed **beef** or chicken **broth**

  About ½ cup **prepared horseradish**

  About ¼ pound **watercress,** rinsed and drained

  **Salt**

**1.** Peel carrots, potatoes, onion, and turnip and cut into about ½-inch dice.

**2.** Rinse ribs, drain, and lay bone-down in a single layer in a 12- by 14-inch casserole (about 5 qt.) at least 2 inches deep. Distribute vegetables evenly around but not over meat. Pour broth and 1¼ cups water into casserole.

**3.** Coat tops of ribs with 6 tablespoons horseradish.

**4.** Cover casserole tightly with foil, tenting if necessary to keep foil from touching ribs. Bake in a 375° oven until meat is very tender when pierced, about 3 hours.

**5.** Meanwhile, break leaves from watercress and finely chop stems. Cover each separately and chill.

**6.** Uncover casserole and bake until ribs brown, about 10 minutes. With a slotted spoon, transfer ribs to a large platter and keep warm. Mix chopped watercress stems with vegetables and return to oven until watercress is slightly wilted, about 5 minutes, stirring once or twice. With slotted spoon, transfer vegetables to platter. Skim and discard fat from pan juices, then pour juices into a bowl.

**7.** Garnish platter with the watercress leaves. Serve the meat and vegetables with pan juices, horseradish, and salt to taste.

Per serving: 539 cal., 38% (207 cal.) from fat; 44 g protein; 23 g fat (9.5 g sat.); 39 g carbo (7.2 g fiber); 205 mg sodium; 114 mg chol.

A TASTE OF THE WEST

# Hurry up and wait

■ In the military, this command is taken seriously—with grumbles. But in the kitchen, it's the secret weapon that puts a glow on lazy cooks (like me) and anyone else who loves tough meat cuts that demand time plus heat to reach melting succulence.

In a half-hour or less, this beef short rib supper—complete with meat, veg-

etables, pan sauce, and salad greens— is organized and all but the salad goes into the oven to be ignored.

While the house fills with appetite-maddening aromas in the several hours it takes to bake, there's time for a satisfying nap, a good chunk of a book, even a preseason ball game televised from spring training.

MARCH 45

JAMES CARRIER (2)

# Blood brothers

■ From roadside stands between Verona and Venice in the late '50s, cut-open blood oranges flashed at me like a battalion of stop signs. Italian is a language that I comprehend only in bits—mostly on menus and food wrappers—but I

did figure out that the hand-lettered posters said something about *sangue,* or blood. One taste of this new fruit quickly banished the image of fruit juice pumping through Italian veins. Clearly, I was eating a unique orange.

In the intervening decades, blood oranges have become a significant Western crop, and the Moro is the dominant variety. Moros have particularly deep ruby-colored flesh and juice, and sweet-tart flavor. Peeled and sliced, blood oranges make brilliant additions to salads and desserts. Juiced, they make a fine beverage. And the juice blends well with everything from sparkling wine to eau-de-vie.

**With bubbles.** Added in about equal proportions, blood-orange juice covers up the faults of inexpensive sparkling wine—and takes gracefully to better champagnes—to make Mimosa Roses.

***Create lush, exotic drinks*** by combining blood-orange juice with floral dessert wine or eau-de-vie from plain, orange, or black Muscat grapes. It's equally compatible with the juice, wine, and late-harvest wine of Gewürztraminer grapes.

***Buying guide:*** A dozen blood oranges (2½ in. wide; about 3½ lb. total) yield 3 to 3½ cups juice.

Per ½ cup plain juice: 56 cal., 3.2% (1.8 cal.) from fat; 0.9 g protein; 0.2 g fat (0 g sat.); 13 g carbo (0.2 g fiber); 1.2 mg sodium; 0 mg chol.

# Buy design for encore use

■ It probably started with gingerbread. Through a snowflake cut from paper, a little powdered sugar was sifted over the gingerbread. The paper snowflake was then carefully lifted off to preserve the pattern. This simple step turned plain gingerbread into a work of art—at least to my young | **TOOL** | eyes. The privilege of making the snowflake was doled out among my brother, my sister, and me. But the more ethereal the design was, the quicker its demise—one use and the stencil was history.

However, there is now a more durable, reusable option. The Kaiser Bakeware decorating kit has 10 round, flexible, 8-inch-wide stencils made of sturdy plastic. The designs include Happy Birthday, Valentine hearts, Easter eggs, and a flag for the Fourth of July, as well as other special greetings. The kit sells for about $10 at cookware stores.

# Beef with feathers

■ Ostrich is no longer a novelty. Growers in this country produce more than 1 million pounds of ostrich meat every year. The meat is available frozen, or it can be ordered at most meat markets and supermarkets. Ostrich is a very red, lean, and mild-tasting meat. Comparing it to beef makes the most flavor sense.

The ostrich has no breast meat—it's mostly leg and thigh, plus a strip from the back called the tenderloin. The tenderloin and some cuts from the thigh (top loin, fan, oyster, and inside and outside strip) are quite tender. Others are chewier. Ostrich meat that is cut into neat slices or reformed into steaks called medallions or mignons cooks quite evenly.

At $10 to $20 a pound, depending on the cut, ostrich isn't cheap. But it's lean, boned, and quick-cooking, and takes well to bold sauces.

## Ostrich with Port and Blue Cheese Glaze

***Prep and cook time:*** About 10 minutes

***Notes:*** Serve on buttered toast with sautéed pear slices.

***Makes:*** 4 servings

    4  **ostrich medallion steaks**
       (¾ in. thick; about 1 lb. total)

    1  tablespoon **butter** or margarine

    ¼  cup **port**

    ¼  cup **whipping cream**

    2  tablespoons **cambozola cheese**
       or creamy blue cheese

Fresh-ground **pepper**

**Salt**

**1.** Rinse ostrich and pat dry.

**2.** In a 10- to 12-inch frying pan over high heat, melt butter. When hot, add ostrich in a single layer. Brown on each side, cooking until rare or medium-rare (red in center, cut to test), 4 to 5 minutes total, or to taste (well-done ostrich is dry).

**3.** Remove pan from heat, quickly transfer the meat to a platter, and keep it warm.

**4.** Add port, cream, and cheese to pan; stir over high heat until reduced to about ⅓ cup. Pour sauce over the meat. Season to taste with pepper and salt.

Per serving: 228 cal., 43% (99 cal.) from fat; 24 g protein; 11 g fat (5.4 g sat.); 2.3 g carbo (0 g fiber); 95 mg sodium; 98 mg chol. ◆

# The Wine Guide

BY KAREN MacNEIL

## Age-old Zins

■ Dry Creek Valley. The first time I heard of the place, I pictured old Texas—unshaven men, scrappy-looking coyotes. If there *was* wine, well, it was probably dusty-smelling and leathery-tasting, like something that had splashed around inside a cowboy boot.

My imagination couldn't have been more wrong.

As it turns out, Dry Creek (which, by the way, is not dry) runs through one of the most idyllic valleys in California's Sonoma County. Time seems to have stood still here. The gentle auburn hills are blanketed with old, gnarled vines that lift their twisted black arms skyward as though imploring the heavens. It is serenely quiet. There are no packed restaurants, no traffic jams of tourists out for a weekend of tasting, no cruising limousines.

There are, however, quite a few well-worn pickups and a seemingly endless number of country roads you'd love to get lost on. Plus, of course, all those gnomelike vines.

Let me explain why they're special.

Dry Creek is known for Zinfandel. In fact, it's been known for Zin since roughly the 1880s, when immigrant vintners—many of them Italian—made the valley their home. In the decades that followed, Dry Creek, like virtually every other region in California, suffered the cumulative ravages of phylloxera (a fatal vine disease), Prohibition, the Great Depression, and two World Wars.

Through it all, winemaking here continued, if sometimes on a far smaller scale. And the grape variety that, in many ways, allowed it to continue was Zinfandel.

First of all, Zin vines are hardy. But they also possess another wonderful trait: Like a person who graduates from Stanford and writes her first novel at age 65, some Zinfandel vineyards just seem to improve the longer they live. In old age, when their branches are wizened and troll-like, Zinfandel vines can produce amazingly lush and concentrated wine.

Today, Dry Creek is full of old Zinfandel vineyards (sometimes called heritage vineyards); it also has scores of newer ones.

So, how old is old if you're a vine?

Dave Rafanelli, winemaker and co-owner of Dry Creek's A. Rafanelli winery, compares vines to people. A 1- to 15-year-old vine, he says, is young. It's actively growing and vigorous—in the training stage of life. A 15- to 40-year-old vine, according to Rafanelli, is mature. It has an established structure. Forty- to 100-year-old vines, he says, are old, on the declining side of life. They grow more slowly and yield smaller and smaller crops. But the flavor of the grapes they do produce can be outrageous.

If Dry Creek were known just for Zinfandel, that would be glory enough. But the valley, some 16 miles long and 2 miles across at its widest, is also known for mellow, lemony Sauvignon Blancs and several delicious wines based on Rhône varieties. (And, yes, Chardonnay and Merlot are made here too.)

Still, it'd be a sin to miss the Zin. ◆

RICK MARIANI

## DRY CREEK STANDOUTS

■ *A. Rafanelli Zinfandel 1995,* $18. Super-intense, super-ripe, super-charged. Begging for a steak.

■ *Lambert Bridge Zinfandel 1996,* $18. Like falling into a pool of blackberry jam. Terrific explosion of fruit.

■ *Peterson Zinfandel Dry Creek Valley 1995,* $15. This wine's wearing pearls with hiking boots—perfectly sophisticated but not fussy.

■ *Pezzi-King Zinfandel 1995,* $22. Lush boysenberries, red currants, blackberries, cherries, and blueberries. Did we leave anything out?

■ *Preston Faux (Rhône Blend) 1996,* $11. An earthy, meaty, sexy, and untamed blend of five reds. Try some with the winery's terrific rustic country breads, baked by Lou Preston himself in a wood-burning brick oven (and usually for sale, with wine, at the tasting room).

■ *Quivira Sauvignon Blanc 1996,* $10. The wine rendition of a light and lemony fig tart.

---

### THE TALK OF THE TOWN

## Go for the scones

Healdsburg, at the southern corner of Dry Creek Valley, is possibly the most charming wine town in Northern California. It has Bistro Ralph, where absolutely scrumptious meals and lots of Dry Creek wines can be had, and—my vote for the best bakery on the West Coast—the Downtown Bakery and Creamery. After careful and repeated analysis, I can vouch that a blackberry scone is the perfect opening act for a tasting of Dry Creek Zins. — *K. M.*

# Our daily bread:
## *easier than you*

BY ANDREW BAKER AND BARBARA GOLDMAN • PHOTOGRAPHS BY JAMES CARRIER

Machines
do the
mixing

you
craft
the loaves

*think!*

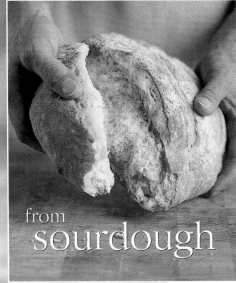

from
sourdough

to brioche

■ New technology doesn't always squelch old traditions—sometimes it leads us back to them. When bread machines arrived on the scene a decade ago, they made homemade loaves an everyday possibility instead of a rare pleasure. Since then, machines are better and cheaper—from $79 up. New models make larger, conventionally shaped loaves, and some turn out quick breads and cakes, even jam and yogurt. Controls are more adjustable and easier to use.

The best news is that the most traditional bread—a hand-shaped loaf—is now an easy option, thanks to dough cycles. The machine does the sticky work; you shape the loaf and pop it in the oven. If you'd like to bake today's wildly popular artisan breads but have been deterred by the time and work they take, these machines are for you.

With more than 70 models on the market, choosing a bread machine can be daunting. To narrow the field, we put 18 of the newest machines to the test, including ones that make 2-pound horizontal loaves, those with the most advanced features, and two just-introduced units that double as ovens. On pages 50 and 51, we compare their performance.

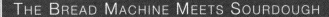

## THE BREAD MACHINE MEETS SOURDOUGH

In 1993, we made our first sourdough in a bread machine, producing a good loaf baked in the machine's pan. Today's machines with dough cycles give even better results. The machines can mix and knead sourdough's hard-to-handle wet dough to perfection—the secret of resilient, springy bread. Then you can hand-shape the dough for baking (photos far left).

*Sunset* has been covering the tangy topic of sourdough since July 1933, starting with recipes for bread, biscuits, pancakes, and muffins. During the next few years, articles included recipes passed down from Gold Rush miners and accounts that blended fact and fantasy. Every reporter held an opinion.

"Sour dough flapjacks," wrote a poetic 1943 commentator, "work better in the open, particularly in the high mountains. When you bring them down into civilization they pine away like a sheep dog."

Early recipes were charmingly vague, and authors brazen: "Notice the indifference I have for exact measurements!" and "Sour dough is an art, not a science." Such cavalier approaches often resulted in a highly hostile sourdough starter, then the bread's sole leavener. "Listen to the hissing noise, and when you know the mixture is working 'good,' keep it from acting like an atomic bomb as you stir appeasingly every day," cautioned a writer in 1947.

No doubt those early stories produced luscious loaves—some of the time. But a quarter of a century ago, *Sunset* food writers realized a quality starter was vital for foolproof results and turned to UC Davis food technologist George K. York, who had pioneered research with the USDA for commercial bakeries to determine what made sourdough, well, sour. In the process, he debunked a few popular myths. For example, good sourdough is not unique to San Francisco—even though the city is renowned for sourdough bread. And most important, sourdough is not activated by wild yeasts captured from the air.

In reality, sourdough's action and flavor come from bacteria. York found that the bacteria in early starters actually came from the flours brought by Italian immigrants. He then identified similar bacteria in yogurt that produce a reliable sourdough starter. This triumphant breakthrough was published in *Sunset* in 1973. But our food writers continued to fiddle with starters, learning what they like to eat and how to keep them happy. Findings published in 1988 included the dramatic resuscitation of a starter neglected for a year and a half.

And along with this update on bread machines, we also introduce *Sunset's* Centennial sourdough bread (see page 52).

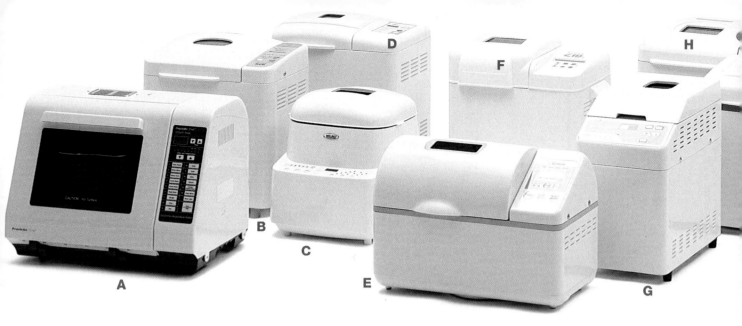

# RATING 18 NEW MACHINES

# The upper crust: larger loaves, new shapes,

| BRAND | A FRANKLIN CHEF | B BREADMAN | C WELBILT | D OSTER | E ZOJIRUSHI | F WEST BEND | G AROMA BREADCHEF | H PILLSBURY | I TOASTMASTER |
|---|---|---|---|---|---|---|---|---|---|
| MODEL | Baker's Oven FBM2000 | TR800 | Baker's Select ABM6200 | Deluxe Bread & Dough Maker 5839 | BBCC-V20 Home Bakery Traditional | 2 lb. Bread & Dough Maker 41072 | ABM-230 | Automatic Bread and Dough Maker 9900 | Corner Bakery Bread and Dessert Maker 1183 |
| PHONE | (800) 480-2610 | (800) 233-9054 | (800) 872-1656 | (800) 526-2832, (800) 667-8623 in Canada | (800) 733-6270 | (414) 334-6949 | (800) 276-6286 | (800) 858-3277 | (800) 947-3744 |
| WEB SITE | None | www. breadman. com | www.wel-bilt. com | None | www.zojirushi. com | www. westbend. com | None | None | www. toastmaster. com |
| PRICE | About $179 | $99 to $149 | About $150 | $90 to $100 | $200 to $250 | $89 to $150 | $79 to $109 | $139 to $179 | About $140 |
| LOAF SHAPE | Horizontal | Horizontal | Horizontal | Vertical | Long horizontal | Vertical | Vertical | Horizontal | Vertical |
| **CYCLES** | | | | | | | | | |
| Basic | 3 hr. 30 min. | 3 hr. 10 min. | 3 hr. 25 min. | 2 hr. 45 min. | 3 hr. 30 min. | 3 hr. 40 min. | 4 hr. | 3 hr. 10 min. | 3 hr. 40 min. |
| Rapid | 3 hr. | 2 hr. 40 min. | 2 hr. 40 min. | None | 1 hr. 58 min. | 3 hr. | 3 hr. | 2 hr. 40 min. | 1 hr. 59 min. |
| Dough | 2 hr. 30 min. | 1 hr. 30 min. | 1 hr. 20 min. | 1 hr. 30 min. | 1 hr. 50 min. | 1 hr. 20 min. | 3 hr. | 1 hr. 30 min. | 1 hr. 3 min. |
| SPECIAL FEATURES | French and sweet cycles; makes cake, jam; oven bakes, broils, toasts; oven light | French, rapid whole-wheat, bagel-, pizza-dough cycles; bake cycle for prepared dough; makes quick bread, cake, jam | French cycle; heats ingredients for whole-wheat cycle; bread ejects from built-in pan | French, sweet, rapid whole-wheat cycles; makes quick bread, cake, jam, jelly | Steps in one complete cycle can be adjusted; rapid whole-wheat cycle; makes cake, jam; heats ingredients | French, sweet, rapid whole-wheat cycles; heats ingredients | Cooks rice; roasts meats; makes yogurt | French, sweet, rapid whole-wheat, bagel-, pizza-dough cycles; bake cycle for pre-pared dough; makes quick bread, jam | French and sweet cycles; butter churn cycle; makes quick bread, cake, cheesecake, pie filling, pudding, fudge |
| RATING (see below) | 🍞🍞🍞 | 🍞🍞🍞 | 🍞🍞 | 🍞🍞🍞 | 🍞🍞 | 🍞🍞 | 🍞🍞 | 🍞🍞🍞 | 🍞🍞 |
| PROS & CONS | Helpful control panel; resumes operation if power fails only 5 to 10 min.; 90-day warranty | Helpful control panel; resumes operation if power fails up to 1 hr.; no keep-warm feature | Smallest machine; rather noisy; kneading blade often bakes into loaf; loaf difficult to remove neatly; won't resume operation after power failure | Fastest basic cycle; quiet; no light-crust setting; won't resume operation after power failure | Resumes operation if power fails no more than 30 sec.; loaves often gnarled; rather noisy | Window doesn't fog; rather noisy; won't resume operation after power failure | No whole-grain cycle; control panel shows time in only 30-min. increments; pan shaft must be oiled; won't resume operation after power failure | No keep-warm feature; noisy; won't resume operation after power failure | Fast dough cycle; quiet; 3-year warranty; won't resume operation after power failure |

## RATING KEY

Fair: 🍞

Better: 🍞🍞

Very Good: 🍞🍞🍞

Best: 🍞🍞🍞🍞

**Our rating** is based on the quality of bread produced (using the manufacturer's recipe for basic white bread, and our own version on page 52) and ease of use.
**Unless noted,** all machines make 1- and/or 1½- and 2-pound loaves and have white and whole-wheat or whole-grain bread cycles; a rapid basic cycle; a dough cycle; a nonstick bread pan; a window (which, unless noted, fogs part of the time and makes viewing difficult); a delayed-start timer (12 to 15 hr.); crust settings for light, medium, and dark; a keep-warm feature; a signal to indicate when ingredients can be added during cycles; a recipe booklet; and a one-year warranty.

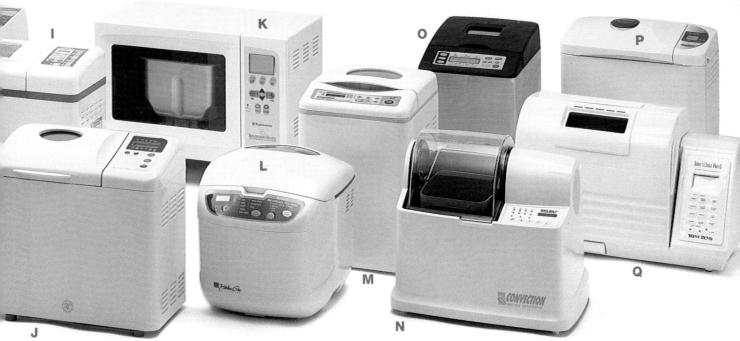

# and hot features

| | J | K | L | M | N | O | P | Q | (not shown) |
|---|---|---|---|---|---|---|---|---|---|
| | WILLIAMS-SONOMA | TOASTMASTER | REGAL | BLACK & DECKER | WELBILT | REGAL | PANASONIC | WEST BEND | GOLDSTAR |
| | Bread Machine WS1094 (max. loaf 1½ lb.) | Breadmaker's Hearth Bread-maker & Cook's Oven 1193 | Kitchen Pro Collection K6725 | All-in-One Deluxe B1630 | Automatic Convection Bread Machine ABM7500 | Kitchen Pro Collection K6780 | Bread Bakery SD-YD205 | Baker's Choice Plus II Automatic Bread & Dough Maker 41090 | Automatic Breadmaker HB-202CE |
| | (800) 858-3277, (714) 434-1515 in Canada | (800) 947-3744 | (800) 998-8809 | (800) 231-9786, (800) 465-6070 in Canada | (800) 872-1656 | (800) 998-8809 | (800) 211-7262, (757) 382-4400 in Canada | (414) 334-6949 | (800) 243-0000 |
| | None | www.toastmaster.com | www.regalware.com | www.blackanddecker.com | www.wel-bilt.com | www.regalware.com | www.panasonic.com | www.westbend.com | www.lgeus.com |
| | $120 to $160 | $150 to $200 | $89 to $99 | $100 to $119 | About $150 | $129 to $169 | About $220 | $219 to $249 | $99 to $119 |
| | Vertical | Horizontal | Horizontal | Vertical | Horizontal | Vertical | Horizontal | Long horizontal | Vertical |
| | 3 hr. 50 min. | 3 hr. 10 min. | 3 hr. | 3 hr. 50 min. | 3 hr. 20 min. | 3 hr. 40 min. | 4 hr. | 3 hr. 40 min. | 3 hr. 40 min. |
| | None | 1 hr. 59 min. | 2 hr. 20 min. | 1 hr. 58 min. | 2 hr. 48 min. | 2 hr. 30 min. | 3 hr. | 3 hr. 20 min. | 1 hr. 59 min. |
| | 1 hr. 40 min. | 1 hr. 25 min. | 1 hr. 30 min. | 2 hr. | 1 hr. 30 min. | 1 hr. 35 min. | 2 hr. 30 min. | 1 hr. 40 min. | 1 hr. 3 min. |
| | French, sweet, pizza-dough cycles; mixes pasta, cookie dough; makes quick bread | French, sweet, rapid whole-wheat, pizza-dough cycles; mixes pasta, cookie dough; makes quick bread, cake; oven bakes, broils, toasts | French, sweet, pasta-dough cycles; bake cycle for prepared dough; makes quick bread | Sweet cycle; mixes pasta dough; heats ingredients | French cycle; can be stopped during kneading to add ingredients; convection heat | French and rapid whole-wheat cycles; makes quick bread, jam; cooks rice; convection heat | Automatic yeast dispenser; heats ingredients | French, sweet, rapid whole-wheat cycles; rising times can be adjusted; heats ingredients; oven light | French cycle; makes quick bread, cake |

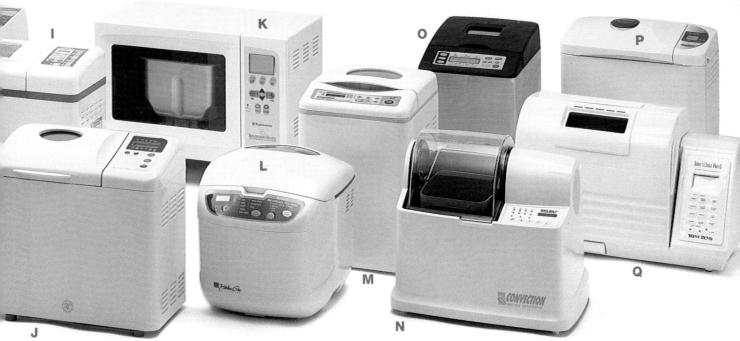

| | | | | | | | | |
|---|---|---|---|---|---|---|---|---|
| This machine was replaced by the 2-lb. model 0797WSR ($149), which arrived too late for us to test. It has a horizontal pan; rapid and French dough cycles; won't resume operation after power failure | Even browning; 3-year warranty; rather noisy; won't resume operation after power failure | Large window; resumes operation if power fails no more than 10 min. | Resumes operation if power fails no more than 20 sec.; 2-year warranty; directions don't have timing chart; no light-crust setting | Large, domed window; easy to view bread-making process; heats ingredients for whole-wheat cycle; won't resume operation after power failure | Helpful control panel; brushed stainless steel finish is attractive but shows smudges; resumes operation if power fails no more than 5 to 20 sec.; no dark-crust setting | Quietest; resumes operation if power fails no more than 10 min.; no window; no crust settings | Window doesn't fog; resumes operation if power fails no more than 10 min.; loaves often uneven, tops gnarled | Fast dough cycle; won't resume operation after power failure |

*Loaf shape.* The *vertical* pans are about 5¼ inches square and 7½ inches high. *Horizontal* pans are about 5¼ inches wide, 7¼ inches long, and 5½ inches high. *Long horizontal* pans (with 2 kneading blades) are about 5 inches wide, 9 inches long, and 4 inches high. *Crust settings* don't produce the same results on different machines. Try them, then tailor to your own taste.

*In our tests,* machines that heat ingredients produced the same results as those that don't.
*Industry terminology* varies. *Cycle, setting,* and *mode* are used interchangeably. A *French* cycle is generally for crustier yeast breads. A *sweet* cycle is for sweet yeast breads. *Rapid* or *insta* are fast cycles. *Quick* may be fast cycle, or a cycle for no-yeast breads.

Baked in a machine, or shaped by hand and baked in the oven, Chili-Cheese Sourdough is a savory, hearty loaf.

## BREADMAKING BY MACHINE

These recipes must be used along with the instructions that come with each bread machine. Results are best if, after the mixing cycle, you scrape the pan sides with a flexible spatula to incorporate all the ingredients. Loaf weights are approximate.

*For crispest crusts* on all the loaves except Tropical Banana Quick Bread, let bread cool, then reheat on a rack in a 350° oven for 5 to 10 minutes.

The nutritional data are averages of the 1½- and 2-pound loaves.

## Sunset Centennial Sourdough

| Ingredients | 1½-pound loaf | 2-pound loaf |
|---|---|---|
| water | 1 cup | 1⅓ cups |
| sourdough starter (see page 54) | 1 cup | 1⅓ cups |
| bread flour | 3 cups | 4 cups |
| rye flour | ½ cup | ⅔ cup |
| sugar | 1 tablespoon | 4 teaspoons |
| salt | 1 teaspoon | 1 teaspoon |
| active dry yeast | 1 package | 1 package |

**1.** Add ingredients to bread machine pan according to manufacturer's directions.

**2.** Select basic cycle.

**3.** Remove baked loaf from pan at once. Cool on a rack at least 15 minutes before slicing. Serve hot, warm, or cool.

Per ounce: 90 cal., 4% (3.6 cal.) from fat; 3.1 g protein; 0.4 g fat (0.1 g sat.); 18 g carbo (0.8 g fiber); 90 mg sodium; 0.2 mg chol.

## Chili-Cheese Sourdough

*1½-pound loaf*
Use ingredients and follow steps for **Sunset Centennial Sourdough,** preceding, adding ⅓ cup shredded **dry jack** or parmesan **cheese** and ¼ cup minced **fresh jalapeño chilies.**

*2-pound loaf*
Use ingredients and follow steps for **Sunset Centennial Sourdough,** preceding, adding ½ cup shredded **dry jack** or parmesan **cheese** and ⅓ cup minced **fresh jalapeño chilies.**

Per ounce: 97 cal., 7.4% (7.2 cal.) from fat; 3.7 g protein; 0.8 g fat (0.3 g sat.); 18 g carbo (0.8 g fiber); 117 mg sodium; 1.4 mg chol.

## Hearth-baked Centennial Sourdough

**1.** Use ingredients for **Sunset Centennial Sourdough,** preceding, and process on dough cycle.

**2.** Scrape dough onto a board coated generously with **bread flour.** Taking care not to puncture or tear dough surface (interior is sticky), pat dough gently with floured hands to form a round loaf about 8 inches wide; do not knead. Sprinkle 2 tablespoons bread flour over dough.

**3.** Slide a pastry scraper or wide spatula under loaf to loosen, then lift quickly and carefully onto a buttered 14- by 17-inch baking sheet. Pat to reshape loaf, if necessary.

**4.** Lightly cover loaf with plastic wrap and let stand until puffy, about 30 minutes. Remove plastic.

**5.** With a floured razor blade or very sharp knife, cut 2 or 3 slashes about ½ inch deep across top of loaf.

**6.** Bake in a 425° oven until richly browned, 25 to 30 minutes.

**7.** Transfer loaf to a rack to cool at least 15 minutes before slicing. Serve hot, warm, or cool.

Nutritional data are the same as for Sunset Centennial Sourdough.

## Hearth-baked Chili-Cheese Sourdough

**1.** Use ingredients and follow directions for **Chili-Cheese Sourdough,** preceding, and process on dough cycle.

**2.** Shape as directed for **Hearth-baked Centennial Sourdough,** preceding.

**3.** After loaf has baked 25 minutes, sprinkle an additional ¼ cup shredded **dry jack** or parmesan **cheese** over it, then continue to bake as directed.

**4.** Transfer loaf to a rack to cool at least 15 minutes before slicing. Serve hot, warm, or cool.

Per ounce: 101 cal., 9.8% (9.9 cal.) from fat; 4.1 g protein; 1.1 g fat (0.5 g sat.); 18 g carbo (0.8 g fiber); 134 mg sodium; 2.1 mg chol.

## Basic White Bread

| Ingredients | 1½-pound loaf | 2-pound loaf |
|---|---|---|
| milk | 1 cup | 1⅓ cups |
| **butter** or margarine | 1 tablespoon | 1 tablespoon |
| **bread flour** | 3 cups | 4 cups |
| sugar | 1 tablespoon | 4 teaspoons |
| salt | ¾ teaspoon | 1 teaspoon |
| active dry yeast | 1 package | 1 package |

**1.** Add ingredients to bread machine pan according to manufacturer's directions.

**2.** Select basic cycle.

**3.** Remove baked loaf from pan at once. Cool on a rack at least 15 minutes before slicing. Serve hot, warm, or cool.

Per ounce: 74 cal., 12% (9 cal.) from fat; 2.5 g protein; 1 g fat (0.5 g sat.); 14 g carbo (0.4 g fiber); 82 mg sodium; 2.5 mg chol.

## Bulgur Wheat Bread

*1½-pound loaf*

**1.** In a small bowl, combine ⅓ cup **water** and ⅓ cup **bulgur wheat**. Let stand until bulgur is soft enough to bite, about 25 minutes. Do not drain.

**2.** Use ingredients and follow steps for **Basic White Bread**, preceding, adding soaked bulgur and liquid with milk.

*2-pound loaf*

**1.** In a small bowl, combine ½ cup **water** and ½ cup **bulgur wheat**. Let stand until bulgur is soft enough to bite, about 25 minutes. Do not drain.

**2.** Use ingredients and follow steps for **Basic White Bread**, preceding, adding soaked bulgur and liquid with milk.

Per ounce: 82 cal., 12% (9.9 cal.) from fat; 2.7 g protein; 1.1 g fat (0.5 g sat.); 15 g carbo (0.7 g fiber); 83 mg sodium; 2.5 mg chol.

## Brioche

| Ingredients | 1½-pound loaf | 2-pound loaf |
|---|---|---|
| water | ⅓ cup | ⅓ cup |
| large eggs | 2 | 3 |
| large egg yolks | 2 | 2 |
| butter or margarine | ½ cup (¼ lb.) | ¾ cup (⅜ lb.) |
| all-purpose flour | 2½ cups | 3⅓ cups |
| sugar | 3 tablespoons | ¼ cup |
| salt | ½ teaspoon | ½ teaspoon |
| active dry yeast | 1 package | 1 package |

**1.** Add ingredients to bread machine pan according to manufacturer's directions.

**2.** Select sweet or basic cycle.

**3.** Remove baked loaf from pan at once. Cool loaf on a rack at least 15 minutes before slicing. Serve hot, warm, or cool.

Per ounce: 101 cal., 45% (45 cal.) from fat; 2.2 g protein; 5 g fat (2.8 g sat.); 12 g carbo (0.4 g fiber); 91 mg sodium; 45 mg chol.

## Venetian Panettone

*1½-pound loaf*

**1.** Use ingredients and follow steps for **Brioche**, preceding, adding 2 tablespoons grated **orange** peel, 1 tablespoon grated **lemon** peel, and 1½ teaspoons **vanilla**.

**2.** When fruit and nut signal sounds (or 5 minutes before end of last kneading), add ¼ cup **golden raisins** and ¼ cup **sliced almonds**.

Per ounce: 111 cal., 43% (48 cal.) from fat; 2.5 g protein; 5.3 g fat (2.7 g sat.); 13 g carbo (0.6 g fiber); 94 mg sodium; 46 mg chol.

## Braided Brioche or Panettone

**1.** Process ingredients for **Brioche** or **Venetian Panettone**, preceding, on dough cycle, according to manufacturer's directions.

**2.** At the end of the cycle, scrape the dough onto a board lightly coated with **all-purpose flour**. Divide dough into 3 equal pieces. If making a 1½-pound loaf, roll each piece to form a rope about 12 inches long. For a 2-pound loaf, roll each piece to form a rope about

14 inches long. Lay ropes parallel about 1 inch apart on a buttered 14- by 17-inch baking sheet. Pinch ropes together at one end, braid loosely, then pinch braid end together.

**3.** Cover loaf lightly with plastic wrap and let stand in a warm place until puffy, about 35 minutes. Remove plastic wrap.

**4.** Beat 1 **large egg** yolk to blend with 1 tablespoon **water**. Brush braid with egg mixture.

**5.** Bake braid in a 350° oven until golden brown, about 30 minutes. Cool on a rack at least 15 minutes before slicing. Serve hot, warm, or cool.

Per ounce braided brioche: 106 cal., 45% (48 cal.) from fat; 2.5 g protein; 5.3 g fat (2.9 g sat.); 12 g carbo (0.4 g fiber); 94 mg sodium; 54 mg chol.

Per ounce braided panettone: 117 cal., 44% (51 cal.) from fat; 2.8 g protein; 5.7 g fat (2.8 g sat.); 14 g carbo (0.6 g fiber); 98 mg sodium; 55 mg chol.

## Five-Seed Wheat Bread

| Ingredients | 1½-pound loaf | 2-pound loaf |
|---|---|---|
| water | 1 cup | 1¼ cups |
| salad oil | 2 tablespoons | 3 tablespoons |
| honey | 2 tablespoons | 3 tablespoons |
| all-purpose flour | 1½ cups | 2 cups |
| whole-wheat flour | 1½ cups | 2 cups |
| sunflower seed | 5 teaspoons | 2 tablespoons |
| millet | 5 teaspoons | 2 tablespoons |
| mustard seed | 5 teaspoons | 2 tablespoons |
| sesame seed | 1 tablespoon | 4 teaspoons |
| poppy seed | 1 tablespoon | 4 teaspoons |
| salt | ½ teaspoon | ¾ teaspoon |
| active dry yeast | 1 package | 1 package |

**1.** Add ingredients to bread machine pan according to manufacturer's directions.

**2.** Select whole-wheat cycle.

**3.** Remove baked loaf from pan at once. Cool on a rack at least 15 minutes before slicing. Serve hot, warm, or cool.

Per ounce: 85 cal., 25% (21 cal.) from fat; 2.4 g protein; 2.3 g fat (0.2 g sat.); 14 g carbo (1.5 g fiber); 52 mg sodium; 0 mg chol.

## Tropical Banana Quick Bread

| Ingredients | 1½-pound loaf | 2-pound loaf |
|---|---|---|
| sweetened flaked dried coconut | ⅓ cup | ½ cup |
| milk | ⅓ cup | ½ cup |
| large egg | 1 | 1 |
| butter or margarine | 3 tablespoons | ¼ cup (⅛ lb.) |
| mashed ripe banana | ½ cup | ¾ cup |
| all-purpose flour | 1½ cups | 2 cups |
| baking powder | ¾ teaspoon | 1 teaspoon |
| baking soda | ¼ teaspoon | ½ teaspoon |
| salt | ½ teaspoon | ½ teaspoon |
| sugar | ½ cup | ¾ cup |
| diced dried papaya | ⅓ cup | ½ cup |

**1.** Toast coconut in an 8- to 9-inch frying pan over medium heat, stirring.

**2.** Add ingredients to bread machine pan according to manufacturer's directions, adding coconut last.

**3.** Select quick-bread cycle.

**4.** Remove baked loaf from pan at once. Cool on a rack at least 15 minutes before slicing. Serve hot, warm, or cool.

Per ounce: 79 cal., 27% (21 cal.) from fat; 1.2 g protein; 2.3 g fat (1.3 g sat.); 14 g carbo (0.5 g fiber); 97 mg sodium; 12 mg chol.

## Sourdough Starter

*Notes:* For best results, use freshly purchased, just-opened milk and yogurt.

*Makes:* About 1⅓ cups

- 1 cup **nonfat** or low-fat **milk**
- 3 tablespoons **plain yogurt**
- 1 cup **all-purpose flour**

**1.** Warm milk to 90° to 100°. Stir in yogurt.

**2.** Pour into a warm 3- to 6-cup container (glass, ceramic, plastic, or stainless steel) with an airtight lid.

**3.** Cover and let mixture stand in a warm (80° to 90°) place until it has the consistency of yogurt, 18 to 24 hours; the mixture should be so thick it doesn't flow readily when container is tilted. A single clot may form or smaller curds may be suspended in clear liquid. Stir to mix in any clear liquid. If liquid turns bright pink, discard the batch and start again.

**4.** Once clot forms, add flour and stir until smooth. Cover airtight and let starter stand in a warm (80° to 90°) place until it is full of bubbles and has a pleasing sour smell, 2 to 5 days. Again, if clear liquid forms, stir to blend mixture. If liquid is pink, discard and start over. To store, cover airtight and refrigerate.

### Using and maintaining the starter

*Notes:* For most active starter, feed at least once a month. *To increase starter supply,* in a large container, add as much as 10 cups *each* of milk and flour to 1 cup of starter. The mixture may need to stand up to 2 days before the clear liquid forms on top.

**1.** Use starter at room temperature. To hasten, set container in warm water.

**2.** Use and/or feed starter.

*To feed,* replenish each 1 cup starter used with 1 cup warm (90° to 100°) **nonfat** or low-fat **milk** and 1 cup **all-purpose flour.** Stir to mix well.

**3.** Cover starter airtight and let stand in a warm (80° to 90°) place until bubbly and sour-smelling, and clear liquid has formed on top, 12 to 24 hours.

**4.** Stir before using. Store airtight in the refrigerator.

# Questions we get asked

*My loaf has an irregular shape. What can I do?*

■ If the loaf is a little wrinkled or bumpy on top, count it a success, as these imperfections are not unusual; results vary with recipes as well as machines.

Defects such as a deeply caved top and gummy, dense texture are serious. The recipe may not work (all *Sunset* recipes are tested, but others may not be), or you may not have followed the recipe accurately. Consult the manual's troubleshooting section or call the toll-free customer service number.

*How can I make my favorite bread recipes in my machine?*

■ Start with a recipe that fits the capacity of your machine. If you have a recipe with a similar volume of ingredients to those of a bread machine recipe that you know works, success is likely. In general, a recipe with a total of 2½ to 3 cups of flour or flours makes about a 1-pound loaf; 3 to 3½ cups of flour, about 1½ pounds; and 3½ to 4 cups of flour, about 2 pounds.

You can process any yeast bread, if scaled for the machine, through the first rising, then shape the loaf in or on a pan, let it rise, and bake in oven.

*What causes sourdough to be dense and heavy?*

■ Most trouble begins with the starter. It naturally grows more acidic with time, and if your loaf is solid and doughy (as if it didn't rise), chances are the starter has become so acidic that, as George York explains, it has destroyed the loaf's ability to rise and hold its shape.

If this happens, neutralize the acidity of your starter:

• Add ½ teaspoon baking soda to 1 cup starter (mixture foams). Then use starter as directed.

• Or feed starter as directed above.

*What if my sourdough bread isn't as tangy as expected?*

■ Wait for the starter to grow more flavorful with time. But flavors from different starter ingredients vary, so if you don't like the one you have, make a new starter (above) using a different brand of yogurt. ◆

# The Low-Fat Cook

## HEALTHY CHOICES FOR THE ACTIVE LIFESTYLE

### BY ELAINE JOHNSON

Hot grapes, whole cooked shallots, and chives garnish sole baked in a delicate sauce.

## Velvety sauces without cream?

■ Like many French classics, sole Véronique and Normandy-style chicken are known for their lavish sauces. Yet they can retain surprisingly rich character even when the sauces are adjusted to meet low-fat criteria. The secret, an unlikely ingredient, is cooked breakfast cereal. It adds more flavor than cornstarch, and the sauce retains its texture with long cooking better than a cornstarch-thickened sauce.

Karen Souther of Monte Sereno, California, uses the cereal to make a simplified version of the sole, and it also works well with this light version of chicken with cider from Jennifer Kirkgaard of Burbank, California.

Use rice cereal that cooks in about 30 seconds.

## Sole with Grapes

*Prep and cook time:* About 30 minutes
*Makes:* 4 servings

- 2 tablespoons minced **shallots**
- 1 cup **dry white wine**
- 1 teaspoon grated **lemon** peel
- 1 tablespoon **lemon juice**
- ¾ cup **nonfat milk**
- 3 tablespoons **quick-cooking rice cereal**
- 1¼ cups **seedless green grapes**
  - **Salt** and **pepper**
- 1 pound **boned, skinned sole fillets** (about ⅓ in. thick), rinsed

1. In an 8- to 10-inch nonstick frying pan over medium-high heat, boil shallots and ¼ cup water until pan is dry. Stir shallots often until light brown, about 5 minutes.
2. Add wine, lemon peel, and lemon juice. Boil over high heat until reduced to ¼ cup, about 5 minutes. Add milk, cereal, and ⅔ cup grapes (mixture will curdle) and stir until boiling.
3. In a blender, purée sauce. Season to taste with salt and pepper.
4. Arrange fish in a shallow 2½- to 3-quart casserole. Pour sauce over fish.
5. Bake in a 450° oven until fish is opaque but still moist-looking in thickest part (cut to test), 8 to 10 minutes.
6. Rinse and dry frying pan. Place over medium-high heat. When hot, add remaining grapes. Shake pan until grapes are hot, about 2 minutes. Pour over fish.

Per serving: 192 cal., 8.3% (16 cal.) from fat; 24 g protein; 1.8 g fat (0.5 g sat.); 19 g carbo (0.9 g fiber); 122 mg sodium; 55 mg chol.

## Cider Chicken

*Prep and cook time:* About 35 minutes
*Makes:* 4 servings

- ½ cup minced **shallots**
- 1 teaspoon **dried thyme**
- 1¼ cups **cider** or apple juice
- ¼ cup **calvados** or brandy
- ⅔ cup **pitted prunes**
- ¾ cup **nonfat milk**
- 3 tablespoons **quick-cooking rice cereal**
  - **Salt** and **pepper**
- 4 **boned, skinned chicken breast halves,** rinsed

1. In an 8- to 10-inch nonstick frying pan over medium-high heat, boil shallots, thyme, and ½ cup water until pan is dry. Stir often until shallots are light brown, 8 to 10 minutes total.
2. Add cider, calvados, and prunes to pan; bring to a boil. Lift out prunes and set aside. Boil liquid down to ¾ cup. Add milk and cereal and stir until boiling.
3. In a blender, purée sauce. Season to taste with salt and pepper.
4. In each of 4 shallow casseroles (5 by 8 in.), place a half breast; cover with sauce.
5. Bake in a 450° oven until meat is white in thickest part (cut to test), about 12 minutes. Add prunes.

Per serving: 251 cal., 6% (15 cal.) from fat; 30 g protein; 1.7 g fat (0.4 g sat.); 29 g carbo (2.1 g fiber); 102 mg sodium; 67 mg chol. ◆

# The grill from Ipanema

## Brazilian barbecue ignites the West; recipes and hot new restaurants

BY ANDREW BAKER • PHOTOGRAPHS BY RICK SZCZECHOWSKI

■ It was in Belém, Brazil, that I had my first restaurant meal abroad—and it was unforgettable. At the Churrascaria Tucuruvi, waiters brandished swords loaded with still-sizzling chunks of meat, which they sliced generously onto my plate. Steps away, a *churrasco* buffet was laden with potato dishes, salads, rice, beans, and even stews for my choosing. Instantly, I fit into this carnivore heaven.

But *farofa*, the condiment the Brazilians sprinkled indulgently over the whole meal, was a new sensation. It looked like sawdust, yet tasted toasty and crunchy—and it was strangely addictive.

The beverage that washed down this feast, *guaraná* (gwar-a-*nah*), made from an unusual South American berry, tasted like a cross between cream soda and champagne. I loved the refreshing flavor. Little wonder that tables were strewn with empty guaraná bottles.

Churrasco is a barbecuing technique from cattle ranches in the south of Brazil. For fiestas not unlike those held on early California ranchos, local cowboys—gauchos—speared big slabs of meat, then drove the tip of the spear or pole into the ground to tilt the meat over an open fire.

In our churrascarias—restaurants that serve churrasco (more and more of which are appearing in the West)—meat cooks on rotisseries or grills and is often served *rodizio*-style—hunks carved at the table. Portions are generous, often all-you-can-eat.

Meats, including beef, pork, poultry, and sausages, are the main attraction. But potatoes—fried, roasted, mashed, and in salads—are always on the menu. So is the ubiquitous farofa (toasted manioc flour), plain or seasoned.

For a simple but festive churrasco menu, serve churrasco misto (mixed grill), farofa, collards, salsas, bread, and dessert. For a grander party, add as many of the buffet dishes (see page 58) as you wish.

Look for guaraná soda and passion fruit (*maracujá* in Portuguese, *maracuyá* in Spanish) beverages in cans or bottles in Latino markets. Passion fruit beverages are also sold at supermarkets—refrigerated, in concentrates, canned, and bottled.

### Brazilian *churrasco* party for 8

**Churrasco Misto (Mixed Grill)**

**Farofa e Couve com Toicinho**
**(Toasted Manioc**
**and Collards with Bacon)**

**Salsa Campanha**
**(Country-style Salsa)**

**Salsa Verde**
**(Green Sauce)**

**Buffet Dishes (see page 58)**

**Country-style Breads**

**Mango Sorbet**

**Guaraná Soda**

**Passion Fruit Drinks**

Hot from the grill, skewers are laden with

### Churrasco Misto

***Prep and cook time:*** About 30 minutes
***Notes:*** If making ahead, cover and chill meats in vinegar mixture up to 2 hours, turning meats over occasionally.
***Makes:*** 8 servings

- 5   tablespoons **white wine vinegar**
- ½   cup **olive oil**
- 2   teaspoons **ground cumin**

churrasco misto meats. Clockwise from front, prosciutto-wrapped turkey tenderloins, sausages, and beef tri-tip.

4 teaspoons **pepper**

2 teaspoons minced **garlic**

1 fat-trimmed **beef tri-tip** (1½ to 2 lb.)

2 **turkey tenderloins** (also called fillets; about 1½ lb. total)

1½ pounds **Italian sausages**

4 ounces **thinly sliced prosciutto**

**1.** In a large bowl, mix vinegar, oil, cumin, pepper, and garlic.

**2.** Rinse beef, turkey, and sausages, pat dry, and coat in vinegar mixture.

**3.** Lift out turkey, drain, and wrap each piece with prosciutto.

**4.** Thread 2 metal skewers (about 13 in. long) parallel and about 2 inches apart through the longest part of the beef. Thread 1 skewer lengthwise through each turkey tenderloin. Thread sausages lengthwise onto 2 or 3 skewers.

**5.** Lay skewered meats on a grill over a solid bed of hot coals or over high heat on a gas grill (you can hold your hand at grill level only 2 to 3 seconds); close lid on gas grill. Brush meats once or twice with remaining vinegar mixture and turn as needed to brown evenly. Cook beef medium-rare, about 20 minutes, or medium, about 25 minutes; cut to center of thickest part to test. Cook turkey and sausages until no longer pink in center of thickest part (cut to test), 13 to 20 minutes for turkey, 12 to 15 minutes for sausages.

6. Place skewered meats on a platter. To serve, slice beef and turkey from skewers. Cut sausages in chunks.

Per serving: 570 cal., 55% (315 cal.) from fat; 58 g protein; 35 g fat (9.2 g sat.); 2.4 g carbo (0.3 g fiber); 918 mg sodium; 167 mg chol.

## Farofa e Couve com Toicinho

*Prep and cook time:* About 45 minutes

*Notes:* Manioc flour, also known as cassava, or yuca, flour, is sold in Latino markets or specialty food stores. Quick-cooking wheat cereal can be used as a substitute. If making ahead, cool, cover, and chill farofa and collards separately up to 1 day. Reheat to serve.

*Makes:* 3½ to 4 cups farofa, about 2¾ cups collards; 8 servings each

- 1¼ to 1½ pounds **collards**
- ½ pound **bacon,** chopped
- 2 **onions** (about 1 lb. total), finely chopped
- 2 cups **manioc flour**
- ¼ cup (⅛ lb.) **butter** or margarine
- ⅓ cup sliced **pimiento-stuffed green olives**

1. Rinse and drain collards. Trim and discard tough stems. Stack collard leaves and slice thinly crosswise.

2. In a 10- to 12-inch nonstick frying pan over high heat, stir bacon and onion until bacon is crisp and onion is lightly browned, about 15 minutes. Pour half the mixture (with drippings) into a bowl.

3. Add manioc and butter to pan. Stir often until manioc is golden and crisp (bite to test), 4 to 6 minutes. Pour into

To go with meats, crunchy farofa is sprinkled over collards and salads.

a bowl at once. Serve hot, warm, or at room temperature, topped with olives.

4. Return remaining bacon-onion mixture to pan. Stir in about half the collards until wilted, 1 to 2 minutes. Add remaining collards and stir until all are wilted, 1 to 2 minutes more.

Per serving farofa: 309 cal., 44% (135 cal.) from fat; 1.7 g protein; 15 g fat (6.8 g sat.); 40 g carbo (1.9 g fiber); 294 mg sodium; 26 mg chol.

Per serving collards: 105 cal., 71% (75 cal.) from fat; 2.3 g protein; 8.3 g fat (3 g sat.); 5.9 g carbo (2 g fiber); 108 mg sodium; 9.5 mg chol.

## Salsa Campanha

*Prep time:* About 10 minutes

*Notes:* If making ahead, cover and chill up to 1 day.

*Makes:* About 2½ cups; 8 servings

- 1 cup diced (¼ in.) **green bell peppers**
- ½ cup diced (¼ in.) **onion**
- ½ cup diced (¼ in.) **tomato**
- ½ cup minced **parsley**
- ¼ cup **white wine vinegar**
- 2 tablespoons **olive oil**
  **Salt** and **pepper**

In a bowl, mix green peppers with onion, tomato, parsley, vinegar, and oil. Add salt and pepper to taste.

Per serving: 42 cal., 74% (31 cal.) from fat; 0.4 g protein; 3.4 g fat (0.5 g sat.); 2.7 g carbo (0.7 g fiber); 3 mg sodium; 0 mg chol.

## Salsa Verde

*Prep time:* About 12 minutes

*Notes:* If making ahead, cover and chill up to 1 day.

*Makes:* About 1 cup; 8 servings

- ¾ cup lightly packed **fresh cilantro**
- 1½ cups lightly packed **parsley**
- 6 tablespoons **lemon juice**
- ¼ cup **olive oil**
- 1½ teaspoons minced **garlic**
  **Salt**
  Fresh-ground **pepper**

In a blender or food processor, purée the cilantro, parsley, lemon juice, olive oil, and garlic until smooth. Add salt and pepper to taste. Pour into a small bowl.

Per serving: 69 cal., 88% (61 cal.) from fat; 0.5 g protein; 6.8 g fat (0.9 g sat.); 2.1 g carbo (0.8 g fiber); 9.7 mg sodium; 0 mg chol.

BUFFET DISHES

- •**Green salad** with an oil and vinegar dressing.
- •**Potato salad.** Use your favorite recipe or purchase.
- •**Black beans.** To quickly replicate long-simmered Brazilian-style beans, prepare 1 package (10 oz.) **instant black beans** as package directs. Drain and add 2 cans (14 to 15 oz. each) **black beans.** Heat.
- •**Rice.** Use long-grain white.

## Churrascarias in the West

These Brazilian churrascarias may be small cafes where foods are grilled and served with the accompanying dishes in the kitchen. Or they may be lavish eateries—with waiters, sometimes clad as gauchos, parading long skewers of meat to your table to carve off portions. Usually there is the Brazilian buffet of side dishes. European culinary influences are evident, since Brazil's heritage is as immigrant-rich as ours. Other Brazilian restaurants often serve churrasco.

DENVER AREA:
*Denver.* Rodizio Grill, 1801 Wynkoop St.; (303) 294-9277.
*Littleton.* Rodizio Grill, 7900 W. Quincy Ave.; (303) 972-0806. Also at 2222 E. Arapahoe Rd.; (303) 347-0650.

LAS VEGAS:
Yolie's Brazilian Steakhouse & Lounge, 3900 Paradise Rd.; (702) 794-0700.

LOS ANGELES AREA:
*Anaheim.* Ginga Brazil, 821 N. Euclid Ave.; (714) 778-0266.
*La Mirada.* Rio Churrascaria, 15122 E. Rosecrans Ave.; (714) 739-2000.
*Long Beach.* Yolie's Brazilian Steakhouse, 300 Oceangate, Suite 150; (562) 491-0221.
*Santa Monica.* By Brazil, 1104 Wilshire Blvd.; (310) 393-0447.
*Westlake Village.* Galletto Caffe & Grill, 982-2 Westlake Blvd.; (805) 449-4300.

SAN FRANCISCO AREA:
*Kensington.* Porto Brasil, 385 Colusa Ave.; (510) 526-1500. ◆

# Good-time buddies

### Team mild asparagus with fresh tarragon for a dynamic combination

BY AMANDA HESSER

Asparagus cooks last in lamb stew.

JAMES CARRIER (2)

■ Their act is a bit like the good cop–bad cop routine. Asparagus is sweet, fresh, and clean-tasting—delicate. Tarragon is racy, aggressive, and prone to take over—bold. Together, they're a classic, with each bringing out the finest in the other. The effect is best when the tarragon is fresh. Unlike the dried herb, which has an aniselike intensity, fresh tarragon can be used with a free hand.

## Braised Lamb with Asparagus and Tarragon

*Prep and cook time:* About 1½ hours
*Makes:* 6 servings

- 2 pounds **boned, fat-trimmed lamb shoulder**, cut into 1-inch cubes
- 1 **onion** (½ lb.), chopped
- 1 **carrot** (3 to 4 oz.), peeled and chopped
- ¼ cup chopped **fresh tarragon**
- ¾ cup **dry white wine**
- 3 cups **chicken broth**
- 1½ pounds **red thin-skinned potatoes** (1 to 1½ in. wide), scrubbed
- 2 pounds **asparagus**
  **Salt** and **pepper**

**1.** In a 6- to 8-quart pan, combine lamb, onion, carrot, 2½ tablespoons tarragon, and 1 cup water. Cover and cook over high heat for 20 minutes.

**2.** Uncover and cook until liquid evaporates and drippings are browned, about 15 minutes; stir often as mixture browns.

**3.** Add wine and broth. Stir to scrape browned drippings free, then cover pan and simmer over low heat 15 minutes. Add potatoes, cover, and simmer until lamb and potatoes are tender when pierced, about 25 minutes.

**4.** Meanwhile, rinse asparagus and snap off and discard tough ends. Cut asparagus diagonally into 1-inch lengths.

**5.** When meat is tender, stir asparagus into stew. Simmer, uncovered, until asparagus is tender when pierced, about 5 minutes. Season to taste with salt and pepper and ladle into wide soup bowls. Sprinkle stew with remaining tarragon.

Per serving: 374 cal., 29% (108 cal.) from fat; 38 g protein; 12 g fat (4.1 g sat.); 31 g carbo (4.1 g fiber); 177 mg sodium; 102 mg chol.

## Asparagus Tarragon Soup

*Prep and cook time:* About 30 minutes
*Makes:* 5 cups; 4 servings

- 1½ pounds **asparagus**
- 2 teaspoons **olive oil**
- ¼ cup chopped **shallots**
- 3 tablespoons chopped **fresh tarragon**
- 1 can (14½ oz.) **vegetable broth**
- ¼ cup **whipping cream**
  **Salt**

**1.** Rinse asparagus and snap off and discard tough ends. Coarsely chop asparagus.

**2.** In a 4- to 5-quart pan over medium heat, stir olive oil and shallots until shallots are limp, about 3 minutes. Add asparagus, 1½ tablespoons tarragon, vegetable broth, and 2 cups water. Bring to boiling over high heat and cook until asparagus is tender-crisp when pierced, about 3 minutes longer.

**3.** Meanwhile, whip cream until it holds soft peaks.

**4.** In a blender, purée soup until smooth, a portion at a time. Season to taste with salt.

**5.** Return soup to pan and stir over high heat until steaming. Ladle into bowls, and sprinkle with remaining tarragon.

**6.** Add an equal portion of whipped cream to each bowl.

Per serving: 122 cal., 55% (67 cal.) from fat; 5.4 g protein; 7.4 g fat (3.2 g sat.); 11 g carbo (1.5 g fiber); 42 mg sodium; 17 mg chol. ◆

# Kitchen Cabinet

## READERS' RECIPES TESTED IN SUNSET'S KITCHENS

### BY LINDA LAU ANUSASANANAN

Beet, carrot, and apple shreds make a crunchy salad.

## Norwegian Beet Salad

### Anore Jones, Three Rivers, California

A beet salad that Anore Jones enjoyed on a trip to Oslo inspired this crisp, fresh version she created in her California kitchen. And as a native Alaskan, she likes to cook a caribou roast to go with the salad.

**Prep time:** About 15 minutes
**Makes:** 4 or 5 servings

- 1 **beet** (6 oz.)
- 1 **carrot** (6 oz.)
- 1 **apple** (6 oz.)
- 1 cup **chopped pecans** or walnuts
- ½ cup **shredded dried coconut,** sweetened or unsweetened
- 2 tablespoons **lemon juice**
- 1 tablespoon minced **fresh ginger**
- 1 tablespoon **Asian** (toasted) **sesame oil** or olive oil

 Chopped **parsley**

 **Salt**

**1.** Peel and shred beet, carrot, and apple. Combine in a bowl.

**2.** Add nuts, coconut, lemon juice, ginger, and oil to beet mixture. Stir and sprinkle with parsley.

**3.** Season salad with salt to taste.

Per serving: 245 cal., 73% (180 cal.) from fat; 2.6 g protein; 20 g fat (3.7 g sat.); 18 g carbo (3.6 g fiber); 47 mg sodium; 0 mg chol.

## Caldo Verde

### Pix Stidham, Exeter, California

"I'm an American of Portuguese descent," says Pix Stidham. "A staple in any Portuguese household is a soup called *caldo verde,* or kale soup. It hit the spot whenever we were feeling bad."

**Prep and cook time:** About 1 hour
**Makes:** 8 to 10 servings

- 1 pound **linguisa** (Portuguese sausages)
- 1 **onion** (8 oz.), chopped
- 2 cloves **garlic,** pressed or minced
- 2½ quarts **chicken broth**
- 1 **cinnamon stick** (3 in. long)
- 1 **dried bay leaf**
- 2 teaspoons **whole allspice**
- 2 pounds **russet potatoes**
- 1 pound **collard greens** or kale
- 1 can (15 oz.) **cannellini** (white beans), rinsed and drained

 **Salt** and **pepper**

**1.** Cut sausages into ¼-inch-thick slices.

**2.** In a 6- to 8-quart pan over medium-high heat, stir sausages often until lightly browned, about 10 minutes. With a slotted spoon, transfer sausages to paper towels to drain. Discard all but 1 teaspoon fat from pan.

**3.** Add onion and garlic to pan. Stir often over medium-high heat until onion is limp, about 5 minutes.

**4.** Add broth to pan. Tie cinnamon stick, bay leaf, and allspice in cheesecloth and add to broth. Cover and bring to a boil over high heat.

**5.** Meanwhile, peel potatoes and cut into ½-inch cubes. Cut out and discard tough parts of collard stems. Rinse leaves well, drain, and stack. Cut stack in half lengthwise, then cut crosswise into thin strips.

**6.** Add collard greens, potatoes, and beans to broth; cover and bring to a boil.

**7.** Simmer, covered, over low heat for 20 minutes. Add sausages and continue simmering, covered, until potatoes are tender when pierced, 5 to 10 minutes longer. Remove and discard wrapped spices.

**8.** Ladle soup into bowls. Add salt and pepper to taste.

Per serving: 292 cal., 43% (126 cal.) from fat; 14 g protein; 14 g fat (5.3 g sat.); 28 g carbo (4.9 g fiber); 663 mg sodium; 34 mg chol.

NOEL BARNHURST (2)

## Chili Beef Loaf

Mary Guzman, Idyllwild, California

To satisfy the fondness her Mexican-American husband and their children have for spicy foods, Mary Guzman uses chili to jazz up simple meat loaf. She serves the meat loaf with boiled red thin-skinned potatoes. And she says she makes a large loaf because "it also makes good sandwiches."

*Prep and cook time:* About 1¼ hours
*Makes:* 8 to 10 servings

- 2 pounds **ground lean** (7% or less fat) **beef**
- 2 **large eggs**
- 1½ cups **red** or green **chili salsa**
- ½ cup **fine dried bread crumbs**
- ½ cup minced **onion**
   About 1 teaspoon **salt**
   About ½ teaspoon **pepper**
- 1 can (4 oz.) **whole green chilies**
- 1 cup (4 oz.) **shredded jack cheese**
   **Sour cream** (optional)

**1.** Mix beef with eggs, ½ cup salsa, bread crumbs, onion, 1 teaspoon salt, and ½ teaspoon pepper.

**2.** Pack half the meat mixture flat into a 5- by 9-inch loaf pan.

**3.** Cut green chilies into ½-inch strips and arrange over the meat. Sprinkle with half the cheese.

**4.** Pack remaining meat mixture over chili-cheese layer.

**5.** Bake in a 400° oven until well browned, 55 to 60 minutes. Sprinkle with remaining cheese and let stand about 10 minutes.

**6.** Cut meat loaf into thick slices and lift out with a wide spatula. Serve with sour cream, remaining salsa, and salt and pepper to taste.

Per serving: 233 cal., 42% (99 cal.) from fat; 23 g protein; 11 g fat (4.8 g sat.); 7.9 g carbo (0.5 g fiber); 694 mg sodium; 107 mg chol.

## Yogurt Pesto Pasta

Denise Naughton,
Colorado Springs, Colorado

Stuck at home on a winter's day, Denise Naughton turned to ingredients on hand in the refrigerator to come up with this tangy pesto sauce.

*Prep and cook time:* About 45 minutes
*Makes:* 6 to 8 servings

- 2 teaspoons **olive oil**
- 1 **onion** (6 oz.), chopped
- 3 cloves **garlic**, sliced
- ⅓ pound **mushrooms**, rinsed and sliced
- ⅔ cup (3 oz.) chopped **cooked ham**
- 1 can (15 oz.) **tomato sauce**
- ⅓ cup (3 oz.) **pesto** or 2 tablespoons dried basil
- 1 package (10 oz.) **frozen chopped spinach**, thawed
- 1 pound **dried vermicelli**
- 1 pint **plain nonfat yogurt**
- 4 teaspoons **cornstarch**
   **Salt** and **pepper**

**1.** In a 10- to 12-inch frying pan, combine oil, onion, garlic, and mushrooms. Stir often over high heat until onion is limp, 3 to 4 minutes.

**2.** Add ham and stir often until mushrooms are lightly browned, about 5 minutes longer.

**3.** Add tomato sauce and pesto to mushroom mixture. Turn heat down to low.

**4.** Squeeze liquid from spinach. Add spinach to pan and heat until simmering.

**5.** Meanwhile, cook vermicelli in about 3 quarts boiling water until just tender to bite, 7 to 9 minutes. Drain and keep warm.

**6.** Mix yogurt and cornstarch. Stir into sauce, then stir over high heat until bubbling, about 3 minutes.

**7.** Pour sauce over pasta. Mix to blend. Add salt and pepper to taste.

Per serving: 372 cal., 21% (79 cal.) from fat; 16 g protein; 8.8 g fat (1.6 g sat.); 57 g carbo (3.5 g fiber); 636 mg sodium; 9.2 mg chol.

## Mega-Ginger Cookies

Jozie Rabyor, Portland

Jozie Rabyor loves ginger, especially in these soft, chewy cookies. She grinds the candied ginger and mixes the dough in her food processor so her cookie jar gets filled quickly.

*Prep and cook time:* About 20 minutes, plus 1 hour to chill
*Makes:* About 4 dozen cookies

- ½ cup chopped **crystallized ginger**
- ¾ cup **sugar**
- 6 tablespoons **butter** or margarine, at room temperature
- ¼ cup **molasses**
- 1 **large egg**
- 2 cups **all-purpose flour**
- 2 teaspoons **baking soda**
- ¾ teaspoon **ground cinnamon**
- ½ teaspoon **ground nutmeg**

**1.** In a food processor (or blender), whirl ginger and ⅓ cup sugar until ginger is finely ground. Pour from container.

**2.** Put butter and ⅓ cup sugar in food processor (or bowl) and whirl (or beat with a mixer) until fluffy.

**3.** Add ginger mixture, molasses, and egg; whirl (or beat) to mix.

**4.** Mix flour, soda, cinnamon, and nutmeg. Add to butter mixture; whirl (or stir, then beat) to blend well.

**5.** Cover dough and chill until firm to the touch, about 1 hour.

**6.** Shape dough into 1-inch balls and coat in remaining sugar. Place balls 2 to 3 inches apart on nonstick or oiled baking sheets.

**7.** Bake in a 350° oven until slightly darker brown, 11 to 12 minutes total (if using 1 oven, switch pan positions after about 6 minutes). Transfer cookies to racks to cool. Serve, or store airtight up to 1 week; freeze to store longer.

Per cookie: 61 cal., 23% (14 cal.) from fat; 0.7 g protein; 1.6 g fat (0.9 g sat.); 11 g carbo (0.1 g fiber); 71 mg sodium; 8.3 mg chol. ◆

These chewy cookies, sparkling with sugar, pack a ginger punch.

Chicken Enchiladas with Salsa Verde combines poblano and serrano chilies, tomatillos, and pumpkin seeds (recipe on page 72).

# April

# foodguide

BY JERRY ANNE DI VECCHIO

## a good egg

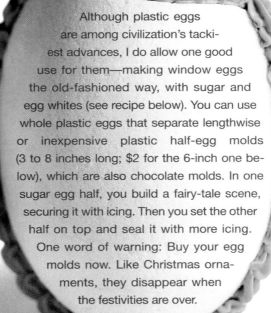

Although plastic eggs are among civilization's tacki-est advances, I do allow one good use for them—making window eggs the old-fashioned way, with sugar and egg whites (see recipe below). You can use whole plastic eggs that separate lengthwise or inexpensive plastic half-egg molds (3 to 8 inches long; $2 for the 6-inch one below), which are also chocolate molds. In one sugar egg half, you build a fairy-tale scene, securing it with icing. Then you set the other half on top and seal it with more icing. One word of warning: Buy your egg molds now. Like Christmas ornaments, they disappear when the festivities are over.

JAMES CARRIER (3)

## Sweet scenes

***Prep and cook time:*** About 1 hour

**1.** In a bowl, mix 3 cups **sugar** and 1 **large egg** white with your fingers until thoroughly blended. This is enough to make 3 to 4 egg halves 6 inches long.

**2.** For 1 egg half, firmly pack sugar mixture into the mold with your hand. Scrape top level with a spatula; save extra sugar mixture.

**3.** To form the window, make a clean cut across the narrow end of the egg, through the sugar mixture straight down to the mold. The closer to the center of the egg you cut, the larger the window. Lift out cut section with the tip of a thin spatula and return to bowl.

**4.** With a spoon, gently scoop sugar mixture from the center of the mold to make a shell. For a 6-inch-long mold, make the shell ½ to ⅝ inch thick—thinner for smaller eggs, thicker for larger ones. Smooth window edge and

rim of egg with a spatula (or it will be rough when baked).

**5.** Invert a small baking sheet on top of mold; holding mold and pan together, invert again. Tap mold gently as you lift it carefully off sugar egg. If egg breaks, wash and dry mold, then fill again, reusing sugar mixture.

**6.** Bake in a 200° oven until egg surface feels hard and solid, 10 to 15 minutes. With a spoon, gently scrape free any loose sugar inside egg. Return egg to oven and bake until well dried, 10 to 15 minutes more.

**7.** Repeat to make matching sugar egg half.

**8.** To make a scene, arrange **decorations** of miniature flora and fauna in 1 egg half, securing with dabs of **icing** (recipe follows).

**9.** Using a pastry bag with rosette tip, generously pipe icing onto rim of egg half with scene. Fit remaining egg half over it, then pipe icing around the seam and window opening. Let dry at least 1 hour. To store, package egg airtight.

***Icing.*** To make about ¾ cup (enough for a 6- to 8-in. egg), whip 1 **large egg** white and ⅛ teaspoon **cream of tartar** with a mixer on high speed until foamy. Gradually beat in 1½ cups **powdered sugar.** Tint icing desired shade with **food coloring.** If needed, beat in more powdered sugar to make icing stiff enough to hold its shape when squeezed through pastry bag with a decorative tip.

## Cheese-stuffed Pork Loin

***Prep and cook time:*** About 1 hour and 25 minutes

***Makes:*** 10 to 12 servings

- 1 **boned center-cut pork loin** (about 3 lb.), fat trimmed
- 6 **mustard-green leaves** (9 to 10 in. long)
- 2 packages (5.2 oz. each) **herb- and garlic-flavor Boursin cheese**
- ½ cup **grated parmesan cheese**
- Fresh-ground **pepper**
- 1 cup fat-skimmed **chicken broth**

**1.** Lay loin fat side down. Make a cut lengthwise down the center of the meat and about ⅔ of the way through it. Push meat flat and, starting from the deepest part of the center cut, make a 1-inch horizontal cut toward each side, running the length of the meat. Push meat flat again.

**2.** Trim stem ends from mustard greens, rinse leaves, and dip in boiling water to wilt; drain briefly.

**3.** Line meat lengthwise with greens, overlapping as needed, extending about 4 inches beyond ends of meat. Spoon Boursin onto leaves down center of roast, then sprinkle evenly with parmesan. Fold extended leaves over cheese flush with ends of meat. Then lap leaves across cheese lengthwise. Gently roll loin back into a log (don't squish out cheese) and tie with cotton string at 2-inch intervals.

**4.** Set loin, cut side down, in a 10- by 15-inch pan and sprinkle generously with pepper.

**5.** Bake in a 375° oven until meat is 150° to 155° in center of thickest part (not in cheese), 50 to 55 minutes. Remove from oven and let stand at least 20 minutes.

**6.** Transfer roast to a platter and keep warm. Skim and discard fat from pan drippings. Add broth and whisk until smooth. Boil over high heat until reduced to about 1¼ cups, about 10 minutes. For a smooth sauce, whirl in a blender.

**7.** Cut loin into ¾- to 1-inch slices, remove string, and serve with sauce.

Per serving: 283 cal., 54% (153 cal.) from fat; 29 g protein; 17 g fat (10 g sat.); 1.5 g carbo (0.2 g fiber); 298 mg sodium; 103 mg chol.

# Spring roast

■ Birds, with their nice body cavities, invite stuffing. But if you want to place a flavorful filling in the center of a solid piece of meat, you need to follow a plan. First, start with an ideal piece of meat, such as the center cut of a boned pork loin.

The loin is from the back ribs—which at my market often sell for more than the loin itself—and is uniformly thick (about 3 inches). Butterflying creates a generous space for a filling of soft cheese wrapped in tender leaves. The cheese oozes just enough as the roast cooks to form the base of a rich brown sauce.

Instead of the Boursin called for in the recipe, you can use an equal weight of herb- and garlic-flavor Rondelé cheese. Serve roast hot or cold with warm sauce.

COOK'S DISCOVERY

# Thin Indian pancakes

■ *Dosas* (or *dosais*) are India's flavorful version of crêpes made with lentil flour and cooked on a grill called a *tava*. To discover these thin pancakes, try a mix. I've come across a few brands in Indian groceries. Most packages weigh 7 ounces and make four 8- or 9-inch-wide pancakes. I often dilute the batter with extra water to make thinner dosas. They are browned on one side only, then typically wrapped around a curry mixture. I like them folded over salad or curried scrambled eggs.

Average per piece: 178 cal., 5.1% (9 cal.) from fat; 6 g protein; 1 g fat (0 g sat.); 37 g carbo (6 g fiber); 645 mg sodium; 0 mg chol.

BACK TO BASICS

# To peel or not to peel

■ Few tasks sound more tedious and affected than peeling asparagus, but I'm all for it. Without that fibrous exterior, you can enjoy each spear to its tender base.

First snap off the tough ends of the asparagus. Then, holding at the tip, peel away scales and the thin outer skin. A plain old vegetable peeler works best, and one glide per cut will do. No point whittling away. Peeling goes faster than you think, especially if you buy fat asparagus.

*To cook asparagus,* immerse in boiling water and cook until tender when pierced, 3 to 4 minutes. Drain at once. Serve hot or cold. To chill, immerse cooked asparagus at once in ice water until cold. Allow about ½ pound asparagus for a serving.

Per serving: 40 cal., 9% (3.6 cal.) from fat; 5.6 g protein; 0.4 g fat (0.1 g sat.); 6.7 g carbo (1.8 g fiber); 3.6 mg sodium; 0 mg chol.

*Norwegian sauce.* Finely mash 1 hard-cooked **large egg** with 6 tablespoons room-temperature **butter.** Spoon onto hot asparagus. Makes ½ cup.

Per tablespoon: 86 cal., 98% (84 cal.) from fat; 0.9 g protein; 9.3 g fat (5.6 g sat.); 0.1 g carbo (0 g fiber); 96 mg sodium; 50 mg chol.

---

AMONG FRIENDS

# Inspiration from the garden

■ Cathrine Sneed raises more than plants. She raises the human spirit, too. She founded the Garden Project, a group of gardening programs sponsored by the San Francisco County Sheriff's Office for jail inmates, recently released inmates, the homeless, the unemployed, and students. These efforts are inspired by her belief in gardening as a way to educate, rehabilitate, and delight. It even works at home. Her son, now 24, grew up requesting this comforting soup made with vegetables that he and his friends helped grow and harvest.

## Cabbage and Lentil Soup

*Prep and cook time:* About 1½ hours

*Notes:* For vegetarian tastes, use water. Cover and chill soup up to 3 days. Thin as desired with broth or water.

*Makes:* 4¾ quarts; 8 to 10 servings

- 1 pound (2 cups) **lentils**
- 6 cups **chicken broth** or water
- 2 tablespoons **cumin seed**
- 1 tablespoon **olive oil**
- 1 head **green cabbage** (about 1 lb.), coarsely shredded
- 6 to 8 leaves **curly kale** (optional; 6 to 7 in. long), stems trimmed, chopped
- 6 **carrots** (about 1½ lb. total), peeled and sliced
- 2 **firm-ripe tomatoes** (¾ to 1 lb. total), rinsed, cored, and chopped
- 6 to 8 **green onions**
  **Salt**

**1.** Sort lentils and discard debris. Rinse lentils and put in a 6- to 8-quart pan. Add 4 cups water, broth, cumin seed, olive oil, cabbage, kale, carrots, and tomatoes.

**2.** Bring to a boil over high heat, then cover and simmer gently, stirring occasionally, until vegetables are soft and flavors well blended, about 1 hour.

**3.** Trim ends from onions and chop onions. Ladle soup into bowls, add onions, and season to taste with salt.

Per serving: 234 cal., 12% (29 cal.) from fat; 16 g protein; 3.2 g fat (0.7 g sat.); 38 g carbo (8.9 g fiber); 103 mg sodium; 2.3 mg chol. ◆

JAMES CARRIER (2)

# The Wine Guide

BY KAREN MacNEIL

RICK MARIANI

## Wild and wise in Santa Barbara

■ Paris, circa 1920. Though no one knew precisely why, the most avant-garde artists and writers in the world gathered here. It was a magical and almost mystical time. Paris had become a mecca for mavericks.

Santa Barbara County, the present. The same thing is happening—but this time the draw is wine. Seemingly inexplicably, dozens of America's most wild and imaginative winemakers have gravitated here. If Steven Spielberg were a winemaker, you can bet he'd be making wine in Santa Barbara County.

Does all of this creativity affect the actual taste of the wines? I think it does. Santa Barbara County wines are sassy, daring, a little reckless and unpredictable. Miss Manners probably wouldn't like them.

Not that any winemaker in the county would care. These are the sort of men and women for whom the phrase *conventional wisdom* is an oxymoron. More often than not, winemaking here means shooting from the hip.

What's amazing about this to me is that it works. On a recent trip to Santa Barbara County, I could not believe the sheer number of fantastic wines I found. Bottle after bottle (I tried some 200 wines) turned up one great surprise after another.

But before I tell you about them, a word about the unique and spectacular geography that helps make these extraordinary wines possible.

Santa Barbara County, about an hour and a half north of Los Angeles, comprises two main valleys—the Santa Maria and the Santa Ynez. These valleys in turn are made up of undulating hills, deep canyons, and windswept mesas.

Most important, both run east to west, opening with total vulnerability right onto the Pacific. You can actually taste the ocean in the air.

Why does this matter? Because the proximity to the sea means that both the soil and the climate are uniquely suited to producing wine. (Bordeaux, for example, would not be Bordeaux were it not for the influence of the nearby Atlantic Ocean.) Cold air sweeps off the sea and barrels down the Santa Maria and Santa Ynez valleys as though they were wind tunnels.

Much to the thrill of the vines. Certain vines, anyway—notably Pinot Noir, Pinot Blanc, Pinot Gris, Chardonnay, and Syrah. These grapes not only thrive in coolness but virtually require it if they are to be made into elegant wines.

Elegance. That's the other thing. The best wines from these valleys exude elegance. No muddled flavors, no overwrought bodies, no components sticking out like sore thumbs. They exist in Zen-like refinement.

Pinot Noir is the leading star. These are earthy, smoky Pinots laced with chocolate, tangerine, and spice flavors. Their texture is pure silk.

Listing every excellent Santa Barbara Pinot Noir would be impossible, so instead I'll give you my personal A+ list of producers whose Pinots I can't get enough of (even at $25 to $50 a bottle):
• Au Bon Climat
• Babcock Vineyards
• Byron Vineyard and Winery
• Foxen Vineyard
• Hartley-Ostini
• Sanford Winery
• Santa Barbara Winery

Pinot Noir, however, is just the tip of the iceberg. The Santa Maria and Santa Ynez valleys also produce some of the world's most devastatingly creamy, lemony versions of Pinot Gris and opulent, honeyed Pinot Blancs. (Both of these white wines make a terrific change of pace from Chardonnay.) The three top producers of Pinot Gris and Pinot Blanc are Babcock, Byron, and Au Bon Climat.

I could write a whole story on the excellent Chardonnays, Merlots, Rieslings, Cabernet Francs, and Cabernet Sauvignons made in the region. And I could write *another* story about the up-and-coming Italian varieties—especially Sangiovese—now being planted in these valleys.

But the one wine I must tell you about here is Syrah. Santa Barbara County is simply packed with sensational Syrahs, as well as other Rhône varieties. These are wildly spicy, howling-with-pepper, full-of-personality Syrahs that detonate on your taste buds with flavor.

Exactly what the winemakers of Santa Barbara had in mind. ◆

## THE MOST OUTRAGEOUS OF ALL

It's almost impossible to choose just a few favorite wines from the Santa Maria and Santa Ynez valleys in Santa Barbara County. But the following are absolute standouts:

■ *Babcock Pinot Gris 1996,* $15. As light and elegant as lemon sorbet.

■ *Byron Pinot Blanc 1996,* $16. Gorgeous, rich. Lemon drops drizzled with honey.

■ *Gainey Chardonnay 1996,* $15. Packed with style, energy, and pizzazz.

■ *Au Bon Climat "Isabelle" Pinot Noir 1995,* $50. Very expensive, but a treat you should have at least once in your life. Earthy, sexy, complex.

■ *Foxen Cabernet Sauvignon "Ma Mere Vineyard" 1995,* $40. Primordially intense, deep, and lush.

■ *Zaca Mesa Syrah 1995,* $20. The delicious confluence of boysenberries, tar, and leather.

■ *Andrew Murray Syrah 1995,* $25. Prototypically sassy and reckless—just right for Clint Eastwood. — *K. M.*

# Hot *on the* chili

All you need to know about buying, cooking, and enjoying the fiery fruit

**Chilies** have shaped the tastes of the West. They're the backbone of Mexican dishes we've embraced, they're integral to the foods of the Southwest, and they're essential to the global cuisines we've adopted.

More chilies are available fresh than ever before, in a rainbow of bright and glossy hues. A typical neighborhood grocery stocks three or four varieties; a trendy supermarket may showcase at least 10, often in various stages of ripeness. Add to these choices the uncommon chilies that show up fresh in farmers' markets—even in flower shops as decorative plants—and the collection grows. We picture 16 varieties here. Most

chilies are available year-round; the season is May through October in the West and Florida, and November through May in Mexico.

When you buy chilies, what you're getting isn't always clear. Varieties often have several common names—and even then, they're apt to be mislabeled because their shapes, colors, and characteristics are notoriously confusing.

Botanically speaking, all chilies are members of the pepper (*Capsicum*) genus and bear fruit that we use like vegetables. Some capsicums—bell peppers and pimientos—are sweet and mild. But chilies, at their sassiest, have heat—gentle enough to bring a glow to the palate or sizzling enough to set it wildly on fire. A chili's

*Santa Fe Grande*

*Chilaca*

*Chiltepín*

*Habanero*

*Dátil*

*Poblano*

# trail

BY ANDREW BAKER

PHOTOGRAPHS BY JAMES CARRIER

*Cayenne*

*Rocoto*

*Chilpequín*

*Anaheim or New Mexico*

*Serrano*

*De Arbol*

*Ají Flor*

*Rocotillo*

*West Indian Hot*

*Jalapeño*

pungency is a compelling and addictive essence. Some of us find euphoria in the pleasure that follows the pain. As we acclimate to each level of warmth, the more we're able to tolerate, up to a dangerous point—chilies actually can burn.

A chili's fieriness is a varietal characteristic that's significantly affected by growing conditions, such as temperature and the amount of water and sun it gets. A single plant may produce chilies with different pungency, different shapes, and different colors all at once. But behind chilies with even the most blaze, rich flavors await discovery.

## TRACKING CHILIES

Although we view chilies as Western, and grow them in large quantities, they haven't always been here. Native to South America, they traveled with traders to Europe and the Far East before they arrived in New Mexico with the Mexican-Spanish settlers of 1598. Later, chili varieties came here with Chinese, Korean, Thai, Indian, and other immigrants, who brought them to make their native dishes.

New Mexico leads the nation in chili production, but California leads in breeding commercial varieties: Santa Fe grande and its look-alike, the Fresno, were born in the Golden State. The city of Anaheim gave its name to a long, mild chili (also called California and New Mexico). Canned as immature green chilies under the Ortega label, they've been a Western staple for more than a century.

In *Sunset,* cooking with chilies has a long history. One reference in 1935 tells how to broil chilies in order to peel them. Another in 1951 explains how to reduce a chili's sizzle by cutting out the veins and seeds. And as early as 1954, we warned cooks to wear gloves for protection from chilies' burn.

*Nuestra Señora de los Chiles*

*The Pepper Lady's POCKET PEPPER PRIMER*

TEXT AND PHOTOGRAPHS BY JEAN ANDREWS

## THE PEPPER LADY'S PASSION

Jean Andrews, an artist and botanist, has made chilies her career. It started with an interest in growing, painting, and cooking chilies, which she calls—with her native-Texan authority and botanical leanings—chilli peppers. Frustrated by scarce information on the *Capsicum* genus, she set off to find answers.

The trail took her to almost every country around the globe where chilies are grown and used. Such is Andrews's passion that she's trademarked herself the Pepper Lady. She routinely propagates chili seeds she's brought back from her travels to paint or photograph, then she eats the chilies. Her first book on the subject, *Peppers: The Domesticated Capsicums* (University of Texas Press, Austin, 1995; $65), is a classic reference,

# At the market

**These chilies, shown on pages 68 and 69,** are a sampling from Western markets and Jean Andrews's book. Her facts, plus our panel's tasting notes, will help you select the chilies you want. Immature chilies have a more vegetal or herbaceous flavor, and ripe chilies have a mellower, richer flavor. Each chili has a pungency rating from 0 (no heat) to 10+ (hottest, which is equivalent to the maximum Scoville units, 100,000+).

■ **Ají flor** (Arawak-Spanish for *flower-shaped chili*), also known as ají orchid or orchid pepper, and often mislabeled rocotillo. Yellow-green, ripens to golden yellow or orange-red; 1½ to 2 in. long, 1 to 2½ in. wide. Flavor: sweet, with grassy to honeylike tones. Substitutes: red bell pepper, pimiento. Heat rating: 0 to 3.
■ **Anaheim/New Mexico** (named for where it grows), also known as California long green chili, chilacate, chile college, chile colorado, chile de ristra, chile verde, Chimayo, Hatch, long green/red

chili, New Mexico 6-4, New Mexico No. 9, or pasado. Bright green, ripens to red; 7 to 10 in. long, 1 to 1¾ in. wide. Flavor: juicy, herbaceous to vegetal and sweet. Substitute: poblano. Heat rating: 3 to 5.
■ **Cayenne** (possibly a French colonial name from Africa or South America). Because this was one of the first chilies transported, and the most widely grown, it has different names in every country. Dark green, ripens to red or yellow; 5 to 6 in. long, ½ to ¾ in. wide. Flavor: vegetal,

mellow and sweet at first, hot later. Substitutes: jalapeño, serrano, Thai. Heat rating: 7 to 9.
■ **Chilaca** (Nahuatl for *old chili*—it's wrinkled and bent), called a pasilla when dried. Dark green–black, ripens to dark brown; 6 to 12 in. long, 1¼ to 1½ in. wide. Flavor: vegetal to sweet. Substitute: poblano. Heat rating: 3 to 5.
■ **Chilpequín** (Nahuatl for *small chili*), also known as amash, amomo, bird, bravo, chilillo, chilipiquín, chilpaya, chiltipiquín, del monte, huarahuao, max, or

piquén. Green, ripens to red, some nearly black; ½ to ¾ in. long, about ¼ in. wide. Flavor: fruity, floral, and mellow if you can separate the thin flesh from the fiery veins. Substitutes: cayenne, Thai, tabasco. Heat rating: 10+.
■ **Chiltepín** (Nahuatl for *flea chili*). Like chilpequín in every respect except size and flavor. About ¼ in. long, ¾ in. wide. Flavor: mainly potent heat.
■ **Dátil** (Spanish for *date*—it's tiny and wrinkled), also known as Mindoran or Minorcan. Yellow-green, ripens to golden yellow; about 2 in. long, ¾ in. wide. Flavor: grassy to fruity. Substitute: habanero. Heat rating: 10.
■ **De árbol** (Spanish for *from the tree*), also known as alfilerillo, bravo, cola de rata, cuauhchilli, ginnie pepper, or pico de pájaro.

relative sizes of 46 peppers (39 fresh) accompanied by the basics of each: multiple names, average sizes, colors, shapes, uses, and substitutes.

As Andrews pursues chilies, she also collects recipes for them, and the following come from her travels. See the list below for varieties that can be used as alternatives in these dishes.

***To minimize the heat of chilies*** in order to savor the more complex underlying flavors, carefully cut away the stem and seeds, then slice off the veins on the interior walls.

## Javanese Sambal with Grilled Shrimp

***Prep and cook time:*** About 25 minutes
***Makes:*** 4 servings

1 cup **sweetened flaked** or shredded **dried coconut**

6 **fresh serrano chilies** (about 1½ oz. total), stemmed, seeded, deveined, and chopped

1½ teaspoons **anchovy paste**

2 cloves **garlic**

5 tablespoons **lime juice**

1 pound (26 to 30 per lb.) **peeled, deveined shrimp**

**1.** In a food processor, whirl coconut, chilies, anchovy paste, garlic, and lime juice until coconut and chilies are minced; scrape container sides frequently.

beautifully and accurately illustrated with her paintings of chilies.

It was the shopper's confusion that inspired her newest book, *The Pepper Lady's Pocket Pepper Primer* (University of Texas Press, 1998; $17.95, 800/252-3206 or 512/471-7233). In this 184-page volume, slim enough to take to the market, she mixes wit with wisdom as she concisely explains more than you've dreamed of asking about capsicums—with and without heat. There is helpful information about nomenclature, cultivars (varieties and hybrids), family groupings, and how to choose and store peppers. Color photographs show

---

Green, ripens to red; about 3 in. long, ⅜ in. wide. Flavor: grassy to sweet-hot, with delayed heat. Substitutes: serrano, green Thai, green cayenne. Heat rating: 7.

■ **Habanero** (Spanish for *from Havana*), also known as Congo, bonda man jacques, bonnie, ginnie pepper, guinea pepper, pimenta do chiero, siete caldos, Scotch bonnet, and pimienta do cheiro (in Brazil). Green, ripens to yellow-orange, orange, or orange-red; 1 to 2½ in. long, about 1 in. wide. Flavor: medicinally sour to florally sweet and hot. Substitutes: jalapeño or dátil (for heat), Scotch bonnet or rocoto (for flavor). Heat rating: 10+.

■ **Jalapeño** (Spanish for *from Jalapa*), also known as acorchado, bola, bolita, candelaria, cuaresmeño, gorda, huachi-

nango, jarocho, mora, or morita. Bright green or deep green–black, ripens to red or yellow; about 3 in. long, 1½ in. wide. Flavor: herbaceous to sweet. Substitutes: caloro, caribe, Fresno, Santa Fe grande, serrano. Heat rating: 4 to 8.

■ **Poblano** (Spanish for *from Pueblo*), also known as ancho, chile para rellenar, joto, Mexican, or mulato, and often mislabeled pasilla (a dried chilaca). Dark green, ripens to red or brown; about 4 in. long, 2½ in. wide. Flavor: mild, mellow, slightly vegetal. Substitutes: Mexi-bell, Anaheim/New Mexico. Heat rating: 3 to 7.

■ **Rocotillo** (Spanish for *little Rocoto*), also known as pimiento. Green, ripens to deep red; 1½ to 2 in. long, 1½ to 2 in. wide. Flavor: sweet and fruity. Substitute: red bell pepper with a dash

of ground dried cayenne. Heat rating: 1 to 3.

■ **Rocoto** (a South American name), also known as caballo, canario, manzana, perón, or jalapeño. Green, ripens to red or golden yellow; 1 to 1½ in. long, 1 to 1½ in. wide. Has black seeds. Flavor: sweet and fruity, with a heat that builds slowly but irrevocably. Substitutes: habanero, jalapeño. Heat rating: 9 to 10.

■ **Santa Fe grande,** also known as caloro, caribe, cera, or güero. Pale green–yellow, ripens to orange, then red; about 3 in. long, 1½ in. wide. Has squarer shoulders than a jalapeño. Flavor: grassy to sweet. Substitutes: any pungent yellow pepper (cascabella, floral gem, Hungarian wax). Heat rating: 5 to 7.

■ **Serrano** (Spanish for *from the foothills* or *mountains*), also

known as balín, chile verde, cora, morita, serranito, or típico. Green, ripens to red; about 2¼ in. long, ½ in. wide. Flavor: herbaceous. Substitutes: chiltepín, Fresno, jalapeño, Thai. Heat rating: 6 to 8.

■ **West Indian hot** (named for where it grows). Green, ripens to red; 1 to 2½ in. long, about 1 in. wide. Flavor: tropical fruit, with mellow heat. Substitutes: dátil, habanero. Heat rating: 10+.

■ **Other chilies** you are apt to find in Western markets include cascabella; cherry (hot cherry, Hungarian cherry, sweet cherry); Fresno; Hungarian wax (Hungarian yellow wax); pepperoncini; peter pepper (penis pepper); romesco; tabasco; Thai/hang prik; tomato pepper (paprika, Spanish paprika, squash pepper).

**2.** Rinse and drain shrimp. Thread onto 4 flat metal skewers (10 to 14 in.).

**3.** Place shrimp on a barbecue grill over a solid bed of medium-hot coals or on a gas grill set at medium-hot (you can hold your hand at grill level only 3 to 4 seconds); close lid on gas grill. Cook shrimp, turning once, until bright pink and opaque but still moist-looking in center of thickest part (cut to test), 3 to 5 minutes total.

**4.** Transfer shrimp to a platter. Serve with sambal paste to add to taste.

Per serving: 221 cal., 33% (73 cal.) from fat; 24 g protein; 8.1 g fat (5.7 g sat.); 12 g carbo (1.4 g fiber); 288 mg sodium; 174 mg chol.

## Chicken Enchiladas with Salsa Verde

***Prep and cook time:*** About 1½ hours

***Notes:*** Green, hulled pumpkin seeds add color to the sauce. If making sauce ahead, cover and chill up to 1 day.

***Makes:*** 6 servings

- 2  pounds **tomatillos,** husks removed
- 1  pound **poblano chilies**
- ½  cup **salted roasted** or raw **shelled pumpkin seeds**
- 4  cloves **garlic**
- ⅓  cup lightly packed chopped **fresh cilantro**
- 2  cups **chicken broth**
- 2  to 4 **fresh serrano chilies** (½ to 1 oz. total), stemmed, seeded, deveined, and chopped
- 1  **red onion** (¾ lb.)
- 15  **corn tortillas** (6 to 7 in.), cut in half
- 3  cups shredded skinned **cooked chicken**
- 3  cups (1½ lb.) **shredded jack cheese**

Green sauce for chicken enchiladas combines poblano and serrano chilies, tomatillos, and pumpkin seeds.

**Cilantro sprigs**

**Salt**

**Sour cream**

**1.** Rinse tomatillos. Place tomatillos and poblanos in a 10- by 15-inch rimmed pan. Broil 4 to 6 inches from heat, turning as needed, until tomatillos and poblanos are blackened all over, about 20 minutes total. Set aside as charred. When cool enough to handle, pull off and discard poblano peels, stems, seeds, and veins.

**2.** In a blender or food processor, whirl (in batches if necessary) tomatillos, poblanos, pumpkin seeds, garlic, cilantro, and broth until chili sauce is smoothly puréed. Add serranos to taste and whirl to purée.

**3.** Meanwhile, peel onion and cut 3 or 4 thin slices from the center. Separate slices into rings and wrap airtight. Finely chop remaining onion.

**4.** Spread 1 cup chili sauce over the bottom of a shallow 3-quart casserole (about 10 by 12 in.). Cover sauce with ⅓ of the tortillas, overlapping them. Scatter ½ the chicken, ½ the chopped red onion, and 1 cup cheese over tortillas. Spoon 1 cup chili sauce over cheese. Cover completely with another ⅓ of the tortillas. Scatter remaining chicken, remaining onion, and 1 cup cheese over tortillas; moisten evenly with 1 cup chili sauce. Cover with remaining tortillas, then coat tortillas evenly with remaining sauce.

**5.** Bake in a 400° oven until sauce is bubbling at edges of casserole, about 15 minutes. Sprinkle remaining cheese on enchiladas and bake until it melts, 2 to 3 minutes.

**6.** Scatter red onion rings over enchiladas and garnish with cilantro sprigs. Cut into rectangles and serve with a wide spatula. Add salt and sour cream to taste.

Per serving: 810 cal., 48% (387 cal.) from fat; 57 g protein; 43 g fat (22 g sat.); 51 g carbo (5.4 g fiber); 824 mg sodium; 183 mg chol.

## Caribbean Habanero Cornbread

***Prep and cook time:*** About 50 minutes

***Makes:*** 9 servings

- 1  cup **yellow cornmeal**
- 1  cup **all-purpose flour**
- 1  tablespoon **sugar**
- 2½  teaspoons **baking powder**

## The name game

**Columbus landed** in the Caribbean in 1492 seeking spices, including black pepper. Convinced that the hot pods the native Arawaks called *ají* were a form of pepper, he called them *pimientos,* after the Spanish word for pepper. The name ají is still used in parts of the Caribbean and South America.

When Hernán Cortés set foot in Mexico in 1518, he was introduced to the local Nahuatl word, *chilli,* which later became the Spanish *chile.* Today aficionados, grudgingly, use chile and chili interchangeably, while botanists prefer chili or chilli peppers.

The popularity of chilies has cursed them with confusion. Their proliferation and inclination to cross-pollinate mean new chilies are always on the horizon—perhaps in your own garden. Add to this the myriad shapes, colors, and names by which many varieties are known and you have a recipe for a spicy etymological mystery.

½ teaspoon **salt**

¼ cup **salad oil**

1 **large egg,** beaten to blend

1 can (8½ oz.) **cream-style corn**

½ cup **plain nonfat yogurt**

½ cup **shredded jack cheese**

2 tablespoons minced **fresh habanero chilies**

2 tablespoons minced **fresh green Anaheim chili**

**1.** In a large bowl, stir to combine cornmeal, flour, sugar, baking powder, and salt.

**2.** Add oil, egg, corn, yogurt, cheese, habaneros, and Anaheims. Stir until ingredients are evenly moistened.

**3.** Pour batter into an oiled 8-inch square pan. Bake in a 375° oven until bread is golden brown and begins to pull from pan sides, 30 to 35 minutes.

**4.** Cut bread into squares and serve hot, warm, or cool.

Per serving: 226 cal., 36% (81 cal.) from fat; 6.2 g protein; 9 g fat (2.1 g sat.); 31 g carbo (1.5 g fiber); 392 mg sodium; 31 mg chol.

## Indian Spiced Potatoes

**Prep and cook time:** About 20 minutes

**Makes:** 4 servings

1 tablespoon **salad oil**

¼ teaspoon **caraway seed**

1 teaspoon **cumin seed**

1 cup finely chopped **red onion**

2 cloves **garlic,** minced

6 **fresh serrano chilies** (about 1½ oz. total), stemmed, seeded, deveined, and minced

2 teaspoons minced **fresh ginger**

2 teaspoons **ground dried turmeric**

3 cups diced cooked **thin-skinned potatoes**

1 to 2 teaspoons minced **fresh cayenne chili** or ground dried cayenne

¼ cup chopped **fresh cilantro**

¼ cup chopped **fresh mint** leaves

2 tablespoons **lime juice**

**Salt**

**1.** In a 10- to 12-inch frying pan over medium-high heat, combine oil, caraway seed, and cumin seed. Stir until seed smells slightly toasted, about 2 minutes.

**2.** Add onion, garlic, serranos, and ginger; stir until onion is limp but not browned, about 2 minutes. Stir in turmeric and potatoes, then add cayenne to taste. Stir often until potatoes are hot, about 2 minutes.

**3.** Add cilantro, mint, and lime juice. Mix, then add salt to taste.

Per serving: 164 cal., 21% (35 cal.) from fat; 3.3 g protein; 3.9 g fat (0.5 g sat.); 31 g carbo (3.1 g fiber); 16 mg sodium; 0 mg chol.

## Portuguese Red Pork

**Prep and cook time:** About 2 hours

**Notes:** Mild red peppers give this dish its color, and fresh jalapeños add a subtle level of heat.

**Makes:** 4 servings

6 **fresh jalapeño chilies** (4 to 6 oz. total), stemmed, seeded, deveined, and chopped

1 jar (about 8 oz.) **peeled red peppers**

3 pounds **fat-trimmed pork shoulder chops** (cut about 1 in. thick)

1 teaspoon **olive oil**

1 **onion** (about 6 oz.), finely chopped

2 cloves **garlic,** minced

¾ cup **dry white wine**

About 1 tablespoon chopped **parsley**

**Salt**

**Fresh-ground pepper**

**1.** In a blender or food processor, smoothly purée jalapeños and red peppers.

**2.** Rinse pork and pat dry.

**3.** Place an 11- to 12-inch nonstick frying pan with an ovenproof handle over medium-high heat. Add oil, onion, and garlic and stir often until mixture is lightly browned, 8 to 10 minutes. Pour onion mixture from pan.

**4.** Add pork chops to pan without crowding and brown evenly, turning once or twice, 3 to 5 minutes per side. Add onion and puréed jalapeño mixtures and wine; stir to blend.

**5.** Cover frying pan tightly (with lid or foil). Bake in a 375° oven until meat is very tender when pierced and pulls from bone easily, about 1½ hours. Uncover, stir, and bake until sauce is slightly thicker, about 10 minutes.

**6.** Transfer chops to a platter and pour sauce over them. Sprinkle with parsley; add salt and pepper to taste.

Per serving: 496 cal., 44% (216 cal.) from fat; 57 g protein; 24 g fat (8.1 g sat.); 9.7 g carbo (1.3 g fiber); 299 mg sodium; 195 mg chol.

## African Hot Sauce

**Prep time:** About 10 minutes

**Notes:** Serve this condiment as you would catsup, with everything from hamburgers to shrimp. To store, cover and chill up to 4 days; stir before using.

**Makes:** About 1¼ cups

1 can (8 oz.) **tomato sauce**

¼ cup chopped **onion**

1 clove **garlic**

About 3 tablespoons **lemon juice**

2 to 8 **fresh red jalapeño chilies** (1½ to 6½ oz. total), stemmed, seeded, deveined, and chopped

In a blender or food processor, whirl tomato sauce, onion, garlic, and lemon juice, adding a few chilies at a time, until smoothly puréed and hot enough to suit your taste.

Per tablespoon: 5.2 cal., 0% (0 cal.) from fat; 0.2 g protein; 0 g fat; 1.2 g carbo (0.2 g fiber); 69 mg sodium; 0 mg chol. ◆

## Fire controls

A chili's taste-temperature comes from capsaicin (cap-*say*-i-sin), a compound found primarily in its veins. Other hot spots are where the seeds and flesh touch the veins. As chilies ripen and develop more flavor, they may seem smoother or sweeter, but they're still hot. Approach with caution.

■ *When handling chilies* (fresh or dried), don't let them touch your skin. Wear rubber gloves or hold chilies with the tines of a fork, then trim with a small, sharp knife.

■ *If chilies burn your skin,* rinse the area with rubbing alcohol. If juice sprays into your eyes or you touch your eyes with capsaicin-coated hands, rinse eyes well with water.

■ *Chopping lots of fresh hot chilies?* Work in a ventilated area. Otherwise your chest may tighten or you'll cough.

■ *To soothe a burning tongue,* try ice cream, milk, or yogurt. All lower the surface temperature of your tongue and contain casein, which washes away the capsaicin.

# Asian noodles take off

## They're making forays into fast-food territory

BY LINDA LAU ANUSASANANAN • PHOTOGRAPHS BY STUART WATSON

■ Asia's answer to the Golden Arches is the noodle house. And in the West, where noodle houses have been dishing up cheap, fast food in ethnic neighborhoods for decades, noodles are establishing fresh turf. Satisfying noodle concoctions—generous enough to make a whole meal—are the essence of a swelling throng of bright, trendy restaurants. But going mainstream doesn't mean that the ethnic magic and good value are selling out.

Modest prices, fresh foods, quick delivery, and good tastes sum up the appeal of these new-wave noodle houses. At Oodles of Noodles in Kailua-Kona, Hawaii, everything on the menu is fresh and freshly made. At TK Noodles in California's Silicon Valley, where Tan Lu owns seven of these establishments, a generous portion of Chinese-style noodles costs as little as $2.75—add 75 cents for a really large serving. Many noodle houses, such as Noodle Planet in Los Angeles and Noodle Ranch in Seattle, feature a Pan-Asian lineup, including Chinese, Japanese, Thai, and Vietnamese noodle dishes.

In restaurants, noodle dishes are expeditiously composed in assembly-line order; they are also easy and relatively quick to make at home. For special ingredients, such as preserved vegetables, black soy sauce, or beef balls, you may need to shop at an Asian market. But a well-stocked supermarket will have all the basics and the Western alternatives.

## Shanghai Delight

*Prep and cook time:* About 35 minutes

*Notes:* At San Francisco's Longlife Noodle Company & Jook Joint, thick, chewy Shanghai-style noodles are seasoned with a savory mix of cabbage and pork.

*Makes:* 3 servings

- 1½ cups (1 oz.) **dried shiitake mushrooms**
- 1 pound **fresh Shanghai-style noodles** or ¾ pound fresh linguine
- 2 teaspoons **salad oil**
- 2 cloves **garlic**, pressed or minced
- ½ pound **fat-trimmed boned pork loin**, cut into matchstick-size slivers
- 4 cups slivered **napa cabbage**
- ¼ cup **mushroom soy sauce** (or 3 tablespoons soy sauce and 1 tablespoon molasses)
- 1½ tablespoons **Chinese black vinegar** or balsamic vinegar
- 1 teaspoon **Asian** (toasted) **sesame oil**
- ½ teaspoon **white pepper**
- ¼ cup thinly sliced **green onions**

**1.** Rinse mushrooms, immerse in hot water, and soak until soft, about 15 minutes. Holding under water, squeeze mushrooms to release grit, then lift mushrooms out and squeeze dry. Cut off and discard stems. Cut mushroom caps into ¼-inch-wide strips.

**2.** In a 5- to 6-quart pan, bring 3 quarts water to a boil over high heat. Add noodles and cook, stirring occasionally, until barely tender to bite, 4 to 6 minutes. Drain well.

**3.** Meanwhile, place a wok or 5- to 6-quart pan over high heat. When pan is hot, add salad oil and tilt pan to coat. Add garlic and pork; stir-fry until pork is lightly browned, about 4 minutes.

**4.** Add cabbage and stir just until it begins to wilt, 1 to 2 minutes.

**5.** Add noodles, mushrooms, soy sauce, vinegar, sesame oil, and pepper. Stir until noodles are hot, about 3 minutes. Transfer to plates. Sprinkle with onions.

Per serving: 664 cal., 18% (117 cal.) from fat; 37 g protein; 13 g fat (2.6 g sat.); 101 g carbo (6.1 g fiber); 1,122 mg sodium; 155 mg chol.

## TK Noodle Soup

*Prep and cook time:* About 25 minutes

*Notes:* This best-selling dish at TK Noodles is made with a broth base of equal parts bony chicken and pork simmered slowly for about 2 hours in water to barely cover. Canned broth is the fast alternative. For a condiment to add to taste to the soup, thinly slice

## THE SALT & PEPPER OF NOODLE HOUSES

**Most noodle houses** offer an assortment of condiments that you use to season the dishes. Some are basics like soy sauces, Asian fish sauce, white pepper, hoisin sauce, vinegars—plain or with sliced hot chilies—and hot chili oils, paste, and sauce. Others, such as the following, are simple to make and enhance most noodle dishes.

### Toasted Garlic Oil

In a 6- to 8-inch frying pan over medium-low heat, combine ½ cup **salad oil** and ¼ cup chopped **garlic**. Stir occasionally until garlic is a light golden color, 5 to 6 minutes, taking care not to scorch garlic. Serve, or cover airtight and store in the refrigerator up to 1 week. Makes about 10 tablespoons.

Per tablespoon: 102 cal., 97% (99 cal.) from fat; 0.2 g protein; 11 g fat (1.4 g sat.); 1.3 g carbo (0.1 g fiber); 0.7 mg sodium; 0 mg chol.

### Vietnamese Nuoc Cham

Mix ½ cup **Asian fish sauce** (*nuoc mam* or *nam pla*), ½ cup **water**, ¼ cup **rice vinegar**, ¼ cup **lime juice**, 2 tablespoons **sugar**, 2 pressed or minced **garlic** cloves, and 1 to 1½ teaspoons (to taste) minced **fresh hot chilies**. Serve, or cover and chill up to 1 week. Makes 1½ cups.

— *Nga Bui, Noodle Ranch, Seattle*

Per tablespoon: 12 cal., 0% (0 cal.) from fat; 0.7 g protein; 0 g fat; 2.3 g carbo (0 g fiber); 230 mg sodium; 0 mg chol.

Fresh, fast, and filling, TK Noodle Soup is protein-charged.

fresh jalapeño chilies and mix with distilled vinegar and Asian fish sauce or soy sauce.

*Makes:* 4 or 5 servings

- ⅓ pound **fat-trimmed boned pork loin**
- ⅓ pound **boned, skinned chicken breast**
- 1 pound **fresh thin Chinese-style egg noodles** or fresh angel hair pasta
- 10 to 12 cups fat-skimmed **chicken broth**
- ½ pound **cooked beef balls** (optional), thawed if frozen
- ½ pound (30 to 35 per lb.) **shrimp,** shelled and deveined

  **Salt** and **pepper**

  About 1 teaspoon **sugar**
- ½ cup thinly sliced **green onions**

  **Fresh cilantro sprigs**
- ½ cup **Tientsin preserved vegetables** (optional)

  **Toasted garlic oil** (see left)

**1.** Cut pork and chicken into 1- by 3-inch slices.

**2.** In a 6- to 8-quart pan over high heat, cook noodles in 3 to 4 quarts boiling water, stirring occasionally, just until hot and barely tender to bite, 2 to 3 minutes. Drain well. Place the hot noodles in 4 or 5 large soup bowls.

**3.** Meanwhile, in a 5- to 6-quart pan, bring broth to a boil over high heat. Add beef balls and return to a boil.

**4.** Stir in shrimp, pork, and chicken; cook until shrimp are opaque in thickest part (cut to test) and pork and chicken are no longer pink in thickest part, 2 to 3 minutes.

**5.** With a slotted spoon, transfer shrimp and meat onto noodles in each bowl.

**6.** Season broth to taste with salt, pepper, and sugar. Ladle hot broth into each bowl. Sprinkle portions equally with green onions, cilantro, and preserved vegetables. Add garlic oil to taste.

Per serving: 450 cal., 9.6% (43 cal.) from fat; 47 g protein; 4.8 g fat (1.1 g sat.); 51 g carbo (2.1 g fiber); 265 mg sodium; 158 mg chol.

In Los Angeles, Noodle Planet crew loads bowls with organized speed.

## Shrimp Tom Yum

***Prep and cook time:*** About 50 minutes
***Notes:*** At Noodle Planet in Los Angeles, thin rice noodles are added to this classic Thai hot-sour shrimp soup.
***Makes:*** 5 or 6 servings

- 1 stalk (12 to 16 in. long) peeled **lemon grass** or 3 strips (½ by 3 in. each) lemon peel (yellow part only)
- 1 or 2 **fresh jalapeño chilies** (2 oz. total)
- 6 slices (quarter-size) **fresh** or dried **galangal** or fresh ginger
- 4 **fresh** or dried **kaffir lime leaves** (optional)
- 2½ quarts fat-skimmed **chicken broth**
- 1 pound **dried rice noodles** (mai fun, rice sticks, or rice vermicelli) or dried angel hair pasta
- 1 pound (30 to 35 per lb.) **shrimp,** shelled and deveined
- ¼ cup **lime juice**
- 2 to 3 tablespoons **Asian fish sauce** (*nuoc mam* or *nam pla*)
- ½ cup **fresh cilantro** leaves
- ½ cup thinly sliced **green onions**

  **Chili oil**

**1.** Crush lemon grass slightly. Cut stalk into about 3-inch lengths.

**2.** Slice chili crosswise into thin rings; discard stem.

**3.** In a 3- to 4-quart pan, combine lemon grass, chili rings, galangal, lime leaves, and broth. Bring to a boil over high heat, cover, and simmer 15 to 20 minutes.

**4.** Meanwhile, in a 6- to 8-quart pan, bring about 3 quarts water to a boil over high heat. Add noodles and cook, stirring occasionally, until barely tender to bite, 3 to 4 minutes. Drain well. Place noodles in 5 or 6 large soup bowls.

**5.** With a slotted spoon, scoop lemon grass, chili rings, galangal, and lime leaves from broth and discard.

**6.** Stir shrimp into broth and cook until they are opaque in thickest part (cut to test), 2 to 3 minutes. Transfer shrimp with a spoon onto noodles in bowls.

**7.** To broth, add lime juice and fish sauce to taste. Ladle into bowls. Sprinkle with cilantro and onions. Add chili oil to taste.

Per serving: 397 cal., 2.5% (9.9 cal.) from fat; 27 g protein; 1.1 g fat (0.2 g sat.); 68 g carbo (0.4 g fiber); 583 mg sodium; 93 mg chol. ◆

# The Low-Fat Cook

## HEALTHY CHOICES FOR THE ACTIVE LIFESTYLE

### BY ELAINE JOHNSON

Creamy red pepper–parmesan sauce seasons salmon and coats angel hair pasta.

RICHARD JUNG

## Lean design for convenience

■ Susan Johnson was trying to shed a few pounds. She was also short on time for cooking, and frustrated by the lack of prepared foods that were fresh, lean, and really good-tasting. Figuring she wasn't alone, Johnson founded Healthy Gourmet, a company that delivers chilled, made-to-order, fat- and calorie-controlled meals directly to customers in Orange and Los Angeles counties.

Some of her recipes are also quick to make at home. And they store well, which is a boon when you want to get a jump-start on dinner or need to keep a meal ready for a late arrival. This pasta and salmon dish reheats perfectly.

### Red Pepper–Salmon Pasta

**Prep and cook time:** About 30 minutes

**Notes:** To reheat, put each serving on a microwave-safe plate, cover with microwave-safe plastic wrap, and warm 1 plate at a time in a microwave oven at full power (100%) until steaming, 2 to 3 minutes. Garnish with cilantro and serve with corn salad (recipe follows).

**Makes:** 4 servings

4   **boned, skinned salmon fillets** (each about $1\frac{1}{2}$ in. thick; 1 lb. total)

2   tablespoons **lemon juice**

$\frac{1}{2}$   cup **canned peeled red peppers**

$\frac{1}{3}$   cup **grated parmesan cheese**

1   tablespoon **cornstarch**

2   teaspoons chopped **fresh jalapeño chili**

1   clove **garlic**

$\frac{1}{4}$   cup chopped **fresh cilantro**

1   cup fat-skimmed **chicken broth**

8   ounces **dried angel hair pasta**

**1.** In an 8-inch baking dish, mix salmon with lemon juice and arrange in a single layer.

**2.** Tightly cover dish with foil. Bake in a 450° oven until fish is opaque but still moist-looking in thickest part (cut to test), 12 to 14 minutes.

**3.** Meanwhile, in a blender or food processor, smoothly purée red peppers, parmesan, cornstarch, chili, and garlic. Add cilantro and broth; whirl to blend.

**4.** Pour pepper mixture into a 10- to 12-inch frying pan. Stir over high heat until boiling; keep warm.

**5.** Meanwhile, cook pasta in 3 quarts boiling water until tender to bite, about 7 minutes. Drain; return to pan.

**6.** Stir juices from the baked salmon into red pepper sauce. Mix $1\frac{1}{3}$ cups sauce with pasta.

**7.** Spoon pasta onto plates. Top with fish and drizzle with remaining sauce. Serve, or cover and chill up to 1 day.

Per serving: 427 cal., 21% (90 cal.) from fat; 35 g protein; 10 g fat (2.5 g sat.); 46 g carbo (1.4 g fiber); 234 mg sodium; 68 mg chol.

### Corn Salad

**Prep time:** 10 minutes

**Makes:** 4 servings

Combine $\frac{1}{4}$ cup **cider vinegar;** 1 tablespoon **Dijon mustard;** 1 teaspoon *each* **sugar, olive oil,** and minced **garlic;** $\frac{1}{4}$ teaspoon **hot sauce** (or to taste); and $\frac{1}{4}$ teaspoon **ground cumin.** Mix with 2 cups thawed **frozen corn,** 1 cup chopped **zucchini,** and $\frac{1}{2}$ cup chopped **green onions.**

Per serving: 102 cal., 16% (16 cal.) from fat; 3.1 g protein; 1.8 g fat (0.2 g sat.); 21 g carbo (2.2 g fiber); 104 mg sodium; 0 mg chol. ◆

# The Quick Cook

JAMES CARRIER

## WHAT'S FOR DINNER?

Golden Onions and Eggs on Toast

Spring Salad Greens with Lemon Juice and Olive Oil Dressing

Strawberries on the Stem Brown Sugar and Sour Cream

## Taking it easy with eggs

■ Faced with a surplus of hard-cooked Easter eggs? Turn them into a quick main dish. Just gently sauté onions to make the mellow base for a creamy sauce, add the eggs, and serve on toast.

The simplicity and speed of this dish are reminders that few staple ingredients are more useful than eggs for emergency meals. Right from the refrigerator, they can be whipped into omelets or soufflés, scrambled into the following light version of the San Francisco classic, Joe's special, or poached in salsa-spiked broth to make a filling soup.

## Golden Onions and Eggs on Toast

**Prep and cook time:** About 30 minutes
**Notes:** Four English muffins, split and toasted, can be used instead of the toast.
**Makes:** 4 servings

| | |
|---|---|
| 1¼ | pounds **onions,** thinly sliced |
| 2 | tablespoons **butter** or margarine |
| 6 | hard-cooked **large eggs** |
| 1 | cup fat-skimmed **chicken broth** |
| ¼ | cup **all-purpose flour** |
| 1 | cup **low-fat milk** |
| 8 | slices **country-style bread** (¾ in. thick; ½ lb. total), toasted |
| | Minced **parsley** |
| | **Salt** |

**1.** In an 11- to 12-inch frying pan over medium-high heat, stir onions and butter often until onions are limp and lightly browned, about 10 minutes.

**2.** Meanwhile, shell eggs and chop.

**3.** Mix a little broth with flour to make a smooth paste, then add to remaining broth and mix into onion mixture. Add milk and stir over high heat until boiling, then stir about 2 minutes more.

**4.** Add eggs to sauce and mix well.

**5.** Spoon sauce onto toast. Sprinkle with parsley and add salt to taste.

Per serving: 438 cal., 35% (153 cal.) from fat; 21 g protein; 17 g fat (6.9 g sat.); 50 g carbo (4.2 g fiber); 537 mg sodium; 337 mg chol.

## Two more fast recipes

*1. Turkey Joe's Special.* In an 11- to 12-inch nonstick frying pan over medium-high heat, combine 1 cup chopped **onion,** ⅓ pound **sliced mushrooms,** and ¼ pound **ground turkey.** Stir often until mushrooms are lightly browned, about 10 minutes. Add ¼ pound (2½ cups packed) **washed spinach leaves;** stir often until wilted, 3 to 4 minutes. Meanwhile, beat 8 **large eggs** to blend. Turn heat to low, pour eggs into pan, and stir until eggs are creamy, 2 minutes, or as set as you like. Sprinkle with 2 to 3 tablespoons **shredded parmesan cheese** and season with **salt** and **pepper.** Serves 4.

Per serving: 231 cal., 51% (117 cal.) from fat; 21 g protein; 13 g fat (4.2 g sat.); 7.5 g carbo (1.9 g fiber); 224 mg sodium; 448 mg chol.

*2. Salsa Soup with Poached Eggs.* Discard fat from 1 can (49 oz.) **chicken broth.** Combine broth and 1½ cups **tomato salsa** in a 5- to 6-quart pan. Cover and bring to a boil over high heat, then reduce heat to just below an active boil. Crack 8 **large eggs,** one at a time; hold each close to soup surface and slip egg into pan. Cover and cook until yolks are as firm as you like, 4 to 5 minutes for slightly soft centers. Ladle 2 eggs into each bowl; fill bowls with soup. Sprinkle 1 cup **shredded cheddar cheese** equally over portions. Serves 4.

Per serving: 344 cal., 50% (171 cal.) from fat; 31 g protein; 19 g fat (9.1 g sat.); 7.6 g carbo (0 g fiber); 1,370 mg sodium; 455 mg chol. ◆

# Kitchen Cabinet

### READERS' RECIPES TESTED IN SUNSET'S KITCHENS

BY LINDA LAU ANUSASANANAN

Kumquat slices, with sour centers and sweet skin, enliven spinach salad.

## Spinach Kumquat Salad

Helen Magid, La Crescenta, California

"This was a mix-and-match evolution with the help of my 6-year-old son, Jake," says Helen Magid. Jake, who loves spinach, also insisted that his mother use kumquats from the tree in their front yard. Her solution became his favorite salad.

*Prep and cook time:* About 15 minutes
*Makes:* 4 to 6 servings

- ¾ cup **pecan halves**
- 1 cup (8 to 10 oz.) **fresh** or drained preserved **kumquats**
- 12 cups (10 oz.) **baby spinach leaves,** rinsed and crisped
- ½ cup chopped **Italian parsley**
- ½ pound **fresh chèvre** (goat) **cheese,** crumbled
- ½ cup **purchased poppy seed** or honey mustard **salad dressing**
  **Salt** and **pepper**

1. In a 6- to 8-inch frying pan over medium-low heat, stir pecans often until toasted, about 5 minutes. Pour from pan into a wide bowl.
2. Thinly slice kumquats crosswise and remove seeds.
3. Put kumquats in bowl with pecans. Add spinach, parsley, and cheese.
4. Add dressing to salad, and mix. Season salad to taste with salt and pepper.

Per serving: 294 cal., 70% (207 cal.) from fat; 9.8 g protein; 23 g fat (7.2 g sat.); 16 g carbo (2.3 g fiber); 254 mg sodium; 17 mg chol.

## Strawberries with Walnut Puffs

Judy Stock, Phoenix

"My husband has always loved this dessert," says Judy Stock. "When I first ate dinner with his family, his mom cut him a piece." But, she adds, instead of eating the piece, he consumed the rest of the dessert. "And he's a thin guy." Stock bakes her meringue as one puff. But we find individual puffs easier to manage—and everyone gets a portion.

*Prep and cook time:* About 45 minutes
*Makes:* 8 servings

- 3 **large egg** whites
- ¼ teaspoon **cream of tartar**
  About 1¼ cups **sugar**
- 1 teaspoon **ground cinnamon**
- ½ teaspoon **baking powder**
- 10 **saltine crackers** (2 in. square)
- ½ cup **chopped walnuts**
- 6 cups **strawberries,** rinsed, hulled, and sliced
- 1 cup **whipping cream,** softly whipped

1. In a large bowl, beat whites and cream of tartar with a mixer on high speed until whites are foamy.
2. Mix 1 cup sugar, cinnamon, and baking powder. Beating on high speed, gradually add sugar mixture to whites. Then continue beating until whites hold stiff, glossy peaks.
3. Crush crackers into pieces about ¼ inch across. Fold crackers and walnuts into whites.
4. Line 2 baking sheets, 12 by 15 inches each, with cooking parchment (or lightly oil nonstick baking sheets). Spoon meringue mixture in 8 equal mounds about 3½ inches wide and well separated.
5. Bake in a 300° oven until meringue walnut puffs are lightly browned, about 30 minutes. Let cool on pan about 10 minutes. With a spatula, transfer to racks to cool. If making ahead, package walnut puffs airtight and hold at room temperature up to 1 day.
6. Mix strawberries and cream with sugar to taste and spoon onto the walnut puffs.

Per serving: 314 cal., 43% (135 cal.) from fat; 4.1 g protein; 15 g fat (6.3 g sat.); 45 g carbo (3.4 g fiber); 112 mg sodium; 33 mg chol.

NOEL BARNHURST (2)

## Spring Thyme Pork Roast with Peanut Sauce

Betty Nichols, Eugene, Oregon

"I experiment a lot with herbs. They can be a wonderful, tantalizing secret ingredient in almost everything, if you use them sparingly," says Betty Nichols. She serves this pork roast with mashed sweet potatoes.

*Prep and cook time:* About 1½ hours, plus marinating

*Makes:* 8 servings

1 **fat-trimmed, boned, tied center-cut pork loin** (about 2½ lb.)

1⅓ cups **apple cider** or juice

⅓ cup **reduced-sodium soy sauce**

¼ cup **peanut butter**

2 teaspoons **fresh thyme** leaves or 1 teaspoon dried thyme

1 teaspoon **hot chili flakes**

2 cloves **garlic**

1. Cut ½-inch-deep slits all over pork; place meat in a large plastic food bag.

2. In a food processor or blender, combine cider, soy sauce, peanut butter, thyme, chili flakes, and garlic. Whirl until well blended.

3. Pour cider marinade over pork, seal bag, turn to coat meat with marinade, then set in a pan. Chill, turning occasionally, for at least 30 minutes or up to 1 day.

4. Lift meat from marinade and set on a rack in a 9- by 13-inch pan. Reserve marinade.

5. Bake pork in a 350° oven until a thermometer inserted in center of thickest part reaches 150° to 155°, 1¼ to 1¾ hours; after 40 minutes, baste with some of the reserved marinade. Transfer pork to platter and let stand 5 to 10 minutes in a warm place.

6. As pork rests, pour remaining marinade into pan with pork juices. (If pork drippings are burned, do not use. Instead pour marinade into a 10- to 12-in. frying pan.) Stir to scrape browned bits free. Then stir often over high heat until the sauce is reduced to about 1 cup, 6 to 8 minutes. Pour into a bowl.

7. Slice the pork and accompany the meat with sauce.

Per serving: 278 cal., 39% (108 cal.) from fat; 33 g protein; 12 g fat (3.4 g sat.); 7.5 g carbo (0.6 g fiber); 509 mg sodium; 84 mg chol.

## Easter Potatoes

Helen M. Wallace, Del Mar, California

For an Easter brunch, Helen Wallace decorated baked potatoes instead of eggs. Though she has mastered creating intricately patterned *pysanky* eggs, a Ukrainian art form, the potatoes were much easier to do. And, Wallace says, "the potatoes were a great centerpiece until it was time to eat them."

*Prep and cook time:* About 1½ hours

*Makes:* 8 servings

8 **Yukon gold**, thin-skinned white, or russet **potatoes** (½ lb. each)

**Blue, red,** and **green food coloring**

**Salad oil**

**Rice vinegar,** butter, or sour cream

**Salt** and **pepper**

1. Scrub potatoes and pat dry. Insert a metal skewer into 1 end of each potato.

2. Pour each food coloring into a separate small bowl. Use colorings full-strength for intense color, or dilute with a few drops of water for paler hues.

3. Hold each potato by its skewer and paint food coloring onto the potato skin in designs, as desired, using small watercolor paintbrushes.

4. Lay potatoes on racks to dry, about 10 minutes. Remove skewers. Rub potato skin with oil and set in a 10- by 15-inch pan.

5. Bake in a 375° oven until potatoes are soft when pressed, 40 to 50 minutes. Pile into a basket and serve hot, split open and seasoned with vinegar, butter, or sour cream, and salt and pepper to taste.

Per serving: 214 cal., 16% (34 cal.) from fat; 4.4 g protein; 3.8 g fat (0.4 g sat.); 41 g carbo (3.8 g fiber); 17 mg sodium; 0 mg chol.

## Grecian Cheese Points

Nancee Melin, Tucson

Greek foods suit the tastes of Nancee Melin. And she uses a Greek touch with filo to make these often-requested cheese-filled triangles.

*Prep and cook time:* About 50 minutes

*Makes:* 18 pieces

3 ounces **neufchâtel** (light cream) or cream **cheese**

1 cup (4 oz.) crumbled **tomato-basil flavor** or plain **feta cheese**

1 cup shredded (3 to 4 oz.) **gruyère cheese**

1 **large egg**

2 tablespoons chopped **parsley**

6 **filo dough sheets** (12 by 17 in.)

**Butter-flavor cooking oil spray**

1. Mix neufchâtel, feta, gruyère, egg, and parsley.

2. Stack filo sheets neatly. From a narrow side, cut filo stack into 3 equal strips. Lift 1 strip from stack and lay flat; cover remaining pieces with plastic wrap to prevent drying. Mist the single strip lightly with cooking oil spray.

3. Place 1 tablespoon of the cheese mixture on one end of strip. Bring a corner end of filo strip over filling to meet opposite edge of filo, forming a triangle, then continue to fold as a triangle (like a flag) until the whole strip is wrapped around filling. As shaped, keep filled triangles covered with plastic wrap. Repeat to use remaining cheese and filo.

4. Place triangles, loose ends beneath, well apart on a nonstick baking sheet. Mist triangles lightly with cooking oil spray. If making ahead, freeze solid, then package airtight.

5. Bake in a 375° oven until golden, 12 to 14 minutes (20 minutes, if frozen). Serve hot or warm.

Per piece: 79 cal., 62% (49 cal.) from fat; 3.8 g protein; 5.4 g fat (2.8 g sat.); 4 g carbo (0 g fiber); 160 mg sodium; 24 mg chol. ◆

Crisp filo triangles contain soft, melting cheese.

Spicy ponzu sauce—a flavoring secret of Pacific Rim cusiine—seasons grilled salmon and salad with Asian flair (see page 101).

# May

Sunset's centennial issue
1898–1998

# Savor

AVOCADO SOUP MEXICANA, with cilantro and chilies, made its debut in *Sunset* in December 1940.

PARTYGOERS ENJOY
a dinner of
selected recipes
from *Sunset's* past.

# the century

BY LINDA LAU ANUSASANANAN

PHOTOGRAPHS BY FRANCE RUFFENACH

After cooking with you for 100 years, we've collected the greatest Western flavors for a most memorable meal

■ For the last 10 decades at *Sunset,* we've eaten oysters up and down the West Coast, and beyond. We explored Pacific salmon, Hawaiian papayas, persimmons, avocados, and artichokes—all the treasures that make our region sublimely delicious. • February 1929 marked the birth of Kitchen Cabinet, to showcase our readers' favorite dishes, and since then, with your help, we've built an enormous legacy of recipes. Each decade brought new discoveries and new ingredients. In the '30s and '40s, for example, fresh chilies, cilantro, and ginger, along with soy sauce and pesto, first appeared in our magazine. Now they're mainstream. • Entertaining in *Sunset* has focused on informality and simplicity—nothing-to-it parties, alfresco dining. Above all, we grilled year-round while our Eastern cousins hibernated in the winter. • In short, *Sunset* has recorded—indeed, shaped—the West's unique regional cuisine and casual lifestyle. And this dinner for 8 to 10, or a walk-around party for 24 to 36, is built on our rich heritage.

## Sunset's Meal of the Century

*Jicama with Chili Salt (November 1968)*

*Indian Relish (September 1934) with Cream Cheese and Crackers*

*Pop-open Barbecue Clams (May 1969)*

NAVARRO VINEYARDS GEWÜRZTRAMINER 1996

•

*Avocado Soup Mexicana (December 1940)*

*Crab and Artichoke Salad (January 1945)*

CHALK HILL ESTATE VINEYARDS AND WINERY SAUVIGNON BLANC 1995

•

*Peppered Salmon (July 1992)*

CHATEAU MONTELENA CHARDONNAY 1995

*or*

*Grilled Merlot Lamb (June 1995)*

BERINGER VINEYARDS MERLOT "HOWELL MOUNTAIN" 1994

*and*

*Mixed Grain Pilaf (April 1980)*

*Asparagus with 10-Second Hollandaise (March 1955)*

*Sheepherder's Bread (June 1976)*

•

*Kona Macadamia-Caramel Torte (February 1984)*

QUADY WINERY ESSENSIA 1995

*Strawberries with Sour Cream Dip (May 1958)*

BONNY DOON VINEYARD FRAMBOISE NONVINTAGE

## Jicama with Chili Salt

**PREP TIME:** About 20 minutes

**NOTES:** We discovered this simple appetizer in Mexico; jicama, now grown in the West, has since added crunch to many of our recipes.

**MAKES:** 8 to 10 servings

- 1 tablespoon **salt**
- ¼ to ½ teaspoon **chili powder**
- 1 **jicama** (1½ to 2 lb.)
- 1 or 2 **limes**

**1.** Mix salt with chili powder to taste. Place in a small, shallow bowl.

**2.** Peel jicama. Rinse and cut into ¼-inch-thick wedges or ½-inch-thick sticks 3 to 4 inches long.

**3.** Cut limes into wedges. Arrange jicama, limes, and chili salt on a platter.

**4.** To eat, rub jicama with lime, then dip in chili salt.

Per serving: 26 cal., 3.5% (0.9 cal.) from fat; 0.5 g protein; 0.1 g fat (0 g sat.); 6.3 g carbo (3.1 g fiber); 662 mg sodium; 0 mg chol.

## Indian Relish

**PREP AND COOK TIME:** About 35 minutes

**NOTES:** Recipes for pickling and canning peppered our early pages. In a modern menu, this colorful relish works perfectly spooned over a mound of cream cheese or a wedge of ripe brie. Scoop onto crackers to eat. Store the relish, covered, in the refrigerator up to 1 month; serve at room temperature.

**MAKES:** About 1½ cups; 8 to 10 servings

- 2 **red bell peppers** (1 lb. total)
- 1 **onion** (½ lb.), finely chopped
- 1 cup **white wine vinegar**
- 1 cup **sugar**
- 1 to 2 tablespoons **hot chili flakes** (optional)
  **Salt**

**1.** Discard bell pepper stems and seeds; finely chop bell peppers.

**2.** In a 2- to 2½-quart pan, combine bell peppers, onion, vinegar, sugar, and chili to taste. Bring to boiling over high heat.

**3.** Stir often over medium-high heat until liquid looks syrupy and is reduced to about 3 tablespoons, about 25 minutes. Add salt to taste.

**4.** Cool and serve.

Per tablespoon: 41 cal., 0% (0 cal.) from fat; 0.2 g protein; 0 g fat; 10 g carbo (0.4 g fiber); 0.7 mg sodium; 0 mg chol.

pluck clams from shells, dip in butter, and eat.

**5.** When all the clams are cooked, dip bread into butter.

Per 2-clam serving: 110 cal., 31% (34 cal.) from fat; 5.9 g protein; 3.8 g fat (1.9 g sat.); 13 g carbo (0.6 g fiber); 184 mg sodium; 18 mg chol.

## Avocado Soup Mexicana

**PREP AND COOK TIME:** About 8 minutes

**NOTES:** Fresh chilies and cilantro initially appeared on our food pages in this refreshing soup.

**MAKES:** 8 to 10 servings

3 or 4 **fresh jalapeño chilies** (about 2 oz. total)

2 **ripe avocados** (1¾ lb. total), peeled and pitted

**Salt**

9 cups **chicken broth**

2 tablespoons minced **fresh cilantro**

**1.** Discard chili stems and seeds (and trim out veins if less heat is desired). Finely mince chilies.

**2.** With a potato masher or fork, mash avocados until almost smooth, leaving a few tiny chunks. Add chilies and salt to taste.

**3.** In a 3- to 4-quart pan, bring broth to a boil over high heat.

**4.** Meanwhile, mound equal portions of the mashed avocado mixture in shallow soup bowls.

**5.** Ladle the hot chicken broth around avocado in the soup bowls. Sprinkle each serving with the chopped cilantro.

Per serving: 124 cal., 73% (90 cal.) from fat; 3.9 g protein; 10 g fat (2.1 g sat.); 6.1 g carbo (1.2 g fiber); 101 mg sodium; 3.4 mg chol.

## Crab and Artichoke Salad

**PREP TIME:** About 20 minutes

**NOTES:** Originally this salad used canned artichoke hearts and bottled French dressing—which was among the first pourable salad alternatives to mayonnaise. Substituting marinated artichoke

## Pop-open Barbecue Clams

**PREP AND COOK TIME:** About 20 minutes

**NOTES:** Guests cook clams on the grill, then dip them in melted butter. This relaxed, do-it-yourself style is a signature of *Sunset* entertaining. The recipe easily expands or shrinks to accommodate any group.

**MAKES:** 8 to 10 appetizer servings

16 to 30 **clams in shells,** suitable for steaming

1 **baguette** (8 oz.), sliced

2½ to 5 tablespoons **butter** or margarine, melted

**1.** Scrub clams under cool running water. Discard any gaping clams that don't close when cleaned.

**2.** Place a bowl with clams, a basket with baguette slices, small forks, and napkins alongside barbecue grill. Place butter in a small pan on a cool section of grill.

**3.** Have guests set clams on grill over a solid bed of hot coals or high heat on a gas grill (you can hold your hand at grill level only 2 to 3 seconds); close lid on gas grill.

**4.** Cook clams until they pop wide open, 6 to 8 minutes. Pick up clams, using tongs or napkins to protect fingers, drain juices into butter, then

INDIAN RELISH (1934) with bell peppers tops cream cheese (above left), while pop-open barbecue clams (1969) go with bread.

CRAB AND ARTICHOKES, indigenous classics, make a dynamic salad (1945).

hearts gives you an updated ready-made dressing.

MAKES: 8 to 10 servings

1 cup minced **celery**

⅓ cup finely chopped **green ripe** or pimiento-stuffed **olives**

About ⅓ cup **mayonnaise** or plain nonfat yogurt

¾ pound **shelled cooked Dungeness crab**

**Salt** and **pepper**

**Lemon juice**

3 jars (6 oz. each) **marinated artichoke hearts**

8 to 10 large **iceberg** or butter **lettuce leaves,** rinsed and crisped

8 to 10 **firm-ripe tomato** slices (about 3½ in. wide and ½ in. thick)

**Paprika**

**1.** Mix celery, olives, and ⅓ cup mayonnaise. Gently mix in crab. Add salt, pepper, and lemon juice to taste.

**2.** Drain artichokes and save marinade. If artichoke hearts are whole, cut lengthwise into halves or quarters.

**3.** Place a lettuce leaf on each plate and lay a slice of tomato on the lettuce. Mound crab mixture equally onto tomato slices and arrange artichokes beside tomatoes. Drizzle salads lightly with artichoke marinade.

**4.** If desired, top crab mixture with a small dollop of mayonnaise. Dust salads lightly with paprika.

Per serving: 151 cal., 66% (99 cal.) from fat; 8.7 g protein; 11 g fat (1.5 g sat.); 6.4 g carbo (2.8 g fiber); 521 mg sodium; 38 mg chol.

## Peppered Salmon

PREP AND COOK TIME: 1½ to 1¾ hours, plus 4 to 24 hours for marinating the salmon

NOTES: We Westerners love our salmon and our grills. This recipe, which puts the fish on the barbecue, was featured on *Sunset's* cover in July 1992.

For mildest flavor, use mainly pink and green peppercorns. The cooked fish can be prepared up to 3 days ahead; cover and chill.

MAKES: 8 to 10 servings

1 cup firmly packed **brown sugar**

6 tablespoons **salt**

1 tablespoon minced **fresh ginger**

2 or 3 **dried bay leaves**

1 teaspoon crushed **whole allspice**

1 **salmon fillet with skin** (2½ to 3 lb.; 1 to 1½ in. thick)

About ⅓ cup mixed **whole peppercorns** (pink, green, white, and black)

About ½ cup **apple** or hickory **wood chips**

1 tablespoon **honey**

2 or 3 thin **red onion** slices

**Dill sprigs**

**1.** In a 1- to 1½-quart pan, bring 1½ cups water, sugar, salt, ginger, bay leaves, and allspice to a boil. Stir until sugar dissolves. Remove from heat and let cool slightly.

**2.** Rinse salmon fillet, pat dry, and lay flat with skin down in a rimmed 12- by 15-inch pan. Pour sugar-salt mixture over salmon. Cover pan tightly and chill fish at least 4 or up to 24 hours, occasionally spooning brine over the fish.

**3.** Mound 16 charcoal briquets on the firegrate of a barbecue with a lid and ignite briquets. Or turn gas grill to high heat and close lid.

**4.** Meanwhile, add peppercorns to enough hot water to make them float; soak at least 15 minutes. Also add wood chips to enough warm water to make them float; soak at least 15 minutes.

**5.** Drain fish and discard brine. Rinse fish with cool water and pat dry. Set fish, skin side down, on a large sheet of foil; cut foil to fit outline of fish.

**6.** Rub honey over top of fish. Drain peppercorns and pat evenly onto fish to set them lightly in place.

**7.** When coals are dotted with gray ash, in about 20 minutes, push half to each side of firegrate.

**8.** Drain wood chips and scatter 2 tablespoons on each mound of coals. For gas grill, put ¼ cup chips in a foil pan and set over heat. Cover barbecue, and heat until chips start to smolder, about 10 minutes.

**9.** Set grill 4 to 6 inches above the firegrate.

**10.** Place salmon on foil in center of grill (not directly over coals); if using gas, turn to lowest setting and adjust for indirect heat (parallel to sides of salmon, not beneath the fish).

**11.** Set an oven thermometer on top of

Peppered Salmon
*July 1992*

PERENNIAL WESTERN
FAVORITES, salmon and
lamb—both barbecued—
provide delectable dining
choices in every decade.

## Patio appetizer party
### for 24 to 36

■ For this casual menu, follow the popular nothing-to-it party concept we pioneered in a 1969 story: Place each dish at a separate station so guests will move and mingle as they serve themselves. All the foods can be picked up to eat, so there's no need for plates or forks.

Double the recipes for the clams and the strawberries. Serve the peppered salmon with drained capers, minced red onion mixed into sour cream, thin toast, and lime or lemon wedges.

Cut the lamb into thin slices and let guests tuck pieces into wedges of pocket bread along with a sauce of yogurt mixed with chopped fresh mint and garlic.

Dip cool asparagus spears into the warm or cool hollandaise, and strawberries into the lemon-flavor sour cream.

---

Jicama with Chili Salt

•

Indian Relish with
Cream Cheese and Crackers

•

Pop-open Barbecue Clams

•

Peppered Salmon with Toast

•

Grilled Merlot Lamb with
Pocket Bread Triangles

•

Cold Asparagus with
10-Second Hollandaise

•

Strawberries with Sour Cream Dip

the center of the fish. Cover barbecue. For charcoal, open vents ¼ inch, and after 30 minutes add 3 briquets to each mound of coals; repeat every 30 minutes of cooking.

**12.** Check thermometer often to be sure temperature stays about 160°. If temperature drops, open vents for charcoal slightly, or turn up heat on gas grill. If temperature rises, close 1 or 2 of the vents, or open lid of gas grill, then prop open slightly. Add wood chips as needed to produce a faint, steady stream of smoke. Moisture that accumulates on fish will evaporate. Cook salmon until a thermometer inserted in center of thickest part reads 140°, from 1 hour to 1 hour and 15 minutes.

**13.** Using wide spatulas, slide fillet with foil onto a rimless baking sheet, then slide fish from sheet onto a platter. Serve salmon warm, cool, or chilled.

**14.** Garnish with onion and dill. Cut fish across grain into wide slices or bite-size chunks; lift fish off skin.

Per serving: 178 cal., 33% (59 cal.) from fat; 21 g protein; 6.6 g fat (1 g sat.); 8.4 g carbo (0.9 g fiber); 839 mg sodium; 56 mg chol.

## Grilled Merlot Lamb

**PREP AND COOK TIME:** About 50 minutes, plus at least 6 hours for marinating the lamb

**NOTES:** Merlot, a recently popular red varietal wine, brings an all-time favorite meat into the '90s.

**MAKES:** 8 to 10 servings

½ cup **soy sauce**

½ cup **Merlot**

½ cup **dry white wine**

4 cloves **garlic,** pressed or minced

½ cup chopped **fresh oregano** leaves or 2 tablespoons dried oregano

2 tablespoons coarsely chopped **fresh rosemary** leaves or 1 tablespoon dried rosemary

1 tablespoon **coarse-ground pepper**

1 **leg of lamb** (5 to 6 lb.), boned, butterflied, and fat-trimmed

**Oregano** and **rosemary sprigs** (optional)

**Salt**

**1.** In a 9- by 13-inch baking dish, combine soy sauce, Merlot, white wine, garlic, chopped oregano, chopped rosemary, and pepper. Add lamb and turn to coat with marinade. Cover and chill at least 6 hours or up to 1 day, turning meat over several times.

**2.** Lift lamb from marinade (reserve marinade) and place on a barbecue grill over a solid bed of medium coals or medium heat on a gas grill (you can hold your hand at grill level only 4 to 5 seconds). Close lid on gas grill. Cook, turning as needed to brown meat evenly, until a thermometer inserted in thickest part of leg reaches 135° to 140° for rare (thinner portions will be well-done), 30 to 45 minutes. Brush meat occasionally with marinade up until the last 10 minutes of cooking.

**3.** Transfer meat to a platter, keep warm, and let rest 5 to 15 minutes. Garnish with oregano and rosemary sprigs. To serve, thinly slice meat. Add salt to taste.

Per serving: 216 cal., 36% (77 cal.) from fat; 31 g protein; 8.5 g fat (3 g sat.); 1.5 g carbo (0.1 g fiber); 487 mg sodium; 97 mg chol.

## Mixed Grain Pilaf

**PREP AND COOK TIME:** About 1 hour

**NOTES:** With characteristic open-mindedness, the West has led the country in experimenting with grains.

You can make this nutty pilaf up to 1 day ahead; cover and chill. Reheat, covered, in a microwave oven at full power (100%), stirring occasionally, about 5 minutes.

**MAKES:** 4½ cups; 8 to 10 servings

⅓ cup chopped **almonds**

2 tablespoons **butter** or margarine

1 **onion** (½ lb.), chopped

2 **carrots** (½ lb. total), chopped

1 clove **garlic,** minced or pressed

⅓ cup chopped **parsley**

½ cup **barley**

½ cup **brown rice**

2¾ cups **beef** or chicken **broth**

¼ cup **dry sherry** or water

¾ teaspoon **dried basil**

¾ teaspoon **dried oregano**

½ cup **bulgur wheat**

**Salt** and **pepper**

**1.** In a 3- to 4-quart pan, stir nuts often over medium heat until lightly toasted, about 3 minutes; pour from pan.

**2.** Turn heat to medium-high and add butter, onion, carrots, garlic, and parsley to pan. Stir often until onion is limp, about 5 minutes.

**3.** Add barley and rice. Stir often until barley is lightly browned, about 4 minutes.

**4.** Add broth, sherry, basil, and oregano. Bring to a boil over high heat, then turn heat to low, cover, and simmer 30 minutes. Stir in bulgur, cover, and simmer until grains are tender to bite, about 15 minutes longer.

**5.** Add salt and pepper to taste. Pour pilaf into a bowl and garnish with toasted nuts.

Per serving: 163 cal., 29% (47 cal.) from fat; 5.5 g protein; 5.2 g fat (1.7 g sat.); 25 g carbo (4.8 g fiber); 56 mg sodium; 6.2 mg chol.

## 10-Second Hollandaise

PREP AND COOK TIME: About 3 minutes to assemble, 10 seconds to blend.

NOTES: Sure, we've gone low-fat in general, but we haven't abandoned the classics for special occasions. In fact, they're coming back. Motto: If you can't trim fat, trim time. Serve this easy hollandaise over hot cooked asparagus or broccoli.

MAKES: About 1¼ cups, enough for 8 to 10 servings (about 2½ lb. of vegetables)

¾ cup (⅜ lb.) **butter** or margarine

3 **large egg** yolks

About 1½ tablespoons **lemon juice**

1 teaspoon **Dijon mustard**

**Cayenne**

**Salt**

**1.** Melt butter in a pan over medium heat or in a microwave oven.

**2.** Put egg yolks, 1 tablespoon lemon juice, 1 tablespoon water, and mustard in a blender or food processor.

**3.** Whirl on high speed to blend, then add butter in a slow, steady stream.

**4.** Add remaining lemon juice, cayenne, and salt to taste; whirl just to blend. Use at once or store in a thermos up to 30 minutes.

Per tablespoon: 71 cal., 99% (70 cal.) from fat; 0.5 g protein; 7.8 g fat (4.6 g sat.); 0.1 g carbo (0 g fiber); 79 mg sodium; 51 mg chol.

## Sheepherder's Bread

PREP AND COOK TIME: About 5 hours, including about 2½ hours to rise and at least 45 minutes to cool

NOTES: With this loaf, Anita Mitchell won the bread-baking contest at the National Basque Festival in Elko, Nevada, in 1975. She used a cast-iron Dutch oven, but a nonstick pan makes the bread easier to manage. Bake the loaf up to 1 day ahead and store, covered, at room temperature. Freeze to store longer.

MAKES: 1 loaf, about 3¾ pounds

½ cup (¼ lb.) **butter,** margarine, or shortening

½ cup **sugar**

2½ teaspoons **salt**

2 packages **active dry yeast**

About 9½ cups **all-purpose flour**

**Salad oil**

**1.** In a large bowl, combine 3 cups very hot tap water with butter, sugar, and

MERLOT LAMB (1995), grain pilaf (1980), and hollandaise with asparagus (1955) make a very Western entrée.

HAWAII'S MACADAMIAS
in a premier torte (1984), plus
berries and sour cream (1958).

salt. Stir until butter melts; let cool until warm (110° to 115°). Stir in yeast; cover and set in a warm place until bubbly, about 15 minutes.

**2.** Add 5 cups of the flour. Beat with a heavy-duty mixer or spoon just until batter is stretchy, 2 to 5 minutes. Mix in enough of the remaining flour, about $3^1/2$ cups, to form a stiff dough.

**3.** *To knead with a dough hook,* beat on medium speed until dough pulls from side of bowl and no longer feels sticky, about 5 minutes. If required, add more flour, 1 tablespoon at a time.

*To knead by hand,* scrape dough out onto a floured board and knead until smooth, about 10 minutes, adding flour as required to prevent sticking. Rinse bowl and rub with oil. Return dough to bowl and turn over to coat with oil.

**4.** Cover bowl with plastic wrap and let dough rise in a warm place until doubled, about $1^1/2$ hours.

**5.** Meanwhile, if using a 5-quart cast-iron Dutch oven, cut a circle of foil to fit bottom of pan; put foil in pan. Rub the foil and sides of pan generously with salad oil. A nonstick pan that is not worn needs no preparation.

**6.** Knead dough with dough hook or on a floured board to expel air, then form into a smooth ball.

**7.** Place dough in baking pan. Cover loosely with plastic wrap and let rise in a warm place until almost doubled again, 45 minutes to 1 hour; watch closely so it doesn't rise too much.

**8.** Bake, uncovered, in a 350° oven until loaf is golden brown and sounds hollow when tapped, 50 to 55 minutes.

**9.** Remove bread from oven and invert onto a rack (you'll need a helper); remove foil and turn loaf right side up. Cool at least 45 minutes. Serve warm or cool, cut into wedges.

Per ounce: 94 cal., 18% (17 cal.) from fat; 2.1 g protein; 1.9 g fat (1 g sat.); 17 g carbo (0.6 g fiber); 108 mg sodium; 4.1 mg chol.

## Kona Macadamia-Caramel Torte

**PREP AND COOK TIME:** About $1^1/2$ hours

**NOTES:** As the westernmost state, Hawaii has been pivotal in introducing us to a whole range of foods and flavors from the Far East and South Seas.

This rich dessert uses Hawaii's signature nut. Make up to 2 days ahead; store airtight at room temperature.

**MAKES:** 16 servings

$2^1/2$ cups ($12^1/2$ oz.) **roasted, salted macadamia nuts**

$2^3/4$ cups **all-purpose flour**

$2^1/2$ cups **sugar**

1 cup ($^1/2$ lb.) **butter** or margarine, cut in chunks

1 **large egg**

1 cup **whipping cream**

1 **large egg** white, beaten until frothy

**1.** Reserve 3 or 4 whole nuts for garnish. Rub remaining macadamias in a towel to remove excess salt; lift nuts from towel and set aside.

**2.** With your fingers or a food processor, mix or whirl flour, $^1/2$ cup sugar, and butter until mixture is fine crumbs. Add egg and mix with a fork or whirl until dough holds together; pat into a ball.

**3.** Press $^2/3$ of the pastry over the bottom and sides of a $1^1/2$-inch-deep,

9-inch-wide round cake pan with removable rim. Cover and chill. Roll remaining pastry between 2 sheets of waxed paper into a 9-inch-wide round. Chill flat.

**4.** Meanwhile, pour remaining 2 cups sugar into a 10- to 12-inch nonstick frying pan. Set over medium-high heat and stir often until sugar melts and turns pale amber, about 7 minutes.

**5.** Pour in cream (mixture will bubble up) and remove from heat. Stir until sauce is smooth, about 5 minutes. Stir in nuts (except those reserved for garnish). Let nut mixture cool 10 to 20 minutes, then pour into pastry shell.

**6.** Peel 1 sheet of waxed paper from pastry round and invert pastry onto nut-filled torte. Peel off remaining paper. Fold edges of top pastry in until flush with pan rim. Press pastry rim with the flour-dipped tines of a fork to seal. Brush top of torte lightly with beaten egg white.

**7.** Bake in a 325° oven until deep golden brown, about 1 hour.

**8.** Cool in pan on a rack 10 to 20 minutes. Run a thin knife between pastry and pan rim. Remove rim and let torte cool.

**9.** Garnish with reserved macadamia nuts. Cut into thin wedges.

Per serving: 509 cal., 58% (297 cal.) from fat; 5.3 g protein; 33 g fat (13 g sat.); 51 g carbo (0.6 g fiber); 227 mg sodium; 74 mg chol.

## Strawberries with Sour Cream Dip

PREP TIME: About 10 minutes

NOTES: Through the years, we've had recipes for endless variations of strawberries and sour cream, but this was the first—it was published in 1958.

MAKES: 8 to 10 servings

1 cup **sour cream**

1 teaspoon grated **lemon** peel

1 teaspoon **lemon juice**

½ cup **powdered sugar**

4 cups **strawberries,** rinsed and drained

**1.** In a small bowl, mix sour cream with lemon peel, juice, and sugar.

**2.** Serve sour cream mixture alongside strawberries as dip, or spoon sauce over the fruit.

Per serving: 91 cal., 49% (45 cal.) from fat; 1.1 g protein; 5 g fat (3 g sat.); 11 g carbo (1.6 g fiber); 13 mg sodium; 10 mg chol.

# WINES WITH HISTORY
## BY KAREN MacNEIL

With the jicama, Indian relish, and barbecue clam appetizers

*Navarro Vineyards Gewürztraminer 1996 (Anderson Valley), $14*

The tangy flavors of the relish (lots of sugar and vinegar) need a dramatic companion. Navarro is widely considered the best Gewürztraminer in America—about three levels above the rest of the pack. The winery, one of the first in the Anderson Valley (Mendocino County, California), was founded in 1974 and specializes in Gewürztraminer; Gewürz was the first variety it planted. The wine is extremely popular; order by calling (707) 895-3686.

With the avocado soup and crab and artichoke salad

*Chalk Hill Estate Vineyards and Winery Sauvignon Blanc 1995 (Chalk Hill, Sonoma), $16*

Chalk Hill makes one of the lushest, most hedonistic Sauvignon Blancs in the West—characteristics necessary to go with these two recipes, with all their bold flavors. The winery, founded in 1980, is the only one in California that is its own appellation. In other words, in the Chalk Hill wine-growing region, there's just one winery: Chalk Hill.

With the peppered salmon

*Chateau Montelena Chardonnay 1995 (Napa Valley), $25*

Chateau Montelena was founded in 1882, but the winery operated only sporadically after Prohibition. In 1972 it was bought and revived by the Barrett family,

and a year later made a Chardonnay that shocked the world by winning the legendary Paris Tasting of 1976. The 1995 is perfect with the flavorful salmon.

With the grilled Merlot lamb

*Beringer Vineyards Merlot "Howell Mountain" 1994 (Howell Mountain, Napa), $40*

Beringer Brothers, founded in 1876, is the oldest continuously operated winery in the Napa Valley. The texture of this Merlot is like that of a cashmere blanket. Outrageous, big fruit oozes out of the glass. In fact, this wine is widely considered one of the best Merlots in California.

With the macadamia-caramel torte

*Quady Winery Essensia 1995 (California), $13.50*

Quady, founded in 1977, is California's dessert-wine specialist. The winery makes sublime wines from two types of Muscats. Muscat is not a single grape varietal, but rather a family of grapes. This wine is made from Orange Muscat, which has orange blossom and nut flavors.

With the strawberries and sour cream

*Bonny Doon Vineyard Framboise nonvintage, $10 (375 ml.)*

Bonny Doon has revolutionized winemaking in California. The avant-garde winery, founded in 1983, has sparked more new trends and more creativity than almost any other winery in America. This wine choice is intended as a berry-berry match, strawberries with raspberries (framboise). ◆

This month, in place of the usual Food Guide, we present
25 Western food contributions to Western civilization.

# foodguide *25*

WESTERN CONTRIBUTIONS TO FOOD • BY JERRY ANNE DI VECCHIO

PHOTOS: JAMES CARRIER (3) ILLUSTRATION: MARINA THOMPSON

## *1* LITERARY LIONESS.

In the late '60s, Mary Frances Kennedy Fisher (1908–1992) moved from her old Victorian in St. Helena, California, to a book-lined, two-room cottage on a knoll in Glen Ellen. Here she often entertained *Sunset* writers. Part of the bargain was food from *Sunset's* kitchen. One of her favorites was this salad—she loved the way the mustard seed popped.

**Lentil and Seed Salad for MFK Fisher**
**Prep and cook time:** About 1 hour
**Notes:** Garnish with more lemon slices and chopped green onions.
**Makes:** 6 servings

**1.** Sort 1 pound (about 2 cups) **lentils** and discard debris. Rinse and drain lentils.

**2.** In a 3- to 4-quart pan, combine lentils, 6 cups fat-skimmed **chicken broth**, ½ teaspoon **cumin seed**, 2 tablespoons minced **fresh ginger**, 3 tablespoons **mustard seed**, ¼ cup **rice vinegar**, and ½ **lemon**, thinly sliced and seeded.

**3.** Bring to a boil over high heat. Cover and simmer until lentils are tender to bite, about 45 minutes. Drain, reserving liquid. Let both mixtures cool.

**4.** Add to lentils 1 cup chopped **green onions** (including tops), about ½ cup reserved liquid (enough to moisten salad), and **salt** to taste.

Per serving: 314 cal., 7% (22 cal.) from fat; 28 g protein; 2.4 g fat (0.2 g sat.); 48 g carbo (9.1 g fiber); 61 mg sodium; 0 mg chol.

You will find you 50 years of good

## *2* FORTUNES TOLD.

David Jung gets credit for making the first fortune cookie, in 1916 in Los Angeles.

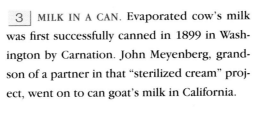

**3** MILK IN A CAN. Evaporated cow's milk was first successfully canned in 1899 in Washington by Carnation. John Meyenberg, grandson of a partner in that "sterilized cream" project, went on to can goat's milk in California.

**4** WESTERN WINES, BEFORE AND AFTER. Amazingly, 183 bonded wineries—177 in California, 2 in Colorado, 1 in Washington, and 3 in Wisconsin—survived Prohibition (1919–1933). Now there are at least 960 bonded wineries in the West.

**5** RECIPE EXCHANGE RATE. Since February 1929, more than 5,000 recipes from *Sunset* readers have made the grade in our test kitchens and appeared in Kitchen Cabinet, a monthly reader-exchange column. The payoff per recipe in 1929 was $1; in 1998, $50.

**6** | SHOP TILL YOU DROP. In 1937 Hollywood's Ranch Market became the first supermarket to keep its doors open round the clock.

**7** | PRE-PESTOMANIA. In 1946 Seattle's Angelo Pellegrini (1903–1991), author, cook, and gardener, shared his pesto recipe with *Sunset*.

**8** | TASTEMAKERS: ONE STATE, TWO WORLDS. In the '40s the McDonald brothers began selling hamburgers in San Bernardino, California. In 1971, Alice Waters opened Chez Panisse in Berkeley. The first event blazed trails in standardizing ingredients; the second sought and supported the best food resources and eschewed standardization.

# 10

**WOK AND ROLL.** Atlas Metal Spinning in South San Francisco began making rolled-steel woks in 1932. When *Sunset* featured it in 1951, the tool—and the stir-frying technique—began moving into everyday use.

# 9

**OREGON GIANT.** One maxim of James Beard (1903–1985) was to honor the quality of food by preparing it simply and with care. One of his favorite ways to cook beef, surprisingly, was to boil it—and the cut he used was tenderloin. It makes perfect sense if you want a quick version of roast beef to slice and serve cold.

**James Beard's Boiled Beef**
Prep and cook time: About 30 minutes, plus at least 1 hour to chill
Makes: 6 or 7 servings
**1.** Trim as much fat as you can from a 1½- to 1¾-pound **center-cut beef tenderloin**. With cotton string, tie beef crosswise at 1- to 1½-inch intervals to make a compact roll (it should be about 3 in. thick).
**2.** In a deep 2½- to 3-quart pan over high heat, bring 5 cups fat-skimmed **beef broth** to a boil. Add beef to the pan and cover. Simmer, turning meat over frequently, until it feels bouncy-firm when pressed and is 100° on a thermometer or pale red in center of thickest part (cut to test), 20 to 25 minutes.
**3.** Lift beef from broth; reserve broth for other uses. Cover and chill beef at least 1 hour or up to 2 days. Slice thin and remove string.

Per 3 ounces: 190 cal., 46% (88 cal.) from fat; 24 g protein; 9.8 g fat (3.7 g sat.); 0 g carbo (0 g fiber); 54 mg sodium; 71 mg chol.

**11** | TATER-TOTS ARE BORN. Oregon Frozen Foods began freezing the bake-and-serve potato nuggets in 1953. In 1961, the firm joined up with an Idaho company to become Ore-Ida.

**12** | KING OF COOKWARE. In 1954 Chuck Williams bought a hardware store in Sonoma, California, and soon converted it to cookware only. Today, the San Francisco–based Williams-Sonoma empire includes more than 275 stores in 40-plus states.

**13** | TV STAR. Pasadena-born Julia Child made her debut as "the French chef" in 1963 on educational television.

**14** | THE REMARKABLE GENEVIEVE. Gen Callahan, *Sunset's* first food editor (1929–1938), defined the West's cuisine in her classic *All-Western Foods Cook Book*. In the '60s, she introduced restaurants to microwave ovens, at the onetime landmark Nut Tree Restaurant in Vacaville, California.

**15** | ADDING TO THE LEXICON. The *Oxford English Dictionary* dates the phrase *tailgate picnic* to 1980. But in 1954, *Sunset* put a picnic on a station-wagon tailgate to forge a dining style.

**16** **BLUE LOBSTERS.**
Kailua-Kona, Hawaii, 1987: Kona Cold Lobsters produces blue-shelled lobsters—rarely found in the wild—from the Maine and European species. They turn red when cooked and taste like any lobster should.

**21** SWEET DEAL. In 1981 Forrest Mars began to produce Ethel M Chocolates in Las Vegas because their liqueur centers are legal in Nevada.

**22** NEW FRONTIERS. In 1995, after much negotiating, Oregon and Washington apples went on sale in Tokyo.

**23** HOLY COW. California is the leading dairy-producing state. If it were a nation, it would be the world's sixth largest country in cheese production.

**24** MARKET BASKET. More than half the nation's fruits, nuts, and vegetables grow in California, including 99 percent or more of the almonds, artichokes, dates, figs, kiwi fruit, olives, persimmons, pistachios, prunes, raisins, and walnuts.

**25** **HAIL TO THE SUPER CHEF.**

In 1975 Austrian-born Wolfgang Puck arrived in Los Angeles. Shortly thereafter, his food was packing the funky phenomenon Ma Maison on Melrose—even with its unlisted phone number. Although Wolf's style was classic French, clearly he was breaking away with fresh ideas. But the "light" in his popular wine sauce pertained only to the wine—little remained in the silken liquid. Ladled over warm lobster or shrimp on frisée (baby curly endive) or slivered Belgian endive, the sauce is a wise investment in calories.

JAMES CARRIER

**Wolf's "Light" Wine Sauce**
**Prep and cook time:** About 15 minutes
**Makes:** About ⅔ cup; 2 or 3 servings
**1.** In a 10- to 12-inch frying pan, combine 1 cup fat-skimmed **chicken broth** and 1 cup **dry white wine.** Boil over high heat until reduced to about ⅔ cup, about 10 minutes.

**2.** Add 2 teaspoons **Dijon mustard** and 6 tablespoons **unsalted butter** in a chunk and whisk until butter is blended into boiling sauce. Continue to boil and stir until sauce is reduced to about ⅔ cup and thick enough to coat a spoon in a velvety layer, 3 to 5 minutes. Add **lemon juice** to taste. Use hot.

Per tablespoon: 66 cal., 94% (62 cal.) from fat; 0.9 g protein; 6.9 g fat (4.3 g sat.); 0.2 g carbo (0 g fiber); 34 mg sodium; 19 mg chol. ◆

**17** PARIS TRIUMPH. In 1976 California wines proved they were world-class. At a blind tasting in Paris, a '73 Stag's Leap Wine Cellars Cabernet Sauvignon and a '73 Château Montelena Chardonnay bested the best French wines.

**18** CELESTIAL CALLING. Red Zinger was an early sensation from Celestial Seasonings, formed in 1969 in Boulder, Colorado.

**19** UNDERSEXED OYSTERS. In the mid-'80s, the triploid oyster was genetically engineered at the University of Washington School of Fisheries. Spawning, which gives other oysters the blahs, has little effect on the triploid.

**20** THE CLIMATE'S RIGHT. Tropical cocoa trees thrive in Hawaii. They were first planted there for domestic chocolate in 1986.

25 WESTERN FOOD CONTRIBUTIONS

# The Wine Guide
BY KAREN MacNEIL

RICK MARIANI

## Then as now: Born great in Napa Valley

■ Let's say someone gave you a million dollars and asked you to buy vineyards in the United States. But not just any vineyards—only those capable of producing legendary, world-class wine.

You could study the soils and climates of this place and that. You could taste wines from all over the country. And in the end, chances are you could find a magical piece of ground—now.

But what if the year were 1840? What if there were no other wineries? No wines to taste? What if no one had any idea where great grapes might grow?

In this realm of the unknown lies one of the biggest miracles of the U.S. wine industry. With virtually nothing to go on, a handful of early Californians just happened to plant vineyards in a place that would ultimately focus worldwide attention on U.S. wines.

Two places, really: the sleepy hamlets of Oakville and Rutherford in the heart of the Napa Valley. Today, they are not only the most richly historic wine regions in California but also where many of the most sensational new wines are made.

At first glance the scene from famous State Highway 29 is utterly serene—a soft green quilt of vines.

But the signposts tell a heady story. Strung together like jewels are some of America's most prestigious wineries: Far Niente, Opus One, Robert Mondavi, Heitz, Cakebread, Niebaum-Coppola (formerly Inglenook), Beaulieu, Franciscan, and Grgich Hills. Tucked in a little farther off the road are other famous names: Caymus, Groth, Flora Springs.

So why Oakville and Rutherford? The story is that of the meteoric rise of the Napa Valley itself. In 1836 the Mexican commander of California, General Mariano Vallejo, gave General George Yount almost 12,000 acres of land in the valley. (To put the enormity of that gift in perspective, consider that a single acre of Napa Valley land today sells for $35,000 to $55,000.)

Yount, in turn, gave his granddaughter Elizabeth and her husband, Thomas Rutherford, 1,040 acres as a wedding present. Rutherford followed in Yount's footsteps, growing more grapes and making wine. Ultimately, Rutherford's estate would become two parcels on which would be founded the most distinguished wineries of the 19th century: Inglenook and Beaulieu Vineyard.

Inglenook (Scottish for *fireside corner*) was the vision of Gustave Niebaum, a Finnish sea captain who'd made a fortune in fur trading and spent it building the majestic Gothic stone château. From the beginning, the wines were considered sensational (half a century later, Inglenook wines would inspire a young man named Robert Mondavi). Today the château and its vineyards are owned by film director Francis Ford Coppola and have been renamed Niebaum-Coppola Estate Winery.

Meanwhile, pioneer H. W. Crabb, who had planted 130 acres of grapes (400 varieties!), was making 50,000 gallons a year of highly praised wine from a vineyard he called To Kalon (Greek for *most beautiful*). Today the To Kalon vineyard is the backbone of several top Robert Mondavi wines. At the same time, Far Niente (Italian for *without a care*) was being built by the same

## SOME OF THE BEST FROM OAKVILLE AND RUTHERFORD

Just because a winery is located in one appellation doesn't necessarily mean all of its wines are made with grapes grown in that appellation. For example, a winery could be in Rutherford but make, say, its Merlot from grapes grown someplace else. That said, all of the wines below come wholly or principally from Oakville or Rutherford vineyards. Alas, since these wines are all highly acclaimed and most are made in small amounts, they are expensive (some are super-expensive)—special treats. If the varietal is not listed, the wine is a blend of Cabernet Sauvignon and Merlot and/or Cabernet Franc.

■ *Beaulieu Vineyard Cabernet Sauvignon "Georges de Latour Private Reserve" 1994,* $50. Utterly soft, sleek, subtle, and refined; no loud flavors here.

■ *Flora Springs Winery & Vineyards Cabernet Sauvignon "Rutherford Hillside Reserve" 1994,* $65. Meaty and masculine, with dramatic toffee and coffee flavors laced with boysenberries.

■ *Groth Vineyards & Winery Cabernet Sauvignon Reserve 1994,* $100. Impeccable. Rich, explosive, dense. A mind-blowing experience—and at the price, it'd better be.

■ *Livingston Wines Cabernet Sauvignon "Moffett Vineyard" 1994,* $36. Outrageous. Leather, chocolate, and mint dance in the mouth with wild abandon.

■ *Opus One 1994,* $90. Beautiful cassis aromas and great depth, but for maximum enjoyment, it should be hidden away and drunk in a few years.

■ *Paradigm Winery Merlot 1995,* $32. Quite possibly the most plush and concentrated Merlot in the Napa Valley.

■ *Quintessa 1994,* $75. One of the most elegant wines of the region. Rose petals, mocha, and blackberries.

■ *Robert Mondavi Winery Cabernet Sauvignon "Oakville" 1995,* $28. Smoky and lush, with sweet, minty blackberry flavors.

■ *Vine Cliff Winery Cabernet Sauvignon 1994,* $36. Almost syruplike in its concentration. Black licorice and cassis.

architect who had designed Inglenook.

By the turn of the century, one of the most important wineries of all was under way—Beaulieu (French for *beautiful place*), founded by Frenchman Georges de Latour. Again, the wines were stunning. De Latour contributed something else of immense impact. In 1937 he hired the young Russian enologist André Tchelistcheff, who would go on to be one of the most influential winemakers in the Napa Valley until his death in 1994. Tchelistcheff, more than anyone else, is credited with improving California wines in the aftermath of Prohibition.

At the time, quality was not exactly on everyone's mind. Prohibition had plunged the industry into a dark era of cheap, sweet wines (with co-opted names like chablis and sauterne). Many of the wineries that held firm on excellence were in Rutherford and Oakville.

The combined impact of Prohibition, the Depression, and World War II brought investments in the wine country to a grinding halt. But when the California wine industry experienced a second golden age, in the 1960s and '70s, the center of the explosive excitement was again Rutherford and Oakville. Many acclaimed wineries were founded: Robert Mondavi Winery, Cakebread, Franciscan, Caymus, and Heitz, among others.

More important, the "soul" of Rutherford and Oakville was discovered to be Cabernet Sauvignon. While other grape varieties did well (especially Cabernet's kinsman Merlot), nothing approached the velvety plushness and heady concentration of the area's Cabs.

Flash forward to the present, California's vinous age of refinement. Once again, Oakville and Rutherford are at ground zero with new top-notch wineries: Screaming Eagle, Paradigm, Harlan Estate, Dalla Valle, Livingston, Vine Cliff.

In the end, what is it about Rutherford and Oakville that makes for such spellbinding wines? No one knows. Of course, climate and soils are exceptional. But the key piece of the puzzle remains a mystery.

The other day in Safeway, I bumped into a young winemaker from Oakville. "What *is* it about those wines?" I asked.

His eyes twinkled, and I knew he was actually tasting the wines in his mind. He shrugged. "Whatever it is," he said happily, "it's pretty awesome." ◆

# Lavender lemonade

## A Western grower shares a favorite summer recipe

BY LAUREN BONAR SWEZEY

■ On a warm summer morning outside Victoria, British Columbia, Lynda Dowling strolls between rows of lavender at her farm, Happy Valley Herbs. Shades from deep purple to violet—from as many as 20 varieties—color the fields. A wonderfully sweet scent fills the air, and bees buzz from flower to flower. It's harvesttime—a moment Dowling has anticipated for months. "Harvest day is a day out of time," she says. "You stand in the middle of a purple field, inhale the intoxicating fragrance, and listen to the bees sing. No faxes or phones nearby."

For Dowling, lavender has become a way of life. She breathes it, eats it, and bathes in it. One whiff of your own homegrown flowers and you'll understand why Dowling looks forward to harvesttime with such gusto. She bundles the lavender into bunches to use in crafts and cooking.

For cooking, Dowling likes *L. angustifolia* 'Hidcote'. "The intense purple flowers color jellies, lemonade, and vinegars beautifully." This variety grows 1 to 2 feet tall. Another favorite is spike lavender (*L. latifolia*), which grows 3 feet tall with violet flowers.

## Lynda Dowling's Lavender Lemonade

PREP AND COOK TIME: 45 minutes

NOTES: 'Hidcote' lavender turns lemonade rosy pink. Other varieties turn it a paler color. Avoid piney-smelling lavenders, such as spike.

MAKES: 6 cups; about 6 servings

1 cup **sugar**

¼ cup (a generous handful) **fresh** or 1 tablespoon dried **lavender blooms** stripped from stems

CONNIE COLEMAN (2)

1 cup **freshly squeezed lemon juice,** strained

**Ice cubes**

**Lavender sprigs** for garnish

**1.** Combine sugar with 2½ cups water in a medium pan. Bring to a boil over medium heat, stirring to dissolve the sugar.

**2.** Add the lavender blooms to the sugar water, cover, and remove from heat. Let stand at least 20 minutes (and up to several hours).

**3.** Strain mixture and discard lavender. Pour infusion into a glass pitcher. Add lemon juice and another 2½ cups water. Stir well and watch lemonade change color.

**4.** Pour into tall glasses half-filled with ice or refrigerate until ready to use. Garnish lemonade with fresh lavender sprigs.

Per serving: 139 cal., 0% (0 cal.) from fat; 0.2 g protein; 0 g fat; 37 g carbo (0.2 g fiber); 0.7 mg sodium; 0 mg chol. ◆

# The Quick Cook

## MEALS IN 30 MINUTES OR LESS

BY ANDREW BAKER

WHAT'S FOR DINNER?

Hungarian Ham Strudel
with Watercress Salad

Sonoma Valley Zinfandel

Sliced Pineapple
with Powdered Sugar

## Getting a feel for filo

■ In the rush of wrapping up a busy day, it's comforting to know that you can also wrap up a meal presentable enough for guests in about half an hour.

This savory filo strudel gets a head start with cooked ham and cooked rice (from a deli or Chinese take-out counter—or use instant rice). While the strudel bakes, stir together a simple mustard sauce and season watercress with rice vinegar to serve as salad.

### Hungarian Ham Strudel with Watercress Salad

PREP AND COOK TIME: About 30 minutes
NOTES: Frozen filo handles best if thawed in the refrigerator at least 8 hours or overnight. If sheets tear, just piece them together. For a zippier flavor, use a hot paprika.

MAKES: 4 servings

- 6 **green onions**
- 1½ cups **cooked rice**
- 1 cup (4 oz.) **shredded Swiss cheese**
- 2 tablespoons **paprika**
- 1 tablespoon **caraway seed**
- 2 tablespoons drained **capers**
- 6 sheets **filo dough** (about 12 by 18 in.)
- ⅓ cup **butter** or margarine, melted
- ½ pound **thin-sliced cooked ham**
- ⅓ cup **reduced-fat sour cream**
- 2 to 3 tablespoons **coarse-grain Dijon mustard**
- ½ pound **watercress**, rinsed and crisped
- 2 tablespoons **seasoned rice vinegar**

**1.** Trim and discard ends of green onions. Chop onions and mix with rice, cheese, paprika, caraway, and capers.

**2.** Lay 1 filo sheet flat (cover remaining filo with plastic wrap to prevent drying) and brush lightly with butter. Top with another filo sheet and brush lightly with more butter. Repeat to stack remaining filo.

**3.** Starting about 1 inch from a narrow edge, lay ham slices over filo (overlap-

ping as needed) to cover about ⅓ of dough, leaving a 1- to 2-inch margin on the sides. Evenly pat rice mixture over ham. Roll filo from ham end to enclose filling. With seam down, gently transfer strudel roll to a buttered baking sheet (at least 11 by 14 in., without side rims). Lightly brush strudel with butter.

**4.** Bake in a 400° oven until golden brown all over, 15 to 17 minutes.

**5.** Meanwhile, mix sour cream with mustard in a small bowl. Mix watercress with vinegar.

**6.** Using 2 wide spatulas, slide strudel onto a platter, cut into thick slices, and accompany with watercress salad. Add sour cream sauce to taste.

Per serving: 582 cal., 51% (297 cal.) from fat; 29 g protein; 33 g fat (18 g sat.); 41 g carbo (2.7 g fiber); 1,775 mg sodium; 107 mg chol.

## THREE MORE QUICK RECIPES FOR FILO MEALS

**1. Spinach, cheese, and sausage packets.** Mix 1 package (10 oz.) **frozen chopped spinach** (thawed and squeezed dry) with ¾ cup shredded **fontina cheese,** ⅛ teaspoon **ground nutmeg,** and ½ cup cooked, crumbled **pork sausage.** Butter and layer filo as directed for strudel. Cut filo stack into 6- by 12-inch strips. Divide filling among strips, mounding at one end; roll from filling end to enclose, tucking sides under. Bake as directed for strudel, 13 to 15 minutes.

Per serving: 398 cal., 68% (270 cal.) from fat; 14 g protein; 30 g fat (16 g sat.); 18 g carbo (1.5 g fiber); 790 mg sodium; 83 mg chol.

**2. Filo-crusted potpie.** Butter and layer filo as directed for strudel. Cut filo to fit the top of a 1- to 2-quart shallow casserole. Bake cut filo as directed for strudel until golden, 3 to 4 minutes. Heat 3 cups **prepared chili** or stew, pour into casserole, and top with crust.

Nutrition information not available.

**3. Filo napoleons.** Butter and layer filo as directed for strudel. Cut into 6 squares. Bake as directed for strudel until golden, 3 to 4 minutes. Top 3 filo squares with ¾ cup of one of the following: **tuna salad,** chicken salad, hummus, or tabbouleh. Top with remaining filo squares. Serve on watercress salad.

Per serving: 259 cal., 63% (162 cal.) from fat; 6.2 g protein; 18 g fat (10 g sat.); 18 g carbo (1.3 g fiber); 433 mg sodium; 43 mg chol. ◆

JAMES CARRIER

MAY 97

CHINESE CLAY POT
holds pork stew
flavored with
hoisin sauce.

# Pacific Rim secrets

## A dozen essential flavorings from the mysterious East that Western chefs have made their own

BY LINDA LAU ANUSASANANAN

PHOTOGRAPHS BY JAMES CARRIER

■ It's a world-class culinary merger: East and West, ancient and innovative. Dubbed Fusion, or Cal-Asia, or Pacific Rim, it's the trendiest cuisine on the restaurant scene, with freewheeling chefs giving it a spin of their own. The results: bold, vibrant dishes born of Eastern ingredients and Western styling.

For such a hot new trend, the Pacific Rim blend has an ingrained heritage.

As long as Westerners have been traveling to the East—and Asian immigrants have been coming to the West—the two culinary worlds have mingled here. By the 1930s, chow mein was a popular West Coast standard, and it was among the first recipes *Sunset* published. Since then, once-exotic dishes such as sushi, *pad Thai*, Vietnamese *pho,* and ginger crab have become familiar favorites. Flavorings like soy sauce have been converted to household staples.

By now we're being seduced by an extensive new spectrum of seasonings that are increasingly available. The selection in Asian markets—Chinese, Japanese, Korean, Thai, Vietnamese—and even in well-stocked supermarkets is bewildering.

Which of these seasoning ingredients belong in your pantry? And which adapt best to contemporary cross-cultural cooking?

We posed these questions to more than a dozen notable chefs who are shaping the personality of Pacific Rim dishes, including European-trained Wolfgang Puck (Spago in Beverly Hills and Chinois in Santa Monica), Rick Yoder (Wild Ginger in Seattle), and Roy Yamaguchi (Roy's Restaurant in Honolulu).

The seasonings that got the most votes made the list that starts at right.

The following recipes have familiar foundations, but Asian seasonings lend a fresh dimension to the finished results.

## PANTRY STAPLES

# Asian basics for a new cuisine

International sections of mainstream urban supermarkets should have most of these items. For more brand choices, shop in Asian groceries.

**ASIAN (TOASTED) SESAME OIL:** Dark oil extracted from toasted sesame seed. For maximum flavor, get a brand that is 100 percent sesame oil; cheaper blends are less intense.
- Use for its rich, nutty, and toasted fragrance. Add at the end of cooking, as heat dissipates flavor and aroma.
- Add to salad dressings, marinades, and soups, and use to season vegetables or noodles.
- *Quick toasted sesame sauce.* In a blender, smoothly purée equal parts **toasted sesame seed** and **Asian (toasted) sesame oil.** Brush the sauce on pan-browned **fish** or use to dress baby salad greens.

— *James McDonald, Pacific'o Restaurant, Lahaina, Hawaii*

Per tablespoon: 103 cal., 96% (99 cal.) from fat; 1 g protein; 11 g fat (1.5 g sat.); 1.3 g carbo (0.6 g fiber); 0.6 mg sodium; 0 mg chol.

**ASIAN FISH SAUCE:** Thin, salty, amber-colored sauce made from fermented fish and salt. Look for *nuoc mam* or *nam pla* on label.
- Use instead of salt or as a light-colored alternative to soy sauce, especially in curries, sauces, dipping sauces, salad dressings, and soups.
- Use the sauce instead of anchovies in dressing for Caesar salad.

— *David Soohoo, Neptune, Sacramento*

**ASIAN RED CHILI PASTE:** A blend of fresh or dried hot red chilies and vinegar. The paste sometimes includes oil, garlic, and other seasonings. Heat level varies with brand and country of origin.
- For pungent heat, add to salad dressings, stir-frys, marinades, and soups.
- Add to dipping sauce for spring rolls.

— *Wolfgang Puck*

**COCONUT MILK:** Made from water pressed through shredded fresh coconut. Thick cream floats to top.

**OYSTER SAUCE:** Thick, brown, salty-sweet sauce made from oyster extract, sugar, and spices. According to David Soohoo, "Chinese call it the magic sauce. It's one of our secrets."
- Use in stir-frys, marinades, and sauces.
- Drizzle over cooked green vegetables—broccoli or green beans.
- For a flavor jolt, add a little to melted butter or cream sauces to pour over meat, vegetables, or fish.
— *Vicky McCaffree, David Soohoo, Larry Tse, House, San Francisco*

- Add to chicken broth and thicken to make an all-purpose gravy or sauce.
— *David Soohoo*

**RICE VINEGAR:** Transparent or golden mellow vinegar made from rice wine. Tastes less acidic than cider, wine, or distilled white vinegars, and does not have a piercing acetic aroma. Seasoned rice vinegar, also called sushi vinegar, contains sugar and salt.
- Use plain or seasoned on salad greens for a no-fat dressing.
- Use instead of butter to season baked potatoes or baked sweet potatoes.

**SOY SAUCE:** Dark, aromatic, full-bodied sauce brewed from fermented soybeans and wheat. There are distinctive flavor differences between Japanese- and Chinese-made soy sauces, and among different brands. Flavored soy sauces, such as mushroom soy (infused with the essence of mushrooms), have unique qualities.
- Use instead of salt in any mixture in which soy sauce's dark color adds an interesting dimension.
- Mix equal parts soy sauce and mushroom-flavor soy for richer flavor.
— *Tim Hartog*

- Substitute salt and pepper at the dinner table with soy sauce and chili pepper water (see facing page).
— *Alan Wong, Alan Wong's Restaurant, Honolulu*

- In dressings made with Asian fish sauce, replace some fish sauce with soy sauce to tone down fish flavor.
— *Roy Yamaguchi*

**THAI CURRY PASTE:** A wet paste made from chilies, spices, and other seasonings. There are many types, including

- Use to deglaze pans in which meat, poultry, or fish has been browned in butter or a mild-flavor oil; reduce slightly to make a velvety coconut sauce. — *Tim Hartog, 301 Folsom, San Francisco*

- Use instead of cream in soups and sauces. — *Roy Yamaguchi*

**FRESH GINGER:** Long-lasting rhizome with pungent and refreshing bite.
- Use in savory and sweet dishes—sauces, dipping sauces, stir-frys, salad dressings, marinades, cakes, cookies, and breads. Especially good with fish.
- Cut in fine slivers and fry crisp. Use to garnish entrees, soups, and salads.
- To crush whole ginger, put in a heavy plastic food bag and smash with a frying pan. — *James McDonald*

**HOISIN SAUCE:** Thick, sweet, red-brown sauce made from soybeans, vinegar, sugar, garlic, and bold spices.
- Use in stir-frys, marinades, and barbecue sauces; brush sauce on near the end of cooking as the sugar makes it brown fast. Especially good with poultry and lamb.
- Sear rack of lamb. Brush with hoisin sauce, press sesame seed onto lamb, and roast. — *James McDonald*

- Mix with garlic, ginger, guava purée, and sambal (Indonesian chili paste) for a sweet-hot, pungent marinade.
— *Mako Segawa-Gonzales, Maui Beach Cafe, Los Angeles*

**LEMON GRASS:** Pale green, woody grass stalks with distinctive lemon aroma. Remove fibrous outer layers and coarse leafy tops, and trim root. Use tender inner stalk. Adds fragrance and flavor but is not acidic.
- Mince for stir-frys and curries.
- To release the maximum amount of flavor, use a hammer or the blunt edge of a cleaver to crush stalk, then toast with ground turmeric, minced fresh ginger, and crushed garlic to make a seasoning base for sauces and marinades. — *James McDonald*

- Add to crab cakes or cook with pan-browned scallops. — *Wolfgang Puck*

- Use instead of lemon juice for flavor in fish marinades where the acid in juice "cooks" the fish, changing its texture and color, such as on tuna.
— *Tim Hartog*

- Simmer with liquid when making chicken or vegetable broth.
— *Serge Burckel, Splash, Los Angeles*

red, green, yellow, panang, and Mussaman—each blend has its own flavor. Comes in packets, envelopes, and jars.

- Mix a yellow curry paste with coconut milk to taste and heat to make a spicy sauce. Or marinate split chickens in the mixture and grill. Serve with Thai sweet chili sauce (see below).
- Steam mussels in broth flavored with red curry paste and coconut milk. — *Vicky McCaffree*

- Use curry paste instead of curry powder. — *Roy Yamaguchi*

**WASABI:** Powerfully pungent, hot green horseradish. Available as a dry powder or paste in a tube. Mix powder with water and let rest for 10 minutes for flavors to "bloom."

- Use as you would horseradish or hot mustard.
- Add dry powder with dry ingredients for sauces and in baking.
- Use in broth for poaching oysters.
  — *Bruce Hill, Waterfront, San Francisco*

## ALSO IN THE RUNNING

# Other ingredients chefs like to use

**BLACK BEAN SAUCE:** Made from salted black beans, rice wine, and seasonings.

**BLACK VINEGAR:** Dark, mildly sweet, smoky vinegar made from rice, wheat, millet, or sorghum.

**CHILI PEPPER WATER:** A mixture of hot red chilies, vinegar, and water. Popular in Hawaii.

**COCONUT OR PALM SUGAR:** Comes in hard chunks to crush or melt. Tastes like sugar boiled with water until thick enough to harden.

**PONZU SAUCE:** A thin, yellow, citrus-flavor Japanese sauce, sometimes called citrus-seasoned sauce.

**THAI SWEET CHILI SAUCE:** Thick, sweet, faintly sour syrup with chilies, sometimes called sweet chili sauce.

## Spicy Ponzu Salmon on Greens

PREP AND COOK TIME: **About 25 minutes**

NOTES: Chef Amiko Gubbins of Cafe Japengo in San Diego uses citrus-flavor ponzu (see lower left) to make an all-purpose sauce. Here the sauce seasons salmon. But if you'd like to try it with other foods as a marinade, basting sauce, salad dressing, or dipping sauce, combine ingredients as directed in step 1; use or cover and chill up to 1 month.

MAKES: **4 to 6 servings**

- ½ cup **soy sauce**
- ¼ cup **ponzu sauce**
- 1 tablespoon **Asian (toasted) sesame oil**
- ¾ teaspoon **oyster sauce**
- ½ teaspoon **black bean sauce**
- ½ teaspoon **Asian red chili paste**
- ½ teaspoon minced **fresh ginger**
- ½ teaspoon minced **garlic**
- 1 **boned salmon fillet** (1½ to 2 lb.)
- 3 quarts (9 oz.) **salad greens,** rinsed and crisped

**1.** Mix soy sauce, ponzu sauce, sesame oil, oyster sauce, black bean sauce, chili paste, ginger, and garlic.

**2.** Rinse fish, pat dry, and coat with half the ponzu mixture. Let stand about 10 minutes. Discard liquid.

**3.** Set salmon, skin up, on an oiled grill over a solid bed of hot coals or high heat on a gas grill (you can hold your hand at grill level only 2 to 3 seconds); close lid on gas grill. Cook salmon, turning once, until opaque but still moist-looking in center of thickest part (cut to test), 6 to 8 minutes. Remove from grill.

**4.** Mix salad greens with remaining ponzu mixture. Present fish on or beside salad.

Per serving: 205 cal., 42% (86 cal.) from fat; 24 g protein; 9.6 g fat (1.4 g sat.); 4.1 g carbo (0 g fiber); 1,500 mg sodium; 1.4 mg chol.

## Thai Salad Dressing

PREP TIME: **About 4 minutes**

NOTES: Jeff McMahon of Saucebox in Portland mixes this dressing with thinly sliced grilled beef and vegetables for a dish he calls Thai beef salad. To store sauce, cover and chill up to 5 days.

MAKES: **About 1¼ cups**

- ½ cup **lime juice**
- ¼ cup **sugar**
- ¼ cup **Asian fish sauce** (*nuoc mam* or *nam pla*)
- 1 to 3 teaspoons minced **fresh hot chilies**

Mix lime juice, sugar, fish sauce, ½ cup water, and chilies to taste.

Per tablespoon: 19 cal., 19% (3.6 cal.) from fat; 0.5 g protein; 0.4 g fat (0.1 g sat.); 3.5 g carbo (0 g fiber); 120 mg sodium; 0 mg chol.

SPICY PONZU seasons grilled salmon and salad with an Asian flair.

## Rick's Pork and Vegetable Hot Pots

PREP AND COOK TIME: About 1½ hours

NOTES: For convenience at home, Rick Yoder of Wild Ginger in Seattle cooks this stew ahead and reheats individual servings in Chinese clay pots.

MAKES: About 4 servings

- 1 pound **fat-trimmed boned pork shoulder** or butt
- ¾ pound **slender eggplant**
- 1 **red bell pepper** (½ lb.)
- 1 **onion** (½ lb.)
- 1 tablespoon **salad oil**
- 2 cloves **garlic**, minced
- 2 **carrots** (6 oz. total), thinly sliced
- ¼ pound **mushrooms**, rinsed and quartered
- 2 tablespoons **hoisin sauce**
- 2 tablespoons **shao hsing wine** (rice wine) or dry sherry
- 1½ cups **chicken broth**
- 1 teaspoon **Asian** (toasted) **sesame oil**
- **Soy sauce**
- Thinly sliced **green onions**

1. Cut meat into ¾-inch chunks.

2. Trim and discard eggplant stems. Cut eggplant into ¾-inch chunks.

3. Stem and seed bell pepper. Cut into ¾-inch chunks.

4. Peel onion and cut into ¾-inch chunks.

5. Place a 5- to 6-quart pan over high heat. Add 2 teaspoons oil and swirl to coat pan. Add pork and garlic; stir occasionally until lightly browned, 10 to 15 minutes. Pour from pan into a bowl.

6. To pan, add 1 teaspoon oil, onion, carrots, and mushrooms; stir-fry over high heat until onion begins to brown, about 10 minutes.

7. Add hoisin sauce, wine, broth, and pork. Stir until boiling to release browned bits in pan. Cover and simmer over low heat 10 minutes; stir often.

8. Add eggplant and bell pepper to pan. Mix, cover, and simmer over low heat until pork is very tender when pierced, 30 to 40 minutes longer; stir occasionally.

9. Add sesame oil and soy sauce to taste. Garnish portions with green onions.

Per serving: 332 cal., 38% (126 cal.) from fat; 26 g protein; 14 g fat (4 g sat.); 24 g carbo (4.6 g fiber); 306 mg sodium; 77 mg chol.

## Roy's Homestyle Chicken Curry

PREP AND COOK TIME: About 50 minutes

NOTES: Roy Yamaguchi of Roy's Restaurant in Honolulu uses mild Thai Mussaman curry paste—one of many prepared Thai curry pastes (see pantry staples, page 100)—to make this simple dish for his family.

MAKES: 4 servings

- 4 **whole chicken legs** (thighs and drumsticks attached, about 2½ lb. total)
- 1 teaspoon **salad oil**
- 1 stalk (12 to 16 in.) **fresh lemon grass**
- 1 can (14 oz.) **coconut milk**
- 1 tablespoon **Mussaman curry paste**
- 1 tablespoon **palm sugar** or firmly packed brown sugar
- 1 to 2 tablespoons **Asian fish sauce** (*nuoc mam* or *nam pla*)
- 4 slices (each about the size of a quarter) **fresh ginger**
- 2 cloves **garlic**, crushed
- 18 **fresh basil** leaves (at least 2 in.)

1. Remove and discard chicken skin. Rinse chicken and pat dry.

2. Place a 10- to 12-inch nonstick frying pan over high heat. Add oil and swirl to coat pan; when hot, add chicken and brown on each side, about 5 minutes total. Transfer chicken to plate.

3. Meanwhile, trim and discard root end and coarse outer lemon grass leaves. Cut the stalk into 4-inch sections and crush with a mallet or the blunt edge of a knife.

4. To pan, add coconut milk, curry paste, and sugar. Stir until mixture is smoothly blended. Stir in 1 tablespoon fish sauce and add lemon grass, ginger, and garlic. Heat until boiling.

5. Set aside 4 of the nicest basil leaves; add remainder to pan along with chicken. Cover and simmer over low heat for 15 minutes. Turn chicken over, cover, and continue to simmer until chicken is no longer pink at bone (cut to test), 10 to 15 minutes longer.

6. Lift chicken from sauce and put on a platter; keep warm. With a slotted spoon, remove lemon grass, garlic, ginger, and basil, if desired. If you want the sauce thick enough to coat chicken in a velvety layer, boil and stir to reduce slightly. Pour sauce over chicken and sprinkle with remaining basil leaves. Season to taste with fish sauce.

Per serving: 444 cal., 59% (261 cal.) from fat; 36 g protein; 29 g fat (21 g sat.); 11 g carbo (0.9 g fiber); 496 mg sodium; 130 mg chol.

## Chili-glazed Shrimp

PREP AND COOK TIME: About 30 minutes

NOTES: Vicky McCaffree of Yarrow Bay Grill in Kirkland, Washington, uses this glaze on firm fish such as halibut. It also complements shrimp. To make sauce only, complete step 1, then use or chill, covered, up to 3 days.

MAKES: 4 servings

- ½ cup **Thai sweet chili sauce**
- 2 tablespoons **lime juice**
- 1 tablespoon **Asian fish sauce** (*nuoc mam* or *nam pla*)
- 2 tablespoons chopped **fresh cilantro**
- 1 pound (30 to 35 per lb.) **shrimp**, shelled, deveined, and rinsed
- **Lime** wedges

1. Mix chili sauce, lime juice, fish sauce, and cilantro; set aside.

2. Divide shrimp into 4 equal portions. Lay each portion of shrimp in a neat row with tails pointed in the same direction. Thread 2 thin wood or metal skewers (8 to 10 in. long) about 1½ inches apart through center of each row of shrimp, pushing the shellfish close together.

3. Place shrimp on an oiled grill above a solid bed of hot coals or high heat on a gas barbecue (you can hold your hand at grill level only 2 to 3 seconds); close lid on gas grill.

4. Cook, turning once, until shrimp are pink, 2 to 3 minutes a side.

5. Brush tops of shrimp with the chili sauce mixture, turn over, and cook just until glaze bubbles and browns slightly, about 30 seconds (watch closely; glaze burns easily). Brush tops with more chili mixture, then turn glaze down and cook just until it darkens slightly, about 30 seconds more.

6. Transfer shrimp to plates or a platter. Season to taste with remaining chili mixture and juice from lime wedges.

Per serving: 191 cal., 12% (22 cal.) from fat; 24 g protein; 2.4 g fat (0.5 g sat.); 14 g carbo (0 g fiber); 558 mg sodium; 173 mg chol. ◆

# The Low-Fat Cook

## HEALTHY CHOICES FOR THE ACTIVE LIFESTYLE

### BY ELAINE JOHNSON

CORNHUSK LINING, spicy filling, and masa dough capture the flavors of tamales.

## Tamale pie gets real, slims down

■ Tamale pie, although inspired by Mexican tamales, is a Western invention. We've traced it back a century in old Los Angeles cookbooks. At *Sunset*, we published our first tamale pie recipe in 1920. Dozens of versions, usually based on cornmeal, have followed.

So what else is there to say? Well, long after the fact, at least one Mexican chef we met in the Yucatán in 1980 generated her own concept of tamale pie. To serve a hotel full of guests, she layered authentic tamale ingredients—lard-rich masa (corn) dough and chicken filling—in a big pan to bake.

Because the pie tasted like tamales and was easy to make, this recipe quickly became one of our favorites. But times demand this lighter touch.

### Trim Tamale Pie

PREP AND COOK TIME: About 1¼ hours

MAKES: 5 or 6 servings

8 to 10 **dried cornhusks,** each 5 to 7 inches wide and long (optional)

1 pound **boned, skinned chicken breasts,** fat trimmed

1 **firm tomato** (½ lb.), cored

1 **onion** (½ lb.)

2 cups plus 2 tablespoons **dehydrated masa flour** (corn tortilla flour)

3¼ cups fat-skimmed **chicken broth**

2 tablespoons **chili powder**

1 tablespoon **distilled white vinegar**

⅛ teaspoon **anise seed**

⅓ cup **raisins**

½ teaspoon **baking powder**

½ teaspoon **salt**

3 tablespoons **olive oil**

Sliced **green onions**

**Guacasalsa** (recipe follows)

**1.** Separate husks, discarding silks and debris. Rinse husks, then soak in warm water until pliable, at least 15 minutes.

**2.** Cut chicken into 1-inch chunks. Cut tomato and onion into slender wedges.

**3.** In a 3- to 4-quart pan, smoothly blend 2 tablespoons masa with ¼ cup broth. Then add 1¼ cups more broth, onion, chili powder, vinegar, anise, and raisins. Stirring, bring mixture to a boil over high heat, then simmer, covered, stirring occasionally, until onion is tender to bite, about 8 minutes. Stir in chicken and tomato, and remove from heat.

**4.** In a bowl, mix remaining 2 cups masa, baking powder, and salt. Stir in oil and remaining 1¾ cups broth.

**5.** Drain husks. Overlapping husks, line a shallow 2½-quart casserole (about 7 by 11 in.), allowing husk tips to extend above casserole rim. (Or lightly oil dish.)

**6.** With damp fingers, pat half the masa dough onto husks in casserole bottom. Add chicken mixture. Drop remaining dough in small spoonfuls onto filling.

**7.** Bake in a 425° oven until casserole is bubbling in center, about 45 minutes. Garnish with green onions.

Per serving: 364 cal., 24% (89 cal.) from fat; 27 g protein; 9.9 g fat (1.4 g sat.); 45 g carbo (5.4 g fiber); 357 mg sodium; 44 mg chol.

Per serving with guacasalsa: 394 cal., 27% (108 cal.) from fat; 27 g protein; 12 g fat (1.7 g sat.); 47 g carbo (5.6 g fiber); 519 mg sodium; 44 mg chol.

**Guacasalsa.** Mix ⅓ cup mashed **ripe avocado,** ⅔ cup **green salsa,** and 3 tablespoons chopped **fresh cilantro.** Makes 1 cup.

Per tablespoon: 11 cal., 57% (6.3 cal.) from fat; 0.1 g protein; 0.7 g fat (0.1 g sat.); 1 g carbo (0.1 g fiber); 61 mg sodium; 0 mg chol. ◆

# Kitchen Cabinet

## READERS' RECIPES TESTED IN SUNSET'S KITCHENS

BY LINDA LAU ANUSASANANAN

DIP ARTICHOKE leaves and fennel chunks in warm anchovy sauce.

## Foods that won the West

### Nonnie's Bagna Cauda

Phyllis Mattson, Fiddletown, California

"Nonnie always served artichokes this old Italian way. She would cook olive oil, butter, garlic, and a little anchovy in a small iron pan and put it in the center of the table. We would dunk artichokes and sweet anise (fennel) in it," reminisces Phyllis Mattson.

PREP AND COOK TIME: About 30 minutes

MAKES: 8 to 10 appetizer servings

- 3  tablespoons **lemon juice**
- 2  **artichokes** (3½ to 4 in. wide)
- 2  heads **fennel** (3 in. wide) or ½ pound **celery hearts**
- ⅓  cup (⅙ lb.) **butter** or margarine
- ⅓  cup **olive oil**
- 2  or 3 cloves **garlic,** pressed or minced
- 2  tablespoons minced **canned anchovies**
- 1  **baguette** (1 lb.), thinly sliced

**1.** In a 5- to 6-quart pan, combine lemon juice and 2 quarts water. Cover and bring to a boil over high heat.

**2.** Meanwhile, cut about 1 inch off artichoke tops; discard tops. With scissors, cut off remaining thorny tips on outer leaves and discard. Slice artichokes in half lengthwise through stems. Rinse and drain.

**3.** Immerse artichokes in boiling water. Return to a boil, cover, and simmer over low heat until artichokes are tender when pierced, about 25 minutes. Drain. Scoop out and discard fuzzy centers.

**4.** As artichokes cook, rinse fennel. Trim and discard stems and any bruised spots. Break segments apart.

**5.** In a 2- to 3-cup pan over low heat, melt butter with oil, garlic, and anchovies to make bagna cauda sauce.

**6.** Put fennel and artichokes on a platter, the bread in a basket, and bagna cauda sauce on an electric or candle warmer; take care not to scorch sauce. Dip fennel and artichoke leaves and bottoms in sauce and hold pieces of bread under vegetables to catch drips as you eat. Also dip the bread in the sauce to eat.

Per serving: 201 cal., 63% (126 cal.) from fat; 4 g protein; 14 g fat (4.9 g sat.); 15 g carbo (2.2 g fiber); 355 mg sodium; 18 mg chol.

### Grilled Salmon with Tomatillo-Avocado Salsa

Phyllis Kidd, Ojai, California

California native Phyllis Kidd was raised with Southwest flavors. Her mother and half-Mexican father were in the restaurant business, and she says, "I grew up around the best chefs in the industry." These influences led her to create dishes that marry Western classics such as salmon and avocado with Latino zest.

PREP AND COOK TIME: About 25 minutes

MAKES: 4 to 6 servings

- ½  pound **tomatillos**
- 2  or 3 unpeeled cloves **garlic**
   About ½ teaspoon **salt**
- 2  tablespoons **olive oil**
- 2  tablespoons **balsamic vinegar**
- 4  to 6 pieces (1 in. thick; about 6 oz. each) **boned salmon fillets**
- 2  **fresh jalapeño chilies,** stemmed
- ½  cup **fresh cilantro** leaves
- 2  tablespoons **lime juice**
- 1  **firm-ripe avocado** (about ½ lb.)
- ⅓  cup minced **onion**

**1.** Pull off and discard tomatillo husks. Rinse and dry tomatillos.

**2.** In a 10- to 12-inch frying pan over medium-high heat, cook tomatillos and garlic until lightly browned, about 5 minutes, turning often. Remove from pan to cool.

**3.** Peel garlic and mash to a paste with ¼ teaspoon salt. Mix with oil and vinegar.

**4.** Rinse fish and pat dry. Coat skinless sides of salmon with garlic mixture. Let stand about 5 minutes.

**5.** For minimum heat, remove seeds and veins from chilies. Coarsely chop chilies.

**6.** In a food processor or blender, combine chilies, tomatillos, ¼ cup cilantro, and lime juice. Whirl until puréed.

**7.** Peel, pit, and coarsely dice avocado. Add half the avocado to tomatillo mixture and whirl just to blend slightly. Pour into a bowl and stir in onion, remaining diced avocado, and salt to taste.

8. Lay fish on an oiled grill over a solid bed of hot coals or high heat on a gas grill (you can hold your hand at grill level only 2 to 3 seconds); close lid on gas grill. Cook salmon, turning once, until opaque but still moist-looking in center of thickest part (cut to test), 6 to 8 minutes.

9. Transfer fish to plates, garnish with remaining cilantro, and top with tomatillo-avocado salsa. Add salt to taste.

Per serving: 415 cal., 59% (243 cal.) from fat; 35 g protein; 27 g fat (5 g sat.); 5.9 g carbo (0.9 g fiber); 299 mg sodium; 100 mg chol.

## Chipotle Honey–Glazed Lamb Chops

### Gretchen Guard, Santa Fe

Gretchen Guard developed her expertise in barbecuing Idaho lamb when she was a caterer in that state. Now she's an artist living in New Mexico, and the lamb she grills has that Santa Fe touch—a glaze of honey and smoky chipotle chilies.

PREP AND COOK TIME: About 25 minutes

MAKES: 3 or 4 servings

- 3 or 4 **dried** or canned **chipotle chilies**
- 3 tablespoons **honey**
- 8 **lamb rib chops** (each about ¾ in. thick; 2 lb. total)

   **Salt** and **pepper**

   **Lime** wedges

1. If chilies are dried, soak in about 1 cup hot water until soft, about 15 minutes. Wearing rubber gloves, remove chili stems and, for minimum heat, discard seeds and veins. Finely chop chilies and mix with honey.

2. Trim excess fat off lamb.

3. Lay chops on a grill over a solid bed of hot coals or high heat on a gas grill (you can hold your hand at grill level only 2 to 3 seconds); close lid on gas grill. Cook chops until lightly browned on each side and still pink in the center (cut to test), turning once, 5 to 6 minutes total.

4. Brush tops of chops with honey mixture, turn over, and cook until glazed sides darken slightly, about 30 seconds (watch closely; honey glaze burns easily). Brush tops with remaining honey mixture, turn glazed sides down, and cook just until slightly darkened, another 30 seconds. Transfer meat to plates. Season to taste with salt, pepper, and lime juice squeezed from wedges.

Per serving: 224 cal., 38% (85 cal.) from fat; 20 g protein; 9.4 g fat (3.4 g sat.); 14 g carbo (0.2 g fiber); 63 mg sodium; 66 mg chol.

## Red Lentil Salad

### Heidi Timmons, Tacoma

When Heidi Timmons moved from Chile to Washington, where the nation's largest crop of lentils is produced in great variety in the Palouse area, she began using quick-cooking, hulled Red Chief legumes in salad.

PREP AND COOK TIME: About 30 minutes

MAKES: 6 to 8 servings

- 1 cup **Red Chief** or regular brown **lentils**
- ⅓ cup **balsamic vinegar**
- 2 tablespoons **olive oil**
- 2 cloves **garlic,** pressed or minced
- ¾ cup coarsely chopped **red** or yellow **bell peppers**
- ¾ cup thinly sliced **green onions**
- ¾ cup halved **cherry tomatoes**
- ¾ cup diced (¼ in.) **cucumber**
- ½ cup chopped **fresh basil** leaves
- ½ cup crumbled **feta cheese**

   **Salt** and **pepper**

1. Sort lentils and discard any debris. Rinse and drain lentils.

2. In a 2- to 3-quart pan, bring about 1 quart water to a boil over high heat. Add lentils, stir to separate, and simmer, uncovered, just until they are tender to bite but not soft, 5 to 10 minutes for Red Chiefs, 20 to 30 minutes for regular lentils. Drain.

3. Mix vinegar, oil, and garlic. Pour over warm lentils and gently mix. Let stand until cool.

4. Add bell peppers, onions, tomatoes, cucumber, basil, and feta cheese. Mix gently with lentils. Pour into a serving bowl. Add salt and pepper to taste.

Per serving: 147 cal., 34% (50 cal.) from fat; 8.5 g protein; 5.6 g fat (1.8 g sat.); 17 g carbo (3.5 g fiber); 105 mg sodium; 7.9 mg chol.

## Chicken and Strawberry Salad

### Erin Smith, Phoenix

A salad with strawberries that Erin Smith's mother enjoyed in a restaurant made such an impression that she frequently described it with flavorful details. Laden with clues, Smith concocted her own version as the surprise for a Mother's Day picnic. She was right on, and the salad was a hit.

PREP AND COOK TIME: About 30 minutes

MAKES: 4 servings

- ¼ cup **sliced almonds**
- 4 **boned, skinned chicken breast halves** (6 oz. each)
- 3 tablespoons minced **fresh** or 2 teaspoons dried **tarragon**
- 1 teaspoon minced **garlic**
- 1 tablespoon **olive oil**
- ½ cup **reduced-fat** or regular **mayonnaise**
- 3 tablespoons **lemon juice**
- 1 tablespoon **sugar**
- 1 tablespoon **poppy seed**
- 3 quarts (about 9 oz.) **salad mix,** rinsed and crisped
- 2 cups **strawberries,** rinsed, hulled, and sliced

   **Salt** and **pepper**

1. Stir almonds just until golden in a 10- to 12-inch nonstick frying pan over medium heat, about 4 minutes. Pour out of pan.

2. Rinse chicken and pat dry. Mix tarragon, garlic, and oil. Rub all over chicken to coat.

3. Set frying pan over medium heat. When hot, add chicken and cook, turning once, until meat is white in center of thickest part (cut to test), 8 to 10 minutes total. Remove from pan. Use warm or let cool.

4. To make the salad dressing, mix mayonnaise with lemon juice, sugar, and poppy seed.

5. Combine salad mix with strawberries and half the dressing. Mound salad equally on dinner plates and set chicken alongside or on top.

6. Drizzle chicken with remaining dressing. Sprinkle with toasted almonds. Add salt and pepper to taste.

Per serving: 402 cal., 36% (144 cal.) from fat; 42 g protein; 16 g fat (2.4 g sat.); 20 g carbo (3.2 g fiber); 369 mg sodium; 99 mg chol.

# Kitchen Cabinet

## Mango-Chili Jam

Theresa M. Liu, Alameda, California

Sweet mangoes from Hawaii spiked with hot chilies produce a jam with a kick. "I love the combination of hot and sweet," says Theresa Liu. She likes the jam with poultry or fish or mixed with cream cheese and served with crackers. If you don't want to can the jam, let it cool and spoon into containers. Cover and chill up to 3 weeks. To store longer, leave about 1 inch headspace in containers, cover airtight, and freeze.

PREP AND COOK TIME: 40 minutes

MAKES: 8 cups

- 6 to 10 (6 to 9 oz.) **fresh red or green jalapeño chilies**
- 6 cups coarsely chopped peeled **ripe mangoes**
- ¾ cup **lemon juice**
- 1 package (1¾ oz.) **dry pectin for lower-sugar recipes**
- 4 cups **sugar**

**1.** Place chilies on a small baking sheet and broil 3 to 4 inches from heat, turning as needed, until chilies are charred and blistered all over, 10 to 12 minutes. Cool. Remove and discard skin, stems, and seeds. Coarsely chop chilies.

**2.** In a 6- to 8-quart pan, combine mangoes, chilies, and lemon juice.

**3.** Mix pectin with ¼ cup sugar. Stir into mangoes. Stirring, bring to a rolling boil over high heat. Add remaining 3¾ cups sugar and stir until mixture returns to rolling boil. Stir and boil exactly 1 minute longer. Remove from heat.

**4.** Ladle into clean canning jars to within ⅛ inch of top. Wipe jar rims. Set clean, flat lids on top. Screw on bands. Invert jars for 5 minutes, then turn upright. Let cool at least 24 hours. Check seals by pressing firmly on centers of the lids. If a lid pops back, it's not sealed; store it in refrigerator.

Per tablespoon: 33 cal., 0% (0 cal.) from fat; 0.1 g protein; 0 g fat; 8.3 g carbo (0.1 g fiber); 25 mg sodium; 0 mg chol.

## Macadamia Pilaf

Ivalee Sinclair, Honolulu

When Ivalee Sinclair's children were growing up, this rich pilaf, lavishly topped with Hawaiian macadamia nuts, was a family tradition. Now her children make it for their families.

PREP AND COOK TIME: About 1 hour

MAKES: 10 or 11 servings

- ⅓ cup (⅙ lb.) **butter** or margarine
- ¾ cup (4 oz.) **salted roasted macadamia nuts,** very coarsely chopped
- 1 **onion** (½ lb.), chopped
- 3 cloves **garlic,** pressed or minced
- 2⅔ cups **short-** or medium-**grain white rice**
- 4 cups **chicken broth**
- ¼ teaspoon **white pepper**
- 2 tablespoons chopped **parsley**

**1.** In a 10- to 12-inch frying pan over medium heat, melt 1 tablespoon butter. Add the macadamia nuts and stir until slightly darker brown, about 3 minutes. Scrape from pan into small bowl and set aside.

**2.** Add remaining butter, onion, and garlic to pan. Stir often over medium-high heat until onion is limp, about 5 minutes.

**3.** Add rice and stir often until grains turn opaque, about 5 minutes.

**4.** Add the broth and pepper. Heat to a simmer. Pour the mixture into a shallow 2½- to 3-quart casserole; cover tightly.

**5.** Bake in a 375° oven until rice is tender to bite, 40 to 45 minutes. Uncover and sprinkle with nuts and parsley.

Per serving: 315 cal., 40% (126 cal.) from fat; 5.4 g protein; 14 g fat (4.9 g sat.); 42 g carbo (0.9 g fiber); 140 mg sodium; 16 mg chol.

## Fresh Raspberry Tart

Ann Brown, Oakland, California

Asked to bring dessert for a dinner, Ann Brown planned to make a fresh berry pie. When she went to the market, the raspberries she found were so exceptional that she chose them to make this open-faced tart in a buttery crust.

PREP AND COOK TIME: About 30 minutes

MAKES: 8 servings

- 1 cup **all-purpose flour**
- 2 tablespoons plus ⅓ cup **granulated sugar**
- ½ cup (¼ lb.) **butter** or margarine, cut into ½-inch chunks
- 5½ cups **raspberries,** rinsed and drained
- 1½ tablespoons **cornstarch**
- 1 cup **whipping cream**
- 1 teaspoon grated **orange** peel
- 2 tablespoons **powdered sugar**

**1.** In a food processor or bowl, combine flour, 2 tablespoons granulated sugar, and butter. Whirl or rub with your fingers until the mixture is crumbly. Whirl until the dough forms a ball, or press dough firmly into a ball. Press dough evenly over bottom and 1 inch up the side of a 9-inch cake pan with a removable rim.

**2.** Bake crust in a 350° oven until golden, about 18 minutes. Cool on a rack.

**3.** Meanwhile, in a 1- to 2-quart pan, mix 6 tablespoons water, ⅓ cup granulated sugar, and ½ cup raspberries. Bring to a boil over medium heat, stirring.

**4.** Blend the cornstarch with 2 tablespoons water and mix with the berries in the pan. Stir until boiling. Cool, stirring occasionally. If making ahead, cover and chill up to 4 hours.

**5.** Up to 1 hour before serving, spread the cool raspberry sauce over bottom of baked crust. Mound remaining berries on sauce.

**6.** Whip cream until soft peaks form. Stir in grated orange peel and powdered sugar. Mound whipping cream onto berries.

Per serving: 335 cal., 56% (189 cal.) from fat; 3 g protein; 21 g fat (13 g sat.); 35 g carbo (3.4 g fiber); 128 mg sodium; 64 mg chol. ◆

BUTTER-TOASTED MACADAMIAS top baked rice pilaf.

# Dive into curried duck

## A classic stew that takes the intimidation out of cooking this bird

BY SANDRA BAKKO CAMERON AND CHRISTINE WEBER HALE

Thai curry pastes are hot, as explained on page 100. And in Thailand, where duck is everyday food, green curry paste is essential to this memorable duck curry, which combines homespun cooking with adventure. Even if you've never tackled duck, there's no need to shy away. Make-ahead steps and no carving eliminate last-minute tensions.

If you can't find green curry paste, whirl smooth in a blender or food processor 6 cloves **garlic**, 3 tablespoons chopped **onion**, 1 packed tablespoon **fresh cilantro**, 2 teaspoons *each* chopped **fresh ginger** and **salad oil**, and 1 teaspoon *each* **hot chili flakes**, grated **lemon** peel, and **anchovy paste**.

## Green Curry Duck and Potatoes

**PREP AND COOK TIME:** About 3 hours, but 2 hours of the work can be done up to 2 days ahead

**NOTES:** Look for Thai green curry paste and fish sauce in Southeast Asian markets or well-stocked supermarkets.

**MAKES:** 6 servings

1   **duck** (about 5 lb.), cut into pieces

6   cups **chicken broth**

1/3   cup **purchased Thai green curry paste**

2   cans (about 14 oz. each) **reduced-fat coconut milk**

1/4   cup **Asian fish sauce** (*nuoc mam* or *nam pla*) or soy sauce

3   tablespoons firmly packed **brown sugar**

1 1/2   tablespoons **curry powder**

1   teaspoon **hot chili flakes**

About 3 pounds **russet potatoes**, peeled and cut into 1 1/2-inch chunks

THE WINNING SECRET of this duck dish is plenty of sauce to mash into potatoes.

1/4   cup minced **fresh cilantro**

**Cilantro sprigs** and **salt**

**1.** *Simmer duck meat.* In a 6- to 8-quart pan, combine duck, broth, and 2 tablespoons curry paste. Cover pan and bring to a boil over high heat. Simmer until leg meat is tender enough to pull from bones, about 2 hours. Lift out duck and let cool to touch. Skim and discard fat from broth. Reserve 1 1/4 cups broth; use remainder for other dishes. Pull meat from bones; discard fat, skin, and bones. Tear meat into bite-size pieces. If making ahead, cover broth and meat airtight and chill.

**2.** *Make green curry sauce.* In a 5- to 6-quart pan, mix the 1 1/4 cups duck broth, remaining curry paste, coconut milk, fish sauce, sugar, curry powder, and chili flakes. Bring to boiling on high heat, then add potatoes. Cover and simmer until potatoes are tender when pierced, about 40 minutes.

**3.** Add duck meat and simmer gently until hot, 5 to 10 minutes. Stir in minced cilantro. Ladle into wide bowls, garnish with cilantro sprigs, and add salt to taste.

Per serving: 579 cal., 28% (162 cal.) from fat; 33 g protein; 18 g fat (8.9 g sat.); 59 g carbo (fiber not available); 874 mg sodium; 99 mg chol. ◆

Flavors of Provence: Chicken breast, French-style, has coarse-grain mustard and herbs under well-browned skin (see page 123).

# June

# foodguide

BY JERRY ANNE DI VECCHIO

JAMES CARRIER (3)

## tree-ripe

When it comes to fragile stone fruit—peaches, plums, pluots, nectarines, and apricots—there's no equal to tree-ripened perfection. But finding fully developed fruit is no small task. True, farmers' markets, overall, have focused on produce harvested at peak quality. But until now, if such a market—or an orchard—wasn't close by, well, too bad. This is changing. Sigona's Farmers Market (run by brothers Joe, John, Mel, and Paul Sigona in Redwood City, California) is initiating a program to put the perfectly ripe in your hands. The market will ship a dozen just-picked, ready-to-eat stone fruit overnight to your door. Varieties will change from week to week as the California harvest moves from the Fresno area in the Central Valley to the choice Placerville high-country orchards. Some varieties the Sigonas expect to offer are new; others are old favorites.

A fruit pack weighs 5 to 9 pounds and is estimated to cost $15 to $29 (plus shipping), although prices were not set as of press time because of weather and harvest variables. For more information and order forms, call (650) 368-6997 or go to www.sigonas.com.

TOOL

## A refined spray

■ Spraying oil in a fine mist onto pans is a practical way to control fat. Until recently, though, you had to buy oils already in spray cans, where they were prone to turn rancid quickly. Now you can buy empty misters and add your own oil, enabling you to control quality, flavor, and freshness. Brushed metal models cost about $25. The all-plastic EcoPump costs $8. You create pressure as needed with the hand pump/lid. Misters are showing up in cookware stores, or you can order the EcoPump from California Olive Oil Co.; (800) 386-6457 or www.olive-oil.com.

1. In a large bowl, mix polenta, flour, baking powder, soda, sugar, and salt.

2. Add egg and buttermilk. Beat with a whisk until batter is smooth. Stir in onions, corn, and butter.

3. Place a griddle or 10- to 12-inch frying pan (nonstick, if desired) over medium heat. When it's hot, spoon batter in ¼-cup portions onto griddle, spacing slightly apart. Cook until edges look dry, turn with a wide spatula, and brown bottoms, 2 to 3 minutes total.

4. Serve pancakes as cooked, or arrange in a single layer on racks on baking sheets and keep warm in a 150° oven up to 15 minutes.

5. Stack pancakes on plates and serve with chipotle sauce added to taste.

Per serving: 310 cal., 15% (46 cal.) from fat; 9.7 g protein; 5.1 g fat (2.5 g sat.); 56 g carbo (6.1 g fiber); 504 mg sodium; 46 mg chol.

## Chipotle Sauce

PREP AND COOK TIME: 20 minutes

NOTES: If making ahead, cover and chill up to 1 day.

MAKES: About 1½ cups

- ½ cup (about 1½ oz.) **dried chipotle chilies**
- 2 tablespoons **butter** or margarine
- ½ cup chopped **onion** or white part of leeks
- 1 cup fat-skimmed **chicken broth**
- 1 tablespoon **lemon juice**
- **Salt**

1. In a bowl, combine chipotles and 2 cups hot water. Let stand until chipotles are soft, 10 to 15 minutes.

2. Pull off and discard chili stems, seeds, and veins. Also discard the soaking water.

3. Meanwhile, in a 10- to 12-inch frying pan, combine 1 teaspoon butter and onion. Stir often over high heat until onion is limp, about 1 minute. Add chipotles and chicken broth.

4. Scrape mixture into a blender. Whirl until very smooth. Return to pan and stir over high heat until simmering, about 3 minutes, then add lemon juice and remaining butter. Remove from heat and stir until butter melts. Season to taste with salt. Use hot, warm, or at room temperature.

Per tablespoon: 17 cal., 71% (12 cal.) from fat; 0.6 g protein; 1.3 g fat (0.6 g sat.); 1.3 g carbo (0.5 g fiber); 14 mg sodium; 2.6 mg chol.

A TASTE OF THE WEST

# Dinner cakes

■ On a warm evening under a star-domed sky at Rancho Encantado north of Santa Fe, we tried these light and slightly crunchy corn pancakes with a mellow chipotle sauce. They were an appetizer that night, but the combination is so satisfying and wholesome, I've moved them into the starring role for an easy lunch or a light dinner. Another good topping: sour cream with fresh salmon caviar.

### Polenta Corn Cakes

PREP AND COOK TIME: About 8 minutes to mix, 3 minutes to cook each batch

NOTES: Serve with thinly sliced prosciutto, sliced tomatoes, and broiled green onions or leeks with some of their green tops. Spoon chipotle sauce onto pancakes or present it in a small cup (one made of lettuce works well). Garnish with slivers of green onions.

MAKES: About 18 pancakes 4 inches wide; 6 main-dish servings

- 1 cup **polenta**
- ⅔ cup **all-purpose flour**
- 1 teaspoon **baking powder**
- 1 teaspoon **baking soda**
- 1 teaspoon **sugar**
- ¼ teaspoon **salt**
- 1 **large egg**
- 1⅔ cups **buttermilk**
- ½ cup sliced **green onions,** including some green tops
- 1 cup **corn kernels** (fresh-cut, frozen, or drained canned)
- 1½ tablespoons melted **butter** or margarine
- **Chipotle sauce** (recipe follows)

### BACK TO BASICS

# The indirect path to a perfect duck

■ For a beautifully browned, crisp-skinned duck, barbecue it over indirect heat, let the duck cool, then reheat it.

PREP AND COOK TIME: About 2 hours and 20 minutes for first cooking, at least 2 hours to cool, and 55 minutes to reheat and crisp

MAKES: 3 cups (at least 1 lb.) lean meat; 4 or 5 servings

1. *If using charcoal briquets,* ignite 40 briquets on the firegrate of a barbecue, let burn until coals are dotted with ash, about 20 minutes, then push half the coals to each side of the grate. Set a foil drip pan (about 8 by 12 in.—slightly longer and wider than duck—and at least 1 in. deep) on firegrate between mounds of coals. Set grill in place. Add 4 briquets to each mound of coals now and every 30 minutes of cooking.

*If using a gas barbecue,* turn heat to high and close lid for at least 10 minutes. Adjust heat to medium and burners for indirect cooking. Put drip pan between ignited burners. Set grill in place.

2. Meanwhile, remove giblets from 1 **duck** (about 5 lb.) and reserve for other uses. Rinse, drain, and pat bird dry. Discard lumps of fat. With a fork, pierce just through skin all over at about 1-inch intervals. Fold wing tips under back. Pin neck skin to back of duck with a metal skewer. Pin body cavity shut and tie legs together.

3. Lay duck, breast up, on grill directly over drip pan. Cover barbecue; open vents for charcoal. Temperature inside barbecue should be about 300°. Cook until duck is lightly browned and a thermometer inserted in thigh against bone at hip joint registers 185°, about 2 hours.

4. Transfer duck to a platter. Let cool at least 2 hours. If making ahead, cover and chill up to 1 day. Discard drippings.

5. Set duck, breast up, in a V-shaped rack in a shallow pan about 8 by 12 inches.

6. Bake duck in a 350° oven until very richly browned, about 55 minutes.

7. Transfer to a platter. Slice skin off in large pieces, trimming fat off the underside. Cut the meat from the duck and season with **salt** and **pepper** to taste; accompany meat with any sauce desired. I like **hoisin** or plum **sauce.**

Per serving: 183 cal., 49% (90 cal.) from fat; 21 g protein; 10 g fat (3.8 g sat.); 0 g carbo (0 g fiber); 59 mg sodium; 81 mg chol.

### FROSTY FACTS

# Smooth-ease

■ Use frozen chunks of fruit—not ice—to make thick, slushy smoothies and other drinks, such as margaritas. Buy individually quick-frozen unsweetened berries or fruit pieces and mix flavors to suit your need. Or, to save space, buy bags of mixed chunks, which I am spotting frequently among the frozen foods at the market. Their labels clearly imply that the purpose of these fruit mixtures is to make smoothies.

Better yet, freeze your own chunks, using up odds and ends of fruit, like a slice of melon, a few berries, or a hunk of banana. Place fruit slightly apart on a baking sheet; when frozen, flex pan to release and slide chunks into a freezer bag to store.

## Pineapple Malt Smoothies

PREP TIME: 5 to 8 minutes

MAKES: 2½ cups; 2 servings

In a blender, combine about 1 cup **frozen pineapple chunks,** ½ cup **frozen unsweetened strawberries,** and 1 peeled **ripe banana** (about 3 oz.) cut into chunks. Add 1 cup **orange juice** and 2 to 3 tablespoons **plain malted milk powder.** Whirl until mixture is very smooth. Pour into 2 tall (at least 10-oz.) glasses.

Per serving: 205 cal., 8.3% (17 cal.) from fat; 3.6 g protein; 1.9 g fat (0.7 g sat.); 47 g carbo (1.9 g fiber); 112 mg sodium; 2.9 mg chol. ◆

# The Wine Guide

BY KAREN MacNEIL

## Good wines ... for a steal

■ Okay, you asked for it. Many of you have written in with a plea: Tell us about inexpensive wines, ordinary Wednesday-night-and-no-one's-coming-for-dinner wines that almost anyone could afford.

I'm thankful for your request. Let me express why by way of a food analogy. It has always seemed to me that the creator (whoever she was) of French onion soup deserves a huge amount of credit compared, say, with a cook who makes a great-tasting foie gras dish. Foie gras (expensive) can't help but taste great. But making stale bread, old cheese, water, and onions taste good? Now *that's* a triumph.

And so it is with wine. Making good-tasting inexpensive wine isn't easy. Great wine is largely a matter of perfect grapes grown in top-notch vineyards by talented viticulturists who then turn the grapes over to skilled winemakers with state-of-the-art equipment. The cost of each of these things—from grapes to equipment—is frighteningly high (French-oak barrels alone cost upwards of $600 apiece!). Which is why dozens upon dozens of cheap wines are, frankly, rank and insipid.

Nonetheless, some wineries do manage to make tasty inexpensive wines. And though finding one is a little like discovering a stunning outfit on the closeout rack—you have to sift through a lot of junk before you uncover a gem—the gems are worth the hunt. Here are a few strategies to simplify your search.

**1. Beware fashionable varietals.** Merlot, Sangiovese, and Syrah are in such

RICK MARIANI

demand that wineries and restaurants can charge uptown prices, even for ultraordinary wines. Instead, look for grapes and wine styles that are (temporarily) out of fashion. Right now, there are excellent rosés on the market (try the terrific Joseph Phelps Vin du Mistral Grenache Rosé, at $10), plus a slew of Rieslings, Chenin Blancs, Petite Syrahs, and Zinfandels. If you do want to drink a fashionable varietal, try strategy 6.

**2. Do a case study.** Most of us instinctively head for a discount store when we want a wine bargain, but a good wine shop can do more to help you avoid the dross. Its knowledgeable merchants can put together a mixed case of 12 inexpensive wines to try (often with a case discount). Discover what you like best, then look for those labels in both discount and top wine shops (the latter often have terrific sales).

**3. Search out second brands.** Many top wineries produce a less expensive wine under another brand name—often made with considerable skill just like the winery's premier wine. Two great second brands: Hawk Crest, from Napa Valley's famous Stag's Leap Wine Cellars, and Michel Lynch, owned by Jean-Michel Cazes, the winemaker of Bordeaux's renowned Chateau Lynch Bages.

**4. Be careful what part of California you buy.** The astronomical cost of vineyard land in a place like the Napa Valley

### THE PRICE IS RIGHT

I tasted more than 75 wines this month to find these eight exciting bottles.

#### WHITE

■ *Columbia Crest Winery Gewürztraminer 1997 (Columbia Valley, WA),* $8. Light and slightly exotic, with fresh apricot flavors.

■ *Fetzer Vineyards Sundial Chardonnay 1997 (California),* $9. Light, soft, and fruity.

■ *Hogue Cellars Chenin Blanc 1996 (Columbia Valley),* $6.50. Lovely spiced apple pie flavors. Would be great with spicy foods.

■ *St. Supéry Vineyards & Winery Sauvignon Blanc 1997 (Napa Valley),* $10. Fresh, crisp, and vibrant.

#### RED

■ *Lindemans Bin 50 Shiraz 1996 (South Australia),* $8. Shiraz is the same grape as Syrah. Supple boysenberry flavors with a hint of pepper. Begging for grilled foods.

■ *Montes Merlot 1996 (Curico Valley, Chile),* $8. Great raspberry-cinnamon flavors. Full of personality.

■ *Napa Ridge Pinot Noir 1996 (North Coast),* $11. Soft, smoky black cherry flavors. Effortless to drink.

■ *Torres Sangre de Toro 1995 (Spain),* $8. One of the best inexpensive wines in the universe. Rustic, with bold cherry flavors. Great with hamburgers and other simple meats.

drives up wine costs. Look instead to less well-known regions, such as Mendocino, Paso Robles, El Dorado County, and Amador County. All produce some stellar Zinfandels that cost peanuts.

**5. Don't forget Washington and Oregon.** Two wineries in Washington—Columbia Crest and Hogue—consistently make inexpensive wines that are rated among the best in the United States. In Oregon look for Pinot Gris (just about every producer makes one), a sensational crisp-yet-creamy white.

**6. Explore foreign ground.** Wines from emerging or less-than-chic places can be a steal. Portugal makes delicious red table wines, as do Argentina, South Africa, Spain, and *southern* Italy (as opposed to Tuscany or Piedmont). Chile's wines are better than ever. And don't overlook Australia (two great wineries to know: Lindemans and Rosemount). The next spot to watch? Eastern Europe—especially Hungary and Bulgaria. ◆

## Memorize a few names

Here is a short, "safe" list of dependably tasty inexpensive brands. From California: *Napa Ridge, Fetzer, Robert Mondavi "Coastal."* Washington: *Columbia Crest, Hogue.* Australia: *Lindemans, Rosemount, Seaview.* Chile: *Montes, Concha y Toro, Caliterra.*

A
Kitchen
in

PHOTOGRAPHS BY
GEORGE OLSON

Each day begins pretty much the same in the big, old stone farmhouse we rent for September in a northern corner of Provence. It's a hideaway we keep filled with a parade of family and friends. • The sun, gliding around the side of bald-peaked, solitary Mont Ventoux, makes the wake-up call, and folks begin to wander downstairs. Breakfast is self-generated at leisure—there are figs to pick, coffee to brew, toast to brown, and small, creamy-colored melons to cut. • David, the den master and host, who is always stirring by the time the neighbor's rooster crows and the dog starts barking, has returned from his morning pilgrimage and greets stragglers with the *International Herald Tribune* and fresh baguettes and croissants. • As we absorb the still morning's golden warmth, sip coffee, swap sections of the paper, admire Crestet—a postcard-perfect medieval walled village perched just below a high ridge across the Ouveze River—the subject of dinner is already upon us. • How, I wonder, do the French manage to work as well as eat? As we plan the meal, an agenda evolves and adventures unfold for a full day. Do we want honey from Brantes in the mountains (population 81) to go with our own figs and crème fraîche? Or those sweet strawberries from the flat fields in Carpentras for a tart? How about squab from the farmer we met at Tuesday market? Who wants to make the winery run? (Shall we drink Gigondas or Châteauneuf-du-Pape tonight? It's 15 minutes to the first group of wineries, 25 to the second. And be sure to pick up a few bottles of that simple rosé that smells like rose petals and crushed berries, from the Puymeras wine co-op.) What time does Crémerie "Lou Canestéou," the cheese shop in Vaison-la-Romaine (20 minutes by foot from our door),

# Provence

open? Madame has set aside several chestnut leaf–wrapped *banons* (goat cheeses) that will be perfectly ripe today. And Hervé Poron, who owns Plantin Cie—the truffle factory just up the road—is stopping by shortly with some of his fabulous dried morels. Let's ask him to come for dinner—and try his morels in a salad. • Bite by savory bite, a menu takes shape. We tally up the chairs that will be filled to decide how much food and wine we need; we survey the sky, check the temperature, and pick the terrace as our dinner setting; then we divvy up duties and roll into action at a pace without pressure. • As den mother, I relish cooking for a tableful of lusty appetites, especially with plenty of help and conversation. • Even though our house is 200 years old, the kitchen, which opens onto the dining

Just outside the kitchen door, a small marble table holds tonight's dinner. The main course is an easy summer version of cassoulet, with white beans, crumb-dusted duck, and a ring of roast sausage. They go with fresh tomatoes and basil from the garden.

One month a year, the **French** countryside is my summer camp. The agenda: Dinner with good **friends**

terrace and lawn, is well equipped. It has a convection oven, a cooktop with gas and electric burners, a microwave oven, a food processor (after all, the French invented it), and a host of other electrified portables. We have ample refrigeration, especially for France, with a spare refrigerator to stockpile dinner ingredients. Only the kitchen sink, a 14-inch square of orange porcelain, presents an inconvenience. We're saved by the deep sink in the laundry room.

Do I try to cook provençal-style? Not really, but the ingredients at hand lend an incontrovertibly provençal essence to our meals. And for tonight's dinner, I'm creating my own version of a warm-weather cassoulet—beans with duck and sausage. Not only is my treatment of duck for confit easier than the traditional process, but the results aren't as salt- or fat-laden.

AT SUNDAY MARKET it takes time to select olives from the huge variety.

The home crew shells fresh dried *coco blancs* (smooth, round white beans similar to dried small whites) in the shade of linden trees as we sip fruity, totally generic, and very young iced red wine the house has dubbed "plunk" (at the local wine co-op, a rubber-booted sommelier in overalls pumps it like gasoline into recycled plastic jugs).

We wander down to the garden for tiny cherry tomatoes and big slicers, then to our trees for perfectly ripe figs.

When the morning reconnaissance team rolls back up the drive with its booty, it's time for lunch. And herein is the best secret of my Provence kitchen: I cook only for dinner, but I cook generously for leftovers. They're available to one and all at any time from the kitchen refrigerator, as is a perpetual supply of sliced ham (hand-cut by the man who cures it); an ever-accumulating array of condiments, from butters to pickles to mustards; and crisp salad greens. There are always cheeses from yesterday, and a big bowl of fruit. Tonight's extras might be tomorrow's bean soup, sausage sandwich, or duck salad.

But who's thinking about tomorrow? The afternoon having passed in pursuit of good food, we gather for appetizers and that chilled rosé on the west side of the house to watch the setting sun glaze the hill-layered horizon with brilliant shades of cerise and fuchsia.

### TO VIEW THE SUNSET
The Cheese Tray:
Brie de Meaux, Banon, Roquefort*

Toast • Radishes

Olives of Provence

Cherry Tomatoes from the Garden
with Coarse Salt

Puymeras Rosé*

### AT THE TERRACE TABLE
Morels with Belgian Endive

Skinned Duck Confit
with Roasted Cracklings

Roast Sausage Ring

Cassoulet White Beans

Sliced Garden Tomatoes
with Fresh Basil

Country Bread

Red Wines from Gigondas*

Fig and Lemon Tart

Muscat de Beaumes-de-Venise*

## Morels with Belgian Endive

PREP AND COOK TIME: About 15 minutes to soak, about 20 minutes to cook

NOTES: If making up to 1 day ahead, complete steps 1 through 5. Let dressing cool, cover, and chill; to use, heat until simmering.

MAKES: 8 to 10 servings

About 1¼ pounds **Belgian endive**

1 ounce (about 1¼ cups) **dried morel mushrooms**

½ cup chopped **shallots**

1½ teaspoons chopped **fresh tarragon** leaves or ½ teaspoon dried tarragon

½ cup **red wine vinegar**

½ cup **whipping cream**

1 cup fat-skimmed **beef broth**

½ cup **dry red wine**

2 tablespoons **brandy**

**Salt**

**1.** Rinse and drain the endive; wrap in towels, enclose in a plastic food bag, and chill.

**2.** Meanwhile, immerse morels in 2 cups hot water. Let stand until cool enough to handle, 10 to 15 minutes. Holding morels in water, squeeze gently to massage grit free. Lift morels from water and squeeze dry. Carefully pour soaking liquid into another container; discard gritty residue.

**3.** Immerse morels in a generous amount of cool water and massage gently again. Lift from water and squeeze dry; discard cool water.

**4.** In a 10- to 12-inch frying pan, combine shallots, tarragon, vinegar, and reserved morel soaking liquid. Boil over high heat, stirring, until liquid evaporates, about 12 minutes. Add morels and ¼ cup cream. Boil, stirring often, until cream evaporates and

---

*NOTE: Brie and Roquefort are available in most stateside supermarkets with good cheese selections. If you can't find banon, serve a ripened goat cheese such as bûcheron. As an alternative to the aromatic Puymeras Rosé, ask for a domestic one that has a good acid level and lots of fruit. The wines of Gigondas and the Muscat de Beaumes-de-Venise are available in well-stocked wine shops. The reds, for the most part, drink well while relatively young. A domestic wine of equivalent seriousness might be a Zinfandel or Merlot.

PROVENCE ROSÉ (top) goes with olives and cheeses. Dinner opens with a toast (right)—the wines are from Gigondas.

vegetables begin to brown, about 1 minute.

**5.** Add remaining cream, beef broth, wine, and brandy and boil until liquid is reduced to about ¾ cup, 4 to 5 minutes.

**6.** Reserve a few endive leaves to garnish each plate; finely sliver remaining endive lengthwise. Arrange endive leaves and slivers on salad plates.

**7.** Bring morel dressing to a boil and ladle over endive. Add salt to taste.

Per serving: 65 cal., 51% (33 cal.) from fat; 2.2 g protein; 3.7 g fat (2.3 g sat.); 5.5 g carbo (1.3 g fiber); 17 mg sodium; 13 mg chol.

## Skinned Duck Confit with Roasted Cracklings

PREP AND COOK TIME: About 2¼ hours

NOTES: **Present duck on a platter with sausages and drained beans (recipes follow).**

MAKES: **8 to 10 servings**

- 4 **boned duck breast halves** (about 1¾ lb. total)
- 4 **whole duck legs** (thighs and drumsticks attached; about 2⅔ lb. total)
- ¼ cup **salt**
- ¼ cup **sugar**
- 2 teaspoons fresh **thyme leaves** or dried thyme

   About 1 teaspoon fresh-ground **pepper**

- 1 cup coarse **bread** crumbs
- ⅓ cup chopped **parsley**

**1.** Pull and cut skin from duck breasts and legs. Slit leg skin open to lie flat. Put skin in a single layer in a pan about 10 by 15 inches.

**2.** Bake in a 350° oven until skin is crisp and golden, about 1 hour, turning pieces over occasionally. Drain skin on towels. Scrape duck fat from pan into a bowl and reserve; wipe pan clean.

**3.** Meanwhile, mix salt and sugar and

rub heavily all over breasts and legs. Put duck in a bowl, cover, and chill at least 30 minutes but no longer than 1 hour.

**4.** Discard liquid that forms and rinse duck well under cool running water, massaging to release salt and sugar. Put duck in the 10- by 15-inch pan. Sprinkle with thyme and pepper. Add ¼ inch of water to pan. Cover pan tightly with foil.

**5.** Bake in a 325° oven until meat is very tender when pierced, about 1¼ hours.

**6.** Meanwhile, in a 10- to 12-inch frying pan over medium-high heat, combine bread crumbs and 2 tablespoons reserved fat from duck skin. Stir until bread is richly toasted. Pour into a bowl. Coarsely chop duck skin.

**7.** Transfer cooked duck to a large platter and keep warm. Put duck skin cracklings on a piece of foil and return to oven to heat, about 5 minutes. Pour into a small bowl.

**8.** Sprinkle toasted bread crumbs and parsley over duck. Add cracklings to portions as desired.

Per serving without cracklings: 227 cal., 38% (87 cal.) from fat; 25 g protein; 9.7 g fat (3.6 g sat.); 8.5 g carbo (0.6 g fiber); 407 mg sodium; 92 mg chol.

Roasted cracklings: Nutrition information not available.

## Roast Sausage Ring

PREP AND COOK TIME: About 1 hour

NOTES: **If you can't get a single piece of sausage or connected links, cook cut-link sausages in pan without skewering together.**

MAKES: **8 to 10 servings**

**1.** Purchase about 2 pounds **mild pork sausages,** such as French-style with white wine and thyme in a single long

piece, or connected links of mild Italian or regular pork sausages.

**2.** Lay sausages flat and coil to form a round disk. Slide a metal skewer horizontally through middle section of sausages, then push another skewer through meat perpendicular to the first, forming an X. Place sausages in a close-fitting rimmed pan about 10 by 15 inches.

**3.** Bake in a 325° oven until well browned, about 55 minutes. Holding the skewers, lift sausages from pan, put on a platter, and pull out skewers. Cut sausages to serve.

**4.** Discard fat from pan, and if desired, add ½ cup water to pan and scrape drippings free; save to add to Cassoulet White Beans.

Per serving: 159 cal., 74% (117 cal.) from fat; 8.5 g protein; 13 g fat (4.6 g sat.); 0.4 g carbo (0 g fiber); 557 mg sodium; 36 mg chol.

## Cassoulet White Beans

PREP AND COOK TIME: 3 to 3½ hours

NOTES: **If making ahead, let cool, cover, and chill up to 1 day. Reheat until steaming, stirring occasionally. Drain beans (you should have about 11 cups) to serve with duck and sausages. Save juice (you should have about 3 cups) and add to leftover beans to make a second-day soup.**

MAKES: **8 to 10 servings, with enough for leftovers**

- 2 pounds **dried small white beans**
- 1 **smoked ham hock** (about ½ lb.)
- 6 cups fat-skimmed **chicken** or beef **broth**
- 4 **carrots** (about 1 lb. total)
- 2 **onions** (about 1 lb. total)

¼ cup **mustard seed**

1½ tablespoons **fresh thyme** leaves or dried thyme

2 teaspoons chopped **fresh sage** leaves or ½ teaspoon dried rubbed sage

2 teaspoons **cumin seed**

½ teaspoon **cardamom seed**

2 tablespoons minced **fresh ginger**

**Salt**

**1.** Sort beans and discard debris. Rinse beans, drain, and put in a 6- to 8-quart pan. Rinse ham hock and add to beans, with broth and 6 cups water. Set over high heat, cover, and bring to a boil.

**2.** Meanwhile, peel and cut carrots and onions into ⅛- to ¼-inch dice. Add to beans, along with mustard seed, thyme, sage, cumin seed, cardamom seed, and ginger. When boiling, reduce heat and simmer, covered, stirring occasionally, until beans are creamy-smooth to bite and meat pulls easily from the ham hock, 2½ to 3 hours.

**3.** Lift out ham hock and let stand until cool enough to touch, about 8 minutes. Discard skin, bone, and fat. Chop meat and return to beans. Stir over medium heat until steaming, about 5 minutes. Drain beans and save liquid. Season beans to taste with salt.

Per 1 cup beans: 359 cal., 6.4% (23 cal.) from fat; 25 g protein; 2.6 g fat (0.4 g sat.); 61 g carbo (11 g fiber); 141 mg sodium; 2.4 mg chol.

## Fig and Lemon Tart

PREP AND COOK TIME: **45 to 50 minutes**

NOTES: **If making ahead, bake crust and filling, let cool, cover, and chill up to 1 day. Then top with figs.**

MAKES: **8 to 10 servings**

CRUST:

1½ cups **all-purpose flour**

¼ cup **granulated sugar**

½ cup (¼ lb.) **butter** or margarine

½ teaspoon grated **lemon** peel

1 **large egg** yolk

FILLING:

3 **large eggs**

½ cup **granulated sugar**

1 **lemon**, sliced, ends and seeds discarded

1 tablespoon **all-purpose flour**

¼ cup (⅛ lb.) **butter** or margarine, in chunks

TOPPING:

4 to 6 cups **ripe figs**, rinsed and stems trimmed

1 to 2 tablespoons **lemon juice**

**Powdered sugar**

**1.** *To make crust:* In a food processor or a bowl, combine flour, granulated sugar, butter, and lemon peel. Whirl or rub with your fingers until mixture has texture of fine crumbs. Add egg yolk and whirl or stir with a fork until a dough forms. Pat dough into a ball, then press evenly over bottom and up sides of a 10-inch tart pan with removable rim.

**2.** Bake crust in a 300° oven until golden, about 30 minutes.

**3.** *Meanwhile, make filling:* In a food processor or blender, whirl eggs, granulated sugar, lemon slices, flour, and butter until lemon is finely chopped.

**4.** Pour filling into hot crust. Continue to bake until filling is firm when pan is gently shaken, about 12 minutes. Let tart cool.

**5.** Cut figs into thin slices and arrange neatly over tart filling. Sprinkle figs with lemon juice and dust with powdered sugar. Cut tart into wedges.

Per serving: 333 cal., 43% (144 cal.) from fat; 4.9 g protein; 16 g fat (9.4 g sat.); 44 g carbo (2.7 g fiber); 164 mg sodium; 123 mg chol. ◆

JUICY FIGS were picked just minutes before being layered over lemon filling baked in a tart.

# Break the bowl and eat it!

It's candy, it's easy, and it's a showstopping sundae

BY ELAINE JOHNSON

The intent isn't to startle, but when you smash this bowl to serve dessert, eyebrows are bound to rise. So you may want to alert guests that the glimmering, transparent container is made of toffee candy.

The bowl is not difficult to make, but you do have to move quickly to shape the cooling, fluid candy before it hardens. To avoid complications, assemble all the equipment and ingredients, and butter pans before you start cooking.

If your first bowl is lopsided, crack it for candy and make another.

## Coconut-Almond Toffee Bowl

PREP AND COOK TIME: About 50 minutes

NOTES: If making bowl and topping ahead, store airtight up to 1 week. Freeze frozen yogurt scoops up to 4 hours.

MAKES: 8 to 10 servings

> About 6 tablespoons **butter** or margarine
>
> $^1/_2$ cup **sweetened shredded dried coconut**
>
> $^1/_3$ cup sliced **almonds**
>
> 1 teaspoon **vanilla**
>
> 1 cup **sugar**
>
> 1 tablespoon **light corn syrup**
>
> 2 quarts **nonfat frozen yogurt** or sorbet, scooped
>
> **Low-fat caramel sauce**

**1.** Butter 2 baking sheets, each 12 by 15 inches, or 1 baking sheet and a 14-inch pizza pan. Also butter the outside of a bowl that's about 4 inches deep and 7 inches wide at top. Invert bowl over a large juice can or other steady object at least 5 inches tall. Gently press an 18-inch square of cooking parchment (or heavy foil) over bowl. Butter a long, slender metal spatula.

RUFFLED toffee bowl holds frozen yogurt and sorbets. Spread most of the hot toffee (left) into a thin round; the extra is for the topping. Shape warm toffee round over an inverted bowl.

**2.** Place coconut and almonds on another 12- by 15-inch baking sheet. Bake in a 350° oven until golden, 5 to 7 minutes; stir 2 or 3 times. Pour coconut and almonds into a bowl, add vanilla, and mix.

**3.** In a $1^1/_2$- to 2-quart pan over high heat, bring $^1/_4$ cup water, sugar, corn syrup, and 6 tablespoons butter to a boil, stirring until butter melts. Boil over medium-high heat without stirring until the mixture reaches 300° on a thermometer, about 10 minutes. Quickly stir in the coconut mixture.

**4.** Working quickly, pour about $^3/_4$ of the toffee, for bowl, onto 1 baking sheet or pizza pan. Pour remaining toffee onto the other sheet. Quickly spread toffee in both pans fairly thin.

**5.** When large piece of toffee is cool enough to touch, pull with your hands into an even, 11- to 12-inch-wide round (a few small holes are not a problem). Let round cool until it starts to firm but is still pliable, 1 to 3 minutes. Slide buttered spatula under round to loosen, then lift round with your hands and center over parchment-draped bowl. Gently press and pinch toffee against bowl to form a fluted bowl. Let toffee cool until rigid, 5 to 10 minutes.

**6.** Gently lift toffee bowl and paper from mold; remove paper. Slide spatula under smaller piece of toffee, and break it into large chunks for topping.

**7.** Fill bowl with frozen scoops and push topping into them. Drizzle with caramel sauce. Break bowl and serve with its contents.

Per serving: 341 cal., 26% (87 cal.) from fat; 4 g protein; 9.7 g fat (5.5 g sat.); 59 g carbo (0.4 g fiber); 155 mg sodium; 19 mg chol. ◆

# A full plate of Mediterranean flavors

From fig pizza to lavender crème brûlée,
transplanted chefs play the classics

BY ELAINE JOHNSON  •  PHOTOGRAPHS BY JAMES CARRIER

■ Just like home ... almost. Mediterranean-born chefs who are now cooking in the West frequently express this sentiment. They say it comes down to the ingredients. With climate similarities that have long lured immigrants from the lands that border this sea—Italy, France, Spain, North Africa, and the Middle East—the West overflows with the foodstuffs they introduced.

Initially, these contemporary professionals were surprised by the availability of ingredients to give their traditional dishes authenticity. Fresh foods, produce in particular, draw praise. Some items, they declare, surpass what they have known.

Mediterranean chefs have also found a receptive audience for their talents. Clearly, Westerners are totally comfortable with Mediterranean dining. Restaurants that feature the concept are everywhere. However, there is nothing common about what's taking place.

Though these chefs can, and do, present their classic dishes, they are falling under the West's inventive spell, and a whole new spectrum of tastes is emerging. In Provence, flavoring crème brûlée with lavender might be considered a stretch. Here, it hits a responsive chord. As a result, most of these chefs confess, it's impossible to resist the temptation to experiment.

Where is it all going? This compilation from five transplanted chefs/restaurateurs promises a very bright future, indeed.

CRISP PIZZA WITH FIGS, arugula, and prosciutto has an Italian lineage.

## Italy in San Francisco

Roman-born chef Giovanni Perticone pronounces the staples he finds in California phenomenal: fresh olive oil and produce, such as organic heirloom tomatoes, which he buys direct from the producer.

With ingredients like these, Perticone lets his imagination take flight. A typical departure is this unconventional pizza with the classic combination of fresh figs and prosciutto presented on crisp, olive oil–flavored crusts.

*Splendido, 4 Embarcadero Center (promenade level), San Francisco; (415) 986-3222.*

### Fig and Prosciutto Pizza

PREP AND COOK TIME: About 1 hour and 20 minutes

NOTES: To make crusts up to 1 day ahead, bake, cool, and wrap airtight.

MAKES: 8 appetizer or 4 main-dish servings

- 1 package **active dry yeast**
- ½ teaspoon **salt**
- ½ cup **extra-virgin olive oil**
  About 3 cups **all-purpose flour**
- ⅓ pound **thinly sliced prosciutto**
- 2½ cups **ripe figs**, stems trimmed, rinsed and quartered
- 2 cups **arugula**, stems trimmed, rinsed and drained
- 1½ tablespoons coarsely chopped **fresh rosemary** leaves
  Fresh-ground **pepper**

**1.** In a large bowl, sprinkle yeast over ¾ cup warm (110°) water. Let stand until softened, about 5 minutes. Stir in salt and ⅓ cup olive oil.

**2.** *If using a dough hook,* add 2½ cups flour and mix until moistened. Beat on high speed until dough no longer feels sticky and pulls cleanly from bowl, about 10 minutes. If dough is still sticky, beat in more flour, 1 tablespoon at a time.

*If mixing by hand,* add 2½ cups flour and beat until dough is moistened and slightly stretchy. Scrape dough onto a lightly floured board. Knead until dough is smooth, elastic, and no longer sticky, 10 to 12 minutes; add flour as required to prevent sticking.

**3.** Cut dough into 4 equal pieces. Place on floured board and cover with plastic wrap to prevent drying. Let rest 10 minutes. Knead 1 piece of dough to expel air. On a floured board, roll out to make an 11-inch round. Put round on a 12- by 15-inch baking sheet and prick dough all over with a fork.

4. Bake on bottom rack of a 500° oven until pale golden, about 3 minutes. Slide crust onto a rack to cool. Repeat to shape and bake remaining dough.

5. To reheat, place baked crusts in a single layer directly on racks in the oven until hot, about 1 minute.

6. Transfer crusts to plates and quickly arrange prosciutto, figs, and arugula equally on each. Sprinkle evenly with remaining oil, rosemary, and pepper.

Per appetizer serving: 387 cal., 40% (153 cal.) from fat; 11 g protein; 17 g fat (2.8 g sat.); 48 g carbo (3.4 g fiber); 494 mg sodium; 15 mg chol.

## Morocco in San Rafael

Brothers Khalid and Mourad Lahlou, restaurant owners in San Rafael, California, note that Moroccan dishes are not as familiar to Westerners as those from France and Italy. But the seasonings they use are—cilantro, garlic, coriander, turmeric, ginger, cumin, and saffron.

Although chef Mourad seasons Moroccan-style, he cooks with less fat and makes meat dishes less sweet than they would be in North Africa. The salads with simple citrus dressings fit in perfectly. *Kasbah Moroccan Restaurant, 200 Merrydale Rd., San Rafael, CA; (415) 472-6666.*

### Lamb in Honey Sauce

PREP AND COOK TIME: About 2¼ hours

NOTES: For a garnish, add about a dozen pitted prunes and apricot halves to boiling pan juices (step 7). When boiling resumes, lift fruit out with a slotted spoon and arrange with toasted almonds around lamb. Garnish meat with mint sprigs, and serve bread to dunk into sauce.

MAKES: 4 servings

- 4 **lamb shanks** (1 lb. each), fat trimmed
- 2 **onions** (1 lb. total), chopped
- 1 tablespoon **olive oil**
- 1 tablespoon **ground coriander**
- 1 tablespoon **ground dried turmeric**
- 1½ teaspoons **ground ginger**
- 1½ teaspoons **ground cumin**
- 1 teaspoon **saffron threads**
- 3½ cups fat-skimmed **beef broth**
- ⅓ cup **honey**

1. Rinse lamb and place in a 2-inch-deep 11- by 17-inch pan. Bake in a 500° oven until well browned, turning shanks over once, about 15 minutes. Discard fat from pan.

2. Meanwhile, in a 10- to 12-inch nonstick frying pan over medium-high heat, frequently stir onions with oil until dark gold, about 15 minutes.

3. Add coriander, turmeric, ginger, cumin, and saffron to onions and stir for 1 minute. Stir in broth and honey.

4. Pour broth mixture over lamb. Cover pan tightly with foil. Bake in a 350° oven until meat is very tender when pierced, 1¼ to 1½ hours; after 30 and 60 minutes, spoon pan juices over lamb.

5. With a slotted spoon, gently transfer shanks to rimmed dinner plates; keep warm.

6. Skim and discard fat from the pan juices.

7. Place pan on 2 burners over high heat and boil juices, stirring often, until reduced to 2 cups, 12 to 15 minutes.

8. Spoon juices equally over the lamb shanks.

Per serving: 613 cal., 29% (180 cal.) from fat; 73 g protein; 20 g fat (6.1 g sat.); 35 g carbo (1.9 g fiber); 224 mg sodium; 205 mg chol.

### Moroccan Carrot Salad

PREP AND COOK TIME: About 20 minutes

MAKES: 4 servings

1. Simmer 6 cups thinly sliced **carrots** in **water** to cover until just tender to bite, 5 to 7 minutes. Drain.

2. Meanwhile, in a 1- to 2-quart pan over medium-high heat, stir ½ teaspoon **ground coriander** and ¼ teaspoon **ground cumin** until fragrant, about 45 seconds.

3. Pour spices into a bowl and mix in ½ teaspoon **cayenne,** 2 tablespoons **lemon juice,** 2 tablespoons **extra-virgin olive oil,** 2 tablespoons chopped **parsley,** ½ teaspoon minced **garlic,** and carrots. Season to taste with **salt,** and if desired, moisten salad with a little more olive oil. Serve at room temperature.

Per serving: 155 cal., 44% (68 cal.) from fat; 2.3 g protein; 7.5 g fat (1.1 g sat.); 22 g carbo (6.9 g fiber); 77 mg sodium; 0 mg chol.

### Roasted Pepper Salad

PREP AND COOK TIME: About 15 minutes

MAKES: 4 servings

1. Drain 2 jars (12 oz. each) **peeled roasted red peppers;** cut into thin strips and put in a bowl.

2. Stir 1½ teaspoons **ground cumin** in a 1- to 2-quart pan over medium-high heat until fragrant, about 45 seconds. Add to peppers along with 1 teaspoon minced **garlic,** 1 tablespoon minced **fresh cilantro,** 1½ tablespoons **lemon juice,** and 1 tablespoon **extra-virgin olive**

SUCCULENT LAMB SHANKS with a Moroccan sauce of spices and honey.

**oil.** Mix, and add **salt** and **pepper** to taste.

Per serving: 75 cal., 44% (33 cal.) from fat; 0.2 g protein; 3.7 g fat (0.5 g sat.); 13 g carbo (1.1 g fiber); 224 mg sodium; 0 mg chol.

## Provence in Los Angeles

Arnaud Palatan's well-traveled customers are eager for the gutsy herb, garlic, and olive oil flavorings of Provence—particularly in dishes that are familiar French classics.

Palatan explains: "Back home, we eat the whole chicken—dark meat, neck, and everything. Americans like boneless chicken breasts." So his chef, Laurent Katgely, obliges with a splendid white meat rendition of *poulet grand-mère*.

On the other hand, Westerners take just fine to experimental desserts, like crème brûlée infused with lavender—the fragrance of Provence.

*Pastis Restaurant, 8114 Beverly Blvd., Los Angeles; (213) 655-8822.*

### Poulet Grand-mère

PREP AND COOK TIME: About 1 hour and 10 minutes

NOTES: Serve with mashed potatoes and a relish made of equal parts chopped and sautéed leeks, sautéed red bell peppers, and chopped pitted niçoise olives.

MAKES: 4 servings

- 2 cups **dry red wine**
- 1 cup minced **shallots**
- 3 cups fat-skimmed **unsalted** or reduced-sodium **chicken broth**
- 1 tablespoon **tomato paste**
- 2 tablespoons minced **fresh sage** leaves or 2 teaspoons dried rubbed sage
- 1 tablespoon plus 2 teaspoons **extra-virgin olive oil**
- ¼ cup **coarse-grain mustard**
- 1 tablespoon minced **fresh thyme** leaves or 1 teaspoon dried thyme
- 1 teaspoon minced **garlic**
- 4 **boned chicken breast halves** (2 lb. total) with skin attached
  **Salt** and **cracked pepper**

**1.** In a 10- to 12-inch ovenproof frying pan over high heat, boil wine and shallots, stirring often, until liquid evaporates, about 12 minutes.

CHICKEN BREAST, French-style, has mustard under well-browned skin.

**2.** Add broth to pan; boil until reduced to 1¾ cups, about 12 minutes. Stir in tomato paste and half the sage; simmer over medium heat for 2 minutes. Pour sauce into a bowl and add 1 tablespoon olive oil. Rinse and wipe pan dry.

**3.** In another bowl, combine remaining sage, mustard, thyme, and garlic.

**4.** From a long side on each breast, pull chicken skin almost free, leaving attached on the opposite edge. Smear exposed areas evenly with mustard mixture. Neatly lay skin back in place.

**5.** Place frying pan over high heat and add 2 teaspoons olive oil. When hot, add chicken, skin down, and brown well, 2 to 3 minutes. Do not turn pieces.

**6.** Place pan in a 450° oven and bake until chicken is no longer pink in thickest part (cut to test), about 15 minutes. Discard fat from pan. Set each chicken piece, skin up, on a dinner plate; keep warm.

**7.** Add sauce to pan and stir over high heat until simmering. Spoon sauce equally around chicken. Season to taste with salt and pepper.

Per serving: 439 cal., 37% (162 cal.) from fat; 53 g protein; 18 g fat (4.2 g sat.); 10 g carbo (0.6 g fiber); 389 mg sodium; 130 mg chol.

### Lavender Crème Brûlée

PREP AND COOK TIME: About 45 minutes, plus at least 1½ hours to chill

NOTES: Some natural-food stores sell dried lavender. You can also order from San Francisco Herb Co. (800/227-4530); 1 pound costs $9.50, plus shipping ($30 minimum order).

MAKES: 4 servings

- 2 cups (1 pt.) **whipping cream**
- 2 tablespoons **dried lavender flowers**
- 1 piece **vanilla bean** (3 in. long), split lengthwise
- 4 **large egg** yolks
  About 1 cup **sugar**

**1.** In a 2- to 3-quart pan over medium-high heat, bring cream, lavender, and vanilla to a boil, stirring often. Remove from heat; let stand 10 minutes.

**2.** In a bowl, beat yolks and ¼ cup sugar to blend.

**3.** Pour cream mixture through a fine strainer into bowl with yolks. Scrape seeds from vanilla bean into the cream mixture; stir. Rinse bean and let dry for other uses. Discard lavender.

**4.** Pour cream custard mixture equally into 4 ovenproof crème brûlée dishes or ramekins (each about 1 in. deep and 5½ in. wide). Set dishes in a 2-inch-deep 11- by 17-inch pan.

**5.** Set pan on rack of a 300° oven. Carefully pour boiling water into pan up to level of custard. Bake until custards jiggle only slightly when shaken gently, 15 to 18 minutes. With a wide spatula, carefully lift dishes from water onto a rack. Let desserts cool, then cover and chill until cold to touch, about 1 hour or up to 1 day.

**6.** In a 6- to 8-inch frying pan over medium heat, shake ⅔ cup sugar until melted and pale amber colored, 8 to 10 minutes. Working quickly, drizzle about a quarter of the hot sugar syrup over 1 custard at a time. Immediately tilt dish so syrup flows evenly over custard. Syrup hardens almost at once. Repeat to glaze remaining custards. Serve, or let desserts chill up to 1 hour so the glaze dissolves a little and gets thinner.

Per serving: 605 cal., 62% (378 cal.) from fat; 5.4 g protein; 42 g fat (25 g sat.); 54 g carbo (0 g fiber); 48 mg sodium; 345 mg chol.

## Lebanon in Seattle

At the Seattle restaurant Phoenicia at Alki, chef-owner Hussein Khazaal uses an ancient recipe with cardamom, cloves, fresh dill, sesame seed, and olive oil to season fish for grilling. At home in Lebanon, the fish was trout. But in the Northwest, he's crazy for wild Copper River (king) salmon. "It's very rich, the flavor is so dense," he says. "Once you eat it, you never forget the taste."

More ancient flavors—orange flower water, saffron, and pistachios—convert vanilla ice cream into an exotic dessert. *Phoenicia at Alki, 2716 Alki Ave. S.W., Seattle; (206) 935-6550.*

GRILLED SALMON, Lebanese-fashion, with lemon, dill, and sesame seed.

### Assyrian Barbecued Salmon

PREP AND COOK TIME: About 20 minutes
NOTES: Garnish with dill sprigs.
MAKES: 4 servings

  2  cloves **garlic**, minced

1½  tablespoons **lemon juice**

1½  tablespoons **extra-virgin olive oil**

  1  teaspoon **ground cardamom**

  ½  teaspoon **ground cloves**

     About ½ teaspoon **salt**

  ¼  cup **sesame seed**

  2  tablespoons minced **fresh dill**

  4  **salmon steaks** (each ¾ to 1 in. thick, 2 to 2⅓ lb. total)
     **Lemon wedges**

**1.** In a bowl, combine garlic, lemon juice, olive oil, cardamom, cloves, and, if desired, ½ teaspoon salt.

**2.** On a plate, mix sesame seed and dill.

**3.** Rinse salmon steaks, drain, add to oil mixture, and turn to coat. Lift out steaks, 1 at a time, and lay each cut side in seed mixture to coat. Place in a single layer on a plate.

**4.** Lightly oil a barbecue grill over a solid bed of medium coals or a gas grill on medium heat (you can hold your hand at grill level only 5 to 6 seconds). Lay fish on grill. Close lid on gas grill.

**5.** Cook fish until browned on bottom, 3 to 4 minutes. Turn with a wide spatula and continue to cook until fish is opaque but still moist-looking in center of thickest part (cut to test), 4 to 6 minutes more.

**6.** With spatula, transfer fish to plates. Season to taste with salt and juice from lemon wedges.

Per serving: 468 cal., 60% (279 cal.) from fat; 42 g protein; 31 g fat (5.7 g sat.); 3.5 g carbo (1.1 g fiber); 411 mg sodium; 118 mg chol.

### Orange-Pistachio Ice Cream

PREP TIME: About 15 minutes, plus at least 3 hours to freeze
NOTES: Shop for orange flower water at a liquor store or in a supermarket wine and liquor section.
MAKES: 4½ cups; 8 servings

**1.** Warm 1 quart **vanilla ice cream** in container with lid on at 30-second intervals in a microwave oven at 30% power until soft enough to scoop easily, about 3½ minutes. (Or let stand at room temperature about 40 minutes.)

**2.** Mix ¼ cup coarsely chopped **roasted, unsalted pistachios**, ⅓ cup **orange flower water**, ½ teaspoon **ground cardamom**, and ¹⁄₃₂ teaspoon **powdered saffron**. Add ice cream and mix quickly. Cover airtight and freeze until firm enough to scoop, at least 3 hours or up to 1 week. Scoop into

ICE CREAM goes Middle Eastern with spices and orange flower water.

bowls and top with more chopped pistachios.

Per serving: 179 cal., 55% (99 cal.) from fat; 4 g protein; 11 g fat (5 g sat.); 18 g carbo (0.9 g fiber); 53 mg sodium; 29 mg chol.

## Spain in Portland

Tapeo restaurant specializes in tapas—Spanish-style appetizers. Ricardo Segura and his staff serve Portlanders foods they already love, such as local Kumamoto oysters. But the Tapeo touch is oysters seasoned with smoked paprika from Segura's hometown of Cáceres, Spain.

Another simple plate Tapeo offers as an appetizer or a dessert combines thin slices of nutty manchego cheese (imported or domestic) and sweet quince paste.

Manchego cheese is relatively easy to find at well-stocked cheese counters, and quince paste (*cajeta de membrillo*) is available at Mexican markets. Or order the paprika, cheese, and quince paste from the Spanish Table in Seattle (206/682-2827). *Tapeo, 2764 N.W. Thurman Ave., Portland; (503) 226-0409.*

### Oysters with Alioli

PREP AND COOK TIME: About 25 minutes
NOTES: Buy shucked oysters in jars or use about 30 freshly shucked oysters. As a substitute for hot smoked Spanish paprika, mix 1½ teaspoons regular paprika with 1½ teaspoons ground dried chipotle chili (whirl to a powder in a blender).
MAKES: 6 servings

$1\frac{1}{2}$  tablespoons **sliced almonds**

2  teaspoons minced **garlic**

$\frac{1}{3}$  cup **mayonnaise**

2  teaspoons **lemon juice**

4  tablespoons **extra-virgin olive oil**

$\frac{1}{3}$  cup **all-purpose flour**

$1\frac{1}{2}$  teaspoons **hot smoked Spanish paprika**

$\frac{1}{2}$  teaspoon **salt**

2  jars (each 10 oz., or 30 total) **shucked oysters,** Kumamotos or small Pacifics, drained and patted dry

**1.** Stir almonds in a 6- to 8-inch frying pan over medium heat until golden, 5 to 6 minutes.

**2.** Pour nuts into a food processor or blender. When slightly cooled, whirl to a fine powder.

**3.** In a bowl, combine nuts, garlic, mayonnaise, lemon juice, and 1 tablespoon olive oil; mix well.

**4.** In a plastic food bag, combine flour, paprika, and salt. Drop in oysters, a few at a time, and shake to coat. Lift from bag, shaking off excess flour mixture.

Lay oysters slightly apart on a sheet of waxed paper. Discard extra flour.

**5.** Place a nonstick 10- to 12-inch frying pan over high heat. When hot, add $1\frac{1}{2}$ tablespoons oil and swirl to coat pan. Add half of the coated oysters and brown well on each side, turning once, about 2 minutes total. Drain on towels and keep warm.

**6.** Add remaining oil to pan and brown remaining oysters.

**7.** Serve the oysters with the almond alioli sauce.

Per serving: 269 cal., 74% (198 cal.) from fat; 8 g protein; 22 g fat (3.4 g sat.); 10 g carbo (0.3 g fiber); 369 mg sodium; 59 mg chol.

CHEESE WITH QUINCE PASTE and sherry is a Spanish tradition.

## Manchego Cheese with Quince Paste

PREP TIME: About 10 minutes

MAKES: 6 servings

Cut $\frac{1}{2}$ pound **manchego cheese** and $\frac{1}{2}$ pound **quince paste** into $\frac{1}{8}$-inch-thick slices, then cut slices into approximately equal triangles.

On a platter, alternate slices of cheese and fruit paste. Eat with a knife and fork.

Per serving: 268 cal., 44% (117 cal.) from fat; 9.3 g protein; 13 g fat (9.3 g sat.); 28 g carbo (1.4 g fiber); 234 mg sodium; 40 mg chol. ◆

# The perfect date shake

## A search from California's Coachella Valley to an L.A. mall

BY AMANDA HESSER

A few years back, a friend from California told me about the sweet, creamy date shakes her family stopped for on their way from Los Angeles to Palm Springs. Dates and the desert—together. To some, the date shake is as quintessentially Southern California as Malibu surf. So when I first moved to this part of the world, I set out in search of the perfect date shake.

Palm Springs was calling. It was summer, but I got into my car, and east to the blazing desert I went. Between San Bernardino and Palm Springs, I stopped at a pharmacy. Even though this isn't the place you'd expect to get the skinny on date shakes, I began asking questions. A round-faced man piped up, "Hadley's. Can't miss it. There's a big sign."

So I went. And at Hadley's Fruit Orchard in Cabazon—just off Interstate

10 on a flat valley floor next to an outlet mall, I experienced my first date shake. It was as thick and smooth as I'd anticipated, with chewy bits of date skin and an intense honey flavor. I realized that Hadley's was just the pearly gate to the date heaven I was seeking. I bought some dates and continued on.

Most of the domestic date industry is in the Coachella Valley east of Indio, but many companies sell shakes at their stores in Palm Springs and Indio (visitor centers can help you locate stores). I had creamy shakes, nutty ones, and others so sweet they were sappy. I gathered tips and recipes, saw a movie on the sex life of date palms (at Shields Date Gardens in Indio), and amassed dates with which to concoct shakes at home.

By the end of my trek in 104° heat, I wondered if this was enlightenment or

punishment. Then in the least expected place—L.A.'s Brentwood district—at another mall, my search bore fruit. At Humphrey Yogart, dates shake with frozen yogurt, balancing the divinely rich, the cloyingly sweet. With frozen yogurt in one hand, and soft, fat Medjool dates in the other, I found date heaven.

## Date Shake Supreme

***Prep time:*** About 5 minutes

***Notes:*** Medjool dates are in supermarket produce sections and produce and health food stores. But any date works.

***Makes:*** 4 cups; 3 to 4 servings

$\frac{1}{2}$  cup **pitted dates**

1  cup **nonfat milk**

3  cups **vanilla nonfat frozen yogurt**

**1.** Coarsely chop dates.

**2.** In a blender, whirl dates with milk until smooth. Add frozen yogurt and whirl until smooth.

**3.** Pour shake into tall, chilled glasses.

Per cup: 233 cal., 0.8% (1.8 cal.) from fat; 5.5 g protein; 0.2 g fat (0.1 g sat.); 52 g carbo (1.1 g fiber); 100 mg sodium; 1.2 mg chol. ◆

BARBECUED PORK SLICES glisten under a sauce made from the citrus marinade.

# One roast, two meals

Let planning, not just leftovers, make dinner easier

BY CHRISTINE WEBER HALE • PHOTOGRAPHS BY JAMES CARRIER

Two for one. The offer that perpetually tempts shoppers also makes good sense when you barbecue a roast. It doesn't take much longer to cook a piece of meat that's twice the size you need for dinner, and it's a time-wise investment when the objective is an easy meal later in the week. To test the theory, start with an economical pork shoulder roast. Marinate it for a half-hour or up to a day ahead. Then, when the meat is cooking, basically untended, you have time to prepare the rest of the meal, perhaps roasted or steamed little Yukon Gold potatoes and asparagus, and a watercress salad. The marinade becomes a flavorful sauce to go with meat and vegetables—truly a bountiful menu to set before guests.

Cut off and set aside half the roast to wrap and chill for the second meal, and serve the rest. A day or two later, cut the reserved pork into shreds and use it to fill enchiladas moistened with two kinds of purchased salsa.

## Citrus-Cumin Barbecued Pork

PREP AND COOK TIME: 2¼ to 2½ hours, plus at least 30 minutes for marinating

NOTES: Have meat tied to form a compact rectangle.

MAKES: 6 servings for first meal, plus extras for enchiladas (recipe follows)

- 1 **fat-trimmed boned and tied pork shoulder** or butt (about 3½ lb.)
- 4 cloves **garlic,** thinly sliced
- 1¼ cups **orange juice**
- ¼ cup **lime juice**
- 1 tablespoon grated **orange** peel
- 2 teaspoons **ground cumin**
- 1 teaspoon minced **fresh oregano** leaves or ½ teaspoon crumbled dried oregano
- ¾ cup fat-skimmed **chicken broth**
- ¼ cup **dry white wine**
- 1½ tablespoons **cornstarch** mixed with 1 tablespoon **water**

   **Salt** and **pepper**

**1.** Without cutting the string, make small slashes all over meat. Tuck garlic slices into slashes.

**2.** In a large bowl, combine orange juice, lime juice, orange peel, cumin, and oregano. Add pork; turn to coat all sides. Cover and refrigerate at least 30 minutes or up to 1 day; turn meat over occasionally.

**3.** In a barbecue with a lid, mound and ignite 60 charcoal briquets on firegrate. When coals are covered with ash, in 20 to 30 minutes, push half to each side of the firegrate. To maintain heat, add 5 briquets to each side now and every 30 minutes of cooking. Lay a drip pan between the mounds of coals. Set grill in place. Or turn gas barbecue on high and heat, covered, 10 minutes, then adjust for indirect, medium heat; set a drip pan beneath grill.

**4.** Place pork on grill over drip pan. Brush with a little of the marinade, then cover barbecue and open vents. Reserve

ENCHILADAS with barbecued pork and two kinds of salsas come together easily.

## Pork Enchiladas

PREP AND COOK TIME: About 1 hour
MAKES: 4 servings

   3  cups slivered ($\frac{1}{4}$ in. thick) cooked **citrus-cumin barbecued pork** (recipe precedes)

$\frac{1}{3}$  cup minced **fresh cilantro**

   1  jar (1 lb., $1\frac{3}{4}$ cups) **tomatillo salsa**

   2  cups **tomato salsa**

   1  cup fat-skimmed **chicken broth**

   8  **corn tortillas** (6 to 7 in. wide)

   2  cups ($\frac{1}{2}$ lb.) **shredded jack cheese**

      **Sour cream** (optional)

**1.** Mix pork, cilantro, and $\frac{1}{2}$ cup tomatillo salsa.

**2.** In a 9- by 13-inch pan, mix tomato salsa and $\frac{1}{2}$ cup broth.

**3.** In an 8- to 10-inch frying pan over medium-high heat, bring remaining $\frac{1}{2}$ cup broth to steaming. Remove from heat. Dip 1 tortilla at a time in broth to slightly soften, about 1 second. As softened, lay each tortilla flat and spoon $\frac{1}{8}$ of the pork mixture down the center. Sprinkle with about 1 tablespoon cheese, then roll tortilla to enclose filling. Set the enchilada seam down in the 9- by 13-inch pan. Repeat to fill remaining tortillas.

**4.** Spoon remaining tomatillo salsa over enchiladas, then sprinkle with remaining cheese.

**5.** Bake in a 400° oven until enchiladas are hot in the center and salsa is bubbling, about 30 minutes. Top portions with sour cream.

Per serving: 653 cal., 47% (306 cal.) from fat; 47 g protein; 34 g fat (16 g sat.); 39 g carbo (2.7 g fiber); 2,471 mg sodium; 159 mg chol.

---

$\frac{1}{2}$ cup marinade to brush over meat occasionally as it cooks. Pour remaining marinade into a 2- to 3-quart pan.

**5.** Cook pork until a thermometer inserted into center of thickest part registers 165°, at least $2\frac{1}{4}$ hours. Brush meat occasionally with the $\frac{1}{2}$ cup of marinade.

**6.** Transfer the roast to a platter and let stand in a warm place at least 20 minutes (the interior is pink, but it will turn white as the meat rests).

**7.** Add broth, wine, and cornstarch mixture to pan with marinade. Stir over high heat until sauce is boiling.

**8.** Remove string and cut meat into thin slices. Offer sauce, salt, and pepper to add to taste.

Per serving, using half the roast: 360 cal., 48% (171 cal.) from fat; 36 g protein; 19 g fat (6.8 g sat.); 9.4 g carbo (0.2 g fiber); 51 mg sodium; 119 mg chol.

---

# Four double-time recipes

Double the planned portion when barbecuing or roasting chicken or a large cut of pork, beef, or lamb. Then stash extras in the refrigerator for up to a week, ready to pull out to make:

•**MU SHU ROLLS.** Use cooked poultry, pork, beef, or lamb. Thinly slice the meat and warm in a microwave oven just until steaming. Lay meat on warm flour tortillas and add to taste shredded cabbage, Asian plum sauce, and sliced green onions. Roll tortillas around fillings and eat out of hand. (No nutrition data available.)

•**PASTA WITH PEANUT SAUCE.** Moisten bite-size pieces of cooked poultry, pork, beef, or lamb with purchased Asian-style peanut sauce and season to taste with seasoned rice vinegar, minced fresh cilantro, and green onions. Mix with hot cooked, drained pasta such as fettuccine or bow ties. (No nutrition data available.)

•**HOT CHUTNEY SALAD.** Thinly slice cooked poultry, pork, beef, or lamb and mound portions onto the cupped side of pocket bread. Sprinkle with shredded jack cheese and heat in a microwave oven until cheese melts. Top with mango chutney and sliced avocados. (No nutrition data available.)

•**RISOTTO.** Prepare risotto (from a mix or recipe). When rice is just cooked, add thin slivers of cooked poultry, pork, beef, or lamb and mix. Sprinkle shredded parmesan or fontina cheese on portions. (No nutrition data available.) ◆

# Kitchen Cabinet

## READERS' RECIPES TESTED IN SUNSET'S KITCHENS
### BY LINDA LAU ANUSASANANAN

PALE GREEN CHAYOTE cubes are the base of this colorful salad.

JAMES CARRIER (2)

## Chayote Salad

Nancy and Don Compton,
Sacramento

While anchored in the Sea of Cortés, Nancy and Don Compton tried pear-shaped chayotes. The tender Mexican squash, quite common in Western supermarkets, is very mild, and the Comptons asked, "Why be bland in the land of hot peppers?" This colorful salad is the result.

PREP AND COOK TIME: About 30 minutes

MAKES: 6 servings

- 2 **chayotes** (1¼ lb. total)
- 1 **fresh jalapeño chili** (¾ oz.)
- 1 **red bell pepper** (6 oz.)
- ¼ pound **cheddar** or mozzarella **cheese**
- 1 **firm-ripe avocado** (10 oz.)
- ⅓ cup **white wine vinegar**
- 2 tablespoons **olive oil**

- 2 tablespoons chopped **fresh cilantro**
- ½ cup thinly sliced **green onions**

  **Salt** and **pepper**

**1.** In a 3- to 4-quart pan over high heat, bring about 1½ quarts water to a boil. Peel chayotes and cut into ½-inch cubes (soft seed is edible). Add chayotes to water, and simmer until tender when pierced, about 10 minutes. Drain. Immerse in cold water until cool; drain again.

**2.** Meanwhile, stem and seed chili and bell pepper. Finely chop chili. Cut bell pepper into ¼-inch squares. Cut cheese into ¼- by 1-inch sticks. Peel and pit avocado and cut into ½-inch cubes. Combine ingredients in a wide bowl.

**3.** In a small bowl, mix vinegar, oil, and cilantro. Add vinegar mixture, chayotes, and onions to vegetables in wide bowl. Mix gently. Add salt and pepper to taste.

Per serving: 207 cal., 70% (144 cal.) from fat; 6.6 g protein; 16 g fat (5.4 g sat.); 11 g carbo (1.3 g fiber); 127 mg sodium; 20 mg chol.

## Rancho Dagwood 1998

Alene Roth, Redmond, Washington

In 1957, Charlene Roth received a booklet distributed by the phone company that contained a *Sunset* recipe for a hot sandwich. The sandwich fit her budget and the tastes of her growing family. Over the years, she made the recipe hundreds of times and gradually streamlined the method and slashed some fat. Now, according to daughter Alene Roth, Charlene's children perpetuate this sandwich legacy for their own families.

PREP AND COOK TIME: About 35 minutes

MAKES: 4 to 6 servings

- 1 loaf (1 lb.) **French sourdough bread**
- 6 thin pieces (each about 4 in. wide; 1½ oz. total) **sliced mozzarella** or provolone **cheese**
- ¾ pound **ground lean** (7% fat) **beef** or ground turkey
- ¼ pound **mushrooms,** sliced
- ½ teaspoon **dried oregano**
- 1 cup **purchased marinara sauce** or pizza sauce
- 1 can (2¼ oz.) **sliced ripe olives,** drained
- 1 cup thinly sliced **green onions**

  **Salt** and **pepper**
- 3 tablespoons **grated parmesan cheese**

**1.** Split loaf in half horizontally. Scoop out soft centers, making top and bottom bread shells about ½ inch thick. Reserve centers for another use. Set bread shells, cupped side up, on a 12- by 15-inch baking sheet. Bake in a 400° oven until bread is toasted, about 8 minutes.

**2.** Line bread shell cavities with mozzarella, overlapping slices as needed, and draping onto the rim of the bread.

**3.** In a 10- to 12-inch nonstick frying pan over high heat, frequently stir meat, mushrooms, and oregano until meat is browned and crumbly, 7 to 8 minutes. Add half the marinara sauce, half the olives, ¾ cup onions, and salt and pepper to taste.

**4.** Fill bread shells equally with meat mixture. Top meat filling with remaining marinara sauce, olives, and onions. Sprinkle with parmesan.

**5.** Bake in a 400° oven until hot throughout, 10 to 15 minutes. Cut crosswise into 2- to 3-inch sections.

Per serving: 297 cal., 30% (90 cal.) from fat; 20 g protein; 10 g fat (3.6 g sat.); 32 g carbo (2.9 g fiber); 754 mg sodium; 40 mg chol.

## Pasta with Fresh Puttanesca Sauce

**Lenore M. Klass, Koloa, Hawaii**

Lenore Klass's family loves Italian food, especially her fresh, light version of the classic anchovy-flavored puttanesca sauce. Instead of using a cooked tomato sauce base, she barely heats diced fresh tomatoes with the seasonings.

PREP AND COOK TIME: About 20 minutes

MAKES: 3 or 4 servings

8 ounces **dried vermicelli**

1 tablespoon **olive oil**

3 cloves **garlic**, pressed or minced

1 can (2 oz.) **anchovies**, drained and minced

1½ pounds **Roma tomatoes**, cored and cut into ½-inch cubes

1 can (2¼ oz.) **sliced ripe olives**, drained

3 tablespoons drained **capers**

¾ to 1 teaspoon **hot chili flakes** (optional)

**Grated parmesan cheese**

**Salt** and **pepper**

**1.** In a 5- to 6-quart pan over high heat, cook vermicelli in about 3 quarts boiling water just until barely tender to bite, about 7 minutes.

**2.** Meanwhile, in a 10- to 12-inch frying pan, combine oil and garlic. Stir over medium-high heat until garlic is soft but not brown, about 1 minute. Mix in anchovies.

**3.** Turn heat to high. Add tomatoes, olives, capers, and hot chili flakes to pan and stir until tomatoes are hot, about 3 minutes.

**4.** Drain pasta and pour into a large bowl. Spoon tomato sauce over pasta and mix. Add cheese, salt, and pepper to taste.

Per serving: 325 cal., 21% (68 cal.) from fat; 12 g protein; 7.6 g fat (1.1 g sat.); 53 g carbo (4.1 g fiber); 854 mg sodium; 6.2 mg chol.

## Seeded Hummus

**Sandy Bowens, Carson City, Nevada**

To save a shopping trip when she was out of sesame seed–based tahini, Sandy Bowens simply toasted sesame seed to use in her quick, garlic-bold version of hummus. Serve hummus as a dip for crisp raw vegetables such as cucumber slices, bell pepper strips, and baby carrots. Or spread it in the cavity of split pocket bread and fill the bread with sliced zucchini, tomato, and sprouts.

PREP AND COOK TIME: About 15 minutes

MAKES: About 1½ cups

2 tablespoons **sesame seed**

2 to 4 cloves **garlic**

3 tablespoons **lemon juice**

2 tablespoons **olive oil**

2 tablespoons **plain nonfat yogurt**

½ teaspoon **ground cumin**

¼ teaspoon **cayenne**

1 can (15½ oz.) **garbanzos**, rinsed and drained

**Salt**

**1.** In a 6- to 8-inch frying pan over medium heat, stir sesame seed until golden, about 5 minutes.

**2.** In a blender or food processor, combine sesame seed, garlic, lemon juice, oil, yogurt, cumin, cayenne, and garbanzos; whirl until smooth, scraping container sides often. Add salt to taste. Scoop into a bowl.

Per tablespoon: 28 cal., 57% (16 cal.) from fat; 0.9 g protein; 1.8 g fat (0.2 g sat.); 2.3 g carbo (0.6 g fiber); 22 mg sodium; 0 mg chol.

## Peach-Cherry Pie

**Amy Groves, Meridian, Idaho**

"I can't believe it! I've come up with one of the best pies I have ever made. It's so easy," writes Amy Groves. The combination must be nature's plan, as peaches and sweet cherries are ripe and ready to join forces right now.

PREP AND COOK TIME: About 1¾ hours, plus at least 2 hours to cool

MAKES: 8 servings

3 pounds **firm-ripe peaches**

1½ cups (12 oz.) **sweet dark cherries**, pitted

¾ cup **sugar**

3 tablespoons **quick-cooking tapioca**

2 tablespoons **lemon juice**

¼ teaspoon **ground nutmeg**

¼ teaspoon **almond extract**

1 package (15 oz.) **refrigerated pastry for double-crust 9-inch pie**, at room temperature

**1.** Peel, pit, and cut peaches into ½-inch-thick slices. You should have 7 to 8 cups fruit.

**2.** In a large bowl, gently mix peaches with cherries, sugar, tapioca, lemon juice, nutmeg, and almond extract.

**3.** Unfold 1 pastry round and ease evenly into a 9-inch pie pan. Fill pastry with fruit mixture.

**4.** Unfold remaining pastry round on a lightly floured board. Roll pastry evenly to make a 13-inch round.

**5.** Center pastry over fruit. Fold top edges of pastry over rim of bottom pastry; flute edges and slash top decoratively. Set pie on a foil-lined baking sheet.

**6.** Bake in a 375° oven until juices bubble near center, 1 to 1¼ hours. If pastry edges get too dark, lightly cover with foil. Filling firms as pie cools; let stand at least 2 or up to 8 hours before cutting into wedges.

Per serving: 408 cal., 33% (135 cal.) from fat; 3.2 g protein; 15 g fat (6 g sat.); 67 g carbo (2.7 g fiber); 285 mg sodium; 14 mg chol. ◆

PEACH SLICES and pitted cherries peek through piecrust.

Mexican Sunrise: A sugar-crusted tortilla tops this stellar low-fat dessert. See page 136 for a 12-page salute to mariachi cuisine.

# July

# foodguide

BY JERRY ANNE DI VECCHIO

## what a honey

The brew of bees has always ranked so-so in my lineup of sweets. That is, until I tried white truffle honey, a Tuscan classic. This luxurious concoction of mild honey with just a touch of fragrant white truffle oil is now made by Restaurant LuLu in San Francisco. • Executive chefs Jody Denton and Marc Valiani use the honey in an appetizer of toast with several cheeses served with nuts and dried fruits. The elusive truffle flavor cuts the cloying sweetness of the honey and is a natural with the cheese. At home, I savor this combination for breakfast: fontina cheese melted on a toasted English muffin, then drenched with the honey, with a piece of fruit on the side. • A 9-ounce jar is about $9.50 in specialty food shops. Or order from Restaurant LuLu Gourmet Product Line; (888) 693-5800.

### Truffle Honey on Cheese Muffins

**PREP AND COOK TIME:** About 10 minutes

**NOTES:** A ripe peach or Bartlett pear really complements this combination, but strawberries and raspberries aren't too shabby as backups.

**MAKES:** 1 serving

- 1 **English muffin**
- 1 ounce **fontina cheese,** thinly sliced
- 2 to 3 teaspoons **white truffle honey**

Split muffin in half and broil 3 to 4 inches from heat until toasted, about 2 minutes. Cover muffin halves with cheese and broil until cheese melts. Drizzle with honey.

Per serving: 287 cal., 31% (88 cal.) from fat; 12 g protein; 9.8 g fat (5.6 g sat.); 38 g carbo (1 g fiber); 492 mg sodium; 33 mg chol.

## TOOL

### Tiny, tidy, and useful

■ I'm always hunting down excuses for cutting up, so when I saw this sheet of plastic peddled on TV, a sample was sent to my office, and a friend pointed it out at the hardware store, my attention was captured. This tough, flexible, washable mat makes a camper happy. It takes up almost no space. And in camp—on the dingiest table, tree stump, or broad rock—it provides a clean space for chopping. Hence the name: Chop & Chop. In the kitchen this work mat protects countertops

not cut out for cutting up, funnels whatever you've sliced or diced into bowl or pan, then pops into the dishwasher for simple cleanup. It comes in three sizes and costs $2 to $6 at kitchen and camping supply stores. You can also order it from New Age Products; (800) 886-2467.

# A mushroom burger

■ When did grilled-vegetable sandwiches become ubiquitous? In my (admittedly faulty) memory, they just popped out of nowhere, full-grown and popular, like Serge Prokofiev's Lieutenant Kije. I suspect the sandwiches were for vegetarians dining in the mainstream. Early models rarely arrived without goat cheese and grilled eggplant, red peppers, and zucchini. But the real talent inside the bun was the big, fat, juicy portabella. This mushroom grills so quickly and is so meaty that a portabella burger now appeals to me as much as a good hamburger.

The secret to a super-juicy portabella burger is gravity. Start grilling the cap with the gill side down until the juices begin to seep. Then turn it over so the flavorful liquid can accumulate. Drop some roasted peppers into the cup, cap it with cheese, and slide the "burger" into a toasted bun. With salad, a glass of Merlot, and the slanting rays of the setting summer sun, dinner's ready.

## Portabella Burgers

**PREP AND COOK TIME:** 15 to 20 minutes

**NOTES:** Buy mushrooms with stems trimmed, or trim the stems and save for other uses.

**MAKES:** 4 servings

- 4 **portabella mushroom caps** (about 5 in. wide; 1 to 1¼ lb. total)
- 1 to 2 tablespoons **olive oil**
- ⅔ to ¾ cup **canned peeled roasted red peppers,** coarsely chopped
- ¼ pound **thin-sliced Swiss cheese**
- 4 **round sandwich buns** (about 4 in. wide; ¾ lb. total)

  **Butter** or margarine (optional)

  **Salt** and **pepper**
- 1 to 2 cups **watercress** leaves, rinsed and drained

**1.** Rinse and drain mushrooms, then rub lightly with oil.

**2.** Lay the mushroom caps, cup (gill) sides down, on a barbecue grill over a solid bed of hot coals or high heat on a gas grill (you can hold your hand at grill level only 2 to 3 seconds); close lid on gas grill.

**3.** Cook until juices start to drip from the mushroom caps, about 5 minutes. Turn caps over and continue to cook until mushrooms are flexible and no longer firm when pressed, 5 to 7 minutes longer.

**4.** Lay an equal portion of the red peppers in each cap and cover with cheese. Continue cooking until cheese melts, about 3 minutes.

**5.** As cheese melts, split buns, butter if desired, and lay cut sides down on grill until lightly toasted.

**6.** Set a mushroom cap on each bun base, season with salt and pepper to taste, add a mound of watercress, and cover with the bun top.

Per serving: 417 cal., 35% (144 cal.) from fat; 18 g protein; 16 g fat (6.6 g sat.); 52 g carbo (3.4 g fiber); 603 mg sodium; 26 mg chol.

SEASONAL NOTE

# Mangoes move in

Exotic is anything you don't have. And that was once the status of mangoes. But now they crowd peaches, plums, and other summer fruits in the fresh produce section of most markets. This is peak season, so mangoes are as moderately priced as they'll ever be—inexpensive enough to use casually, as in this quick supper dish. I came across it in a little Indian restaurant on the outskirts of San Diego. For all its complex flavors, the dish is surprisingly easy to make. Major Grey, just one of the multitude of chutney mixtures used in Indian cuisine, is an English-influenced version of mango chutney, and it accentuates the fruity flavor of the fresh mango.

## Mango Chutney Chicken

PREP AND COOK TIME: About 45 minutes
NOTES: Garnish with cilantro leaves, if desired.
MAKES: 4 servings

- 1 pound **boned, skinned chicken thighs**, fat-trimmed
- 1 teaspoon **curry powder**
- ¼ cup **Major Grey chutney**
- 2 teaspoons minced **fresh ginger**
- 1 tablespoon **lemon juice**
- ½ cup fat-skimmed **chicken broth**
- 1 **firm-ripe mango** (about 1 lb.), pitted, peeled, and cut into ½-inch chunks
- 4 cups hot cooked **white basmati rice**
  **Salt**

**1.** Cut chicken into about 2-inch chunks. Put in a 10- to 12-inch nonstick frying pan over medium-high heat. Turn pieces as needed until lightly browned, about 10 minutes.

**2.** Add curry powder to pan and stir about 30 seconds, then mix in chutney, ginger, lemon juice, and chicken broth. Scatter mango over chicken. Cover and simmer, stirring occasionally, until chicken is tender when pierced, about 30 minutes.

**3.** With a slotted spoon, transfer chicken to a bowl and keep warm. Boil sauce, uncovered, over high heat, stirring to prevent sticking, until reduced to about 1¼ cups, 2 to 4 minutes. Pour sauce over chicken.

**4.** Serve chicken mixture on rice; add salt to taste.

Per serving: 564 cal., 10% (57 cal.) from fat; 34 g protein; 6.3 g fat (1.2 g sat.); 100 g carbo (2 g fiber); 320 mg sodium; 94 mg chol.

# For crunch, put the bite on jicama

■ As far as looks are concerned, jicama borders on boring. It's tan outside, snowy white inside, and shaped like a turnip.

Jicama's real bonus is its refreshing texture—juicy-cool and crisp, and it stays crunchy when cooked (diced jicama and potatoes pan-browned together make an interesting dish).

I first enjoyed jicama slices dipped into hot chili powder and salt at street stands in Mexico. Finally jicama came to northern markets. Donna Nordin, chef-owner of Café Terra Cotta in Scottsdale, Arizona, makes the immigrant root into slaw with a pungent horseradish dressing. This recipe is inspired by her presentation. Serve it as you would coleslaw, as a salad or a relish for sandwiches.

## Jicama Slaw

PREP AND COOK TIME: About 10 minutes
NOTES: For fastest results, use a food processor to shred the jicama (although you can shred it by hand).
MAKES: About 6 cups

- About 1¾ pounds **jicama**
- ¾ cup **reduced-fat** or regular **sour cream**
- ¾ cup chopped **green onions** with tops
- ¼ cup chopped **parsley**
- 2 tablespoons **rice vinegar**
- 2 to 3 tablespoons **prepared horseradish**
  **Salt**

**1.** Peel and coarsely shred jicama. Put shreds in a colander and rinse with cool water until water runs clear. Drain well.

**2.** Put jicama in a bowl; mix in sour cream, green onions, parsley, rice vinegar, and horseradish. Season to taste with salt.

Per ½ cup: 52 cal., 37% (19 cal.) from fat; 1.6 g protein; 2.1 g fat (1 g sat.); 7.1 g carbo (3.2 g fiber); 14 mg sodium; 5 mg chol. ◆

# The Wine Guide

BY KAREN MacNEIL

RICK MARIANI

## Wines on the noir edge in Carneros

■ Here's my version of Public Radio International's Geoquiz: Name a famous wine region without a single town, not one hotel, nary a boutique—not even a restaurant, unless you count the rundown truck stop. Yet one whose serene landscape of loping hills has become one of California's most renowned appellations for sensual Pinot Noirs, sensational Chardonnays, and hypnotic sparkling wines. Hint: Until recently, it was almost exclusively the domain of sheep.

Carneros (Spanish for *sheep*) was reborn as a wine region a mere 26 years ago when schoolteacher-turned-winemaker Francis Mahoney looked around at the barren, sandy hills, the remote ranches, the forlorn cloud-swept sky and decided they were perfect. Mahoney, now proprietor of Carneros Creek Winery, had Pinot Noir on his mind, and even then suspected the counterintuitive key to its success—adversity.

Let me explain. Pinot Noir is a little bit like a great artist for whom the angst of the world is the lifeblood of his creativity. For the artist—and for Pinot Noir—hardship is not oppressive, it's essential. Cold climate, shallow soils, wind, fog—it's all a blessing. More than

almost any other grape, Pinot thrives when it lives on the edge.

And you can't get much more on the edge (literally or metaphorically) than Carneros. The region begins about 40 miles north of San Francisco and straddles the lower reaches of both Napa and Sonoma counties. It's a small place, with only about a fifth as many acres of vines as the Napa Valley, which is itself a small region.

Yet more than 35 top California wineries now get their grapes from Carneros. Many of these are among the state's most prestigious small and medium-size wineries (Etude, Acacia, Saintsbury); others are new, tiny, and on the cutting edge (Siduri, Talisman, Ancien).

Carneros's success is grounded in the area's close proximity to San Pablo Bay, the northernmost part of San Francisco Bay. The conjoined bays act as a giant funnel for the cool ocean air and fog that surge through the region.

The effect on Carneros's vineyards is profound. The grapes get enough sun but never become scorched. Because of the constant caress of cool air, there's virtually no risk of flavors being baked out of the grapes (a definite danger in some parts of California). Ripening happens the best way—slowly and incrementally.

The wines, as a result, often have gorgeous balance. They aren't big and blowsy, but have a proclivity toward that all-too-rare commodity, elegance.

This scenario is perfect for the enfant terrible, Pinot Noir. But Carneros is also famous for Chardonnay, which isn't nearly as persnickety as Pinot. Indeed, it's grown nearly everywhere on the planet, from Texas to the Golan Heights. But in lots of places, Chardonnay grapes make oafish, one-dimensional wines. Chardonnays with nuance and grace generally come from cool areas. Enter Carneros.

And any place that manages to produce graceful, refined Pinot Noirs and Chardonnays can produce something else: top-notch sparkling wines. (Champagne, after all, is a blend of Pinot Noir and Chardonnay grown in a cold climate.) So Carneros has also become synonymous with first-class sparkling

## SENSATIONAL SIPPING

Because of Carneros's small size, the huge demand for its grapes, and the high cost of producing Pinot Noir in general, many of the best wines from this region are pricey.

■ *Domaine Carneros "Le Reve" Blanc de Blancs Brut 1992,* $35. The California subsidiary of Champagne Taittinger makes stunningly elegant, complex sparklers. *Le reve* means *the dream,* and this is!

■ *Acacia Winery Carneros Chardonnay 1996,* $20. As soft as cashmere, with rich honey and toasted nuts.

■ *Saintsbury Chardonnay 1996,* $17. Gorgeously vibrant flavors of ripe pears and golden apples.

■ *Shafer Vineyards "Red Shoulder Ranch" Chardonnay 1996,* $30. Opulent honeysuckle and tropical fruit flavors.

■ *Carneros Creek Winery Pinot Noir Reserve 1995,* $35. Rich, with sophisticated hints of menthol, leather, and strawberry.

■ *Etude Wines Pinot Noir 1995,* $30. Scrumptious and refined, with mouth-filling berry jam and grenadine flavors.

■ *Siduri Wines Pinot Noir 1996,* $26. Zingy, earthy, and alive with dried leaves, pomegranates, and rose petals.

wines—wines with such clarity and polish that most of California's leading makers of sparkling wines (Domaine Carneros, Mumm Napa Valley, Codorníu Napa, Gloria Ferrer, Domaine Chandon) are in or buy grapes from the region.

I'm totally hooked on Carneros sparkling wine, and whenever Carneros Chardonnay is mentioned, my eyes light up. But for outright hedonism, Pinot Noir takes the cake. Taste a sampling of Carneros Pinot Noirs side by side and inevitably a flavor emerges throughout the lineup. Winemakers here know it well—red berry (strawberry, raspberry) jam. Carneros Pinots almost always have a telltale, lip-smacking whoosh of it. Scott Rich, winemaker at the highly respected Etude winery, says that he's always on the lookout for this "sweet spot" in the middle of a great Pinot.

If only the early settlers had known. Maybe all the sheep ranches would have been ringed with vineyards. ◆

COOL PRICKLY PEAR
margarita goes well with
jicama grapefruit salad.

LOW-FAT MEXICAN

# Mariachi Cuisine

The tempo is quick, the taste is bold, and—
even though the foods sound rich—fat's out and
flavor's in for these great Mexican dishes

BY LINDA LAU ANUSASANANAN,
ANDREW BAKER & ELAINE JOHNSON

■ With flavors as exciting and compelling as a throbbing blast of "Guadalajara" from a mariachi band, Mexican foods are so popular in the West that they border on being basic. In fact, items like salsa, beans and bean dips, chilies, hot and not-as-hot sauces, and tortillas already are. It seems ages since tomato salsa outstripped catsup as the nation's favorite condiment and established itself as the ideal low-fat dip, sauce, and ingredient. And tortilla chips, used to scoop up salsa, are no longer naughty: when baked, not fried, they are guilt-free, nutritious nibbles.

Sure, temptations like deep-fried, cheese-filled *chiles rellenos* and tamales full of rich pork and lard still exist—to be enjoyed now and then. But for most tastes, there's satisfaction in a leaner approach. Try Norman Fierros's Sonoran fiesta, with turkey (a native ingredient) instead of beef as the cornerstone of a bountiful *carne asada* (grilled meat) party menu. Savor the beautiful soups that *Sunset's* well-traveled senior writer Linda Anusasananan found in Oaxaca, Mexico, and the main-dish huaraches she discovered in a little Mexican restaurant in Redwood City, California. Enjoy the versatile, playful nature of typical Mexican ingredients in our collection of salads and desserts, from chicken salad in a taco shell to caramelized tortillas with a fruit sundae.

Overall, most dishes are ready to serve in less than three-quarters of an hour. Very few ingredients will challenge the supermarket shopper. And the results will keep you safely and deliciously within the boundaries of light and lean. *Buen provecho.*

PHOTOGRAPHS BY GEOFFREY NILSEN

FRANCE RUFFENACH

JUGGLING FRESHNESS is Norman Fierros's secret for great, light menus.

# Sonoran fiesta

## From the Arizona desert, a gala party for 6 to 8

Norman Fierros's interest in Sonoran food took hold when he was a small boy cooking with his mother. And what he learned goes way back—his ancestors lived in Arizona when it was still part of Mexico. As Norman grew, other cuisines joined his repertoire. Now, as owner of a Phoenix restaurant called Norman's Arizona, he uses Chinese and French techniques to prepare Sonoran favorites, describing the dishes as *nuéva Mexicana.*

His carne asada uses turkey breast, vegetables, and a multipurpose tangy citrus dressing. The jicama salad is much like the relish *pico de gallo.*

### SONORAN FIESTA

Prickly Pear Margaritas
(Margaritas de Tunas)

Jicama Grapefruit Salad
(Ensalada de Jicama con Toronja)

Grilled Turkey and Vegetable Platter
(Pavo Asado con Verduras)

Roasted Tomato Salsa
(Salsa con Tomates Asados)

Roasted Yams (Camotes Asados)

Warm Flour or Corn Tortillas
(Tortillas de Harina o Maiz)

Hibiscus Tea  (Té de Jamaica)

## Prickly Pear Margaritas

PREP TIME: **About 15 minutes**

NOTES: **Look for prickly pears (also called cactus pears, Indian figs, and tunas) with fresh produce in supermarkets and Latino markets. Wear heavy cotton or rubber gloves or use a thick towel to hold them when peeling.**

MAKES: **About 7 cups; 8 servings**

- 1¼ pounds **green** or red **prickly pear fruit**
- 1 cup **lime juice**
- 1 cup **tequila**
- ¾ cup **orange-flavor liqueur**
- 2 tablespoons **sugar**
- 4 cups crushed **ice**
- Thin **lime** slices (optional)

1. Cut ends from prickly pears. Cut a ⅛-inch-deep lengthwise slit through peel on each fruit. Pull back peel and remove from pulp; discard peel. Cut fruit pulp into ½-inch chunks.

2. In a blender, combine half of all these ingredients: prickly pear chunks, lime juice, tequila, orange liqueur, and sugar; whirl until smooth. Add half the ice and whirl until blended. Pour into glasses slowly, leaving seeds behind. Discard seeds.

3. Repeat step 2 with remaining pear chunks, lime juice, tequila, liqueur, sugar, and ice.

4. Garnish with lime slices.

Per serving: 176 cal., 1.5% (2.7 cal.) from fat; 0.5 g protein; 0.3 g fat (0 g sat.); 17 g carbo (0 g fiber); 7.6 mg sodium; 0 mg chol.

## Jicama Grapefruit Salad

PREP TIME: **About 20 minutes**

NOTES: **Jicama, onion, grapefruit, and radishes can be sliced, covered, and refrigerated up to 4 hours ahead.**

MAKES: **8 servings**

- 1 **jicama** (1 lb. or a 1-lb. piece)
- ½ cup thinly sliced **red onion**

- 2 **red** or pink **grapefruit** (1¼ lb. each)
- ¼ cup **red wine vinegar**
- 2 tablespoons chopped **fresh basil** leaves or 2 teaspoons dried basil
- 1 clove **garlic,** pressed or minced
  About ¼ teaspoon **salt**
- ½ cup sliced **red radishes**
- 1 firm-ripe **avocado** (½ lb.)
  **Pepper**

1. Rinse jicama. Cut off and discard skin and any tough fibers. Cut jicama into matchstick-size sticks 2 to 3 inches long.
2. Rinse onion slices with cool water and drain.
3. With a knife, cut off and discard grapefruit peel and membrane. Over a wide serving bowl, cut between inner grapefruit membranes and lift out fruit segments. Put fruit in bowl. Squeeze remaining membrane over bowl to collect juice.
4. Drain grapefruit segments; save ½ cup juice and keep the rest to drink. Combine the ½ cup juice with vinegar, basil, garlic, and ¼ teaspoon salt; return to grapefruit. Add jicama, radishes, and onion and mix.
5. Peel, pit, and thinly slice avocado onto jicama salad. Gently mix and add salt and pepper to taste.

Per serving: 73 cal., 30% (22 cal.) from fat; 1.7 g protein; 2.4 g fat (0.3 g sat.); 13 g carbo (2.1 g fiber); 75 mg sodium; 0 mg chol.

## Grilled Turkey and Vegetable Platter

PREP AND COOK TIME: **About 40 minutes**

NOTES: **Up to 4 hours ahead, prepare the vegetables and turkey for cooking.**

MAKES: **6 to 8 servings**

- 1 **boned, skinned turkey breast half** (2 to 2½ lb.)
- ¾ cup **orange juice**
- ½ cup **lemon juice**
- 1 tablespoon **pepper**
- 4 cloves **garlic,** minced
  About 1 teaspoon **salt**
- 1 tablespoon **olive oil**
- 2 **red onions** (½ lb. each)
- 2 **oranges** (½ lb. each)
- 2 **red bell peppers** (½ lb. each)
- 2 **zucchini** (6 oz. each)
- 3 **ears corn** (each about 8 in.)

1. Rinse turkey breast and pat dry.

MIXED-GRILL MAIN DISH includes turkey breast, vegetables, and oranges.

Make a lengthwise cut about ⅔ through the thickest part of the breast. Pat out meat to make evenly thick. If still uneven, make more cuts parallel to first, through thickest parts, and again press to flatten turkey.

**2.** To make sauce, mix orange juice, lemon juice, pepper, garlic, and 1 teaspoon salt. Mix ½ cup of the sauce with oil; cover and chill remaining sauce.

**3.** In a bowl, coat turkey with ¼ cup of the sauce with oil.

**4.** Peel and cut onions crosswise into ¾-inch-thick slices. Cut oranges crosswise into ¾-inch-thick slices. Discard ends. Thread onions through the width of the rounds onto thin metal skewers to hold them flat. Thread oranges the same way onto more skewers.

**5.** Stem and seed bell peppers; cut lengthwise into quarters.

**6.** Trim off zucchini ends, then cut squash in halves crosswise and lengthwise. Thread pieces lengthwise onto thin metal skewers.

**7.** Remove and discard husks and silk from corn. With a heavy knife, tapping with a mallet if needed, cut corn crosswise into 2-inch rounds.

**8.** Brush all vegetables and orange slices with remaining sauce with oil.

**9.** Place turkey, all the vegetables, and orange slices on a barbecue grill over a solid bed of hot coals or on a gas grill over high heat (you can hold your hand at grill level only 2 to 3 seconds). Close lid on gas grill.

**10.** Turn vegetables and orange slices, turning as needed to brown evenly, about 5 minutes for oranges, 10 to 12 minutes for vegetables. As done, transfer to a large platter.

**11.** Cook turkey, turning once, just until meat is 160° on a thermometer or white in center of thickest part (cut to test), 15 to 20 minutes.

**12.** Transfer turkey to platter. Cut meat into pieces and pull skewers from vegetables and oranges. Pour reserved sauce over foods on the platter; add salt to taste.

Per serving: 257 cal., 12% (30 cal.) from fat; 32 g protein; 3.3 g fat (0.6 g sat.); 27 g carbo (4.5 g fiber); 349 mg sodium; 70 mg chol.

## Roasted Tomato Salsa

PREP AND COOK TIME: **About 10 minutes**

NOTES: **Make up to 2 days ahead, cover, and chill.**

MAKES: **About 1 cup; 8 servings**

- 3 **firm-ripe tomatoes** (6 oz. each)
- 2 to 3 **yellow wax chilies** (½ to ¾ oz. total)

  **Salt**

**1.** Place tomatoes and chilies in a pan about 10 by 15 inches. Broil about 2 inches from heat, turning as needed, until vegetables are charred on all sides, 6 to 8 minutes. Let stand until cool enough to touch.

**2.** Pull off and discard skin of tomatoes and chilies. Coarsely dice tomatoes. Remove seeds from chilies for less heat. Finely chop chilies. Mix tomatoes and chilies; add salt to taste.

Per serving: 22 cal., 12% (2.7 cal.) from fat; 0.8 g protein; 0.3 g fat (0 g sat.); 4.9 g carbo (1.3 g fiber); 5.9 mg sodium; 0 mg chol.

## Hibiscus Tea

PREP AND COOK TIME: **About 20 minutes, plus 1 hour to steep**

NOTES: **Look for dried hibiscus blossoms (*jamaica*) in Latino markets. Or use Celestial Seasonings' hibiscus-flavor Red Zinger tea as directed on package to make 3 quarts. If making ahead, cover and chill tea up to 2 days.**

MAKES: **About 2¼ quarts; 6 to 8 servings**

- 1 cup (1½ oz.) **dried hibiscus blossoms**
- 1 **cinnamon stick** (about 1 in.)

  **Ice cubes**

  About ⅓ cup **sugar**

**1.** In a 4- to 5-quart pan on high heat, bring 3 quarts water to boiling. Add hibiscus blossoms and cinnamon stick. Cover and simmer over low heat for 15 minutes. Let cool about 1 hour.

**2.** Pour tea through a strainer, lined with a double thickness of cheesecloth, into a pitcher. Discard residue in strainer. Pour tea, hot or cold, into ice-filled glasses. Add sugar to taste.

Per serving: 32 cal., 0% (0 cal.) from fat; 0 g protein; 0 g fat; 8.4 g carbo (0 g fiber); 0.1 mg sodium; 0 mg chol. — *L. L. A.*

### FIESTA GAME PLAN

UP TO 1 DAY AHEAD:
Make tea and salsa.

UP TO 4 HOURS AHEAD:
Marinate turkey and prepare vegetables for the salad and the grill.

ABOUT 45 MINUTES BEFORE SERVING: Bake yams in the oven. Grill meats and vegetables, then warm tortillas on the grill.

JUST BEFORE SERVING:
Blend margaritas.

# Summer soups from Oaxaca

## With a palette of fresh vegetables, low-fat cooking comes naturally

A pair of brilliantly painted fantasy dogs, sculpted in wood and displayed on a friend's mantel, first stirred my curiosity about Oaxaca. This region, in the highlands of southeast Mexico, is justly famous for folk art like these pooches. And when my art interest turned into a visit, I discovered the foods of Oaxaca to be as richly imaginative.

The backbone of the cooking comes from the Zapotec and Mixtec cultures, which weave together corn, squash, and beans—the revered trinity for ancient peoples of the Americas—with seemingly infinite variety, particularly in soups. In Oaxaca's historic Hotel Stouffer Presidente, a memorable dish was starkly simple—wheels of corn on the cob and chunks of zucchini floating in broth. At the rug-filled Restaurant Tlaminalli in the nearby weaving village of Teotitlán del Valle, a soup thickened with masa flour (corn tortilla flour) and laced with golden squash blossoms, chayote squash, and corn was garden-fresh with flavor. And in a restaurant overlooking the broad plaza of the lively *zócalo*, a chili-infused soup studded with beans, potatoes, carrots, and tortillas left a lingering memory.

These satisfying soups are naturally light, healthful, and easy to make. In generous portions, each makes a meal, while smaller servings make a stylish first course. Accompany with soft warm tortillas or crusty *bolillos* (hard rolls).

## Corn Wheels and Zucchini Soup

PREP AND COOK TIME: **About 25 minutes**

NOTES: To cut the corn, use a mallet or hammer to gently drive a heavy knife or cleaver through the cob.

MAKES: 6 or 7 servings

$\frac{1}{2}$ cup **dehydrated masa flour** (corn tortilla flour)

CORN WHEELS float in broth with dumplings made of corn tortilla flour.

2 quarts fat-skimmed **chicken** or vegetable **broth**

2 cloves **garlic,** pressed or minced

$\frac{3}{4}$ pound **zucchini**

3 **ears corn** (each about 6 in.)

$\frac{1}{4}$ cup chopped **fresh cilantro**

**Lime** wedges

**Salt** and **pepper**

**1.** In a 4- to 5-quart pan, mix masa flour with 1 cup broth until smooth. Stir over high heat until mixture boils, then reduce heat to medium-low and stir until masa is thick, 2 to 3 minutes. Pour onto a flat plate. Spread evenly to make a $\frac{3}{4}$-inch-thick cake; let cool.

**2.** Meanwhile, rinse pan and add remaining broth and garlic. Cover and bring to a boil over high heat.

**3.** Trim and discard zucchini ends. Cut zucchini into $\frac{3}{4}$-inch cubes. Add zucchini to pan; cover and simmer for 5 minutes.

**4.** Meanwhile, discard husks and silks from corn. Cut corn crosswise into 1-inch-thick wheels. Also cut masa into $\frac{3}{4}$-inch chunks. Add corn and masa chunks to broth.

**5.** Cover pan and return to boiling over high heat; simmer until corn is hot, about 3 minutes.

**6.** Ladle into bowls. Sprinkle with cilantro. Serve with lime wedges, salt, and pepper to season portions to taste.

Per serving: 118 cal., 6.9% (8.1 cal.) from fat; 12 g protein; 0.9 g fat (0.1 g sat.); 17 g carbo (2.4 g fiber); 95 mg sodium; 0 mg chol.

## Chayote Corn Soup

PREP AND COOK TIME: **About 20 minutes**

NOTES: Use squash blossoms from your garden or buy them at a farmers' market. At peak season during the summer, some supermarkets carry squash blossoms. If desired, serve soup with triangles of pan-grilled corn tortilla quesadillas filled with squash blossoms and low-fat jack cheese.

MAKES: 6 servings

1½ quarts fat-skimmed **chicken** or vegetable **broth**

1 **dried hot red chili** (3 in.), such as chile de arból

1 **chayote squash** (¾ lb.)

18 **squash blossoms** (about 6 oz. total; optional)

½ cup **dehydrated masa flour** (corn tortilla flour)

1½ cups **corn kernels,** fresh or frozen

2 cups chopped **spinach**

About ⅓ cup crumbled **cotija** or feta **cheese**

**Salt** and **pepper**

**1.** In a covered 3- to 4-quart pan over high heat, bring 5 cups broth and chili to a boil.

**2.** Meanwhile, peel chayote and cut into ½-inch cubes (include edible seed). Gently rinse and drain blossoms. Leave baby squash stems (female flowers); if desired, trim off fuzzy stems (male flowers). Set aside 6 of the prettiest blossoms; chop the remainder.

**3.** Add chayote to boiling broth. Mix masa flour with remaining 1 cup broth and stir into pan. Stir until boiling. Reduce heat to medium-low, cover, simmer, and stir occasionally, until chayote is tender when pierced, about 10 minutes.

**4.** Stir corn, spinach, and chopped squash blossoms into soup, turn heat to high, and cook until corn is hot, about 2 minutes.

**5.** Ladle soup into bowls and lay 1 blossom in each. Add cheese, salt, and pepper to taste.

Per serving: 146 cal., 18% (26 cal.) from fat; 13 g protein; 2.9 g fat (1.3 g sat.); 19 g carbo (2.5 g fiber); 222 mg sodium; 5.6 mg chol.

## Red Chili Vegetable Soup

PREP AND COOK TIME: **About 45 minutes**

NOTES: Mild dried California or slightly hotter New Mexico chilies are ground and sold as chili powder. They are 100% chili, unlike most chili powder blends, which contain spices.

MAKES: **6 servings**

1½ quarts fat-skimmed **chicken** or vegetable **broth**

1 **onion** (½ lb.), chopped

1 clove **garlic,** pressed or minced

1½ tablespoons **ground dried New Mexico** or California **chilies,** or ¼ teaspoon cayenne

½ teaspoon **ground cumin**

½ teaspoon **dried oregano**

½ pound **carrots,** peeled

½ pound **thin-skinned potatoes,** scrubbed

½ pound **green beans,** ends trimmed

About ⅓ cup crumbled **cotija** or feta **cheese**

About ½ cup **nonfat** or reduced-fat **sour cream**

**Crisp corn tortilla strips** (see recipe below)

**Salt** and **pepper**

**1.** In a 4- to 5-quart pan over medium-high heat, combine ¼ cup broth, onion, and garlic. Cover and stir occasionally until onion is limp, 5 to 6 minutes.

**2.** Add chili, cumin, and oregano; stir about 30 seconds. Add remaining broth, cover, and bring to boiling over high heat.

**3.** Meanwhile, cut carrots diagonally into about ¼-inch-thick slices. Cut potatoes into ½-inch cubes. Cut beans into 2-inch lengths.

**4.** Add carrots and potatoes to pan; cover. When boiling, reduce heat to medium-low and simmer 10 minutes.

**5.** Turn heat to high, uncover, add beans, and when boiling, reduce heat to medium-low. Simmer until vegetables are tender to bite, 5 to 7 minutes.

**6.** Ladle into bowls. Add cheese, sour cream, tortilla strips, salt, and pepper to taste.

Per serving: 159 cal., 13% (21 cal.) from fat; 13 g protein; 2.3 g fat (1.3 g sat.); 21 g carbo (3.3 g fiber); 234 mg sodium; 7.6 mg chol.

## Crisp Corn Tortilla Strips

PREP AND COOK TIME: **About 15 minutes**

NOTES: If making up to 2 days ahead, package cool strips airtight.

MAKES: About 2½ ounces, 1 cup

**1.** Stack 3 **corn tortillas** (6 in.) and cut into ¼-inch-wide strips. Spread strips slightly apart on a nonstick 12- by 15-inch baking sheet.

**2.** Bake in a 400° oven until crisp and lightly browned, 10 to 15 minutes.

Per ½ ounce: 33 cal., 11% (3.6 cal.) from fat; 0.9 g protein; 0.4 g fat (0 g sat.); 7 g carbo (0.8 g fiber); 24 mg sodium; 0 mg chol. — **L. L. A.**

OPTIONAL SQUASH BLOSSOMS are tender-sweet additions to chayote corn soup.

**3.** Put watermelon chunks into bowl along with jicama, vinegar, and basil. Peel cucumber, cut into ½-inch chunks, and add to bowl. Mix and season to taste with salt.

**4.** Spoon salad mixture equally onto watermelon slices; sprinkle portions with toasted coconut.

Per serving: 99 cal., 20% (20 cal.) from fat; 2 g protein; 2.2 g fat (1.2 g sat.); 20 g carbo (2.8 g fiber); 304 mg sodium; 0 mg chol.

## Crunchy Chicken Taco Salad

PREP AND COOK TIME: About 35 minutes
NOTES: If you don't have a V-shaped rack, bake tortillas flat on a baking sheet and top with salad.
MAKES: 2 main-dish servings

- 2 **flour tortillas** (10 in.)
- 2 **boned, skinned chicken breast halves** (5 to 7 oz. each)
- 3 tablespoons **jalapeño jelly**
- ⅓ cup finely crushed **corn chips**
- 1 can (15 oz.) **black beans**, rinsed and drained
- ½ cup **refrigerated tomato salsa**
- 2 cups shredded **iceberg lettuce**

  About ¼ pound **firm-ripe avocado**, peeled, pitted, and thinly sliced

  **Reduced-fat sour cream**

  **Salt**

**1.** Adjust a V-shaped roasting rack so each side is at a 45° angle to the base. Cut 2 sheets of foil, each 12 inches long. Fold each sheet lengthwise to make a strip that is about 3 inches wide. Drape 1 strip from center of the V over and down to the base of the rack. Fold foil at each end to secure to rack. Repeat to secure second piece of foil to other side of the rack. Drape each flour tortilla with its center over the highest point on one side of the rack (foil keeps tortilla from curling inward as it bakes).

**2.** Bake tortillas in a 450° oven until lightly browned, about 5 minutes, then lift off racks and set aside (they continue to crisp as they cool). If making more than 1 hour or up to a day ahead, package airtight.

**3.** As tortillas bake, rinse chicken and pat dry. Melt 1 tablespoon jelly (in a microwave oven or in a small pan over medium heat, stirring occasionally). Brush all the melted jelly onto the

BRILLIANT, JUICY SLICE of watermelon is the base for refreshing salad.

# South-of-the-border salads

Authentic, adapted, or invented, these salads take their inspiration from tacos, Caesars, and street-vendor snacks

All dressed up but traveling light, these streamlined salads tackle the fat in old favorites. A street snack turns into watermelon salad. Tradition takes a new twist with Crunchy Chicken Taco Salad—big and lavish, but as lean as can be. Mexico's flag inspires a tricolor blend of tomatoes, tomatillos, and cheese. A classic gets trimmed when Caesar trades oil-soaked croutons for oven-crisped tortilla strips. Some salads are full-fledged main dishes; others can play the game either way, as the star or in a supporting position.

## Watermelon, Cucumber, and Jicama Salad

PREP AND COOK TIME: About 30 minutes
MAKES: 4 servings

- 2 tablespoons **sweetened shredded dried coconut**
- 1 piece **seedless watermelon** (about 2¾ lb.)
- ½ cup diced (⅛ in.) **jicama**
- ¼ cup **seasoned rice vinegar**
- ¼ cup slivered **fresh basil** leaves
- 1 **cucumber** (about 1 lb.)

  **Salt**

**1.** In an 8- to 10-inch frying pan over medium-high heat, stir coconut until lightly toasted, 3 to 4 minutes. Pour from pan.

**2.** Cut 4 equal slices, each ½ inch thick, from watermelon piece. Lay each slice on a plate. Cut off and discard rind from remaining watermelon; cut watermelon into ½-inch chunks.

smooth sides of breast halves. Put corn chips on a small plate and press jelly-coated side of chicken into chips so they stick. Set breasts, chips up, in an 8- or 9-inch square pan. Pat any remaining chips onto chicken.

**4.** Bake in a 450° oven until chicken is no longer pink in thickest part (cut to test), 15 to 20 minutes.

**5.** Meanwhile, in a bowl, mix beans, salsa, and remaining jalapeño jelly.

**6.** Lift breasts from pan with a wide spatula. If desired, cut each piece crosswise into 4 or 5 equal slices.

**7.** Set each tortilla shell on a plate. Put half the lettuce into each shell. Top lettuce equally with the bean mixture. Use the spatula to transfer a breast onto beans in each tortilla shell. Garnish with avocado and add sour cream and salt to taste.

Per serving: 701 cal., 23% (162 cal.) from fat; 50 g protein; 18 g fat (2.8 g sat.); 85 g carbo (9.5 g fiber); 1,164 mg sodium; 82 mg chol.

## Tomatillo, Tomato, and Panela Salad

PREP AND COOK TIME: **About 25 minutes**

NOTES: **Panela is a mild Mexican-style cheese found in many supermarkets; if you can't find it, use mozzarella cheese instead.**

MAKES: **4 servings**

½ pound **tomatillos**

¼ cup **orange juice**

¼ cup **lime juice**

About ¼ teaspoon **salt**

About ¼ teaspoon **pepper**

½ pound **firm-ripe tomatoes**

⅛ pound **panela cheese**

1 tablespoon chopped **fresh cilantro leaves**

**Chili-cumin chips** (see recipe below)

**1.** Pull off and discard the tomatillo husks. Rinse tomatillos and thinly slice into a bowl.

**2.** Add orange juice, lime juice, ¼ teaspoon salt, and ¼ teaspoon pepper; mix gently.

**3.** Rinse, core, and thinly slice tomatoes. Cut cheese into very thin slices. Arrange both on a flat plate.

**4.** Spoon tomatillo mixture over tomatoes and cheese. Sprinkle with cilantro; season to taste with salt and pepper.

Accompany with chili-cumin chips.

Per serving: 160 cal., 27% (43 cal.) from fat; 6.3 g protein; 4.8 g fat (2.6 g sat.); 26 g carbo (1.7 g fiber); 492 mg sodium; 5.2 mg chol.

## Chili-Cumin Chips

PREP AND COOK TIME: **About 15 minutes**

MAKES: **8 pieces**

2 **fat-free flour tortillas** (10 in.)

1 tablespoon **lime juice**

1 teaspoon **chili powder**

½ teaspoon **ground cumin**

¼ teaspoon **salt**

**1.** Brush each flour tortilla on 1 side with lime juice. Mix chili powder, ground cumin, and salt. Sprinkle seasoning mixture over lime-moistened side of tortillas. Cut tortillas into quarters.

**2.** Arrange quarters in a single layer, chili side up, on a 12- by 15-inch baking sheet. Bake in a 400° oven until chips are crisp and lightly browned, about 10 minutes.

Per piece: 41 cal., 2.2% (0.9 cal.) from fat; 1.1 g protein; 0.1 g fat (0 g sat.); 8.8 g carbo (0.5 g fiber); 195 mg sodium; 0 mg chol.

## Mexican Caesar Salad

PREP AND COOK TIME: **About 30 minutes**

NOTES: **Use flavored or plain flour tortilla.**

MAKES: **6 servings**

1 **chili-** or tomato-**flavor flour tortilla** (10 in.)

⅔ cup **nonfat** or reduced-fat **sour cream**

1 clove **garlic,** chopped

2 tablespoons **lemon juice**

1½ teaspoons **anchovy paste**

2 tablespoons **fresh cilantro**

8 cups rinsed, crisped **romaine lettuce** in bite-size pieces

2 tablespoons **shelled, roasted pumpkin seed**

3 tablespoons crumbled **cotija** or feta **cheese**

**1.** Cut tortilla into strips about ¼ inch wide and 2 inches long. Arrange in single layer in pan about 10 by 15 inches.

**2.** Bake in a 400° oven until strips are crisp, about 10 minutes.

**3.** Meanwhile, in a blender or food processor, whirl the sour cream, garlic,

TOMATILLOS, TOMATOES, and mild cheese make a cooling combo with lime dressing.

lemon juice, anchovy paste, and cilantro until cilantro is finely chopped.

**4.** Place lettuce in a wide bowl, add dressing, and mix. Top with tortilla strips, pumpkin seed, and cheese. Mix to serve.

*Per serving: 98 cal., 18% (18 cal.) from fat; 5.5 g protein; 2 g fat (0.6 g sat.); 14 g carbo (2.3 g fiber); 198 mg sodium; 5.1 mg chol.*

### Shrimp and Scallop Ceviche Salad

PREP AND COOK TIME: **35 to 40 minutes**

NOTES: **If making ahead, cover and chill shrimp and scallops up to 4 hours, then add dressing.**

MAKES: **4 main-dish servings**

- ½ pound **bay scallops**
- ½ pound (35 to 40 per lb.) **peeled, deveined shrimp**
- ¼ pound **tomatillos,** husked and rinsed
- 2 tablespoons **lime juice**
- ½ cup lightly packed **fresh cilantro**
- ½ cup finely chopped **red onion**
- 1 cup chopped **yellow bell pepper**
- 2 cups **cold cooked white rice**
  **Salt**
  **Hot sauce**
- 8 cups **baby spinach leaves** or salad mix (about ½ lb.), rinsed and drained

**1.** In a 2- to 3-quart pan over high heat, bring 4 cups water to a boil. Add scallops and shrimp, cover pan, and remove from heat. Let stand until scallops and shrimp are opaque in thickest part (cut to test), about 5 minutes. Drain shellfish and pour into a bowl; nest bowl in ice water. Stir occasionally.

**2.** Meanwhile, coarsely chop tomatillos. In a blender or food processor, whirl tomatillos, lime juice, and cilantro until puréed. Pour over scallops and shrimp. Add onion and bell pepper. Mix occasionally until ceviche is lukewarm or cool, 20 to 30 minutes.

**3.** Add rice; mix and season to taste with salt and hot sauce.

**4.** Arrange spinach on dinner plates and top with ceviche mixture.

*Per serving: 253 cal., 8% (20 cal.) from fat; 27 g protein; 2.2 g fat (0.3 g sat.); 31 g carbo (4.1 g fiber); 269 mg sodium; 105 mg chol.*

### Ancient Grains Salad

PREP AND COOK TIME: **About 35 minutes**

NOTES: **Quinoa and amaranth, both native to the Americas, are sold packaged or in bulk in natural-food stores or well-stocked supermarkets. If amaranth is unavailable, use a total of ⅔ cup quinoa.**

MAKES: **4 servings**

- 1 **dried New Mexico** or California **chili** (about 6 in.)
- 1 teaspoon **salad oil**
- 1 **onion** (½ lb.), finely chopped
- 1 clove **garlic,** minced or pressed
- ⅓ cup **amaranth**
- ⅓ cup **quinoa,** rinsed and drained
- 1 cup **corn kernels,** fresh or frozen
- 1 cup fat-skimmed **chicken broth**
- 2 tablespoons **lime juice**
- ⅓ cup chopped **fresh cilantro**
- 4 large **butter lettuce leaves,** rinsed and crisped
  **Salt**
  **Fresh-ground pepper**

**1.** Wipe chili with a damp cloth. Using scissors, cut off and discard chili stem end; remove and discard seeds. Cut chili crosswise into ¼-inch strips.

**2.** In a 10- to 12-inch nonstick frying pan over medium-low heat, stir chili in oil until it smells toasted and feels slightly crisp (avoid scorching), 1 to 2 minutes. With a slotted spoon, transfer chili pieces to towels to drain (they crisp as they cool).

**3.** Add onion and garlic to pan. Stir often over medium-high heat until onion is lightly browned, about 5 minutes.

**4.** Add amaranth and quinoa. Stir until grains are slightly toasted, about 1 minute. Mix in corn and broth. Bring to a boil over high heat; cover and simmer over medium heat until liquid is absorbed, about 15 minutes.

**5.** Let cool to room temperature. Or nest pan in ice water and stir occasionally with a fork until cool, about 10 minutes.

**6.** Mix lime juice and cilantro with grains. Spoon onto plates lined with lettuce leaves. Top salads with the crisp chili pieces. Add salt and pepper to taste.

*Per serving: 213 cal., 20% (43 cal.) from fat; 9.1 g protein; 4.8 g fat (0.8 g sat.); 38 g carbo (8.5 g fiber); 43 mg sodium; 0 mg chol.*

*— A. B.*

# Hooray for *huaraches*

Mexico's "sole" food, main-dish tostadas take their name from a sandal

**M**ention huaraches, and squeaky leather sandals are the first image that pops into most heads. But Mexicans know another huarache, a special kind of tostada. It's a bountiful main-dish presentation of vegetables, meat, salsa, and cheese mounded on a thick, toasted tortilla that's shaped like the sole of a shoe. Traditionally, the tortilla is made from masa dough, whipped up in seconds from dehydrated masa flour and laden with lard. But a little baking powder used instead of lard produces lean, tender results as easily and quickly.

PAT MASA DOUGH on waxed paper to make oval huaraches. Toast on a dry griddle and add toppings.

TOASTED HUARACHES make a solid foundation for hearty toppings.

## Huaraches

PREP AND COOK TIME: **About 40 minutes**

NOTES: If making ahead, cover and chill the masa dough up to 2 hours. If you find full-size huaraches hard to turn on the griddle, make them half as big and divide toppings equally.

MAKES: **4 servings**

2 cups **dehydrated masa flour** (corn tortilla flour)

1 teaspoon **baking powder**

$\frac{1}{4}$ teaspoon **salt**

$1\frac{3}{4}$ cups fat-skimmed **chicken broth**

1 can (15 oz.) **refried beans**

**Chicken,** beef, pork, or mushroom **topping** (recipes follow)

2 cups shredded **cabbage**

About $\frac{1}{2}$ cup **tomato** or green tomatillo **salsa**

About $\frac{1}{4}$ cup crumbled **cotija** or feta **cheese**

About $\frac{1}{4}$ cup **nonfat** or reduced-fat **sour cream**

**Salt** and **pepper**

**1.** In a bowl, stir masa flour, baking powder, salt, and broth until dough holds together well, adding a little water if needed.

**2.** Divide dough into 4 equal portions. Shape each portion into a 6-inch-long log on a sheet of waxed paper. Pat each log into a $\frac{1}{8}$-inch-thick oval, about 4 by 8 inches. (If shaped ahead, stack with waxed paper, wrap airtight, and refrigerate up to 2 hours.)

**3.** Place a griddle or 2 frying pans (10 to 12 in.) over medium-high heat. When pan is hot, flip masa dough onto pan and peel off paper. Cook until bottom of masa is light brown, about 3 minutes. Use a wide spatula to turn huaraches over.

**4.** Spread about $\frac{1}{4}$ of the beans over each huarache. Cover beans with $\frac{1}{4}$ of the chicken topping. Cook until huarache bottoms are lightly browned, 2 to 3 minutes. With a wide spatula, transfer to plates.

**5.** Top huaraches equally with shredded cabbage, salsa, cheese, sour cream, salt, and pepper to taste.

Per huarache without topping: 392 cal., 11% (42 cal.) from fat; 19 g protein; 4.7 g fat (1.6 g sat.); 72 g carbo (5.1 g fiber); 1,040 mg sodium; 5.5 mg chol.

CILANTRO CHICKEN TOPPING. Mix 2 cups shredded **cooked chicken breast,** $\frac{1}{3}$ cup thinly sliced **green onion,** and $\frac{1}{4}$ cup chopped **fresh cilantro.** Use warm or cool. Makes 2 cups.

Per $\frac{1}{2}$ cup: 120 cal., 19% (23 cal.) from fat; 22 g protein; 2.5 g fat (0.7 g sat.); 0.6 g carbo (0.2 g fiber); 54 mg sodium; 60 mg chol.

BEEF AND CHILI TOPPING. Lay 3 **fresh poblano** (also called pasilla) **chilies** (9 oz. total) and $\frac{3}{4}$-pound piece **boned, fat-trimmed top round** or top sirloin **beef** (about 1 in. thick) on a barbecue grill over a solid bed of hot coals or on a gas grill over high heat (you can hold your hand at grill level only 2 to 3 seconds); close lid on gas grill. Turn chilies as needed to brown and blister all sides, 5 to 7 minutes. Cook beef, turning once, until browned and rare in center of thickest part (cut to test), 8 to 10 minutes, longer for medium or well done. Pull stems, seeds, and skins off chilies and discard. Coarsely chop beef and chilies, and mix together. Add **salt** and **pepper** to taste. Use warm or cool. Makes 2 cups.

Per $\frac{1}{2}$ cup: 133 cal., 22% (29 cal.) from fat; 21 g protein; 3.2 g fat (1.1 g sat.); 4.4 g carbo (0.7 g fiber); 42 mg sodium; 53 mg chol.

CHILI PORK TOPPING. Thinly slice $\frac{1}{2}$ pound **fat-trimmed pork tenderloin** or boned pork loin into strips about $\frac{1}{4}$ by 2 inches. Thinly slice 1 **onion** ($\frac{1}{2}$ lb.). Mince 3 cloves **garlic.** In a 10- to 12-inch nonstick frying pan over high heat, stir-fry pork until lightly browned, about 3 minutes. Pour into a bowl. Add onion and garlic to pan; stir-fry until onion begins to brown, about 2 minutes. Add $1\frac{1}{2}$ teaspoons **chili powder,** $\frac{1}{2}$ teaspoon **cumin seed,** $\frac{1}{4}$ teaspoon **cayenne,** and pork. Stir-fry until meat is hot and coated with spices, about 1 minute. Add **salt** and **pepper** to taste. Use warm. Makes 2 cups.

Per $\frac{1}{2}$ cup: 97 cal., 21% (20 cal.) from fat; 13 g protein; 2.2 g fat (0.7 g sat.); 6.3 g carbo (1.3 g fiber); 40 mg sodium; 37 mg chol.

MUSHROOM TOPPING. Rinse and drain 1 pound **mushrooms** ($1\frac{1}{2}$ in. wide) and cut into quarters. Thinly slice 1 **onion** (6 oz.). In a 10- to 12-inch nonstick frying pan over high heat, frequently stir mushrooms, onion, 2 cloves minced **garlic,** and $\frac{1}{2}$ teaspoon **dried oregano** until mushrooms brown, 12 to 15 minutes. Add **salt** and **pepper** to taste. Use warm. Makes 2 cups.

Per $\frac{1}{2}$ cup: 47 cal., 9.6% (4.5 cal.) from fat; 3 g protein; 0.5 g fat (0.1 g sat.); 9.5 g carbo (2.2 g fiber); 6.1 mg sodium; 0 mg chol.

— L. L. A.

**3.** Run a thin-bladed knife between meringue cake and pan rim to release. Cool cake on a rack, about 20 minutes.

**4.** Thinly slice peaches; mix 2 cups slices with ½ cup raspberries, 1 tablespoon sugar, lemon peel, and 1 tablespoon lemon juice.

**5.** In a blender or food processor, whirl smooth remaining peaches, raspberries, 2 tablespoons sugar, and 2 tablespoons lemon juice. Rub purée through a fine strainer into a bowl; discard residue.

**6.** Remove pan rim and set meringue cake on a plate. Spoon sliced peaches and whole berries onto cake and drizzle with about 2 tablespoons fruit sauce. Cut cake into wedges and add remaining sauce to taste.

Per serving: 159 cal., 1.1% (1.8 cal.) from fat; 2.8 g protein; 0.2 g fat (0 g sat.); 38 g carbo (1.8 g fiber); 36 mg sodium; 0 mg chol.

### Pineapple and Papaya with Tequila Syrup

PREP AND COOK TIME: **About 35 minutes**

NOTES: Large Mexican-style papaya, Meridol, is often sold as cut pieces. If a peeled, cored pineapple isn't available, buy and trim a 3½- to 3¾-pound fruit. For garnish, cut long thin shreds of lime peel, green part only.

MAKES: **4 servings**

- 1  peeled and cored **pineapple** (about 1⅔ lb.)
- 1  piece **Meridol papaya** (about ½ lb.), peeled
- 1  **lime**
- 3  tablespoons **corn syrup**
- 3  tablespoons **lime juice**
- ⅛  teaspoon **cayenne**
- 2  tablespoons **tequila**

**1.** Cut pineapple crosswise into 8 to 12 slices. Cut papaya crosswise into thin slices. Cut lime crosswise into paper-thin slices, discarding ends. Arrange fruit on plates.

**2.** In a 1- to 2-quart pan over high heat, stir corn syrup, lime juice, and cayenne until boiling, 1 to 2 minutes. Add tequila and immediately ignite (not near a vent, fan, or inflammables). Shake pan until flames die down. Spoon syrup over fruit.

Per serving: 177 cal., 4.6% (8.1 cal.) from fat; 1.1 g protein; 0.9 g fat (0.1 g sat.); 42 g carbo (2.6 g fiber); 24 mg sodium; 0 mg chol.

PAPAYA AND PINEAPPLE endure trial by fire when tequila syrup adds a blazing finish.

# Frutas fantásticas

## Dramatic, easy, and refreshingly simple desserts

Desserts are as light as a summer breeze when you put sweet, ripe fruit to work. And in these Mexican-inspired creations, color and design are bonuses.

Usually, a cloud cake is swathed in whipped cream; our version is unadorned, but the soft-baked meringue base is as velvety as cream and it's drenched with peaches and raspberries. Papaya and pineapple are flamed with a tequila syrup; a crisp caramelized glazed tortilla goes with mangoes and melons; the sweet sangria is full of fruit; and grapes get a low-fat topping of cream and brown sugar.

### Peach and Raspberry Cloud Cake

PREP AND COOK TIME: About 30 minutes, plus at least 1 hour and 35 minutes to bake and cool

NOTES: Use a flat-bottomed glass to crush anise seed.

MAKES: 6 to 8 servings

- 5  **large egg** whites
- ½  teaspoon **cream of tartar**
- 1  cup plus 3 tablespoons **sugar**
- 1  teaspoon **vanilla**
- 1  teaspoon **anise seed**, crushed (see notes)

- 3  **firm-ripe peaches** (about 1 lb. total), peeled
- 1½  cups **raspberries**
- ½  teaspoon grated **lemon** peel
- 3  tablespoons **lemon juice**

**1.** In a deep bowl, beat egg whites and cream of tartar with a mixer on high speed until frothy. Add 1 cup sugar, about 1 tablespoon every 30 seconds, beating whites until they hold stiff peaks. Beat in vanilla and anise.

**2.** Lightly butter and flour-dust an 8-inch cheesecake pan with removable rim. Spread meringue level in pan. Bake in a 275° oven until pale golden, 1¼ to 1½ hours.

## Mexican Sunrise

PREP AND COOK TIME: About 45 minutes

NOTES: Before you start to cook, make scoops of frozen yogurt and set on a flat pan in the freezer; if making ahead, cover airtight up to 1 day.

MAKES: 4 servings

- ½ cup **sugar**
- 1 teaspoon **ground cinnamon**
- 2 **reduced-fat flour tortillas** (10 in.)
- 1 **firm-ripe mango** (about 1¼ lb.)
- 1 piece **honeydew melon** (about 1 lb.)
- 3 tablespoons **lemon juice**
- 2 cups **nonfat frozen vanilla yogurt,** in frozen scoops (see notes)

**1.** On a flat plate, mix ¼ cup of the sugar with cinnamon.

**2.** Stack tortillas, and with a small knife, notch edges to make sunburst rim (see photo below); reserve scraps for other uses. Cut tortillas in half, rub sides lightly with water, and coat, 1 piece at a time, with cinnamon sugar. Arrange pieces in a single layer on 2 baking sheets (12 by 15 in.).

**3.** Bake in a 400° oven until tortillas are lightly browned and crisp, about 10 minutes; switch pans halfway through baking.

**4.** Meanwhile, peel and pit mango. Seed and peel melon. Cut mango and melon into ½- to ¾-inch cubes, or cube half of each and thinly slice remainder. Mix fruit with lemon juice.

**5.** Arrange fruit equally on salad or dessert plates.

**6.** In a 6- to 8-inch frying pan over high heat, melt remaining ¼ cup sugar, shaking and tilting pan to mix dry sugar into syrup until liquid is amber color; remove from heat. At once, put frozen yogurt beside fruit, lean tortillas against frozen yogurt, and quickly drizzle desserts with melted sugar.

Per serving: 362 cal., 1.5% (5.4 cal.) from fat; 5.8 g protein; 0.6 g fat (0.1 g sat.); 86 g carbo (3 g fiber); 285 mg sodium; 0 mg chol.

## Sangria Fruit Soup

PREP AND COOK TIME: About 30 minutes

NOTES: Use a combination of berries such as sliced strawberries and whole blackberries and blueberries. Garnish with mint sprigs.

MAKES: 5 cups; 4 servings

- 1 cup **dry red wine**
- ½ cup **sugar**
- ⅓ cup **lemon juice**
- ¼ cup **orange-flavor liqueur**
- 1 teaspoon **vanilla**
- 4 cups mixed **berries** (see notes)
- ½ cup diced **cantaloupe** or honeydew melon

**1.** In a 2- to 3-quart pan, combine wine, 1 cup water, sugar, and lemon juice. Boil over high heat, stirring occasionally, until reduced to 1¼ cups, 10 to 15 minutes.

**2.** Remove from heat and stir in liqueur, vanilla, berries, and cantaloupe.

**3.** Nest pan in a bowl of ice and stir often until cool, about 10 minutes.

**4.** Ladle soup into bowls.

Per serving: 257 cal., 2.5% (6.3 cal.) from fat; 1.3 g protein; 0.7 g fat (0 g sat.); 49 g carbo (4.6 g fiber); 12 mg sodium; 0 mg chol.

## Crema-Grape Parfaits

PREP TIME: About 10 minutes

MAKES: 4 servings

**1.** Combine ½ cup **reduced-fat sour cream** and ½ teaspoon grated **orange** peel.

**2.** Divide 2 cups rinsed and drained **red seedless grapes** among 4 stemmed glasses or small bowls. Spoon sour cream over grapes and sprinkle equally with 2 tablespoons (total) firmly packed **brown sugar.** Garnish with thin strips of orange peel.

Per serving: 133 cal., 31% (41 cal.) from fat; 2.5 g protein; 4.5 g fat (2.2 g sat.); 23 g carbo (1.3 g fiber); 20 mg sodium; 10 mg chol.

— *E. J.* ◆

SNIPPED TO STELLAR SHAPE, sugar-crusted tortilla rises over fruit and frozen yogurt.

# The Quick Cook

MEALS IN 30 MINUTES OR LESS

BY CHRISTINE WEBER HALE

of each crêpe. Smash cheese down slightly (crêpes tear easily). Mound ⅛ of the mushroom mixture over cheese on each crêpe and sprinkle mushrooms equally with parmesan.

**5.** Fold crêpes in half over filling, then in half again to make a triangle. Set triangles, 3-layer side down, slightly apart in 2 nonstick or lightly oiled 10- by 15-inch pans.

**6.** Bake in a 400° oven until filling is hot in the center and crêpe edges are crisp, about 6 minutes; switch pan positions after 3 minutes. Transfer crêpes to plates.

Per serving: 317 cal., 68% (216 cal.) from fat; 12 g protein; 24 g fat (16 g sat.); 16 g carbo (2.2 g fiber); 584 mg sodium; 65 mg chol.

## 4 more dinner crêpes

### Chicken-Mango Crêpes

PREP AND COOK TIME: About 30 minutes
MAKES: 4 servings

**1.** In a bowl, gently mix 1 cup chopped **mango**, 2 tablespoons chopped **fresh cilantro**, 3 cups (about ¾ lb.) shredded, skinned, **cooked chicken,** ½ cup **Major Grey chutney,** and 1 tablespoon **lime juice.**

**2.** Spoon mixture equally onto a quarter section of each of 8 **packaged crêpes** (9 in.). Sprinkle equally with ½ cup crumbled **feta cheese.**

**3.** Fold crêpes and bake as directed in steps 5 and 6, above.

**4.** If desired, garnish crêpes with mango slices and cilantro leaves.

Per serving: 463 cal., 15% (71 cal.) from fat; 27 g protein; 7.9 g fat (2.4 g sat.); 71 g carbo (2.5 g fiber); 510 mg sodium; 81 mg chol.

### Chili Relleno Crêpes

PREP AND COOK TIME: About 20 minutes
MAKES: 4 servings

**1.** Drain 2 cans (4 oz. each) **whole green chilies** and lay an equal portion on a quarter section of each of 8 **packaged crêpes** (9 in.). Mound 3 tablespoons **shredded cheddar cheese** (you'll need 2 cups, ½ lb. total) onto chilies on each crêpe.

**2.** Fold crêpes and place on pans as directed in step 5 above. Top crêpes

## MENU

Mushroom and Arugula Crêpes
Bulgur Wheat Pilaf
Sliced Summer-ripe Tomatoes
Sugared Raspberries and Sliced White Nectarines
Crisp Orange Wafer Cookies

## Under wraps

■ France's favorite ultra-thin pancake, the crêpe, is found packaged and ready to use in produce sections this time of year. Crêpes are usually promoted for use in quick fruit desserts, but they also make handy wraps to dress up simple dinners quickly. Just fold them around a savory filling and bake briefly. Typically, a package of 10 crêpes (9 in. wide; 4 oz. total) costs $4 to $5; they last for months on the shelf. Once opened, store airtight in the refrigerator for weeks. Order from Frieda's by Mail, (800) 241-1771, ext. 151, or Melissa's World Variety Produce, (800) 588-0151.

## Mushroom and Arugula Crêpes

PREP AND COOK TIME: About 30 minutes
NOTES: Reserve a few mushroom slices and arugula leaves for garnish.
MAKES: 4 servings

- 1 pound **sliced mushrooms**
- 1 tablespoon **butter** or margarine
- 6 cups (about 6 oz.) **arugula,** rinsed and drained
- 1 package (5.2 oz.) **Boursin cheese**
- 8 **packaged crêpes** (9 in.)
- ½ cup shredded **parmesan cheese**

**1.** In a covered 10- to 12-inch nonstick frying pan over high heat, frequently stir mushrooms and butter until mushrooms are juicy, about 5 minutes.
**2.** Uncover and stir often until liquid evaporates and mushrooms are lightly browned, about 5 minutes more.
**3.** Stir chopped arugula with mushrooms just until wilted, about 2 minutes. Remove from heat.
**4.** Stir Boursin cheese to soften. Spoon ⅛ of the cheese onto a quarter section

148 JULY

with remaining cheese and bake as directed in step 6 on page 132.

Per serving: 293 cal., 61% (180 cal.) from fat; 16 g protein; 20 g fat (12.5 g sat.); 13 g carbo (0.6 g fiber); 788 mg sodium; 65 mg chol.

### Ham-Gouda Crêpes

PREP AND COOK TIME: About 25 minutes

MAKES: 4 servings

1. Lay equal portions of **thinly sliced cooked ham** ($^1/_2$ lb. total) and **thinly sliced gouda cheese** (7 oz. total) on a quarter section of each of 8 **packaged crêpes** (9 in.), then sprinkle lightly with **ground nutmeg.**

2. Fold the crêpes and bake them as directed in steps 5 and 6 on page 132. Serve crêpes topped with **Dijon mustard** (about 3 tablespoons total) and chopped **parsley.**

Per serving: 321 cal., 50% (162 cal.) from fat; 25 g protein; 18 g fat (10 g sat.); 11 g carbo (0 g fiber); 1,449 mg sodium; 92 mg chol.

### Turkey-Pesto Crêpes

PREP AND COOK TIME: About 25 minutes

MAKES: 4 servings

1. Mix all but 3 tablespoons of 1 package (7 oz.) **pesto** with 4 cups (about 1 lb.) shredded, skinned **cooked turkey** and spoon an equal portion of the mixture on a quarter section of each of 8 **packaged crêpes** (9 in.). Top turkey mixture on each crêpe with 1 tablespoon **shredded jack cheese** (you'll need 1 cup total).

2. Fold crêpes, place on pans as directed in step 5 on page 132, and top with remaining cheese. Bake as directed in step 6 on page 132; dot crêpes with remaining pesto.

Per serving: 656 cal., 58% (378 cal.) from fat; 54 g protein; 42 g fat (12 g sat.); 13 g carbo (0 g fiber); 721 mg sodium; 151 mg chol. ◆

# Picnic panoramas

## Scenic sites where you can enjoy food with a view

BY CHRISTINE COLASURDO

KAREN STRELECKI

■ So you can enjoy the midsummer sunshine, we've brought you a sampling of the many scenic picnic spots the West has to offer. All the following places are either in or near cities.

**Washington Park, Portland.** With its 550 varieties of roses blooming this month, the International Rose Test Garden in Washington Park might be one of the most fragrant places on the planet. If the roses don't intoxicate you, try gazing out over Portland for a view of Mount Hood. WHERE: 400 S.W. Kingston Ave. (just west of downtown Portland). WHEN: 7 A.M.–9 P.M. CONTACT: (503) 823-3636.

**Sandia Crest, near Albuquerque.** To view all of Albuquerque and half of New Mexico, head into the Cibola National Forest to the crest of the Sandia Mountains. WHERE: On State 536, 25 miles east of Albuquerque. WHEN: Open 24 hours. COST: Parking $3. CONTACT: (505) 281-3304.

**Discovery Park, Seattle.** A $^1/_2$-mile stroll to the Sand Bluffs through this former military fort (now Seattle's largest park) rewards you with views of Puget Sound and the glacier-etched Olympic Mountains. WHERE: The south entrance to the park lies at the end of Magnolia Blvd. WHEN: Open to vehicles 6 A.M.–11 P.M. CONTACT: (206) 386-4236.

**Marin Headlands, near San Francisco.** One of the most dizzying roads of the entire West Coast takes you to Point Bonita Lighthouse. Or stop along the way for breathtaking shots of the Golden Gate Bridge and San Francisco. WHERE: From San Francisco, take U.S. 101 north across the Golden Gate Bridge and exit at Alexander Ave. WHEN: Open 24 hours, but the road is dangerously dark after sunset. CONTACT: (415) 331-1540.

**South Mountain Park/Preserve, Phoenix.** The world's largest city park offers 16,500 acres of rugged desert mountains. Check out the vistas from either Dobbin's Lookout or Gila Valley. WHERE: 7 miles south of downtown Phoenix. WHEN: 5:30 A.M.–10:30 P.M. CONTACT: (602) 495-0222.

**Chautauqua Park, Boulder.** This 100-year-old Colorado park lies smack-dab at the base of the Flatirons with their red sandstone faces. Summer concerts fill the mountain air, and trails through pines and meadows take you to higher ground. WHERE: At the intersection of Baseline Rd. and Grant Place, 1 mile west of U.S. 36. WHEN: Open to vehicles 9 A.M.–10 P.M. CONTACT: (303) 441-3408.

**Earthquake Park, Anchorage.** Enjoy stunning views of Cook Inlet, Mount Susitna, the Alaska Range, and Mount McKinley from the coastal picnic areas of Earthquake Park. Interpretive signs explain the history of the massive 1964 quake—a full 9.2 on the Richter scale. WHERE: On Northern Lights Blvd., 4 miles south of downtown. To reach the picnic area, take the trail in 100 yards from the west side of the parking lot. WHEN: Open 24 hours. CONTACT: (907) 274-3531.

**Sunset Cliffs Park, San Diego.** Watch miles of coastline glow in the setting sun from this 60-foot-high sandstone bluff overlooking the grand Pacific. Go during low tide so you can take a nearby staircase to hidden beaches and tidepools. WHERE: From I-8 west, exit south onto Sunset Cliffs Blvd. WHEN: Open to vehicles 4 A.M.–11 P.M. FYI: Beware of high tides and crumbling cliffs. CONTACT: (619) 581-9976. ◆

# Kitchen Cabinet

## READERS' RECIPES TESTED IN SUNSET'S KITCHENS

### BY LINDA LAU ANUSASANANAN

CHILI-TINTED TORTILLAS, wrapped snugly around a cream cheese and turkey filling, are cut in half and served upright—ready for lunch. Follow with sliced peaches.

4 **chili-flavor** or plain **flour tortillas** (about 10 in.), at room temperature

2 cups finely slivered **romaine lettuce**

3 to 4 cups skinned, shredded **cooked turkey** or chicken

$^{1}/_{2}$ cup thinly sliced **green onions**

$^{1}/_{4}$ cup chopped **fresh cilantro**

1 can ($2^{1}/_{4}$ oz.) **sliced ripe olives**, drained

**1.** Smoothly mix cream cheese with chili sauce to taste.

**2.** Spread $^{1}/_{4}$ of the cheese mixture evenly onto 1 side of each tortilla.

**3.** Down the center of each tortilla, spoon $^{1}/_{4}$ of the lettuce, turkey, onions, cilantro, and olives.

**4.** Roll tortilla snugly to enclose filling, then cut each roll in half. If desired, stand rolls upright on flat end.

Per serving: 445 cal., 22% (99 cal.) from fat; 45 g protein; 11 g fat (2.4 g sat.); 40 g carbo (3 g fiber); 925 mg sodium; 87 mg chol.

## Seed-spiced Potato Salad

### Kathleen Grice, Berkeley

For a lighter, leaner potato salad, Kathleen Grice uses nonfat yogurt instead of mayonnaise, and laces it with mustard and cumin seeds.

**PREP AND COOK TIME:** About 25 minutes

**MAKES:** 5 servings

$1^{1}/_{2}$ pounds **thin-skinned potatoes**

$^{3}/_{4}$ pound **carrots**

2 teaspoons **salad oil**

1 teaspoon **black** or yellow **mustard seed**

1 teaspoon **cumin seed**

1 or 2 cloves **garlic,** minced

$^{1}/_{4}$ teaspoon **pepper**

1 cup **plain nonfat yogurt**

$^{1}/_{4}$ cup chopped **parsley**

**Salt**

**1.** Peel potatoes and carrots and cut into $^{3}/_{4}$-inch chunks. Place vegetables on a rack at least 1 inch above boiling water in a 5- to 6-quart pan. Cover and steam over medium heat until vegetables are tender when pierced, 8

## Chili Turkey Wraps

### Marilou Robinson, Portland

Wraps make a quick lunch for Marilou Robinson and her family. They favor turkey in their wraps, but almost any cooked or leftover meat can be used. If chili-flavor tortillas are not available, mix $^{1}/_{2}$ teaspoon chili powder into the cheese mixture. For best re-

sults, use very fresh tortillas so they don't crack, and let them warm to room temperature before rolling.

**PREP TIME:** About 25 minutes

**MAKES:** 4 servings

1 package (8 oz.) **nonfat cream cheese**

3 to 4 tablespoons **tomato-based chili sauce**

to 10 minutes. Let stand until cool, or to cool quickly, immerse vegetables in cold water. When vegetables are cold, drain well.

**2.** Meanwhile, pour oil into a 6- to 8-inch frying pan over high heat. When oil is hot, stir in mustard and cumin seeds. Cover pan, remove from heat, and shake (holding lid on) until popping subsides, about 40 seconds. Add garlic and pepper.

**3.** In a wide bowl, combine seed mixture, yogurt, drained vegetables, and parsley; mix gently. Add salt to taste. Serve salad, or cover and chill up to 6 hours.

Per serving: 188 cal., 12% (23 cal.) from fat; 6.3 g protein; 2.6 g fat (0.3 g sat.); 36 g carbo (4.7 g fiber); 71 mg sodium; 0.9 mg chol.

## Peach-Pear Salsa

Rose Ann Koffler,
West Hollywood, California

Rose Ann Koffler recommends fresh salsa to perk up even the plainest meats. And for pork or poultry, she uses this spiced fresh fruit concoction. It holds well at room temperature up to 2 hours.

PREP TIME: About 15 minutes

MAKES: About 2¾ cups

- 1 cup diced (½ in.) peeled **firm-ripe peach** or nectarine
- 1 cup diced (½ in.) peeled **firm-ripe pear**
- ½ cup chunks (½ in.) **red bell pepper**
- ½ cup chopped **red onion**
- ¼ cup **cider vinegar**
- 2 teaspoons **honey**
- 3 tablespoons chopped **fresh basil** leaves
- ¼ teaspoon **ground cinnamon**
- ¼ teaspoon **cayenne**
- ⅛ teaspoon **ground allspice**

Mix peach, pear, bell pepper, onion, vinegar, honey, basil, cinnamon, cayenne, and allspice.

Per ¼ cup: 25 cal., 3.6% (0.9 cal.) from fat; 0.3 g protein; 0.1 g fat (0 g sat.); 6.4 g carbo (0.8 g fiber); 1 mg sodium; 0 mg chol.

## Cabernet-Soy Tri-Tip

Cary Yoshio Mizobe, Gardena, California

At a friend's house in California's Central Valley, Cary Yoshio Mizobe was served what he rates as the best marinated tri-tip ever. It became the model for this version. Mizobe says his comes "pretty darn close" to the original.

PREP AND COOK TIME: About 40 minutes, plus at least 30 minutes to marinate

MAKES: 6 servings

- ½ cup **Cabernet Sauvignon**
- ⅓ cup **sugar**
- ¼ cup **soy sauce**
- 3 slices **fresh ginger** (each the size of a quarter)
- 2 cloves **garlic**
- 1 fat-trimmed **beef tri-tip** (about 2 lb.)

**1.** In a plastic food bag (at least 1 gal.), combine wine, sugar, and soy sauce.

**2.** With the flat side of a knife, crush ginger and garlic. Add to wine mixture.

**3.** Wipe beef with a damp towel and put in bag, seal, and shake to mix. Set bag in a pan and chill, turning occasionally, at least 30 minutes or up to 1 day.

**4.** Lift beef from bag, reserving the marinade. Lay meat on a grill above a solid bed of medium coals or on a gas barbecue on medium heat (you can hold your hand at grill level only 4 to 5 seconds). Cover gas grill. Turning beef as needed to brown evenly, cook until a thermometer inserted in center of thickest part registers 125° for rare, 20 to 30 minutes total for a 1½- to 2-inch-thick piece.

**5.** Transfer meat to a carving board, keep warm, and let rest 5 to 10 minutes.

**6.** Meanwhile, pour reserved marinade into a 1- to 2-quart pan. Over high heat, boil marinade until reduced to about ½ cup, about 5 minutes. With a slotted spoon, discard ginger and garlic. Pour marinade sauce into a bowl and add juices that have drained from meat.

**7.** Slice meat thinly across the grain and accompany with sauce.

Per serving: 263 cal., 27% (70 cal.) from fat; 33 g protein; 7.8 g fat (2.7 g sat.); 13 g carbo (0 g fiber); 761 mg sodium; 92 mg chol.

## Alaska Mocha

Marti Bradley, Anchorage

"It does get hot in Alaska—really—and when it does we like to sit on the deck, sip a cold drink, and enjoy the flowers before the moose eat them," says Marti Bradley of Anchorage. She whizzes up this low-fat drink using leftover breakfast coffee frozen in ice cube trays.

PREP TIME: About 10 minutes, plus at least 3 hours to freeze coffee

MAKES: About 3 cups; 2 servings

- About 1½ cups cold **strong coffee**
- ⅓ cup **chocolate syrup**
- ⅓ cup **nonfat dried milk**

**1.** Pour 1¼ cups coffee into an ice cube tray or trays and freeze until solid, at least 3 hours.

**2.** To a blender (through opening in lid) or food processor with motor running, add frozen coffee cubes, chocolate syrup, nonfat dried milk, and ¼ cup cold coffee. Whirl until mixture is a thick slush; if thicker than you like, add a little more cold coffee. Pour into tall glasses.

Per serving: 152 cal., 3% (4.5 cal.) from fat; 5 g protein; 0.5 g fat (0.3 g sat.); 36 g carbo (0 g fiber); 113 mg sodium; 2 mg chol. ◆

**FROZEN COFFEE**
whirled with chocolate
makes a cool drink.

For the coolest desserts, we round up 27 easy recipes, the newest machines, and favorite ice cream parlors (see page 158).

# August

# foodguide

BY JERRY ANNE DI VECCHIO

## hot snack

Ruth Waltenspiel at Timber Crest Farms in Healdsburg, California, has dried all kinds of local produce—including kiwi fruit and persimmons—without preservatives. Her latest offering is mangoes. She dries unsweetened strips, seasons them with chili and lime, and labels the results Macho Mango. The fruit is smooth but chewy, and the seasonings are sharp enough to warm your tongue but not hot enough to start a fire. For munching, it's hard to find anything more wholesome—or more satisfying. 1½-ounce bags of strips cost about $1.50, 4-ounce tubs of slices about $4.50; (707) 433-8251.

JAMES CARRIER (3)

### BACK TO BASICS

## Grape expectations

■ Occasionally, I've extolled the virtues of giving green seedless grapes a touch of heat to brighten their color and intensify their flavor. Swirl them in a single layer in a frying pan over high heat for about 30 seconds and you have a beautiful, refreshing garnish for fish, chicken, pork, or lamb.

But if you take the process one step further and cook the grapes way down, they turn sweet-sour, golden, and sticky. *Sunset* senior food writer

Linda Anusasananan came back from a Mediterranean visit with this extremely simple sausage dish. I liked it so much, it's become a regular on my table.

### Sausages with Shallots and Grapes

**PREP AND COOK TIME:** About 45 minutes
**NOTES:** Serve with an arugula salad and polenta (boiled, or sliced and broiled) topped with shaved parmesan.
**MAKES:** 6 servings

- 2½ pounds **green seedless grapes**
- ½ pound **shallots** or red onion
- 6 **Italian sausages** (about 1¾ lb. total)
- **Salt** and **pepper**

**1.** Pull grapes from stems, rinse, and set aside about 2 cups. Put remaining grapes in an 11- to 12-inch nonstick frying pan.
**2.** Peel shallots and coarsely chop. Add to frying pan.
**3.** Cover pan and cook over medium-high heat until mixture is juicy, about

10 minutes. Uncover and boil over high heat, stirring often, until grapes begin to collapse and most of the liquid has evaporated, about 5 minutes longer.
**4.** Push grape mixture to one side and lay sausages in pan. Cover and cook over medium heat until mixture is juicy, about 10 minutes. Uncover, turn heat to high, and stir grape mixture often as it thickens and concentrates. Also turn sausages as needed to brown lightly. When grape mixture is richly browned, in about 10 minutes more, transfer with sausages to a platter and keep warm. Cut sausages in half lengthwise if desired.
**5.** Pour reserved grapes into pan, return to high heat, and shake pan frequently to rotate grapes; heat until they turn slightly brighter green, about 30 seconds. Pour over sausages. Season to taste with salt and pepper.

Per serving: 611 cal., 63% (387 cal.) from fat; 21 g protein; 43 g fat (15 g sat.); 39 g carbo (3.3 g fiber); 976 mg sodium; 101 mg chol.

## Purple Potato Salad

PREP AND COOK TIME: 40 minutes

NOTES: Dark green poblano chilies are often called pasillas. This nonfat citrus dressing is good on white potatoes too.

MAKES: About 8 cups

- 2 pounds **purple potatoes** (about 1½ in. thick)
- 2 **yellow crookneck squash** (about ¼ lb. each)
- ¼ pound **tomatillos**
- 1 **red bell pepper** (½ lb.)
- 1 **poblano chili** (about 3 oz.)
- 1 cup **orange juice**
- ½ cup **lime juice**
  **Sugar** (optional)
- ¼ cup chopped **fresh cilantro**
  **Salt**

**1.** Scrub potatoes and place on a rack in a 5- to 6-quart pan over about 1 inch boiling water. Cover and steam over medium-high heat until potatoes are almost tender when pierced, about 15 minutes.

**2.** Rinse squash and trim stem ends. Cut squash in half lengthwise. Set squash on potatoes, cover, and continue to steam until vegetables are tender when pierced, about 5 minutes more. Add boiling water to pan as needed to maintain water level. Let vegetables cool.

**3.** Meanwhile, husk, rinse, and thinly slice the tomatillos. Stem, seed, and dice the red bell pepper and the poblano chili.

**4.** When the potatoes are cool enough to touch, peel and cut into pieces no thicker than ½ inch. Put potatoes in a wide salad bowl. Add orange and lime juices; mix gently, taste, and if desired add about 1 teaspoon sugar (or to taste).

**5.** Add tomatillos, red bell pepper, chili, and cilantro to potatoes; mix gently. Cut squash halves in half lengthwise, add to salad, and mix gently again. Season potato salad to taste with salt. Serve while still warm or at room temperature.

Per cup: 127 cal., 2.8% (3.6 cal.) from fat; 3.3 g protein; 0.4 g fat (0 g sat.); 29 g carbo (2.5 g fiber); 13 mg sodium; 0 mg chol.

## A TASTE OF THE WEST

# Potato salad surprise

■ Potato salads are like a favorite relative: they can be plain or they can be fancy, but it's nice when they show up for a picnic. This particular salad always reminds me of my Aunt Stell, who used a blue rinse on her snow-white hair. Mostly, the blue enhanced the white, but on one occasion, she mismeasured and her coif turned purple. At age 6, I loved the result. At 60-plus, she hated it.

Well, even potatoes can be purple. But naturally so. Incas were serving them long before Pizarro came along to help himself to their gold.

Now purple potatoes are in most supermarkets, looking just like … potatoes. They have the same coloring compounds that make cabbage red, however. And like red cabbage, they get brighter in an acid dressing. (Creamy mixtures mask the color.) The potatoes are positively brilliant when seasoned with this see-through lime and orange juice dressing. I think Aunt Stell would've loved purple in her salad as much as I liked it on her hair.

## SEASONAL NOTE
# A ristra for all reasons

■ The basic function of a dark red New Mexico chili ristra is to store chilies, not to be admired. I break off chilies to cut into strips and toast in oil to add to salads and to garnish mashed potatoes and vegetables.

When the ristra gets too ratty-looking, I break off the remaining chilies and make a big batch of this sauce to freeze. Use it in any recipe that calls for canned chili sauce, or add it as part of the liquid when making chili with beans or meats.

Bueno Foods in Albuquerque sells ristras for $26; (800) 888-7336. CHILI SAUCE. Wipe off **dried New Mexico chilies.** Lay in single layer in a rimmed pan. Toast in a 350° oven just until chilies begin to get fragrant, 3 to 5 minutes. Let chilies cool, then discard stems and seeds. Put chilies in a bowl and pour 1 quart boiling **water** over each ½ pound chilies (about 36). Let stand until chilies are soft, at least 10 min-

utes. Whirl chilies and soaking water in a blender until smoothly puréed. Cover and refrigerate up to 3 days, or package airtight and freeze up to 6 months. Thin with water or broth to use; ½ pound of chilies makes 4½ cups sauce.

Per ½ cup: 80 cal., 50% (40 cal.) from fat; 3 g protein; 4.4 g fat (0.8 g sat.); 14 g carbo (6.9 g fiber); 7.6 mg sodium; 0 mg chol.

SAUTÉED CHILI STRIPS. Wipe off **dried New Mexico chilies.** Discard stems and seeds. Cut chilies into thin slivers. Put 2 teaspoons **salad oil** for each 1 cup (about ½ oz.) chili strips in a 10- to 12-inch frying pan over medium heat. Add chilies; stir until they smell toasted (they scorch easily). Pour onto towels and drain; chilies crisp as they cool. Use or store airtight up to 1 week.

Per tablespoon: 7.8 cal., 81% (6.3 cal.) from fat; 0.1 g protein; 0.7 g fat (0.1 g sat.); 0.5 g carbo (0.2 g fiber); 0.3 mg sodium; 0 mg chol.

---

## CLASSIC UPDATE
# Caramel, Latin-style

■ Recently at Loews Coronado Bay Resort in Southern California, I sat in on a think tank with chefs from all the Loews Hotels. The day included a little competition for refreshments. The chefs presented brunch concepts that reflected the flavors of their home base. My mental blue ribbon went to Jim Makinson from Loews Ventana Canyon Resort in Tucson. He served hot, frothy cinnamon-flavor Mexican chocolate and sweetly seasoned warm tortillas topped with a fruit salsa and mellow cajeta, Latin America's tangy caramel sauce. Makinson made his own cajeta with canned evaporated goat's milk from the supermarket. It's wonderful on waffles with fruit, and makes a fabulous sundae spooned over vanilla ice cream or mango sorbet.

## Cajeta Sauce

PREP AND COOK TIME: 15 minutes
NOTES: If making ahead, cool and store airtight in the refrigerator up to 2 weeks. Reheat to use.
MAKES: About 2 cups

  1  can (12 oz.) **evaporated goat's milk**

  ½  cup **whipping cream**

  1  cup **sugar**

  2  tablespoons **lemon juice**

**1.** Scrape goat's milk into a bowl, add whipping cream, and whisk until smooth.

**2.** In a 10- to 12-inch frying pan, melt sugar over high heat, tilting pan to mix dry sugar into the syrup that forms, and cook until amber-colored, 3 to 5 minutes.

**3.** Remove from heat and add ½ cup water to caramel (it spatters), then return to heat and stir until caramel dissolves.

**4.** Add goat's milk mixture and lemon juice. Boil over high heat, stirring often and scraping pan sides, until reduced to 2 cups, about 10 minutes.

**5.** Serve warm to pour or cold to spread.

Per ¼ cup: 201 cal., 34% (68 cal.) from fat; 3.3 g protein; 7.6 g fat (4.8 g sat.); 30 g carbo (0 g fiber); 44 mg sodium; 27 mg chol. ◆

# The Wine Guide

RICK MARIANI

## Wine matters

■ Last week, for the first time in my life, I had a dinner party at my house catered. As the caterer began to prep, I, being an inquisitive sort, stood watching her. First the eggplant. She peeled it quickly and chopped the flesh into perfect cubes before sautéing them.

"Wait a minute," I said. "What about the part where you're supposed to sprinkle salt over the eggplant and let it sit to remove the bitterness?"

"That old idea," she sighed. "I never do that anymore. It doesn't matter."

Next came the shrimp. She peeled them with lightning speed. But when it came to removing the stringlike "intestine," forget it. I looked at her in disbelief.

"Not necessary," she proclaimed.

Her refreshing irreverence got me thinking. When it comes to wine, what sorts of things matter and what don't?

### SMELLING THE CORK
The waiter puts the cork down on the table beside you. Are you supposed to sniff it? Poke it? Ignore it? Despite all those cartoons of cork-sniffing sommeliers, the answer is the last one. The practice of placing the cork on the table dates from the 19th century when wineries began branding corks to prevent unscrupulous restaurateurs from filling an empty bottle of Château Expensive with inferior wine, recorking the bottle, then reselling it. In honest restaurants the cork was placed on the table so the diner could see that the name on it matched that on the label.

Admittedly, a moist and pliable cork is a good sign: the wine bottle has probably been stored correctly on its side. So touch tells you *something*. But a moist cork is no guarantee that the wine is in good condition, and a dry cork doesn't necessarily portend a wine gone awry.

### ONE GLASS, TWO WINES
If you're serving a white wine with the shrimp, then a red with the chicken, should you rinse the glass between courses? No. Water has a powerful diluting effect on wine. A drop of white in the red does far less harm to the red's flavor than water.

### THE FREEZER—FAUX PAS?
We've all done it. Dinner's about ready and (oops) the white wine is warm. We toss it in the freezer. Bad idea? No. Most wines will be fine (just pull them out well before they start to get slushy—check every 10 minutes). It takes only a little more time, however, to chill wine in a gentler manner: in a bucket filled half with ice and half with cold water (an especially good method for an older, somewhat fragile wine). The bucket should be deep enough so the bottle can be submerged up to its neck in the ice-water bath. To chill a white wine down to 55° takes about:
• 20 minutes in an ice-water bath
• a little more than an hour in ice alone
• three hours in the refrigerator.

### CHILLING REDS
The notion that red wines should *not* be chilled is actually extremely out of date. It stems from a century ago, when red wines were brought up from cold underground cellars. But in many restaurants—and homes—today, red wines come to the table so warm they taste like high-octane cough syrup. At high temperatures a wine's alcohol dominates and the wine tastes harsh and unbalanced. So chilling a red is often a good idea. Just five minutes can do the trick.

### TO BREATHE OR NOT TO BREATHE
Letting a wine "breathe" simply means exposing it to oxygen so its flavors and aromas can "open up" and become more expressive. In particular, young, tight red wines benefit from breathing. It makes them softer, more compelling.

But to breathe, a wine must be poured out of the bottle into a carafe or decanter (or even generous-size glasses). Simply pulling out the cork and letting the bottle stand there does nothing. There just isn't enough airspace in the neck of a wine bottle to make any difference. ◆

---

## WHAT WOULD I SERVE?
Here are a few of the bottles (among many) I love to open for guests.

■ *A. Rafanelli Winery Zinfandel 1996 (Dry Creek Valley),* $19. No home should be without a generous, mouth-filling Zinfandel.

■ *Domaine Carneros by Taittinger Brut 1993 (Carneros),* $18. These bubbles are my favorite reward after a really tough day.

■ *Joseph Phelps Vineyards Vin du Mistral Grenache Rosé 1996 (California),* $11. Pretend you're in Paris (where rosé is chic) with this stunning wine.

■ *Navarro Vineyards Gewürztraminer 1996 (Anderson Valley),* $14. Exotic personality unbeatable with spicy foods.

■ *Santa Barbara Winery Pinot Noir Reserve 1995 (Santa Barbara County),* $40. Alas, great Pinot is expensive, but this one, with chocolate-cedar notes, is irresistible.

■ *Shafer Vineyards Cabernet Sauvignon 1995 (Napa Valley Stags Leap District),* $30. As rich and soft as butter, and indispensable with grilled steak.

■ *St. Supéry Vineyards & Winery Sauvignon Blanc 1997 (Napa Valley),* $10. Fresh-lime pizzazz! Just right on a hot night.

# Get your licks

27 easy recipes,
the newest
machines, and the
West's best
ice cream parlors

BY ANDREW BAKER, BARBARA GOLDMAN
& ELAINE JOHNSON

■ It's the tiny ice crystals that form when the cream hits the cold metal container. It's the rhythmic circling of the dasher. It's the giddy anticipation. But most of all, it's that first sweet, cooling lick that makes homemade ice cream one of summer's most addictive indulgences. • Of course, there's more than ice cream, and flavors go far beyond vanilla. Frozen yogurts and intense fruit sorbets also tempt languid palates. • To make these frosty desserts, you need a good ice cream maker. An old favorite may do the job very well, thank you. But today's frozen-canister and self-refrigerated models make ice cream easier to churn than ever. We review and compare nine makers on page 160. • With the mechanics under control, dip into the 27 recipes that follow. Start with our Ultimate Vanilla Ice Cream as the base for flavor variations, from playful habanero to a sublime caramel and luxurious hazelnut truffle. Or go low-fat with tangy frozen yogurts and fruit-rich sorbets. As toppers, choose sinfully smooth chocolate or caramel sauce. And for more elaborate presentations, try the six desserts on page 164.

PHOTOGRAPHS BY JAMES CARRIER

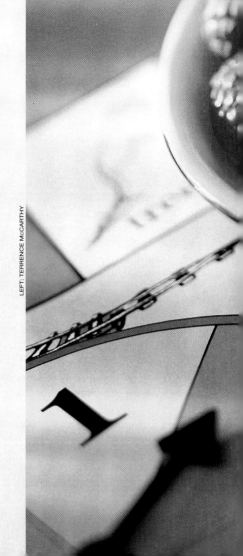

LEFT: TERRENCE McCARTHY

## What's the ultimate in vanilla?

How much better is ice cream made with the richest cream? How much smoother is ice cream made with a cooked custard? To determine the optimum starting point for the ice cream recipes on these pages, we tested 18 variations of vanilla ice cream. The bases for these ice creams were whipping cream, half-and-half, whole milk, and nonfat milk. The number of eggs ranged from zero to four. Some recipes used only yolks, some used whole eggs. The vanilla came from a bean or extract. And all were sweetened the same.

The final products were rated by a *Sunset* taste panel, and the winner crowned as the Ultimate Vanilla Ice Cream. Surprisingly, we found all-whipping-cream ice cream to be too dense—almost like frozen butter. Nonfat-milk ice creams tasted watery and icy. Cooked-custard ice creams were the smoothest. Too many eggs imparted an eggy flavor. Without eggs, the ice cream wasn't quite as smooth, but it was easier to make. Vanilla bean or extract? It's a matter of taste.

## Ultimate Vanilla Ice Cream

PREP AND COOK TIME: About 30 minutes, plus 20 to 40 minutes to freeze

NOTES: To use a vanilla bean instead of vanilla extract, slit pod (about 7 in.) open lengthwise with a small, sharp knife. Scrape seed from pod, add seed and pod to the cream mixture, and heat (step 1). Remove pod from cold custard, rinse, let dry, and save for other uses.

MAKES: About 1 quart

¾  cup **sugar**

3  cups **half-and-half** (light cream)

2  **large eggs**

2  teaspoons **vanilla**

1. In a 2- to 3-quart pan, combine sugar and half-and-half. Stir over high heat until bubbles form at pan edge (scalding, about 180°), 5 to 8 minutes.

2. In a small bowl, whisk eggs to blend.

TAKE VANILLA FOR A SPIN: Turn our basic recipe into Very Berry Ice Cream (page 162) or Habanero Ice Cream (page 161).

Then whisk about ½ cup of the hot cream mixture into eggs. Return egg mixture to pan and stir over medium-low heat with a flexible spatula-scraper, scraping pan bottom and sides thoroughly for even cooking, until custard thickly coats a metal spoon (about 190°), 8 to 10 minutes.

3. Add vanilla to custard.

4. At once, nest pan in ice water and stir custard often until mixture is cold, 10 to 15 minutes.

5. Pour cold custard through a fine strainer into a bowl, then pour mixture into an ice cream maker (1-qt. or larger capacity), or strain directly into the maker; discard residue. Freeze as directed on page 162 until mixture is firm enough to scoop, dasher is hard to turn, or machine stops.

6. Serve softly frozen, or freeze airtight (see page 162).

Per ½ cup: 211 cal., 51% (108 cal.) from fat; 4.2 g protein; 12 g fat (6.8 g sat.); 23 g carbo (0 g fiber); 53 mg sodium; 86 mg chol.

## No-Cook Ultimate Vanilla Ice Cream

PREP TIME: About 5 minutes, plus 20 to 40 minutes to freeze

NOTES: To use a vanilla bean (about 7 in.), slit pod lengthwise with a sharp knife. Scrape seed into sugar, mix, then add cream; do not heat.

MAKES: About 1 quart

Follow directions for **Ultimate Vanilla Ice Cream,** preceding, but omit eggs and do not heat. Instead, mix sugar, half-and-half, and vanilla in a bowl, pour into an ice cream maker (or mix in the maker), and freeze as directed (step 5).

Per ½ cup: 193 cal., 47% (90 cal.) from fat; 2.7 g protein; 10 g fat (6.4 g sat.); 23 g carbo (0 g fiber); 37 mg sodium; 33 mg chol.

## Malted Caramel Ice Cream

PREP AND COOK TIME: About 30 minutes, plus 20 to 40 minutes to freeze

NOTES: Because this mixture is high in sugar, it takes longer to freeze.

MAKES: About 1 quart

Follow directions for **Ultimate Vanilla Ice Cream** (see page 159), omitting sugar. Instead, add 1 recipe's worth of **Caramel Powder** (at right) and 6 tablespoons **malted milk powder** to half-and-half (step 1); caramel powder lumps, then melts when heated.

Per ½ cup: 312 cal., 38% (117 cal.) from fat; 5.6 g protein; 13 g fat (7.3 g sat.); 45 g carbo (0 g fiber); 135 mg sodium; 89 mg chol.

## Hazelnut Truffle Ice Cream

PREP AND COOK TIME: About 1½ hours, plus at least 3½ hours to freeze

NOTES: Put a 2- to 3-quart metal bowl in the freezer before starting to cook. With the liqueur, the mixture has to get colder than usual to freeze.

MAKES: About 1¼ quarts

# Fabulous sauces & toppings

## Deep, Dark Chocolate Sauce

PREP AND COOK TIME: **10 minutes**

NOTES: If making ahead, chill airtight up to 1 month. To soften, reheat.

MAKES: About 1 cup

- 5 ounces **bittersweet** or **semisweet chocolate,** chopped
- ⅔ cup **whipping cream**

Combine chocolate and cream in a 1- to 2-quart pan. Stir over low heat just until chocolate melts, 5 to 7 minutes. Use hot, warm, or cool.

Per tablespoon: 72 cal., 78% (56 cal.) from fat; 0.8 g protein; 6.2 g fat (3.6 g sat.); 5.2 g carbo (0.2 g fiber); 3.4 mg sodium; 11 mg chol.

## Caramel Powder

PREP AND COOK TIME: **50 minutes**

1. In a 350° oven, bake 1 cup **hazelnuts** in an 8- or 9-inch square pan until nuts are golden beneath skins, about 12 minutes. Pour nuts onto a towel and rub to remove loose skins. Discard skins and let nuts cool. Coarsely chop ½ cup nuts.

## Ice cream makers: power + convenience = price . . .

Models use ice and salt or frozen canisters, or are self-refrigerated. Some work with the flick of a switch; others take elbow power.

| BRAND | White Mountain | White Mountain | Cuisinart | Donvier | Krups |
|---|---|---|---|---|---|
| MODEL | Ice Cream Freezer F64304 or F64306 | Ice Cream Freezer F69204 or F69206 | Frozen Yogurt–Ice Cream & Sorbet Maker, ICE-20 | Ice Cream Maker 837407 or 837409W | La Glacière 358 |
| FREEZING METHOD | Ice and salt | Ice and salt | Frozen canister | Frozen canister | Frozen canister |
| POWER | Hand crank | Electric | Electric | Hand crank | Electric |
| PHONE | (800) 343-0065 or (800) 363-8144 | (800) 343-0065 or (800) 363-8144 | (800) 726-0190; call for nearest retail source | (800) 243-0852 (Sur La Table) | (800) 526-5377 |
| PRICE | $135 or $143 | $194 or $204 | $85 | $50 or $60 | $95 or less |
| CAPACITY (MAX.) | 4 or 6 quarts | 4 or 6 quarts | 1½ quarts | 1 quart | 1½ quarts |
| FREEZING TIME (APPROX. FOR 1 QT.) | 30 minutes | 30 minutes | 30 minutes | 20 minutes | 25 minutes |
| PROS & CONS | Mixtures freeze evenly, smoothly. Labor-intensive. Set in a tray to catch leaking brine. Fill 6-quart machine to at least the 2-quart level. | Mixtures freeze evenly, smoothly. Very noisy. Set in a tray to catch leaking brine. Fill 6-quart machine to at least the 2-quart level. | Mixtures freeze evenly. Easy to use. In testing, motor occasionally stopped before ice cream was frozen and had to rest 10 minutes before restarting. | Mixtures freeze evenly. Model 837409W has more insulation. Easy to use and clean; few parts. Quiet. Makes the densest ice cream. | Mixtures freeze evenly and smoothly. Among frozen canisters, this machine makes the creamiest product. Easy to use and clean; few parts. |

DON'T PASS GO without trying silky chocolate and rich caramel sauces.

NOTES: Mixture is fluffier than sugar, so you get more than you start with. For a simple treat, sprinkle onto servings of ice cream.

MAKES: About 1 cup and 6 tablespoons

1⅓ cups **sugar**

1. Line a 10- by 15-inch pan with foil.
2. In a 10- to 12-inch nonstick frying pan over medium-high heat, shake sugar often until melted and amber-colored, 8 to 10 minutes.
3. Pour melted sugar onto foil. Let stand until hard, about 30 minutes. Peel off foil and break caramel into chunks.
4. With motor running, drop chunks into a food processor and whirl into a fine powder. Or whirl chunks in batches in a blender. Immediately store in airtight container. Powder keeps indefinitely, but absorbs moisture quickly if exposed to air.

Per tablespoon: 47 cal., 0% (0 cal.) from fat; 0 g protein; 0 g fat; 12 g carbo (0 g fiber); 0.1 mg sodium; 0 mg chol.

## Caramel Velvet Sauce

PREP AND COOK TIME: About 10 minutes, plus at least 10 minutes to cool
NOTES: If making ahead, chill airtight up to 1 month. Reheat to soften.
MAKES: About 2 cups

2 cups **whipping cream**
1 recipe **Caramel Powder** (preceding)

In a 6- to 8-quart pan, bring cream and caramel powder to a rolling boil, stirring (powder lumps, then melts). Serve warm or cool.

Per tablespoon: 76 cal., 54% (41 cal.) from fat; 0.3 g protein; 4.6 g fat (2.9 g sat.); 8.7 g carbo (0 g fiber); 5.2 mg sodium; 17 mg chol.

2. Prepare **Deep, Dark Chocolate Sauce** (see page 160) using **semisweet**, not bittersweet, **chocolate**. Pour sauce into a blender and add whole hazelnuts, 6 tablespoons **Frangelico** or other hazelnut-flavor liqueur, and 2 tablespoons **corn syrup**. Whirl until chocolate truffle sauce is very smoothly puréed.
3. Return chocolate truffle sauce to pan and nest pan in ice water. Stir often until sauce is cold, about 20 minutes. Scrape into chilled bowl (see notes) and freeze while making ice cream.
4. Follow directions for **Ultimate Vanilla Ice Cream** (see page 159), adding reserved chopped nuts to cold custard in ice cream maker (step 5).
5. When ice cream is frozen (step 5), remove bowl with truffle sauce from freezer. Stir sauce briefly to soften, then quickly scoop ice cream into bowl. With a flexible spatula-scraper, swirl chocolate through ice cream, using 4 or 5 strokes.
6. Return to freezer for at least 3 hours to firm. Package airtight if storing longer.

Per ½ cup: 393 cal., 60% (234 cal.) from fat; 5.8 g protein; 26 g fat (12 g sat.); 35 g carbo (1.8 g fiber); 55 mg sodium; 87 mg chol.

## Habanero Ice Cream

PREP AND COOK TIME: About 30 minutes, plus 20 to 40 minutes to freeze
NOTES: For flavor variations, try jellies made with jalapeños, Scotch bonnets, or other hot chilies.
MAKES: About 1 quart

Follow directions for **Ultimate Vanilla Ice Cream** (see page 159). When ice cream is firm enough to scoop (step 5), add ¼ cup **habanero chili jelly**. Close container and turn dasher just until jelly is streaked through ice cream. Serve or store as directed.

Per ½ cup: 236 cal., 46% (108 cal.) from fat; 4.2 g protein; 12 g fat (6.8 g sat.); 29 g carbo (0 g fiber); 55 mg sodium; 86 mg chol.

## sometimes, but not always

| | Sunbeam | Lello | Lello | Simac |
|---|---|---|---|---|
| |  |  |  |  |
| | Home Soft Serve Ice Cream & Frozen Yogurt Machine 4742 and 4743 (with stand) | Lucina 6607 | Dream Ice Cream Machine 12422 | Gelataio Magnum Plus 2758 |
| | Frozen canister | Self-refrigerated | Self-refrigerated | Self-refrigerated |
| | Electric | Electric | Electric | Electric |
| | (800) 528-7713 | (800) 338-3232 (Chef's Catalog) | (800) 243-0852 (Sur La Table) | (800) 338-3232 (Chef's Catalog) |
| | $150 or $159 | $600 | $1,195 | $500 |
| | 1 quart | 1½ quarts | 2 quarts | 1⅓ quarts |
| | 25 minutes | 35 minutes | 40 minutes | 30 minutes |
| | Use only smooth mixtures or dispenser clogs. Even freezing. Introduces air for soft-serve texture. If mixture gets too firm, machine may stall or stop dispensing. Complicated to assemble and clean. | Mixtures freeze evenly. Easy to operate. Nonremovable freezing chamber. Cleaning is awkward. | Mixtures freeze evenly, smoothly. Machine very easy to operate. Fill chamber to at least the 1½-quart level. Nonremovable freezing chamber. | Mixtures freeze evenly, smoothly. Machine very easy to operate. Removable freezing chamber makes |

## Freezing facts

**HOW TO USE ICE CREAM MAKERS.** Before you start, read the manufacturer's instructions for assembly and use. Each machine operates differently. Canisters that are frozen need to sit upright in the freezer 8 to 24 hours (depending on maker and freezer temperature); many find it convenient to store empty canisters in the freezer. If salt and ice are used, the ratio for freezing is 5 parts ice (crushed or small cubes) to 1 part rock salt (also called ice cream salt) or 3 parts table salt. A higher ratio of salt to ice freezes faster but produces a coarser-textured frozen dessert. Keep machines that are self-refrigerated upright at all times.

**HOW LONG DOES IT TAKE TO FREEZE ICE CREAM?** Machines vary, but it takes 20 to 40 minutes to freeze a quart of chilled ingredients until firm enough to scoop into a bowl (not onto a cone). Mixtures with high proportions of sugar or liqueurs take longer to freeze.

If you can see the mixture as the dasher turns, you can tell when it's frozen. Some machines give other indications— the dasher becomes hard to turn or stops.

**VOLUME.** Yields vary depending upon the maker. All introduce some air as the dasher turns, but self-refrigerated machines incorporate the most.

**FIRMING AND STORING.** To get frozen desserts hard enough to scoop onto a cone, or to store them, transfer when frozen to an airtight container and put in the freezer at least 3 hours or up to 1 week.

If freezing with ice and salt, leave the frozen dessert in ice and salt up to 3 hours.

For best flavor and texture, serve frozen desserts within a week. On longer standing, icy crystals develop.

## Lemon Meringue Ice Cream

**PREP AND COOK TIME:** About 30 minutes, plus about 3½ hours to freeze
**NOTES:** Buy hard meringues at a supermarket or a bakery. Put a 2- to 3-quart metal bowl in the freezer before starting to cook.
**MAKES:** About 1½ quarts

Follow directions for **Ultimate Vanilla Ice Cream** (see page 159). Quickly transfer frozen mixture to a chilled bowl (see notes) and add ¾ cup **lemon curd** and 1½ cups 1- to 2-inch broken chunks **baked hard meringues** (about 1½ oz. total). With a flexible spatula-scraper, swirl through ice cream, then cover airtight and freeze until firm enough to scoop, at least 3 hours.

Per ½ cup: 205 cal., 39% (79 cal.) from fat; 4 g protein; 8.8 g fat (4.5 g sat.); 31 g carbo (0 g fiber); 55 mg sodium; 58 mg chol.

## Espresso Thyself Ice Cream

**PREP AND COOK TIME:** About 40 minutes, plus 20 to 40 minutes to freeze
**NOTES:** You can buy brewed espresso at a coffee shop.
**MAKES:** About 1 quart

**1.** Put 6 tablespoons **finely ground espresso roast** or other dark-roast **coffee** in a paper-lined coffee filter set over a pitcher. Pour 1⅓ cups **hot** (about 190°) **water** into filter and let drip through. Measure and add water if needed to make 1 cup coffee.

**2.** Follow directions for **Ultimate Vanilla Ice Cream** (see page 159), reducing half-and-half to 2 cups. Add coffee to cream mixture (step 1). Continue as directed.

Per ½ cup: 173 cal., 43% (74 cal.) from fat; 3.4 g protein; 8.2 g fat (4.7 g sat.); 22 g carbo (0 g fiber); 41 mg sodium; 75 mg chol.

## Mozambique Spice Ice Cream

**PREP AND COOK TIME:** About 30 minutes, plus 20 to 40 minutes to freeze
**MAKES:** About 1 quart

Follow directions for **Ultimate Vanilla Ice Cream** (see page 159), mixing ⅛ teaspoon *each* **ground nutmeg, ground cloves,** and **ground cinnamon** with sugar (step 1).

Per ½ cup: 212 cal., 51% (108 cal.) from fat; 4.2 g protein; 12 g fat (6.8 g sat.); 23 g carbo (0 g fiber); 53 mg sodium; 86 mg chol.

## Biscotti Crunch Espresso Ice Cream

**PREP AND COOK TIME:** About 30 minutes, plus 20 to 40 minutes to freeze
**MAKES:** About 1 quart

**1.** Follow directions for **Ultimate Vanilla Ice Cream** (see page 159) and add coffee as directed in **Espresso Thyself Ice Cream** (below left).

**2.** When ice cream is almost firm enough to scoop (step 5), open freezer container and add 1 cup chopped (about ½-in. chunks) **almond biscotti** and ⅔ cup coarsely chopped **chocolate-covered coffee beans.** Close container and continue as directed.

Per ½ cup: 287 cal., 44% (126 cal.) from fat; 5.5 g protein; 14 g fat (7.2 g sat.); 38 g carbo (1.5 g fiber); 76 mg sodium; 81 mg chol.

## Double-Ginger Dried Cherry Ice Cream

**PREP AND COOK TIME:** About 35 minutes, plus 20 to 40 minutes to freeze
**MAKES:** About 1 quart

**1.** Follow directions for **Ultimate Vanilla Ice Cream** (see page 159), reducing sugar to ⅔ cup. In a blender or food processor, whirl sugar, half-and-half, and ⅓ cup **crystallized ginger** until ginger is minced. Continue as directed (step 1).
**2.** To cold custard in ice cream maker (step 5), add 2 to 4 tablespoons minced **fresh ginger** and ⅓ cup finely chopped **dried sour cherries.** Freeze as directed.

Per ½ cup: 254 cal., 43% (108 cal.) from fat; 4.3 g protein; 12 g fat (6.8 g sat.); 34 g carbo (0.4 g fiber); 61 mg sodium; 86 mg chol.

## Very Berry Ice Cream

**PREP AND COOK TIME:** About 30 minutes, plus 20 to 40 minutes to freeze
**MAKES:** About 1 quart

**1.** In a blender, whirl 1 cup *each* rinsed **raspberries** and **blackberries** until smoothly puréed. Rub purée through a fine strainer into a bowl; discard seeds. Mix ⅔ cup finely mashed **strawberries** and 6 tablespoons **sugar** with purée.
**2.** Follow directions for **Ultimate Vanilla Ice Cream** (see page 159), reducing half-and-half to 2 cups. Add berry mixture to cold custard in ice cream maker (step 5). Freeze as directed.

Per ½ cup: 229 cal., 33% (75 cal.) from fat; 3.7 g protein; 8.3 g fat (4.7 g sat.); 36 g carbo (1.9 g fiber); 41 mg sodium; 75 mg chol.

## Hello Hawaii Ice Cream

**PREP AND COOK TIME:** About 30 minutes, plus 20 to 40 minutes to freeze
**NOTES:** Unsweetened sliced dried coconut (also called coconut chips) is sold in Asian markets and some natural-food stores. Or use sweetened shredded dried coconut.
**MAKES:** About 1 quart

1. Follow directions for **Ultimate Vanilla Ice Cream** (see page 159), but reduce half-and-half to 1¼ cups and add 1 can (10 oz.) **coconut milk** to cream mixture (step 1).

2. As ice cream churns, stir ¾ cup **unsweetened sliced dried coconut** in a 10- to 12-inch frying pan over medium-high heat until toasted, about 4 minutes. Pour from pan and let cool.

3. When ice cream is almost firm enough to scoop (step 5), add coconut and ¾ cup chopped **roasted, salted macadamia nuts.** Continue as directed.

Per ½ cup: 340 cal., 69% (234 cal.) from fat; 4.8 g protein; 26 g fat (15 g sat.); 25 g carbo (0.4 g fiber); 93 mg sodium; 67 mg chol.

## Peach Frozen Yogurt

PREP TIME: About 10 minutes, plus 20 to 40 minutes to freeze

MAKES: About 1 quart

- 1½ cups peeled, coarsely chopped **ripe peaches**
- ⅔ cup **sugar**
- 3 cartons (8 oz. each; about 2½ cups total) **peach-flavor whole-milk** or low-fat **yogurt**
- 2 tablespoons **lemon juice**
- 2 teaspoons **vanilla**

1. In a bowl, use a potato masher or fork to finely crush peaches with sugar.

2. Add yogurt, lemon juice, and vanilla and mix well.

3. Nest bowl in ice water and stir often until mixture is cold, about 5 minutes.

4. Pour yogurt mixture into an ice cream maker (1-qt. or larger capacity). Freeze as directed on page 162 until mixture is firm enough to scoop or dasher is hard to turn or stops.

5. Serve softly frozen, or freeze airtight (see page 162).

Per ½ cup: 165 cal., 13% (21 cal.) from fat; 4 g protein; 2.3 g fat (1.8 g sat.); 32 g carbo (0.5 g fiber); 54 mg sodium; 7.5 mg chol.

## Plum-Cardamom Frozen Yogurt

PREP AND COOK TIME: About 35 minutes, plus 20 to 40 minutes to freeze

MAKES: About 1 quart

1. Follow directions for **Peach Frozen Yogurt**, preceding, but instead of peaches, use unpeeled **ripe plum slices.** Instead of peach-flavor yogurt, use **vanilla-flavor whole-milk** or low-fat **yogurt.** Omit vanilla.

2. In a 2- to 3-quart pan over medium heat, simmer plums, sugar, and 1½

NUMBERS ADD UP to flavor, not fat, in plum-cardamom and peach frozen yogurts.

teaspoons **ground cardamom,** stirring often, until plums are soft enough to mash, 8 to 10 minutes. In pan, finely mash fruit with a potato masher or fork.

3. Chill plums (step 3), then add yogurt and lemon juice (step 2); continue as directed.

Per ½ cup: 164 cal., 13% (22 cal.) from fat; 4 g protein; 2.4 g fat (1.8 g sat.); 32 g carbo (0.6 g fiber); 53 mg sodium; 7.5 mg chol.

## Lemon Cheesecake Frozen Yogurt

PREP TIME: About 25 minutes, plus 20 to 40 minutes to freeze

MAKES: About 1 quart

1. In bowl with a mixer, beat 1 package (8 oz.) **neufchâtel** (light cream) **cheese** and ⅔ cup **sugar** to blend. Add 1 teaspoon grated **lemon peel,** ¼ cup **lemon juice,** and 3 cartons (8 oz. each; 2½ cups total) **vanilla-flavor whole-milk** or low-fat **yogurt.** Beat to blend.

2. Follow directions for **Peach Frozen Yogurt** (above left), starting at step 3.

Per ½ cup: 223 cal., 36% (80 cal.) from fat; 6.6 g protein; 8.9 g fat (6 g sat.); 30 g carbo (0 g fiber); 167 mg sodium; 29 mg chol.

## Raspberry-Blueberry Sorbet

PREP AND COOK TIME: About 35 minutes, plus 20 to 40 minutes to freeze

NOTES: In the freezer, sorbet gets very hard. To serve, thaw partially, break into chunks, and beat to a slush with a mixer or a food processor.

MAKES: About 1 quart

- 1½ cups **blueberries,** rinsed
  About ⅔ cup **sugar**
- 3 cups **raspberries,** rinsed
  About 1 tablespoon **lemon juice**

1. In a 1½- to 2-quart pan over high heat, frequently stir blueberries, ⅔ cup sugar, and ¼ cup water until berries begin to pop, 4 to 5 minutes.

2. In a blender or food processor, purée blueberry mixture, raspberries, and 1 tablespoon lemon juice. Rub through a fine strainer into a bowl; discard residue. Add more sugar and lemon juice if desired. Nest bowl in ice water; stir often until mixture is cold, 15 to 20 minutes.

3. Pour chilled purée into an ice cream maker (1-qt. or larger capacity). Freeze as directed on page 162 until sorbet is firm enough to scoop, the dasher is

# Gilding the lily: six cool recipes

**TOASTED POUND CAKE SANDWICH.** For each serving, toast 2 slices (½ in. thick) **pound cake.** Drizzle 2 to 3 tablespoons **Deep, Dark Chocolate Sauce** around cake. Add ¼ cup rinsed, drained **raspberries** and/or blackberries. Top slice with ⅔ cup **Ultimate Vanilla Ice Cream,** then set remaining cake on ice cream.

Per serving: 526 cal., 48% (252 cal.) from fat; 6.8 g protein; 28 g fat (17 g sat.); 64 g carbo (2 g fiber); 271 mg sodium; 215 mg chol.

**TROPICAL SUNDAE.** For each serving, set 1 or 2 **pineapple** slices on a plate. Top with ⅔ cup **Hello Hawaii Ice Cream.** Pour 2 to 3 tablespoons **Caramel Velvet Sauce** over ice cream, then sprinkle with 1 to 2 tablespoons coarsely chopped **roasted macadamia nuts.**

Per serving: 476 cal., 62% (297 cal.) from fat; 4.8 g protein; 33 g fat (16 g sat.); 45 g carbo (1.3 g fiber); 73 mg sodium; 77 mg chol.

**FROSTY LEMON PIE.** For 8 servings, fill a 9-inch **purchased graham cracker crumb crust** with about 1 quart **Lemon Meringue Ice Cream** or Lemon Cheesecake Frozen Yogurt. Cover airtight and return to freezer until firm, at least 2 hours or up to 2 days. Unwrap and drizzle pie with 2 to 4 tablespoons stirred **lemon curd.** Sprinkle pie with 1½ cups rinsed, drained **raspberries.** Cut into wedges.

Per serving: 441 cal., 39% (171 cal.) from fat; 7.4 g protein; 19 g fat (7.8 g sat.); 65 g carbo (1.8 g fiber); 221 mg sodium; 86 mg chol.

**BERRY BROWNIE SUNDAE.** For each serving, place a **brownie** (2 oz.) on a plate. Top with ½ cup **Very Berry Ice Cream** or Raspberry-Blueberry Sorbet. Pour about 3 tablespoons **Deep, Dark Chocolate Sauce** over ice cream, then top with 2 tablespoons **whipped cream** and curls of **semi-sweet chocolate.**

Per serving: 734 cal., 51% (378 cal.) from fat; 9.3 g protein; 42 g fat (21 g sat.); 90 g carbo (4 g fiber); 231 mg sodium; 135 mg chol.

**FROZEN S'MORE.** For each sandwich, set 1 **mini fudge-coated graham cracker** on a plate, top with 1 tablespoon **Mozambique Spice Ice Cream** or Espresso Thyself Ice Cream and 1 tablespoon **marshmallow cream.** Gently press another mini fudge-coated graham cracker onto the ice cream.

Per serving: 151 cal., 37% (56 cal.) from fat; 1.2 g protein; 6.2 g fat (3.9 g sat.); 23 g carbo (0.5 g fiber); 82 mg sodium; 11 mg chol.

**SPARKLING FLOAT.** To make each serving, pour about ¾ cup chilled **sparkling Muscat wine,** such as an Italian asti spumante or domestic Ballatore, into a tall glass (at least 1¼-cup size). Add ⅔ cup **Honeydew Sorbet** or Raspberry-Blueberry Sorbet. Garnish with a **mint sprig.**

Per serving: 167 cal., 0.5% (0.9 cal.) from fat; 0.5 g protein; 0.1 g fat (0 g sat.); 14 g carbo (0.6 g fiber); 15 mg sodium; 0 mg chol.

FOR A GOOD DEAL, sandwich ice cream with pound cake.

---

hard to turn, or the machine stops.

**4.** Serve, or freeze airtight (see page 162).

Per ½ cup: 103 cal., 3.5% (3.6 cal.) from fat; 0.6 g protein; 0.4 g fat (0 g sat.); 26 g carbo (2.8 g fiber); 2.2 mg sodium; 0 mg chol.

## Honeydew Sorbet

**PREP TIME:** About 25 minutes, plus 20 to 40 minutes to freeze

**NOTES:** Buy a honeydew melon or piece weighing about 3½ pounds. To store and serve, see Raspberry-Blueberry Sorbet notes preceding.

**MAKES:** About 1 quart

> About ⅓ cup **sugar**
>
> 2 tablespoons grated **lime** peel (green part only)
>
> About ½ cup **lime juice**
>
> 4½ cups diced (about ½ in.) **honeydew melon**

**1.** In a bowl, mash ⅓ cup sugar and lime peel with a spoon to release oils. Let stand 5 to 10 minutes.

**2.** Stir ½ cup lime juice into sugar mixture. Pour mixture through a fine strainer into a blender or food processor; discard lime peel.

**3.** Add melon, a portion at a time, and whirl until smooth. Return purée to bowl. Taste, and if desired, add more sugar and lime juice. Nest bowl in ice and stir often until mixture is cold, 5 to 10 minutes.

**4.** Pour chilled purée into an ice cream maker (1-qt. or larger capacity). Freeze as directed on page 162 until sorbet is firm to scoop, dasher is hard to turn, or machine stops.

**5.** Serve, or freeze airtight (see page 162).

Per ½ cup: 71 cal., 1.3% (0.9 cal.) from fat; 0.5 g protein; 0.1 g fat (0 g sat.); 19 g carbo (0.9 g fiber); 9.9 mg sodium; 0 mg chol.

## Nectarine-Gewürztraminer Sorbet

**PREP TIME:** About 20 minutes, plus 20 to 40 minutes to freeze

**NOTES:** To store and serve, see Raspberry-Blueberry Sorbet notes (page 163).

**MAKES:** About 1 quart

> About 2 pounds **ripe nectarines,** rinsed and sliced
>
> About 3 tablespoons **lemon juice**
>
> ¾ cup **late-harvest Gewürztraminer** or late-harvest Johannisberg Riesling
>
> About 3 tablespoons **sugar**

**1.** In a bowl, mix nectarine slices with 3 tablespoons lemon juice. Whirl, a portion at a time, in a blender or food processor until very smooth. Return purée to bowl.

**2.** Add Gewürztraminer, sugar to taste, and more lemon juice if desired. Nest bowl in ice water and stir often until mixture is cold, 5 to 10 minutes.

**3.** Pour chilled purée into an ice cream maker (1-qt. or larger capacity). Freeze as directed on page 162 until sorbet is firm enough to scoop, dasher is hard to turn, or machine stops.

**4.** Serve, or freeze airtight (see page 162).

Per ½ cup: 85 cal., 5.3% (4.5 cal.) from fat; 1 g protein; 0.5 g fat (0 g sat.); 17 g carbo (1.7 g fiber); 2.3 mg sodium; 0 mg chol. ◆

# Emperors of ice cream

*Sunset's* readers pick
the West's best

BY PETER FISH

FAIR OAKS PHARMACY—Where the sweet-toothed meet in South Pasadena.

When we asked *Sunset* readers to choose their favorite ice cream parlors and soda fountains, we received a triple dip of votes— hundreds of letters, postcards, and e-mails. We learned that when it comes time to determine where the rocky meets the road, different people have different priorities. Some of you will not settle for anything less than ice cream churned right on the premises. Others demand a patina of history—tin ceilings and malted milk canisters dating back to somewhere around the Harding administration.

We listened. We tallied votes. We performed intensive legwork—or, more accurately, spoonwork and strawwork.

Our judgment is that the best ice cream parlors mix hedonism and restraint. They appear innocent at first, with their cool marble counters and their demure wrought-iron chairs. But in their hot fudge hearts, they are temples to sensual abandon. In a world wearied by the grim arithmetic of calorie and cholesterol counts, the best ice cream parlors and soda fountains whisper, "Go ahead, live a little." Sure, you could be somewhere sensible, eating lentils and plotting out your 401(k). Instead you command a vinyl booth and debate the larger questions. Mocha almond or cookie vanilla? Two scoops or three?

"The only emperor is the emperor of ice-cream," poet Wallace Stevens wrote. Below, we happily present 40 such emperors—your choices for the best ice cream parlors and soda fountains in the West. Did we miss your favorite? Let us know. This is a topic that may require much additional research.

## Northwest

**GOODY'S SODA FOUNTAIN, BEND, OR.** "This is just a really great place," a Bend friend advised. We agree. In an old brick building downtown, Goody's makes its own ice cream, toppings, and chocolates, including smashing coconut clusters. Goody's also has shops in Sunriver, Oregon (541/593-2155), and Boise (see mountain listing). *957 N.W. Wall St.; (541) 389-5185.*

**MARY LOU'S MILK BOTTLE, SPOKANE.** Old photos decorate the art deco interior of this historic city landmark— a three-story concrete rendition of an old-fashioned milk bottle. Mary Lou's makes 20 luscious flavors of ice cream and yogurt, and also serves reasonably priced burgers, sandwiches, and Greek food. *802 W. Garland Ave.; (509) 325-1772.*

**MUSEUM SODA FOUNTAIN, YAKIMA, WA.** The Yakima Valley Museum's re-creation of the 1930s Jordan's drugstore soda fountain—the last of many such old-time establishments in Yakima— features soda jerks, neon signs, and salvaged fountain stools, syrup pumps, and glassware. Hits here are the fizzy Green River phosphates, hot fudge sundaes, and lush banana splits. The fountain also serves hot dogs, chili, and soup. *2105 Tieton Dr.; (509) 248-0747.*

**POULSBO DRUG STORE, POULSBO, WA.** This fountain is pretty much the same as it was when it was founded in 1929. Milk shakes and Green River sodas are popular. But raves go to the old-style hand-stirred ice cream sodas. They come in 30 flavors—chocolate, strawberry, and vanilla are tops. "Some things in life don't change," says owner Sally Kvam. *18911 Front St. N.E.; (360) 779-2737.*

**SNOHOMISH VALLEY ICE CREAM AND CANDY COMPANY, SNOHOMISH, WA.** No marble top, but wrought-iron chairs, thick shakes bearing an outrageous mound of whipped cream, handmade waffle cones, and hard candies in glass jars. *902 First St.; (360) 568-1133.*

**TAYLOR'S FOUNTAIN & GIFTS, INDEPENDENCE, OR.** Run by four generations of the Taylor family, the fountain serves the same style of ice cream sodas, phosphates, and even sarsaparillas that were all the rage when the family purchased the fountain in 1943. *296 S. Main*

Street.; (503) 838-1124.
**TOLLY'S, OAKLAND, OR.** This place serves traditional soda fountain treats made with local Umpqua ice cream, plus homemade pie and cinnamon rolls, at a milk-glass counter surrounded by tall jars of sweets. *115 Locust St.; (541) 459-3796.*

## Northern California

**AUBURN DRUG CO., AUBURN.** Choose one of 12 stools at the marble counter of this drugstore—active since 1896—and enjoy a lime-flavor Irish Soda. *815 Lincoln Way; (530) 885-6524.*

**BIG AL'S DRIVE IN, CHICO.** For folks nostalgic about cruising *American Graffiti*–style, Big Al's is a dying breed—a stopping place for classic car buffs and people who like to hang out. The signs boast "Happy Burgers" and "Our Shakes Are Triple Thick." Many combinations of shakes and malts are on the menu, but nothing costs more than $5. *1844 Esplanade; (530) 342-2722.*

**BIG DIPPER, ST. HELENA.** One block off the touristy main drag, the Big Dipper is a museum of ice cream parlor memorabilia. A wall display shaped like a giant vanilla cone contains a triangular ice cream dipper from 1908, a circa-1920 square ice cream sandwich dipper, and an oval scoop specifically for banana splits. Early milk shake blenders and Coca-Cola

WHAT TIME IS IT? Time for ice cream, of course.

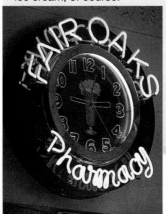

paraphernalia are exhibited. The Big Dipper also features a tempting penny-candy counter, old-fashioned coin-operated games, and a working jukebox. *1336A Oak Ave.; (707) 963-2616.*

**FENTONS CREAMERY AND RESTAURANT, OAKLAND.** This beloved East Bay institution proves that quantity and quality are not mutually exclusive: portions are big enough to satisfy any UC Berkeley lineman, and often have. *4226 Piedmont Ave.; (510) 658-7000.*

> " In their hot fudge hearts, they are temples to sensual abandon. "

**GAIL'S OLDIES & GOODIES CAFE, ST. HELENA.** Gail's blends the ambience of a vintage ice cream emporium with the sophisticated fare of a wine country cafe. In addition to ice cream concoctions, Gail's serves homemade fudge, espresso drinks, and menu items like omelets, pizzas, steaks, salads, and local wines. A coin-operated player piano emits cheerful melodies, and the walls are plastered with metal advertising signs touting Nehi soda and Peter Pan ice cream—plus autographed photos of Mickey Mantle, Frank Sinatra, and Barbara Stanwyck. *1347 Main St.; (707) 963-3332.*

**LASSEN DRUG CO., CHESTER.** This little-bit-of-everything store, in business since 1946, houses an old-fashioned soda fountain framed with stained glass and curios. Pull up a stooll for a banana split, milk shake, or sundae with friendly folks in this sleepy mountain town near Lake Almanor. *220 Main St.; (530) 258-2261.*

**PENINSULA FOUNTAIN & GRILL, PALO ALTO.** An oasis of

homespun values (and superior milk shakes) in this growingly glitzy town. *566 Emerson St.; (650) 323-3131.*

**SHUBERT'S ICE CREAM AND CANDY STORE, CHICO.** The Shubert family has owned this Chico landmark since 1938, and today the third generation sells homemade ice cream to eat on the benches out front, or hand-packed to go. Candies range from colorful rock candy on a stick to sugar-free chocolates. On summer nights, the lines of families and college students overflow onto the sidewalks. *178 E. Seventh St.; (530) 342-7163.*

**ST. FRANCIS FOUNTAIN, SAN FRANCISCO.** A wonderful, venerable sundae-lovers' hangout in the Mission District. *2801 24th St.; (415) 826-4200.*

**TOY BOAT DESSERT CAFE, SAN FRANCISCO.** Good sundaes and Xena Warrior Princess action figures decking the walls. 401 Clement St. at Fifth Ave.; (415) 751-7505.

**VIC'S ICE CREAM, SACRAMENTO.** Owned by the Rutledge family since 1947; try the cinnamon-chocolate-almond jik jak. *3199 Riverside Blvd.; (916) 448-0892.*

## Southern California

**BURNARDO'Z ICE CREAM PARLOR-DELI AND JUICE BAR, ARROYO GRANDE.** Homemade ice cream on a Central Coast town's pretty main street; our fave is the Mexican chocolate. *114 W. Branch St.; (805) 481-2041.*

**DEWAR'S CANDY SHOP, BAKERSFIELD.** It's not large, it's not ornate. But Dewar's—just down the road from Bakers-

field High—has been making fine ice cream for almost 90 years. A bag of its peanut butter chews will keep your mouth happy for hours. *1120 Eye St.; (805) 322-0933.*

**FAIR OAKS PHARMACY AND SODA FOUNTAIN, SOUTH PASADENA.** This joint garnered so many votes we almost suspect ballot stuffing. But the Fair Oaks deserves the applause. Meredith and Michael Miller took a pharmacy (in business since 1915), added an early 1900s soda fountain (moved here from Joplin, Missouri), and began mixing up magnificent shakes, sundaes, and sodas. And—a rarity—you can still get a prescription filled once you're done slurping that last droplet of root beer float. *1526 Mission St.; (626) 799-1414.*

**FOSSELMAN'S, ALHAMBRA.** Homey but proud, with walls displaying 70 years' worth of gold medals for ice cream artistry. Green tea and other Asian flavors of ice cream testify to the changing demographics of Alhambra and environs, while a knockout lemon custard proves Fosselman's reverence for the classics. *1824 W. Main St.; (626) 282-6533.*

**JULIAN DRUG STORE & SODA FOUNTAIN, JULIAN.** This San Diego County town is famous for its apples—so order the Rosemarie sundae with apple pie filling. *2134 Main St.; (760) 765-0332.*

**SODA JERKS, PASADENA.** Phosphates and egg creams served with Andy Hardy élan. *219 S. Fair Oaks Ave.; (626) 583-8031.*

**SUPERIOR DAIRY, HANFORD.** Why do we love the Superior Dairy? The homemade ice cream helps, of course. But so does the fact that the dairy's strawberry pink booths overlook one of the prettiest town squares in California's San Joaquin Valley. *325 N. Douty St.; (209) 582-0481.*

**WATSON DRUG AND SODA FOUNTAIN, ORANGE.** Everything about Watson Drug, which has been the center of activity in Old Towne Orange since 1899, is comfortably familiar, from red swivel counter seats to ice cream dreams like old-fashioned malts and cola floats. And don't overlook the old-time special meals— liver and onions, ham and lima beans, country fried steak. *116 E. Chapman Ave.; (714) 633-1050.*

## Southwest

**CLARKDALE ANTIQUE EMPORIUM & SODA FOUNTAIN, CLARKDALE, AZ.** If you're of a certain age, sitting on the stools at the Clarkdale Antique Emporium's old-fashioned fountain will make you feel like a teenager again. Sundaes, sodas, and homemade pie à la mode are the specialties. *907 Main St.; (520) 634-2828.*

**MARY COYLE ICE CREAM, PHOENIX.** A new location and nonfat yogurt may be two concessions to modern times, but Mary Coyle Ice Cream is still scooping out homemade ice cream in flavors such as butter brittle and lemon custard, just the way it did when it opened in 1951. Kill yourself with Suicide (four scoops of ice cream layered with hot fudge, caramel, and marshmallow sauces) or share a Mountain (7 pounds of ice cream and toppings) with a few friends. *5521 N. Seventh Ave.; (602) 265-0405.*

**MODEL PHARMACY, ALBUQUERQUE.** Turquoise awnings and lavender window frames set off the ice cream parlor inside, where patrons sit at the counter or at small round tables for banana splits, shakes, or sundaes. Lunch and espresso drinks are also available. *3636 Monte Vista Blvd.; (505) 255-8686.*

**PLAZA DRUGS, LAS VEGAS, NM.** This longtime fixture on a corner of the historic plaza still serves classic sundaes, cones, and shakes. Wood floorboards creak reassuringly as you make your way to a stool at the fountain or a table with white wire-backed chairs. Try the banana split. *178 Bridge St.; (505) 425-5221.*

**SUGAR BOWL, SCOTTSDALE, AZ.** For 40 years, the pink-and-white Sugar Bowl has been the place to go to satisfy an ice cream craving in Scottsdale. Try a Camelback soda or an extra-luscious malt, in which the glass is lined with fudge, caramel, or marshmallow sauce. Sandwiches and salads are also served. *4005 N. Scottsdale Rd.; (602) 946-0051.*

## Mountain

**BLUEBIRD RESTAURANT, LOGAN, UT.** The bluebird of happiness has lived in Logan since 1914. Here is the parlor nonpareil: marbled and mirrored and gilded, offering treats like the vanilla-ice-cream-and-brownie-chunk Double Devil. *19 N. Main St.; (435) 752-3155.*

**GOODY'S SODA FOUNTAIN, BOISE.** Goody's makes its own ice cream, toppings, and chocolates; try its smashing coconut clusters. It also has shops in Oregon. *1502 N. 13th St.; (208) 367-0020.*

**MAD DOG RANCH FOUNTAIN CAFE, CRAWFORD, CO.** A passion for vanilla milk shakes inspired singer Joe

SUNDAES STAR at Bluebird Restaurant in Logan, Utah.

Cocker and his wife, Pam, to open the cafe. "When we moved here, Joe used to go all the way to Hotchkiss for shakes," laughs Pam. "I said, 'Why don't we just open a soda fountain so you don't have to drive so far?'" Customers perch on hide-covered bar stools at a granite counter, while sweet local ladies blend Colorado-made ice cream into thick shakes, malts, and floats (based on turn-of-the-century recipes) and top them with fresh whipped cream and Oreo cookies. For a buzz, try Java Joe's Cappuccino Brain Freeze, made with cappuccino ice cream and a shot of espresso. Check out Cocker's collection of gold albums on the walls of the back room. *131 Hwy. 92; (970) 921-7632.*

**PARROT CONFECTIONERY, HELENA, MT.** Unchanged since 1935, the Parrot features 12 mahogany booths, a fountain counter with red leather stools, parrot and elephant knickknacks, and glass showcases of handmade chocolate-covered toffee and parrots (a candy like Turtles). It serves homemade ice cream and toppings, such as the Parrot special: scoops of chocolate, vanilla, and the flavor of

the week covered with fudge, caramel, and marshmallow toppings. *42 N. Main St.; (406) 442-1470.*

**SNELGROVE'S, SALT LAKE CITY.** To more than a few Utahans, this, the original Snelgrove's with its lavish sundaes, is a Beehive State treasure equal to the Great Salt Lake or the Mormon Tabernacle. *850 East 2100 South; (801) 485-8932.*

**SNYDER DRUG, GREAT FALLS, MT.** At the 78-year-old soda fountain in the back corner of Snyder Drug, you sit on stools at a marble-topped counter or in wire-backed chairs at ice cream tables next to antique posters and calendars. Try the phosphates or locally made ice cream served in thick glass dishes. *2515 Sixth Ave. N.; (406) 452-6461.*

**WALRUS ICE CREAM, FORT COLLINS, CO.** Rich homemade ice cream earns this landlocked marine mammal a special place in the hearts of Colorado State University students. *125 W. Mountain Ave.; (970) 482-5919.*

**YELLOWSTONE DRUG STORE, SHOSHONI, WY.** One reader said it all: "An old-fashioned ice cream parlor in a tiny, old-fashioned town." Established in 1909. *127 Main St.; (307) 876-2539.* ◆

## SANTA MARIA BARBECUE

Drive the streets of Santa Maria, California, on most any weekend and you're apt to see a Santa Maria–style barbecue. Schools and charity groups frequently host these unpretentious barbecues, usually in parking lots. The cooking is done on giant grills over glowing beds of red oak coals. The foods are easy and homegrown: beef tri-tip from a local cattle ranch seasoned with garlic salt and pepper; a simple salsa; and pinquitos, small pink beans grown in the Santa Maria Valley. For a new spin, check it out at www.ci.santa-maria.ca.us/geninfo/smbbq.html.

# barbecue's all-time greatest hits

■ YOU NAME IT, *Sunset* has grilled it.

From barracuda to banana splits and beyond, if we can get it in our hands, it'll end up on the barbecue. On our patio, a battalion of barbecues stand at attention, ready to fire. It's a rare day of recipe testing when they aren't in action.

Why all this pyromania? We're just doing what comes naturally in the West. Eight of the nation's 10 sunniest cities are here—prime turf for outdoor cooking. But even snow and rain don't stop Westerners from grilling year-round. In fact, most have a wardrobe of barbecues—big, small, built-in, portable, charcoal, gas, or electric. Barbecuing is to a Western cook what John Wayne is to a Western movie: vital.

At fiestas on grand ranchos, Spanish and Mexican settlers roasted beef, pigs, and lambs over—or under—hot coals. In fact, *barbecue* comes from the Spanish word *barbacoa,* wrapped meats buried under hot coals to cook. At Pacific Northwest potlatches, Native Americans celebrated tribal wealth with salmon cooked on wood frames in front of flames. On the range, cowboy "cookies" seared steaks over campfires.

> From the **hottest** chicken to the **jazziest** steak—here are recipes **most requested** by our readers

*Sunset* inherited barbecuing as a Western right, and codified every aspect to make it a predictable art, telling readers how to build, buy, and cook on barbecues.

Since the 1920s, *Sunset* has reported on gracious patios with barbecues. City folks who were required to burn their own trash often incorporated barbecues into handsome backyard incinerators built of stone or brick. *Sunset* gave plans for these solid structures, as well as other, less demanding ones. Inventiveness ran rampant. Some ideas were simple, some were simply silly. Barbecues and smokers were made from woks, wine barrels, wheelbarrows, metal roofing, water heater tanks, water pipes, oil drums, trash cans, flowerpots, and steel plow disks. A 1942 design from a Hollywood home featured flame-shaped lights and a waterwheel-turned spit, à la Rube Goldberg.

*Sunset* has explored barbecue techniques and dishes from every continent except Antarctica. For this retrospective of barbecue classics, we've updated old favorites using the foods and flavor combinations that reappear decade after decade—and remain fresh today.

BY ANDREW BAKER • PHOTOGRAPHS BY JAMES CARRIER

## Hot topics

The ashes of the past reveal landmarks, of sorts, that fueled the West's barbecue frenzy. **1911** *Sunset's* first barbecue story by Bertha H. Smith actually involves pit-cooked bulls' heads. **1921** A division of Ford Motors produces charcoal briquets, widely available by 1935 under the Kingsford label. **1931** *Sunset* gives how-to steps for barbecues built from old bricks, steel doormats. **1934** We offer plans that "the family patriarch can knock together of a Sunday morning" using cement blocks. **1938** Wood-covered *Sunset Barbecue Book* published. **1942** Wine barrel barbecue construction is a seasoned subject. **1943** Trader Vic restaurateur Victor Bergeron shows us how to build a Chinese oven; shares many recipes through the years. **1948** Wok (we call it a "chop suey bowl") on a war surplus metal stand makes a barbecue. **1951** Electric barbecue wagon, a *Sunset*-GE project, has power outlets, holds an electric roaster. **1952** George Stephen introduces precursor of the Weber-Stephen Weber Kettle, which lists for $46.95 in the first catalog—pricey for the time; it becomes a classic. **1956** We introduce how to judge cooking heat with your hand at grill level. **1957** Hibachis and portable grills soar in popularity; we show 15 models priced from $3 to $16. **1967** Barbecued turkey, a *Sunset* Thanksgiving trademark, is explored in encyclopedic depth. **1970** Our writers build a rack to grill a whole lamb and dig a pit to roast a pig. First test brings fire department. **1973** A $5 garbage can, an electric hot plate, and a grill make a slow-cook smoker. **1985** Mesquite charcoal is the hot fuel; *Sunset* demystifies the fables. **1986** Outdoor kitchens even include built-in Japanese teppan griddles. **1989** Gas barbecues profiled; cooking techniques honed. **1995** Barbecue Industry Association reports gas grills are outselling charcoal models.

# Barbecue how-to

There are two ways to arrange the heat when cooking on a barbecue grill. For direct heat, the fuel source is directly beneath the foods. For indirect heat, the fuel source is parallel to the foods and not beneath them.

## Direct heat

**Step 1**

IF USING CHARCOAL BRIQUETS, cover firegrate with a single, solid layer of ignited coals.

IF USING A GAS BARBECUE, turn all burners to high and close lid for 10 minutes.

**Step 2**

IF USING CHARCOAL BRIQUETS, let them burn down to desired heat (following).

IF USING A GAS BARBECUE, adjust burners to desired heat (following).

Set grill in place and measure heat: •Very hot (you can hold your hand at grill level only 1 to 2 seconds) •Hot (you can hold your hand at grill level only 2 to 3 seconds) •Medium-hot (you can hold your hand at grill level only 3 to 4 seconds) •Medium (you can hold your hand at grill level only 4 to 5 seconds) •Medium-low (you can hold your hand at grill level only 5 to 6 seconds) •Low (you can hold your hand at grill level only 6 to 7 seconds)

TO OIL GRILL, brush lightly with salad oil. Lay food on grill and cook as recipe directs. Cover gas barbecue. Do not cover charcoal barbecue unless recipe specifies.

## Indirect heat

**Step 1**

IF USING CHARCOAL BRIQUETS, mound and ignite 60 briquets on the firegrate of a barbecue with a lid. When briquets are dotted with gray ash, in 15 to 20 minutes, push equal amounts to opposite sides of firegrate. Add 5 more briquets to *each* mound of coals now and every 30 minutes while cooking. Set a drip pan on firegrate between coals.

IF USING A GAS BARBECUE, turn all burners to high and close lid for 10 minutes. Adjust burners for indirect cooking (no heat down center) and keep on high unless recipe specifies otherwise.

Set barbecue grill in place.

**Step 2**

TO OIL GRILL, brush with salad oil. Lay food on grill, but not over heat source. Cover grill (open vents for charcoal). Cook as recipe directs.

## Barbecued Tri-Tip

PREP AND COOK TIME: About 25 minutes

NOTES: Tri-tip is a triangular piece cut from the bottom of beef sirloin.

MAKES: 8 to 10 servings

1 **beef tri-tip** (2 to 2½ lb.)
½ teaspoon **garlic salt**
½ teaspoon fresh-ground **pepper**

**1.** Trim and discard fat from beef. Wipe meat with a damp towel, then sprinkle with garlic salt and pepper.

**2.** Prepare barbecue for *direct heat* (left, step 1). When grill is *very hot* (step 2), lay meat on barbecue. Cook, turning as needed to brown evenly, until meat is rare in center of thickest part (cut to test) and 125° to 130° on a thermometer, about 20 minutes, or until it has reached desired doneness.

**3.** Transfer the tri-tip to a board and cut meat across the grain into thin, slanting slices.

Per serving: 126 cal., 33% (42 cal.) from fat; 20 g protein; 4.7 g fat (1.6 g sat.); 0.1 g carbo (0 g fiber); 116 mg sodium; 55 mg chol.

## Pinquito Beans

PREP AND COOK TIME: About 35 minutes

MAKES: 8 to 10 servings

4 slices (about ¼ lb.) **bacon,** chopped
2 **onions** (1 lb. total), coarsely chopped
1 clove **garlic,** minced or pressed
½ cup chopped **green bell pepper**
⅔ cup **canned red chili sauce** (about ½ of a 10-oz. can)
1 can (6 oz.) **tomato paste**
3 tablespoons firmly packed **brown sugar**
1 teaspoon **dry mustard**
3 cans (15 oz. each) **pinquito beans**

**1.** In a 4- to 5-quart pan over high heat, frequently stir bacon until crisp, about 4 minutes. Lift out the bacon with a slotted spoon and drain on towels. Discard all but 1 teaspoon of the drippings from pan.

**2.** Add onions and garlic to pan. Stir often until onion is lightly browned, about 5 minutes. Add green pepper, chili sauce, tomato paste, sugar, mustard, beans, and bacon. Stir often until

boiling, then reduce heat and simmer 5 to 10 minutes to blend flavors.

Per serving: 167 cal., 19% (32 cal.) from fat; 7.4 g protein; 3.5 g fat (1 g sat.); 28 g carbo (5 g fiber); 645 mg sodium; 3.6 mg chol.

## Fresh Salsa

PREP AND COOK TIME: About 10 minutes

MAKES: 8 to 10 servings

1 cup thinly sliced **green onions**
1 can (4 oz.) **diced green chilies**
2 **firm-ripe tomatoes** (1 lb. total), rinsed, cored, and chopped
2 tablespoons **red wine vinegar**
**Salt**
Fresh-ground **pepper**

In a bowl, mix green onions, chilies, tomatoes, and vinegar. Add salt and pepper to taste.

Per serving: 15 cal., 12% (1.8 cal.) from fat; 0.6 g protein; 0.2 g fat (0 g sat.); 3.4 g carbo (0.9 g fiber); 75 mg sodium; 0 mg chol.

PLATE-SIZE margherita pizza overflows with melting cheese.

## Barbecued pizza

**PREP AND COOK TIME:** About 35 minutes
**NOTES:** Barbecued pizza made the cover of *Sunset* in July 1987, and flat breads from the barbecue followed frequently, often finished as pizzas. These topping choices pull together several popular flavor combinations.
**MAKES:** 4 pizzas; 4 servings

  1  loaf (1 lb.) **frozen white** or whole-wheat **bread dough,** thawed

    About 1 tablespoon **olive oil**

    **Toppings** (choices follow)

    **Salt** and **pepper**

**1.** On a floured board, divide dough into 4 equal pieces; shape each into a ball. Roll out each ball into a 5- to 6-inch-wide round. Brush tops lightly with about half the olive oil. Place each round, oiled side down, on a 10- by 12-inch piece of foil (4 total). With your hands, flatten rounds to ⅛ inch thick and 7 to 8 inches wide. Lightly brush with remaining oil. Let stand, uncovered, at room temperature until slightly puffy, 15 to 25 minutes.

**2.** As dough stands, prepare barbecue for *direct heat* (facing page, step 1).

**3.** When grill is *medium* (step 2), lift 1 piece of foil and flip dough round over onto grill. Peel off and discard foil. Repeat to place remaining dough on grill, keeping rounds slightly apart. Cook until pizza crusts are golden brown on bottom, about 2 minutes.

**4.** With a wide spatula, transfer crusts to baking sheets, browned sides up. Cover crusts with topping choice and slide from baking sheet back onto grill. Cover barbecue with lid (open vents for charcoal), and cook until topping is hot and pizza bottoms are crisp and brown, 3 to 4 minutes. Remove from grill; add salt and pepper to taste.

Per pizza crust: 334 cal., 24% (81 cal.) from fat; 8.5 g protein; 9 g fat (1.8 g sat.); 54 g carbo (2.3 g fiber); 547 mg sodium; 5.7 mg chol.

## Toppings

**NECTARINE AND BASIL TOPPING.** For each pizza, thinly slice 1 small pitted **firm-ripe nectarine** (about 6 oz.) and mix with ½ teaspoon **balsamic vinegar.** Sprinkle pizza crust with ⅓ cup **shredded jack cheese** and 2 tablespoons **finely shredded parmesan cheese.** Lay nectarine over cheese. Top with 1 tablespoon **pine nuts.** When pizza is removed from grill, scatter with 2 tablespoons finely shredded **fresh basil** leaves.

Per pizza: 655 cal., 40% (261 cal.) from fat; 27 g protein; 29 g fat (11 g sat.); 75 g carbo (6.2 g fiber); 976 mg sodium; 55 mg chol.

**PROVENÇAL TOPPING.** For each pizza, spread ⅓ cup **fresh chèvre** (goat) **cheese** onto pizza crust; sprinkle with ¼ teaspoon **dried thyme.** Lay ½ cup thinly sliced **canned peeled red peppers** on cheese and sprinkle with 2 tablespoons **finely shredded parmesan cheese.** When pizza is removed from grill, mound ½ cup **salad mix** on it.

Per pizza: 539 cal., 37% (198 cal.) from fat; 22 g protein; 22 g fat (11 g sat.); 63 g carbo (3.2 g fiber); 1,073 mg sodium; 36 mg chol.

**SAUSAGE-GRUYÈRE TOPPING.** For each pizza, sprinkle ⅓ cup shredded **gruyère cheese** and 2 tablespoons **finely shredded parmesan cheese** onto pizza crust. Lightly grate **nutmeg** over cheese. Thinly slice 1 **cooked chicken-apple sausage** (3½ to 4 oz.) and lay meat on pizza crust.

Per pizza: 750 cal., 44% (333 cal.) from fat; 40 g protein; 37 g fat (15 g sat.); 62 g carbo (2.9 g fiber); 1,449 mg sodium; 69 mg chol.

**PEKING DUCK TOPPING.** For each pizza, spread 1 to 2 tablespoons **hoisin sauce** over pizza crust. Top with ½ cup shredded boned, skinned **barbecued duck** (from a Chinese market) or roast chicken and 2 tablespoons finely chopped **green onion.** When pizza is removed from grill, scatter with 2 tablespoons **fresh cilantro** leaves.

Per pizza: 548 cal., 28% (153 cal.) from fat; 25 g protein; 17 g fat (4.7 g sat.); 68 g carbo (2.7 g fiber); 1,068 mg sodium; 69 mg chol.

**MARGHERITA TOPPING.** For each pizza, sprinkle ⅓ cup **shredded mozzarella cheese** over pizza crust. Top with 2 tablespoons **finely shredded parmesan cheese** and ½ cup chopped **tomatoes.** When pizza is removed from grill, scatter with small whole **fresh basil** leaves.

Per pizza: 517 cal., 37% (189 cal.) from fat; 22 g protein; 21 g fat (9.1 g sat.); 60 g carbo (3.9 g fiber); 922 mg sodium; 45 mg chol.

CHICKEN—seasoned and cooked Thai-style—is skewered to lie flat on grill.

ens, push another skewer parallel to the first through skin of outstretched wing into breast, over the backbone, through breast, and out through skin of opposite wing.

**3.** In a blender or food processor, whirl garlic, onions, ginger, coriander, pepper, and fish sauce until a coarse paste. Rub paste all over chickens.

**4.** Prepare barbecue for *indirect heat* (page 170, step 1). Lay chickens, skin up, on grill as directed (step 2). Cook until meat at thighbone is no longer pink (cut to test), about 1¼ hours.

**5.** Pull skewers from chickens, cut chickens into pieces, and serve with Thai chili sauce.

Per serving: 777 cal., 50% (387 cal.) from fat; 85 g protein; 43 g fat (12 g sat.); 8 g carbo (0.7 g fiber); 846 mg sodium; 264 mg chol.

***Thai chili sauce.*** In a blender or food processor, combine 1 can (8 oz.) **tomato sauce,** 3 tablespoons firmly packed **brown sugar,** 2 tablespoons chopped **garlic,** 1 teaspoon chopped **fresh serrano chili,** ¼ cup **vinegar,** 1¼ cups **golden raisins,** and ⅓ cup **water;** whirl until raisins are coarsely chopped. Pour into a 10- to 12-inch frying pan. Stir sauce over high heat until reduced to 1½ cups, about 10 minutes. Serve warm, at room temperature, or cold, adding **salt** to taste.

Per serving: 202 cal., 1.3% (2.7 cal.) from fat; 2.6 g protein; 0.3 g fat (0.1 g sat.); 53 g carbo (3.4 g fiber); 354 mg sodium; 0 mg chol.

## Teriyaki Dinosaur Bones

PREP AND COOK TIME: About 25 minutes, plus at least 3 hours to marinate

NOTES: We featured Dinosaur Bones, named for their size and prehistoric appearance, in September 1971. Beef back rib bones are trimmed from the rib roast. Some butchers call them beef spare ribs. Don't confuse back ribs with beef short ribs, a tougher cut suited to braising.

MAKES: 6 servings

 6 pounds **beef back rib bones** (6 to 8 in.), fat trimmed

 ¾ cup **soy sauce**

 ⅓ cup **sugar**

 2 cloves **garlic,** minced or pressed

 2 teaspoons minced **fresh ginger**

 2 tablespoons **tomato-based chili sauce**

## Bangkok Birds

PREP AND COOK TIME: About 1½ hours

NOTES: In Bangkok and across Southeast Asia, skewered, grilled chickens are sold by street vendors. This recipe, from August 1990, is served with a Thai chili sauce from September 1982.

MAKES: 4 servings

 2 **chickens** (3 to 3½ lb. each)

 ¼ cup chopped **garlic**

 ½ cup thinly sliced **green onions**

 2 tablespoons chopped **fresh ginger**

 1 teaspoon ground **coriander**

 1 teaspoon **coarse-ground pepper**

 ¼ cup **Asian fish sauce** (*nuoc mam* or *nam pla*) or soy sauce

 **Thai chili sauce** (recipe follows)

**1.** Remove giblets and necks; save for another use. Rinse chickens. With poultry shears or a knife, split chickens lengthwise through breastbones. Pull

birds open and place, skin up, on a flat surface. Press down firmly, cracking bones, until birds lie flat.

**2.** Insert a metal skewer (you need 4, each 10 to 12 in.; see above), across 1 chicken through drumstick (knee bent), then thigh, over backbone, through opposite thigh and its drumstick (knee bent). Repeat step with remaining chicken. Then, on both chick-

PLATE: WINSLOW HARRIS COMPANY, SAN FRANCISCO  FLATWARE: THE GARDENER, BERKELEY

Salt

Fresh-ground **pepper**

**1.** Cut ribs into 4- to 6-rib sections. Wipe with a damp towel.

**2.** In a heavy-duty gallon-size plastic food bag, combine ¾ cup water, soy sauce, sugar, garlic, ginger, and chili sauce. Pour half this mixture into another heavy-duty gallon-size plastic food bag. Put ½ the ribs in each bag, seal, and turn over several times to mix well. Set bags in a bowl and refrigerate at least 3 hours or up to 1 day, turning bags over several times.

**3.** Prepare barbecue for *indirect heat* (page 170, step 1). Lift ribs from marinade and lay on grill as directed (step 2). If there is not enough space for all the ribs, cook in sequence. Discard marinade. Cook until ribs are browned and have reached desired doneness, about 25 minutes for rare (red at bone, cut to test), 35 minutes for medium-well (no longer pink at bone).

**4.** Serve with salt and pepper to season to taste.

Per serving: 669 cal., 69% (459 cal.) from fat; 41 g protein; 51 g fat (21 g sat.); 8.1 g carbo (0 g fiber); 1,192 mg sodium; 149 mg chol.

## Rubbed Ribs

PREP AND COOK TIME: About 2½ hours

NOTES: These ribs were part of an August 1993 story on Texas barbecue, where barbecue means slow-cooked smoked meats with sauce. Back ribs are cut from the pork loin; sometimes they're called baby back ribs. Metal rib racks are available where barbecue equipment is sold.

MAKES: 6 servings

> 3  cups **hickory** or apple **wood chips**
>
> 3  tablespoons ground **California** or New Mexico **chilies**
>
> 3  tablespoons **paprika**
>
> 1½  tablespoons **pepper**
>
> 1  teaspoon **salt**
>
> About 4 pounds **pork back ribs**
>
> **Sweet and tangy sauce**

**1.** In a bowl, pour enough hot water over wood chips to make them float. Drain chips to add to barbecue.

**2.** Mix ground chilies, paprika, pepper, and salt.

PORK BACK RIBS, rubbed with spices, cook slowly over indirect heat.

**3.** Wipe ribs with a damp towel, then rub all over with the chili mixture.

**4.** Prepare barbecue for *indirect heat* (page 170, step 1), with these changes: if using charcoal, start with 40 briquets; when adjusting gas grill for indirect cooking, reduce heat to low. For charcoal smoke, add ½ cup soaked wood chips with the 5 briquets every 30 minutes of cooking. For gas smoke, as soon as you turn on heat, place 1 cup soaked wood chips in the barbecue's metal smoking box or in a small, shallow foil pan directly on heat in a corner of the firegrate; add 1 more cup chips after each hour of cooking.

**5.** Lay ribs on grill but not directly over heat. If there is not enough space for all the ribs, set them upright in a metal rib rack on grill but not directly over heat. Cover barbecue (open vents for charcoal) and cook until meat pulls easily from bones, about 2½ hours. You don't need to turn ribs on a charcoal barbecue, but on a gas barbecue turn ribs occasionally, even in metal rack.

**6.** Transfer ribs to a large platter; cut between bones and serve with sweet and tangy sauce (following).

Per serving: 563 cal., 70% (396 cal.) from fat; 36 g protein; 44 g fat (16 g sat.); 4.5 g carbo (1.1 g fiber); 539 mg sodium; 172 mg chol.

***Sweet and tangy sauce.*** In a 1½- to 2-quart pan, combine ¾ cup **catsup**, 6 tablespoons **beef broth** or water, 6 tablespoons **Worcestershire**, ¼ cup **lemon juice**, 3 tablespoons firmly packed **brown sugar**, ¼ cup chopped **onion**, and 1 teaspoon **hot sauce.** Simmer until reduced to 1½ cups, about 10 minutes. Add more hot sauce to taste. Serve warm or cool. If making ahead, chill airtight up to 2 weeks. Makes 1½ cups.

Per serving: 78 cal., 1.2% (0.9 cal.) from fat; 1.6 g protein; 0.1 g fat (0 g sat.); 19 g carbo (0.6 g fiber); 552 mg sodium; 0 mg chol.

## Grilled Corn

**PREP AND COOK TIME:** 15 to 20 minutes

**NOTES:** Grilled corn has been a *Sunset* standard since the 1930s.

**MAKES:** 6 servings

**1.** Strip husks and silks from 6 **ears corn** (7 to 8 in.).

**2.** Prepare barbecue for ***direct heat*** (page 170, step 1). When grill is ***medium-hot*** (step 2) lay corn on barbecue and turn ears as needed until hot and speckled with brown, 10 to 12 minutes.

**3.** Rub corn with **lime** wedges and sprinkle with **salt** to taste.

Per serving: 108 cal., 13% (14 cal.) from fat; 4.1 g protein; 1.5 g fat (0.2 g sat.); 24 g carbo (4 g fiber); 19 mg sodium; 0 mg chol.

## Skirt Steak with Mustard Sauce

**PREP AND COOK TIME:** About 20 minutes

**NOTES:** An elegant sauce is "all a fine steak needs," according to this August 1968 recipe. The sauce warms at the side of the grill as the steak cooks.

**MAKES:** 5 servings

- 1 fat-trimmed **skirt steak** (about 1¼ lb.)
- ¼ cup (⅛ lb.) **butter** or margarine
- 1 tablespoon **coarse-grain Dijon mustard**
- 2 tablespoons **dry vermouth** or dry white wine
- ½ teaspoon **Worcestershire**
- 3 cups (about 6 oz.) **watercress,** rinsed and crisped

**1.** Wipe meat with a damp towel, then cut crosswise into 2 or 3 equal pieces.

FIRM FISH CHUNKS alternate on skewers with aromatic lemon and bay.

**2.** Prepare barbecue for ***direct heat*** (page 170, step 1). When grill is ***medium-hot*** (step 2), lay steak on barbecue. Cook, turning as needed to brown evenly, until meat is pink in center of thickest part (cut to test), 7 to 10 minutes.

**3.** Meanwhile, in a shallow pan (at least 9 in. wide) on grill, combine butter, mustard, vermouth, and Worcestershire; stir occasionally until butter melts, then push to a cool area of grill and keep warm.

**4.** Set cooked steak in pan, slice, and stir meat juices into sauce. Divide watercress among plates, lay meat on it, and spoon sauce over portions.

Per serving: 275 cal., 59% (162 cal.) from fat; 24 g protein; 18 g fat (9.7 g sat.); 0.6 g carbo (0.8 g fiber); 260 mg sodium; 83 mg chol.

## Skewered Swordfish with Bay and Lemon

**PREP AND COOK TIME:** About 25 minutes

**NOTES:** Simple flavors made this May 1959 recipe memorable.

**MAKES:** 4 servings

- 1 pound **boned, skinned swordfish**
- 2 **lemons**
- 10 **fresh** or dried **bay leaves** (3 to 4 in.), cut in half crosswise
- 2 tablespoons **butter** or margarine, melted
- **Coarse salt** (sea or kosher)

**1.** Rinse swordfish, drain, and cut into 1-inch chunks. Cut 1 lemon in half

## Barbecued Salmon Fillet

PREP AND COOK TIME: About 35 minutes

NOTES: This July 1970 Kitchen Cabinet recipe is an excellent version of many similar preparations through the years that use lemon and soy with salmon.

MAKES: 10 to 12 servings

- 1 **salmon fillet with skin** (3½ to 4 lb.)
- 2 tablespoons **butter** or margarine, melted
- ½ cup **dry white wine**
- ¼ cup **lemon juice**
- ¼ cup **soy sauce**
    Chopped **parsley**
    **Lemon** wedges

**1.** Rinse fish and pat dry. Set fish, skin down, on a sheet of heavy foil and trim foil to make a rim about 2 inches wider than fish. Fold excess foil up to create a lip around fish.

**2.** In a bowl, combine butter, wine, lemon juice, and soy sauce.

**3.** Prepare barbecue for *indirect heat* (page 170, step 1). Set fish, foil down, on grill as directed (step 2). Brush fish generously with butter mixture, then again about every 5 minutes, until fish is opaque but still moist-looking in center of thickest part (cut to test), 20 to 30 minutes.

**4.** Slide a large, rimless baking sheet under foil, then slide fish from pan onto a platter. Sprinkle with parsley. Cut fish into portions and lift from skin. Season with juice from lemon wedges.

Per serving: 267 cal., 54% (144 cal.) from fat; 27 g protein; 16 g fat (4.1 g sat.); 0.9 g carbo (0 g fiber); 442 mg sodium; 83 mg chol.

## Shrimp with Chili Paste

PREP AND COOK TIME: About 30 minutes

NOTES: Chilies are winners with shrimp in *Sunset*. This recipe appeared in August 1987.

MAKES: 4 or 5 servings

- ⅓ cup **lemon juice**
- 2 tablespoons **salad oil**
- 1 **onion** (½ lb.), chopped
- ½ cup lightly packed **fresh cilantro**
- 2 tablespoons minced **garlic**
- 1 tablespoon **fresh ginger**
- 1 to 2 tablespoons chopped **fresh jalapeño chilies**

- 1 cup **plain nonfat yogurt**
- 1½ pounds **colossal shrimp** (10 to 15 per lb.), shelled and deveined
    **Salt**

**1.** In a blender or food processor, whirl lemon juice, oil, onion, cilantro, garlic, ginger, and chilies until smooth.

**2.** Mix ⅓ cup chili mixture with yogurt.

**3.** In a bowl, mix the remaining chili mixture with shrimp and let stand at least 10 or up to 30 minutes, then thread shrimp onto metal skewers.

**4.** Prepare barbecue for *direct heat* (page 170, step 1). When grill is *hot* (step 2) lay skewered shrimp on it. Turn to cook shrimp evenly until they are opaque but still moist-looking in thickest part (cut to test), 5 to 8 minutes.

**5.** Push shrimp off skewers and serve with yogurt sauce and salt to taste.

Per serving: 220 cal., 31% (68 cal.) from fat; 26 g protein; 7.6 g fat (1.1 g sat.); 11 g carbo (0.9 g fiber); 205 mg sodium; 169 mg chol.

## Queso al Horno

PREP AND COOK TIME: About 20 minutes

NOTES: An easy appetizer, this Mexican classic debuted in August 1966. For a spicier version, add hot sauce, or use chili- or pepper-flavor jack cheese.

MAKES: 6 servings

- ¾ pound **asadero** or jack **cheese**
- 1 **fresh Anaheim** (California or New Mexico) **chili** (3 oz.)
- ⅓ cup finely chopped **red onion**
- 12 **corn tortillas** (6 in.)
- 2 tablespoons crumbled **cotija** or feta **cheese**
- 1 **firm-ripe tomato** (6 oz.), rinsed, cored, and chopped

**1.** Cut asadero cheese into ⅛- to ¼-inch slices and lay in an overlapping layer to cover bottom and sides of a shallow 1½-quart pan (about 9 by 12 in.).

**2.** Remove and discard stem, seeds, and veins from chili. Cut chili crosswise into ¼-inch slices. Scatter chili and onion over cheese.

**3.** Stack tortillas, cut stack in half, and set halves together on a sheet of heavy foil (about 12 by 24 in.); seal tortillas in foil.

**4.** Prepare barbecue for *direct heat* (page 170, step 1). When grill is *medium* (step 2), set tortilla packet and pan with cheese on barbecue. Turn packet over often until tortillas are hot

---

lengthwise, then cut halves crosswise into ¼-inch slices. Discard seeds. Cut remaining lemon into wedges.

**2.** Thread swordfish onto metal skewers (10 to 12 in.), separating each piece alternately with a lemon slice then a bay leaf half.

**3.** Brush skewered foods with butter and sprinkle lightly with salt.

**4.** Prepare barbecue for *direct heat* (page 170, step 1). When grill is *hot* (step 2), lay fish on barbecue. Turn fish as needed, until opaque but still moist-looking in center of thickest part (cut to test), about 8 minutes.

**5.** Push foods from skewers and add salt and juice from lemon wedges to taste.

Per serving: 203 cal., 49% (99 cal.) from fat; 23 g protein; 11 g fat (4.9 g sat.); 5.4 g carbo (0 g fiber); 162 mg sodium; 60 mg chol.

in the center, about 5 minutes; wrap in a thick towel and put in a basket. Heat asadero cheese until melted, 10 to 15 minutes; sprinkle with cotija cheese.

**5.** To eat, spoon cheese mixture onto tortilla pieces and add tomatoes to taste. Wrap tortillas to enclose filling.

Per serving: 308 cal., 47% (144 cal.) from fat; 18 g protein; 16 g fat (9.5 g sat.); 26 g carbo (3.2 g fiber); 513 mg sodium; 51 mg chol.

## Beef Platter Burger

PREP AND COOK TIME: 30 to 35 minutes, plus 15 minutes for toppings

NOTES: A staff member remarked that this burger, popularized in July 1981, has garnered so many reader requests that it needs its own zip code. The original recipe was for rare beef; this is a well-done but juicy version with a ground turkey option. You can serve it plain; top it with mustard, pickles, catsup, and lettuce leaves; or try the Mexican and Italian variations that follow.

MAKES: 8 servings

    1   **round French bread** (1½ lb., about 11 in. wide)
    2   tablespoons **butter** or margarine
    2   **large eggs**
    2½  pounds **ground lean beef**
    1   cup minced **onion**
    ½   cup **fine dried bread crumbs**
    ½   cup fat-skimmed **beef broth**
    2   cloves **garlic,** minced or pressed
    ½   teaspoon **dried oregano**

**1.** Using a long, serrated knife, cut bread in half horizontally. Spread butter evenly over cut sides.

**2.** In a large bowl, beat eggs to blend, then add beef, onion, bread crumbs, broth, garlic, and oregano and mix well. Line a 12- by 15-inch baking sheet with waxed paper. Scrape meat mixture onto paper and pat into a 12-inch-wide round (or 1 in. wider than bread).

**3.** Prepare barbecue for **direct heat** (page 170, step 1). When grill is **hot** (step 2), lay meat on barbecue: holding both ends of baking sheet, invert patty onto grill. Pull waxed paper off the patty and discard.

**4.** Cook patty until browned on bottom, about 7 minutes. To turn, use 2 rimless baking sheets, one as a pusher to slide patty onto the second sheet. When patty is on the baking sheet, invert first sheet onto it. Hold baking sheets together, turn over, and slide patty, browned side up, back onto grill. Continue to cook

until well-done (no longer pink in the center, cut to test), 7 to 9 minutes.

**5.** During the last few minutes the meat cooks, if there is space, lay bread, cut side down, on grill to toast. If there is not enough room, toast bread after removing patty. Slide a baking sheet under the meat, then slide meat onto the bottom half of the toasted bread. Cut the top half of the bread into 8 wedges. Arrange bread wedges on burger. Cut burger and the bottom of the bread into wedges.

Per serving: 588 cal., 40% (234 cal.) from fat; 35 g protein; 26 g fat (10 g sat.); 51 g carbo (2.9 g fiber); 704 mg sodium; 148 mg chol.

## Turkey Platter Burger

Follow directions for Beef Platter Burger (preceding), but use 2½ pounds **ground lean turkey** instead of beef.

Per serving: 551 cal., 34% (189 cal.) from fat; 36 g protein; 21 g fat (6.7 g sat.); 51 g carbo (2.9 g fiber); 713 mg sodium; 132 mg chol.

## Mexican Platter Burger

**1.** Make **Beef** or Turkey **Platter Burger** (preceding) as directed, but omit broth in step 2 and instead add ½ cup **prepared taco sauce,** 2 teaspoons **chili powder,** and 1 teaspoon **ground cumin.**

**2.** In step 4, sprinkle 1½ cups (6 oz.) **shredded jack cheese** over burger for the last 3 to 4 minutes of cooking.

Per serving with beef: 675 cal., 43% (288 cal.) from fat; 40 g protein; 32 g fat (14 g sat.); 53 g carbo (3.1 g fiber); 931 mg sodium; 171 mg chol.

Per serving with turkey: 638 cal., 39% (252 cal.) from fat; 41 g protein; 28 g fat (10 g sat.); 53 g carbo (3.1 g fiber); 939 mg sodium; 155 mg chol.

**3.** Top burger with 1 or more of the following:

***Guacamole.*** Peel, pit, and slice 2 **firm-ripe avocados** (¾ lb. total) and mash with a fork. Stir in 3 tablespoons **lime juice,** ¼ cup thinly sliced **green onions,** 2 tablespoons minced **fresh cilantro,** 1 tablespoon minced **fresh jalapeño chili,** and **salt** to taste.

Per serving: 54 cal., 81% (44 cal.) from fat; 0.7 g protein; 4.9 g fat (0.8 g sat.); 3.1 g carbo (0.7 g fiber); 4.7 mg sodium; 0 mg chol.

***Pickled tomatillos.*** Pull off and discard husks from ½ pound **tomatillos.** Rinse and thinly slice tomatillos. In a bowl, mix tomatillo slices with ¼ cup **orange juice,** ⅓ cup **lime juice,** 1 teaspoon **hot chili flakes,** and ¼ tea-

spoon **salt.** Lift tomatillos from juices and lay on burger.

Per serving: 8.4 cal., 11% (0.9 cal.) from fat; 0.4 g protein; 0.1 g fat (0 g sat.); 1.5 g carbo (0 g fiber); 18 mg sodium; 0 mg chol.

***Green chilies and tomatoes.*** Arrange 1 can (7 oz.) **diced green chilies,** drained, and 2 thinly sliced **firm-ripe tomatoes** (1 lb. total) on burger.

Per serving: 18 cal., 10% (1.8 cal.) from fat; 0.7 g protein; 0.2 g fat (0 g sat.); 4.1 g carbo (1 g fiber); 157 mg sodium; 0 mg chol.

## Italian Platter Burger

**1.** Make **Beef** or Turkey **Platter Burger** (left) as directed, but omit broth in step 2 and instead add ½ cup **prepared pasta sauce.**

**2.** In step 4, sprinkle 1½ cups (6 oz.) shredded **fontina cheese** over burger for the last 3 to 4 minutes of cooking.

Per serving with beef: 686 cal., 43% (297 cal.) from fat; 41 g protein; 33 g fat (14 g sat.); 54 g carbo (2.9 g fiber); 947 mg sodium; 173 mg chol.

Per serving with turkey: 650 cal., 40% (261 cal.) from fat; 41 g protein; 29 g fat (11 g sat.); 54 g carbo (2.9 g fiber); 956 mg sodium; 157 mg chol.

**3.** Top burger with 2 or more of the following:

***Sautéed mushrooms.*** Rinse and drain 1 pound **mushrooms** (shiitake, portabella, oyster, common, or a combination of these). Trim off and discard the discolored stem ends (or tough shiitake stems). Thinly slice mushrooms. In a 10- to 12-inch nonstick frying pan over high heat, frequently stir 2 tablespoons **butter** or margarine and sliced mushrooms until their juices evaporate and the mushrooms are lightly browned, about 15 minutes.

Per serving: 39 cal., 72% (28 cal.) from fat; 1.2 g protein; 3.1 g fat (1.8 g sat.); 2.6 g carbo (0.7 g fiber); 31 mg sodium; 7.8 mg chol.

***Pasta sauce.*** Heat ½ cup **prepared pasta sauce** until warm.

Per serving: 17 cal., 37% (6.3 cal.) from fat; 0.3 g protein; 0.7 g fat (0.1 g sat.); 2.5 g carbo (0 g fiber); 77 mg sodium; 0 mg chol.

***Bitter greens.*** Rinse and drain 2½ cups (about 2 oz.) lightly packed **curly endive,** frisée, escarole, or arugula.

Per serving: 1.2 cal., 0% (0 cal.) from fat; 0.1 g protein; 0 g fat; 0.2 g carbo (0.2 g fiber); 1.6 mg sodium; 0 mg chol. ◆

# Say cheese!

## The Northwest's dairy products are rising to the top

BY JENA MACPHERSON

LARRY'S MARKETS in the greater Seattle area carry hundreds of varieties of cheese, including such Northwest signatures as Oregon Blue, Tillamook White, and Cougar Gold, an eastern Washington cheese that's sold in a can.

Think of the great Pacific Northwest and what's the first thing that comes to mind? Snow-capped volcanoes? Computer software? Towering stands of Douglas firs? Cheese?

Cheese? Well, maybe not, but for those of us who consider a hunk of sourdough and a thick slice of fresh cheddar just this side of sublime, the Northwest does us right. That fancy stuff from France is fine, but we prefer a wheel of Pleasant Valley Gouda, Cougar Gold in a can, a pound or so of Tillamook Vintage White, and perhaps a bit of Oregon Blue.

And we're not the only fans of our cheese—in recent years Tillamook and Darigold cheddars and Cougar Gold have won national contests.

### CHEESE HEADQUARTERS

Visiting a cheese production site is a fun—and tasty—lesson in cheesemaking. In addition to getting a close-up view of the many steps in the handcrafting process, you can pick up a pound or two of a company's best. At some places you can even buy cheese curds—cheddar that's still in chewy, bite-size pieces before being packed and aged. That's a good thing.

*Pleasant Valley Dairy.* In the late 1970s, George and Dolores Train started making classic goudas on their farm in dairy-rich northwest Washington. Their goudas are available during the summer—for something that's a little different, try the cumin-flavor variety. You can expect the dairy's farmstead cheese to be a little tarter and firmer, while the Mutschli tastes a lot like the cheese used in a Swiss raclette. *6804 Kickerville Rd., Ferndale, WA; (360) 366-5398.*

*Washington State University Creamery.* In the early 1940s, Washington State University began transforming the output from its dairy herds into a distinctively Northwest cheese called Cougar Gold, a version of white cheddar that's sold in a can. You probably won't find Cougar Gold at your favorite cheese shop (few places carry it), but you can order it by mail. Although it will arrive in its trademark flat, 30-ounce can, it should be refrigerated, since the cheese continues to age in the can. You can also head to the source and visit the brightly colored campus creamery. While you're there, watch cheesemaking, eat great ice cream cones, and try Cougar Gold or Viking (a mild white cheese). *In the Food Quality Building, WSU campus, South Fairway Lane, Pullman, WA; (800) 457-5442.*

*Tillamook County Creamery Association.* In 1909 the Tillamook County Creamery Association was formed to produce and market that area's cheese. Today, the association's facility is probably the most visitor-friendly cheesemaking plant in the Northwest. Guests of the association can take advantage of an elaborate viewing area, dine at a restaurant, and peruse a large gift-and-cheese shop. Besides cheddar (including a special aged white), the association sells colby and jack. *On U.S. Highway 101, 2 miles north of Tillamook, OR; (503) 842-4481.*

*Rogue River Valley Creamery.* Italian-born Thomas Vella began making cheddar and jack at his Rogue River Valley Creamery in southern Oregon in 1935. In 1957 he opened another plant, this one devoted solely to blue cheese. The plant, says Vella, closely duplicates the conditions found in the Roquefort caves in France; it also keeps the highly invasive blue mold from spreading to the cheddar and jack that he produces in his other plants. You can watch the cheese being made and then taste the end result. *311 N. Front St., Central Point, northwest of Medford, OR; (541) 664-2233.*

## Portland and Seattle cheeseries

No time for a trip into cheese country? You can visit any of these well-stocked cheese shops.

In Portland, PASTAWORKS has a fine selection of Northwest and Mediterranean cheeses, at 3735 S.E. Hawthorne Blvd. (503/232-1010) and 735 N.W. 21st Ave. (221-3002). THE CHESHIRE CAT specializes in blue cheeses, in the Irvington Market across from Lloyd Center, at 1409 N.E. Weidler St. (284-5226).

In the Seattle area, the cheese departments of the five LARRY'S MARKETS carry more than 400 kinds of cheeses, including Cougar Gold; call (425) 453-5031 for the market nearest you. You'll also find Cougar at DE-LAURENTI SPECIALTY FOOD MARKET in Pike Place Market (206/622-0141). ◆

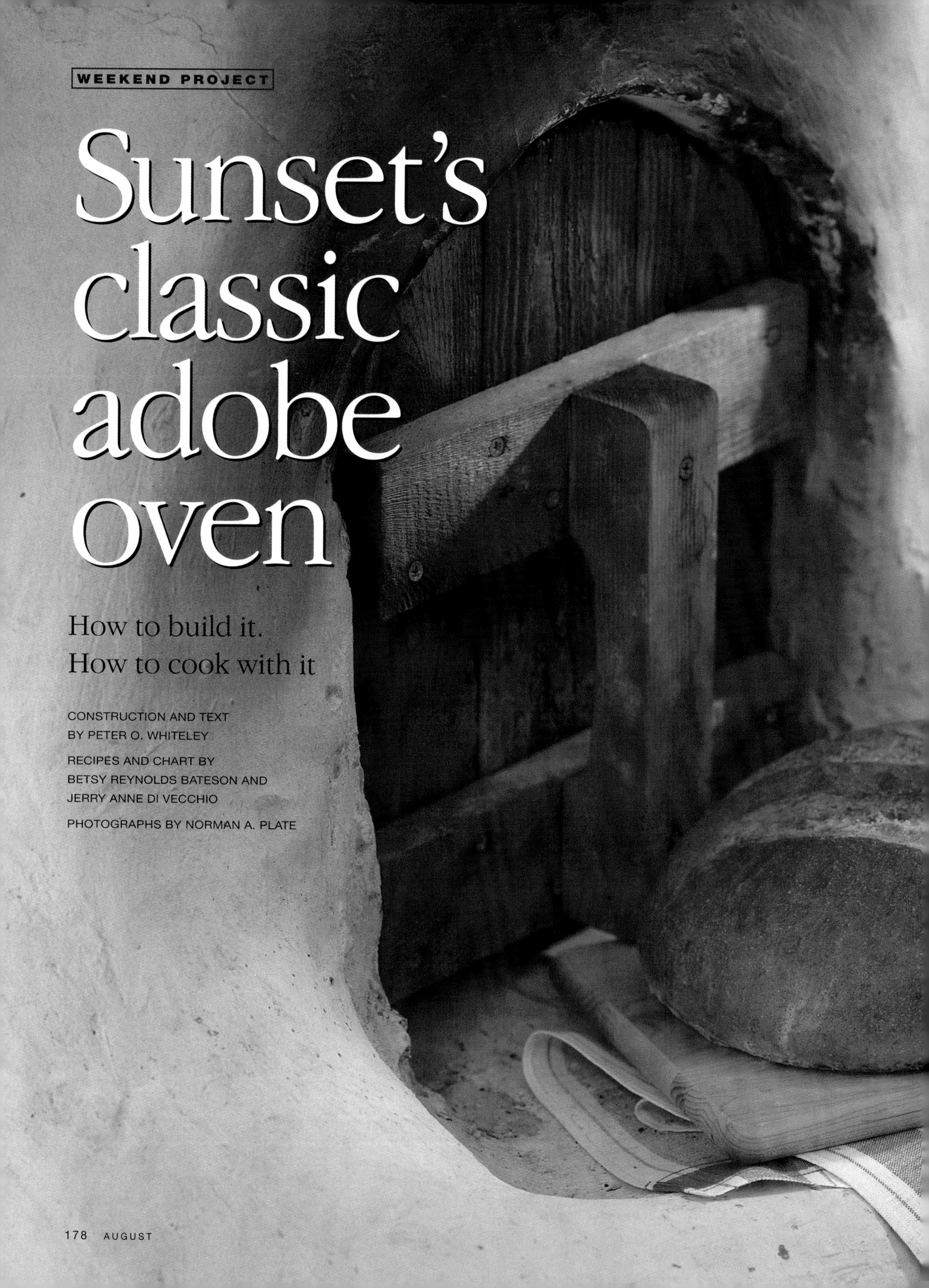

WEEKEND PROJECT

# Sunset's classic adobe oven

How to build it.
How to cook with it

CONSTRUCTION AND TEXT
BY PETER O. WHITELEY

RECIPES AND CHART BY
BETSY REYNOLDS BATESON AND
JERRY ANNE DI VECCHIO

PHOTOGRAPHS BY NORMAN A. PLATE

In response to reader requests, we decided to bring back one of our most popular projects: the adobe oven, featured in our August 1971 issue. It's modeled after mud-brick ovens used around the world, from the Southwest to Mexico, Italy, and France. With the rising interest in wood-fired cooking, it was time to revisit the article and build a new version in our editorial test garden.

The project takes about two days of grubby work; it speeds up building to have two or three people making the thick-walled adobe shell, the mass of which stores the heat of the fire. It's great for pizza, roasts, vegetables, and crusty loaves of bread. (We give recipes to try on page 183.)

## Materials and tools

You'll find most of the materials you need at a home center or building supply yard, except for the cardboard barrel, often used by movers. (You cut it in half lengthwise and use it to form the oven's curving top.) Look in the yellow pages under Barrels & Drums for a local source.

- 14 concrete building blocks (8 by 8 by 16)
- 14 concrete cap blocks (8 by 2 by 16)
- 68 firebricks (2½ by 4½ by 9)
- One 28- to 30-gallon cardboard barrel
- One empty 1-quart can
- 6-foot square of 6-inch wire mesh (used to reinforce concrete driveways)
- 10 feet of 30-inch-wide chicken wire
- 4 feet of rough-sawed redwood 2-by-4
- 2 feet of redwood 1-by-3
- 16 1½-inch deck screws
- 3 feet of 6-inch-wide aluminum flashing
- Eight large wheelbarrow loads of adobe soil
- Three bags Portland cement
- 1-foot square of ¼-inch galvanized wire mesh (see sidebar, page 181)
- Exterior latex paint
- Optional: 24 precast 1- by 2-foot concrete steppingstones

You'll also need a tape measure, hacksaw, pencil, circular saw with masonry bit, wire cutters, saber saw, drill, screwdriver, large wheelbarrow, hoe, shovel, sturdy rubber gloves, sponge, small piece of scrap lumber or plywood, old towels, and plastic tarp.

# Building the adobe oven

## Step-by-step directions

Find a safe, level location in your garden for the oven. Building code requires oven to be a minimum of 10 horizontal feet from any combustible surface, such as fences or walls. Also, check with local officials on property line setback requirements.

We built our oven on a 6- by 8-foot base of red concrete steppingstones—an optional layer. The rest of the base is stacked but mortarless, which allows for easy disassembly at some point in the future.

**1.** Arrange the 8 by 8 by 16 blocks on the ground to make a 32- by 54-inch base.

**2.** Cover with an identical layout of cap blocks.

**3.** Add layer of firebricks.

**4.** Cut the barrel in half lengthwise with a hacksaw. Center empty quart can on closed end of a half-barrel; trace and cut out circular shape. This hole will be the vent.

**5.** Score and cut two firebricks in half with a circular saw (halves measure $4\frac{1}{2}$ inches square).

**6.** Starting at back end of base, make three U-shaped layers of firebricks to support the half-barrel. Each layer is three bricks long and $2\frac{1}{2}$

bricks wide at back end. Position barrel on bricks.

**7.** Cut a 3- by 4-foot piece of the 6-inch wire mesh and shape it so it arcs over the barrel by about 1 inch. Bend and tuck excess under bricks at side. Repeat with at least one layer of chicken wire, bending and folding edges over the rear and open end of barrel.

**8.** Make door (shown on page 178): Cut three 14-inch-long pieces from redwood 2-by-4. Join them together with screws running through two parallel lengths of redwood 1-by-3 across the front. Cut top into an arch that measures 14 inches tall at the peak and conforms to the basic shape of the open end of the barrel. Shape handle from excess 2-by-4, and screw

FRONT

BACK

to 1-by-3s. Center and tack flashing around door perimeter. Insert the can in the hole cut in rear of barrel.

**9.** Mix 3 parts adobe soil to 1 part Portland cement, add water, and mix with a hoe and shovel to the consistency of thick oatmeal. Be warned: it's tiring and muddy work. Test that the mix holds together by squeezing it.

**10.** Working from the base up, pack the adobe-cement mixture firmly over and through the layers of mesh, leaving no air pockets. Pack mixture around the can, wiggling and rotating it to keep it from being trapped in place. Form arch for door by squeezing mixture into the chicken wire, and periodically inserting the door (with flashing attached) to check fit. Continue adding mixture until the coat is 4 to 5 inches thick overall. Let it dry slightly, then smooth the surface with a damp sponge and a wood "float" made with scrap lumber.

**11.** Wiggle the door and can, then cover the oven with damp towels and plastic tarp. Keep towels damp and oven covered for at least a week while adobe hardens and cures (check daily). Remove flashing from door.

**12.** Paint adobe shell after building first fire (see sidebar, at right).

## How to heat the oven

The first time you build a fire in the oven is exciting. Remove the can from the rear vent, and cut and fit a piece of the ¼-inch wire mesh over vent to act as a spark arrester. Build a small fire and keep it burning steadily so the adobe warms slowly and bakes out any remaining moisture. Hairline cracks will likely develop when the oven is heated, but they can be sealed with coats of exterior latex paint later.

The next time, build a fire as directed for cooking (page 182) to test how the oven holds heat. The oven's surface will become hot to the touch. Let the fire die down, use a hoe or shovel to pull out the coals into a metal bucket partially filled with water, sweep off the brick surface with a damp broom, and check the temperature with an oven thermometer. Initial temperatures will often be about 700°—too hot for cooking.

Block the vent hole with the can or a damp rag, and remove and soak the door in water. Replace the door and periodically monitor the temperature for several hours to get an idea of how your oven performs. Leave oven door open for cooling.

# Cooking in the adobe oven

## The first three hours, heat oven

**1** **0 to 10 minutes:** Screen vent and open door. In center of oven, mound 6 to 8 sheets of crumpled newspaper. Lean 2 or 3 handfuls of kindling wood, including some 1-inch-thick pieces, tepee-style against the paper. Ignite paper, and when kindling is burning well, lay 2 or 3 more handfuls of kindling on the fire and top with 3 or 4 logs (3 to 4 in. thick and about 1½ ft.).

**2** **20 to 40 minutes:** When logs begin to burn, add 6 more logs (4 to 5 in. thick), but be careful of heat from oven door—it can singe hair. Toss about half a 10-pound bag of charcoal briquets between logs. Let fire burn about 1 hour, then add remaining briquets. Burn until most wood is gone, about 3 hours total. Occasionally poke fire to keep air circulating.

**At about 2 hours and 50 minutes:** With a shovel, scoop hot ashes into a fireproof metal container partially filled with water. Quickly clean oven floor with a wet mop or wet towel tied to a pole.

**3** **2 hours and 50 minutes to 3 hours:** Set oven thermometer on floor just inside door. Close door; block vent. Check after 10 minutes. Temperature should be between 700° and 650°; then it drops quickly to 600°.

## The next four hours, bake

During the brief period of high heat, bake pizzas. In the next phase, put meats and vegetables in to roast. Bake bread when oven heat is most constant.

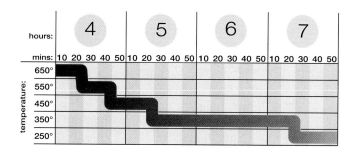

COOKING TIP: Meats brown best when oven starting temperature is 500° to 450° and heat is regulated by the oven door (see chart above). But for roasting that requires less attention, wait until temperature drops to about 400° to allow more time for meats to cook.

## Adobe oven vegetables
Starting oven temperature: 500° to 450°

| | Size | Approx. time | Doneness test |
|---|---|---|---|
| Beets | 2 to 2½ in. | 1 to 1¼ hr. | Give when pressed |
| Bell peppers | 6 to 8 oz. | ½ to 1 hr. | Black spots, collapsed |
| Chilies | 3 to 6 oz. | ½ to 1 hr. | Black spots, collapsed |
| Corn | 6 to 8 in. | 20 to 30 min. | Husks slightly charred |
| Eggplant | 1 to 2 in. thick | 1 to 1¼ hr. | Very soft when pressed |
| Garlic heads | 2 to 3 oz. | About 1 hr. | Soft when pressed |
| Onions | 6 to 8 oz. | 1¼ to 1½ hr. | Give when pressed |
| Potatoes | 6 to 8 oz. | 1¼ to 1½ hr. | Give when pressed |
| Sweet potatoes | 6 to 8 oz. | 1 to 1¼ hr. | Give when pressed |
| Tomatoes, Roma | 3 to 4 oz. | ¾ to 1 hr. | Black spots, soft when pressed |

**1.** Rinse or scrub vegetables, as appropriate, but do not peel. Pierce eggplant, potatoes, and sweet potatoes.
**2.** Set vegetables slightly apart in a shallow rimmed pan (or pans).
**3.** Push pan to center or back of oven. Leave door open until temperature drops to 350°, then close door. Check in 5 minutes; if above 400°, open door and let cool to 350°. Close door, then check every 30 minutes.

**4.** Remove vegetables as cooked. Peel beets. Pull skins, stems, and seeds from peppers and chilies. Pull husks and silks from corn. Cut stems from eggplant. Cut tops off garlic heads and squeeze out pulp. Peel onions. Slit open potatoes and sweet potatoes. Pull off tomato skins and cut out cores. Season vegetables to taste with salt, pepper, and olive oil or butter. Or use as suggested in the recipes on the facing page.

## Adobe oven meats
Starting oven temperature: 500° to 450°

| | Weight | Approx. time | Doneness (cut to test) |
|---|---|---|---|
| Chicken | 3 to 4 lb. | 45 min. to 1¼ hr. | Breast white at bone in thickest part |
| Turkey | 12 to 14 lb. | about 2 hr. | 160° at breastbone in thickest part |
| Leg of lamb | 5½ to 6½ lb. | 1¼ to 1½ hr. | 135° at bone in thickest part (medium-rare) |
| Beef rib roast | about 10 lb. | 2½ to 2¾ hr. | 135° in center (medium-rare) |

**1.** Rinse meat, pat dry, sprinkle with salt and pepper, and set poultry (breast up) or roasts (fat side up) on a rack in a close-fitting shallow pan.
**2.** Push meat in pan to center or back of oven. Cook with door open until temperature drops to 350°, then close door. Check in 5 minutes; if over 400°, open door and let cool to 350° again. Close door. Check every 30 minutes during last hour. For more meat, use 2 cuts the same size.

## Second-Generation Adobe Oven Bread

PREP AND COOK TIME: About 3¼ hours, including about 1½ hours for rising

MAKES: 1 loaf, about 2½ pounds

- 2 cups warm (about 110°) **water**
- 2 teaspoons **sugar**
- 1 package **active dry yeast**

  About 4½ cups **all-purpose flour**
- ¾ cup **whole-wheat flour**

  About ½ cup **cornmeal**
- 1 teaspoon **salt**
- 1 tablespoon **olive oil**
- 1 **large egg,** beaten with 1 tablespoon water

**1.** In a large bowl, combine warm water and sugar. Sprinkle the yeast over the water; let stand until yeast softens, about 5 minutes.

**2.** Stir together 4 cups all-purpose flour, the whole-wheat flour, ¼ cup cornmeal, and salt. Add ½ the flour mixture to bowl. Beat with a spoon or mixer until dough is well moistened. Stir in remaining flour.

**3.** *To knead with a dough hook,* beat at medium speed until dough begins to pull from bowl sides and is not sticky when lightly touched, 10 to 15 minutes. If dough sticks, beat in more all-purpose flour, 1 tablespoon at a time. Remove dough hook.

*To knead by hand,* scrape dough onto a well-floured board. Knead until very elastic and no longer sticky, 10 to 15 minutes. Add flour as required to keep dough from sticking to the board. Wash and oil bowl, then return dough to bowl.

**4.** Cover bowl with plastic wrap and let dough rise in a warm place until doubled, 1 to 1¼ hours.

**5.** Briefly knead dough with dough hook or on a lightly floured board to expel air. Shape dough into a smooth ball or oval loaf. Set smooth side up on a baking sheet dusted with about 2 tablespoons all-purpose flour. Dust loaf top lightly with more flour, drape with plastic wrap, and let stand until puffy, 30 to 40 minutes. Refrigerate loaf if it is ready before adobe oven is.

**6.** When adobe oven has cooled to about 350°, transfer loaf to a cornmeal-coated bread paddle. Make slashes about ½ inch deep across the loaftop in

GLAZE BREAD DOUGH with beaten egg.

several places with a very sharp knife or razor, then brush with beaten egg; take care not to let egg run onto paddle.

**7.** Slip loaf from paddle onto clean oven floor. Close oven door. Check temperature in 5 minutes; if above 450°, remove door until oven drops to 350°, then close. After 10 minutes, spray loaf all over with water; close door. After another 10 minutes, spray loaf with more water; close door.

**8.** Continue baking until loaf is rich golden brown and sounds hollow when tapped, 40 to 60 minutes more. Pull loaf onto oven hearth to cool. Serve warm or cool.

Per ounce: 71 cal., 7.6% (5.4 cal.) from fat; 2.1 g protein; 0.6 g fat (0.1 g sat.); 14 g carbo (0.8 g fiber); 60 mg sodium; 5.3 mg chol.

## Flat Bread Salt Pizzas

PREP AND COOK TIME: About 20 minutes

MAKES: 4 servings

**1.** Cut a thawed 1-pound loaf of **frozen bread dough** into quarters. Shape each portion into a ball.

**2.** On a lightly floured board, pat each ball into an 8-inch-wide round and rub lightly with **olive oil** (about 4 teaspoons total). Sprinkle rounds with **kosher** or coarse **salt** (½ to ¾ teaspoon total).

**3.** If desired, cut **1 head roasted garlic** (see Adobe Oven Vegetables, facing page) in half, squeeze out pulp, and pat equally over bread rounds. Sprinkle lightly with **dried thyme** (about ½ teaspoon total).

**4.** Set rounds, 1 at a time, on a cornmeal-dusted bread paddle.

**5.** When adobe oven is at 550°, slip rounds directly onto clean oven floor.

Leave door open and cook until bread is browned, about 5 minutes. Rotate with paddle if necessary to brown evenly. (You can bake pizzas at cooler oven temperatures, but they take longer to cook and don't brown as well.)

Per pizza: 352 cal., 26% (90 cal.) from fat; 8.7 g protein; 10 g fat (1.9 g sat.); 55 g carbo (2.4 g fiber); 730 mg sodium; 5.7 mg chol.

## Adobe Oven Ratatouille

PREP AND COOK TIME: About 1¼ hours

NOTES: If roasting meat in the adobe oven, skim fat from juices and mix with the ratatouille.

MAKES: 4 cups; 6 to 8 servings

**1.** Following directions for Adobe Oven Vegetables (facing page), roast 8 **Roma tomatoes** (1½ lb. total), 2 **slender eggplant** (¾ lb. total), 2 **bell peppers** (1 lb. total), 1 **onion** (6 oz.), and 1 **head garlic** (2½ oz.).

**2.** Peel, core, and chop tomatoes; put tomatoes and juice in a bowl. Stem eggplant. Pull skin, stems, and seeds from peppers. Peel onion. Chop eggplant, peppers, and onion and add to bowl. Cut garlic heads in half crosswise and squeeze pulp into bowl.

**3.** Heat ½ cup **chicken broth** and ¾ teaspoon **dried thyme** until boiling. Mix with vegetables and add 1 tablespoon **lemon juice** and **salt** and **pepper** to taste.

Per ½ cup: 60 cal., 6% (3.6 cal.) from fat; 2.3 g protein; 0.4 g fat (0 g sat.); 14 g carbo (2.9 g fiber); 12 mg sodium; 0 mg chol.

## Adobe Oven Roasted Salsa

PREP AND COOK TIME: About 1½ hours

NOTES: To avoid discomfort, wear plastic gloves when handling chilies.

MAKES: 2 cups

**1.** Following directions for Adobe Oven Vegetables (facing page), roast 8 **fresh poblano chilies** (about 1½ lb. total; also called pasillas), 4 **fresh Anaheim chilies** (about ½ lb. total; also called California or New Mexico), 2 **red bell peppers** (about ¾ lb. total), and 1 **onion** (6 oz.). Pull off and discard chili and bell pepper skins, stems, and seeds. Peel onion. Dice vegetables and scoop, with juices, into a bowl.

**2.** Season salsa with 3 tablespoons **lime juice** and **salt** to taste.

Per ¼ cup: 52 cal., 5.2% (2.7 cal.) from fat; 2.2 g protein; 0.3 g fat (0 g sat.); 12 g carbo (2.1 g fiber); 8.1 mg sodium; 0 mg chol. ◆

# Kitchen Cabinet

## READERS' RECIPES TESTED IN SUNSET'S KITCHENS

### BY LINDA LAU ANUSASANANAN

SPLIT A CRISP BAGUETTE and fill with roasted garlic and vegetables.

## Veggie Sandwich with Roasted Garlic-Shallot Spread

### Anita Behnke, Oakley, California

With two small kids and a daily two-hour commute to a full-time job, Anita Behnke is always looking for fast meals—especially low-fat ones. In this main-dish sandwich, roasted garlic and shallots replace mayonnaise. Sometimes Behnke adds sliced roast turkey instead of the cucumber.

PREP AND COOK TIME: About 50 minutes

MAKES: 3 or 4 servings

- 2 heads (each 3 in. wide) **garlic**
- 4 **shallots** (each 3 in. wide)
- 1 **baguette** (8 oz.)
- 1 **firm-ripe avocado** (6 oz.)
  **Salt** and **pepper**
- 1 cup thinly sliced **cucumber**
- ½ pound **Roma tomatoes,** rinsed and thinly sliced
- 1 cup lightly packed **fresh basil** leaves

**1.** Set garlic heads and shallots in an 8- or 9-inch pan. Bake in a 375° oven until garlic and shallots are very soft when pressed, 35 to 40 minutes. Let cool.

**2.** Split baguette in half lengthwise.

**3.** Cut root end off garlic and squeeze out soft pulp; discard skin. Cut root end off shallots, peel, and discard skin; chop soft interior. Mix garlic and shallots and spread onto cut sides of baguette.

**4.** Peel, pit, and thinly slice the avocado. Lay slices over bottom baguette half and sprinkle lightly with salt and pepper.

**5.** Arrange cucumber, tomatoes, and basil leaves on avocado. Cover with top half of baguette. With a serrated knife, carefully cut sandwich into 3 or 4 portions.

Per serving: 287 cal., 22% (64 cal.) from fat; 9.3 g protein; 7.1 g fat (1.2 g sat.); 49 g carbo (5.1 g fiber); 363 mg sodium; 0 mg chol.

## Mango Chicken Salad

### Sherbonné Barnes-Anderson, San Francisco

A legal secretary by day and a coloratura soprano at night, time-pressed Sherbonné Barnes-Anderson throws this salad together after work while she warms up her voice. "It travels to rehearsals at room temperature and doesn't contain any garlic or onion to torture my tenors with," she says. For a speedier version, use a purchased mango dressing instead of the nectar and vinegar mixture.

PREP AND COOK TIME: About 45 minutes

MAKES: 6 servings

- ½ cup coarsely chopped **pecans**
- 2 packages (4 oz. each) **brown and wild rice mix with seasonings**
- 1 **firm-ripe mango** (1 lb.)
- ⅔ cup **refrigerated** or canned **mango nectar**
- ½ cup **rice vinegar**
- 2 cups shredded skinned **cooked chicken**
- ⅓ cup chopped **fresh mint** leaves
  **Salt** and **pepper**
  **Mint sprigs**

**1.** In a 3- to 4-quart pan over medium-low heat, stir pecans often until lightly browned, 3 to 4 minutes. Pour into a small bowl.

**2.** In the same pan, cook rice in water as directed on package, until tender to bite, about 25 minutes. Reserve season-

RICHARD JUNG

ing packets for another use.

**3.** Meanwhile, slice mango lengthwise down each side of pit to remove fleshy cheeks. On the flesh side of each cheek, cut down to the peel (but not through it) in a crosshatch pattern to make ³/₄-inch cubes. With a large metal spoon, scoop cubes from peel. Also trim fruit off pit and dice it.

**4.** Mix mango nectar and vinegar. Add to warm or cool rice and mix lightly. Add pecans, mango, chicken, and chopped mint; gently mix. Add salt and pepper to taste.

**5.** Spoon into bowl and garnish with mint sprigs.

Per serving: 333 cal., 30% (99 cal.) from fat; 18 g protein; 11 g fat (1.8 g sat.); 43 g carbo (3.5 g fiber); 55 mg sodium; 42 mg chol.

## Spinach and Bulgur Salad

### Nan Kelley Lofas, Bainbridge Island, Washington

During the walk home from a belly-dancing class, Nan Kelley Lofas stopped at a deli for dinner. The spinach and feta salad she ordered didn't taste as good as she thought it could, so she experimented at home. The result is this salad.

PREP AND COOK TIME: About 25 minutes

MAKES: 5 or 6 servings

- ²/₃ cup **bulgur wheat**
- 12 cups (about 10 oz.) **spinach** leaves, rinsed and drained
- ¹/₂ cup thinly sliced **green onions**
- ¹/₃ cup chopped **fresh dill**
- ³/₄ cup (4 oz.) crumbled **feta cheese**
- ¹/₄ cup **red wine vinegar**
- 2 tablespoons **olive oil**
  - **Salt** and **pepper**

**1.** In a small bowl, combine bulgur and 1¹/₂ cups boiling water. Let stand until bulgur is tender to bite, about 15 minutes.

**2.** Meanwhile, stack spinach leaves and cut into ¹/₄-inch-wide strips.

**3.** Place spinach, onions, dill, and cheese in a wide bowl. Pour bulgur into a fine strainer and press out the excess water. Add bulgur to bowl with spinach.

**4.** Mix vinegar and oil. Add to salad

and mix. Season with salt and pepper to taste.

Per serving: 158 cal., 51% (80 cal.) from fat; 6.1 g protein; 8.9 g fat (3.5 g sat.); 15 g carbo (4.3 g fiber); 253 mg sodium; 17 mg chol.

## Hungarian Peppers and Eggs

### Liz Ashford, Coquitlam, British Columbia

Ever since Liz Ashford was a child, a Hungarian dish called lecsó has been a treasured tradition in her family. Her father made it with a combination of sweet and hot yellow peppers. Now Ashford cooks lecsó for Labor Day when she and her family are on their annual camping trip. In the market, sweet peppers for this dish may be sold as yellow banana peppers, which are mild like bell peppers, or Hungarian wax peppers, which have more pungency.

PREP AND COOK TIME: About 30 minutes

MAKES: 4 servings

- ³/₄ pound **yellow banana peppers** or yellow bell peppers
- 1 **yellow Hungarian wax pepper** (4 oz.) or 2 yellow Fresno chilies (also called Santa Fe Grande or wax; 2 oz. total)
- 2 **firm-ripe tomatoes** (¹/₂ lb. total)
- 1 tablespoon **olive oil**
- 1 **onion** (6 oz.), finely chopped
- 8 **large eggs**
  - About ¹/₂ teaspoon **salt**
  - About ¹/₈ teaspoon **pepper**

**1.** Stem and seed yellow banana and Hungarian peppers (or chilies). Cut banana peppers into ¹/₂-inch squares. Finely chop Hungarian pepper.

**2.** Rinse tomatoes, core, and cut in half crosswise. Gently squeeze out and discard seeds and juice; coarsely chop tomatoes.

**3.** In a 10- to 12-inch nonstick frying pan over high heat, combine oil, onion, all the peppers, and half the tomatoes. Stir often until vegetables are tinged with brown and all liquid evaporates, 7 to 9 minutes.

**4.** Meanwhile, in a bowl, beat eggs to blend with 2 tablespoons water, ¹/₂ teaspoon salt, and ¹/₈ teaspoon pepper.

**5.** Add egg mixture to vegetables and reduce heat to medium-low. With a wide spatula, lift cooked portion of eggs to allow uncooked portion to flow underneath until eggs are softly set, 1 to 2 minutes. Transfer to plates. Garnish with remaining tomatoes. Add salt and pepper to taste.

Per serving: 237 cal., 53% (126 cal.) from fat; 15 g protein; 14 g fat (3.6 g sat.); 15 g carbo (3 g fiber); 425 mg sodium; 425 mg chol.

## Sweet Zucchini Pickles

### Chuck Allen, Palm Springs

Because Chuck Allen is a retired chef, hostesses expect more from him than a bouquet. He finds these zucchini pickles make a fine house gift. They are almost as pretty as flowers and last a lot longer—up to six weeks in the refrigerator.

PREP AND COOK TIME: About 40 minutes, plus at least 1 day to age

MAKES: About 6 cups

- 4 **zucchini** (¹/₄ lb. each)
- 1 **red onion** (¹/₂ lb.)
- 1 teaspoon **salt**
- 2 **red** or yellow **bell peppers** (or 1 of each; ¹/₂ lb. total)
- 2 cups **cider vinegar**
- ²/₃ cup **sugar**
- 2 tablespoons **pickling spice**

**1.** Trim and discard zucchini ends. Thinly slice zucchini.

**2.** Peel onion and cut in half lengthwise, then vertically into thin slivers.

**3.** Mix zucchini, onion, and salt. Let stand 30 minutes. Rinse well and drain.

**4.** Meanwhile, stem, seed, and cut red bell peppers into thin slivers about 2 inches long.

**5.** In a 4- to 5-quart pan over high heat, bring vinegar, sugar, and pickling spice to a boil. Add bell peppers and zucchini-onion mixture. Remove from heat and mix well.

**6.** Spoon vegetables and liquid into jars, cover, and let cool. Chill at least 24 hours or up to 6 weeks.

Per ¹/₄ cup: 33 cal., 0% (0 cal.) from fat; 0.4 g protein; 0 g fat; 8.6 g carbo (0.3 g fiber); 99 mg sodium; 0 mg chol. ◆

Prizewinning recipes from Sunset's centennial cook-off (see page 192) showcase classic Western ingredients.

# September

# foodguide

BY JERRY ANNE DI VECCHIO

## mexican cheeses

Two aromatic Mexican herbs, epazote and *hoja santa,* have arrived here with cheeses made by Paula Lambert's Mozzarella Company in Dallas. Epazote, a bitter herb used sparingly, is mixed with green chilies in *queso blanco* (top in photo)*,* a mild, fresh, squeaky-textured white cheese that

gets squeakier, not softer, when heated ($10 per lb.). Hoja santa, a big leaf with a mint-anise-tarragon fragrance, is wrapped around a chunk of soft, fresh chèvre (goat) cheese (left and right in photo), imparting to it a subtle taste and smell ($14 per lb.). To order, call (800) 798-2954. Shipping costs extra.

Try the hoja santa goat cheese on toasted tortilla chips or dried banana chips. Slice the queso blanco to eat plain or use it in this simple salad.

**Black bean salad.** Drain 2 **cans** (15 oz. each) **black beans.** In a bowl, mix beans with 2 tablespoons **sherry vinegar** and 2 tablespoons chopped **red onion.** Thinly shave about 2 ounces **queso blanco cheese with green chilies and epazote** and mix with salad. Makes 4 servings.

Per serving: 211 cal., 24% (50 cal.) from fat; 15 g protein; 5.6 g fat (2.5 g sat.); 28 g carbo (12 g fiber); 795 mg sodium; 13 mg chol.

JAMES CARRIER (3)

## FOOD NEWS
# What will George say?

■ When President Bush declared he didn't like it, broccoli made headlines. Now, Cruciferae is making news again.

A new broccoli hybrid has appeared on the Western scene, and you can expect to find it in many markets from now through spring. The hybrid, developed by Sakata Seed America in Morgan Hill, California, is slimmer and milder-tasting than regular broccoli. Its long stems are about as thick as plump asparagus, and its shape and flavor reveal its relationship to Chinese kale. The vegetable may be labeled *broccolini* or *asparation,* but if you ask for baby broccoli, your produce dealer will know what you want.

In its tender stage (the stem skin pierces easily), the flavor is mild and sweet, making raw broccolini delightful for munching. Or you can cook it as you would broccoli—boil, steam, stir-fry, or grill it until tender-crisp.

rant in San Francisco, Reed Hearon makes a version he calls sage farinata (a roasted chickpea cake). The sage looks pretty and adds a faint crunch. For lunch or a light supper, enjoy wedges of sage farinata with olives, some feta cheese, and a cold, bold rosé wine.

## Sage Farinata

**PREP AND COOK TIME:** About 30 minutes

**NOTES:** Garbanzo flour is sold in many supermarkets and natural-food stores, as well as Indian and Middle Eastern food markets.

**MAKES:** 6 appetizer, 2 main-dish servings

- 2 tablespoons **olive oil**
- ¼ cup **fresh sage** leaves, rinsed and drained
- 1 **onion** (6 oz.)
- 1 cup **garbanzo flour**

  About ¼ teaspoon **salt**

**1.** Put oil in a 9- to 10-inch ovenproof frying pan. Add sage leaves and mix to coat with oil, then lift out leaves and put in a small bowl.

**2.** Peel and thinly slice onion. Put onion in frying pan over medium-high heat and stir often until golden and sweet-tasting, about 10 minutes.

**3.** Meanwhile, in a bowl, whisk garbanzo flour and ¼ teaspoon salt with 1½ cups water until smooth.

**4.** Reduce heat under onions to medium-low. Push onion slices to center of pan and pour garbanzo mixture around them, then lift onions so batter can flow under them. Sprinkle socca with sage leaves. Cook until socca feels dry when lightly touched and is browned on the bottom (lift carefully with a spatula to check), 12 to 14 minutes.

**5.** Broil 6 to 8 inches from heat until top is lightly browned, 3 to 4 minutes.

**6.** Cut into wedges and serve with a wide spatula. Add salt to taste.

Per appetizer serving: 124 cal., 42% (52 cal.) from fat; 4.2 g protein; 5.8 g fat (0.7 g sat.); 15 g carbo (1.7 g fiber); 101 mg sodium; 0 mg chol.

## A TASTE OF THE WEST

# Out of Africa

■ I first tasted *socca* long ago—in the shaded, open-air market by the sea in Nice. The flat cake sizzling in olive oil atop a wood-fired oil drum smelled so good that I sidled right up and bought a chunk. Had I known that garbanzo flour and water were the essence of what I'd just snatched up, I'd have brushed socca aside as boring. What a mistake that would have been. There's a Mother

Earth simplicity about socca. One tender, slightly nutty bite leads to another. Its flavor is unemphatic, but it seeps right into the bones of taste memory.

No doubt the dish arrived in France by way of North Africa, where garbanzo (also known as chickpea) flour is a staple. And apparently, socca also migrated down the coast into Italy. At his Italian-influenced Rose Pistola Restau-

*Canned option.* If garbanzo flour isn't available, omit it from preceding recipe. Instead, drain 1 **can** (15½ oz.) **garbanzos,** reserving 6 tablespoons of the liquid. Whirl garbanzos, reserved liquid, and 1 tablespoon **all-purpose flour** in a blender until very smooth. Use in step 3. Mixture will still feel moist on top when browned on bottom, step 4, and will take 3 to 4 minutes longer to brown when broiled, step 5.

# Freshly minted

■ Mint and lamb are partners of long standing. If, however, you fancy lamb with mint *jelly,* you may have to smuggle your own jar of the now passé condiment into hoity-toity restaurants and risk condescending stares. To be culinarily correct and still relish your lamb, you could demand fresh mint. This aromatic combination of rib chops and risotto is how I put new life into the old food marriage at home.

## Lamb Chops with Mint Risotto

PREP AND COOK TIME: About 35 minutes

NOTES: If risotto is ready before lamb, it can be kept warm for a few minutes.

MAKES: 4 servings

    2  teaspoons **butter** or margarine
 ¼  cup chopped **shallots**
 1½  cups **medium-grain white rice** such as arborio or pearl
 1½  teaspoons grated **lemon** peel
      About 4½ cups fat-skimmed **chicken broth**
    4  **fat-trimmed double-bone lamb rib chops** (about 1¾ in. thick, 1½ lb. total)
    1  teaspoon minced **garlic**
 ¼  cup **balsamic vinegar**
    1  teaspoon **sugar**
    1  cup slivered **fresh mint** leaves
    3  tablespoons **lemon juice**

**1.** In a 3- to 4-quart pan over high heat, combine butter and shallots and stir until shallots are limp, about 1 minute. Add rice and stir until some of the grains are opaque, about 2 minutes longer.

**2.** Add lemon peel and 4 cups broth to pan and bring to a boil. Reduce heat and simmer, stirring often, until rice is tender to bite, about 15 minutes.

**3.** Meanwhile, in a 10- to 12-inch ovenproof frying pan over

JAMES CARRIER (2)

high heat, rub fatty side of chops in pan to lightly oil, then lay chops in pan and brown on all sides, about 5 minutes.

**4.** Put pan with chops in a 400° oven. Bake until meat is medium-rare (pink) in center of thickest part (cut to test), about 15 minutes, or medium (only slightly pink), about 20 minutes. Skim and discard fat from pan.

**5.** Return pan with chops to high heat. Add garlic, vinegar, and sugar. Shake pan and stir to release browned bits, then stir in ¼ cup mint and remove from heat.

**6.** If rice is cooked before lamb is ready, turn heat to very low and stir in about ¼ cup broth. Stir lemon juice and most of the remaining mint into rice, and if you want a creamier texture, a little more broth. Serve rice with lamb and pan juices, sprinkled with the final bits of mint.

Per serving: 463 cal., 21% (99 cal.) from fat; 33 g protein; 11 g fat (4.3 g sat.); 56 g carbo (6.1 g fiber); 171 mg sodium; 65 mg chol.

---

MORE BABY BUZZ

## No-fuzz kiwi

■ This year, little kiwi fruit are a big deal at Hurst's Berry Farm in Sheridan, Oregon (www.hursts-berry.com). That is, the crop of miniature kiwi fruit is big enough to attract attention. Each grape-size fruit makes a single bite, and its thin, red-green skin is smooth—no more peeling.

Baby kiwi fruit are harvested from mid-September to late October, but you may find them in markets into November. Healthy fruit keep well in containers in the refrigerator for up to two weeks.

Inside, baby kiwi fruit are as brilliant green as the big guys. Cut into halves for a beautiful addition to this simple dessert.

## Pineapple, Blueberry, and Kiwi Fruit Dessert

PREP TIME: 3 to 4 minutes

MAKES: 1 serving

Cut 2 crosswise slices (about ½ in. thick) from a peeled, cored **pineapple.** Place on plate; scatter with ¼ to ⅓ cup rinsed, drained **blueberries.** Rinse, drain, and trim ends from 3 to 4 **baby kiwi fruit.** Cut in half; arrange on pineapple. Drizzle with 2 tablespoons **orange-flavor liqueur,** such as Cointreau (or orange juice sweetened with honey), and 1 to 2 teaspoons **lemon juice.**

Per serving: 204 cal., 4% (8.1 cal.) from fat; 1.4 g protein; 0.9 g fat (0 g sat.); 39 g carbo (4.8 g fiber); 7.1 mg sodium; 0 mg chol. ◆

# The Wine Guide

BY KAREN MacNEIL

## Nature vs. nurture in Oregon

■ One of the unforeseen consequences of living in New York for a few years was that Woody Allen films got a lot funnier. That's because there are some places you can never truly understand until you live there. Like Oregon. Oregonians seem to share a secret enchantment not bestowed on the world at large. There's a kind of private glee in the state.

This goes a long way toward explaining the perplexing behavior of Oregon vintners. There is probably only one group of outsiders who might comprehend the nail-biting, nerve-racking gratification of Oregon viticulture—the Cistercian monks of the Middle Ages (who, coincidentally, planted the same grapes as Oregonians do today—in the equally unforgiving climate of Burgundy).

Admittedly, Oregon wines can achieve a delicacy rarely found in other U.S. wines, and that is a compelling reward. But can results alone propel one to take on the nearly impossible? Do people climb Kilimanjaro to see snow?

Consider this basic reality: without sunlight and warmth, grapes don't ripen, and unripe grapes make mean wine. In Oregon, as fate would have it, sunlight and warmth can be in short supply. Moreover, rain (about 40 inches a year) and frost are ubiquitous threats during spring and fall, when grapes are most susceptible to rot or damage. To top it off, weather patterns here are so erratic from year to year that a given producer's wines can be great one year, disappointing the next. In short, Oregon grapes live on the edge, sometimes hanging on by the skins of their teeth.

Though seemingly counterintuitive, Oregon winemakers wouldn't have it any other way. For the vines' struggle against these harsh vagaries of climate is precisely the key to the wines' success. Grapes here cannot explode into ripeness (which often results in simple wines); they must make their way slowly toward maturity, ideally developing finesse and nuances of flavor along the way. Every year is a gamble with nature, but when the grapes (and winemaker)

RICK MARIANI

do win, a wine of utter beauty emerges.

A number of small wineries struggled along prior to Prohibition, but the modern Oregon wine industry was born in the mid-1960s when David Lett planted the state's first Pinot Noir, at Eyrie Vineyards in the Willamette Valley. (Eyrie still makes some of the best Pinot in the state.) Local farmers thought he was crazy. And in a way, he *was* possessed—by an idea. Namely, that complexity in wine is related to the marginality of the climate in which the grapes are grown; grapes that receive barely enough sun to cross the finish line of ripeness have a better chance of making graceful wine than grapes that bake in full sun.

Winemakers who followed Lett, like

Dick Erath of Erath Vineyards, agreed. Today there are more than 100 wineries in Oregon, and virtually all of them grow Pinot Noir, the great red of Burgundy and one of the world's most fragile, persnickety grapes. Oregon, in fact, is the only place outside of Burgundy that specializes in this variety.

To no one's surprise, the results are mixed. Depending on the year and the winemaker's judgment calls, an Oregon Pinot Noir can be loaded with personality—or something you'd really rather pour down the drain.

Even a devastatingly good Oregon Pinot, though, is almost never powerful. Because big, syrupy flavors and textures (such as in a Zinfandel, Syrah, or Cabernet Sauvignon) are not the province of Pinot Noir. To appreciate Pinot, you must turn the binoculars around and go looking for elegance.

Oregon is also well known for Chardonnay, but the white grape that winemakers here are most smitten with is Pinot Gris, an ancestral sister of Pinot Noir, which in good-weather years is fresh, lemony, and irresistible.

Those Oregon winemakers are a story in themselves. Almost all are renegade dropouts or exes. College dropouts. Ex-professors. Counterculture dropouts. Even ex-theologians. These are the modern-day monks who have renounced easier winemaking conditions and take pleasure in the hard lessons of the greatest teacher of all—nature herself.

## OREGON WINES TO TRY

There are so many great producers in Oregon—Adelsheim, Amity, Beaux Frères, Broadley, Chehalem, Cristom, Domaine Drouhin, Eyrie, Ken Wright, Ponzi, and many more—that it is nearly impossible to narrow the field to a few favorites. Experiment on your own, because every year Oregon, which is packed with small and new wineries, is full of surprises.

■ *Archery Summit Winery "Vireton" 1997 (Oregon),* $25. A rich, intriguing white made from Pinot Gris, Pinot Blanc, and Chardonnay.

■ *Hamacher Wines Chardonnay 1995 (Oregon),* $20. Vivid, gorgeous, and perfectly balanced. The best Chardonnay from anywhere in the United States I've had this year.

■ *Willakenzie Estate Pinot Gris 1996 (Willamette Valley),* $15. Lovely rich pear and almond cake flavors.

■ *Broadley Vineyards Pinot Noir "Claudia's Choice" 1996 (Willamette Valley),*

$30. The intensity of fruit in this wine is stunning. Chocolate-covered cherries!

■ *Chehalem Pinot Noir "Rion Reserve" 1995 (Willamette Valley),* $35. Rich pomegranate, cherry spice, and earth flavors.

■ *Eyrie Vineyards Pinot Noir Reserve 1990 (Willamette Valley),* $35. Owner David Lett has an intuitive ability to bring out femininity and elegance in every wine he makes.

■ *Thomas Winery Pinot Noir 1994 (Willamette Valley),* $27. Fascinating cola, berry, and wild mushroom flavors. ◆

# Sunset's Centennial Cook-off

## Prizewinning recipes showcase classic Western ingredients

BY ELAINE JOHNSON • FOOD PHOTOGRAPHS BY JAMES CARRIER • PORTRAITS BY TERRENCE McCARTHY

■ A CENTURY AGO, *Sunset's* raison d'être was to lure Easterners west. And part of that mission was to establish the region's bragging rights about food. After all, with our abundant agriculture and spirit of discovery, food trends have a natural way of starting here. From 1915 on, recipes rich with local products—artichokes, citrus, cranberries, olives, raisins, and wine—appeared regularly on our pages.

Then *Sunset* shifted gears. In 1929, we became a magazine about the West for Westerners. And our view of regional foods became even more commanding when we invited readers to share their recipes in a monthly feature called Kitchen Cabinet. More than 5,000 recipes later, the column is still going strong.

So it seemed fitting to honor our Centennial year by extending another invitation—this one to a cooking contest. Last September we asked you to send your best recipes built around five great Western foods: artichokes, avocados, berries, chilies, and seafood.

Responses poured in. *Sunset's* food staff evaluated more than 800 recipes, winnowing the entries to the 75 most promising. These we prepared in our test kitchens, and a tasting panel narrowed the field to 15 finalists, three in each food category.

They were guests last March at *Sunset's* headquarters in Menlo Park, California, where they prepared their entries for judges (see page 10) who rated the dishes for flavor, use of ingredients, creativity, and presentation. Wonderful dishes all, they had a neck-and-neck race to the finish line.

And here are the winners: the grand prize, five best-of-category, and remaining finalists. Some of the recipes are fresh spins on old favorites, others make innovative leaps. But all 15 make a delicious start for our second century.

---

## Helen Wolt
### Colorado Springs

### GRAND PRIZE

"In Colorado Springs, we like flavors of the Southwest, such as pine nuts and cornmeal," says Wolt. "But I'm a native Seattleite, so I remembered the lush berry fields at home." To create her winning recipe she mixed the flavors of her two homes. Judges applauded the delicate crunch and flavor of Wolt's shortcakes. She serves them with berries and a lime cream sauce.

As a hobby, Wolt enters about 10 cooking contests a year. "Cooking is my creative outlet," she says. "And though I cook all kinds of foods, baking desserts is my original love."

## Cornmeal Piñon Shortcakes with Berries and Lime Cream

PREP AND COOK TIME: About 1½ hours

NOTES: To gild the lily, top shortcakes with whipped cream sweetened with a little caramel syrup and curled strips of lime peel.

MAKES: 8 servings

About 1½ cups **all-purpose flour**

¾ cup **cornmeal**

2 teaspoons **baking powder**

¼ teaspoon **salt**

About 5 tablespoons **butter** or margarine

⅓ cup **caramel ice cream topping**

⅓ cup plus 1 tablespoon **half-and-half** (light cream) or milk

1 **large egg**

¼ cup **pine nuts**

2 tablespoons firmly packed **brown sugar**

⅛ teaspoon **ground cinnamon**

1 can (14 oz.) **sweetened condensed milk**

½ cup **sour cream**

1½ teaspoons grated **lime** peel (green part only)

¼ cup **lime juice**

2 cups **raspberries,** rinsed and drained

2 cups **blueberries,** rinsed and drained

2 cups **blackberries,** rinsed and drained

**1.** In a bowl, mix 1½ cups flour, cornmeal, baking powder, and salt. With pastry blender or fingers, cut or rub in 5 tablespoons butter until largest lumps are ¼-inch pieces.

**2.** In another bowl, beat to blend caramel topping, ⅓ cup half-and-half, and egg. Pour into flour mixture and stir just until moistened.

**3.** Pat dough into a ball. Knead on a lightly floured board just until smooth,

GRAND PRIZE piñon shortcakes overflow with sweet lime cream and berries.

**What did the winners win?** Grand prize winner Helen Wolt received $2,500; a Kitchen-Aid KSM5 mixer; butter for a year, courtesy of Land O'Lakes; and Woodbridge wine by Robert Mondavi. Best-of-category winners—Dottie Lyons (artichokes), Fran Jenkins (avocados), Roxanne Chan (berries), Kristen Farrar (chilies), and Sharon Tobin (seafood)—each received a Spirit 500 Weber gas grill and Woodbridge wine. All contestants received a trip to *Sunset* headquarters, accommodations, gift certificates from Safeway and Land O'Lakes, Woodbridge wine, and a 1998 *Sunset Recipe Annual*.

about 10 turns; add flour to board as required to prevent sticking.

**4.** Pat dough into a 6½-inch round. Cut into 8 wedges and place pieces about 1 inch apart on a nonstick or lightly buttered 12- by 15-inch baking sheet.

**5.** Brush shortcake wedges with remaining 1 tablespoon half-and-half. Combine pine nuts with sugar and cinnamon; gently pat onto shortcakes.

**6.** Bake in a 375° oven until dark gold, 22 to 25 minutes. Cool on a rack.

**7.** In a bowl, mix sweetened condensed milk, sour cream, and lime peel with lime juice to make lime cream.

**8.** Split shortcakes in half. Place each bottom on a dessert plate. Combine raspberries, blueberries, and blackberries and spoon equally over shortcake bottoms. Spoon lime cream over berries, then place shortcake tops on cream.

Per serving: 542 cal., 33% (180 cal.) from fat; 11 g protein; 20 g fat (11 g sat.); 84 g carbo (5.7 g fiber); 402 mg sodium; 74 mg chol.

## ARTICHOKES

### Dottie Lyons
Santa Maria, California
BEST-OF-CATEGORY

"I grew up in Oklahoma and was very poor," Lyons reflects. "When I was 14, we came to California—the land of opportunity. As the oldest girl of 11 kids, I always helped out. We canned and had a garden." Lyons still loves fresh vegetables, which are abundant in her agricultural community. "I came up with this recipe to use all my favorite foods—fennel, artichokes, spicy Italian sausage, and pasta."

### Baby Artichokes and Sausage Rigatoni

PREP AND COOK TIME: **About 1 hour**

NOTES: To be completely edible, small artichokes must be peeled down to tender leaves that are pale green to the tip. Save fennel leaves to garnish pasta.

MAKES: **8 servings**

TINY ARTICHOKES, fennel, and sausage highlight sauce for rigatoni.

1½ pounds **artichokes** (1½ in. wide)
1 head **fennel** (3½ in. wide)
1 pound **mild** or hot **Italian sausages,** casings removed
1½ cups chopped **onion**
2 teaspoons **fennel seed**
1 teaspoon minced **garlic**
1 cup thinly sliced **red bell pepper**
½ cup **dry white wine**
1 cup fat-skimmed **chicken** or vegetable **broth**
½ cup **whipping cream**
1 pound **dried rigatoni pasta**
½ cup **grated parmesan cheese**
  **Salt**

**1.** Break off and discard artichoke leaves down to the pale green, tender inner leaves. Cut off and discard thorny tips. Trim bottoms. Quarter artichokes (they will discolor). Trim out and discard fuzzy centers. Rinse and drain artichokes.

**2.** Trim and discard stems and any bruised portions from fennel. Rinse fennel and thinly slice crosswise.

**3.** In a 5- to 6-quart pan over medium-high heat, frequently stir sausages, breaking up meat with spoon, until brown, about 10 minutes.

**4.** Add artichokes, fennel, onion, fennel seed, garlic, and bell pepper to pan. Stir often until onion is limp, about 10 minutes.

**5.** Pour wine, broth, and cream into pan. Bring to a boil over high heat,

then reduce heat and simmer, stirring occasionally, until artichokes are tender when pierced, about 10 minutes.

**6.** Meanwhile, cook pasta in 4 quarts boiling water until tender to bite, 10 to 12 minutes.

**7.** Drain pasta, put in a serving bowl, and top with artichoke sauce.

**8.** Offer cheese and salt to add to taste.

Per serving: 526 cal., 43% (225 cal.) from fat; 20 g protein; 25 g fat (10 g sat.); 52 g carbo (4.3 g fiber); 711 mg sodium; 64 mg chol.

### Kristen Farrar
Davis, California
FINALIST

Farrar is relatively new to cooking, and *Sunset's* cook-off was her first recipe contest. Nonetheless, she was a finalist in two ingredient categories, artichokes and chilies. Judges liked the juxtaposition of flavors in Farrar's paella: tangy marinated artichokes, sweet crab, and pungent olives.

### Artichoke Crab Paella

PREP AND COOK TIME: **About 50 minutes**

NOTES: For a creamier texture, add up to 1 cup more chicken broth to cooked risotto and stir over high heat until steaming. Garnish with chopped parsley and lemon wedges.

MAKES: **6 servings**

3 tablespoons **olive oil**
2 cups **white arborio** or pearl **rice**
2 cups chopped **red onions**

1 cup chopped **red bell pepper**

1 tablespoon minced **garlic**

1 cup **dry white wine**

1 quart fat-skimmed **chicken broth**

2 jars (6 oz. each) **marinated artichokes**

¼ cup chopped **parsley**

1 cup (½ lb.) **shelled, cooked crab**

½ cup pitted, chopped **oil-cured olives**

**Pepper**

**1.** In an ovenproof 14-inch-wide, 2- to 3-inch-deep frying pan (or 5- to 6-quart pan) over medium heat, frequently stir oil and rice until rice is opaque, about 5 minutes.

**2.** Add onions, bell pepper, and garlic; stir often until onions are limp, 5 to 8 minutes.

**3.** Add wine, broth, and artichokes with marinade. Bring to a boil over high heat, stirring occasionally.

**4.** Cover tightly with lid or foil and bake in a 350° oven until liquid is absorbed, 20 to 30 minutes.

**5.** Stir in parsley. Arrange crab and olives on risotto. Season to taste with pepper.

Per serving: 447 cal., 34% (153 cal.) from fat; 20 g protein; 17 g fat (2 g sat.); 56 g carbo (7.5 g fiber); 851 mg sodium; 38 mg chol.

### Allan Levy and Pamela Pierson
Oakland, California
FINALIST

Husband and wife contestants Levy and Pierson first tasted grilled artichokes at a restaurant four years ago. "They wouldn't share the recipe, so we started experimenting," Levy explains. "We're both vegetarians, and we're fearless about putting anything on the grill." Cooked artichokes, marinated in an unusual combination of balsamic vinegar, soy, and dill, get sweeter as they char slightly on the barbecue.

### Grilled Artichokes

PREP AND COOK TIME: About 50 minutes

NOTES: Garnish with more chopped fresh dill.

MAKES: 6 servings

6 **artichokes** (each 3½ in. wide)

⅔ cup **balsamic vinegar**

½ cup coarsely chopped **fresh dill**

⅓ cup **reduced-sodium soy sauce**

¼ cup chopped **fresh ginger**

¼ cup chopped **garlic**

1 tablespoon **olive oil**

**1.** Slice artichoke tops off crosswise to remove tips; discard. Pull small leaves from artichokes. With scissors, cut off and discard thorny tips from remaining outer leaves. With a knife, trim fibrous exterior from bottoms and stems.

**2.** Half-fill an 8- to 10-quart pan with water. Cover and bring to a boil over high heat. Add artichokes, cover, and simmer until bottoms pierce easily, about 20 minutes.

**3.** Drain artichokes and let stand until cool enough to handle. Cut each one in half lengthwise and scrape out and discard fuzzy center.

**4.** In a large bowl, combine vinegar, ¼ cup water, dill, soy, ginger, garlic, and oil. Spoon half of the vinegar sauce into a small bowl.

**5.** Roll artichokes in large bowl of sauce.

**6.** Lift artichokes from bowl, draining, then lay them, cut side down, on a barbecue grill over a solid bed of medium coals or a gas grill on medium (you can hold your hand at grill level only 4 to 5 seconds); close lid on gas grill.

**7.** As artichokes cook, baste every few minutes with sauce from large bowl. Grill until lightly browned on bottom, 5 to 7 minutes. Turn artichokes over and spoon remaining basting sauce into them. Grill until leaf tips are lightly charred, 3 to 4 minutes more.

**8.** Arrange artichokes on a platter. Break off leaves and cut up bottoms to dunk into the small bowl of sauce.

Per serving: 98 cal., 23% (23 cal.) from fat; 5 g protein; 2.5 g fat (0.3 g sat.); 17 g carbo (6.1 g fiber); 638 mg sodium; 0 mg chol.

### A V O C A D O S

#### Fran Jenkins
Valley Center, California
BEST-OF-CATEGORY

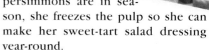

Cooking has been a lifelong passion for Jenkins. At age 5 she baked her own birthday cake—from scratch. Now she teaches cooking at her home, a 40-acre grapefruit and avocado ranch near San Diego. "For our family we also grow persimmons and all sorts of subtropicals, including sapotes and bananas," notes Jenkins. When persimmons are in season, she freezes the pulp so she can make her sweet-tart salad dressing year-round.

### Avocado, Citrus, Jicama, and Persimmon Salad

PREP TIME: About 30 minutes

MAKES: 6 servings

AVOCADO, jicama, and grapefruit are dressed with a golden persimmon-citrus sauce.

1 pound **jicama**

2 **pink** or red **grapefruits** (2 lb. total)

2 **oranges** (1¾ lb. total)

2 **firm-ripe avocados** (1¼ lb. total)

1 head (¾ lb.) **red-leaf lettuce,** rinsed and crisped

½ cup thinly sliced **red onion**

**Persimmon dressing** (recipe follows)

**Salt**

**1.** Rinse and peel jicama, then cut into ⅛- by 2-inch sticks.

**2.** Cut off and discard peel and white membrane from grapefruits and oranges. Working over a bowl to catch juices, cut between inner membranes and fruit to free segments, dropping fruit into bowl.

**3.** Pit, peel, and thinly slice avocados.

**4.** Line a platter or salad plates with lettuce. With a slotted spoon, lift fruit from bowl; reserve 2 tablespoons juice for persimmon dressing and the rest for other uses. Arrange fruit, avocados, onion, and jicama on lettuce.

**5.** Spoon about ¼ cup of dressing over salad. Offer remaining dressing and salt to add to taste.

Per serving: 267 cal., 54% (144 cal.) from fat; 4 g protein; 16 g fat (2.3 g sat.); 33 g carbo (8.4 g fiber); 25 mg sodium; 0.9 mg chol.

## Persimmon Dressing

PREP TIME: About 10 minutes

NOTES: For pulp, cut stem from 1 rinsed soft-ripe Hachiya persimmon (about ½ lb.). Whirl fruit in a blender or food processor until smooth. Makes about ¾ cup pulp; chill extra pulp airtight up to 2 days, or freeze.

MAKES: ¾ cup; 6 servings

6 tablespoons **Hachiya persimmon pulp** (see notes)

1 tablespoon **rice vinegar**

1 teaspoon minced **fresh sage** leaves

½ teaspoon minced **garlic**

2 tablespoons **mayonnaise**

2 tablespoons **citrus juice** (see preceding recipe, step 4)

¼ cup **avocado** or salad **oil**

**Salt** and **pepper**

**1.** In a food processor or blender, whirl persimmon pulp, vinegar, sage, garlic,

mayonnaise, and juice until smooth and blended.

**2.** With motor running, pour in oil. Add salt and pepper to taste.

Per tablespoon: 65 cal., 89% (58 cal.) from fat; 0.1 g protein; 6.4 g fat (0.8 g sat.); 2.2 g carbo (0 g fiber); 13 mg sodium; 1.4 mg chol.

## Sharlee Foster
### Rogue River, Oregon
### FINALIST

"In Southern Oregon we can grow anything *except* avocados and citrus," laughs Foster, who has a huge garden at her home near the Rogue River. "We were in California visiting relatives, and I became intrigued with the combination of avocados and citrus." She uses them in a salad with spinach and rice accented by smoked almonds and sweet dates.

## Sunshine Salad

PREP TIME: About 45 minutes

MAKES: 6 servings

3 **firm-ripe avocados** (2½ lb. total)

4 **navel oranges** (3¾ lb. total)

2 cups cooked **long-grain brown rice,** at room temperature

¾ cup coarsely chopped **salted smoked almonds**

¾ cup chopped **pitted dates**

**Sunshine dressing** (recipe follows)

4 quarts **spinach leaves,** rinsed and crisped

**Salt**

**1.** Pit and peel 2 avocados. Cut peel and white membrane from 2 oranges. Cut peeled avocados and oranges into ¾-inch cubes and put in a bowl. Add rice, almonds, dates, and ⅓ cup dressing; mix.

**2.** Arrange spinach around rims of salad plates. Mound rice mixture in center of spinach.

**3.** Pit, peel, and thinly slice remaining avocado lengthwise. Cut peel and membrane off remaining oranges, cut fruit in halves, then slice crosswise. Arrange avocado and orange slices around rice mixture. Moisten salads with remaining dressing. Season to taste with salt.

Per serving: 737 cal., 60% (441 cal.) from fat; 15 g protein; 49 g fat (6.5 g sat.); 74 g carbo (15 g fiber); 257 mg sodium; 0 mg chol.

## Sunshine Dressing

Mix ½ cup **salad oil,** 3 tablespoons **rice vinegar,** 2 tablespoons thawed **frozen orange juice concentrate,** 1 teaspoon **hot sauce,** and ¼ teaspoon *each* **pepper, cayenne,** and **curry powder.** Makes about ¾ cup; 6 servings.

Per serving: 171 cal., 95% (162 cal.) from fat; 0.2 g protein; 18 g fat (2.3 g sat.); 2.4 g carbo (0.1 g fiber); 22 mg sodium; 0 mg chol.

## Joan Takayama-Ogawa
### Pasadena
### FINALIST

"My husband is a produce distributor. Last summer we had a lot of avocados," recounts Takayama-Ogawa, who is a professional ceramist. "I like to cook low-fat, and was experimenting with ways to stretch avocado in guacamole. Anything green went into it. Brussels sprouts and cabbage were horrible. But milder green onion, peas, and artichokes were great."

## Enlightened Guacamole

PREP TIME: About 10 minutes

NOTES: Use a cooked, trimmed artichoke bottom or a canned artichoke bottom packed in water. Instead of tortilla chips, you can serve guacamole with raw vegetables.

MAKES: About 1½ cups; 6 servings

1 **green onion** (ends trimmed), cut into 2-inch pieces

1 **fresh jalapeño chili,** stemmed, seeded, and coarsely chopped

2 tablespoons coarsely chopped **fresh cilantro**

¼ cup thawed **frozen peas**

3 tablespoons coarsely chopped **cooked artichoke bottom** (see notes)

1 **soft-ripe avocado** (¾ lb.), pitted, peeled, and coarsely chopped

2 tablespoons **lime juice**

**Salt**

8 cups (about 4½ oz.) **low-fat baked tortilla chips**

**1.** In a food processor, whirl onion, chili, cilantro, peas, artichoke, avocado, and lime juice until a chunky paste. (Or with a knife, finely chop vegetables; add lime juice in step 2.)

**2.** Scrape mixture into a bowl and add salt to taste. Serve with chips for dunking.

Per serving: 161 cal., 41% (66 cal.) from fat; 2.9 g protein; 7.3 g fat (1 g sat.); 23 g carbo (2.7 g fiber); 179 mg sodium; 0 mg chol.

## B E R R I E S

### Roxanne Chan
Albany, California

BEST-OF-CATEGORY

Chan was no stranger when she arrived for the cook-off. Since 1974, *Sunset* has published more than 50 of her recipes. She has made recipe contests a serious hobby, entering several thousand and receiving awards from many. "My strategy? I get a feel for what kind of recipes the sponsor publishes, and try to know what current food trends are," Chan explains. "I use a catchy name, and maybe do an unusual twist on a familiar dish. For this recipe I had golden and red raspberries in the garden and incorporated them with white chocolate."

### Red-Gold Raspberry White Chocolate Tart

PREP AND COOK TIME: About 50 minutes, plus 1½ hours to chill

MAKES: 8 servings

- 2 cups **blanched almonds**
- ¼ cup **sugar**
- ¼ cup (⅛ lb.) melted **butter** or margarine
- ½ cup **seedless raspberry jam**
- ⅔ cup **whipping cream**
- 8 ounces **white chocolate,** chopped
- 2 tablespoons **lemon juice**
- ½ teaspoon **almond extract**
- 2¼ cups **red raspberries,** rinsed and drained
- 2 cups **golden raspberries,** rinsed and drained (or use red raspberries)
- 1 tablespoon **almond-flavor liqueur**

RASPBERRIES top white chocolate filling with jam in an almond crust tart.

**1.** In a blender or food processor, whirl almonds with 2 tablespoons sugar until finely ground; if using a blender, whirl half of the mixture at a time.

**2.** Pour nut mixture into a 9-inch tart pan with a removable rim. Add butter and rub with fingers until mixture forms fine crumbs. Press nut mixture evenly over bottom and up side of pan until flush with rim.

**3.** Bake crust in a 325° oven until dark gold, about 20 minutes.

**4.** Spread crust bottom with jam. Cool on a rack.

**5.** In a 1- to 2-quart pan over medium heat, stir cream and chocolate until smoothly melted, about 2 minutes. Stir in lemon juice and almond extract. Evenly spoon into crust.

**6.** Chill tart until filling is firm to touch, 1 to 1¼ hours.

**7.** Arrange red raspberries in a single layer on filling.

**8.** In a blender or food processor, whirl golden raspberries, remaining 2 tablespoons sugar, and liqueur until smoothly puréed. Press mixture through a fine strainer into a bowl; discard seeds. Evenly spread golden raspberry sauce in center of dessert plates.

**9.** Remove pan rim. Cut tart into wedges and place a wedge in sauce on each plate.

Per serving: 584 cal., 62% (360 cal.) from fat; 10 g protein; 40 g fat (14 g sat.); 52 g carbo (7.4 g fiber); 103 mg sodium; 38 mg chol.

### Buzz Baxter
Florence, Oregon

FINALIST

"I'm of Armenian descent, and grew up with yogurt cheese and mint— that's soul food to me," says Baxter. So these ingredients were a natural base for his creamy tart, which he covers with berries picked on friends' property. When Baxter is out of yogurt cheese, he uses sour cream; in testing, we liked either choice.

### The Queen of Tarts

PREP AND COOK TIME: About 35 minutes, plus 1 hour to cool. Allow at least 24 hours to drain yogurt cheese

NOTES: *To make yogurt cheese,* position a strainer over a deep bowl at least 2 inches from bowl bottom. Line strainer with 2 layers cheesecloth. Dump 2 cups low-fat yogurt into cloth. Wrap strainer and bowl airtight with plastic wrap. Chill at least 24 hours or up to 4 days. Pour off whey as it accumulates in bowl. Makes about ³⁄₄ cup yogurt cheese. Garnish tart with mint sprigs and edible flowers such as pansies.

MAKES: 8 servings

About 1 cup **all-purpose flour**

¹⁄₄ cup firmly packed **brown sugar**

¹⁄₂ cup (¹⁄₄ lb.) **butter** or margarine

²⁄₃ cup (6 oz.) **mascarpone** or neufchâtel (light cream) cheese

¹⁄₂ cup **yogurt cheese** (see notes) or sour cream

1 teaspoon grated **lemon** peel

1¹⁄₂ teaspoons minced **fresh mint** leaves

¹⁄₄ cup **powdered sugar**

1 teaspoon **vanilla**

2 cups **mixed berries** such as marionberries, blueberries, raspberries, and boysenberries, rinsed and drained

¹⁄₄ cup **seedless blackberry**, huckleberry, or salal **jam**

1. In a bowl, mix 1 cup flour and the brown sugar. With a pastry blender or fingers, cut or rub in butter to make fine crumbs. Add 1 tablespoon water and stir with a fork until evenly moistened.

2. Gather dough into a ball.

3. On a lightly floured board, roll dough into an 11-inch round. Ease dough into a 9-inch tart pan with a removable rim; if dough tears, overlap edges slightly and press to seal. Gently press dough against bottom and side of pan. Fold excess dough down and flush with pan rim; press against pan side.

4. Bake crust in a 325° oven until golden brown, about 20 minutes. Cool on a rack.

5. In a bowl with a mixer, beat mascarpone, yogurt cheese, lemon peel, mint, powdered sugar, and vanilla until smooth. Spread evenly in crust.

6. Arrange berries in a single layer over filling.

7. In a 1- to 1¹⁄₂-quart pan over medium heat, stir jam until melted, 2 to 3 minutes. Drizzle over berries.

8. Remove pan rim and cut tart into wedges.

Per serving: 351 cal., 54% (189 cal.) from fat; 4.9 g protein; 21 g fat (14 g sat.); 35 g carbo (1.7 g fiber); 145 mg sodium; 49 mg chol.

## CHILIES

### Kristen Farrar
Davis, California

#### BEST-OF-CATEGORY

"I used to be a vegetarian," says Farrar, a plant pathologist at the University of California at Davis, "and I was looking for a quick way to do something similar to tamales without messing with the cornhusks. I decided to make a pseudo-tamale mixture and stuff it in poblanos, the largest chili I could find that was fairly mild." The delicious result is a cross between chiles rellenos and a Mexican-style polenta.

### Chilies with Corn Tamale Filling

PREP AND COOK TIME: About 1¹⁄₄ hours

NOTES: Chilies that are straight are easiest to fill. Serve with Spanish rice made from a mix or favorite recipe.

MAKES: 4 servings

³⁄₄ cup **cornmeal**

¹⁄₂ cup **milk**

6 tablespoons **butter** or margarine

1 cup **fresh** or frozen **corn kernels**

¹⁄₂ cup chopped **red bell pepper**

1 **fresh jalapeño chili**, stemmed, seeded, and chopped

1¹⁄₂ cups (6 oz.) shredded **jack cheese**

¹⁄₃ cup chopped **fresh cilantro**

**Salt** and **pepper**

8 **fresh poblano chilies** (2 lb. total; also called pasillas)

³⁄₄ cup chopped **onion**

1 can (4 oz.) chopped **green chilies**

¹⁄₂ cup **half-and-half** (light cream)

1. In a 2- to 3-quart pan over medium-high heat, stir cornmeal, 1¹⁄₂ cups water, milk, 3 tablespoons butter, ¹⁄₂ cup corn, red bell pepper, and jalapeño until mixture bubbles and cornmeal no longer feels gritty, about 5 minutes.

2. Stir ³⁄₄ cup cheese and cilantro into cornmeal mixture. Let stand until just cool to touch. Season to taste with salt and pepper.

3. About ¹⁄₂ inch below stems, cut tops crosswise off poblanos; save tops. With a fork, scrape out and discard seeds and pith. Holding a chili upright, spoon in cornmeal mixture, pushing gently with spoon and shaking gently to fill chili to rim. Replace poblano tops and secure with toothpicks.

4. Lay poblanos on their sides in a shallow 10- by 15-inch casserole. Cover tightly with foil and bake in a 375° oven until chilies are tender when pierced, 40 to 45 minutes.

5. Meanwhile, in a 1- to 2-quart pan over medium heat, frequently stir onion in remaining butter until limp, 8 to 10 minutes. Add canned chilies, remaining ¹⁄₂ cup corn, remaining ³⁄₄ cup cheese, and half-and-half; stir until cheese melts, 1 to 2 minutes.

6. Remove toothpicks from poblanos and spoon sauce over chilies. Add salt and pepper to taste.

Per serving: 560 cal., 55% (306 cal.) from fat; 18 g protein; 34 g fat (20 g sat.); 52 g carbo (6.1 g fiber); 586 mg sodium; 99 mg chol.

### Ann Beck
Tucson

#### FINALIST

"I have a sweet niece in Phoenix, Karen McMahon, who's crazy about pepper jelly," says Beck. "I make food gifts for Christmas, and I developed this hotter chili marmalade (flavored with habaneros) for her. It's very versatile, and good spooned on soft lahvosh or cucumbers, brushed over meats during the last few minutes of barbecuing, even melted and poured over ice cream." Judges enjoyed the marmalade with cream cheese and crackers.

### Habanero Marmalade

PREP AND COOK TIME: About 45 minutes, plus at least 3 hours to cool

NOTES: These jars of marmalade seal without water-bath canning.

MAKES: 7 jars; 1 cup each

1³⁄₄ ounces (4 to 5) **fresh habanero chilies**

1¹⁄₂ pounds **red bell peppers**

1¹⁄₂ cups **distilled white vinegar**

6¹⁄₂ cups **sugar**

2 pouches (3 oz. each) **liquid pectin**

MELLOW POBLANO chilies with corn tamale filling are served on Spanish rice.

1. Place 7 clean canning jars (1-cup size), rings, and new lids in a 6- to 8-quart pan. Cover with water and bring to a boil over high heat. Remove from heat; leave in water until ready to use.

2. Wearing rubber gloves, remove and discard stems and seeds from chilies.

3. Cut off curved tops and bottoms from bell peppers; discard stems and save pieces. Cut off and discard white membranes; save seeds. Slice straight pepper sides into ⅛- by 2½-inch strips.

4. In a blender, whirl chilies, bell pepper tops and bottoms, and ½ cup vinegar until a smooth purée.

5. In an 8- to 10-quart pan over high heat, bring chili purée, bell pepper seeds and slices, remaining 1 cup vinegar, and sugar to a full, rolling boil, stirring constantly, then boil for exactly 3 minutes.

6. Add pectin to pan. Stirring constantly over high heat, return to a full, rolling boil, then boil for exactly 1 minute.

7. Drain jars, rings, and lids. Ladle chili mixture into hot jars to within ⅛ inch of top. (Let any extra marmalade cool, then serve or chill airtight up to 2 weeks.) Wipe jar rims clean. Cover with hot rings and lids.

8. Protecting hands with pot holders, invert filled jars on a towel for 5 minutes. Turn right side up. Every 5 minutes, turn jars over until marmalade has set and seeds are evenly distributed, 45 to 60 minutes.

9. Let marmalade cool at least 2 more hours. Serve, or store up to 2 years.

Per tablespoon: 47 cal., 0% (0 cal.) from fat; 0.1 g protein; 0 g fat; 12 g carbo (0.1 g fiber); 0.3 mg sodium; 0 mg chol.

## Richard Baxter
Edmonds, Washington
FINALIST

"During the summer when I was a first-year medical student, I took a Spanish immersion program. I got interested in mole while staying with a family in Mexico," Baxter remembers. "Their mole took two days to make and had 30 ingredients. I simplified the recipe, figuring out the common elements."

## Turkey Mole

PREP AND COOK TIME: About 55 minutes

NOTES: Crush anise seed with the bottom of a glass. To use leftover cooked turkey or chicken, omit raw turkey and oil. Add 4 cups shredded cooked meat to prepared sauce and simmer until warm. Serve with warm tortillas.

MAKES: 4 to 6 servings

- 3 **dried New Mexico** or California **chilies** (1 oz. total)
- 1 **dried pasilla chili** (¼ oz.)
- 4 to 6 **dried small hot red chilies** (⅛ oz. total)
- 2 tablespoons **peanut butter**
- 2 teaspoons **sesame seed**
- 1 **corn tortilla** (6 in.), torn into pieces
- ⅓ cup minced **onion**
- 1 can (6 oz.) **tomato paste**
- 1 ounce **unsweetened chocolate**, grated
- ⅛ teaspoon **anise seed**, crushed (see notes)
- ⅛ teaspoon **ground cinnamon**
- ⅛ teaspoon **ground cloves**
- ⅛ teaspoon **ground coriander**
- 1¾ cups fat-skimmed **chicken broth**
- 2 pounds **boned**, **skinned turkey breast** or thighs, cut into ¾-inch chunks

  About 2 teaspoons **salad oil**

  **Salt**

1. Wipe New Mexico, pasilla, and small chilies clean with a damp cloth. Stem and seed chilies, then place in a bowl with hot water to cover. Let stand until chilies are pliable, 5 to 10 minutes.

2. Drain chilies, reserving liquid.

3. In a food processor or blender, whirl chilies, peanut butter, sesame seed, tortilla, onion, tomato paste, chocolate, anise seed, cinnamon, cloves, coriander, and broth until smoothly ground.

4. In a 5- to 6-quart pan (preferably nonstick) over medium-high heat, brown half of the turkey in 1 teaspoon oil, turning as needed, about 8 minutes. (With a regular pan, you may need a little more oil.) Pour into a bowl; repeat to cook remaining turkey in oil and pour into bowl.

5. Add chili mixture to pan. Stirring often, bring to a simmer over medium heat, then reduce heat and simmer, covered, 15 to 20 minutes to blend flavors; stir often.

6. Add turkey and any juices to sauce. Stir in about ½ cup reserved chili water to thin sauce. Season to taste with salt.

Per serving: 313 cal., 28% (89 cal.) from fat; 44 g protein; 9.9 g fat (2.8 g sat.); 14 g carbo (4.6 g fiber); 355 mg sodium; 94 mg chol.

## S E A F O O D

## Sharon Tobin
Seattle
BEST-OF-CATEGORY

On a trip to Singapore 12 years ago, Tobin tried black pepper crab. "The restaurant made it with small blue swimmer crabs," she remembers. "It had the pepper, but it really wasn't hot. It had the sweetness of honey. We couldn't stop licking our fingers. Later I could not find a recipe anywhere. So I kept fiddling until I got it right."

## Black Pepper Dungeness Crab

PREP AND COOK TIME: **About 45 minutes**
NOTES: Tobin starts with live crabs that she catches. If you start with live crabs, have your fishmonger kill 3 (5¼ to 6 lb. total), and clean and crack them. Marinate pieces (step 1), then lift out and add to hot oil (step 3), cover, and stir often for 5 minutes. Add marinade and 1½ tablespoons pepper to pan and stir often until crab shells are bright red, about 5 minutes more. Serve with steamed white rice.

MAKES: **4 servings**

- 1 tablespoon chopped **fresh cilantro**
- 1½ tablespoons finely chopped **garlic**
- ⅓ cup minced **green onions**
- 1 teaspoon minced **ginger**
- ¾ cup **soy sauce**
- ½ cup **honey**
- 3 cooked **Dungeness crabs** (4¾ to 5½ lb. total), cleaned and cracked
- ¼ cup **peppercorns**
- 3 tablespoons **peanut oil** or salad oil

**1.** In a large bowl, combine cilantro, garlic, onions, ginger, soy, and honey. Add crab pieces. Cover and chill 15 minutes to 1 hour, turning crab often.

**2.** Coarsely grind pepper in a coffee grinder or crush with a rolling pin.

**3.** Pour oil into a 14-inch wok or 6- to 8-quart pan over medium-high heat. Pour crab, marinade, and 1½ tablespoons pepper into wok. Stir often until crab is steaming hot, about 5 minutes.

**4.** Sprinkle remaining pepper over crab and mix well. Ladle crab and juices into bowls.

Per serving: 403 cal., 29% (117 cal.) from fat; 30 g protein; 13 g fat (2 g sat.); 46 g carbo (2 g fiber); 3,453 mg sodium; 129 mg chol.

## Robin Bolton
### Seward, Alaska
### FINALIST

During a recent stint as chef at Wilderness Lodge on Alaska's Lake Clark, Bolton came up with this creamy, Thai-style curried seafood soup. "I usually make it with Dungeness crab, but it's good with king crab too," she notes. Bolton now serves the soup at Seward Windsong Lodge, where she is executive chef.

COMPELLING BLEND of soy, honey, and pepper glazes Dungeness crab.

## Curried Sweet Potato Soup with Crab

PREP AND COOK TIME: **About 30 minutes**
NOTES: Garnish soup with toasted, unsweetened shredded dried coconut.
MAKES: **5 cups; 4 servings**

- 1 **sweet potato** or yam (¾ lb.)
- 1 can (13½ oz.) **coconut milk**
- 1 tablespoon **olive oil**
- 1 cup diced **onion**
- 1 tablespoon minced **garlic**
- 1 tablespoon **Thai red curry paste** or regular curry powder
- 1 teaspoon **ground coriander**
- 1 teaspoon **ground cumin**
- 2 cups fat-skimmed **chicken broth**
- 1 cup (⅓ lb.) **shelled, cooked crab**
- ½ cup diced **canned, peeled, roasted red pepper**
- **Salt**

**1.** Scrub sweet potato and pierce with a fork. Cook in a microwave oven at full power (100%) for 4 minutes. Turn over and cook until tender when pressed, 2 to 4 minutes more. (Or bake in a 400° oven until tender when pressed, about 45 minutes.)

**2.** Slit potato, then let stand until cool enough to handle. Scoop flesh into a blender. Add coconut milk and whirl until smoothly puréed.

**3.** Meanwhile, in a 10- to 12-inch frying pan over medium heat, frequently stir oil, onion, and garlic until onion is limp, 8 to 10 minutes.

**4.** To onion, add curry paste, coriander, cumin, broth, and sweet potato mixture, mixing well. Bring to a boil over high heat, stirring, then reduce heat and simmer, covered, to blend flavors, about 20 minutes.

**5.** Stir crab and red pepper into pan. Ladle soup into bowls. Season to taste with salt.

Per serving: 380 cal., 62% (234 cal.) from fat; 15 g protein; 26 g fat (19 g sat.); 25 g carbo (2.7 g fiber); 521 mg sodium; 37 mg chol.

## Cheryl Laurance
### Parkdale, Oregon
### FINALIST

"We live at the base of Mount Hood and are fruit tree growers," Laurance says. "My parents came visiting from Alaska and brought salmon. After a long day harvesting fruit, we needed something fast. We treated the salmon like fajitas and added feta for spark." And thus her tacos were born.

## Salmon Avocado Tacos

PREP AND COOK TIME: **About 50 minutes**
MAKES: **8 tacos; 8 servings**

- 1 **boned salmon fillet with skin** (1 in. thick, 2 lb.)
- 1 **onion** (6 oz.), cut into rings
- 2 tablespoons **lime juice**
- 1 tablespoon minced **garlic**
- ¼ teaspoon **pepper**
- 1 tablespoon **olive oil**
- 8 **flour tortillas** (8 in.)

**Avocado salsa** (recipe follows)

2 cups finely shredded **cabbage**

1 cup crumbled **feta cheese** or queso fresco

**Salt**

**1.** Place salmon in a heavy-duty plastic food bag. Add onion, lime juice, garlic, pepper, and oil. Seal bag. Turn fish often for 30 minutes.

**2.** Meanwhile, stack the tortillas and seal in foil.

**3.** Cut a piece of heavy-duty foil the same size as salmon. Lift fish from marinade and place skin down on foil.

**4.** Lay foil with fish on a barbecue grill over a solid bed of medium coals or gas grill on medium (you can hold your hand at grill level only 4 to 5 seconds). Evenly distribute onion from marinade over fish. Close lid on grill; open vents for charcoal.

**5.** After 5 minutes, place tortilla packet next to salmon. Turn tortillas every few minutes. Cook until salmon is no longer translucent but is still moist-looking in center (cut to test) and tortillas are hot in center, about 8 minutes more.

**6.** Pull off salmon skin and discard. Cut fish into 1-inch chunks and put in a bowl.

**7.** To assemble tacos, wrap chunks of salmon, salsa, cabbage, and feta in tortillas. Add salt to taste.

Per serving: 503 cal., 54% (270 cal.) from fat; 30 g protein; 30 g fat (7 g sat.); 28 g carbo (3 g fiber); 435 mg sodium; 82 mg chol.

## Avocado Salsa

PREP TIME: About 20 minutes

MAKES: 2⅔ cups; 8 servings

1¾ cups diced (½-in. chunks) **firm-ripe avocados**

¾ cup chopped **firm-ripe Roma tomato**

⅔ cup minced **green onions**

⅓ cup chopped **fresh cilantro**

3 tablespoons **olive oil**

2 tablespoons **lemon juice**

1 tablespoon minced, seeded **fresh jalapeño chili**

1 tablespoon minced **garlic**

**Salt**

In a bowl, combine avocados, tomato, onions, cilantro, oil, lemon juice, chili, and garlic. Add salt to taste.

Per serving: 107 cal., 84% (90 cal.) from fat; 1.1 g protein; 10 g fat (1.5 g sat.); 5 g carbo (1.2 g fiber); 7.5 mg sodium; 0 mg chol. ◆

# Why?

### ANSWERS TO COMMON COOKING QUESTIONS
BY LINDA LAU ANUSASANANAN

## The realities of E. coli

■ Fresh apple juice and cider, crisp green salad, a plump, juicy burger—are these taste pleasures in jeopardy? Since a deadly strain of bacteria *E. coli*—*Escherichia coli* 0157:H7—has been found in these foods, such treats carry potential danger.

Human and animal waste contains *E. coli,* and the bacteria can spread to food that comes into contact with the waste—including fallen apples that touch animal droppings, or salad greens exposed to contaminated water.

Meat presents an even greater risk because manure on the animal's hide or hair may spread bacteria to the carcass during processing. Any *E. coli* on the surface of meat is easily killed by cooking. But if contaminated raw meat is ground, bacteria is mixed throughout.

### WHAT KEEPS FOODS SAFE?

At home, store foods at 40° or below to restrict bacterial growth. Between 40° and 160°, bacteria can multiply to dangerous levels in just a few hours.

Wash raw produce, such as salad greens and alfalfa sprouts, in chlorinated water (1 teaspoon chlorine bleach to 1 quart water), drain, and, if chlorine odor is noticeable, rinse well.

Pasteurization kills bacteria in apple juice and cider, but it changes their flavor. If you want fresh taste with some degree of safety, buy from a manufacturer that bans the use of fallen apples (grounders) and cleans all fruit with an antimicrobial agent before pressing it.

Irradiating meat, recently approved by the FDA, destroys bacteria. Until this process is used, however, ground meat must be thoroughly cooked to be absolutely safe. The USDA recommends cooking it to the fail-safe temperature of 160°. George K. York, extension food technologist at the University of California at Davis, points out that the bacteria begin to die at 140° and if you hold food at this temperature for four minutes, all are killed. He advises checking with an accurate instant-read thermometer.

Unfortunately, ground meat patties

Well-done but still juicy—a good burger can be safe.

JAMES CARRIER

get hard and dry when cooked to an internal temperature of 160°. But if you add crumbs to the raw meat, it will stay moist when safely cooked.

## Safe & Juicy Burgers

***Prep and cook time:*** About 15 minutes
***Makes:*** 4 servings

1 pound **ground lean beef**

1 **large egg**

½ cup minced **onion**

¼ cup **fine dried bread crumbs**

1 clove **garlic,** minced

About ½ teaspoon **salt**

About ¼ teaspoon **pepper**

4 **hamburger buns,** split and toasted

**1.** Mix beef with egg, onion, bread crumbs, garlic, ½ teaspoon salt, and ¼ teaspoon pepper. Form into 4 equal patties about ½ inch thick.

**2.** Place an 11- to 12-inch nonstick frying pan over medium-high heat.

**3.** When pan is hot, add beef patties and brown on each side, cooking until a thermometer inserted in center of thickest part reads 160° (no pink in the center), 7 to 8 minutes total.

**4.** With a spatula, transfer beef patties to buns. Add salt and pepper to taste.

Per serving: 402 cal., 43% (171 cal.) from fat; 26 g protein; 19 g fat (7.1 g sat.); 29 g carbo (1.4 g fiber); 668 mg sodium; 122 mg chol. ◆

# Pomegranate delights

### As brilliant as rubies, and rich with flavor

ICY, REFRESHING pomegranate granita is topped with juicy orange segments.

■ "Color is everything for determining ripeness," says Jim Simonian as he picks a softball-size pomegranate during harvest on a sweltering day in the San Joaquin Valley. Using a pocketknife, he cuts the pomegranate open and takes a bite, as if it was an apple. "Don't try to eat every seed," he advises.

Indeed, an onlooking farmer says, "you need to get into a bathtub naked when you eat these. They sure stain."

For more than 20 years, Simonian has grown pomegranates in the hot, dusty fields near Mendota, California. His brother and partner, David, is president of the Pomegranate Council. Their orchards and others in the Golden State produce 100 percent of the U.S. commercial crop.

Pomegranate season is late August to late December. Foothill, the first harvested variety, has a mild taste and pink seeds. Early Wonderful, which appears in mid-September, is tarter with light red seeds. Wonderful, the biggest crop, is available from late September to Christmas. It's the sweetest, with dark red seeds.

More than 800 gemlike seeds, completely edible, cluster beneath the thick, red, leathery hide of a pomegranate. Technically, each seed is an aril (sort of a tender pip sealed in a juicy packet).

## Pomegranate Granita

**PREP TIME:** About 30 minutes, plus 6 hours to freeze

**NOTES:** This coarsely textured frozen dessert is a favorite of Paul Bertolli, chef and co-owner of Oliveto Cafe & Restaurant in Oakland, California. To make pomegranate juice, see notes for Pomegranate Margaritas; for pomegranate seeds, see notes for Pomegranate-Ginger Muffins (page 204). For a smooth texture, freeze the mixture in an ice cream maker.

**MAKES:** 6 servings

 2   cups **pomegranate** juice
 1/3 cup **orange juice**
 1½  teaspoons **lemon juice**
 ¼   cup **sugar**
 1   **orange** (about ½ lb.)
 6   tablespoons **pomegranate** seeds

**1.** In a 9- by 13-inch pan, stir pomegranate juice, orange juice, lemon juice, and sugar. Cover airtight.

**2.** Freeze mixture until solid, 3 to 4 hours. Break frozen mixture into chunks. Beat with a mixer just until pieces are pea-size. Return granita to pan and freeze, covered airtight, until firm, at least 3 hours or up to 2 days.

**3.** Meanwhile, using a zester or grater, cut about 1 tablespoon peel from orange in long, thin shreds.

**4.** With a sharp knife, cut remaining peel and membrane from orange. Hold fruit over a bowl and cut between membrane and fruit to release segments into bowl.

**5.** Spoon equal portions granita into chilled stemmed glasses or small bowls, sprinkle each with 1 tablespoon pomegranate seeds, and garnish with orange segments and orange peel.

Per serving: 108 cal., 0.8% (0.9 cal.) from fat; 0.4 g protein; 0.1 g fat (0 g sat.); 27 g carbo (0.7 g fiber); 4.1 mg sodium; 0 mg chol.

## Chilies Stuffed with Pomegranate Salad

**PREP AND COOK TIME:** 35 to 40 minutes

**NOTES:** For a refreshing salsa, omit poblano (sometimes called pasilla) chilies and serve pomegranate-avocado mixture with tortilla chips.

**MAKES:** 4 servings

 4   **fresh poblano chilies** (3 to 4 oz. each)
 5   tablespoons **orange juice**
 ¼   cup **lime juice**
 1   **firm-ripe avocado** (about 10 oz.)
 1   to 2 teaspoons minced **fresh jalapeño chili**
 1/3 cup chopped **green onions**
 1/3 cup chopped **fresh cilantro**
 1   cup **pomegranate** seeds
     **Salt**
 ¼   cup crumbled **cotija** or feta **cheese**

**1.** In a 10- by 15-inch pan, broil poblano chilies 4 to 6 inches from heat, turning as needed, until skins blister and blacken all over, 15 to 20 minutes.

**2.** When chilies are cool enough to touch, gently pull off and discard skin. Cut a lengthwise slit through 1 side of each chili. Gently scoop out and discard seeds and veins; leave stems on chilies.

**3.** In a bowl, mix orange juice and lime juice.

**4.** Peel and pit avocado. Cut into ¼- to ½-inch chunks and add to bowl. Add jalapeño chili, green onions, cilantro, and pomegranate seeds. Stir gently to mix salad. Add salt to taste.

**5.** Lay chilies on plates, slit side up. Spoon equal amounts of salad into each chili; some of the salad will overflow. Sprinkle cotija cheese evenly over stuffed chilies.

Per serving: 163 cal., 53% (86 cal.) from fat; 4.2 g protein; 9.6 g fat (2.1 g sat.); 19 g carbo (2.4 g fiber); 102 mg sodium; 4 mg chol.

## Pomegranate-Ginger Muffins

**PREP AND COOK TIME:** About 30 minutes

**NOTES:** *For seeds,* cut ends off pomegranates. Score skin from end to end with several evenly spaced cuts. Immerse fruit in a bowl of water, then pull apart and rub seeds free. The skin and most of the membrane float; skim off and discard. Drain seeds.

**MAKES:** 12 (2½-in.) or 24 (1¾-in.) muffins

- 2 cups **all-purpose flour**
- About ⅔ cup **sugar**
- 1 tablespoon **baking powder**
- ½ teaspoon **salt**
- ⅓ cup minced **crystallized ginger**
- 1 teaspoon grated **lemon** peel
- 1¼ cups **pomegranate** seeds
- 1 cup **milk**
- 1 **large egg**
- About ¼ cup (⅛ lb.) **butter** or margarine, melted and cooled

**1.** In a bowl, mix flour, ⅔ cup sugar, baking powder, and salt. Stir in crystallized ginger, lemon peel, and pomegranate seeds. Make a well in the center.

**2.** In a measuring cup, blend milk, egg, and ¼ cup butter. Pour liquid all at once into well. Stir just until batter is moistened; it will be lumpy.

**3.** Spoon batter into 12 (2½-in.-wide) or 24 (1¾-in.-wide) buttered muffin cups, filling each almost to the rim. Sprinkle with 1 to 2 teaspoons sugar.

**4.** Bake in a 425° oven until lightly browned, about 16 minutes for large muffins, 13 minutes for small. Remove

POMEGRANATE seeds dot tender muffins.

### POMEGRANATE CONCENTRATE

The concentrate, a tart, brownish syrup sometimes labeled pomegranate molasses, is made from the fruit's juice but, unlike most concentrates, cannot be reconstituted with water. A staple in Middle Eastern cuisines, pomegranate concentrate is used in meat marinades and *fesenjoon,* a dip or meat condiment. Try fesenjoon as a dunk for carrots, cucumbers, and pocket bread; spread it in chicken sandwiches; or serve with roast leg of lamb.

### FESENJOON SAUCE

In a 10- to 12-inch nonstick frying pan over medium-high heat, stir 2 cloves **garlic** in ½ teaspoon **olive oil** until garlic is lightly browned and soft when pressed, about 2 minutes. Remove from pan. To pan, add 2 cups **walnuts;** stir until toasted, about 6 minutes. In a blender or food processor, purée walnuts, garlic, 1 to 2 tablespoons minced **fresh jalapeño chili,** ¼ cup **pomegranate concentrate,** and ¾ cup **water;** scrape container sides often. Add **salt** to taste. Serve, or cover and chill up to 1 day. Makes 2 cups.

Per tablespoon: 54 cal., 78% (42 cal.) from fat; 1.1 g protein; 4.7 g fat (0.4 g sat.); 2.6 g carbo (0.4 g fiber); 0.8 mg sodium; 0 mg chol.

muffins from pan at once. Serve hot or set on a rack and serve warm or cool.

Per 2½-inch muffin: 215 cal., 27% (57 cal.) from fat; 3.5 g protein; 6.3 g fat (3.6 g sat.); 37 g carbo (0.9 g fiber); 290 mg sodium; 34 mg chol.

## Sticky Red Wings

**PREP AND COOK TIME:** About 1¼ hours

**MAKES:** 4 main-dish or 8 appetizer servings

- 3 pounds **chicken wings**
- ½ teaspoon **salad oil**
- 2 teaspoons minced **garlic**
- 3 tablespoons minced **fresh jalapeño chilies**
- 1 cup **pomegranate** juice
- 1 cup **cranberry juice blend**
- ⅓ cup **sugar**
- 2 tablespoons **cider vinegar**
- 3 tablespoons **pomegranate** seeds
- **Salt**

**1.** Rinse wings, drain, and cut apart at joints; reserve tips for other uses. Place remaining chicken in a single layer in a 10- by 15-inch nonstick pan.

**2.** Bake in a 400° oven until brown and crisp, about 1 hour, turning pieces occasionally with a wide spatula.

**3.** Meanwhile, in a 10- to 12-inch nonstick frying pan over high heat, stir oil, garlic, and chilies until vegetables are limp, 2 to 3 minutes. Add pomegranate juice, cranberry juice, sugar, and vinegar. Bring to a boil, stirring until sugar dissolves. Boil until reduced to ⅔ cup, about 15 minutes.

**4.** Drain and discard fat from chicken wings. Pour pomegranate sauce over wings and turn pieces with spatula. Bake until sauce thickens and sticks to wings, about 12 minutes, turning pieces often to prevent scorching.

**5.** Place wings on a platter. Sprinkle with pomegranate seeds. Add salt to taste. Serve hot.

Per main-dish serving: 465 cal., 43% (198 cal.) from fat; 29 g protein; 22 g fat (5.9 g sat.); 38 g carbo (0.2 g fiber); 93 mg sodium; 91 mg chol.

## Pomegranate Margaritas

**PREP TIME:** About 10 minutes, plus about 2 hours to freeze

**NOTES:** *For juice,* whirl pomegranate seeds in a blender or food processor, then pour through a fine strainer into a container. Serve margaritas in salt-rimmed glasses.

**MAKES:** About 3½ cups; 4 servings

- 2 cups **pomegranate** juice
- ½ cup **lime juice**
- 2 tablespoons **orange-flavor liqueur**
- ½ cup **tequila**

**1.** Pour pomegranate juice into ice cube trays. Freeze until solid, about 2 hours. Pop cubes from tray.

**2.** In a blender, combine lime juice, liqueur, and tequila. Turn blender to highest speed and gradually drop in juice cubes, whirling until slushy.

**3.** Pour margaritas into glasses.

Per serving: 176 cal., 0.5% (0.9 cal.) from fat; 0.1 g protein; 0.1 g fat (0 g sat.); 23 g carbo (0 g fiber); 9.9 mg sodium; 0 mg chol. ◆

# Celebrate the harvest

Fun towns for enjoying autumn's bounty in grand style

BY CHRISTINE COLASURDO

■ The West has some of the world's most prolific growing regions. Potatoes, pears, wine, apples, and chilies all have their capitals here, in rich valleys and on fertile coastal plains. Below are some of the biggest, oldest, and most scenic farmlands, where the harvest is toasted in grand style, and visitors can enjoy parades, markets, and festivals of every variety. (Dates given are for 1998 festivals.)

**Hood River, OR.** Nearly 400 farms harvest fruits and vegetables this month. Sample the bounty at the annual Hood River Valley Harvest Fest, which also features local crafts and entertainment. WHERE: Expo Center, at 405 Portway Ave. Take exit 63 off I-84 and head toward the Columbia River. WHEN: October 16–18. COST: $2. CONTACT: (800) 366-3530.

**Sonoma, CA.** California's oldest wine festival began in 1897. You can join wine tasters (and even stomp grapes) at the Valley of the Moon Vintage Festival in Sonoma, then tour more than 20 nearby wineries during the harvest. WHERE: Sonoma Plaza, at State 12 (Broadway) and Napa St. WHEN: September 26–27. COST: Free (with charge for tastings). CONTACT: (707) 996-1090.

**Cranberry Coast, WA.** Cranberries are picked each fall on approximately 130 peat-bog farms, many nestled in valleys between Grayland and Tokeland. The picking culminates with the annual Cranberry Harvest Festival in Grayland, which boasts a cranberry cook-off and tours of the bogs. WHERE: Grayland Community Hall, one block off State 105 at Grange Rd. WHEN: October 10–11. COST: Free. CONTACT: (800) 473-6018.

**Okanagan Valley, B.C.** The bountiful Okanagan region explodes each fall with a dizzying number of tours, farmers' markets, and festivals. Tour 17 orchards as well as the B.C. Orchard Industry Museum in Kelowna; attend three apple festivals (in Vernon, Keremeos, and Kelowna); sample wines

from more than 35 of the continent's northernmost wineries at the 10-day Okanagan Fall Wine Festival. CONTACT: For a map and listing of all regional events, call (800) 567-2275.

**Hatch, NM.** Farmers have been growing chilies in the Rio Grande valley for 400 years. More than a dozen varieties are grown near Hatch, renowned as the chili capital of the world. During September farmers are harvesting jalapeños and other hot green varieties. At the 27th Annual Hatch Chile Festival, growers display their roasting skills and visitors sample such treats as chili honey and salsa. WHERE: Hatch Airport, on State 26. WHEN: September 5–6. COST: $2 for parking. CONTACT: (505) 267-5050.

**Shelley, ID.** More potatoes are grown in Idaho than anywhere else in the world. The humble tuber's phenomenal harvest takes place this month along I-15. Idaho Annual Spud Day comes complete with free baked potatoes, a tug-of-war over a pit of mashed potatoes, and contests for picking, peeling, and cooking. WHERE: Shelley's City Park, just north of downtown on U.S. 91. WHEN: September 19. COST: Free. CONTACT: (208) 357-3390.

**Brigham City, UT.** The town has been celebrating its reputation as Utah's finest peach-producing region since 1905 with its Peach Days Festival. Buy produce at its Fruit Row, watch a parade, enjoy a carnival, view the antique car show—or cheer for Miss Peach Queen and Mr. Peach Pit. WHERE: Main St. at Forest St. downtown. WHEN: September 10–12. COST: Free. CONTACT: (435) 723-3931.

**Arroyo Grande, CA.** For 61 years the town has honored its diverse cornucopia (broccoli, bok choy, celery, snow peas, lettuce, and grapes) with its annual Arroyo Grande Valley Harvest Festival. Spectacles run the range from the largest zucchini competition to arts and crafts booths to a parade. WHERE: Historic village area downtown. WHEN: September 25–26. COST: Free. CONTACT: (805) 489-1488. ◆

Sunset's

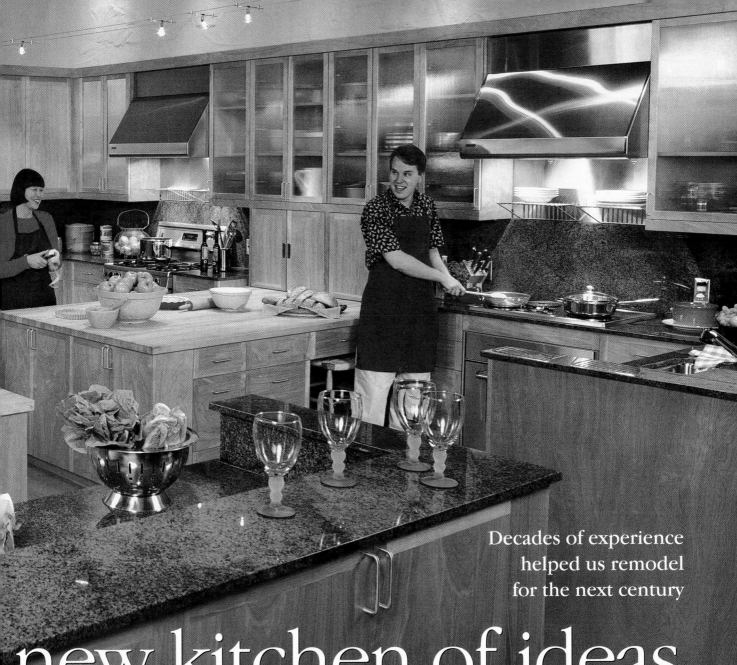

Decades of experience
helped us remodel
for the next century

# new kitchen of ideas

BY DANIEL GREGORY

■ After 32 years, it was time to refine and update the test kitchen here at our headquarters in Menlo Park, California. As senior food editor Jerry Anne Di Vecchio recalls, "The original kitchen—really four kitchens in one—was built in 1966. It served us well. But we have learned a lot since then and felt we could build a space better suited to our current needs." Those needs include more work and storage space, better separation between work zones, improved lighting, and a more open plan to allow for magazine

PHOTOGRAPHS BY JAMES CARRIER

BEFORE: The old kitchen looked tired after years of use.

photography and television production.

One of the challenges was to create an up-to-date room that would be compatible with the original Cliff May–designed structure. Architect Chris Wasney says, "The space had great bones; it was just a little dowdy." His firm preserved the architectural shell while installing new working parts. The architects moved the tasting area into an adjacent glass-walled corridor, which made it possible to expand the work centers and consolidate support functions like cleanup and storage of food and props. The idea was to create a "front stage, back stage" layout to make the kitchen as versatile as possible.

*Sunset* and the architects chose a simple, elegant palette of materials to complement the original building's classic,

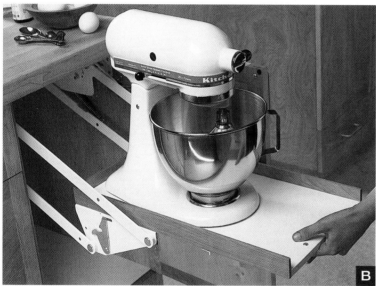

**A)** Flour and sugar bins built into drawers are a necessity for us because they help keep counters clear for working and photography.
**B)** The mixer stand pivots up to counter height for easy use; by Hafele America, Archdale, NC (336/889-2322).
**C)** Warming racks (under heat lamps) are conveniently located above the ranges.
**D)** Refrigerated drawers put cold storage at our fingertips.

adobe-and-terra-cotta ranch house character: green granite near sinks, butcher block for food preparation, stainless steel appliances, red birch cabinetry, and linoleum and quarry tile for the floor. A two-tiered counter separates the cooking and tasting zones without cutting off sight lines. The counter puts the cooking zone "on stage" by framing it.

The architects improved the ventilation and lighting with four tiers of lights to heighten the theatrical effect. Warm fluorescents behind a plastic diffuser create an artificial skylight; they're supplemented by halogen cable, soffit, and under-cabinet lights.

DESIGN: Cody Anderson Wasney Architects, Palo Alto (650/328-1818)
CONTRACTOR: Blach Construction Company, Santa Clara, CA (408/244-7100)

**E)** We installed a small drawer for compost materials at each workstation, since wet refuse should be removed daily. **F)** No more in-counter tracks for cabinet doors: they were dirt catchers. Our new doors are hinged over a continuous counter surface.

### PRODUCTS (partial listing)

•**Lighting.** Recessed downlights and compact fluorescents: Halo, Elk Grove, IL (847/956-8400); track mounted and compact fluorescent quadrant squares: Lightolier (800/215-1068); low-voltage halogen cable system: Kabel Light, Tech Lighting, Chicago (773/883-6110); under-cabinet strips: Creative Systems Lighting (800/642-2286); ceiling diffuser: double-skinned acrylic sheet, Cyro Canada, Mississauga, Ontario (905/677-1388).•**Resilient floor covering.** Linoleum Marmorette, distributed by Gerbert (800/828-9461).•**Wood countertops.** Michigan maple butcher block, MacBeath Hardwood Company, San Francisco (415/647-0782).•**Granite countertops.** Tunas Green, Marble Unlimited, Hayward, CA (510/785-9940).•**Appliances.** Electric cooktops: 30-inch KitchenAid (800/422-1230); 30-inch GE (800/626-2000). Ovens: 30-inch electric convection, Bosch (800/944-2904); 30-inch Monogram double electric convection, GE; 30-inch under-counter, Thermador (800/656-9226). Ranges: 30-inch freestanding, Kenmore (800/469-4663); 48-inch six-burner gas, Jenn-Air (800/536-6247). Hoods: Thermador and custom-made. Microwaves: GE and KitchenAid. Freezer: 36-inch-wide, 24-inch-deep, Sub-Zero Freezer Co. (800/444-7820). Under-counter refrigerated drawers: Sub-Zero.•**Sinks.** Undertone, Kohler Company (800/456-4537).•**Faucets.** Pull-out spray Europlus, Grohe America (800/201-3407).

## Kitchen-design ideas from senior food editor Jerry Anne Di Vecchio

•RANGES. When we planned the first kitchen, there was a big difference between commercial and residential cooking equipment. Now, as then, we use residential equipment. But today commercial-quality equipment designed to work well in a home is available, and that's what we've chosen. It's quiet and well insulated. Also, most manufacturers now have a stainless steel or brushed-chrome line that makes it easy to coordinate a number of different brands at different prices, which we wanted to do in order to approximate the range of equipment *Sunset* readers use.

•REFRIGERATED DRAWERS. These handy and efficient products give each work area its own cold storage compartment. They save a lot of steps and are easier to use than conventional refrigerators because you can see everything at a glance as you look into them from the top.

•COUNTERS. We had butcher-block counters before, and they were perfect for chopping and other food preparation, but it was a mistake to use them near water—spills or splashes invariably caused spotting and discoloration. So this time we put the butcher block on counters away from the sinks.

•ACCESSIBILITY. Elbow space is very important when four cooks are working at the same time, so each work center's butcher-block counter is accessible from at least three sides.

•FLEXIBLE STORAGE. Shallow storage is very useful. Some of our drawers are just 2 inches deep—perfect for skewers and crab crackers.

•CABINET DOOR VARIATION. Translucent glass for some cabinet doors adds texture and depth without revealing clutter.

•FOOD STORAGE. We use our pantry to store food, tools, and serving pieces. Because some foodstuffs need to be kept cool, not cold, we considered building a cooler; it turned out to be much less expensive just to buy another refrigerator, install it in the pantry, and select its warmest setting. ◆

# Kitchen Cabinet

### READERS' RECIPES TESTED IN SUNSET'S KITCHENS

BY LINDA LAU ANUSASANANAN

PINK SHRIMP and pea pods dress up pasta.

KARL PETZKE

**3.** Meanwhile, in a wide bowl, mix soy sauce, vinegar, sesame oil, sugar, and chili oil.

**4.** When water boils, stir in pasta. Cook, uncovered, 3 minutes. Stir in peas and shrimp. Cook until pasta is just tender to bite and shrimp are pink, 1 to 2 minutes longer. Drain well.

**5.** Add pasta mixture, cilantro, and green onions to soy dressing and mix well. Sprinkle with nuts.

Per serving: 451 cal., 26% (117 cal.) from fat; 24 g protein; 13 g fat (1.9 g sat.); 60 g carbo (3.8 g fiber); 913 mg sodium; 84 mg chol.

## Summer Garden Squash Soup

Margaret Mallory, Walnut Creek, California

When Margaret Mallory was a newspaper food editor, winemakers she dined with often shared their recipes. She has added her own touches to this favorite. It's good hot or cold, and works as a starter or for lunch.

**PREP AND COOK TIME:** About 25 minutes, 45 minutes for chilled soup.

**MAKES:** 2 quarts; 6 servings

- 1 tablespoon **olive oil** or butter
- 1 **red onion** (6 oz.), thinly sliced
- 2 **carrots** ($\frac{1}{2}$ lb. total), peeled and thinly sliced
- 1 clove **garlic**, pressed or minced
- $\frac{1}{4}$ cup **dry white wine**
- 4 cups fat-skimmed **chicken** or vegetable **broth**
- $\frac{1}{2}$ cup **dry vermouth**
- 6 cups ($1\frac{3}{4}$ lb.) chopped **zucchini,** crookneck, or pattypan squash (use 1 or several kinds)

    **Salt** and **pepper**

**1.** In a 3- to 4-quart pan over medium-high heat, stir oil, onion, carrots, and garlic until onion is limp, 5 to 7 minutes. Stir in white wine and bring to a boil. Pour mixture into a large bowl.

**2.** To pan, add broth and vermouth. Place over high heat, cover, and bring

## Asian Angel Hair Pasta

Patti Pope, Woodside, California

"I can get my son to do anything if I tell him I'm going to make this pasta," says Patti Pope. The recipe she shares makes a handsome, colorful whole-meal main course.

**PREP AND COOK TIME:** About 35 minutes

**MAKES:** 4 or 5 servings

- $\frac{1}{4}$ cup **pine nuts** or slivered almonds
- $\frac{1}{4}$ cup **soy sauce**
- 3 tablespoons **rice vinegar**
- 2 tablespoons **Asian** (toasted) **sesame oil**
- 1 tablespoon **sugar**
- 2 teaspoons **hot chili oil**
- $\frac{3}{4}$ pound **dried angel hair pasta**
- $\frac{1}{2}$ pound **edible-pod peas,** stem ends and strings removed
- $\frac{3}{4}$ to 1 pound (51 to 60 per lb.) **shrimp,** shelled and deveined
- $\frac{1}{4}$ cup chopped **fresh cilantro**
- $\frac{1}{4}$ cup thinly sliced **green onions**

**1.** In a 5- to 6-quart pan over medium heat, stir nuts often until golden, 4 to 5 minutes. Pour out of pan.

**2.** Pour $2\frac{1}{2}$ to 3 quarts water into pan, cover, and bring to a boil over high heat.

to a boil. Add squash. Cover and simmer over low heat until squash is tender when pierced, 10 to 12 minutes.

**3.** A portion at a time, whirl squash mixture in a blender until smooth. As puréed, add to onion mixture.

**4.** To serve hot, return soup to pan and stir over high heat until hot, 2 to 3 minutes. To serve cool, chill quickly by nesting pan in ice water; stir frequently until cold, 20 to 25 minutes. If making ahead, cover and chill up to 1 day. Add salt and pepper to taste.

Per serving: 117 cal., 27% (32 cal.) from fat; 4.4 g protein; 3.5 g fat (0.8 g sat.); 12 g carbo (2.2 g fiber); 91 mg sodium; 2.5 mg chol.

## Vegetable Pizza with Rice Crust

Pat Patnode-Edwards, Woodland Park, Colorado

Instead of bread dough, the crust for this knife-and-fork pizza is made with rice and cheese. For variety, Pat Patnode-Edwards frequently changes the vegetable topping.

PREP AND COOK TIME: About 50 minutes

MAKES: 8 servings

- 1½ cups **long-grain white rice**
- 2 **large eggs**
- 1 cup (4 oz.) **shredded sharp cheddar cheese**

  About 1 tablespoon **olive oil**
- 1 cup thinly slivered **red** or yellow **bell pepper**
- 1 cup thinly sliced **mushrooms**
- 1 cup thinly sliced **zucchini**
- 1 cup thinly sliced **onion**
- 1 can (2¼ oz.) **sliced ripe black olives,** drained
- ¾ cup **prepared pizza sauce**
- 1½ cups **shredded mozzarella cheese**
- ¼ cup **grated parmesan cheese**

  **Salt** and **pepper**

**1.** In a 2- to 2½-quart pan, combine rice and 2¾ cups water. Bring to a boil over high heat and cook until most of the water is absorbed, 7 to 10 minutes. Reduce heat to low, cover, and simmer until rice is tender to bite, 10 to 15 minutes longer. Scrape rice into a large bowl. Cool about 5 minutes, stirring occasionally with a fork.

**2.** In another bowl, beat eggs to blend. Add eggs and cheddar cheese to rice and mix well. Scrape rice mixture into an oiled 9- by 13-inch pan and pat into an even layer.

**3.** Bake in a 400° oven until rice begins to brown around edge, 15 to 20 minutes.

**4.** Meanwhile, in a 10- to 12-inch frying pan over high heat, frequently stir 1 tablespoon olive oil, bell pepper, mushrooms, zucchini, and onion until mushrooms begin to brown, 3 to 5 minutes. Stir in olives. Remove from heat.

**5.** Spread pizza sauce evenly over baked rice and sprinkle with mozzarella cheese. Spoon vegetable mixture over crust and top with parmesan cheese.

**6.** Return to oven and bake until parmesan begins to brown, 8 to 10 minutes. Add salt and pepper to taste. Cut into rectangles and lift from pan with a spatula.

Per serving: 326 cal., 41% (135 cal.) from fat; 14 g protein; 15 g fat (7 g sat.); 34 g carbo (1.6 g fiber); 398 mg sodium; 87 mg chol.

## Indian Summer Salad

Rosa G. Dierks, Flagstaff, Arizona

More than 20 years ago, Rosa Dierks discovered this corn salad in Chile. She makes it often and, because it holds up well, in double portions for summer barbecues. To cook fresh corn, cut kernels from about 6 cobs (8 in.), combine with ¼ cup water in a 10- to 12-inch frying pan over high heat, and stir for 3 to 4 minutes. Drain.

PREP AND COOK TIME: About 30 minutes for fresh corn, 20 minutes for frozen

MAKES: 5 or 6 servings

- ¼ cup **red wine vinegar**
- 1 tablespoon **olive** or salad **oil**
- ½ teaspoon **coarse-ground pepper**
- ½ teaspoon **dried basil**
- 1 clove **garlic,** pressed or minced
- 3 cups cooked **fresh** or thawed frozen **corn** kernels
- 2 **firm-ripe tomatoes** (½ lb. total), rinsed, cored, and chopped
- 1 cup chopped **sweet onion** (such as Maui or Walla Walla), rinsed and drained
- 1 **green bell pepper** (½ lb.), stemmed, seeded, and chopped
- ¼ cup chopped **parsley** or fresh cilantro

  **Salt**
- ¼ pound (about 6 cups) **baby spinach leaves,** rinsed and crisped

**1.** In a large bowl, mix vinegar, oil, pepper, basil, and garlic.

**2.** Add corn, tomatoes, onion, bell pepper, and parsley. Mix well. If desired, cover and chill up to 4 hours. Add salt to taste.

**3.** Line a wide bowl with spinach. Pour corn salad into bowl; mix.

Per serving: 120 cal., 26% (31 cal.) from fat; 4.1 g protein; 3.4 g fat (0.5 g sat.); 22 g carbo (4.5 g fiber); 34 mg sodium; 0 mg chol.

SWEET CORN SALAD can partner a summer

KARL PETZKE

# Kitchen Cabinet

## Pearsauce à la Devlin

Patti Devlin, Lafayette, California

**B**ecause the Devlin children love applesauce, Patti Devlin figured pears from the trees in their garden might fare well given similar treatment. *Voilà*—pearsauce! Serve this red-hued sauce by the bowl, with roast pork or poultry, or over vanilla ice cream. For adult occasions, Devlin adds crème de cassis.

PREP AND COOK TIME: About 20 minutes
MAKES: 3 cups; 4 servings

- 2 pounds **ripe pears**
- 1 teaspoon grated **lemon** peel
- 1 tablespoon **lemon juice**
- 1 cup **fresh** or frozen **cranberries** or raspberries
- 1 tablespoon grated **fresh ginger**
- About ¼ cup **sugar**
- 1 tablespoon **vanilla**
- ¼ cup **crème de cassis** (optional)

1. Peel and core pears. Cut fruit into ½-inch chunks.

2. Place pears in a 2- to 3-quart pan. Add lemon peel, lemon juice, cranberries, ginger, and ¼ cup sugar. Mix, cover, and stir occasionally over medium heat until fruit is tender when pierced, 10 to 15 minutes.

3. Add vanilla, crème de cassis, and more sugar, if desired. Serve warm or cool. If making ahead, cover and chill up to 3 days.

Per serving: 197 cal., 4.1% (8.1 cal.) from fat; 0.9 g protein; 0.9 g fat (0 g sat.); 48 g carbo (6 g fiber); 1.7 mg sodium; 0 mg chol.

## Pronto Scallop Risotto

Betty J. Nichols, Eugene, Oregon

**B**etty Nichols loves the creaminess of risotto but refuses to be slowed down by the old-fashioned technique that requires adding the broth a portion at a time. She just pours in the liquid, and when the risotto is almost ready, she adds scallops, frozen peas, and fresh ginger.

PREP AND COOK TIME: About 30 minutes
MAKES: 4 servings

- 1 tablespoon **olive oil**
- ⅓ cup chopped **celery**
- ⅓ cup chopped **red onion**
- 1¼ cups **medium-grain white rice** such as pearl or arborio
- About 4 cups fat-skimmed **chicken broth**
- ¾ pound **bay scallops**, rinsed and drained
- 1 cup **frozen petite peas**
- 2 teaspoons grated **fresh ginger**
- 1 tablespoon **lemon juice**
- 2 tablespoons finely shredded **fresh basil** leaves
- **Lemon** wedges
- **Salt** and fresh-ground **pepper**

1. In a 3- to 4-quart pan over medium heat, combine oil, celery, and onion. Stir often until onion is limp, 4 to 5 minutes. Add rice and mix well.

2. Add 4 cups broth and bring to a boil over high heat, stirring often. Reduce heat to simmering and stir often until rice is tender to bite, 12 to 15 minutes.

3. Add scallops, peas, and ginger. Stir until scallops are opaque but still moist-looking in center of thickest part (cut to test), 5 to 7 minutes. Add lemon juice, and a little more broth if a creamier texture is desired; mix well.

4. Spoon risotto into wide bowls. Sprinkle with basil and garnish with lemon wedges. Add salt and pepper to taste.

Per serving: 401 cal., 10% (41 cal.) from fat; 29 g protein; 4.6 g fat (0.6 g sat.); 58 g carbo (4.1 g fiber); 286 mg sodium; 28 mg chol.

## Sweet-Sour Baked Chicken Legs

Mickey Strang, McKinleyville, California

**M**ickey Strang cooks with what she has on hand. One day she paired an orange and some chicken with Asian seasonings. The resulting citrusy sweet-sour sauce enhances the chicken and goes well with rice.

PREP AND COOK TIME: About 1 hour and 20 minutes
MAKES: 4 servings

- 1 **orange** (½ lb.)
- 4 **whole chicken legs with thighs** (about 2⅓ lb. total)
- ¼ cup **mirin** (rice wine) or ¼ cup cream sherry plus 1 tablespoon sugar
- ¼ cup **rice vinegar**
- 1 tablespoon **cornstarch**
- 1 tablespoon **oyster sauce**
- 1 tablespoons **tamari** or soy sauce
- 1 tablespoon minced **fresh ginger**
- 2 tablespoons sliced **green onion**

1. Slice orange crosswise into ¼-inch-thick rounds; discard seeds. Line a shallow 2½- to 3-quart casserole with orange slices.

2. Pull skin and fat off chicken and discard. Rinse chicken; lay in casserole.

3. Mix mirin, vinegar, cornstarch, oyster sauce, tamari, and ginger. Pour evenly over chicken.

4. Bake, uncovered, in a 375° oven, basting occasionally with pan juices, until chicken is no longer pink at bone (cut to test), 50 to 60 minutes.

5. Sprinkle with green onion.

Per serving: 228 cal., 23% (53 cal.) from fat; 32 g protein; 5.9 g fat (1.5 g sat.); 14 g carbo (1.2 g fiber); 563 mg sodium; 121 mg chol. ◆

# The Low-Fat Cook

## HEALTHY CHOICES FOR THE ACTIVE LIFESTYLE
### BY ELAINE JOHNSON

FOR A COOL entrée, serve yellow tomato gazpacho with shrimp.

RICHARD JUNG

## Rainbow soups

■ Loaded with vegetables, gazpacho easily ranks high in healthfulness. To make the most of its flavor, select ripe, peak-season tomatoes. And for fun, use yellow tomatoes. Gazpacho also can be made with cream, but think slim and use lighter buttermilk for its refreshing effect.

### Yellow Tomato Gazpacho with Shrimp

PREP TIME: About 50 minutes

NOTES: Brian Whitmer, chef at Moose's Restaurant in San Francisco, contributed this recipe. Garnish with yellow cherry tomatoes and sliced cucumbers, if desired.

MAKES: 7 to 8 cups; 4 to 6 servings

- 3 pounds **ripe yellow tomatoes** (about 6), rinsed, cored, and cut into chunks
- ²⁄₃ cup **tomato juice**
- 3 tablespoons **red wine vinegar**
- 3 tablespoons **lemon juice**
- 2 teaspoons **Worcestershire**
- 1 teaspoon **hot sauce**
- 1 cup diced **red bell pepper**
- ¹⁄₃ cup peeled, seeded, diced **cucumber**
- 1 clove **garlic,** minced
- 1¹⁄₂ tablespoons chopped **fresh cilantro**
- ¹⁄₂ pound (70 to 90 per lb.) **shelled cooked rock shrimp** or tiny shrimp
- **Salt** and **pepper**

**1.** In a food processor or blender, coarsely purée tomatoes, a portion at a time. Pour into a large bowl.

**2.** Stir in tomato juice, vinegar, lemon juice, Worcestershire, hot sauce, bell pepper, cucumber, garlic, and cilantro.

**3.** Serve soup at room temperature, or nest bowl in ice and stir often until cold, about 15 minutes. Ladle into wide bowls and add shrimp. Season to taste with salt and pepper.

Per serving: 96 cal., 10% (9.9 cal.) from fat; 10 g protein; 1.1 g fat (0.2 g sat.); 13 g carbo (3.1 g fiber); 244 mg sodium; 74 mg chol.

### Buttermilk Gazpacho

PREP TIME: About 15 minutes

NOTES: Mickey Strang of McKinleyville, California, shares this recipe. Garnish with cilantro sprigs.

MAKES: About 1 quart; 2 or 3 servings

- 1 **cucumber** (³⁄₄ lb.), peeled and cut into chunks
- ²⁄₃ cup coarsely chopped **sweet onion** such as Maui or Walla Walla
- 1 cup coarsely chopped **ripe tomato**
- 1 tablespoon chopped **fresh jalapeño chili**
- 1¹⁄₂ cups **buttermilk**
- **Salt** and **pepper**

**1.** In a food processor or with a knife, mince cucumber, onion, tomato, and jalapeño.

**2.** Scrape vegetable mixture into a large bowl, stir in buttermilk, and season to taste with salt and pepper.

**3.** Serve soup with a few ice cubes added to each bowl. Or nest mixing bowl in ice and stir often until cold, about 10 minutes, then ladle into bowls.

Per serving: 91 cal., 14% (13 cal.) from fat; 5.8 g protein; 1.4 g fat (0.7 g sat.); 15 g carbo (1.9 g fiber); 144 mg sodium; 4.9 mg chol. ◆

Chili-and-cheddar frittata is a specialty at Windy Point, one of five featured bed-and-breakfast inns (article begins on page 224).

# October

# foodguide

BY JERRY ANNE DI VECCHIO

## A TASTE OF THE WEST

# One fine fish

### Move over, king salmon: Chilean seabass is heir to the throne

What's in a name? For Chilean seabass, not much fact. This firm, flavorful, snowy-flesh fish is not a bass, nor is it exclusively from Chile (it's also caught off the coast of Argentina). But in 1994, Chilean seabass was officially accepted by the FDA as the name of *Dissotichus eleginoides*. When this fish was introduced to the West in the '80s, it was a big hit right from the start. It has few bones and is about as fatty as king salmon and therefore more tolerant of overcooking than most fish.

## Oven-roasted Chilean Seabass

PREP AND COOK TIME: About 30 minutes

NOTES: Salted fermented black beans are available in bags or jars in Asian food markets and some supermarkets.

MAKES: 5 or 6 servings

- 1½ pounds **Chilean seabass,** cut into 1-inch-thick pieces
- 1 tablespoon **salted fermented black beans**
- 1 tablespoon minced **fresh ginger**
- ¼ cup **rice vinegar**
- 2 tablespoons **butter** or salad oil
- ¼ cup slivered **shallots** or red onion
- 2 **ruby grapefruit** (1 lb. each)

  About 1 pound **mustard greens,** rinsed and drained

  About 2 tablespoons **soy sauce**

## Cultivated taste

PRODUCE

Pompon mushrooms appear in markets in fall—football season—conjuring up images of cheerleaders. But pompon, not pom-pom, is its generally accepted label. It has others, too: pom pon blanc, lion's mane, bearded tooth, goat's beard, bear paw, and sea sponge. This shaggy ivory puff tastes like a cross between sweet fresh crab and delicate bone marrow.

**Oven-fried pompons for 4:** Discard dark or soft spots from ¾ pound **pompon mushrooms.** Quickly swish mushrooms in cool water to rinse, then drain. Cut into ½- to ¾-inch-thick slices. Melt 6 tablespoons **butter** or margarine in a 10- by 15-inch rimmed pan. Turn mushrooms over in butter; arrange side by side. Bake in a 400° oven about 10 minutes. Turn slices over; bake until browned, 10 to 15 minutes more. If making ahead, let cool in pan, then reheat in oven 4 to 5 minutes. Season with **salt** and **pepper.** Per serving: 174 cal., 93% (162 cal.) from fat; 2 g protein; 18 g fat (11 g sat.); 4 g carbo (1.1 g fiber); 179 mg sodium; 47 mg chol.

1. Rinse fish and pat dry.

2. Rinse beans, drain, then mash slightly with ginger and vinegar.

3. Put 1 tablespoon butter in a 9- by 13-inch pan. Set pan in a 500° oven until butter melts and begins to brown, about 2 minutes. Remove pan from oven, tilt to spread butter, then lay fish in pan and turn over. Mix shallots with butter. Pour black bean mixture over fish.

4. Bake until fish is opaque but still moist-looking in center of thickest part (cut to test), about 10 minutes. Baste occasionally with pan juices.

5. Meanwhile, with a sharp knife, cut peel and white membrane from grapefruit, then cut between membrane and fruit to release segments. Squeeze juice from membrane. Measure 3 to 4 tablespoons juice and pour over fish as it bakes. Reserve fruit.

6. Trim and discard coarse stems from mustard greens; coarsely chop greens.

7. In an 11- to 12-inch frying pan over high heat, melt remaining butter. Add greens and 2 tablespoons soy sauce. Stir often until wilted, 2 to 5 minutes.

8. Transfer fish to a platter; pour juices over it. Arrange wilted greens around fish. Garnish with grapefruit segments. Season with more soy sauce to taste.

Per serving: 196 cal., 30% (58 cal.) from fat; 24 g protein; 6.4 g fat (3 g sat.); 11 g carbo (0.9 g fiber); 550 mg sodium; 57 mg chol.

# A retro dessert

■ Who eats quince anymore? This old-fashioned fruit—hard, astringent, and inedible raw—came West with pioneers. They made the effort because, cooked, quince is quite another story—tender, sweet, and moist, much like cooked apples (there's one interesting quirk: quince turns more golden or pink), with a pleasant musky, floral flavor. Bruce Naftaly, chef and owner of Le Gourmand restaurant in Seattle, shares his recipe for an old-time dessert worth remembering.

## Quince-Apple Crisp

PREP AND COOK TIME: About 1 hour and 20 minutes

MAKES: 8 servings

1. In a bowl, mix 1 cup **sugar,** 1 cup **all-purpose flour,** and 1 teaspoon **baking powder.** Cut ½ cup (¼ lb.) **butter** or margarine into chunks and add to bowl, along with 1 tablespoon **vanilla.** Rub mixture with fingers until it forms coarse crumbs. Then squeeze mixture to make small lumps.

2. Peel and core 3 **quinces** (about 1½ lb. total) and 3 **Golden Delicious apples** (about 1½ lb. total). Cut fruit into ⅓-inch-thick slices and mix in a shallow 2-quart baking dish. Pour sugar-flour lumps evenly over fruit.

3. Bake in a 350° oven until fruit is very tender when pierced, 55 to 60 minutes. Serve with ice cream.

Per serving: 331 cal., 33% (108 cal.) from fat; 2 g protein; 12 g fat (7.2 g sat.); 56 g carbo (1.8 g fiber); 181 mg sodium; 31 mg chol.

EMERGENCY MEASURES

# Cheese ease

## Hot over potatoes, it's a cozy Alpine dish

Raclette is a cheese from Switzerland. It's also the name of the wonderfully simple main dish made by scooping the melted cheese onto hot potatoes and adding onions and pickles.

The Swiss melt raclette in an elaborate portable electric gizmo. At home, just use a fireplace or the broiler. The fireplace is my preference. Just put a hunk of cheese in a shallow pan and push it close to the flames. Pull it away to scrape off the melted cheese, then push it back to melt some more.

### Raclette

PREP AND COOK TIME: About 30 minutes
NOTES: Any smooth-melting cheese—cheddar, fontal, fontina, gouda, gruyère, jack, Swiss, taleggio, or teleme, even brie—can stand in for raclette. You can bake or boil potatoes.
MAKES: 4 servings

- 2 pounds **thin-skinned potatoes** (1 to 1½ in. wide), scrubbed
- 1 **red onion** (½ lb.)
- 1 tablespoon **lemon juice**
  About 1 pound **raclette cheese** (see notes)
  About 1 cup **cornichon pickles**
  **Salt** and **pepper**

1. Put potatoes in a 4- to 5-quart pan. Barely cover with water, put lid on

pan, and place over high heat. When boiling, reduce heat and simmer until potatoes are tender when pierced, about 20 minutes.

2. Meanwhile, peel onion and thinly slice lengthwise. Mix with lemon juice.

3. Slice cheese; arrange in a shallow 8- by 11-inch casserole or 4 individual casseroles, each about 5 inches wide.

4. When potatoes are cooked, drain off most of the water and keep warm.

5. Broil cheese about 6 inches below heat until melted, about 5 minutes.

6. To eat, put potatoes, onion, and pickles on dinner plates. Spoon hot cheese, a few bites at a time, over potatoes. Add salt and pepper to taste. If cheese in casserole gets hard, return to broiler to soften, 3 to 4 minutes.

Per serving: 687 cal., 50% (342 cal.) from fat; 40 g protein; 38 g fat (21 g sat.); 48 g carbo (4.7 g fiber); 1,217 mg sodium; 125 mg chol.

## HOT TOPPER

# Spreadable heat

Add chilies to a simple jelly to wake up taste buds

Why make chili-flavor jellies from scratch when there's a quicker way? Start with apple jelly. It's mild and unobtrusive, so you can jazz it up, even with fireball habaneros. You can easily control the heat of this chili by trimming out its veins. In doing so, you'll allow the unique floral taste of the habaneros to come through and make a jelly that's gentle enough to enjoy on breakfast toast. It's also a great house gift.

### Hasty Habanero Jelly

**PREP AND COOK TIME:** About 25 minutes

**NOTES:** Other fresh chilies that work are West Indian hot (as hot as habaneros); milder but still hot cayenne, Fresno, jalapeño, Santa Fe grande, and serrano; and milder-still Hungarian wax. If desired, double the amount of milder ones.

**MAKES:** 4 jars; 10 ounces each

About 1½ ounces **habanero chilies**

1 cup **rice vinegar**

¼ cup **sugar**

4 jars (10 oz. each) **apple jelly**

JAMES CARRIER (4)

## Easier than pie

A. Fork prevents chili burns.

B. Melt jelly with cooked chilies.

C. Pour jelly back into original jars.

**SUSPENDED STRANDS** of deep orange habanero chilies announce that this jelly is anything but tame. Bright paper caps tied with raffia or ribbon wrap it up.

**1.** Rinse chilies and cut off stem ends. Wearing gloves or holding chilies with a fork (do not touch with bare hands), cut chilies in half lengthwise. Slice out and discard veins and seeds. Cut chilies into ⅛- to ⅙-inch slivers.

**2.** Put chilies, vinegar, and sugar in a 4- to 5-quart pan. Bring to a boil over high heat, stirring often, and boil until mixture is reduced to about ⅓ cup, about 7 minutes.

**3.** Scrape jelly from jars into pan. Stirring often, boil until jelly melts. Ladle hot jelly back into the unwashed jars to within ¼ inch of rims. Wipe rims clean and screw lids onto jars. (If there is a little extra jelly, pour into a small dish and cover when cool.)

**4.** After 1½ hours, gently shake jelly in jars to redistribute chili pieces if they have floated to the top. When jelly is cool, use or store in the refrigerator up to 3 months.

Per tablespoon: 51 cal., 0% (0 cal.) from fat; 0.1 g protein; 0 g fat; 13 g carbo (0.1 g fiber); 6.4 mg sodium; 0 mg chol. ◆

# The Wine Guide

BY KAREN MacNEIL

RICK MARIANI

## Restaurant etiquette uncorked

■ Ten years ago, I wrote a piece for the *New York Times* on how New York waiters size up guests based on their wine savvy. The leading pet peeve among servers back then? Guests who "stare at the waiter the whole time he's pouring, casting a deadly pall over the table."

Well, I suspect we guests have a few laments of our own these days, including servers who challenge our knowledge, shower us with bits of broken cork, and inadvertently pour wine into our sleeve (all of which have happened to me).

A little knowledge of wine etiquette—on the part of both waiters and diners—can make a restaurant meal more comfortable, even downright special.

### SPENDING STRATEGIES

Just because there are expensive wines on a restaurant's list doesn't mean you should be intimidated into spending a lot. It's perfectly acceptable to seek out an easy-drinking bargain.

When you ask for a suggestion, beware the server who proposes a $90 bottle! A truly professional waiter will always offer several wines in different price brackets. I like to end run this situation entirely by stating from the outset how much I want to spend: "I'm looking for something light and crisp that costs around $25 a bottle."

### ASKING FOR BETTER GLASSES

Do it! Drinking a great wine out of a badly designed, meager glass is just not acceptable. Admittedly, you don't need fine crystal, but a generous-size glass is critical for the wine to open up so you can smell and taste it better.

Many restaurants have a stash of bigger wineglasses, and your wine doesn't need to cost a zillion dollars to warrant your requesting one. It's a matter of appreciation, not money.

### SENDING THE WINE BACK

Sure, there are uppity customers who abuse this privilege. But if you genuinely believe the wine tastes wrong, by all means send it back—politely—and ask for a different wine. There's no need on your part to name the defect—that is, you don't have to know if the wine is corked or oxidized, or has a hydrogen sulfide problem.

Corked wines, by the way, are not commonplace, but neither are they rare, because cork is subject to contamination. A corked wine smells slightly moldy, like damp newspapers or a wet dog. It won't hurt you; it's just unpleasant.

You needn't ask the waiter to taste the wine for confirmation, and risk getting into a confrontation over whether or not it's bad. Most good restaurants will graciously take it back, no questions asked.

What should you do if the wine is in sound condition but you just don't like it? Clearly this isn't the restaurant's problem, so the restaurant shouldn't be penalized. In this case, it's good form to order a different bottle but offer to pay for the wine you didn't care for.

### TOPPING UP

The server has poured your wine, put the bottle on the table, and disappeared. After 15 minutes or so, you're ready for a little more. Is it tacky to grab the bottle and top up your own glasses?

### CHOICE RHÔNES

Some of the most exciting wines on restaurant lists these days are Rhône varieties, both white (Viognier, Roussanne, and Marsanne) and red (Grenache, Mourvèdre, Cinsault, Syrah, and Petite Syrah, among others). Some of my favorites among those I've recently tasted from California and Australia:

■ **d'Arenberg Grenache "The Custodian" 1996 (McLaren Vale, South Australia),** $21. Like an ultra-rich boysenberry pie.

■ **Edmunds St. John "Les Côtes Sauvages" 1996 (California),** $20. A howling blend of Grenache, Mourvèdre, Syrah, and other grapes. Very primal, even savage.

■ **Guenoc and Langtry Estate Vineyards and Winery Petite Syrah 1995 (California),** $16. Chocolate-covered boysenberries and exotic spices.

■ **McDowell Valley Vineyards Marsanne 1997 (Mendocino County),** $16. Super appley, fresh, and snappy. A fantastic aperitif.

■ **Qupé Wine Cellars Syrah "Bien Nacido" Reserve 1996 (Santa Barbara County),** $25. Can raspberries be rich and elegant?

---

Twenty years ago a good waiter would have been mortified if you poured your own (a sign he was not doing his job). But increasingly, it's fine, especially in casual restaurants. Lots of guests, in fact, like to be in charge of the rate—and amount—of wine poured.

### TIPPING

Historically, waiters were tipped only on the food portion of the bill, not on wine or other beverages. You were expected to tip the sommelier separately.

These days it's more common for a single waiter to recommend and serve both food and wine. And it's customary to tip 15 to 20 percent on the entire bill minus the tax. But if a separate server has been especially helpful in finding and pouring your wine, you may want to tip that person an additional 10 to 15 percent of the cost of the bottle.

In the end, wine etiquette comes down to honesty, common sense, and respect. There's really only one hard-and-fast rule: Trust your judgment. ◆

Halloween
'98

# trick or
# treat

BY LINDA LAU ANUSASANANAN

icked witches, creepy creatures, sinister monsters, even Batman and petite ballerinas can't survive on candy alone. And whether the Halloween hordes gather after ringing doorbells or simply for fun and games while admiring one another's devilish styles, an easy supper is in order to enhance the fantasy of the evening. Sure, you could have a buffet, but how about turning it into a "boo! fête"? Dreadful names and ghoulish shapes turn dishes suited to all ages into party fare.

## how 'bout something good to eat?

GAME PLAN: Up to 1 day ahead, make the tortilla cutout crisps, sausage and vegetable soup, bread, and apple ghosts. Also, freeze berries that will chill the punch. Up to 3 hours ahead, rinse radishes (you'll need 20 to 30), cut jicama bones, and make guacamole. Use guacamole as a dip for the spook crisps, radishes, and bleached bones. Shortly before serving, reheat soup and bread, pour the punch together, and set out your favorite bloody Mary mixtures.

PHOTOGRAPHS BY RICHARD JUNG

## A Wicked Boo! Fête

Spook Crisps

Bleached Bones • Guacamole

Bloodshot Eyes

(Red Radishes and Pimiento-stuffed Olives)

Boil and Bubble Soup Cauldron

Jack-o'-Lantern Bread • Butter

Apple Ghosts

Bleeding Hearts Punch • Bloody Marys

JAMES CARRIER

STAMP OUT wild creatures from flour tortillas using Halloween cookie cutters.

APPLES turn ghostly pale with white candy coating. Licorice slices make them expressive.

## Spook Crisps

**PREP AND COOK TIME:** About 30 minutes

**NOTES:** If making ahead, store cool crisps airtight at room temperature.

**MAKES:** About 48 (3- to 4-in. size) or 12 (6- to 8-in. size); 10 to 12 servings

- 6 plain or flavored **flour tortillas** (10 in.)
- ¾ cup **grated parmesan cheese**
- 2 teaspoons **chili powder**
- ⅓ cup (⅙ lb.) melted **butter** or margarine

**1.** Use Halloween cookie cutters to cut tortillas into shapes such as ghosts, goblins, witches, and jack-o'-lanterns.

**2.** Lay the cutouts slightly apart on 2 nonstick baking sheets about 14 by 17 inches.

**3.** Mix cheese and chili powder.

**4.** Brush tortillas with butter. Sprinkle with cheese mixture.

**5.** Bake in a 350° oven until golden and crisp, about 15 minutes; if using 1 oven, switch pan positions halfway through baking.

**6.** Transfer crisps to racks. Serve warm or cool.

Per serving: 158 cal., 49% (77 cal.) from fat; 4.6 g protein; 8.6 g fat (4.4 g sat.); 16 g carbo (1 g fiber); 280 mg sodium; 18 mg chol.

## Bleached Bones

**PREP TIME:** About 15 minutes

**NOTES:** Chill cut jicama airtight if making ahead.

**MAKES:** 10 to 12 servings

- 3 pounds **jicama**
  **Salt**

Peel jicama, rinse, and cut into ½-inch-thick slices. With cookie cutters or a knife, cut jicama into bone shapes or ½-inch-wide sticks. Arrange on a tray or in a bowl. Season to taste with salt.

Per serving: 40 cal., 2.3% (0.9 cal.) from fat; 0.8 g protein; 0.1 g fat (0 g sat.); 9.2 g carbo (5.1 g fiber); 4.2 mg sodium; 0 mg chol.

## Guacamole

**PREP TIME:** About 25 minutes

**NOTES:** Cover and chill guacamole if making ahead.

**MAKES:** 10 to 12 servings

- 3 or 4 **firm-ripe** to ripe **avocados** (about 2 lb. total)
- ¼ cup **lime juice**
- 2 tablespoons minced **green onion**
- 2 tablespoons chopped **fresh cilantro**
- 1 to 2 tablespoons minced **fresh jalapeño chilies**
- 1 or 2 cloves **garlic**, pressed or minced
  **Salt**

Peel, pit, and coarsely mash avocados. Add lime juice, onion, cilantro, chilies, garlic, and salt to taste, mixing well. Serve in a bowl.

Per serving: 92 cal., 84% (77 cal.) from fat; 1.1 g protein; 8.6 g fat (1.4 g sat.); 4.7 g carbo (1.1 g fiber); 6.7 mg sodium; 0 mg chol.

## Boil and Bubble Soup Cauldron

**PREP AND COOK TIME:** About 50 minutes

**NOTES:** The hominy can pass for teeth and the green peas as beady little eyes. If making soup ahead, don't add peas; cover soup when cool and chill, then add peas when reheating. For a tureen, use a rustic pan, such as a cast-iron Dutch oven. Or you can use a pumpkin shell. You'll need a pumpkin at least 12 to 16 inches tall and wide. Cut off top and scoop out seeds. About 10 minutes before serving, fill shell with boiling water to warm. Drain and fill with hot soup. Use top as lid for the pumpkin tureen.

**MAKES:** About 5 quarts; 10 to 12 servings

- 1 tablespoon **salad oil**
- 2 pounds **raw turkey Italian sausages**
- 1 **onion** (8 oz.), chopped
- 1 **red bell pepper** (8 oz.), stemmed, seeded, and chopped
- 2 cloves **garlic**, pressed or minced
- 1 tablespoon **chili powder**
- 2 teaspoons **cumin seed**
- 1 teaspoon **dried oregano leaves**
- 2 quarts fat-skimmed **chicken broth**
- 2 pounds **banana** or Hubbard **squash**
- 3 cans (15 oz. each) **hominy**, drained
- 1 box (10 oz.) **frozen peas**
  **Salt** and **pepper**

**1.** Place oil in an 8- to 10-quart pan over medium-high heat. Squeeze sausages from casings into pan; discard casings. Break sausage into bite-size chunks. Stir occasionally until lightly browned, about 5 minutes.

**2.** Add onion, bell pepper, and garlic. Stir over high heat until onion is limp, about 5 minutes.

**3.** Stir in chili powder, cumin seed, and oregano. Add broth, cover, and bring to a boil over high heat.

**4.** Meanwhile, peel squash and cut into ½-inch cubes. Add to broth. Return to a boil. Reduce heat, cover, and simmer until squash is tender when pierced, about 15 minutes, stirring occasionally.

**5.** Add hominy. If peas are frozen in a block, whack container against counter to separate, then pour peas into soup. Turn heat to high and bring soup to a boil, about 3 minutes.

**6.** Pour soup into a tureen and ladle into mugs or bowls. Add salt and pepper to taste.

Per serving: 286 cal., 38% (108 cal.) from fat; 19 g protein; 12 g fat (3.1 g sat.); 29 g carbo (5.2 g fiber); 826 mg sodium; 43 mg chol.

## Jack-o'-Lantern Bread

**PREP AND COOK TIME:** About 45 minutes, plus about 1 hour to rise

**NOTES:** Follow package directions for thawing bread dough. If making ahead,

wrap cool bread airtight and hold at room temperature up to 1 day or freeze to store longer. Reheat (thawed, if frozen), loosely covered with foil, in a 350° oven until warm, 10 to 15 minutes.

**MAKES:** 1 loaf or 4 small loaves (2 lb. total); 10 to 12 servings

- 2 loaves (1 lb. each) **frozen bread dough**, thawed
- 1 tablespoon beaten **egg**
- 1½ teaspoons **milk**

**1.** Place loaves in a bowl. Cover bowl with plastic wrap and let rise until doubled, 45 minutes to 1 hour.

**2.** Punch dough down, knead loaves together in bowl, and shape into a ball.

**3.** Transfer ball to an oiled 12- by 15-inch baking sheet. With oiled hands or a lightly floured rolling pin, flatten ball into an 11- by 13-inch oval. Cut out eyes, nose, and mouth; openings should be at least 1½ to 2 inches wide. (To make small loaves, divide dough into 4 equal pieces, roll into 4- by 6-in. ovals; eye, nose, and mouth openings should be at least 1 to 1½ in. wide.) Lift out cutout dough and bake on another pan or use for decorations.

**4.** Cover shaped dough lightly with plastic wrap and let rise until puffy, about 20 minutes.

**5.** Mix egg with milk; brush over dough.

**6.** Bake in a 350° oven until well-browned, 30 to 35 minutes. Cool on a rack. Serve warm or cool.

Per serving: 211 cal., 19% (41 cal.) from fat; 5.8 g protein; 4.6 g fat (1.1 g sat.); 36 g carbo (1.6 g fiber); 367 mg sodium; 9.2 mg chol.

## Apple Ghosts

**PREP AND COOK TIME:** About 30 minutes

**NOTES:** Use small apples, such as those for lunch boxes. If making ahead, let coating firm, then enclose apples with plastic wrap and refrigerate. Look for the wood craft sticks at hobby shops; they're also sold with caramel for coating apples. Save leftover white candy for other uses.

**MAKES:** 10 to 12 servings

- 10 to 12 **green** or red **apples** (4-oz. size, about 2¼ in. at widest point)
- 10 to 12 **wood craft** or caramel apple **sticks**
- 3 cups (18 oz.) **white candy chips** or chunks, suitable for melting (not all kinds will melt)
- 2 tablespoons **solid shortening**

- 2 **black licorice sticks** (6 in.), cut crosswise into thin slices (optional)

**1.** Rinse apples, wipe dry, and firmly insert a stick into stem end of each fruit until secure.

**2.** In a 1-quart glass measure or small deep microwave-safe bowl, combine candy and shortening. Place in a microwave oven and heat at half power (50%) until chips are soft, 2½ to 3 minutes. Stir until smooth. If still lumpy, return to microwave and heat for 20-second intervals until candy is smooth.

**3.** Quickly dip apples, 1 at a time, into coating to cover, letting excess drip back into bowl. Set apples, sticks up, in a 10- by 15-inch pan lined with waxed paper or cooking parchment. If desired, make ghost faces by pressing licorice slices into soft coating. If coating on apple is too firm, use melted coating to glue licorice in place. If coating gets too thick, reheat it briefly in the microwave at 50% power and stir.

**4.** Let apples stand until coating is firm to touch, at least 30 minutes at room temperature or 10 minutes if chilled.

Per serving: 236 cal., 42% (99 cal.) from fat; 0.2 g protein; 11 g fat (8 g sat.); 36 g carbo (2.3 g fiber); 30 mg sodium; 0 mg chol.

## Bleeding Hearts Punch

**PREP TIME:** About 15 minutes, plus 1 hour to freeze fruit

**NOTES:** If freezing fruit ahead, transfer berries when solid to a freezer container and freeze up to 2 weeks.

**MAKES:** 10 to 12 servings

- 4 cups **strawberries**, rinsed and drained
- 2 cans (12 oz.) **frozen cranberry juice cocktail concentrate**, thawed
- 1 bottle (67.6 oz.) **sparkling water**, chilled

**1.** Cut a V shape under stem of each strawberry and discard. Cut berries in half lengthwise across the V to form a heart. Lay berries in a single layer on baking sheets. Freeze until solid, at least 1 hour; flex pan to release frozen fruit.

**2.** In a 4½-quart or larger bowl, mix cranberry juice cocktail concentrate with sparkling water. Add frozen berries.

Per serving: 159 cal., 2.3% (3.6 cal.) from fat; 0.3 g protein; 0.4 g fat (0 g sat.); 40 g carbo (1.3 g fiber); 5.7 mg sodium; 0 mg chol. ◆

## G R E A T
## E S C A P E S

# Bed, breakfast, and hiking boots

From British Columbia to an Arizona oasis, these inns offer wilderness adventure and creature comforts, too

■ IT IS A CONFLICT as old as human-kind—the passion for adventure versus the equally powerful desire to be coddled. Think of the luxury-loving Athenians versus the rugged if grumpy Spartans, or, on a different note, Eva Gabor and Eddie Albert sparring about stores and chores on *Green Acres.*

In truth, most of us want both adventure and a little luxury in our lives. And, especially on vacation, why can't we get exactly what we want? No reason at all. That's why *Sunset* scoured the West for bed-and-breakfast inns that offer unbeatable access to great hiking. At the same time, these inns know that even stalwart wilderness fans appreciate starting the day with a wonderfully prepared breakfast and ending it by sinking into a comfortable bed.

Each of these inns lies an easy stroll (or in some cases, a very short drive) from trails that offer some of the best hiking in the West. Each knows how to pamper guests. And they prepare such good breakfasts we knew we had to share their best recipes with you. After all, we can use some adventure and a bit of pampering when we return home, too.

RIVERSONG guests hit the trail in Estes Park, Colorado; above, boots await the next hike at Aravaipa Farms.

NATALIE FOBES

## Durlacher Hof, Whistler, British Columbia

■ "Peter's a mountain goat," says Erika Durlacher of her husband, who first came to Canada with a group of Austrian mountain climbers. But a love of hiking is in Austrian-born Erika's genes, too. The couple keep their Alpine heritage alive at Durlacher Hof, a bed-and-breakfast they built 10 years ago near Whistler Village, in the Coast Mountains of southwestern British Columbia.

Modeled after the farmhouses that dot the Austrian Alps, the inn serves a generous breakfast buffet with Austrian specialties such as apple pancakes or ricotta-filled crêpes, along with frittatas or omelets and plenty of fresh fruit. It's ample fuel for hiking the dozens of nearby trails, which are their most inviting when autumn color is popping out.

WHERE: Whistler, 75 miles northeast of Vancouver, B.C.

CONTACT: (604) 932-1924.

RATES: $150–$255 Canadian. Two-night minimum on weekends.

SUGGESTED HIKE: For superb mountain vistas, head up Blackcomb Mountain via Whistler's high-speed ski lifts, which start about a ½-mile walk from the inn and will carry you up to the Rendezvous Lodge. From here a 3-mile nature trail runs through alpine meadows along the mountain crest. The route is only moderately difficult—but remember you'll be above 7,000 feet. Lifts operate 10–5 daily through mid-October; tickets $20 Canadian, about $15 U.S.

FYI: Whistler Resort; (604) 932-3434.

*— Jena MacPherson*

### Durlacher Hof Austrian Ricotta Crêpes

PREP AND COOK TIME: About 1 hour

NOTES: At Durlacher Hof in Whistler, Erika Durlacher makes *topfen palatschinken*, German for crêpes filled with curd cheese. Serve them with cranberry sauce (following), a sweetened purée of fresh raspberries, or a poached fruit compote. If making ahead, fill crêpes, cover, and

CRANBERRY-cheese crêpes await guests at Durlacher Hof.

chill up to 1 day, then pour custard over them just before baking.

MAKES: 8 crêpes; 4 servings

#### Crêpes

1¼ cups **milk**

1 **large egg**

⅔ cup **all-purpose flour**

About 2 teaspoons **butter** or margarine

#### Filling and custard

½ cup **raisins**

1 carton (15 oz., 1¾ cups) **part-skim ricotta cheese**

About ½ cup **sugar**

1 **large egg** yolk

1 **large egg**

1 cup **half-and-half** (light cream) or milk

1 teaspoon finely shredded **lemon** peel

**Cranberry sauce** (recipe follows)

**Sour cream** (optional)

1. *To make crêpes,* whirl 1¼ cups milk, 1 egg, and flour in a blender until smooth.

2. Place over medium heat a nonstick frying pan that measures 7 to 8 inches across bottom. When hot, add ¼ teaspoon butter and swirl to coat pan. Pour in ¼ cup batter, quickly tilting pan so batter flows over entire flat surface. Cook until crêpe is dry on top and edge is browned, about 30 seconds. Turn crêpe with a spatula and brown other side, about 15 seconds. Invert from pan onto a plate. Repeat, stacking crêpes as made. You need 8 crêpes; reserve any extras for another use.

3. *To make filling,* soak raisins in hot water for 2 to 3 minutes.

4. Beat ricotta, ¼ cup sugar, and egg yolk until well mixed. Drain raisins and stir into ricotta mixture.

5. Spoon ⅛ of the filling (about ¼ cup) across lower third of each crêpe, and roll to enclose. Place filled crêpes, seam side down, in a lightly buttered shallow 9- by 13-inch baking dish or shallow casserole.

6. *To make custard,* whisk ¼ cup sugar and 1 egg with half-and-half. Pour evenly over filled crêpes.

7. Bake in a 375° oven until custard at casserole edge no longer jiggles when gently shaken, about 20 minutes.

8. Sprinkle casserole with about 1 teaspoon sugar and shredded lemon peel. Lift out crêpes with a wide spatula. Serve warm with cranberry sauce and sour cream added to taste.

Per serving without cranberry sauce: 568 cal., 38% (216 cal.) from fat; 23 g protein; 24 g fat (14 g sat.); 67 g carbo (1.5 g fiber); 251 mg sodium; 230 mg chol.

### Cranberry Sauce

PREP AND COOK TIME: About 10 minutes

MAKES: 1 cup; 4 servings

In a 2- to 3-quart pan, combine 1⅓ cups rinsed and drained **fresh** or frozen **cranberries,** ⅓ cup **sugar,** and ⅓ cup **water.** Bring to a boil over high heat, cover pan, and reduce heat to medium. Stir occasionally just until berries begin to pop, about 5 minutes. Serve warm or cool.

Per serving: 82 cal., 1.1% (0.9 cal.) from fat; 0.1 g protein; 0.1 g fat (0 g sat.); 21 g carbo (1.3 g fiber); 0.5 mg sodium; 0 mg chol.

*— Linda Lau Anusasananan*

RECIPES

CLIMBING GEAR FROM REI, SAN CARLOS, CA

TERRENCE McCARTHY

APRÈS-HIKE picnic spreads across Mangels House lawn.

## Mangels House, Aptos, California

■ It looks as though it might be made from spun sugar, and that is appropriate: the Mangels House was built by a relative of Claus Spreckles, California's 19th-century sugar king. Plunked in a green meadow at the foot of the Santa Cruz Mountains, the 1886 Italianate Victorian served the Mangels family as a summer retreat.

The Mangels House's current owner, Jackie Fisher, has done a notably good job with the inn's decor. As a result, a guest's inclination might be to loll around in the sitting room. That would be a big mistake. For the single best thing about the Mangels House may be its location, adjacent to Forest of Nisene Marks State Park. This snake-skinny 10,000-acre park runs along Aptos Creek deep into the second-growth red-woods of the Santa Cruz Mountains. Its trails will call you— and as you hike, chances are good you'll run into owner Fisher and shepherd-mix Dieter.

WHERE: Aptos, 6 miles south of Santa Cruz and 90 miles south of San Francisco.

CONTACT: (800) 320-7401 or www.innaccess.com/mangels.

RATES: $120–$160. Six bedrooms. Two-night minimum weekends.

SUGGESTED HIKE: Start at Forest of Nisene Marks's Aptos Creek Rd. entrance, a short walk from the inn. From here you can grab a map and do an 11-mile loop that takes you north on the road, then west along the Aptos Creek Trail up the Big Slide Trail, then back down Aptos Creek Fire Rd. to your start.

FYI: Forest of Nisene Marks State Park; (831) 763-7063. Park entrance $3 per car. — *Peter Fish*

RECIPES

## Mangels House English Scones

PREP AND COOK TIME: About 35 minutes

NOTES: Jackie Fisher uses her mother's recipe to make these tender, currant-studded scones at Mangels House in Aptos. Serve with raspberry jam and butter.

MAKES: 4 to 8 servings

- ¼ cup **dried currants**
- 1 tablespoon **brandy**
- ½ teaspoon grated **orange** peel
- About 2 cups **all-purpose flour**
- About 6 tablespoons **sugar**
- 1 tablespoon **baking powder**
- ¼ teaspoon **salt**
- About ½ cup (¼ lb.) **butter** or margarine
- About ½ cup **buttermilk**

**1.** In a small microwave-safe bowl, mix currants, brandy, and orange peel. Heat in a microwave oven at full power (100%) just until warm, 15 to 20 seconds.

**2.** In another bowl, mix 2 cups flour, 6 tablespoons sugar, baking powder, and salt. With a pastry blender, cut in ½ cup butter until no lumps are larger than ¼ inch. Stir in currant mixture.

**3.** Add ½ cup buttermilk; stir just enough to evenly moisten dough. If dough is crumbly, sprinkle a little more buttermilk over mixture and stir. Pat dough into a ball and knead in bowl just until dough holds together.

**4.** Set dough on a lightly buttered 12- by 15-inch baking sheet. Flatten into a ½-inch-thick round. With a floured knife, cut round in quarters or eighths, leaving wedges in place. Brush dough with about 2 teaspoons buttermilk and sprinkle with about ½ teaspoon sugar.

**5.** Bake scones in a 400° oven until golden brown, 20 to 25 minutes. Transfer to a rack. Serve warm or cool. Break round into wedges.

Per serving: 276 cal., 36% (108 cal.) from fat; 4 g protein; 12 g fat (7.6 g sat.); 38 g carbo (1.1 g fiber); 394 mg sodium; 33 mg chol.

— *Linda Lau Anusasananan*

FLAKY, citrus-scented scones are a Mangels House specialty.

JAMES CARRIER (2)

## Windy Point Inn, Big Bear Lake, California

■ Jutting into the Big Bear's blue waters, high in the San Bernardino Mountains, Windy Point is sleekly sybaritic in a particularly Southern California way—with whirlpool spas and CD players tucked into the stylish rooms, it's the kind of nest into which some *Melrose Place* vixen might lure her latest conquest, preferably her best friend's husband.

That just goes to show that looks can be deceiving. Stylish it is, but the Windy Point Inn is also wholesomely outdoorsy. Innkeepers Kent and Val Kessler, who built the inn seven years ago, know Big Bear and the surrounding San Bernardino Mountains well. (They even supply each inn guest with a San Bernardino National Forest activity pass, mandatory for hiking in the forest.) They steer hikers down the road to nearby Gray's Peak Trail and guide bicyclists to the lakeshore Alpine Pedal Path. No matter which option you choose, you know that at day's end you can return to the inn with its expansive lake views and soothing spas and dream not of *Melrose Place* but of the miles you've covered.

WHERE: Big Bear Lake, about 110 miles east of Los Angeles.

CONTACT: (909) 866-2746.

RATES: $125–$245. Two-night minimum on weekends and holidays.

SUGGESTED HIKE: The 6-mile round trip hike up Gray's Peak offers superb views of Big Bear Lake and the surrounding San Bernardinos. It also leads into a bald eagle breeding area (and for that reason is closed December through April). The trailhead lies off State 18 about 1/3 mile east of the inn.

FYI: San Bernardino National Forest Big Bear Discovery Center; (909) 866-3437. — *Peter Fish*

LAKESIDE retreat: Windy Point Inn lies near trails in the San Bernardino Mountains.

CHILI-and-cheddar frittata is a specialty of Windy Point innkeepers Kent and Val Kessler.

## Windy Point Inn Spanish Frittata

PREP AND COOK TIME: About 1 hour, plus 8 hours to chill
MAKES: 8 servings

- 1/2 pound **cheese onion** or cheese jalapeño **bread,** cut into 1/2-inch cubes
- 9 **large eggs**
- 2 cups **milk**
- 1 cup (4 oz.) **shredded jack cheese**
- 1 cup (4 oz.) **shredded cheddar cheese**
- 1 can (7 oz.) **diced green chilies**
- 1/2 cup chopped **onion**
- 1/4 cup chopped **fresh Anaheim chili**
- 1/4 cup chopped **fresh cilantro**
- 2 tablespoons chopped **parsley**
- 1 teaspoon **seasoned** or plain **salt**
- **Fresh cilantro** sprigs
- **Avocado** slices
- **Fruit salsa** (recipe follows)

1. Spread bread evenly in a buttered 9- by 13-inch pan.

2. In a bowl, beat eggs and milk just to blend. Add jack cheese, cheddar cheese, canned chilies, onion, fresh chili, chopped cilantro, parsley, and salt. Pour evenly over bread. Cover and chill at least 8 hours or overnight.

3. Uncover and bake in a 350° oven until center barely jiggles when gently shaken and top is lightly browned, about 45 minutes.

4. Garnish servings with cilantro sprigs and avocado slices. Add fruit salsa to taste.

Per serving with salsa: 389 cal., 46% (180 cal.) from fat; 21 g protein; 20 g fat (10 g sat.); 31 g carbo (2.5 g fiber); 799 mg sodium; 285 mg chol.

FRUIT SALSA. Pit, peel, and coarsely chop 1 **firm-ripe mango** (1 lb.). Coarsely chop 3 **Roma tomatoes** (3/4 lb. total). Mix mango, tomatoes, 1/2 cup sliced **green onion,** 2 tablespoons minced **fresh Anaheim chili,** 1 clove pressed **garlic,** 3 tablespoons **lime juice,** 1/2 cup chopped **fresh cilantro,** and **salt** to taste.

—*Linda Lau Anusasananan*

## Across the Creek at Aravaipa Farms, Winkelman, Arizona

■After several hours of hiking through Aravaipa Canyon, your boots or tennis shoes will have sluiced off enough creek water to irrigate the Sahara, and your head will spin trying to remember how many species of birds you've seen. This remote riparian wilderness area in southeastern Arizona hosts eagles and herons and other more rarely seen birds that congregate here for the year-round water.

If you wanted to rough it, you could camp near the trailhead. But since you don't, you can make the 5-mile drive back to Across the Creek at Aravaipa Farms.

Carol Steele bought the apricot, pear, and peach orchard in 1995. She renovated the main house for herself, and set up two nearby cottages for guests. (She kept the business in the family when she sold it to her son and daughter-in-law, Larry and Susan.) Each cabin comes with a private bath, fireplace, queen and twin bed, patio, and plenty of art.

Breakfast is a do-it-yourself proposition. Cottage refrigerators are stocked with yogurt, fruit, muffins—and often Steele's superb morning banana cake. She provides hearty picnic lunches for hikers; in the evening, guests dine with her in the main house. After dinner, you can recover from your day of hiking in a hammock slung beneath a mesquite tree.

WHERE: Winkelman, 70 miles north of Tucson.

CONTACT: (520) 357-6901.

RATES: $200 a day, including all meals. Two cottages.

SUGGESTED HIKE: From the inn, it's a 5-mile drive to Aravaipa Canyon Wilderness. From the trailhead, follow Aravaipa Creek east, then return the same way; total distance is 11 miles. Many creek crossings are required—don't set out if flash floods are forecast.

FYI: Hiking permits required for Aravaipa Canyon Wilderness: $5 per person per night. Contact the Bureau of Land Management, Safford, AZ; (520) 348-4400.

— *Nora Burba Trulsson*

EDWARD McCAIN

RETREAT for wilderness buffs, Aravaipa Farms offers cozy rooms and morning banana cake.

### Across the Creek at Aravaipa Farms Morning Banana Cake

PREP AND COOK TIME: About 1 hour and 20 minutes

NOTES: At Across the Creek at Aravaipa Farms, Carol Steele presents a self-serve breakfast buffet of yogurt, fresh fruit, and this sugar-crusted, flavor-dense, moist banana cake.

MAKES: 16 to 20 servings

2⅓ cups **all-purpose flour**

1 cup **pecan** or walnut **halves**

1 cup **dried cranberries**

1 teaspoon **baking powder**

1 teaspoon **baking soda**

¼ teaspoon **salt**

2½ cups **sugar**

1 cup mashed **ripe banana**

2 teaspoons **vanilla**

2 **large eggs**

1 cup (½ lb.) melted **butter** or margarine

1 cup **buttermilk**

1. Mix flour, pecans, cranberries, baking powder, baking soda, and salt.

2. In a large bowl, mix sugar, banana, vanilla, and eggs until well blended.

Add butter and buttermilk; mix well.

3. Add flour mixture to bowl and stir until evenly moistened.

4. Butter and flour-dust a nonstick 10-inch decorative tube pan. Pour batter into pan.

5. Bake in a 350° oven until a long wood skewer, inserted in the thickest part, comes out clean, and cake pulls from pan sides, about 1 hour.

6. Cool cake in pan on a rack for 15 minutes. Lay a rack on top of pan. Holding pan and rack together, invert to release cake. Lift off pan. Serve cake warm or cool.

Per serving: 314 cal., 40% (126 cal.) from fat; 3.2 g protein; 14 g fat (6.5 g sat.); 45 g carbo (1.3 g fiber); 234 mg sodium; 48 mg chol.

— *Linda Lau Anusasananan*

RUSTIC, elegant rooms
pamper RiverSong guests.

STEVE MOHLENKAMP

## RiverSong Inn, Estes Park, Colorado

■ On the edge of Rocky Mountain National Park in Estes Park, RiverSong Inn is the kind of hostelry you'd expect to find in Aspen or Vail, not in this modest little tourist town. A central inn and several guest houses cluster at the end of a private, unpaved road. All are elegantly detailed, with extra-deep whirlpool tubs, wood-burning stoves, and tall windows that look out on pines and the nearby mountains.

Every room has a theme. The Cowboy's Delight features collections of branding irons, barbed wire, and other Western memorabilia. More extra touches: plush slippers shaped like horses, and luxuriant plaid flannel robes.

Breakfast is served in a room the size of a small cafe. Socializing is generally done in a common room with a large fireplace, a huge sectional sofa, and pots of coffee and tea, plus an extensive display of Western folk art.

RiverSong's 27-acre grounds include a new beaver pond and a herd of deer that visits daily for apples provided by inn owners Gary and Sue Mansfield. The land makes for good hiking and, come winter, snowshoeing. For longer adventures, the trails of Rocky Mountain National Park are minutes away.

WHERE: Estes Park, 65 miles northwest of Denver.
CONTACT: (970) 586-4666.
RATES: $135–$250. Two-night minimum; no children under 12.
SUGGESTED HIKES: Simplest option is to wander the inn's grounds. Within adjacent Rocky Mountain National Park, a good easy hike is the 6-mile loop past Cub Lake. Trailhead is near Moraine Park—also the site of a good museum. From here the trail runs through Elk Meadows (look for elks in spring and fall), then continues to the lake, where you'll find lily pads in an alpine marsh, rare in Colorado's dry mountains.
FYI: Rocky Mountain National Park; (970) 586-1206.

— *Claire Martin*

## RiverSong Giddy-Up Grits

PREP AND COOK TIME: About 1 hour
NOTES: At RiverSong Inn, breakfast starts with Continental Divide Strawberries (berries topped with a mixture of equal parts sweetened whipped cream and plain yogurt), followed by hearty baked grits.
MAKES: 8 servings

    1 pound **bulk pork sausage**
    1 clove **garlic,** pressed or minced
  ³/₄ teaspoon **pepper**
      About 1 teaspoon **hot sauce**
    1 cup **quick-cooking grits**
    2 tablespoons **butter** or margarine
    2 **large eggs**
    2 cups (½ lb.) shredded **sharp cheddar cheese**
    1 can (7 oz.) **diced green chilies**
  ½ cup diced **red bell pepper**
  ⅓ cup **fresh cilantro** leaves

**1.** Crumble sausage into a 10- to 12-inch frying pan over high heat. Stir often until browned and crumbly, about 6 minutes. Drain off and discard fat. To sausage, add garlic, pepper, and hot sauce to taste. Set aside.
**2.** In a 2- to 3-quart pan, blend grits with 4 cups water. Bring to a boil over high heat, stirring. Add butter. Cover pan; reduce heat to low. Stir often until grits are tender, 5 to 6 minutes.
**3.** In a large bowl, beat eggs to blend. Stirring, add cheese, chilies, sausage mixture, and grits. Pour mixture into a buttered shallow 9- by 13-inch baking dish or 2½- to 3-quart casserole.
**4.** Bake, uncovered, in a 350° oven until lightly browned, 40 to 45 minutes. Let stand about 5 minutes. Sprinkle with red bell pepper and cilantro. Cut into pieces and serve with a wide spatula.

Per serving: 331 cal., 60% (198 cal.) from fat; 16 g protein; 22 g fat (11 g sat.); 17 g carbo (1.4 g fiber); 734 mg sodium; 113 mg chol.

— *Linda Lau Anusasananan*

RIVERSONG mornings start with chili-and-cheese grits.

JAMES CARRIER (2)

# Why?

ANSWERS TO COMMON COOKING QUESTIONS

BY LINDA LAU ANUSASANANAN

## High altitude wreaks havoc on breads, cakes. Why?

■ Climb every mountain and you're apt to find a frustrated baker, like Barbara Kittelson of Volcano, California. Recipes she once used at the coast "now turn out a mess" at 3,900 feet. Because most baking recipes, including those in *Sunset Magazine,* are written and tested for use from sea level to about 3,000 feet, we enlisted the help of high-altitude baking authorities Pat Kendall of the Colorado State University Cooperative Extension and Nancy Feldman from the University of California Cooperative Extension.

What does high altitude mean to the baker? Liquids boil at lower temperatures (below 212°), and moisture evaporates more quickly—both of which significantly impact the quality of baked goods. If you live at 3,000 feet or below, Kendall and Feldman suggest that you first try a recipe as is. Sometimes few, if any, changes are needed. But as you go higher, ingredient adjustments become necessary. Unfortunately, variables in recipes make it impossible to give across-the-board advice. Use the following suggestions as guidelines.

**"Why do my attempts at making sourdough end up with bread so heavy it could be used as boat anchors? We live at 5,800 feet."**
— *Al Hansen*

Flours tend to be drier and will take up more liquid in the low humidity of high altitudes. You may need less flour than the recipe calls for, so mix in about two-thirds, then check the dough before adding more.

Sourdough and yeast doughs rise more quickly—sometimes twice as fast—in the reduced pressure of higher altitudes. If dough rises much more than double, its structure may be affected.

If a short rising time doesn't produce enough sourdough or yeast flavor, punch the dough down after the first fast rise and let it rise a second time before shaping.

As wheat products bake, they are lightened, or leavened, as the heated moisture in them swells and forms tiny bubbles encased by thin dough walls. The bubbles expand until the flour mixture gets hot enough to become rigid and retain their impression. When bubbles form at lower temperatures, the flour mixture isn't hot enough to firm up, and these walls break, producing bread with an uneven, coarse texture.

Two safeguards for baking breads at high altitudes: proof shaped yeast loaves less (until barely puffy) and bake them at a higher temperature (see chart below). Also, store baked goods airtight at high altitudes to keep them from drying out.

**"Why do I end up with a layer of yellow rubberlike substance on the bottom of my six-egg chiffon cake?"**
— *Shelia Gumerman, Santa Fe*

At higher elevations, delicate cakes are especially fragile. The adjustments you need to make depend on what makes the cakes rise.

**Cakes leavened by trapped air.** Cakes such as chiffon, angel food, and sponge are leavened by air bubbles trapped in whipped eggs or egg whites. At higher altitudes, egg mixtures whipped to the maximum can't stretch much before they get rigid and break.

Whip a little less—to soft peaks instead of stiff ones—to allow for expansion. Also reduce sugar slightly so the whipped mixture firms up at a lower temperature.

If the egg foam breaks, drainage forms a rubbery layer—and the cake usually falls. A little additional flour will strengthen the cake, and baking at a slightly higher temperature firms up the egg mixture faster.

**Cakes leavened by baking powder or soda.** At high altitudes, a slight increase in egg and flour (along with the changes noted in the chart below) produces effective results. Most cake mixes have adjustments on the package.

**Cookies.** Those high in fat tend to need more adjustments. Slightly decrease leavening, sugar, and fat. Or slightly increase liquid, flour, and baking temperature.

**Quick breads: muffins, pancakes, and biscuits.** These batters and doughs contain less fat and sugar, and a minor reduction in baking powder may be all that is needed. But if results are unsatisfactory, try the other modifications for cakes suggested in the chart.

### NEED MORE HELP?

Cooperative extension services have booklets or recipes for high-altitude cooking and baking. Call your county extension office or, for a good selection, write or call the Other Bookstore—Cooperative Extension Resource Center, 115 General Services Building, Colorado State University, Fort Collins, CO 80523; (970) 491-6198. ◆

## Ups and downs for baking at high altitudes

| CHANGE | 3,000 FEET | 5,000 FEET | 7,000 FEET |
|---|---|---|---|
| **Baking powder:** reduce each teaspoon | by ⅛ to ¼ tsp. | by ⅛ to ¼ tsp. | by ¼ tsp. |
| **Sugar:** reduce each cup | up to 1 tbsp. | up to 2 tbsp. | by 1 to 3 tbsp. |
| **Liquid:** increase each cup | by 1 to 2 tbsp. | by 2 to 4 tbsp. | by 3 to 4 tbsp. |
| **Oven temperature:** increase | 3° to 5° | 15° | 21° to 25° |

# Olive harvest party

### An homage to the olive and its oil

BY ANDREW BAKER

■ In 1990, Nan McEvoy (right), former chairman of the board of the Chronicle Publishing Co., bought a 550-acre ranch near Petaluma, California, to give her city-dwelling grandchildren a place to play. And to make the property productive, she planted olive trees, which now give 300 of her friends a reason to play here too.

On a cloudy November afternoon last year, they lent a hand, gathering the fruit. Duties done, the guests trekked back to the ranch house and celebrated the harvest with a feast produced by Paul Bertolli, chef and co-owner of Oliveto Cafe & Restaurant in Oakland. The menu was saturated with olives and olive oil, of course—cured olives bathed in a citrus-infused olive oil, mushrooms sautéed in olive oil and spooned onto toast, beans perfumed with olive oil, and several spit-roasted pigs stuffed with fennel cooked in olive oil.

And at every table, rustic breads sat alongside bowls of McEvoy's olive oil, ready to soak up the taste of the day.

Such olive oil celebrations are widespread and growing. On page 234, learn what's new with the West's hottest liquid commodity; on page 235, how to taste it; and on page 236, how to find it. Then host your own festivities with a tasting of oils followed by Bertolli's menu, featuring a succulent stuffed pork loin instead of the whole hog.

THE BEST OIL comes from unbruised olives crushed just after picking. A ton of olives makes up to 40 gallons of oil.

## Olives with Orange, Fennel, and Chili

PREP AND COOK TIME: About 10 minutes
MAKES: About 3¼ cups; 8 servings

  1  teaspoon **fennel seed**
  ¼  cup **olive oil**
  2  tablespoons long, thin shreds of **orange** peel
  1  teaspoon **hot chili flakes**
  2  cans (each about 7½ oz.; 3¼ cups total) **ripe green olives,** drained

**1.** In a 10- to 12-inch frying pan over medium-high heat, stir fennel until seeds are slightly darker, 1 to 2 minutes. Add oil, peel, chilies, and olives. Stir until olives are hot, about 2 minutes.
**2.** Serve olives hot, warm, or at room temperature. If making ahead, store airtight up to 2 weeks.

Per serving: 124 cal., 94% (117 cal.) from fat; 0.8 g protein; 13 g fat (1.7 g sat.); 1.3 g carbo (1.5 g fiber); 1,276 mg sodium; 0 mg chol.

## An olive feast for 8

OLIVES WITH ORANGE, FENNEL, AND CHILI

CROSTINI OF CHANTERELLES

*Napa Valley Sauvignon Blanc*

FENNEL-STUFFED PORK ROAST

TUSCAN BEANS

SALAD GREENS WITH OLIVE OIL AND
BALSAMIC VINEGAR

*Italian Chianti*

RUSTIC PEAR TART

*French Muscat*

WHAT'S HAPPENING

## Olive oil in the West

■ By global standards, Nan Mc-Evoy's production is a drop in the olive-oil bucket—California generates only 0.1 percent of the world's supply. But by domestic standards, it is part of a tidal wave of new interest in all things olive.

California's first olive oils came from trees brought over and planted by Spanish padres at the missions in the late 1700s. In the following century, olives and olive oils were significant products.

But in the early 1900s, various factors, including the arrival of cheap and plentiful oils, shrank the market for domestic olive oil. Olive oil became a sideline, as olive ranchers turned to the more profitable venture of curing and canning the fruit.

A few oil makers, however, stuck it out through those lean years. And now they have been joined by many newcomers, as interest in high-quality olive oil has surged during the past decade. Research in all aspects of olive oil production, from variety selection through oil making, focuses on the creation of a superior product.

Even an Arizonan, Perry Rea, has joined in. At Friendly Corners, about 45 miles south of Phoenix, he has planted 43,000 olive trees, from which he expects a harvest in three to four years.

## Crostini of Chanterelles

PREP AND COOK TIME: About 45 minutes
MAKES: 8 servings

- 1½ pounds **fresh chanterelle** or common **mushrooms**
- 4 tablespoons **olive oil**
- 5 teaspoons **champagne vinegar** or white wine vinegar
- 1 tablespoon **fresh thyme** leaves or dried thyme
  **Salt** and **pepper**
- 16 slices (¼ in. thick) **sourdough baguette**
- 4 teaspoons minced **fresh chives**

**1.** Rinse chanterelles, gently rubbing mushroom gills with fingers to release any grit; drain. Repeat if necessary. Trim and discard bruised parts and discolored ends. Slice mushrooms ¼ inch thick.

**2.** In a 10- to 12-inch pan over high heat, stir mushrooms, 1 tablespoon olive oil, 1 teaspoon vinegar, and thyme until liquid is evaporated and mushrooms are browned, 15 to 20 minutes. Add 2 tablespoons olive oil, the remaining vinegar, and salt and pepper to taste.

**3.** Meanwhile, brush bread slices with remaining 1 tablespoon olive oil and lay on a 14- by 17-inch baking sheet. Bake in a 350° oven until crisp and brown, about 15 minutes.

**4.** Top toast pieces equally with mushroom mixture and sprinkle with chives.

Per serving: 159 cal., 45% (72 cal.) from fat; 4.3 g protein; 8 g fat (1.1 g sat.); 19 g carbo (1.9 g fiber); 176 mg sodium; 0 mg chol.

## Fennel-stuffed Pork Roast

PREP AND COOK TIME: About 2¾ hours
NOTES: At the market, have the backbone (chine) of roast left on but have it cut through to the ribs to make carving easy.
MAKES: 8 to 10 servings

- 2 heads **fennel** (3½ to 4 in. wide)
- 3 cloves **garlic,** minced or pressed
- 1 teaspoon **olive oil**
- 1 teaspoon **hot chili flakes**
- 1 **fat-trimmed shoulder-end pork loin** (about 6 lb.)
  **Salt** and **pepper**

**1.** Rinse and drain fennel. Trim tops, discard tough stalks, and save feathery greens. Coarsely chop enough greens to make ½ cup; save extras for garnish. Trim and discard root ends and bruised areas from fennel heads. Using a slicer, cut fennel into ¹⁄₁₆-inch-thick pieces.

JUICY AND RICHLY browned, pork roast with Tuscan-style beans is the main course. Pocket between bone and pork holds mellow chili-fennel stuffing.

ABOVE: TERRENCE McCARTHY. LEFT: JAMES CARRIER

**2.** In a 10- to 12-inch frying pan over high heat, mix fennel, garlic, oil, and ¼ cup water. Stir often until liquid evaporates and fennel is lightly browned, about 6 minutes. Stir in ½ cup fennel greens and chilies. Remove from heat.

**3.** Wipe roast with a damp towel. With a paring knife, make a cut the length of the roast and parallel to the backbone to create a pocket that is about 3 inches deep. Spoon fennel mixture evenly into the pocket, packing it in to use all.

**4.** With cotton string, tie roast crosswise at every rib to hold fennel stuffing in place. Set meat, rib side down, on a rack in an 11- by 17-inch pan.

**5.** Bake at 375° until a thermometer inserted in the center of the thickest part registers 150° to 155°, about 2¼ hours.

**6.** Transfer roast to a platter; snip string and remove. Skim and discard fat from roast drippings. Scrape drippings free with 2 to 3 tablespoons water, and pour over meat. Garnish roast with reserved fennel greens. Slice between ribs to serve. Add salt and pepper to taste.

Per serving: 289 cal., 34% (99 cal.) from fat; 42 g protein; 11 g fat (3.8 g sat.); 2.2 g carbo (0.7 g fiber); 163 mg sodium; 113 mg chol.

## Tuscan Beans

PREP AND COOK TIME: About 2½ hours
NOTES: Instead of cannellinis, you can use Great Northern beans.
MAKES: About 9 cups

- 1½ pounds **dried cannellini** (white) **beans**
- 6 ounces **thin-sliced prosciutto**
- ¾ cup chopped **carrot**
- ¾ cup chopped **celery**
- ¾ cup chopped **onion**
- 1 clove **garlic,** minced or pressed
- 2 teaspoons **olive oil**
- 1½ tablespoons **fresh rosemary** leaves, minced
- About 6 cups fat-skimmed **chicken broth**
- 2 **Roma tomatoes** (about 6 oz. total), rinsed, cored, and chopped
- **Salt**

**1.** Sort beans and discard debris. Rinse and drain beans.

**2.** Finely chop prosciutto.

**3.** In a 5- to 6-quart pan over high heat, stir carrot, celery, onion, and garlic in oil until onion is limp, about 4 minutes. Add prosciutto and stir just until

# Understanding olive oil
Learn the lingo of olive oil labels to identify the best

Olive oil is made by crushing olives to a paste. **Freerun** oils are those that drip from the paste. But most are extracted by pressing or spinning the paste in a centrifuge. For **cold press,** no heat is applied. The finest oil, extra-virgin, is often described as a **first cold press** and **unrefined.** Additional pressings, often with heat or chemicals, produce lesser-quality oils. Oils may be **filtered** to make them clear; however, unfiltered oils may clarify on standing. A **California** olive oil must be made only with olives grown in the Golden State. If it's an **estate** oil, all the olives were grown on the owner's land. If the olive oil is labeled **organic,** the trees are chemical-free.

The label may specify when the fruit was picked. Usually, **early harvest** means fall to winter, **late harvest** winter to spring. Early oils tend to be green and taste grassy, while late oils are typically gold and buttery-tasting. The olive varieties may or may not be identified on the label. Store olive oil airtight in a cool, dark place. Do not refrigerate.

### HOW SHOULD OLIVE OIL TASTE?
The California Olive Oil Council (COOC) seal "Certified Extra Virgin" on the label means the COOC has tasted and approved the oil's quality. Approved oils rate as close to flawless as possible. Descriptions of tastes or aromas include *fruity, grassy, fresh, clean,* and *pungent.* Oils may have have a slightly bitter flavor, reminiscent of raw artichokes, but they shouldn't be harsh. Nor should they taste or smell *musty, fermented, muddy, vinegary, metallic,* or *rancid.*

Three experts—Darrell Corti of Corti Brothers specialty food and wine merchants in Sacramento; Maggie Klein, author of *Feast of the Olive: Cooking with Olives and Olive Oil* and co-owner of Oliveto Cafe & Restaurant in Oakland; and Giovanna Passalacqua, a COOC-trained olive oil taster—explain how to evaluate oils: First check for aromas, then taste (on cubes of bread). An olive oil should taste good—a judgment anyone can make.

STONE MILL at McEvoy Ranch crushes just-picked olives to release their treasure flow of green-gold oil.

mixture is lightly browned, 2 to 3 minutes.

**4.** Add beans, rosemary, 6 cups broth, 2 cups water, and tomatoes; bring to a boil. Cover, reduce heat, and simmer until beans are tender to bite, 2 to 2½ hours; stir occasionally.

**5.** Purée 1 cup beans in a food processor or blender, then stir into beans. Add broth if beans are too thick. If making ahead, cool, cover, and chill up to 1 day. Reheat, thinning with more broth. Add salt to taste.

Per serving: 347 cal., 12% (41 cal.) from fat; 28 g protein; 4.6 g fat (1.1 g sat.); 51 g carbo (31 g fiber); 424 mg sodium; 15 mg chol.

A RUSTIC PASTRY ripples around pears and almonds.

JAMES CARRIER

### Rustic Pear Tart

PREP AND COOK TIME: About 1 hour
MAKES: 8 to 10 servings

¼  cup sliced **almonds**

About 2¼ cups **all-purpose flour**

About ½ cup **sugar**

About ⅞ cup (about ½ lb.) **butter** or margarine

1½  pounds **Bosc pears**

**1.** In a blender or food processor, finely grind 1 tablespoon almonds, 1 tablespoon flour, and 2 teaspoons sugar. Pour into a small bowl.

**2.** In a food processor or another bowl, combine 2 cups flour and ¼ cup sugar. Add ¾ cup butter, cut into small pieces. Whirl or rub with your fingers until fine crumbs form. Add ¼ cup water; whirl or stir with a fork just until the dough holds together. Pat the dough into a flat disk.

**3.** On a lightly floured board, roll dough into a 15-inch-wide round, about ⅛ inch thick. Slide onto a 14- by 17-inch baking sheet; press any tears back together.

**4.** Sprinkle almond mixture onto pastry, leaving about a 3-inch rim.

**5.** Peel, core, and cut pears into ¼-inch slices. Neatly overlap pear slices on pastry to cover almond mixture, leaving a 3-inch rim. Lift rim up and lay over pears, folding neatly to incorporate excess pastry. Sprinkle 2 teaspoons sugar and remaining slivered almonds over pears.

**6.** Melt 1 tablespoon butter (in a small pan over direct heat or in a microwave-safe bowl in a microwave oven). Brush pastry rim with butter and sprinkle with 1 teaspoon sugar.

**7.** Bake on center rack in a 400° oven until pastry is golden brown, about 40 minutes.

**8.** Slide tart onto a platter. Cut into wedges and serve hot, warm, or cool.

Per serving: 355 cal., 51% (180 cal.) from fat; 3.8 g protein; 20 g fat (12 g sat.); 41 g carbo (2.4 g fiber); 188 mg sodium; 50 mg chol.

## Finding California olive oil

WHERE TO BUY

Look for olive oil in fancy-food stores and well-stocked supermarkets. Or order estate-grown olive oils from the following producers (the asterisk denotes at least one COOC-certified oil).

Not all highly regarded olive oils are estate-produced. Among other skilled producers are Chappellet*, Critelli, Frantoio*, and Jaeger.

As an artisan product, extra-virgin olive oil is expensive to make and pricey—up to $30 for a 275-milliliter bottle (about 9 oz.); that's $1.64 per tablespoon. Prices listed are for the producer's smallest bottle and do not include shipping; prices and availability vary.

*Aeolia Organics,* Cedar Ridge. $7.50–$9 (8.5 oz.). (530) 268-6563.

*Bariani Olive Oil,* Sacramento. $6 (375 ml.). (916) 689-9059.

*Beltane Ranch,* Glen Ellen. $15 (500 ml.). At Olive Press, Glen Ellen; (800) 965-4839.

*B. R. Cohn Winery,* Glen Ellen. $50 (500 ml.). (800) 330-4064, ext. 24, or www.brcohn.com.

***Calaveras Olive Oil Co.,*** Copperopolis. $10 (250 ml.). (209) 785-1000.

***Calio Groves,*** St. Helena. $16.95 (750 ml.). (707) 963-8888.

***Corbett Vineyards,*** St. Helena. $14.95 (375 ml.). (707) 963-8808.

***DaVero,*** Healdsburg. $24 (375 ml.). (707) 431-8000 or www.davero.com.

***Dodici Giardini,*** Pacific Palisades. $25 (⅓ l.). 1475 Chastain Pkwy. W., Pacific Palisades, CA 90272.

***Figone's of California,*** Tracy. $10 (250 ml.). (877) 434-4663.

***Graber Olive House,*** Ontario. $9.95 (12.7 oz.). (800) 996-5483 or www.graberolives.com.

*Grace Family Vineyards,* St. Helena. $33.50 (375 ml.). (707) 967-9980 or www.digitalchef.com.

*Harrison Vineyards,* St. Helena. $30 (275 ml.). (800) 913-9463.

*Henwood Estate,* Marysville. $12–$18 (500 ml.). (530) 639-2400.

***Long Meadow Ranch,*** St. Helena. $45 (500 ml.). (877) 627-2645.

*Lunigiana,* Glen Ellen. $15 (250 ml.). (707) 939-8900.

***McEvoy of Marin,*** Petaluma. $15 (250 ml.). At Oakville Grocery; (800) 736-6602.

*Pinnacles Olive Orchard,* Monterey. $18 (250 ml.); (707) 939-8900.

***Preston Vineyards,*** Healdsburg. $18 (500 ml.). (800) 305-9707.

*Sadeg Organic,* Palermo. $10 (8.5 oz.). (800) 400-8851.

*Sciabica's,* Modesto. $5 (5 oz.). (800) 551-9612, ext. 15, or www.sciabica.com.

***Stutz,*** Berkeley. $14.50 (375 ml.). At Pasta Shop; (510) 528-1786.

*V. G. Buck California Foods,* Kenwood. $10 (16 oz.). (707) 833-6548.

***Wente Vineyards,*** Livermore. $25 (375 ml.). (925) 456-2305. ◆

# The Quick Cook

MEALS IN 30 MINUTES OR LESS

BY CHRISTINE WEBER HALE

Hoisin Chicken

White, Brown, and Wild Rice Blend

Steamed Sugar Snap Peas
with Lemon Butter

Purchased Chocolate Torte

## Fast thaw for chicken

■ Real bargains at supermarket and discount stores are big bags (4 lb. and up) of individually frozen boned, skinned chicken breast halves. You can bake or poach this meat ice-hard from the freezer. But one caveat: breast halves tend to vary in weight, from 6 to 10 ounces, and you'll get best results if you cook pieces that are about the same size together. While the chicken is underway, prepare a rice mix and steam peas.

## Basics for baking and poaching

*To bake:* Place 4 **frozen boned, skinned chicken breast halves** (about 2 lb. total) in a single layer in a 9- by 13-inch pan. Bake in a 400° oven until meat is no longer pink in center of thickest part (cut to test), 25 to 30 minutes.

*To poach:* Place 4 **frozen boned, skinned chicken breast halves** (about 2 lb. total) in an 11- to 12-inch frying pan. Add specified **liquid** and other **seasonings** (recipes follow), cover, and bring to a boil over high heat. Reduce heat and simmer until meat is no longer pink in center of thickest part (cut to test), **15 to 20 minutes total.**

## Hoisin Chicken

PREP AND COOK TIME: About 30 minutes

MAKES: 4 servings

¼ cup **hoisin sauce**

¼ cup **apricot jam**

4 **frozen boned, skinned chicken breast halves** (about 8 oz. each)

¼ cup minced **fresh mint** leaves

¼ cup minced **fresh cilantro**

¼ cup minced **green onions**

1 tablespoon minced **lemon** peel

1. Mix hoisin sauce and jam.
2. Bake chicken as directed at left. After 15 minutes, spread hoisin mixture onto chicken. Baste once with juices. Transfer meat and juices to a platter.
3. Meanwhile, mix mint, cilantro, onions, and lemon peel. Sprinkle mixture over and around chicken.

Per serving: 349 cal., 7.4% (26 cal.) from fat; 53 g protein; 2.9 g fat (0.8 g sat.); 23 g carbo (0.8 g fiber); 474 mg sodium; 132 mg chol.

## Caper Chicken

MAKES: 4 servings

1. Bake 4 **frozen boned, skinned chicken breast halves** as directed.
2. Meanwhile, in a 1½- to 2-quart pan over medium heat, stir 3 cups chopped **ripe tomatoes** and 3 tablespoons drained **capers** until hot; keep warm.
3. Transfer chicken to a platter and top with tomato mixture. Sprinkle with ½ cup slivered **fresh basil** leaves and ¼ cup **shredded parmesan cheese.** Add **salt** to taste.

Per serving: 307 cal., 14% (43 cal.) from fat; 56 g protein; 4.8 g fat (1.8 g sat.); 7.6 g carbo (2.2 g fiber); 538 mg sodium; 136 mg chol.

## Jeweled Chicken

MAKES: 4 servings

1. Poach 4 **frozen boned, skinned chicken breast halves** as directed in this liquid: 1¼ cups fat-skimmed **chicken broth**, 1 teaspoon grated **orange** peel, 1 cup **orange juice**, ¼ cup **dry white wine**, ¾ cup **mixed dried fruit bits**, and ⅓ cup **dried cranberries.** Transfer chicken to a platter; keep warm.
2. Boil pan juices over high heat, uncovered, until reduced to 1 cup, 3 to 4 minutes. Mix 1 tablespoon **cornstarch** with 3 tablespoons **water,** pour into sauce, and stir until boiling.
3. Moisten chicken with some of the sauce and pour remainder into a bowl. Sprinkle chicken with ¼ cup minced **green onions.** Serve with remaining sauce and **salt** to add to taste.

Per serving: 408 cal., 6.9% (28 cal.) from fat; 56 g protein; 3.1 g fat (0.8 g sat.); 35 g carbo (2.3 g fiber); 179 mg sodium; 132 mg chol.

## Mango Chicken

MAKES: 4 servings

1. Poach 4 **frozen boned, skinned chicken breast halves** as directed in this liquid: 1¼ cups **mango nectar**, 1 cup fat-skimmed **chicken broth**, ¼ cup **lime juice**, 1 tablespoon minced **fresh ginger**, and 1 teaspoon **ground cinnamon.** Transfer chicken to a platter and keep warm.
2. Boil pan juices over high heat, uncovered, until reduced to 1 cup, about 5 minutes. Mix 1 tablespoon **cornstarch** with 3 tablespoons **water,** pour into sauce, and stir until boiling. Pour over chicken. Add **salt** to taste.

Per serving: 314 cal., 8.3% (26 cal.) from fat; 55 g protein; 2.9 g fat (0.7 g sat.); 14 g carbo (0.2 g fiber); 175 mg sodium; 132 mg chol. ◆

JAMES CARRIER

# Kitchen Cabinet

### READERS' RECIPES TESTED IN SUNSET'S KITCHENS

BY LINDA LAU ANUSASANANAN

VELVETY CHOCOLATE frosting has a nutritious base: tofu.

## Chocolate Tofu Frosting

Lori Peterkin, Albuquerque

Lori Peterkin uses high-protein, shelf-stable tofu instead of butter in chocolate frosting. The frosting is so smooth, cool, and creamy that her kids also like it as a pudding.

PREP AND COOK TIME: About 20 minutes, including chilling

MAKES: 2 cups, enough for a 2-layer 8- or 9-inch cake, a 9- by 13-inch cake, or 2 dozen cupcakes

- 1 package (6 oz., 1 cup) **semisweet chocolate chips**
- 1 box (12.3 oz.) **nonrefrigerated extra-firm regular** or low-fat **tofu**
- 2 tablespoons **rum**, orange- or coffee-flavor liqueur, or water
- 1 tablespoon **vanilla**

**1.** Pour chocolate into a microwave-safe bowl. Heat in a microwave oven on half power (50%) until chocolate is soft, 2 to 2½ minutes.

**2.** Meanwhile, in a blender combine tofu, rum, and vanilla. Whirl until smoothly puréed.

**3.** Stir chocolate until smooth. Scrape into blender with tofu mixture. Whirl until smoothly puréed. Pour into a bowl and nest in ice water. Stir often until frosting is cold, 10 to 12 minutes. Use or cover airtight and chill up to 2 days; stir before spreading.

Per tablespoon: 39 cal., 49% (19 cal.) from fat; 1.5 g protein; 2.1 g fat (0.9 g sat.); 3.7 g carbo (0 g fiber); 1.3 mg sodium; 0 mg chol.

## Spaghetti Squash Stir-Fry

Jane Shapton, Portland

"My mom introduced me to spaghetti squash when I was a girl growing up in Spokane. I liked it so much that years later I prepared it for my boyfriend, who is now my husband," says Jane Shapton.

PREP AND COOK TIME: About 25 minutes

MAKES: 6 servings

- 1 **spaghetti squash** (3 lb.)
- 1 **green bell pepper** (6 oz.)
- 1 **red bell pepper** (6 oz.)
- 2 **carrots** (6 oz. total)
- ½ cup **vegetable broth**
- 1 tablespoon **dried basil**
- ¼ teaspoon **pepper**
  **Salt**
- ¼ cup grated **parmesan cheese**

**1.** Pierce squash in several places with a sharp knife. Set squash in a microwave oven and cook at full power (100%) until soft when pressed, 10 to 12 minutes; turn squash over after 5 minutes.

**2.** Meanwhile, rinse, stem, and seed bell peppers. Peel carrots. Cut bell peppers and carrots into matchstick-size slivers.

**3.** When squash is tender, cut open and scoop out and discard seeds. Scoop out tender squash strands and reserve.

**4.** Set a 10- to 12-inch nonstick frying pan over high heat. Add bell peppers and carrots. Stir often until carrots are tender-crisp, 5 to 7 minutes.

**5.** Add broth, basil, pepper, and squash strands. Stir until squash is hot. Add salt to taste.

**6.** Pour vegetables into a dish. Sprinkle with cheese.

Per serving: 97 cal., 20% (19 cal.) from fat; 3.2 g protein; 2.1 g fat (0.8 g sat.); 18 g carbo (4.1 g fiber); 105 mg sodium; 2.6 mg chol.

## Beef Stew with Almonds and Olives

Linda Tebben, Menlo Park, California

While living in Denmark, Linda Tebben found exchanging recipes a way to get acquainted. One of the good cooks she met, Merete Corneliussen, shared this hearty beef stew—and became a good friend.

PREP AND COOK TIME: About 2¼ hours

MAKES: About 6 servings

- 2 pounds fat-trimmed **boned beef chuck**
- 1 **onion** (8 oz.), peeled and chopped
- 2 cloves **garlic**, pressed or minced

LENDON FLANAGAN

2 **fresh** or dried **bay leaves**

2 cups fat-skimmed **beef broth**

⅔ cup **dry sherry**

⅓ cup **blanched almonds**

½ cup **calamata olives**, pitted

1 teaspoon **cornstarch**

2 tablespoons chopped **parsley**

**1.** Cut beef into 1-inch cubes. Place meat, onion, garlic, bay leaves, and ⅓ cup water in a 5- to 6-quart pan. Bring to a boil over high heat, cover, reduce heat to medium, and boil 20 minutes. Uncover and boil over high heat, stirring often, until juices evaporate and a dark brown film forms in pan, 10 to 15 minutes.

**2.** Add broth, ⅓ cup sherry, and almonds; stir to release brown film from pan. Return to a boil. Cover, reduce heat, and simmer 1 hour. Add olives. Cover and simmer until beef is tender when pierced, 10 to 15 minutes longer.

**3.** If more than 1 cup liquid is in pan, boil, uncovered, over high heat until reduced to 1 cup. Mix ⅓ cup sherry with cornstarch. Add to pan; stir until boiling. Pour into a bowl; sprinkle with parsley.

Per serving: 335 cal., 48% (162 cal.) from fat; 33 g protein; 18 g fat (5 g sat.); 8 g carbo (1.5 g fiber); 347 mg sodium; 98 mg chol.

## Potato Pizza

Sandra Krist, Edmonds, Washington

When Sandra Krist and her sister toured Europe in the 1960s, they discovered potato pizza in Rome. They loved it then and still do—Krist now makes her own version, starting with purchased or homemade dough.

**PREP AND COOK TIME:** About 30 minutes

**MAKES:** 4 servings

2 **red thin-skinned potatoes** (6 oz. each)

1 pound thawed **frozen bread dough** or 1 tube (10 oz.; 12 in.) refrigerated pizza crust dough

About 1 tablespoon **olive oil**

1 cup (¼ lb.) **shredded mozzarella cheese**

1 cup (¼ lb.) **shredded jack cheese**

**Salt** and fresh-ground **pepper**

1 teaspoon **fresh rosemary** leaves or dried rosemary, crushed or crumbled

½ cup thinly sliced **onion**

2 tablespoons drained **capers**

¼ cup crumbled **feta cheese**

**1.** Scrub potatoes and cut crosswise into ¼-inch-thick slices. Lay potatoes on a rack in a pan over at least 1 inch boiling water. Cover and steam potatoes over medium-high heat just until tender when pierced, 10 to 12 minutes.

**2.** Meanwhile, pat dough evenly to fit a lightly oiled 12-inch pizza pan.

**3.** Scatter mozzarella and jack cheese over crust. Lay potato slices in a single layer over cheese. Lightly sprinkle potatoes with salt and pepper. Scatter rosemary, onion, capers, and feta over pizza. Drizzle with 1 tablespoon olive oil.

**4.** Bake on lowest rack in a 500° oven until bottom of crust is well browned, 12 to 15 minutes for bread dough, 9 to 10 minutes for pizza crust dough. Cut into wedges.

Per serving: 621 cal., 38% (234 cal.) from fat; 24 g protein; 26 g fat (12 g sat.); 72 g carbo (4.1 g fiber); 1,096 mg sodium; 65 mg chol.

## Crab Lasagna Rolls

Wendy Nankeville, San Francisco

A delicate crab sauce rolled up in noodle pinwheels makes an attractive casserole. Wendy Nankeville finds it perfect for a make-ahead party entrée. We're inclined to agree.

**PREP AND COOK TIME:** About 1 hour

**MAKES:** 8 servings

1 package (8 oz.) **dried lasagna**

2 teaspoons **olive oil**

1 **onion** (8 oz.), peeled and chopped

¼ pound **sliced mushrooms**

1 clove **garlic,** pressed or minced

1 teaspoon **dried basil**

½ cup fat-skimmed **chicken broth**

1½ teaspoons **cornstarch**

1 package (8 oz.) **neufchâtel** (light cream ) **cheese,** cut into chunks

½ cup **reduced-fat sour cream**

1 can (14 oz.) **artichoke hearts,** drained and chopped

¾ pound **shelled cooked crab**

**Salt** and **pepper**

⅔ cup **shredded jack cheese**

2 tablespoons thinly sliced **green onion**

**1.** In a 5- to 6-quart pan over high heat, bring about 3 quarts water to a boil. Add lasagna and cook just until tender to bite, 10 to 12 minutes. Drain and rinse with warm water.

**2.** Meanwhile, in an 11- to 12-inch frying pan over medium-high heat, frequently stir oil, onion, mushrooms, garlic, and basil until onion is limp, 6 to 8 minutes.

**3.** Mix broth and cornstarch. Pour into pan and stir until boiling. Add cream cheese and stir until melted.

**4.** Mix in sour cream, artichokes, and crab. Add salt and pepper to taste. Remove from heat.

**5.** Lay noodles flat. Divide all the crab mixture equally among noodles and spread the length of each strip. Roll noodles from a narrow end around filling. Set seam down, in a single layer, in a shallow 3- to 3½-quart casserole. Cover with foil. If making ahead, chill up to 1 day.

**6.** Bake, covered, in a 350° oven until hot in center, 20 to 25 minutes (if chilled, 25 to 30 minutes). Uncover and sprinkle with jack cheese. Return to oven until cheese melts, about 5 minutes. Sprinkle with green onion.

Per serving: 323 cal., 39% (126 cal.) from fat; 20 g protein; 14 g fat (7.2 g sat.); 29 g carbo (1.7 g fiber); 299 mg sodium; 79 mg chol. ◆

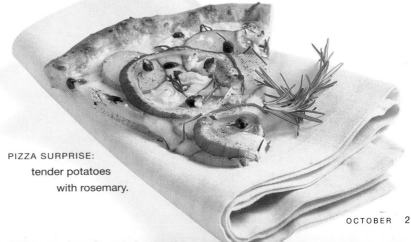

PIZZA SURPRISE: tender potatoes with rosemary.

JULIE TOY

Aromatic fresh bay leaves and steamed baby squash surround juicy, lightly smoked turkey (article begins on page 266).

# November

# foodguide

BY JERRY ANNE DI VECCHIO

A TASTE OF THE WEST

## Sweet and savory indulgence

*Foie gras foiled again—by the Fuyu persimmon (and a good thing, too)*

Extremely rich foods, from blue cheese to foie gras, fare well with sweet companions that have enough underlying acid to counter the foods' unctuousness. Several kinds of fruit do the job very well—pear and pineapple, for instance. My favorite for a blowout occasion is firm, orange Fuyu persimmon, served like a slice of the sun with warm foie gras.

Order fresh foie gras several days ahead from an upscale supermarket. And for a simple sauce with rich body, start with a shelf-stable or frozen reduction (demi-glace), also from a well-stocked supermarket.

Once the ingredients are assembled, this first course is easy to engineer. And it's stunning.

### Fuyu Persimmons with Foie Gras

**PREP AND COOK TIME:** About 30 minutes
**NOTES:** Foie gras is easiest to handle when cold and firm. Make sauce (step 3) up to a day ahead; cover and chill, then reheat. As a less costly alternative to fresh foie gras, buy ½ pound duck or chicken liver pâté or mousse. Cut pâté into 6 equal parts and spread on toast, then broil about 6 inches from heat just until pâté begins to sizzle, about 2 minutes. Top with sauce.
**MAKES:** 6 servings

- 6 to 8 ounces chilled **fresh duck foie gras**

- 2 **firm-ripe Fuyu persimmons** (5 to 6 oz. total), rinsed

  About 2 cups **watercress** sprigs, rinsed and drained

- 1 package (1½ oz.; 2 tablespoons) **shelf-stable demi-glace** (any flavor)

- ½ cup **madeira**

- 3 tablespoons **sherry vinegar**

- ¼ cup **whipping cream**

- 6 slices (about ½ in. thick; 6 oz. total) **dense white bread** or slightly sweet egg bread such as brioche or challah

  **Salt**

**1.** Rinse foie gras, pat dry, and discard any tough membrane. Cut foie gras crosswise into ½-inch-thick slices. Cover and chill.
**2.** Trim off stems and bottom ends of

A GOLDEN ORB of crisp Fuyu persimmon makes a perfect foil for lavish seared fresh duck foie gras on toast.

JAMES CARRIER (3)

persimmons. Cut each crosswise into 3 equal pieces. Lay a slice on each plate with a cluster of watercress sprigs.

**3.** In a 10- to 12-inch frying pan, mix demi-glace, madeira, vinegar, and cream. Boil over high heat, stirring often, until ⅔ cup, about 5 minutes. Put sauce in a small bowl; keep warm. Rinse and dry pan.

**4.** Lay bread slices, side by side, in a 10- by 15-inch pan. Broil about 6 inches from heat until toasted on both sides, about 3 minutes total. Keep toast warm.

**5.** Place frying pan over high heat; when very hot, add foie gras. Brown slices lightly, turning once, about 1 minute total (fat spatters, so partially cover pan). Take off heat.

**6.** Put toast on plates and top each slice with about 2 teaspoons of foie gras fat. Top equally with foie gras.

**7.** Drizzle warm sauce equally over foie gras. Season to taste with salt.

Per serving (not including foie gras, which is approximately 98% fat): 170 cal., 23% (39 cal.) from fat; 3 g protein; 4.3 g fat (2.1 g sat.); 25 g carbo (0.9 g fiber); 188 mg sodium; 11 mg chol.

# Tried-and-true tricks on a roll

Aunt Nora, my homesteading great-aunt, never wasted a thing, even worn-out cotton socks: she snipped off the tops and slipped them onto her rolling pin. The flour clung lightly to the fabric, not the pastry, and made rolling dough much easier. This great idea has stuck, but socks are out. Instead, at cookware and hardware stores, you can buy knit cotton tubing cut to fit a rolling pin. A companion aid is a pastry cloth made of firm canvas. Toss both in the wash between uses. Together, these cloths roll right over sticky dough problems.

# A taste for taro

## This island sleeper is worth rooting out

■ Visitors to a Hawaiian luau usually come away with two impressions: the pit-roast pig is amazing, and poi tastes like library paste. But the ingredient that is beaten up to make poi—taro—is another story. In other forms it's very easy to like. A starchy, tuberous root (technically a corm), taro tastes much like a sweet potato, doesn't fall apart when cooked, and soaks up flavor like a sponge.

Hundreds of varieties of *Colocasia esculenta* grow around the world, often beyond the tropical latitudes where the plant originated.

*One important detail: Don't eat, or even peel, taro raw. It contains crystals of calcium oxalate, an irritant deactivated by heat. So blanch in boiling water before peeling, then cook.*

This casserole for lazy cooks isn't a dish you'd find at a luau, but it does bring pork and taro together in a flavorsome way.

### Roast Pork and Taro

PREP AND COOK TIME: About 3½ hours
MAKES: 6 servings

1¼ to 1½ pounds **taro** (2 to 3 in. long)

1 piece **fat-trimmed, boned and tied pork butt** or shoulder (2 to 2½ lb.)

1 **onion** (½ lb.), peeled and chopped

2 tablespoons chopped **fresh ginger**

2 cups fat-skimmed **chicken** or beef **broth**

4 cups chopped **washed spinach leaves**
**Salt**

**1.** In a 4- to 5-quart ovenproof pan over high heat, bring 2 quarts water to a boil. Add taro and cook 5 minutes. Drain and let cool. With a knife, peel taro and cut away any bruised or decayed spots. Cut taro into 1-inch chunks. Rinse pan.

**2.** Rinse pork and set, fatty side up, in pan. Add taro, onion, ginger, and broth.

**3.** Cover and bake in a 375° oven until meat is very tender when pierced, about 2½ hours. Uncover and stir spinach into juices. Bake until meat is lightly browned, about 30 minutes more. Then broil about 8 inches from heat until meat is richly browned, about 5 minutes longer.

**4.** Cut strings from pork, slice meat (it tends to tear apart), and serve with taro mixture and juices. Add salt to taste.

Per serving: 356 cal., 30% (108 cal.) from fat; 35 g protein; 12 g fat (4.2 g sat.); 26 g carbo (1.6 g fiber); 171 mg sodium; 103 mg chol.

# Another way to skin a nut

■ I've noticed packaged roasted skinned hazelnuts from Oregon at the market of late. But they aren't plentiful everywhere yet, so it's still useful to know how to skin the nuts. You can toast hazelnuts to loosen most of the brown papery, slightly bitter skin. But a more efficient process is to blanch the nuts with baking soda to soften the skin so it slips off easily. The downside is that water also softens the nuts, so you still need to toast them. When they're crisp, season them for a handy appetizer.

STEP BY STEP

**1.** To blanch: In a 2- to 3-quart pan over high heat, bring 4 cups water and 1 tablespoon baking soda to a boil. Add up to 4 cups hazelnuts. Cook 3 minutes.

**2.** Drain nuts, immerse in cold water, and rub between your hands to loosen most of the skins. Drain again and spread nuts on a towel to dry. Scrape off any clinging skin with the tip of a small, sharp knife.

**3.** Put nuts in a single layer in a rimmed pan. Bake in a 300° oven to dry nuts well, 8 to 10 minutes. Cool in pan at least 15 minutes. Return to oven and toast until nuts are golden brown, shaking pan occasionally. Use, or cool and chill airtight up to a week; freeze to store longer.

JAMES CARRIER (4)

## Spiced Hazelnuts

In an 8- or 9-inch square pan, combine 1 cup skinned, toasted **hazelnuts** (preceding), 2 teaspoons **butter** or margarine, and ¼ teaspoon *each* **ground coriander, pepper,** and **salt**. Bake in a 300° oven, shaking pan frequently to mix well, until butter is melted and nuts are hot and coated with spice mixture, 3 to 5 minutes. Serve warm or cool. Makes 1 cup.

Per ¼ cup: 199 cal., 90% (180 cal.) from fat; 3.8 g protein; 20 g fat (2.5 g sat.); 4.5 g carbo (2.4 g fiber); 164 mg sodium; 5.2 mg chol.

# Wasabi makes new contacts
## Networking with potatoes

■ My friend Vaughn Davis, who came by his taste for wasabi honestly—from his Japanese mother—was recently surprised to find this potent green horseradish on a restaurant menu, mixing it up with mashed potatoes. The wasabi potatoes were served with roast chicken. Intrigued by this defection from tradition, he tried an even bolder version, enhancing wasabi's green presence with parsley. He serves his potatoes with salmon. Use refrigerated wasabi paste in tubes or canned wasabi powder.

### Green Wasabi Potatoes

Peel 3 pounds **thin-skinned potatoes** (red, white, or Yukon gold), rinse, and cut into 2-inch chunks. In a 3- to 4-quart pan, combine potatoes and 3 cups fat-skimmed **chicken broth.** Cover and bring to a boil over high heat. Simmer until potatoes mash easily, 20 to 25 minutes. Drain, reserving broth. Put ¾ cup broth and 1 cup rinsed, chopped **parsley** in a blender. Whirl until smooth. Add parsley mixture and 1 tablespoon **wasabi paste** or powder to potatoes. Beat with a mixer or mash with a potato masher until smooth, adding more broth to make potatoes as creamy as you like. Season to taste with **salt** and more wasabi (I like 2 tablespoons total). And for a smoother texture, mix in ¼ cup **whipping cream.** Makes 6 cups; 6 servings.

Per serving: 186 cal., 1.9% (3.6 cal.) from fat; 8.2 g protein; 0.4 g fat (0 g sat.); 38 g carbo (3.9 g fiber); 57 mg sodium; 0 mg chol. ◆

# The Wine Guide

BY KAREN MacNEIL

RICK MARIANI

## Match point

■ There's only one thing about food and wine that makes me nervous—matching them.

Several years ago I listened to a famous food and wine writer elaborately describe why a steak should never be paired with Zinfandel unless the meat was cooked rare and liberally seasoned with black pepper. Medium steak minus black pepper, he said, married best with Cabernet. Furthermore, Champagne and caviar were an awful match. And so his talk went—acidity contrasts with salt; salt fights with fat. Or maybe it was salt suits sweetness. By the end of his presentation, I was dizzy from so many "rules."

Then, all of a sudden, I thought to myself, "Wait a minute. Did Italian grandmothers 100 years ago stop to consider the acidity level of their spaghetti sauce before choosing a wine for dinner?" I doubted it. In fact, I'd never seen anyone in Europe be so neurotic about putting food and wine together as that American writer. And I wasn't quite ready to swallow such intricate pairing regulations.

But in the next instant, I was hit by another realization: flavor affinities *do* exist. If I were given, say, a leg of lamb and a choice of rosemary or basil to season it with, I'd choose rosemary. Why?

Because over time, lamb and rosemary have proved themselves a classic combination. Similarly, wouldn't it make sense that certain wines would naturally taste good with certain foods?

The answer is, they do. A particular wine combined with the right dish can be magic—a taste bud epiphany.

Alas, these "wow" moments are not the norm. Most food and wine matches are neither awesome nor awful. Which is as it should be. After all, what makes a great dinner great is not solely the synergy between the food and the wine. It's the whole gestalt—the food, the wine, the people, the atmosphere.

You can understand my dilemma, then, when a few months ago I got a call from *Sunset* senior food editor Jerry Di Vecchio. Would I suggest wines for *Sunset's* Thanksgiving menus (page 246), she wanted to know. I took a deep breath (Jerry can be very convincing). "I'll try," I said hesitantly.

There are, it seems to me, a few broad principles involved in creating a tasty match. These drove my choices.

1. RELAX AND BE PLAYFUL. Food and wine pairing is not a science. Any one of countless variables (a different herb, more lemon juice, less sugar) can change the whole equation. Perfection (when it happens) is usually a happy accident.

2. PAIR GREAT WITH GREAT, HUMBLE WITH HUMBLE. A leftover-turkey sandwich doesn't need an expensive, complex Merlot to set it off. Foods and wines of the same "status" seem to partner best.

3. MATCH INTENSITIES—delicate with delicate, robust with robust. My notes to Jerry for the Turkey Loco (page 262), for example, said, "Lots of bold, piquant, spicy, and hot flavors going on. Needs a real zinger of a wine—a spicy Gewürztraminer or a massive Petite Syrah."

4. MIRROR A GIVEN FLAVOR. The light smokiness of the Hot-smoked Hickory Turkey (A Traditional Feast, page 248) called out for a wine with a rich, smoky meatiness of its own, like a Syrah. A good wine merchant can suggest a wine with flavors that echo those in your meal.

## OLD CLASSICS

For centuries in Europe, people have paired local wines with local foods. And though that isn't necessarily a prescription for success, some of these combinations have proved to be among the world's great matches. Here are several—plus a few long-standing cross-country marriages.

- Oysters and Chablis
- Lamb and Cabernet Sauvignon
- Shellfish and fino sherry
- Smoked fish and Riesling
- Stilton cheese and port
- Foie gras and sauterne
- Choucroute and Gewürztraminer

## NEW DISCOVERIES

America, with its vast array of ethnic influences and wines from all over the world, is now the leading laboratory for food and wine experimentation. Some potential classics:

- Grilled salmon and Pinot Noir
- Salad and Sauvignon Blanc
- Hearty pastas and Zinfandel
- Risotto and Chardonnay
- Steak and Petite Syrah
- Asian dumplings and fruity Riesling

---

5. CREATE A CONTRAST. Instead of mirroring a flavor, it can be fun to go in the opposite direction. The Ginger-Caramel Macadamia Tart (An Almost-No-Recipe Thanksgiving, page 255) needed something contrapuntal. Bonny Doon's lush raspberry wine, Framboise, would challenge the chocolate and nuts.

6. OPT FOR FLEXIBILITY. Ironically, though Chardonnay is the most popular white varietal, it's the least versatile with food. The toasty oak and high alcohol of most Chardonnays make them very hard to pair. In countless matches they end up tasting like big, clumsy oafs. Instead, go with Sauvignon Blanc or a dry Riesling; both have a cleansing acidity. In reds, opt for wines with loads of fruit, such as Zinfandel and Rhône blends, or with light acidity, such as Pinot Noir.

To me, this is as close to science as food and wine pairing should get. The Europeans were right all along: the most important thing a wine needs to match is not the food—it's the mood. ◆

# Centennial Thanksgiving

Choose one of Sunset's most popular dinners, or mix and match our treasured holiday recipes for your own menu

**A TRADITIONAL FEAST:** From left, Green Beans in a Mist (page 260), Artichoke-Parmesan Sourdough Dressing (page 256), and Garlic Mashed Potatoes (page 263) go with Chili-Orange-glazed Turkey (page 254).

■ One hundred years of Thanksgivings has given *Sunset* a treasured legacy of menus and recipes. Some are inspired by the bounty of Western markets, some by our rich ethnic-cultural influences, and others by our weather, which can be kindly.

To honor this heritage in our Centennial year, we offer this collection of *Sunset's* most enduring Thanksgiving recipes. You can choose one of the four menus, each with its own game plan. One is unsparingly lavish, another generous but low in fat. And two are the most popular Thanksgiving dinners in our history: the Turkey Loco meal, in which a butterflied bird cooks on the grill and zings with Mexican style, and the Almost-No-Recipe Thanksgiving, which delivers a great meal with a minimum of work.

PHOTOGRAPHS BY JAMES CARRIER

MENUS

## A Traditional Feast
for 10 to 12

Candied Cranberries with Cheese and Crisp Crusts *(page 249)*

*Calera Viognier 1997 (Mt. Harlan) $30*

Acorn Squashes with Boursin Custard *(page 250)*

*Saintsbury "Garnet" Pinot Noir 1997 (Carneros) $15*

Hot-smoked Hickory Turkey *(page 268)* or
Chili-Orange-glazed Turkey *(page 254)*

Giblet Gravy Supreme *(page 254)*

Butter-browned Baby Squash Wreath *(page 259)*

Artichoke-Parmesan Sourdough Dressing *(page 256)*

Red Pepper Relish with Aromatics *(page 257)*

Baked Fennel with Cambozola *(page 260)*

Green Beans in a Mist *(page 260)*

Garlic Mashed Potatoes *(page 263)*

*Fess Parker Syrah 1996 (Santa Barbara County) $18, or
A. Rafanelli Zinfandel 1996 (Dry Creek Valley) $19*

Marbled Pumpkin Cheesecake *(page 264)*

*Quady Essensia 1996 (California) $12*

Candied Cranberries with Cheese and Crisp Crusts

## APPETIZERS, FIRST COURSES & SALADS

*Crisp tip.* For a head start, crisp salad greens such as watercress, Belgian endive, spinach, and lettuces: rinse in cold water, drain well, wrap in towels, enclose in a plastic bag, and chill 30 minutes or up to 2 days.

### Gorgonzola and Belgian Endive (1987)

PREP TIME: About 5 minutes
MAKES: 10 to 12 servings

1. Trim discolored stem ends from 5 or 6 heads (1¼ to 1½ lb. total) rinsed and drained **Belgian endive.** Separate endive leaves down to small centers. Cut centers in half lengthwise.

2. Place a ½-pound chunk of **gorgonzola** or other blue-veined **cheese** in the center of a platter. Arrange endive, tips pointing out, around cheese.

3. To eat, cut off a small bit of cheese and put it on a piece of endive.

Per serving: 73 cal., 74% (54 cal.) from fat; 4.4 g protein; 6 g fat (4 g sat.); 1.3 g carbo (0.9 g fiber); 263 mg sodium; 17 mg chol.

### Antojitos Tray (1984)

PREP TIME: 15 to 20 minutes
NOTES: If making up to 4 hours ahead, cover tray and let stand at room temperature.
MAKES: 10 to 12 servings

1. Rinse and drain 4 **oranges** (about ½ lb. each). Cut each into 8 wedges. Rinse and drain 1 **pineapple** (about 4 lb.). Cut crosswise through peel into ½-inch-thick slices. Cut each slice into quarters. Save pineapple crown for decoration or discard. Scrub and peel 1½ pounds **jicama.** Cut into ¼- to ½-inch-thick sticks.

2. Arrange fruit and jicama (and pineapple crown, if desired) on a rimmed platter. Drizzle fruit and jicama with about ½ cup **lime juice.** Cut 2 **limes** into wedges and put on platter.

3. In a small dish, mix ¼ cup **salt,** 1 tablespoon **paprika,** and 1 teaspoon **cayenne.** Place seasoned salt on platter.

4. To eat, dip foods in salt to taste, squeeze juice from lime wedges over pieces, or do both.

Per serving without salt: 84 cal., 5.4% (4.5 cal.) from fat; 1.1 g protein; 0.5 g fat (0 g sat.); 21 g carbo (4.8 g fiber); 2.9 mg sodium; 0 mg chol.

Per ½ teaspoon salt: 1.1 cal., 0% (0 cal.) from fat; 0 g protein; 0 g fat; 0.2 g carbo (0 g fiber); 1,163 mg sodium; 0 mg chol.

### Candied Cranberries with Cheese and Crisp Crusts (1986)

PREP AND COOK TIME: 45 to 55 minutes
NOTES: Up to 3 days ahead, make, cover, and chill candied cranberries. Up to 2 days ahead, crisp lettuce (see crisp tip, left). Up to 1 day ahead, slice, cover, and chill cheese; make crusts, cool, and store airtight at room temperature.
MAKES: 10 to 12 servings

2 cups **cranberries,** fresh or thawed frozen
About ¾ cup **sugar**
¼ teaspoon **mixed whole pickling spice**
1 **baguette** (8 oz.)
2 tablespoons **butter** or margarine, melted
1 teaspoon **kosher salt**
About ½ pound **cheddar cheese**
30 to 36 inner **butter lettuce** leaves, rinsed and crisped
6 **glacéed chestnuts,** cut into quarters (optional)

1. Sort cranberries and discard any soft or decayed fruit. Rinse berries. In a 1½- to 2-quart pan, combine cranberries, ¾ cup sugar, and pickling spice. Cover and set over low heat. Stir occasionally until cranberries are translucent, sugar dissolves, and a syrup forms, about 30 minutes. Remove from heat, uncover, and let stand until cranberries are warm or cool.

2. Meanwhile, cut baguette diagonally into 30 to 36 slices. Lightly brush 1 side of each slice with butter. Set slices, buttered side up, in a 10- by 15-inch pan. Mix salt with 1 teaspoon sugar and lightly sprinkle over bread.

3. Bake baguette slices in a 325° oven until bread is dry and golden at edges, about 20 minutes. Use warm or cool.

4. With a cheese spade or vegetable slicer, cut cheese into thin slices and mound lightly in a dish. Put cranberries, lettuce, and chestnuts in sep-

## A TRADITIONAL FEAST GAME PLAN

☐ UP TO 1 WEEK AHEAD:
*Make* red pepper relish (1 or 2 batches).

☐ AT LEAST 3 DAYS AHEAD:
*Thaw* frozen turkey in refrigerator. *Cook* candied cranberries.

☐ UP TO 2 DAYS AHEAD:
*Bake* cheesecake. *Crisp* lettuce.

☐ UP TO 1 DAY AHEAD:
*Finish* cranberry appetizer. *Assemble* fennel and cambozola. *Steam* acorn squash and make filling for 12. *Steam* baby squash. *Make* artichoke-parmesan dressing. *Cook* green beans and onion mixture for 12. *Prepare* mashed potatoes. *Make* gravy.

☐ *4 HOURS AHEAD:
*Soak* turkey in brine. *Soak* wood chips.

☐ 3 HOURS AHEAD:
*Ignite* briquets for charcoal barbecue, or

☐ 2 HOURS AND 50 MINUTES AHEAD:
*Heat* gas barbecue and add wood chips.

☐ *2 HOURS AND 40 MINUTES AHEAD:
*Arrange* briquets for indirect heat and add wood chips. *Rinse* turkey, pat dry, and set in barbecue. *Add* briquets to charcoal and add wood chips to charcoal or gas barbecues.

☐ 1 HOUR AHEAD:
*Bake* artichoke-parmesan dressing.

☐ 35 MINUTES AHEAD:
*Reheat* mashed potatoes. *Bake* fennel.

☐ 30 MINUTES AHEAD:
*Transfer* turkey to platter; keep warm. *Set out* cranberry appetizer.

☐ 20 MINUTES AHEAD:
*Place* garlic on mashed potatoes.

☐ 15 MINUTES AHEAD:
*Steam* acorn squash with filling.

☐ 10 MINUTES AHEAD:
*Reheat* gravy, add turkey drippings, and keep hot. *Bring* water to a boil to reheat green beans. *Spoon* relish into a bowl.

☐ 5 MINUTES AHEAD:
*Reheat* green beans and onion mixture. *Reheat* baby squash in butter. *Garnish* turkey.

*Timetable based on a 15-pound turkey; adjust for other sizes.

Acorn Squash with Boursin Custard

arate small bowls. Arrange baked baguette slices in a basket.

**5.** To eat, set a baguette slice on a lettuce leaf and top with a slice of cheese, candied cranberries, and a chestnut piece.

Per serving: 205 cal., 39% (79 cal.) from fat; 6.8 g protein; 8.8 g fat (5.3 g sat.); 25 g carbo (1.4 g fiber); 376 mg sodium; 25 mg chol.

## Acorn Squash with Boursin Custard (1990)

**PREP AND COOK TIME:** 45 to 50 minutes

**NOTES:** Miniature pumpkins such as Jack Be Little or Munchkin also work well in this recipe. Up to 1 day ahead, steam vegetables and make filling; cover and chill separately. To make 12 servings, prepare recipe twice.

**MAKES:** 6 servings

- 3 **acorn squash** (about 10 oz. each) or 6 miniature pumpkins (7 to 8 oz. each), rinsed

- 1 package (4 to 5 oz.) **herb-flavor Boursin** or Rondelé **cheese**

- 1 package (3 oz.) **cream cheese**

- 1 **large egg**

At least 6 to 12 **fresh sage** leaves

**1.** Cut squash in half lengthwise (or slice top quarter off each pumpkin). Place squash, cut side down (or pumpkins with tops sitting on them), on a rack over 1 inch boiling water in a 5- to 6-quart pan or 14-inch wok. Cover and steam over high heat until vegetables are tender when pierced (don't cut through skin), about 20 minutes. Lift from rack; let stand until cool enough to handle, 5 to 8 minutes.

**2.** With a small spoon, gently scoop out and discard seeds, taking care not to break skin. You may need to set squash halves cut side up and press down gently so they sit steady.

**3.** In a food processor or with a mixer,

beat herb cheese, cream cheese, and egg until smooth. Pour filling equally into each squash half (or pumpkin). Lay 1 or 2 sage leaves on filling.

**4.** In the same pan, set filled vegetables on rack over 1 inch boiling water. Cover and steam over high heat until filling puffs slightly and is firm when jiggled, about 10 minutes. (After 5 minutes, fit pumpkin tops onto rack to heat. To serve pumpkins, place tops on or alongside.) Garnish with sage leaves.

Per serving: 181 cal., 70% (126 cal.) from fat; 4.2 g protein; 14 g fat (9 g sat.); 12 g carbo (3.8 g fiber); 169 mg sodium; 73 mg chol.

## Shrimp and Watercress Salad (1987) with Hot Mustard Dressing (1986)

**PREP TIME:** About 15 minutes

**NOTES:** Up to 2 days ahead, crisp Belgian endive and watercress (see crisp tip, page 249). Up to 4 hours ahead, make dressing (step 1), cover, and chill.

MAKES: 10 to 12 servings

- 1½ tablespoons **dry mustard**
- ½ cup **lemon juice**
- 2 teaspoons **Worcestershire**
- 6 tablespoons **extra-virgin olive** or salad **oil**
- ⅓ cup freshly grated **parmesan cheese**
- 6 heads **Belgian endive** (3 to 4 oz. each), rinsed and crisped
- 6 cups (about 6 oz.) **watercress sprigs**, rinsed and crisped
- ¾ pound **shelled cooked tiny shrimp**, rinsed and drained

  **Salt** and fresh-ground **pepper**

1. In a large bowl, mix mustard with 1½ tablespoons water. Add lemon juice, Worcestershire, oil, and cheese.
2. Trim discolored stem ends from endive. Break off 30 to 36 outer leaves and arrange 3 leaves on each salad plate.
3. Cut remaining endive into fine slivers. Add slivered endive, watercress, and shrimp to dressing in bowl. Mix well.
4. With a slotted spoon, mound salad mixture equally on endive leaves and season to taste with salt and pepper.

Per serving: 113 cal., 65% (73 cal.) from fat; 8 g protein; 8.1 g fat (1.5 g sat.); 2.4 g carbo (1.2 g fiber); 133 mg sodium; 57 mg chol.

## Spinach Salad with Pine Nut Dressing (1966)

PREP AND COOK TIME: About 10 minutes
NOTES: Up to 2 days ahead, crisp spinach (see crisp tip, page 249). Up to 1 day ahead, toast nuts and make dressing; cover and chill separately.
MAKES: 10 to 12 servings

- ½ cup **pine nuts**
- ½ teaspoon **dried tarragon**
- ½ teaspoon grated **lemon** peel
- ¼ teaspoon **ground nutmeg**
- ⅓ cup **extra-virgin olive** or salad **oil**
- ⅓ cup **white wine vinegar**
- 1½ pounds (about 4 qt.) **baby spinach leaves**, rinsed and crisped

  **Salt**

1. Pour nuts into a 10- to 12-inch frying pan over medium heat. Shake pan and stir nuts often until pale gold, about 2 minutes. Pour from pan, let cool, and coarsely chop.
2. In a large bowl, combine nuts, tarragon, lemon peel, nutmeg, oil, and vinegar.
3. Add spinach leaves, mix well, and season to taste with salt. Spoon onto salad plates.

Per serving: 98 cal., 87% (85 cal.) from fat; 3.1 g protein; 9.4 g fat (1.4 g sat.); 3.1 g carbo (2.1 g fiber); 45 mg sodium; 0 mg chol.

## Green Bean and Jicama Salad (1989)

PREP AND COOK TIME: About 25 minutes
NOTES: Up to 2 days ahead, crisp watercress (see crisp tip, page 249). Up to 1 day ahead, cover and chill onion in liquid, cold cooked beans, jicama, and dressing separately.
MAKES: 10 to 12 servings

- ⅔ cup thinly slivered **red onion**
- 6 tablespoons **white wine vinegar**
- ¾ pound **green beans**, ends trimmed
- 1 pound **jicama**, scrubbed and peeled
- ¼ cup **extra-virgin olive oil**
- 1 tablespoon **Dijon mustard**
- 1 teaspoon **dried oregano**
- 6 cups (about 6 oz.) **watercress sprigs**, rinsed and crisped

  **Salt** and **pepper**

1. In a small bowl, mix onion, 1 tablespoon vinegar, and 1½ cups cold water; let stand at least 20 minutes.
2. Rinse beans and cut into julienne strips with a food processor, French bean cutter (slicing bars in the handle of some vegetable peelers), or knife. In a 3- to 4-quart pan over high heat, bring 2 quarts water to a boil. Add beans and cook just until tender-crisp, 2 to 5 minutes. Drain beans and immerse at once in ice water until cold. Drain well.
3. Meanwhile, cut jicama into ¼-inch-thick sticks.
4. In a large bowl, mix remaining vinegar with oil, mustard, and oregano. Drain onion. Add onion, beans, jicama, and watercress to bowl. Mix well and add salt and pepper to taste.

Per serving: 69 cal., 59% (41 cal.) from fat; 1.2 g protein; 4.6 g fat (0.6 g sat.); 6.2 g carbo (2.6 g fiber); 40 mg sodium; 0 mg chol.

## Fall Fruit Salad (1995)

PREP AND COOK TIME: About 35 minutes
NOTES: As an alternative to frisée, use tender inner leaves of curly endive. Up to 2 days ahead, crisp frisée (see crisp tip, page 249). Up to 1 day ahead, toast nuts and segment grapefruit; cover and chill separately.
MAKES: 10 to 12 servings

- 2 to 4 tablespoons **pine nuts**
- 4 **ruby grapefruit** (1 lb. each)
- 4 **firm-ripe Fuyu persimmons** (½ lb. each)
- 2 **Asian pears** (about ¾ lb. each)
- 6 tablespoons **lime juice**
- 6 tablespoons **rice vinegar**
- ¼ cup **honey**
- 4 to 6 cups **frisée**, rinsed and crisped
- 1½ cups **pomegranate seeds**

  **Salt**

1. Cook pine nuts in a 6- to 8-inch frying pan over medium heat, shaking pan often to stir nuts until pale gold, 2 to 3 minutes. Pour from pan.
2. With a knife, cut peel and membrane from grapefruit. Holding fruit over a bowl, cut between segments and inner membrane to release fruit into bowl. Squeeze juice from membrane into bowl; discard membrane.
3. Rinse Fuyu persimmons, trim off and discard stem ends, then slice fruit crosswise into thin rounds.
4. Rinse Asian pears and discard stems. Cut fruit crosswise into thin rounds through center seeds. Coat pear slices with grapefruit juice.
5. In a small bowl, mix 6 tablespoons grapefruit juice (reserve remainder for other uses) with lime juice, rice vinegar, and honey.
6. Line a salad bowl or salad plates with frisée. Arrange Fuyu persimmons, Asian pears, and grapefruit on frisée. Sprinkle with pomegranate seeds and pine nuts, then moisten with the grapefruit-lime dressing. Add salt to taste.

Per serving: 170 cal., 7.1% (12 cal.) from fat; 1.9 g protein; 1.3 g fat (0.1 g sat.); 43 g carbo (3.1 g fiber); 6.3 mg sodium; 0 mg chol.

## SOUPS

### Chestnut Soup (1994)

**PREP AND COOK TIME:** About 40 minutes

**NOTES:** To use fresh chestnuts, you'll need about 1½ pounds. Cut an X through shell on flat side. Immerse in boiling water and simmer 10 minutes. Drain, and while nuts are warm and wet, use a small knife to pull off shell and dark membrane. Or buy peeled, cooked chestnuts canned (in water), frozen, or in shelf-stable packaging. Up to 3 days ahead, make soup, cover, and chill. Reheat to serve, thinning, as desired, with more broth—soup thickens on standing. To make 12 servings, double the recipe and use a 6- to 8-quart pan.

**MAKES:** 6 servings

1 cup minced **shallots** or onions

¾ teaspoon **dried thyme**

About 7 cups fat-skimmed **chicken broth**

4 cups **peeled cooked chestnuts** (see notes)

**Sour cream**

1½ tablespoons slivered **fresh chives** or parsley

**Salt**

**1.** In a 5- to 6-quart pan over high heat, frequently stir shallots, thyme, and ½ cup broth until vegetables are lightly browned, 5 to 7 minutes. Add 6½ cups broth and chestnuts. Cover, bring to a boil, then reduce heat and simmer until chestnuts mash easily, about 30 minutes.

**2.** Whirl mixture, a portion at a time, in a blender until very smooth. Or, with a slotted spoon, skim chestnuts and vegetables from broth and purée in a food processor, then mix with broth in pan.

**3.** Measure soup. If you have less than 6 cups, add broth to make this amount and return to pan and stir until hot. If you have more, boil and stir until reduced.

**4.** Ladle hot soup into bowls. Add a spoonful of sour cream to each and sprinkle with chives. Season with salt to taste.

Per serving: 182 cal., 6.6% (12 cal.) from fat; 12 g protein; 1.3 g fat (0.2 g sat.); 30 g carbo (0.2 g fiber); 116 mg sodium; 0 mg chol.

**Shrimp and Watercress Salad with Hot Mustard Dressing**

### Winter Squash Soup with Sage (1996)

**PREP AND COOK TIME:** About 1¼ hours

**NOTES:** Choose a squash with deep orange, sweet flesh, such as butternut, kabocha, red kuri, or buttercup. If making up to 3 days ahead, start at step 2, using plain olive oil. Continue through step 4. Cover and chill. Up to 1 day ahead, fry sage leaves, wrap in paper towels, seal in a plastic bag, and hold at room temperature. Cover and chill sage-flavor oil. Reheat soup, thinning, if desired, with more broth—it thickens on standing. Add sage oil. To make 12 servings, double the recipe and use a 5- to 6-quart pan.

**MAKES:** 6 servings

2 tablespoons **olive oil**

18 **fresh sage** leaves (about 1½ in.)

2¾ to 3 pounds **winter squash**

2 unpeeled **onions** (about 6 oz. each), cut in half

6 unpeeled cloves **garlic**

¼ cup chopped **parsley**

1 tablespoon chopped **fresh sage** leaves

¾ teaspoon **fresh thyme** leaves or dried thyme

4 cups fat-skimmed **chicken** or vegetable **broth**

**Salt**

½ cup diced **fontina cheese**

**Pepper**

**1.** Pour oil into a 6- to 8-inch frying pan over medium-high heat. When oil is hot, add whole sage leaves and stir until they turn darker green, 45 seconds to 1 minute. With a slotted spoon, lift out leaves and drain on paper towels. Reserve the oil.

**2.** Rinse squash and, if whole, cut in half and scoop out and discard seeds. Brush cut surfaces of squash and onions with a little of the reserved oil. Lay vegetables, cut side down, in a 10- by 15-inch pan. Slip garlic under squash.

**3.** Bake in a 375° oven until all vegetables are soft when pressed, 45 to 60 minutes. Reserve juices. Scrape squash from skin. Peel and chop onions. Peel

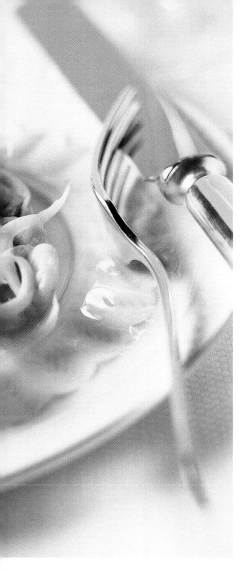

## Best-ever Roasted or Barbecued Turkey (1985 to present)

**PREP AND COOK TIME:** About 10 minutes, 20 minutes if stuffing the bird; see chart below for cooking times

**MAKES:** Allow ¾ pound uncooked turkey per serving, at least 1 pound if you want leftovers

1 **turkey** (10 to 30 lb.)

**Olive** or salad **oil**

**1.** Remove and discard leg truss from turkey. Pull off and discard lumps of fat. Remove giblets and neck. Rinse bird inside and out; pat dry with towels.

**2.** Rub turkey skin with oil. Insert a meat thermometer straight down through the thickest part of the breast to the bone. (If using an instant-read thermometer, insert when checking temperature.)

**3.** Cook turkey until the meat thermometer registers 160°; see chart below for details.

***To roast,*** place turkey, breast up, on a V-shaped rack in a 12- by 17-inch roasting pan (or one that is at least 2 in. longer and wider than the bird). Roast in a 325° or 350° oven, as determined by bird size; see chart below.

***To barbecue with charcoal,*** use a barbecue (20 to 22 in. wide) with a lid. Mound and ignite 40 charcoal briquets on firegrate. When coals are spotted with gray ash, in about 20 minutes, push equal portions to opposite sides of firegrate. Place a foil or metal drip pan between coals. To each mound of coals, add 5 briquets now and every 30 minutes while cooking.

***To barbecue with gas,*** use a barbecue with indirect heat controls at least 11 in. between burners. Turn all burners to high, close lid, and heat for about 10 minutes. Adjust gas for indirect cooking (heat parallel to sides of bird and not beneath) and set a foil or metal drip pan in center (not over direct heat; if drippings flare when lid is open, add a little water to pan).

Set grill in place. Set turkey, breast up, on grill over drip pan. Cover barbecue and open vents for charcoal. If edges of turkey close to gas heat begin to get too dark, slide folded strips of foil between bird and grill.

**4.** Transfer cooked turkey to a platter. Keep warm and let stand 15 to 30 minutes.

**5.** Carve bird. If thighs are still slightly pink at the joint (typical, if oven-roasted), put thighs on a microwave-safe plate in a microwave oven at full power (100%) until pink disappears, 1 to 3 minutes.

Per ¼ pound boned cooked turkey with skin, based on percentages of white and dark meat in an average bird: 229 cal., 39% (90 cal.) from fat; 32 g protein; 10 g fat (3 g sat.); 0 g carbo (0 g fiber); 82 mg sodium; 93 mg chol.

## Turkey Loco (1984)

**PREP AND COOK TIME:** About 1½ hours
**NOTES:** Up to 1 day ahead, butterfly turkey (step 1), then cover and chill.
**MAKES:** Allow ¾ pound uncooked turkey per serving, 1 pound for leftovers.

1 **turkey** (10 to 12 lb.)

About 4 **limes,** cut into halves

About 4 teaspoons **dried oregano**

**Salt** and **pepper**

---

garlic. Discard skin and peels.

**4.** In a 3- to 4-quart pan, combine squash, onions, garlic, parsley, chopped sage, and thyme. Mash squash mixture with a potato masher. Stir in reserved juices and broth. Stirring often, bring to a boil over high heat. Cover, reduce heat to low, and stir occasionally to blend flavors, 15 to 20 minutes.

**5.** Add the remaining sage cooking oil and season soup with salt to taste. Distribute cheese equally among individual bowls. Add soup, top with fried sage, and sprinkle with pepper.

Per serving: 187 cal., 41% (77 cal.) from fat; 11 g protein; 8.6 g fat (2.9 g sat.); 18 g carbo (3.5 g fiber); 153 mg sodium; 14 mg chol.

## TURKEY

***Turkey tips.*** Thaw frozen turkey in its wrapper in the refrigerator for at least 72 hours. Reserve giblets, neck, and drippings for gravy (pages 254 and 255). If stuffing the bird with dressing, do so just before bird is cooked. Spoon dressing from the hot bird into a serving dish.

## BIRD BASICS

### Oven-roasted or barbecued whole turkey

See **Best-ever Turkey** (above), step 3, for charcoal and gas barbecuing directions.

| Turkey weight with giblets | Oven temp. | Internal temp.* | Cooking time |
|---|---|---|---|
| 10–13 lb. | 350° | 160° | 1½–2¼ hr. |
| 14–23 lb. | 325° | 160° | 2–3 hr. |
| 24–27 lb. | 325° | 160° | 3–3¾ hr. |
| 28–30 lb. | 325° | 160° | 3½–4½ hr. |

*To measure the internal temperature of the turkey, insert a thermometer through the thickest part of the breast to the bone.

Times are for unstuffed birds. A stuffed bird may cook at the same rate as an unstuffed one; however, be prepared to allow 30 to 50 minutes more.

Turkey Loco

1. At the meat market, have turkey backbone sawed through lengthwise. Or at home, use spring-loaded poultry shears to cut through length of backbone. Lay turkey on its breast; pull open from back, pressing to flatten (some bones will crack). Pull off and discard lumps of fat.

2. Rinse turkey and pat dry with towels. Squeeze and rub 1 or 2 lime halves over turkey; sprinkle with oregano, then season lightly with salt and pepper.

3. Follow step 3 from Best-ever Turkey (preceding), to barbecue with charcoal or gas. Lay bird, bones down, on grill over drip pan.

4. Cook turkey until thermometer registers 160° at thickest part of breast at bone, about 1½ hours. Start checking at 1 hour.

5. Transfer turkey to a large platter. Keep warm and let stand 15 to 30 minutes, then carve. Accompany with remaining limes to add juice to taste.

Per ¼ pound boned cooked turkey with skin, based on percentages of white and dark meat in an average bird: 233 cal., 39% (90 cal.) from fat; 32 g protein; 10 g fat (3 g sat.); 0.9 g carbo (0 g fiber); 82 mg sodium; 93 mg chol.

## Chili-Orange Glaze (1993)

PREP AND COOK TIME: About 5 minutes, plus about 20 minutes to cook with turkey

NOTES: Up to 3 days ahead, mix glaze, cover, and chill.

MAKES: Enough for a 10- to 24-pound turkey, oven-roasted or barbecued

1. In a small bowl, combine 3 tablespoons **ground dried New Mexico** or California **chilies** or 3 tablespoons chili powder, 1 can (12 oz.; 1½ cups) thawed **frozen orange juice concentrate,** 2 tablespoons grated **orange** peel, and 1 teaspoon **ground cumin.**

2. When **turkey** has about 20 more minutes to cook (the breast temperature at the bone will be about 150° for birds up to 18 lb., about 155° for birds over 18 lb.), coat generously with the chili-orange glaze.

3. Continue to cook until the meat thermometer registers 160°; see chart page 253 for details. If glaze starts to get quite dark, drape dark areas with foil.

Per tablespoon: 44 cal., 4.1% (1.8 cal.) from fat; 0.7 g protein; 0.2 g fat (0 g sat.); 10 g carbo (0.5 g fiber); 1.3 mg sodium; 0 mg chol.

## Brown Sugar Crackle Glaze (1993)

PREP TIME: About 5 minutes, plus about 45 minutes to cook with turkey

NOTES: Up to 3 days ahead, mix glaze, cover, and chill.

MAKES: Enough for a 10- to 24-pound turkey, oven-roasted or barbecued

1. In a small bowl, mix 2 cups firmly packed **brown sugar,** 5 tablespoons **Di-**

jon **mustard,** and 2 teaspoons **coarse-ground pepper.**

2. When **turkey** has about 45 more minutes to cook (breast temperature at bone will be about 135° for birds up to 18 lb., about 145° for birds over 18 lb.), spread with half the glaze.

3. Cook 20 minutes. Brush with remaining glaze. Continue to cook until the meat thermometer registers 160°; see chart page 253 for details. If glaze starts to get quite dark, drape dark areas with foil.

Per tablespoon: 46 cal., 0% (0 cal.) from fat; 0 g protein; 0 g fat; 11 g carbo (0 g fiber); 52 mg sodium; 0 mg chol.

## GRAVY

### Giblet Gravy Supreme (1968)

PREP AND COOK TIME: About 2 hours

NOTES: Up to 1 day ahead, make gravy, cover, and chill. Add drippings from turkey and reheat, stirring often.

MAKES: About 8 cups without giblets; 10 to 12 servings

**Giblets and neck** from a 10- to 24-pound turkey

About 10 cups fat-skimmed **chicken broth**

2½ cups **dry white wine** or chicken broth

2 **onions** (1 lb. total), peeled and quartered

4 **carrots** (1 lb. total), sliced

1¾ cups sliced **celery**

8 **parsley sprigs**

½ teaspoon **dried marjoram**

1 cup **all-purpose flour**

Fat-skimmed **oven-roasted** or barbecued **turkey drippings** (optional)

**Salt** and **pepper**

1. Rinse giblets and neck. Wrap liver airtight and chill to add later, or save for other uses.

2. In a 5- to 6-quart pan over high heat, combine giblets, neck, 10 cups broth, wine, onions, carrots, celery, parsley, and marjoram. Cover and bring to a boil. Reduce heat and simmer until gizzard is very tender when pierced, about 1½ hours. If desired, add the liver and simmer 10 more minutes.

3. Meanwhile, in a 10- to 12-inch frying pan over high heat, stir flour until it's

## An Almost-No-Recipe Thanksgiving

### for 10 to 12 (1982)

Shrimp and Watercress Salad with Hot Mustard Dressing *(page 251)*

*St. Supéry Sauvignon Blanc 1997 (Napa Valley) $10*

Best-ever Roasted Turkey *(page 253)*

Rich Brown Giblet Gravy *(page 255)*

Cranberry–Meyer Lemon Relish *(page 258)*

Italian Chard Dressing *(page 256)*

Whole Roasted Onions *(page 261)* and Whole Roasted Bell Peppers *(page 262)*

Baked Sweet Potatoes *(page 262)*

Thanksgiving Chestnuts *(page 262)*

*Shafer Cabernet Sauvignon 1995 (Napa Valley/Stags Leap District) $30,
Columbia Crest Cabernet Sauvignon 1995 (Columbia Valley, Washington) $12,
or St. Francis old vine Zinfandel 1996 (Sonoma County) $20*

Ginger-Caramel Macadamia Tart *(page 264)*

*Bonny Doon Framboise (Infusion of Raspberries)
nonvintage (California) $10, 375 ml.*

---

## AN ALMOST-NO-RECIPE THANKSGIVING GAME PLAN

(Roast potatoes, onions, bell peppers, and chestnuts in oven with turkey.)

☐ **UP TO 1 WEEK AHEAD:**
*Make* cranberry-lemon relish.

☐ **AT LEAST 3 DAYS AHEAD:**
*Thaw* frozen turkey in refrigerator.

☐ **UP TO 2 DAYS AHEAD:**
*Crisp* salad greens.

☐ **UP TO 1 DAY AHEAD:**
*Make* Italian chard dressing. *Bake* ginger-macadamia tart. *Make* chocolate sauce. *Make* broth for gravy.

☐ **UP TO 4 HOURS AHEAD:**
*Make* salad dressing.

☐ **\*2½ HOURS AHEAD:**
*Roast* turkey. *Scrub* sweet potatoes.

☐ **1½ HOURS AHEAD:**
*Put* onions and sweet potatoes in oven with turkey. *Add* chestnuts to turkey roasting pan.

☐ **1 HOUR AHEAD:**
*Put* chard dressing on bottom rack of oven or another oven. *Put* bell peppers in oven. *Open* wines.

☐ **30 MINUTES AHEAD:**
*Transfer* turkey and chestnuts to serving platter; keep warm. *Continue* to bake vegetables and dressing. *Thicken* and finish gravy; keep hot. *Spoon* cranberry relish into a bowl.

☐ **10 MINUTES AHEAD:**
*Assemble* salad.

☐ **5 MINUTES AHEAD:**
*Remove* vegetables and dressing from oven. *Arrange* vegetables around turkey.

☐ **AT DESSERT TIME:**
*Warm* chocolate sauce.

*\*Timetable based on a 15-pound turkey; adjust for other sizes.*

---

golden brown and smells richly toasted (but not scorched), 12 to 15 minutes. Pour into a bowl.

**4.** Pour broth through a fine strainer into a bowl. Discard vegetables. Measure broth. If you have more than 8 cups, boil to reduce; if you have less, add more chicken broth.

**5.** Pull meat off neck; discard bones. Finely chop meat and giblets (optional).

**6.** With a whisk, smoothly mix about 3 cups of the simmered broth into flour. Pour into the 5- to 6-quart pan and add remaining broth. If desired, scrape turkey drippings free from roasting or barbecue drip pan and add to broth. Stir over high heat until boiling, then reduce heat and simmer, stirring often, for about 5 minutes. Add giblets, if desired, and stir 1 to 2 minutes more. Pour into a bowl. Add salt and pepper to taste.

Per serving: 135 cal., 14% (19 cal.) from fat; 16 g protein; 2.1 g fat (0.6 g sat.); 11 g carbo (0.9 g fiber); 114 mg sodium; 74 mg chol.

### Rich Brown Giblet Gravy (1985)

**PREP AND COOK TIME:** About 2½ hours

**NOTES:** Up to 1 day ahead, complete through step 4. Cover and chill broth and giblets.

**MAKES:** About 8 cups without giblets; 10 to 12 servings

**Giblets and neck** from a 10- to 24-pound turkey

2 **onions** (about ¾ lb. total), peeled and quartered

2 **carrots** (about ½ lb. total), cut into chunks

¾ cup sliced **celery**

About 10 cups fat-skimmed **chicken broth**

1 **dried bay leaf**

½ cup **port**, sherry, or dry white wine

½ teaspoon **pepper**

⅔ cup **cornstarch**

Fat-skimmed **oven-roasted** or barbecued **turkey drippings** (optional)

**Salt**

**1.** Rinse giblets and neck. Wrap liver airtight and chill to add later, or save for other uses. Chop giblets and cut neck into 3 or 4 pieces.

**2.** In a 5- to 6-quart pan over high heat, combine chopped giblets, neck, onions, carrots, celery, and ½ cup broth. Boil and stir often until meat and vegetables are very well browned, 15 to 20 minutes. Add another ½ cup broth, scrape drippings free, and repeat step.

**3.** Add 9 cups broth, bay leaf, port, and pepper, stirring to scrape browned bits free. Cover and simmer until giblets are very tender when pierced, about 1½ hours. If desired, add the liver and simmer 10 more minutes.

**4.** Pour broth through a fine strainer into a bowl. Discard vegetables. Measure broth. If you have more than 8 cups, boil to reduce; if you have less, add more chicken broth.

**5.** Pull meat off neck; discard bones. Finely chop meat and giblets (optional).

**6.** Smoothly blend cornstarch with ²⁄₃ cup water. Add to broth in pan and stir over high heat until gravy is boiling, about 5 minutes. If desired, scrape turkey drippings into gravy and stir until boiling. Add giblets, if desired, and stir 1 to 2 minutes more. Pour into a bowl. Add salt to taste.

Per serving: 107 cal., 17% (18 cal.) from fat; 15 g protein; 2 g fat (0.6 g sat.); 3.4 g carbo (0.4 g fiber); 106 mg sodium; 74 mg chol.

## DRESSINGS

## Italian Chard Dressing (1966)

PREP AND COOK TIME: About 1½ hours
NOTES: Up to 1 day ahead, make dressing, put in casserole, cover, and chill.
MAKES: About 11 cups; 10 to 12 servings

- ¾ loaf (¾ lb.) **French bread**
- 2 cups **nonfat milk**
- 2 pounds **Italian sausages**
- 1 cup chopped **parsley**
- 1 **garlic** clove, minced or pressed
- 1 **onion** (about 6 oz.), peeled and chopped
- ½ cup finely chopped **celery**
- 1½ cups **grated parmesan cheese**
- 1½ teaspoons **dried basil**
- ¼ teaspoon **dried rubbed sage**
- ¼ teaspoon **dried rosemary**
- 2 packages (10 oz. each) thawed **frozen Swiss chard**
- **Salt**

**1.** Cut bread into ½-inch slices. Place in a bowl and add milk. Mix to saturate with milk and let stand about 30 minutes. Stir occasionally.

**2.** Meanwhile, place a 10- to 12-inch frying pan over high heat. Squeeze sausages from casings into pan. Discard casings. Stir meat often to crumble and lightly brown, 10 to 15 minutes; discard fat. Add parsley, garlic, onion, and celery. Stir often until vegetables are lightly browned, 5 to 8 minutes.

**3.** With your hands, squeeze bread to break into tiny pieces. Add cooked meat mixture, cheese, basil, sage, and rosemary.

**4.** Squeeze moisture from chard and add to bowl. Mix dressing and add salt to taste.

**5.** Spoon into a shallow 3-quart (9- by 13-in.) casserole. For moist dressing, cover with foil; for crusty dressing, do

not cover. Bake in a 325° to 350° oven (use temperature turkey requires; see chart on page 253) until hot (at least 150° in center) or lightly browned, about 50 minutes (1 hour if chilled).

Per serving: 422 cal., 60% (252 cal.) from fat; 20 g protein; 28 g fat (11 g sat.); 21 g carbo (2.4 g fiber); 1,084 mg sodium; 67 mg chol.

## Artichoke-Parmesan Sourdough Dressing (1994)

PREP AND COOK TIME: About 1½ hours
NOTES: Up to 1 day ahead, make dressing, put in casserole, cover, and chill.
MAKES: About 10 cups; 10 to 12 servings

- 1 loaf (1 lb.) **sourdough bread,** cut into ½-inch cubes
- 1 pound **mushrooms,** rinsed
- 1 tablespoon **butter** or margarine
- 2 **onions** (about ¾ lb. total), peeled and chopped
- 1 cup chopped **celery**
- 2 tablespoons minced **garlic**
- About 2 cups fat-skimmed **chicken broth**
- 2 jars (6 oz. each) **marinated artichoke hearts,** drained
- ½ cup **grated parmesan cheese**
- 1½ teaspoons **poultry seasoning**
- 1½ tablespoons minced **fresh rosemary** leaves or ¾ teaspoon crumbled dried rosemary
- **Salt** and **pepper**
- 1 **large egg**

**1.** Spread bread cubes in a single layer in 2 pans, each 10 by 15 inches. Bake in a 350° oven until toasted golden brown, about 25 minutes. Turn cubes over with a wide spatula occasionally. After 15 minutes, switch pan positions.

**2.** Trim and discard discolored mushroom stem ends. Slice mushrooms.

**3.** In a 10- to 12-inch frying pan over high heat, combine butter, mushrooms, onions, celery, and garlic. Stir often until vegetables are lightly browned, about 15 minutes. Pour into a large bowl. Add a little broth to pan and stir to scrape browned bits free. Add to bowl.

**4.** Pour 2 cups broth into bowl and add toasted bread, artichoke hearts, cheese, poultry seasoning, and rosemary; mix well. Add salt and pepper to taste. Make a well in dressing, add egg, beat with a fork to blend, then mix egg with dressing.

**5.** Spoon into a shallow 3-quart (9- by 13-in.) casserole. For moist dressing, cover with foil; for crusty dressing, do not cover. Bake in a 325° to 350° oven (use temperature turkey requires; see chart on page 253) until hot (at least 150° in center) or lightly browned, about 50 minutes (1 hour if chilled).

Per serving: 190 cal., 28% (53 cal.) from fat; 8.5 g protein; 5.9 g fat (1.9 g sat.); 27 g carbo (3.3 g fiber); 477 mg sodium; 23 mg chol.

## Oyster and Sausage Cornbread Dressing (1985)

PREP AND COOK TIME: About 1½ hours
NOTES: Up to 1 day ahead, make dressing, put in casserole, cover, and chill. Use cornbread recipe that follows, or prepare a cornbread mix (1 package, about 14 oz.).
MAKES: About 10 cups; 10 to 12 servings

- 2 tablespoons **butter** or margarine
- 2 **onions** (about ¾ lb. total), peeled and chopped
- ¾ cup chopped **celery**
- 1 cup **corn kernels,** fresh or frozen
- ¾ pound **bulk pork sausage**
- ½ cup **shucked fresh** or canned **oysters**
- 1 teaspoon **dried rubbed sage**
- 1 teaspoon **dried thyme**
- **Cornbread** (recipe follows)
- **Salt** and **pepper**

**1.** In a 10- to 12-inch frying pan over high heat, combine butter, onions, celery, and corn. Stir often until vegetables are lightly browned, 5 to 8 minutes. Pour into a large bowl.

**2.** Crumble sausage in frying pan and stir often until lightly browned, about 5 minutes. With a slotted spoon, transfer sausage to onion mixture. Discard fat.

**3.** Pour oysters and liquid into frying pan. Stir to free browned bits and bring to a boil. With slotted spoon, lift out oysters and cut into ½-inch chunks. Add to onion mixture. Boil oyster liquid until reduced to 2 tablespoons and add to onion mixture. Add sage, thyme, and cornbread; mix well, breaking cornbread into small pieces. Season to taste with salt and pepper.

**4.** Pat into a shallow 3-quart (9- by 13-in.) casserole. For moist dressing, cover with foil; for crusty dressing, do not cover. Bake in a 325° to 350° oven

Wild Rice and Porcini Mushroom Dressing

1 **garlic** clove, minced or pressed

¾ teaspoon **ground cumin**

½ teaspoon **dried oregano**

½ pound **mushrooms,** rinsed

2 packages (10 oz. each) thawed **frozen spinach**

2 cups **soft bread crumbs**

½ cup **shredded jack cheese**
    **Salt**

1 **large egg**

10 to 12 **fresh Anaheim** (California or New Mexico) or poblano **chilies** (about 2 oz. each)

**1.** Remove and discard sausage casings. Crumble meat in a 12- to 14-inch frying pan over medium-high heat. Add garlic, cumin, and oregano. Stir often until sausage is lightly browned, 8 to 10 minutes. Drain and discard fat.

**2.** Meanwhile, trim and discard discolored mushroom stem ends. Chop mushrooms. Add to sausage mixture. Squeeze moisture from spinach and add to sausage mixture. Stir often over high heat until mixture begins to brown, about 10 minutes longer. Remove from heat. Stir in bread crumbs and cheese. Season to taste with salt. Add egg and mix well.

**3.** Rinse and drain chilies. From stem to tip, cut each chili open lengthwise. Ease open chili and carefully pull out and discard seeds and veins. Fill chilies equally with chorizo stuffing, packing it in firmly. Lay chilies, slit side up, in a single layer in a 10- by 15-inch pan.

**4.** Bake in a 400° oven until chilies are soft and tinged with brown, about 25 minutes. With a wide spatula, transfer to a platter.

Per serving: 161 cal., 53% (86 cal.) from fat; 9.4 g protein; 9.6 g fat (3.8 g sat.); 10 g carbo (1.9 g fiber); 340 mg sodium; 40 mg chol.

## RELISHES

## Red Pepper Relish with Aromatics (1993)

PREP AND COOK TIME: About 30 minutes

NOTES: Up to 1 week ahead, make relish; cool, cover, and chill. For 12 servings, make 2 batches.

MAKES: About 1½ cups; 6 servings

1 to 1¼ pounds **red bell peppers**

1 **lemon**

1 cup **rice vinegar**

---

(use temperature turkey requires; see chart on page 253) until hot (at least 150° in center) or lightly browned, about 50 minutes (1 hour if chilled).

Per serving: 246 cal., 48% (117 cal.) from fat; 7.3 g protein; 13 g fat (4 g sat.); 26 g carbo (1.8 g fiber); 449 mg sodium; 43 mg chol.

**Cornbread.** In a bowl, mix 1 cup *each* **yellow cornmeal** and **all-purpose flour,** 2 tablespoons **sugar,** 1 tablespoon **baking powder,** and ½ teaspoon **salt.** Stir in 1 cup **milk,** ¼ cup **salad oil,** and 1 **large egg;** beat just until well blended. Pour batter into a buttered 8-inch square pan. Bake in a 425° oven until golden brown and edges just begin to pull from pan sides, about 25 minutes. Let cool at least 10 minutes. Use, or cool, cover, and store at room temperature up to 1 day. Cut into ¾- to 1-inch chunks.

## Wild Rice and Porcini Mushroom Dressing (1993)

PREP AND COOK TIME: About 1¾ hours

NOTES: Up to 2 days ahead, cook dressing, drain, and separately cover and chill dressing and cooking liquid. Combine dressing and liquid, heat, then drain and serve.

MAKES: About 10 cups; 10 to 12 servings

¾ cup (¾ oz.) **dried porcini mushrooms**

3 **onions** (1½ lb. total), peeled and finely chopped

1 teaspoon **dried thyme**

¼ teaspoon fresh-grated or ground **nutmeg**

6 cups fat-skimmed **chicken broth**

3 cups **wild rice,** rinsed and drained

3 tablespoons **dry sherry** (optional)
    **Salt**

**1.** In a bowl, pour 2 cups boiling water over porcini mushrooms. Let stand until water is cool enough to touch, about 20 minutes. Squeeze mushrooms gently to release grit, then lift from water. Finely chop mushrooms. Carefully pour soaking liquid into another container, leaving grit behind. Add water to soaking liquid to make 1½ cups. Discard gritty residue.

**2.** In a 5- to 6-quart pan, combine onions, thyme, nutmeg, and ¾ cup of the mushroom soaking liquid. Stir often over high heat until onions begin to brown, 10 to 15 minutes. Add remaining soaking liquid, mushrooms, broth, wild rice, and sherry.

**3.** Cover and bring to a boil. Reduce heat and simmer until rice is tender to bite and beginning to split, about 1 hour. Drain, reserving liquid for other uses. Season dressing with salt to taste.

Per serving: 187 cal., 2.4% (4.5 cal.) from fat; 11 g protein; 0.5 g fat (0.1 g sat.); 35 g carbo (3.3 g fiber); 42 mg sodium; 0 mg chol.

## Chilies with Chorizo Stuffing (1984)

PREP AND COOK TIME: About 1¼ hours

NOTES: Up to 1 day ahead, stuff chilies, cover, and chill. Uncover to bake.

MAKES: 10 to 12 servings

½ pound **chorizo sausage** or bulk pork sausage

Viva Cranberry

1 cup **sugar**

**Aromatic spice mix**
(recipe follows)

1. Rinse, stem, seed, and thinly slice peppers. Rinse lemon, trim ends, and discard. Thinly slice lemon and cut slices into quarters; discard seeds.

2. In a 4- to 5-quart pan, combine 1 cup water, peppers, lemon, vinegar, sugar, and aromatic spice mix. Bring to a boil over high heat and boil rapidly, stirring often, until liquid is almost evaporated, about 20 minutes; take care not to scorch. Serve warm or cool. Stir before serving.

Per serving: 160 cal., 4.5% (7.2 cal.) from fat; 1.3 g protein; 0.8 g fat (0 g sat.); 40 g carbo (1.4 g fiber); 2.5 mg sodium; 0 mg chol.

***Aromatic spice mix.*** Combine 1 tablespoon **mustard seed**, 1 teaspoon **coriander seed**, $^1/_4$ teaspoon **fennel seed**, $^1/_8$ teaspoon **cardamom seed**, $^1/_8$ teaspoon **ground nutmeg**, and 3 or 4 **whole cloves**.

## Cranberry–Meyer Lemon Relish (1964)

PREP AND COOK TIME: 12 to 15 minutes

NOTES: Up to 1 week ahead, make relish; cool, cover, and chill.

MAKES: About 3 cups; 10 to 12 servings

1. Sort 3 cups (12-oz. package) **fresh** or thawed frozen **cranberries**, discarding any soft or decayed fruit. Rinse and drain berries. Rinse 2 **Meyer lemons** (about $^1/_4$ lb. each), trim and discard ends. Cut lemons into 1-inch chunks and discard seeds.

2. In a food processor, whirl cranberries and lemon chunks until finely chopped. Or grind through a food

chopper with a fine blade.

3. Mix fruit and 1 cup **sugar** (or to taste) in a 2- to 3-quart pan. Bring to a boil over high heat. Reduce heat and simmer, stirring often, until mixture is reduced to about 3 cups, 8 to 10 minutes. Serve warm or cool.

Per serving: 82 cal., 1.1% (0.9 cal.) from fat; 0.3 g protein; 0.1 g fat (0 g sat.); 22 g carbo (1 g fiber); 1 mg sodium; 0 mg chol.

## Viva Cranberry (1987)

PREP TIME: 10 to 15 minutes

NOTES: Up to 1 week ahead, make relish; cover and chill. Stir before serving.

MAKES: About 3 cups; 10 to 12 servings

3 cups (12-oz. package) **fresh** or thawed frozen **cranberries**

1 **fresh jalapeño chili**, stemmed, seeded, and chopped

$^3/_4$ cup chopped **onion**

2 tablespoons chopped **fresh ginger**

$^1/_2$ cup **fresh cilantro**

5 tablespoons **lime juice**

2 teaspoons grated **orange** peel

$^1/_4$ cup **tequila** (optional)

3 tablespoons **orange-flavor liqueur** or 1 more tablespoon grated orange peel

**Salt**

1. Sort cranberries and discard any soft or decayed fruit. Rinse berries.

2. In a food processor, whirl cranberries, chili, onion, ginger, cilantro, lime juice, orange peel, tequila, and orange liqueur until finely chopped. Or grind through a food chopper with a fine blade. Add salt to taste.

Per serving: 31 cal., 2.9% (0.9 cal.) from fat; 0.3 g protein; 0.1 g fat (0 g sat.); 6.3 g carbo (1.2 g fiber); 2 mg sodium; 0 mg chol.

## Pineapple-Pepper Relish (1987)

PREP TIME: About 10 minutes

NOTES: Up to 1 day ahead, cover relish and chill. Stir before serving.

MAKES: About 4 cups; 10 to 12 servings

In a bowl, combine $3^1/_2$ cups coarsely chopped **pineapple**, $^3/_4$ cup chopped **red onion**, $^1/_4$ cup **lime juice**, and 2 to 3 tablespoons rinsed, drained **canned green peppercorns** (to taste). Season to taste with **salt**.

Per serving: 27 cal., 6.7% (1.8 cal.) from fat; 0.3 g protein; 0.2 g fat (0 g sat.); 6.9 g carbo (0.7 g fiber); 52 mg sodium; 0 mg chol.

### VEGETABLES

## Artichokes and Spinach au Gratin (1987)

PREP AND COOK TIME: About 1 hour and 20 minutes

NOTES: Up to 1 day ahead, assemble casserole, cover, and chill. If you can find frozen artichoke bottoms at a well-stocked supermarket, simmer 6 of them in seasoning liquid (step 2) for 10 minutes. For 12 servings, make 2 casseroles.

MAKES: 6 servings

6 **artichokes** (4 to $4^1/_2$ in. wide) or 2 packages (9 oz. each) frozen artichoke hearts

1 teaspoon **dried thyme**

1 teaspoon **coriander seed**

1 teaspoon **dried basil**

$^1/_2$ teaspoon coarsely crushed **black peppercorns**

**Spinach filling** (recipe follows)

$^3/_4$ cup shredded **gruyère** or Swiss **cheese**

1. Rinse and drain fresh artichokes. Trim leaves off just above artichoke bottoms. Discard leaves or save to cook separately.

2. In a 3- to 4-quart pan over high heat, bring $1^1/_2$ quarts water, thyme, coriander, basil, and peppercorns to a boil. Add fresh artichoke bottoms, cover, reduce heat, and simmer until bottoms are tender when pierced, about 30 min-

**MENU**

## Thanksgiving on the Lighter Side
### for 10 to 12*

Fall Fruit Salad *(page 251)*

*Jekel Johannisberg Riesling 1996 (Monterey) $10*

Best-ever Barbecued Turkey *(page 253)*

with Brown Sugar Crackle Glaze *(page 254)*

Giblet Gravy Supreme *(page 255)*

Wild Rice and Porcini Mushroom Dressing *(page 257)*

Pineapple-Pepper Relish *(page 258)*

Scorched Corn Pudding *(page 260)* or Roasted Sweet and
White Potatoes with Hazelnuts *(page 262)*

Sugar Snap Peas with Mint and Bacon Dressing *(page 261)*

*Grgich Hills Chardonnay 1996 (Napa Valley) $30, or
Chateau St. Jean Merlot 1995 (Sonoma County) $18*

Chestnut Tiramisu *(page 265)*

*McDowell Syrah Port 1994 (Mendocino) $20, 375 ml.*

*\*Per dinner without wines, with corn pudding: 1,288 cal., 20% (261 cal.) from fat,
29 g fat; or with sweet and white potatoes: 1,419 cal., 23% (324 cal.) from fat, 36 g fat.
Both include turkey with light and dark meat and skin.*

## THANKSGIVING ON THE LIGHTER SIDE GAME PLAN

(Cook turkey on a charcoal or gas barbecue or roast in the oven.)

☐ **AT LEAST 3 DAYS AHEAD:**

*Thaw* frozen turkey in refrigerator. *Make* brown sugar crackle glaze.

☐ **UP TO 2 DAYS AHEAD:**

*Crisp* salad greens. *Cook* wild rice and porcini dressing.

☐ **UP TO 1 DAY AHEAD:**

*Toast* pine nuts for salad. *Segment* grapefruit for salad. *Make* pineapple relish. *Make* gravy. *Cook* sugar snap peas, bacon, and sauce. *Assemble* corn pudding. Make tiramisu.

☐ **4 HOURS AHEAD:**

*Partially roast* sweet and white potatoes.

☐ **3 HOURS AHEAD:**

*Ignite* briquets for charcoal barbecue, or

☐ **2 HOURS AND 50 MINUTES AHEAD:**

*Heat* gas barbecue.

☐ **\*2 HOURS AND 30 MINUTES AHEAD:**

*Rinse* turkey and pat dry. *Set* turkey in oven or on barbecue. *Add* briquets to charcoal now and every 30 minutes.

☐ **2 HOURS AHEAD:**

*Set* out ingredients for peas to warm.

☐ **1¼ HOURS AHEAD:**

*Glaze* turkey. *Open* wines.

☐ **55 MINUTES AHEAD:**

*Glaze* turkey again.

☐ **45 MINUTES AHEAD:**

*Bake* corn pudding.

☐ **30 MINUTES AHEAD:**

*Transfer* turkey to platter; keep warm. *Spoon* relish into bowl. *Finish* baking sweet and white potatoes.

☐ **15 MINUTES AHEAD:**

*Assemble* salad.

☐ **10 MINUTES AHEAD:**

*Reheat* dressing and drain. *Reheat* gravy and add drippings. *Set out* salad.

☐ **5 MINUTES AHEAD:**

*Remove* corn pudding and potatoes from oven. Garnish turkey. Assemble peas.

☐ **AT DESSERT TIME:**

*Garnish* tiramisu with orange slices.

*\*Timetable based on a 15-pound turkey; adjust for other sizes.*

---

utes. (Or add frozen artichoke hearts and simmer until thawed and seasoned, about 10 minutes.) Drain artichokes. Trim coarse fibers from artichoke bottoms, break off remaining leaves, and scoop out and discard fuzzy centers.

**3.** Place artichokes in a shallow 8- or 9-inch-wide casserole; turn bottoms cup side up. Cover artichokes with spinach filling and sprinkle with cheese.

**4.** Bake in a 350° oven until cheese is lightly browned, about 35 minutes (45 minutes if chilled).

Per serving: 192 cal., 47% (90 cal.) from fat; 12 g protein; 10 g fat (5.9 g sat.); 17 g carbo (7.9 g fiber); 194 mg sodium; 32 mg chol.

***Spinach filling.*** Thaw 2 packages (10 oz. each) **frozen leaf spinach** and squeeze out as much liquid as possible. Coarsely chop spinach. Peel and chop 1 **onion** (½ lb.). In a 10- to 12-inch frying pan, frequently stir onion, ¼ cup **water,** and 1 tablespoon **butter** or margarine until onion is slightly browned, about 5 minutes. Remove from heat and mix 2 tablespoons **all-purpose flour** with onion, then smoothly stir in 1 cup fat-skimmed **chicken broth** and ¼ cup **whipping cream** or half-and-half (light cream). Season with ¼ teaspoon fresh-grated or ground **nutmeg.** Stir over high

heat until boiling, about 2 minutes. Add spinach, mix well, and season to taste with **salt** and **pepper.** Use hot or cold.

## Butter-browned Baby Squash Wreath (1998)

**PREP AND COOK TIME:** 12 to 15 minutes

**NOTES:** Up to 1 day ahead, steam squash, then immerse in ice water. Drain when cool and chill airtight. Re-heat in butter (step 2) until hot, 5 to 6 minutes. Spoon around cooked turkey or serve in a bowl.

**MAKES:** 12 servings as a garnish, 6 servings as a side dish

1½ pounds **baby yellow** or **green pattypan, zucchini,** or **crookneck squash** (or a combination)

2 tablespoons **butter** or margarine

½ teaspoon **dried thyme** (optional)

**Salt** and **pepper**

**1.** Rinse squash and trim off stem ends. Set on a rack over about 1 inch boiling water in a 14-inch wok or 5- to 6-quart pan. Cover and steam over high heat until vegetables are tender when pierced, about 8 minutes.

**2.** In an 11- to 12-inch frying pan over high heat, melt butter. Add squash and thyme. Shake pan, gently mixing ingredients until butter begins to brown, 2 to 3 minutes. Season to taste with salt and pepper.

Per garnish serving: 27 cal., 67% (18 cal.) from fat; 0.7 g protein; 2 g fat (1.2 g sat.); 2.1 g carbo (0.3 g fiber); 20 mg sodium; 5.2 mg chol.

## Green Beans in a Mist (1974)

PREP AND COOK TIME: About 25 minutes

NOTES: Use wide Italian, skinny haricot vert, plump blue lake, or Chinese long beans. Up to 1 day ahead, cook beans, drain, immerse in ice water until cold, drain, and chill airtight. Reheat in boiling water for 2 to 3 minutes. You can also cover and chill cooked onion mixture, then reheat. To serve 12, double the recipe and allow about 10 minutes for onions to cook.

MAKES: 6 servings

> 1 tablespoon **olive oil**
>
> 1 **onion** (½ lb.), peeled and finely chopped
>
> 1 clove **garlic,** finely chopped
>
> 2 ounces **thin-sliced prosciutto** or bacon (omit oil), finely chopped
>
> 1½ pounds **green beans,** ends trimmed
>
> **Salt**

**1.** In a 10- to 12-inch frying pan over high heat, frequently stir oil, onion, garlic, and prosciutto until onion is lightly browned, 5 to 8 minutes; keep warm.

**2.** Meanwhile, in a 4- to 5-quart covered pan, bring 3 quarts water to a boil over high heat. Add beans and cook, uncovered, until tender-crisp when pierced, 6 to 12 minutes, depending on variety. Drain beans and put in a shallow serving dish.

**3.** Pour onion mixture over beans. Add salt to taste.

Per serving: 86 cal., 38% (33 cal.) from fat; 4.9 g protein; 3.7 g fat (0.7 g sat.); 10 g carbo (2.3 g fiber); 182 mg sodium; 7.7 mg chol.

## Green Beans with Mushroom Duxelles (1990)

PREP AND COOK TIME: 20 to 25 minutes

NOTES: For varieties, see notes for Green Beans in a Mist, preceding. Up to 1 day ahead, cover cool sauce and chill. Reheat to serve. To serve 12, double recipe and allow about 30 minutes.

MAKES: 6 servings

> 1 tablespoon **butter** or margarine
>
> ½ cup finely chopped **onion**
>
> 2 cups finely chopped **mushrooms** (about ½ lb.)
>
> 1½ pounds **green beans,** ends trimmed
>
> 1 teaspoon **cornstarch**
>
> ¼ cup **dry sherry**
>
> About 2 teaspoons **soy sauce**
>
> 2 teaspoons **Asian** (toasted) **sesame oil** (optional)

**1.** In a 10- to 12-inch frying pan over medium-high heat, melt butter. Add onion and stir often until tinged with brown, 3 to 5 minutes. Add mushrooms. Stir often until mushrooms are lightly browned, 5 to 8 minutes.

**2.** Meanwhile, in a 4- to 5-quart covered pan, bring 3 quarts water to a boil over high heat. Add beans and cook, uncovered, until tender-crisp when pierced, 6 to 12 minutes, depending on variety. Drain beans and put in a shallow serving dish.

**3.** Blend cornstarch with ⅓ cup water, dry sherry, and 2 teaspoons soy sauce. Add to mushroom mixture and stir over high heat until boiling. Add sesame oil.

**4.** Pour sauce over beans. Add soy sauce to taste.

Per serving: 78 cal., 26% (20 cal.) from fat; 2.9 g protein; 2.2 g fat (1.2 g sat.); 11 g carbo (2.5 g fiber); 143 mg sodium; 5.2 mg chol.

## Scorched Corn Pudding (1989)

PREP AND COOK TIME: 40 to 45 minutes

NOTES: Up to 1 day ahead, cover unbaked pudding and chill. For an attractive presentation, line the casserole with dried cornhusks, tips rising above the rim. Buy husks (available in 1-lb. bags; husks keep indefinitely) in Mexican grocery stores and some supermarkets. Select 8 to 12 large husks, discard silks, and cover with boiling water. Let stand about 30 minutes to soften. Drain and pat dry.

MAKES: 10 to 12 servings

> 7 cups **corn kernels,** fresh or frozen (3 packages, 10-oz. size)
>
> About 1 tablespoon **butter** or margarine
>
> ¼ cup **all-purpose flour**
>
> 2¼ cups **low-fat milk**
>
> 5 teaspoons **sugar**
>
> About ¼ teaspoon **cayenne**
>
> **Salt**
>
> 2 **large eggs**
>
> 2 **large egg** whites

**1.** In a 12- to 14-inch nonstick frying pan over high heat, stir corn often until about ¼ of the kernels are tinged with brown, 10 to 12 minutes. Add 1 tablespoon butter. When melted, add flour and mix well. Remove from heat and stir in milk, sugar, and cayenne and salt to taste.

**2.** In a small bowl, beat eggs and egg whites to blend. Stir into corn mixture.

**3.** Butter a shallow 2½-quart casserole (if desired, line with husks in a single layer; see notes). Pour in pudding.

**4.** Bake in a 350° oven until center feels firm when lightly pressed, about 30 minutes (40 to 45 minutes if chilled).

Per serving: 139 cal., 24% (33 cal.) from fat; 6.3 g protein; 3.7 g fat (1.5 g sat.); 23 g carbo (2.9 g fiber); 69 mg sodium; 41 mg chol.

## Baked Fennel with Cambozola (1993)

PREP AND COOK TIME: 45 to 50 minutes

NOTES: Up to 1 day ahead, prepare through step 4. Cover and chill casserole. Wrap fennel leaves in a paper towel, seal in a plastic bag, and chill.

MAKES: 10 to 12 servings

**1.** Trim stalks from 5 or 6 heads **fennel** (about 3½ in. wide). Reserve about 1 cup of the feathery green fennel leaves. Trim root ends, bruised areas, and coarse fibers from fennel heads. Rinse, then cut each head in half from stem through root end.

**2.** Lay fennel in an 11- to 12-inch frying pan; add 2 cups fat-skimmed **chicken broth.** Cover and bring to a boil over high heat; simmer until fennel is tender when pierced, about 20 minutes. With a slotted spoon, transfer fennel, cut side up, to a shallow 2- to 2½-quart casserole.

**3.** Boil broth, uncovered, over high heat until reduced to about ⅓ cup. Coarsely chop fennel leaves and add about half to the broth. Spoon mixture evenly over fennel.

**4.** Mash ⅓ pound (¾ cup) **cambozola** or gorgonzola **cheese** with 3 table-

Baked Fennel with Cambozola

spoons **fine dried bread crumbs.** Dot evenly over fennel.

**5.** Bake in a 375° oven until cheese begins to brown and fennel is hot, 25 to 30 minutes (35 minutes if chilled). Garnish with remaining fennel leaves; season to taste with **salt.**

Per serving: 76 cal., 50% (38 cal.) from fat; 5.6 g protein; 4.2 g fat (2.7 g sat.); 4.5 g carbo (1.2 g fiber); 313 mg sodium; 11 mg chol.

## Buttered Hominy (1984)

PREP AND COOK TIME: About 8 minutes

MAKES: 10 to 12 servings

In a 12- to 14-inch frying pan over high heat, stir 2 tablespoons **butter** or margarine with 2 teaspoons **cumin seed** until butter melts. Add 4 **cans** (14½ oz. each) drained **golden** or white **hominy.** Stir hominy often until hot, about 5 minutes. Season to taste with **salt** and **pepper.** Pour into a serving bowl.

Per serving: 117 cal., 25% (29 cal.) from fat; 2.1 g protein; 3.2 g fat (1.4 g sat.); 20 g carbo (3.5 g fiber); 308 mg sodium; 5.2 mg chol.

## Balsamic Roasted Onions (1984)

PREP AND COOK TIME: About 1 hour

NOTES: Up to 1 day ahead, bake onions, cool, cover, and chill. Serve at room temperature.

MAKES: 10 to 12 servings

**1.** In a 12- by 17-inch pan, combine 1 cup **balsamic vinegar,** 1¼ cups **water,** 3 tablespoons firmly packed **brown sugar,** ½ teaspoon **salt,** and ¼ teaspoon **pepper.**

**2.** Cut 5 or 6 unpeeled **onions** (½ lb. each) in half lengthwise. Lay onions cut side down in pan.

**3.** Bake in a 400° oven until onions give readily when gently squeezed and most of the liquid has evaporated, 50 to 60 minutes. If liquid cooks away, add a little water to prevent scorching. Arrange onions cut side up on a platter and pour pan juices over them. Serve hot or at room temperature. Add salt to taste.

Per serving: 59 cal., 3.1% (1.8 cal.) from fat; 1.3 g protein; 0.2 g fat (0 g sat.); 14 g carbo (1.8 g fiber); 102 mg sodium; 0 mg chol.

## Sugar Snap Peas with Mint and Bacon Dressing (1993)

PREP AND COOK TIME: 25 to 30 minutes

NOTES: Up to 1 day ahead, complete through step 3; cover and chill the bacon, sauce, and peas separately. Serve at room temperature.

MAKES: 10 to 12 servings

- ¼ pound **sliced bacon,** chopped
- 4 teaspoons **sugar**
- 1 tablespoon **cornstarch**
- ¾ cup fat-skimmed **chicken broth**
- ⅔ cup **rice vinegar**
- 2 to 2¼ pounds **sugar snap peas** or Chinese pea pods, rinsed
- 3 tablespoons minced **fresh mint** leaves

**1.** In a 10- to 12-inch frying pan over medium-high heat, stir bacon often until browned; drain on towels. Discard fat in pan and wipe clean.

**2.** In frying pan, mix sugar and cornstarch, then stir in chicken broth and vinegar. Bring to a boil over high heat, stirring often. Use warm or at room temperature.

**3.** Meanwhile, break ends off peas and pull off strings. In a 5- to 6-quart pan over high heat, bring 3 quarts water to a boil. Add peas and cook until tender-crisp, about 1 minute. Drain and immerse in ice water until cold to preserve color. Drain and serve at room temperature.

**4.** Arrange the peas in a bowl. Stir mint into sauce and pour over peas. Sprinkle with bacon.

Per serving: 57 cal., 21% (12 cal.) from fat; 3.1 g protein; 1.3 g fat (0.5 g sat.); 7.5 g carbo (1.9 g fiber); 47 mg sodium; 2.2 mg chol.

## Whole Roasted Onions (1982)

PREP AND COOK TIME: About 1½ hours

NOTES: Roast with the turkey; serve with gravy.

MAKES: 10 to 12 servings

Place 5 or 6 unpeeled **onions** (½ lb. each) in a 9- by 13-inch pan. Bake in a 325° to 350° oven until onions give readily when gently squeezed, about 1½ hours. Lift from pan and cut each onion in half lengthwise. Season to taste with **salt** and **pepper.**

Per serving: 43 cal., 4.2% (1.8 cal.) from fat; 1.3 g protein; 0.2 g fat (0 g sat.); 9.8 g carbo (1.8 g fiber); 3.4 mg sodium; 0 mg chol.

MENU

## Turkey Loco
### for 10 to 12 (1984)

Antojitos Tray *(page 249)* Spanish Peanuts

*Montevina Aleatico 1996 (Amador County) $7.50, 375 ml.*

Turkey Loco *(page 253)*

Chilies with Chorizo Stuffing *(page 257)*

Viva Cranberry *(page 258)*

Balsamic Roasted Onions *(page 261)*

Buttered Hominy *(page 261)*

Sweet Potatoes with Tequila and Lime *(page 263)*

Warm Corn Tortillas

*Hogue Gewürztraminer 1997 (Columbia Valley, Washington) $7, or Hidden Cellars Petite Syrah 1996 (Mendocino) $18*

Crisp Persimmon Pie *(page 264)*

*Chateau St. Jean Johannisberg Riesling "Belle Terre" Special Select Late Harvest 1994 (Alexander Valley) $25, 375 ml.*

## TURKEY LOCO GAME PLAN

☐ **UP TO 1 WEEK AHEAD:**
*Make* Viva Cranberry.

☐ **AT LEAST 3 DAYS AHEAD:**
*Thaw* frozen turkey in refrigerator.

☐ **UP TO 1 DAY AHEAD:**
*Butterfly* turkey. *Stuff* chilies. *Roast* balsamic onions. *Bake* persimmon pie.

☐ **UP TO 4 HOURS AHEAD:**
*Assemble* antojitos tray.

☐ **2 HOURS AND 30 MINUTES AHEAD:**
*Ignite* briquets for charcoal barbecue or,

☐ **2 HOURS AND 20 MINUTES AHEAD:**
*Heat* gas barbecue.

☐ **2 HOURS AHEAD:**
*Arrange* coals for indirect cooking on charcoal barbecue; add briquets now and every 30 minutes. *Adjust* gas for indirect heat. *Rub* turkey with lime and place on grill. *Set* balsamic onions out to warm. *Shred* sweet potatoes.

☐ **1½ HOURS AHEAD:**
*Bake* sweet potatoes. *Open* wines.

☐ **30 MINUTES AHEAD:**
*Transfer* turkey to platter, garnish, and keep warm. *Remove* sweet potatoes from oven and keep warm. *Spoon* Viva Cranberry into bowl.

☐ **25 MINUTES AHEAD:**
*Bake* chilies.

☐ **10 MINUTES AHEAD:**
*Stack* tortillas, wrap in foil, and heat in oven or on covered barbecue. Wrap in a thick towel to keep warm. *Heat* hominy and keep warm. *Return* sweet potatoes to oven with chilies.

☐ **5 MINUTES AHEAD:**
*Transfer* chilies and potatoes to serving dishes; keep warm. *Set out* antojitos tray and peanuts.

## Whole Roasted Bell Peppers (1982)

**PREP AND COOK TIME:** About 1 hour

**NOTES:** Roast with the turkey.

**MAKES:** 10 to 12 servings

Rinse 5 or 6 **red** and/or **yellow bell peppers** (½ lb. each). Cut out stems and remove seeds and pith. Place peppers in a 9- by 13-inch pan. Bake in a 325° to 350° oven until wrinkled and tender when pierced, about 1 hour. Cut in half lengthwise and season with **salt** and **pepper.**

Per serving: 25 cal., 7.2% (1.8 cal.) from fat; 0.8 g protein; 0.2 g fat (0 g sat.); 6 g carbo (1.5 g fiber); 1.9 mg sodium; 0 mg chol.

## POTATOES AND SUCH

## Baked Sweet Potatoes (1982)

**PREP AND COOK TIME:** About 1½ hours

**NOTES:** Roast with the turkey; serve with gravy.

**MAKES:** 10 to 12 servings

Scrub 10 to 12 **sweet potatoes** or yams (1½ to 2 in. thick and about 6 in. long) and pierce in several places with a fork. Place potatoes on oven rack or in a single layer on a baking sheet.

Bake in a 325° to 350° oven until potatoes give readily when gently squeezed, about 1½ hours. Slit open; season to taste with **turkey gravy, butter** or margarine, and **salt** and **pepper.**

Per serving: 172 cal., 2.6% (4.5 cal.) from fat; 2.7 g protein; 0.5 g fat (0.1 g sat.); 40 g carbo (4.9 g fiber); 21 mg sodium; 0 mg chol.

## Thanksgiving Chestnuts (1982)

**PREP AND COOK TIME:** About 1 hour

**NOTES:** For choice of chestnuts, see chestnut soup notes, page 252. The chestnuts roast in the turkey drippings.

**MAKES:** 10 to 12 servings

Place 3 cups **cooked, peeled chestnuts** in pan around Best-ever Roasted Turkey (page 253) during the last hour the turkey roasts. Bake in 325° to 350° oven about 1 hour, turning chestnuts occasionally in juices. With a slotted spoon, transfer to a serving dish. Season to taste with **salt** and **pepper.**

Per serving: 94 cal., 12% (11 cal.) from fat; 1.7 g protein; 1.2 g fat (0.2 g sat.); 19 g carbo (4.2 g fiber); 0.7 mg sodium; 0.4 mg chol.

## Roasted Sweet and White Potatoes with Hazelnuts (1989)

**PREP AND COOK TIME:** 1 hour and 20 minutes

**NOTES:** Up to 4 hours ahead, partially roast potatoes and let stand uncovered.

**MAKES:** 12 cups; 10 to 12 servings

**1.** Rinse and peel 3 pounds **sweet potatoes** or yams and 3 pounds **russet potatoes.** Cut potatoes into 1-inch chunks. Put in a 2-inch-deep 12- by 17-inch pan. Add 12 peeled cloves **garlic** and ¼ cup (⅛ lb.) **butter,** melted, or olive oil.

**Roasted Sweet and White Potatoes with Hazelnuts**

**2.** Bake in a 475° oven for 45 minutes; turn vegetables with a wide spatula every 15 to 20 minutes. Stir in ¾ cup coarsely chopped **hazelnuts.**

**3.** Continue to bake potatoes until very tender when pierced and edges are well browned, about 20 minutes (30 minutes if cool); occasionally turn pieces with wide spatula. Stir in 2 more tablespoons melted butter. Add **salt** to taste.

Per serving: 270 cal., 37% (99 cal.) from fat; 4.5 g protein; 11 g fat (4 g sat.); 40 g carbo (4.8 g fiber); 79 mg sodium; 16 mg chol.

## Sweet Potatoes with Tequila and Lime (1984)

PREP AND COOK TIME: About 1½ hours

NOTES: The original recipe used three times as much butter, but the dish works well with less. If using only one oven for Turkey Loco menu, bake sweet potatoes, keep warm up to 30 minutes, then reheat in a 400° oven for 5 to 10 minutes

MAKES: 10 to 12 servings

5 pounds **sweet potatoes** or yams

½ cup (¼ lb.) **butter** or margarine

¼ cup **sugar**

⅓ cup **tequila** or orange juice

¼ cup **lime juice**

    **Salt** and **pepper**

    **Lime** wedges

**1.** Rinse and peel sweet potatoes. Shred with coarse blade of a food processor or a hand grater.

**2.** Put a 2-inch-deep 12- by 17-inch baking pan in a 475° oven. Add butter, cut into chunks. When butter melts, in about 3 minutes, add sweet potatoes and sugar. Mix well with a wide spatula. Bake, turning occasionally with the spatula (taking care not to mash mixture), until about half the sweet potatoes are browned and remainder are tender to bite, 50 to 60 minutes. Add tequila and lime juice and mix well. Bake 5 minutes more.

**3.** Pour sweet potatoes into a bowl. Season to taste with salt and pepper. Ac-

company with lime wedges to squeeze over potatoes.

Per serving: 244 cal., 30% (73 cal.) from fat; 2.3 g protein; 8.1 g fat (4.9 g sat.); 38 g carbo (4.1 g fiber); 97 mg sodium; 21 mg chol.

## Garlic Mashed Potatoes (1993)

PREP AND COOK TIME: About 55 minutes

NOTES: For a quick version, omit garlic and neufchâtel cheese. Mash potatoes with 2 packages (4 to 5 oz. each) garlic-flavor Boursin, Rondelé, or Alloutte cheese. Up to 1 day ahead, put mashed potatoes in casserole, cool, cover, and chill. Wrap the reserved half-head of garlic airtight and chill. Reheat potatoes, uncovered, in a 375° oven until hot in center, 30 to 40 minutes; after 15 minutes set garlic on potatoes.

MAKES: 10 to 12 servings

3 tablespoons **olive oil**

4 heads **garlic** (12 to 14 oz. total)

6 pounds **Yukon gold** or russet **potatoes**

1½ cups (a 3-oz. and an 8-oz. package) **neufchâtel** (light cream) **cheese** or cream cheese

    About 1 cup fat-skimmed **chicken broth** or milk

    **Salt** and **pepper**

**1.** Pour olive oil into a 9- to 10-inch square pan. Cut garlic heads in half crosswise through cloves and lay cut sides down in pan.

**2.** Bake in a 375° oven until garlic is golden brown on the bottom and oozing sticky juices, about 35 minutes. Slip a thin spatula under garlic to release from pan. Reserve 1 half-head of garlic; pluck or squeeze cloves from remaining garlic.

**3.** Meanwhile, rinse and peel potatoes. Cut into 2-inch chunks. Set on a rack over 1 inch boiling water in a 14-inch wok or a 5- to 6-quart pan. Cover pan and steam over high heat until potatoes mash very easily when pressed, 20 to 25 minutes.

**4.** Transfer potatoes to a large bowl. Add loose garlic cloves and cheese. With a potato masher or mixer, mash potatoes, adding enough broth to make them as soft and creamy as you like. (If you plan to serve potatoes as soon as they are mashed, heat broth before adding.) Season to taste with salt and swirl into a shallow 2½- to 3-quart casserole.

**5.** Serve garnished with reserved roasted garlic. Sprinkle with pepper.

Per serving: 302 cal., 30% (90 cal.) from fat; 8.7 g protein; 10 g fat (4.3 g sat.); 46 g carbo (3.9 g fiber); 130 mg sodium; 20 mg chol.

## DESSERTS

## Cranberry Linzer Torte (1987)

PREP AND COOK TIME: About 1½ hours, plus at least 2 hours to cool

NOTES: Up to 1 day ahead, bake and cool torte, then wrap airtight and hold at room temperature.

MAKES: 10 to 12 servings

- 3 cups (12-oz. package) **fresh** or thawed frozen **cranberries**
- 1 cup **sugar**
- 1 tablespoon grated **orange** peel
- **Linzer crust** (recipe follows)

**1.** Sort cranberries and discard any soft or decayed fruit. Rinse berries.

**2.** In a 2- to 2½-quart pan over high heat, stir cranberries, ¼ cup water, sugar, and peel until boiling. Boil, stirring often, until mixture has the consistency of soft jam, about 4 minutes. Let cool about 15 minutes, stirring occasionally.

**3.** Pour cranberry mixture into crust. Break reserved dough into almond-size lumps and scatter over filling.

**4.** Bake on the lowest rack in a 350° oven until crust is richly browned at edges, about 1 hour. Serve cool.

Per serving: 412 cal., 48% (198 cal.) from fat; 4.6 g protein; 22 g fat (10 g sat.); 52 g carbo (2.8 g fiber); 160 mg sodium; 77 mg chol.

***Linzer crust.*** In a food processor or blender, finely grind 1 cup **almonds.** If using a blender, pour ground nuts into a bowl. To almonds, add 1½ cups **all-purpose flour,** 1 cup (½ lb.) **butter** or margarine, 1 cup **sugar,** 2 **large egg** yolks, 1 tablespoon grated **orange** peel, 1 tablespoon **unsweetened cocoa,** 2 teaspoons **ground cinnamon,** and ½ teaspoon **ground cloves.** Whirl in food processor or rub with your fingers until dough holds together. Pack into a firm ball, then pinch off and reserve ½ cup dough. Firmly press remaining dough evenly over bottom and 1½ inches up sides of a 9-inch cake pan with removable rim.

## Crisp Persimmon Pie (1981)

PREP AND COOK TIME: About 1¼ hours, plus at least 3 hours to cool

NOTES: Two pies will serve 10 to 12 with leftovers. Up to 1 day ahead, wrap cool pie airtight and hold at room temperature. Serve with ice cream such as eggnog or vanilla, plain or with toffee bits.

MAKES: 8 or 9 servings

- 2½ pounds **firm-ripe Fuyu persimmons**
- ⅓ cup **granulated sugar**
- ⅓ cup firmly packed **brown sugar**
- 2½ tablespoons **quick-cooking tapioca**
- 1 teaspoon **ground cinnamon**
- ½ teaspoon grated **orange** peel
- ½ teaspoon grated **lemon** peel
- 3 tablespoons **lemon juice**
  **Refrigerated pastry for a double-crust 9-inch pie** (15-oz. package), at room temperature
- 1 tablespoon **butter** or margarine, cut into small pieces

**1.** Rinse Fuyu persimmons. Trim and discard stem ends. Slice persimmons crosswise into thin rounds; you should have 8 cups.

**2.** In a large bowl, combine persimmons, granulated sugar, brown sugar, tapioca, cinnamon, orange peel, lemon peel, and lemon juice; stir gently to blend.

**3.** Fit 1 pastry round into a 9-inch pie pan. Pour in persimmon mixture and dot with butter.

**4.** Lay remaining pastry round over fruit. Fold pastry edges together and crimp to seal. Cut decorative slits in top pastry.

**5.** Bake on the lowest rack in a 375° oven until juices bubble in center of pie and pastry is well browned, about 1 hour. If pastry edges brown before pie is done, drape dark areas with foil. Cool pie on a rack. Serve at room temperature.

Per serving: 424 cal., 32% (135 cal.) from fat; 2.5 g protein; 15 g fat (6 g sat.); 74 g carbo (0 g fiber); 268 mg sodium; 16 mg chol.

## Marbled Pumpkin Cheesecake (1979/1996)

PREP AND COOK TIME: About 1 hour and 20 minutes, plus 2½ hours to cool

NOTES: Up to 2 days ahead, cover cool cheesecake and chill. Serve with sweet-ened softly whipped cream flavored to taste with Chinese five spice seasoning or chopped crystallized ginger.

MAKES: 10 to 12 servings

- About 8 ounces **gingersnap cookies**
- 2 tablespoons **granulated sugar**
- 3 tablespoons melted **butter** or margarine
- 2 packages (8 oz. each) **neufchâtel** (light cream) **cheese** or cream cheese
- ¾ cup firmly packed **brown sugar**
- 2 **large eggs**
- 1½ teaspoons **Chinese five spice seasoning** or pumpkin pie spice
- 1 can (1 lb.) **pumpkin**

**1.** Crush enough cookies to make 1¾ cups crumbs. In a 9-inch cheesecake pan with removable rim, mix cookie crumbs, granulated sugar, and butter. Press over bottom and about 1 inch up pan sides.

**2.** Bake crust in a 325° oven until slightly browner, about 15 minutes.

**3.** Meanwhile, in a food processor or in a bowl with a mixer, blend cheese, brown sugar, and eggs until smooth. Spoon ½ cup of the cheese mixture into a small bowl. Add five spice and pumpkin to remaining cheese mixture and mix well.

**4.** Pour pumpkin filling into hot or cool crust. Drop rounded tablespoons of the reserved cheese mixture onto the pumpkin filling. With a knife tip, swirl to marble the white and orange mixtures.

**5.** Bake in a 325° oven until the center barely jiggles when cake is gently shaken, about 50 minutes. Cool on a rack. Cover and chill until cold, at least 2½ hours or up to 1 day. Run a knife between cake and pan rim; remove rim.

Per serving: 288 cal., 47% (135 cal.) from fat; 6.3 g protein; 15 g fat (8 g sat.); 34 g carbo (1.2 g fiber); 322 mg sodium; 72 mg chol.

## Ginger-Caramel Macadamia Tart (1992)

PREP AND COOK TIME: About 1 hour

NOTES: Up to 1 day ahead, wrap cool tart airtight and chill. Cover chocolate sauce and chill; reheat to serve.

MAKES: 10 to 12 servings

**Butter pastry** (recipe follows)

3 **large eggs**

1 cup firmly packed **brown sugar**

½ cup minced **crystallized ginger**

1 tablespoon minced **fresh ginger**

1 teaspoon **vanilla**

3 cups **salted, roasted macadamia nuts**

**Warm chocolate sauce** (recipe follows)

**Vanilla ice cream** or sweetened whipped cream (optional)

**1.** Press butter pastry evenly over bottom and up sides of an 11-inch plain or fluted tart pan with removable rim.

**2.** Bake in a 300° oven until pale gold, 12 to 15 minutes. Use hot or cool.

**3.** Meanwhile, in a bowl, beat to blend eggs, sugar, crystallized ginger, fresh ginger, and vanilla.

**4.** Rub macadamia nuts in a towel to remove excess salt. Lift nuts from towel and put in bowl. Mix and pour into pastry.

**5.** Bake on lowest rack in a 350° oven until top is golden and filling set when pie is gently shaken, 35 to 40 minutes. Cool tart on a rack. Remove pan rim and cut tart into wedges. Spoon warm chocolate sauce onto portions and accompany with ice cream.

Per serving: 618 cal., 61% (378 cal.) from fat; 7.4 g protein; 42 g fat (13 g sat.); 61 g carbo (0.7 g fiber); 262 mg sodium; 97 mg chol.

*Butter pastry*. In a food processor or a bowl, combine 1⅓ cups **all-purpose flour** and ¼ cup **sugar**. Add ½ cup (¼ lb.) **butter** or margarine, in chunks, and whirl or rub with your fingers until fine crumbs form. Add 1 **large egg** yolk; whirl or mix with a fork until dough holds together.

*Warm chocolate sauce*. In a microwave-safe bowl or a 1- to 1½-quart pan, melt 1½ cups **semisweet chocolate chips** with ¾ cup **half-and-half** (light cream) or milk in a microwave oven or over low heat, stirring often until smooth. Serve warm. Makes about 2 cups.

## Chestnut Tiramisu (1993)

**PREP TIME:** 35 to 40 minutes

**NOTES:** Up to 1 day ahead, separately wrap orange slices and dessert airtight, without touching the dessert top; chill.

Marbled Pumpkin Cheesecake

Uncover and decorate with fruit.

**MAKES:** 10 to 12 servings

12 ounces **ladyfingers** or pound cake

1 can (17½ oz., 1½ cups) **sweetened chestnut spread**

2 tablespoons **rum** or orange juice

**Orange syrup** (recipe follows)

1 cup **whipping cream**

2 cups **plain nonfat yogurt** or regular sour cream

2 to 4 ounces **semisweet chocolate**

3 or 4 thin round peeled **orange** slices

**1.** Separate ladyfingers (or thinly slice cake) and lay pieces side by side (or overlap, as needed) to cover a 14- to 15-inch-wide rimmed platter or very shallow bowl; leave a 1-inch rim.

**2.** Mix chestnut spread with rum and 2 tablespoons of the orange syrup. Pour remaining syrup over ladyfingers to moisten evenly. Gently spread chestnut mixture over ladyfingers, leaving 1 inch at rim of the cookies uncovered.

**3.** In a bowl with a mixer on high speed, beat whipping cream until it holds distinct peaks; whisk in the yogurt. Swirl over chestnut spread and most of the exposed ladyfinger rim.

**4.** Pare chocolate with a vegetable peeler to make curls, or finely chop with a knife or in a food processor. Scatter chocolate over tiramisu. Top chocolate with orange slices. Scoop portions with a spoon.

Per serving: 298 cal., 30% (90 cal.) from fat; 5.8 g protein; 10 g fat (5.5 g sat.); 41 g carbo (1.8 g fiber); 78 mg sodium; 126 mg chol.

*Orange syrup*. In a 1- to 1½-quart pan over high heat, boil 1 cup **water**, ½ cup **sugar**, and 1 tablespoon finely shredded **orange** peel until reduced to ¾ cup. Let cool slightly and add ¼ cup **rum** or orange juice. Use hot or cool. ◆

## Hickory perfumes
## Western barbecue classic

# Smoked Turkey

BY ANDREW BAKER • PHOTOGRAPHS BY JAMES CARRIER

■ When it comes to turkey, where there's smoke, there's flavor. But unlike birds smoked the slow traditional way, this magnificent barbecued turkey picks up a sweet, smoky taste and a rich, dark color in short order. The secret is a seasoned brine. Resting a couple of hours in a salt-and-sugar liquid results in an exceptionally moist and succulent bird. The brine also attracts the delicate, not the bitter, flavors of smoldering wood chips.

Barbecuing has other benefits, too. The bird browns beautifully, and the thigh joint, which tends to stay pink in oven-roasted birds, cooks through. (The pink just beneath the turkey skin is a natural result when brined meats are smoked.)

Through the years, cooking turkey on the barbecue has been a favorite *Sunset* technique—it frees up the oven, not only at Thanksgiving but for any season or occasion.

For a meal to match this handsome, plump bird, turn to page 248 for menu suggestions and all-time favorite *Sunset* holiday recipes.

AROMATIC
FRESH BAY
leaves and
steamed baby
squash surround
juicy, lightly
smoked turkey.

## Hot-smoked Hickory Turkey

PREP AND COOK TIME: 2 hours to brine, plus 2 to 3 hours to cook, depending on size of bird

NOTES: You can brine the bird the day before, then rinse well, cover, and refrigerate until time to cook. Hickory wood chips are sold beside charcoal briquets in markets and hardware stores.

MAKES: Allow ¾ pound uncooked turkey per person, more for leftovers

- 1 **turkey** (15 to 20 lb.)
- 1 cup firmly packed **brown sugar**
- ¾ cup **salt**
- 1 tablespoon minced **garlic**
- 1 teaspoon **black peppercorns**
- 2 **dried bay leaves**
- 2 to 3 cups **hickory wood chips**

**1.** Remove and discard leg truss from turkey. Pull off and discard lumps of fat. Remove giblets and neck (reserve for other uses). Rinse bird well.

**2.** In a bowl or pan (at least 12 to 14 qt.), combine 3 quarts water, brown sugar, salt, garlic, peppercorns, and bay leaves. Stir until sugar and salt are dissolved. Add turkey, cover, and chill for 2 hours, turning bird over occasionally.

**3.** In a bowl, combine wood chips and 2 to 3 quarts hot water.

**4.** Lift turkey from brine and rinse thoroughly under cold running water, rubbing gently to release salt; pat dry with towels. Discard brine. Insert a meat thermometer straight down through the thickest part of the turkey breast to the bone.

**5.** *On a charcoal barbecue* (20 to 22 in. wide) with a lid, mound and ignite 40 charcoal briquets on firegrate. When coals are spotted with gray ash, in about 20 minutes, push equal portions to opposite sides of firegrate. Place a foil drip pan between mounds of coals. To each mound, add 5 briquets and ½ cup drained soaked wood chips now and every 30 minutes (until all chips are used). Set grill in place. Set turkey, breast up, on grill over drip pan. Cover barbecue and open vents.

*On a gas barbecue* (with at least 11 in. between indirect-heat burners), place 1 cup drained soaked wood chips in the metal smoking box or in a foil pan directly on heat in a corner. Turn heat to high, close lid, and heat for about 10 minutes. Adjust gas for indirect cooking (heat parallel to sides of bird and not beneath) and set a metal or foil drip pan in center (not over direct heat). Set grill in place. Set turkey, breast up, on grill over drip pan. Close barbecue lid. Add another cup of wood chips (sprinkle through or lift grill) every 30 minutes until all are used. If edges of turkey close to heat begin to get too dark, slide folded strips of foil between bird and grill. Fat in drippings may flare when barbecue lid is opened; quench by pouring a little water into the pan.

**6.** Cook turkey until thermometer registers 160°, in 2 to 3 hours; start checking after 1 hour.

**7.** Drain juices from cavity into drippings and reserve for other uses. Transfer turkey to a large platter; let rest 15 to 30 minutes before carving.

Per ¼ pound boned cooked turkey with skin, based on percentages of white and dark meat in an average bird: 232 cal., 39% (90 cal.) from fat; 32 g protein; 10 g fat (3 g sat.); 0.7 g carbo (0 g fiber); 315 mg sodium; 93 mg chol. ◆

BRINING: Chill turkey in seasoned brine; turn bird over several times.

SMOKING: Smoldering wood chips flavor turkey as it cooks on covered grill.

# The Quick Cook

## MEALS IN 30 MINUTES OR LESS
### BY ANDREW BAKER

### WHAT'S FOR DINNER
Pilaf with Baked Eggs

Arugula with Balsamic Vinaigrette

Biscotti      Espresso

## Going with the grain

■ Grains in minutes? The smallest ones just naturally cook fast. Others may be specially treated in processing to make them speedy.

Bulgur (cracked) wheat is steamed when processed. It gets soft enough to eat when soaked but stays chewy when cooked.

Quinoa (pronounced *keen*-wah), a fine, round, high-protein grain, is native to the Andes and was prized by ancient farmers because it grows at high altitudes. It has a slightly bitter natural coating that needs to be rinsed off.

Barley labeled quick-cooking has had its outer hull removed so that moisture penetrates faster.

Quick-cooking brown rice has been cooked and dried, and needs to be rehydrated. It's ready to eat in three-quarters the time it takes to cook regular brown rice.

### Pilaf with Baked Eggs

PREP AND COOK TIME: About 30 minutes

NOTES: For an interesting grain mix, combine equal parts quick-cooking barley, quick-cooking brown rice, bulgur, and rinsed quinoa.

MAKES: 4 servings

- 1 tablespoon **butter** or margarine
- 2/3 cup finely chopped **shallots**
- 1 1/3 cups **grain mix** or any individual quick-cooking grain (see notes)
- 2 cups fat-skimmed **chicken broth**
- 3/4 teaspoon **dried marjoram**
- 1 cup (1/4 lb.) **shredded Swiss cheese**
- 4 **large eggs**

  About 1/2 cup 1/4-inch-thick **Roma tomato** slices

**1.** In a 10- to 12-inch ovenproof frying pan over high heat, stir butter and shallots often until shallots are lightly browned, about 3 minutes.

**2.** Add grain mix; stir until grains are lightly toasted, about 2 minutes. Add broth and marjoram, stir, and bring to a boil. Cover, reduce heat, and simmer until grains are tender to bite, about 12 minutes; stir pilaf occasionally.

**3.** Mix 1/2 cup cheese with pilaf. Using the back of a spoon, make 4 deep wells in mixture. Slide 1 egg into each well. Lay tomato slices around eggs.

**4.** Bake in a 400° oven until egg whites are opaque and yolks are desired texture, 8 minutes for liquid yolks. About 3 minutes before eggs are cooked, sprinkle mixture with remaining cheese.

**5.** Use a wide spatula to scoop under pilaf and lift out eggs, 1 at a time. Put portions on plates.

Per serving: 413 cal., 37% (153 cal.) from fat; 24 g protein; 17 g fat (8.5 g sat.); 42 g carbo (6.1 g fiber); 223 mg sodium; 246 mg chol.

## 3 More Quick Grain Recipes

**Lamb Soup.** In a 4- to 5-quart pan over high heat, stir 1 pound **ground lean lamb,** 1 cup chopped **onion,** and 1 cup chopped **carrots** until lamb is well browned, 8 to 10 minutes. Spoon off and discard any fat. Add 1 1/3 cups **grain mix** (see notes, left), 5 1/2 cups fat-skimmed **beef broth,** and 1 cup **dry sherry.** Bring to a boil, cover, reduce heat, and simmer until grains are tender to bite, about 12 minutes. Stir in 1/4 cup chopped **parsley.** Makes about 9 cups; 4 servings.

Per serving: 521 cal., 29% (153 cal.) from fat; 32 g protein; 17 g fat (6.5 g sat.); 44 g carbo (7.5 g fiber); 194 mg sodium; 76 mg chol.

**Shrimp Tumble with Lettuce.** In a 10- to 12-inch frying pan over high heat, combine 1 1/3 cups **grain mix** (see notes, left) and 2 cups fat-skimmed **chicken broth.** Bring to a boil. Cover, reduce heat, and simmer until grains are tender to bite, about 12 minutes, stirring occasionally. Meanwhile, rinse and finely chop 1/2 pound **shelled cooked tiny shrimp.** Stir shrimp, 1/2 cup minced **green onions,** 2 tablespoons **oyster sauce,** and 1 tablespoon minced **fresh ginger** into grains. Spoon into 8 rinsed and crisped large **iceberg lettuce** leaves (about 1/2 lb. total). Roll to eat. Makes 4 servings.

Per serving: 263 cal., 7.6% (20 cal.) from fat; 23 g protein; 2.2 g fat (0.3 g sat.); 39 g carbo (6.5 g fiber); 543 mg sodium; 111 mg chol.

**Sausage Pilaf.** In a 10- to 12-inch frying pan over high heat, frequently turn 3 or 4 **cooked sausages** (about 14 oz. total) until lightly browned. Set aside. Add to pan 1 1/3 cups **grain mix** (see notes, left), 2 cups fat-skimmed **chicken broth,** and 1/2 cup minced **parsley.** Bring to a boil. Cover, reduce heat, and simmer about 8 minutes, stirring occasionally. Push sausages down into grains, cover, and continue simmering until liquid is absorbed and grains are tender to bite, about 5 minutes more; stir occasionally. Sprinkle with about 2 tablespoons **shredded parmesan cheese** and fresh-ground **pepper** to taste. Makes 3 or 4 servings.

Per serving: 562 cal., 53% (297 cal.) from fat; 30 g protein; 33 g fat (11 g sat.); 36 g carbo (5.9 g fiber); 1,385 mg sodium; 84 mg chol. ◆

# Kitchen Cabinet

## READERS' RECIPES TESTED IN SUNSET'S KITCHENS
### BY LINDA LAU ANUSASANANAN

IT LOOKS—and tastes—like pumpkin pie, but it stars carrots.

JULIE TOY

Per serving: 264 cal., 38% (99 cal.) from fat; 5.8 g protein; 11 g fat (4.9 g sat.); 37 g carbo (2 g fiber); 329 mg sodium; 66 mg chol.

## Armenian Fruit and Nut Pilaf

Christine Vartanian Datian, Las Vegas

From her Armenian mother and grandmother, Christine Vartanian Datian learned how to prepare this festive nut- and fruit-topped pilaf. This family favorite is in demand, especially during the holidays.

PREP AND COOK TIME: About 25 minutes
MAKES: 8 servings

- 5 tablespoons **butter** or margarine
- 3 ounces **dried angel hair pasta**
- 2 cups **long-grain white rice**
- 1 quart fat-skimmed **chicken broth**
- $\frac{1}{2}$ teaspoon **ground allspice**
- $\frac{1}{4}$ teaspoon **white pepper**
- $\frac{3}{4}$ cup coarsely chopped **almonds**
- $\frac{3}{4}$ cup coarsely chopped **golden raisins**
- $\frac{3}{4}$ cup **frozen petite peas**
- 2 tablespoons chopped **parsley**
- 1 teaspoon **lemon juice**

**1.** In a 5- to 6-quart pan over medium heat, melt 4 tablespoons butter. Break pasta into 1-inch lengths. Add pasta and rice to butter and stir often until golden, about 8 minutes.

**2.** Add broth, allspice, and pepper. Bring to a boil over high heat, then cover, reduce heat to low, and simmer until rice is tender to bite, 15 to 20 minutes; stir occasionally.

**3.** Meanwhile, in an 8- to 10-inch frying pan over medium heat, melt remaining 1 tablespoon butter. Add almonds and stir often until golden, about 5 minutes. Add raisins and stir until they puff, about 2 minutes. Remove from heat.

**4.** Stir peas, parsley, and lemon juice into rice. Cover and simmer until peas are hot, about 3 minutes. Pour into a serving bowl and sprinkle with nut and raisin mixture.

Per serving: 415 cal., 30% (126 cal.) from fat; 12 g protein; 14 g fat (5.2 g sat.); 61 g carbo (3.9 g fiber); 141 mg sodium; 19 mg chol.

## Joy's Creamy Carrot Pie

Joy Taylor, Sylmar, California

When friends gave Joy Taylor a huge bag of homegrown carrots, she was stumped as to how to use them creatively. Her husband suggested trying a carrot dessert. The result was this pumpkin pie taste- and look-alike.

PREP AND COOK TIME: About 1¼ hours
MAKES: One 9-inch pie; 8 or 9 servings

- 1¼ pounds **carrots**
- 1 **refrigerated pastry for single-crust 9-inch pie** (half of a 15-oz. package), at room temperature
- 1 can (12 oz.) **evaporated milk**
- $\frac{1}{2}$ cup **honey**
- 2 **large eggs**
- 1 teaspoon **ground cinnamon**
- $\frac{1}{2}$ teaspoon **ground ginger**
- $\frac{1}{2}$ teaspoon **salt**
- $\frac{1}{4}$ teaspoon **ground cloves**

**1.** In a 3- to 4-quart pan over high heat, bring about 1 quart water to a boil. Peel carrots, cut into ½-inch slices, and add to water. Cover and return to a boil, then reduce heat and simmer until carrots are tender when pierced, 10 to 12 minutes. Drain.

**2.** Meanwhile, gently fit pastry into a 1½-inch-deep, 9-inch pie pan. Fold under any excess pastry at rim and decoratively flute edge. Prick pastry with a fork several times. Bake on the bottom rack of a 350° oven until pastry is golden, 13 to 15 minutes.

**3.** Mash cooked carrots and measure 1½ cups. Reserve any extra carrots for another use.

**4.** In a blender, combine the 1½ cups carrots, milk, honey, eggs, cinnamon, ginger, salt, and cloves; whirl until very smooth.

**5.** Set pie pan on a foil-lined baking sheet on bottom rack of oven. Carefully pour carrot mixture into pastry. Bake until filling barely jiggles in the center when pie is gently shaken, 50 to 55 minutes. If crust rim starts to get too dark, drape affected areas with foil.

**6.** Cool pie on rack at least 1 hour. Serve warm or cool. If making up to 1 day ahead, cover and chill.

## Curried Joes

Maureen Valentine,
Normandy Park, Washington

Maureen Valentine likes to update old favorites. With curry and vegetables, she brightens and lightens that enduring cafeteria sandwich, the sloppy joe. The result is comfort food with a fresh perspective.

PREP AND COOK TIME: 30 minutes

MAKES: 6 sandwiches; 3 or 6 servings

- 1 pound **ground lean turkey** or ground lean beef
- 1 **onion** (6 oz.), peeled and chopped
- 1 **red bell pepper** (6 oz.), stemmed, seeded, and chopped
- 1 teaspoon **curry powder**
- ½ teaspoon **ground coriander**
- ½ teaspoon **ground ginger**
- ½ teaspoon **dried tarragon**
- 1 can (8 oz.) **tomato sauce**
- 2 tablespoons **apricot jam** or orange marmalade
  **Salt** and **pepper**
- 3 **pocket breads** (7 in.)
- 3 cups (3 oz.) **baby spinach leaves**, rinsed and crisped
  **Plain nonfat yogurt** (optional)

**1.** In an 11- to 12-inch nonstick frying pan over high heat, crumble turkey with a spoon and stir often until lightly browned, about 4 minutes. With a slotted spoon, transfer meat to a bowl. Discard fat in pan.

**2.** Add onion and bell pepper to the pan. Stir over high heat until the onion begins to brown, about 4 minutes. Reduce heat to low. Add curry powder, coriander, ginger, and tarragon, stirring until the spices are fragrant, about 30 seconds. Stir in tomato sauce, apricot jam, and turkey with its juices. Stir often until hot, about 2 minutes. Add salt and pepper to taste. Spoon into a bowl.

**3.** Cut pocket breads in half crosswise and fill each half equally with the turkey mixture and spinach. Add yogurt to taste.

Per piece: 259 cal., 29% (74 cal.) from fat; 18 g protein; 8.2 g fat (2.1 g sat.); 29 g carbo (2.4 g fiber); 451 mg sodium; 38 mg chol.

CHEESE-CRUSTED yeast rolls are intensely perfumed by garlic.

## Easy Cheese-Garlic Rolls

Lynn Evans, Anza, California

In lieu of garlic bread, Lynn Evans invented these garlic rolls using dough made in her bread machine. The rolls are so popular, they often disappear before the meal begins.

PREP AND COOK TIME: 40 minutes, plus at least 25 minutes to rise

MAKES: 16 rolls

- 6 tablespoons **butter** or margarine, at room temperature
- ⅓ cup chopped **garlic**
- ¼ cup grated **parmesan cheese**
- 1 pound (1 loaf) thawed **frozen white** or whole-wheat **bread dough** or homemade bread dough
- ⅔ cup shredded **longhorn cheddar** or sharp cheddar **cheese**

**1.** Mix butter, garlic, and 2 tablespoons parmesan cheese.

**2.** On a lightly floured board, pat, roll, and stretch dough into a 12- by 16-inch rectangle. If dough springs back, let rest a few minutes, then continue to shape.

**3.** Spread garlic-butter mixture evenly over dough. Sprinkle with ⅓ cup cheddar cheese.

**4.** From a 16-inch edge, roll dough to enclose filling. Cut log of dough crosswise into 16 equal rolls.

**5.** Setting on cut sides, evenly space rolls in a buttered 9- by 13-inch pan.

**6.** Cover pan lightly with plastic wrap. Let rolls rise in a warm place until almost doubled in size, 25 to 35 minutes. Remove wrap; sprinkle rolls with remaining parmesan and cheddar cheeses.

**7.** Bake in a 350° oven until golden brown, 30 to 35 minutes. Let cool in pan on a rack about 5 minutes. With a wide spatula, lift rolls from pan and serve warm or cool.

Per roll: 144 cal., 48% (69 cal.) from fat; 4.1 g protein; 7.7 g fat (4.2 g sat.); 15 g carbo (0.6 g fiber); 234 mg sodium; 19 mg chol.

## Liz's Spicy Ribs

Liz Patrick, Eureka, California

Inspired by a succulent dish of pork ribs cooked San Salvadoran–style by a friend, Liz Patrick experimented and created her own mildly spicy version. There is plenty of sauce to spoon over rice.

PREP AND COOK TIME: About 2¾ hours

MAKES: 8 servings

- 3 pounds **country-style pork ribs,** surface fat trimmed off
- 1 tablespoon **salad oil**
- 3 **onions** (6 oz. each), chopped
- 1 **bell pepper** (½ lb.), stemmed, seeded, and chopped
- 5 cloves **garlic,** pressed or minced
- 1 can (15 oz.) **diced tomatoes**
- 1 can (4 oz.) **diced green chilies**
- 1 cup **thick, chunky salsa**
- 1 teaspoon **hot chili flakes**
- ½ teaspoon **pepper**
  **Salt**

**1.** Wipe off pork with a damp cloth. Pour oil into a 2-inch-deep, 12-inch frying pan or a 5- to 6-quart pan and set over high heat. When oil is hot, fill pan with a single layer of pork and brown well on all sides, 8 to 10 minutes. Lift out pork as browned, place in a bowl, and add more meat to pan. When all the meat is browned and in the bowl, discard all but 1 tablespoon fat from pan.

**2.** Add onions, bell pepper, and garlic to pan. Stir often until onions are lightly browned, about 8 minutes. Stir in tomatoes (including juices), green chilies, salsa, hot chili flakes, and pepper.

**3.** Return pork and accumulated juices to pan, pushing meat down into sauce. Bring to a boil, then reduce heat to low, cover, and simmer until pork is tender when pierced, 1½ to 2 hours, stirring occasionally. If sauce begins to stick, stir in a little water.

**4.** With a slotted spoon, transfer pork to a wide bowl. Skim off and discard any fat from sauce. Pour sauce over meat. Add salt to taste.

Per serving: 223 cal., 40% (89 cal.) from fat; 20 g protein; 9.9 g fat (3 g sat.); 13 g carbo (2.1 g fiber); 560 mg sodium; 61 mg chol. ◆

JULIE TOY

California winemakers share some of their favorite holiday appetizers in this month's Kitchen Cabinet (see page 308).

JAMES CARRIER

272

# December

# food guide

BY JERRY ANNE DI VECCHIO

## A TASTE OF THE WEST

# Carols and crab

A holiday supper that crackles with flavor

■ Once upon a time, Dungeness crab had a season—winter. And in the face of emergency, it became our habit for Christmas Eve supper. With gifts yet to wrap, we stopped at the fish stand north of town seeking a primitive form of HMR (home-meal replacement) just as a big basket of red-shelled Dungeness crab was being hauled out of a deep vat of boiling water. Our menu was clinched, requiring only one more quick stop, at the Italian bakery on Main Street for a loaf of sourdough.

Now, with live tanks for Alaskan crustaceans, Dungeness is available year-round. But it's still our Christmas Eve tradition—plain, as cioppino, or warmed up in this steamy, fragrant broth.

JAMES CARRIER (3)

**DELICATELY AROMATIC SAUCE** clings lightly to Dungeness crab, letting the sweet, fresh flavor of this fine shellfish shine through.

## Vermouth Crab

**PREP AND COOK TIME:** 15 minutes

**NOTES:** For convenience, have the crab cleaned and cracked at the market.

**MAKES:** 4 or 5 servings

- 2 tablespoons **cornstarch**
- 2 cups fat-skimmed **chicken broth**
- 1¼ cups **dry vermouth**
- 1 tablespoon **soy sauce**
- 1 tablespoon chopped **fresh ginger**
- 1 teaspoon grated **lemon** peel
- 2 tablespoons **lemon juice**
- ½ teaspoon **dried thyme**
- 2 cooked **Dungeness crab** (about 2 lb. each), cleaned and cracked
- ¼ cup chopped **parsley**

**1.** In a 5- to 6-quart pan, mix cornstarch with a little of the broth. Then add remaining broth, vermouth, soy sauce, ginger, lemon peel, lemon juice, and thyme.

**2.** Stirring often, bring the broth mixture to a boil over high heat. Add crab, reduce heat, and simmer, continuing to stir often, until crab is hot, about 5 minutes. Sprinkle with parsley.

**3.** Ladle crab and broth equally into wide bowls.

Per serving: 181 cal., 7.7% (14 cal.) from fat; 21 g protein; 1.6 g fat (0.2 g sat.); 4.7 g carbo (0.2 g fiber); 484 mg sodium; 87 mg chol.

# Try tubes of tubers

■ *Sunset* food writer Andrew Baker is an avid collector of kitchen tools. He justifies his expensive interest by constantly devising new functions for old gadgets. Recently, Andrew discovered a speedy way to make crisp potato tubes and cones by baking thin slices wrapped around metal pastry forms such as cannoli tubes. You can salt and serve the potatoes like fancy chips, scooping them gently through a dip (they're fragile), or tilt them on a dinner plate as an unexpected garnish. After all, potatoes do go with almost everything.

## Potato Cannoli

PREP AND COOK TIME: About 15 minutes per potato

MAKES: 15 to 20 pieces

**1.** Cut an 8- to 10-ounce (6- to 8-in.-long) peeled **potato** in half lengthwise. From the center of the potato, cut even, full-length $\frac{1}{16}$-inch or thinner slices on an Asian slicer or mandoline. You should get 15 to 20 full-size slices. Reserve extra potato for other uses.

**2.** Wrap each potato slice around a buttered cannoli tube (about 1 in. wide) or the tip of a metal pastry cone. Set, seam down, on a buttered baking sheet. Brush each slice lightly with melted **butter** or margarine (about $\frac{1}{2}$ teaspoon per slice).

**3.** Bake in a 400° oven until browned, 7 to 8 minutes. Let stand until metal forms are cool enough to touch, then gently twist and slide potatoes off forms. If making ahead, seal airtight and keep at room temperature up to 1 week.

Per piece: 32 cal., 75% (24 cal.) from fat; 0.2 g protein; 2.7 g fat (1.7 g sat.); 1.8 g carbo (0.2 g fiber); 28 mg sodium; 7.2 mg chol.

---

PRESERVING TRADITION

# A cure for kumquats

■ Preserving lemons with salt, a common practice in the Middle East and North Africa, makes them a powerful seasoning agent. Treated the same, little orange kumquats undergo a similar metamorphosis. They also become particularly attractive, making a tasteful gift. Use them in any recipe that calls for preserved lemon, or in the simple red pepper relish at right, to serve with chicken, pork, beef, lamb, fish—or salad.

## Preserved Kumquats

PREP TIME: About 15 minutes to assemble, about 2 days to develop flavor

Rinse 1 pound (about 3 cups) **kumquats.** On 1 side, slit each lengthwise to the center. Put in a $3\frac{1}{2}$- to 4-cup jar with 2 to 3 tablespoons drained **large capers.** Add $\frac{1}{4}$ cup **kosher salt.**

Cover airtight and freeze at least 8 hours. Place jar upside down in the refrigerator and let stand 24 hours. Use, or chill up to 1 month, turning jar over every 2 or 3 days to keep salt distributed. MAKES: About 3 cups.

Per kumquat: 6.2 cal., 0% (0 cal.) from fat; 0.1 g protein; 0 g fat; 1.6 g carbo (0 g fiber); 108 mg sodium; 0 mg chol.

## Kumquat–Red Pepper Relish

PREP TIME: 5 to 10 minutes

Rinse 4 preserved **kumquats** (preceding) with 3 or 4 **capers.** Coarsely chop kumquats, discarding seeds. Drain and chop 1 jar (7 to 8 oz.) **peeled roasted red peppers.** Mince 1 clove **garlic.** In a bowl, mix kumquats and capers with peppers, garlic, $\frac{3}{4}$ teaspoon **ground cumin,** and $\frac{1}{4}$ teaspoon **pepper.** Serve, or cover and chill up to 2 days. MAKES: $\frac{3}{4}$ cup.

Per tablespoon: 6.9 cal., 0% (0 cal.) from fat; 0.1 g protein; 0 g fat; 1.9 g carbo (0.1 g fiber); 59 mg sodium; 0 mg chol.

## Spinach Salad with Preserved Kumquat Relish

PREP TIME: About 10 minutes

In a wide bowl, combine 6 cups **washed baby spinach leaves,** $\frac{1}{4}$ cup chopped **fresh cilantro,** 2 tablespoons **lemon juice,** 1 tablespoon **olive oil,** and 1 recipe's worth of **kumquat–red pepper relish** (preceding). MAKES: 6 to 8 servings.

Per serving: 35 cal., 49% (17 cal.) from fat; 1.3 g protein; 1.9 g fat (0.2 g sat.); 4.5 g carbo (1.3 g fiber); 123 mg sodium; 0 mg chol.

# The Midas touch

Gold-frosted chocolate leaves
dress up holiday desserts

■ In India, ethereal wisps of real gold and silver have decorated desserts since ancient times. Impossibly thin flecks of gold float in every glass of the German liqueur Goldwasser. And a few chocolate makers here in the West brush streaks of gold dust onto elegant confections. Although the FDA has not approved gold or silver as a food, nontoxic forms are available in a few specialty food, cookware, and baking supply shops. And you can order edible "lustre dust" in metallic colors from Sur La Table's catalog service; (800) 243-0852. (The dust costs $3.95 for 0.7 oz.; it goes a long way.)

Gold and silver don't make any flavor impression. But a gold-frosted leaf can turn a simple scoop of ice cream into an event. For even more drama, arrange a cluster of the leaves over a satin-smooth chocolate-frosted cake.

## STEP BY STEP

**1.** Select firm, nontoxic leaves such as camellia or citrus. Rinse and wipe dry. With a small brush, paint back sides of leaves almost but not quite to edges with melted semisweet or bittersweet chocolate. Let stand until chocolate is firm, about 1 hour; or chill about 15 minutes.

**2.** Starting at the tip, peel leaf quickly away from chocolate. Don't touch more than necessary; hands melt chocolate.

**3.** Put 1 teaspoon clear liquor such as gin or vodka (or use lemon juice) in a small bowl. Carefully open the nontoxic gold (or silver) lustre dust and measure about ¼ teaspoon into the liquor. Mix with the tip of a small watercolor paintbrush. Paint the gold mixture onto the firm chocolate leaves. Let leaves stand until gold is dry, about 10 minutes. Use, or chill airtight up to 1 month. If you have paint left, let mixture dry completely. Cover airtight and keep at room temperature indefinitely, then revive with a little more liquor when you're ready to use it again.

JAMES CARRIER (5)

F O O D   N E W S

# Caviar dreams

■ With New Year's Eve just weeks away, my plans are full of wild and crazy notions. Ringing in the last year of the millennium calls for a magical reception. Maybe I'll indulge in a fresh caviar buffet.

Stolt Sea Farm California near Sacramento is raising sturgeon and producing caviar similar to the famous—and pricey—product from Russia's Caspian Sea. But roe from other fish is being used to make tasty caviars, too (unlike sturgeon caviar's, their labels must name the fish they came from)—spoonbill (paddlefish), hackleback, and whitefish (tiny, slightly crunchy golden caviar) from Montana and the Great Lakes; and salmon (brilliant red-orange caviar, the *ikura* for sushi) from Alaska and Washington. Seattle Caviar Company (888/323-3005; www.caviar.com) ships domestic and imported sturgeon as well as other fresh caviars. Prices range from about $6 to $60 an ounce. ◆

# The Low-Fat Cook

## HEALTHY CHOICES FOR THE ACTIVE LIFESTYLE

### BY ELAINE JOHNSON

CHICKEN, ALMONDS, and spices are handsomely wrapped in filo.

ROBERT OLDING

## Is it a gift or dinner?

■ As a private chef—for notables such as George Lucas of *Star Wars* fame—Cheryl Forberg has earned a reputation for extravagant-looking but light entrées.

One dish that she often chooses for her own parties is the Moroccan pie *bastilla.* She makes individual servings, easily packaged in purchased filo dough, exotically finished with a topknot.

Traditionally, the heart of the pie is pigeon, eggs, nuts, a souk's worth of spices, and lots of butter. Forberg manages a lighter touch by using poached chicken breasts and egg whites in the filling. A fine mist of cooking oil, not butter, makes the pastry flaky and crisp. The lean, flavorful poaching broth becomes a smooth, sweet-hot sauce.

### Low-Fat Chicken Bastillas

PREP AND COOK TIME: About 1¼ hours

MAKES: 4 servings

1 cup thickly sliced **onion**

2 cloves **garlic,** minced

1½ tablespoons minced **fresh ginger**

1½ teaspoons **ground turmeric**

1 teaspoon **ground coriander**

⅛ teaspoon **ground saffron**

¾ teaspoon **hot chili flakes**

1¼ teaspoons **ground cinnamon**

3 cups fat-skimmed **unsalted** or reduced-sodium **chicken broth**

1 pound **boned, skinned chicken breasts,** cut into ⅓- by 2-inch slices

4 **large egg** whites

¼ cup chopped **fresh cilantro**
**Salt**

⅓ cup finely chopped **almonds**
About 1½ tablespoons **powdered sugar**

6 sheets (12 by 17 in.) **filo dough**
**Cooking oil spray**

2 tablespoons **red jalapeño jelly**

1 tablespoon **cornstarch**

**1.** In a 3- to 4-quart pan over high heat, bring onion, garlic, ginger, turmeric, coriander, saffron, chili flakes, ¼ teaspoon cinnamon, and broth to a rolling boil. Add chicken, cover, remove from heat, and let stand until chicken is no longer pink in center (cut to test), about 2 minutes. With a slotted spoon, transfer chicken, but not onion, to a bowl.

**2.** Whisk ¼ cup of the cooking broth with egg whites just to blend. Place an 8- to 10-inch nonstick frying pan over medium heat. Pour egg mixture into pan and stir just until softly set, 3 to 5 minutes.

**3.** With a flexible spatula, gently combine egg mixture and cilantro with chicken. Season to taste with salt.

**4.** In another bowl, combine almonds, 1½ tablespoons sugar, and remaining cinnamon.

**5.** Working quickly so dough doesn't dry out, lightly spray each filo sheet with oil and make 3 stacks of 2 sheets each. From a 17-inch edge, cut each stack of filo into 3 equal parts; you'll have 9 stacks. Lay 1 stack of 2 strips at right angles across another. With 6 more stacks, make 3 more crosses; reserve remaining stack for other uses.

**6.** Using a slotted spoon, mound a quarter of the chicken mixture (add any accumulated liquid to cooking broth) onto center of each cross. Sprinkle mounds equally with almond mixture. For each bundle, gather filo strips up over filling and gently squeeze and twist to enclose. Set filo bundles well apart on an oiled 12- by 15-inch baking sheet.

**7.** Pull back tips of filo strips to make "petals." Lightly spray bundles with oil.

**8.** Bake bastilla pastries in a 400° oven until deep golden color, 15 to 18 minutes.

**9.** Meanwhile, boil reserved broth mixture over high heat until reduced to 2 cups, 8 to 10 minutes. Pour through a fine strainer into a bowl; discard residue. Rinse pan and return broth to it. Add jelly. Mix cornstarch with 1 tablespoon water and add to pan. Set pan over high heat and stir with a whisk until boiling.

**10.** With a spatula, transfer bastillas to plates. Dust with powdered sugar and accompany with sauce.

Per serving: 385 cal., 28% (108 cal.) from fat; 37 g protein; 12 g fat (1.7 g sat.); 33 g carbo (1.9 g fiber); 352 mg sodium; 69 mg chol. ◆

# MOTHER LODE TRADITIONS

# indoors & out

BY LINDA LAU ANUSASANANAN

■ These days, the hills of California's Gold Country are yielding a treasure of good eating. The fertile soil nourishes foods from wine grapes to ranch-raised beef and, most important, good cooks who know how to use them.

To reap the spirit of the Gold Country season, we tagged along with two families who celebrate the holidays with easy-to-prepare party meals. The Easton clan of Fiddletown traditionally cuts the Christmas tree in the nearby woods, and finishes the ceremony by enjoying a warming outdoor picnic that might suit one of your family outings. If indoors is more your style, try the handsome and very achievable dinner that Jenny Burnsworth of Arnold serves for Christmas or New Year's Day.

These tradition-filled parties can bring a golden glow to your own celebrations.

## Indoor Mother Lode dinner:
Above, the Burnsworth clan toasts the holidays. At right, Jenny Burnsworth and granddaughter Victoria share a few secrets over plates laden with slices of beef tenderloin stuffed with fresh herbs, rosemary potato fans, and lemony green beans.

Outdoor tree-cutting picnic: Bill Easton and Jane O'Riordan's family gathers at the tailgate of his venerable '49 Chevy pickup for mugs of hot homemade soup, ham and cheese sandwiches, and varietals from their Terre Rouge Winery. When the meal is done, the felled tree is loaded aboard for the trip home.

# on the first day of...

## The countdown to Christmas begins with tree-cutting and hot soup

It wouldn't be Christmas for the Easton family without a trek to Farnham Ridge Tree Farm. The first weekend in December, three generations of Eastons canvas the acreage, looking for the perfect white fir. After the tree is cut, Bill Easton's wife, Jane O'Riordan, unpacks sandwiches while he uncorks the wine. The heart of the menu is a warming soup transported in a widemouthed thermos. Only when the picnic's eaten, the tree loaded, and the family on the road is the season officially ushered in.

Throughout the West, tree-cutting expeditions are a rediscovered tradition. And a soup picnic like the Eastons' fits in well. Three choices follow, adapted from O'Riordan's *Rhône Appétit* (Toyon Hill Press, Woodside, CA, 1998; $17.95).

### Tree-cutting Picnic

Soup of choice: Soupe au Pistou; Butternut Squash Soup with Sage; Lamb, Sausage, and Bean Soup • Ham and Herb Cream Cheese Sandwiches • Apples and Christmas Cookies • Terre Rouge Zinfandel, Barbera, and Syrah • Cider and Hot Chocolate

### Soupe au Pistou

PREP AND COOK TIME: About 1¼ hours
NOTES: Soup can be made up to 2 days ahead. Reheat, covered, over high heat. Transport in a thermos or a tightly covered container in an insulated chest. Carry pistou in a separate covered jar.
MAKES: 12 to 14 servings

- 3½ quarts **vegetable** or fat-skimmed chicken **broth**
- 1 pound **butternut** or Hubbard **squash**
- 2 **carrots** (6 oz. total), peeled
- 1 **red thin-skinned potato** (5 oz.), scrubbed
- 3 stalks **celery** (½ lb. total), rinsed
- 1 **onion** (½ lb.), peeled and chopped
- 3 cloves **garlic,** minced
- ½ pound **zucchini,** ends trimmed
- 1 **red bell pepper** (½ lb.), rinsed, stemmed, and seeded
- 2 tablespoons chopped **fresh basil leaves** or 1 teaspoon dried basil
- 5 cans (15 oz. each) **cannellini** (white) **beans,** rinsed and drained
  **Pistou** (recipe follows)
  **Salt** and **pepper**

**1.** In an 8- to 10-quart pan over high heat, bring broth to a boil.
**2.** Meanwhile, cut skin from butternut squash. Cut squash, carrots, potato, and celery into ½-inch cubes.
**3.** Add butternut squash, carrots, potato, celery, onion, and garlic to boiling broth. Cover, return to a boil, then reduce heat and simmer 10 minutes.
**4.** Meanwhile, cut zucchini and red bell pepper into ½-inch cubes.
**5.** Add zucchini, bell pepper, basil, and beans to broth. Cover and return to a boil over high heat. Reduce heat and simmer until all vegetables are tender when pierced, about 20 minutes longer.
**6.** Stir ¼ cup pistou into soup, then ladle soup into bowls or mugs. Add salt and pepper and more pistou to taste.

Per serving: 211 cal., 18% (39 cal.) from fat; 10 g protein; 4.3 g fat (0.6 g sat.); 34 g carbo (8 g fiber); 303 mg sodium; 0.9 mg chol.

### Pistou

PREP TIME: About 5 minutes
NOTES: If making pistou up to 1 day ahead, cover and chill. Serve cool or at room temperature. Top may darken as pistou stands; just stir to blend.
MAKES: 1 cup

- 5 cloves **garlic,** peeled
- 2½ cups **fresh basil** leaves
- ⅔ cup **olive oil**
- ⅔ cup **grated parmesan cheese**

In a food processor or blender, purée garlic, basil, and oil. Add cheese and whirl until blended, scraping container sides often. Pour into a bowl.

Per tablespoon: 104 cal., 87% (90 cal.) from fat; 2.1 g protein; 10 g fat (2 g sat.); 1 g carbo (0.5 g fiber); 77 mg sodium; 3.2 mg chol.

### Butternut Squash Soup with Sage

PREP AND COOK TIME: About 1 hour
NOTES: Soup can be made up to 2 days ahead. Reheat, covered, over low heat, stirring occasionally.
MAKES: 4 or 5 servings

2 to 3 cups **vegetable** or fat-skimmed chicken **broth**

1 cup **apple juice** or cider

3 pounds **butternut squash**

1 **onion** (6 oz.), peeled and chopped

6 **fresh sage** leaves (about 3 in. long)

**Crème fraîche** or sour cream

About 2 tablespoons minced **fresh sage** leaves

**Salt** and **pepper**

**1.** In a 3- to 4-quart pan over high heat, bring 2 cups broth and juice to a boil.

**2.** Meanwhile, peel squash, seed, and cut into 1-inch chunks (you need 7 to 8 cups).

**3.** Add squash, onion, and whole sage leaves to pan, cover, and return to a boil. Reduce heat and simmer until squash is very tender when pierced, about 30 minutes.

**4.** With a slotted spoon, transfer about half the vegetables to a food processor or blender. Purée, adding just enough broth to facilitate. Pour purée into a bowl and repeat to purée remaining vegetables.

**5.** Return puréed vegetables to broth in pan. If soup is thicker than you like, thin with more broth. Stir over medium heat until soup is hot.

**6.** Ladle into bowls or mugs. Add crème fraîche, minced sage, and salt and pepper to taste.

Per serving: 153 cal., 2.9% (4.5 cal.) from fat; 3 g protein; 0.5 g fat (0.1 g sat.); 38 g carbo (4.7 g fiber); 40 mg sodium; 0 mg chol.

## Lamb, Sausage, and Bean Soup

PREP AND COOK TIME: About 2 hours

NOTES: You can make soup up to 2 days ahead. Offer toasted coarse bread crumbs or coarsely crushed croutons to sprinkle onto each serving.

MAKES: 8 servings

1½ pounds **boned, fat-trimmed lamb shoulder**

¼ teaspoon **dried thyme**

6 cups fat-skimmed **chicken broth**

2 **dried bay leaves**

1 **head garlic** (2 oz.)

MUGS OF CHUNKY Soupe au Pistou and ham sandwiches reward tree-cutters.

FOR DESSERT, taste the first Christmas cookies of the season.

1 can (14 oz.) **diced tomatoes**

½ pound **andouille** or kielbasa (Polish) **sausages**, sliced ¼ inch thick

4 cans (15 oz. each) **small white beans**, rinsed and drained

**Salt** and **pepper**

**1.** Cut lamb into 1-inch chunks.

**2.** In a 5- to 6-quart pan, combine lamb, thyme, and 1 cup water. Cover and bring to a boil over high heat. Reduce heat and simmer for 20 minutes.

**3.** Uncover and boil over high heat, stirring often, until a brown film forms on pan bottom, about 15 minutes. Add ⅓ cup broth and stir to loosen browned bits, then stir often until lamb is lightly browned, about 4 minutes.

**4.** Add remaining broth and bay leaves; bring to a boil.

**5.** Cut ¼ of the top off the garlic head. Add garlic head to broth. Cover, reduce heat, and simmer until lamb is tender when pierced, about 1 hour.

**6.** With a slotted spoon, lift out garlic and set aside. To pan, add tomatoes (including juice), sausages, and beans.

**7.** Squeeze garlic cloves from the head and add cloves to soup. Reduce heat, cover, and simmer to blend flavors, about 5 minutes, stirring occasionally.

**8.** If soup is thicker than you like, thin with a little water and simmer 2 to 3 more minutes to blend flavors. Ladle into bowls or mugs and add salt and pepper to taste.

Per serving: 371 cal., 39% (144 cal.) from fat; 31 g protein; 16 g fat (5.5 g sat.); 26 g carbo (6.3 g fiber); 869 mg sodium; 78 mg chol.

HEATHER MONAHAN (3)

# Crowning the Season

## A holiday meal worth

BEEF FOR Christmas dinner is Jenny Burnsworth's traditional choice. This year it's tenderloin.

"People eat with their eyes. If it looks good, they'll try it," says caterer Jenny Burnsworth. But her choice of beautifully presented foods is not based on appearance alone; taste figures into the calculation, as does savvy time-use: her cooking has to fit around a full-time teaching job.

Burnsworth's food philosophy comes together in this sumptuous, stylish menu she serves her family and friends. Many ingredients—cranberries, roast beef, and potatoes—resonate tradition, but there's a delicious freshness to these versions: this is not your standard fruitcake, for instance. Best of all, the meal is easy enough for a new cook to manage comfortably.

its weight in gold

## Cranberry-Wine Aperitif

PREP TIME: **About 15 minutes**

NOTES: Make at least 1 week ahead; flavor and color intensify with 3 to 4 weeks' storage.

MAKES: 7 cups; 8 servings

- 2 cups **cranberries,** fresh or thawed frozen
- 2 tablespoons finely shredded **orange** peel
- 2 cups **sugar**
- 2 bottles (750 ml. each) **Chardonnay**

**1.** Sort cranberries and discard soft or decayed fruit. Rinse berries and put in a 2- to 3-quart glass jar, crock, or bowl. Add peel, sugar, and wine; mix well.

**2.** Cover and chill at least 1 week or up to a month; stir several times. Pour aperitif through a fine strainer into a pitcher, or return to jar. Serve cold. Reserve cranberry–orange peel mixture to dress up muffins and pancakes.

Per serving: 328 cal., 0% (0 cal.) from fat; 0.2 g protein; 0 g fat; 53 g carbo (0 g fiber); 10 mg sodium; 0 mg chol.

## Belgian Endive with Crab

PREP TIME: **About 15 minutes**

NOTES: Up to 1 day ahead, assemble appetizers, cover, and chill.

MAKES: 32 pieces; 8 appetizer servings

- 1 package (8 oz.) **cream cheese**
- 3 tablespoons minced **green onions**
- 1 tablespoon **lemon juice**
- 1 tablespoon **white wine Worcestershire**
- ¼ teaspoon **white pepper**
- ¼ pound **shelled cooked crab**
- 32 **red** or white **Belgian endive** leaves (from about 1¼ to 1½ lb. total), rinsed and crisped

**1.** Mix cheese with 1 tablespoon onions, lemon juice, Worcestershire, and pepper. Add crab and stir to mix.

**2.** Mound 2 teaspoons crab filling at

CATHERINE LEDNER (3)

DINNER BEGINS with crab appetizers and cranberry aperitifs.

stem end of each endive leaf. Garnish with remaining green onions. Set leaves, filling side up, on a platter.

Per serving: 127 cal., 71% (90 cal.) from fat; 5.7 g protein; 10 g fat (6.3 g sat.); 3.6 g carbo (1.6 g fiber); 145 mg sodium; 45 mg chol.

## From-Scratch Shrimp Bisque

PREP AND COOK TIME: **About 1¼ hours**

NOTES: Up to 1 day ahead, make soup, cool, cover, and chill. To reheat, stir often over medium heat. Set aside 8 cooked shrimp for garnish.

MAKES: 8 servings

- 1½ pounds (31 to 35 per lb.) **shrimp**
  About 5 cups fat-skimmed **chicken broth**
- 1 **onion** (½ lb.), quartered
- 4 stalks **celery** (¾ lb. total), cut into chunks
- 1 **carrot** (3 oz.), peeled and cut into chunks
- 2 **dried bay leaves**
- 1 tablespoon **white peppercorns**
- 6 tablespoons **butter** or margarine
- 4 cloves **garlic,** pressed or minced
- ½ cup **all-purpose flour**
- 3 cups **half-and-half** (light cream)
  **Salt** and **pepper**
  **Fresh dill** sprigs

**1.** Shell and devein shrimp; save shells. Rinse shrimp. Cut into ½-inch pieces.

**2.** In a 5- to 6-quart pan, combine shrimp shells, 5 cups broth, onion, celery, carrot, bay leaves, and white

### Holiday Dinner in the Mother Lode

Cranberry-Wine Aperitif • Belgian Endive with Crab • From-Scratch Shrimp Bisque
1997 Milliaire Chardonnay • Butter Lettuce Salad with Balsamic Vinaigrette
Beef Tenderloin with Fresh Herbs • Rosemary Potato Fans • Lemony Green Beans
1994 Milliaire Cabernet Sauvignon • St. Nicholas Dried-Fruit Cake •
Vanilla Ice Cream with Rum-soaked Raisins

SHRIMP BISQUE (far left) is followed by butter lettuce salad with homemade croutons (center), then sliced tenderloin with potatoes and green beans (below).

peppercorns. Bring to a boil over high heat, cover, and simmer for 30 minutes. Pour broth through a strainer into a 2-quart glass measure or bowl. If needed, add more broth to make 5 cups.

**3.** Melt butter in same pan over medium heat. Add garlic and stir just until limp, 1 to 2 minutes. Stir in flour.

**4.** Off the heat, whisk broth and half-and-half into flour mixture. Stir over medium-high heat until boiling, then boil for about 2 minutes. Add shrimp and stir until pink, about 1 minute.

**5.** Add salt and pepper to taste. Ladle into bowls; garnish with dill and shrimp.

Per serving: 342 cal., 55% (189 cal.) from fat; 20 g protein; 21 g fat (13 g sat.); 18 g carbo (1.7 g fiber); 335 mg sodium; 164 mg chol.

## Butter Lettuce Salad with Balsamic Vinaigrette

PREP AND COOK TIME: About 25 minutes

NOTES: Up to 1 day ahead, make croutons, cool, wrap airtight, and hold at room temperature. Cook bacon, wrap, and chill. Wrap lettuce pieces in towels, seal in a plastic bag, and chill. Make dressing, cover, and chill.

MAKES: 8 servings

¹⁄₂  pound **sourdough bread**

3  tablespoons plus ¹⁄₂ cup **olive oil**

4  cloves **garlic,** pressed or minced

¹⁄₄  cup **grated parmesan cheese**

¹⁄₂  pound **bacon**

¹⁄₄  cup **balsamic vinegar**

1  tablespoon **red wine vinegar**

2  teaspoons **Dijon mustard**

1¹⁄₄  pounds **butter lettuce,** rinsed and crisped

**Salt** and **pepper**

**1.** Cut bread into ³⁄₄-inch cubes. In a 10-by 15-inch baking pan, mix bread with 3 tablespoons oil, half of the garlic, and cheese.

**2.** Bake in a 375° oven until bread is golden, stirring occasionally, about 20 minutes. Let cool.

**3.** Cut bacon into ¹⁄₄-inch-wide strips. Stir bacon often in a 10- to 12-inch frying pan over medium heat until crisp, 6 to 8 minutes. Lift out bacon with a slotted spoon and drain on paper towels.

**4.** In a food processor or blender, whirl remaining garlic, balsamic vinegar, wine vinegar, and mustard, and with motor running, pour in remaining ¹⁄₂ cup oil.

**5.** Tear lettuce into bite-size pieces and place in a wide serving bowl.

**6.** Add croutons, bacon, and garlic dressing. Mix to coat greens. Add salt and pepper to taste.

Per serving: 313 cal., 69% (216 cal.) from fat; 6.9 g protein; 24 g fat (4.6 g sat.); 17 g carbo (1.5 g fiber); 380 mg sodium; 8.7 mg chol.

## Beef Tenderloin with Fresh Herbs

PREP AND COOK TIME: About 1 hour

NOTES: Up to 4 hours ahead, prepare meat to roast.

MAKES: 8 servings

1  **center-cut beef tenderloin** (3 to 4 lb.)

2  tablespoons **Dijon mustard**

6  **fresh basil** leaves (about 4 in.)

6  **fresh sage** leaves (about 3 in.)

1  tablespoon **fresh thyme** leaves

3  to 6 cloves **garlic,** minced

Fresh-ground **pepper**

2  tablespoons **butter** or margarine, at room temperature

**Sage,** basil, or thyme sprigs

**Salt**

**1.** Trim any excess fat from meat and discard. Cut through tenderloin lengthwise to within ¹⁄₂ inch of other side. Lay meat open like a book.

**2.** Spread meat with mustard. Lay basil and sage leaves on mustard. Sprinkle with thyme leaves, garlic, and pepper.

**3.** Bring cut sides together and tie roast with cotton string at about 1-inch intervals to secure. Coat surface of beef with butter and sprinkle with more pepper. Lay roast, cut to the side, on a rack in a 12- by 17-inch pan.

**4.** Bake in a 425° oven until a thermometer inserted in center of thickest part registers 130° to 135° for rare, 40 to 50 minutes. Let rest in a warm place up to 20 minutes.

**5.** Transfer meat to a platter. Remove strings. Garnish with herb sprigs. Slice and add salt and pepper to taste.

Per serving: 241 cal., 52% (126 cal.) from fat; 26 g protein; 14 g fat (5.9 g sat.); 0.6 g carbo (0.1 g fiber); 177 mg sodium; 86 mg chol.

## Rosemary Potato Fans

PREP AND COOK TIME: About 1 hour

NOTES: Potatoes can be baked in oven with beef tenderloin. To make fan cuts, set equally thick wood dowels or pencils on each side of potato so you won't cut all the way through. Cut perpendicular to dowels.

MAKES: 8 servings

2½ to 3 pounds **red thin-skinned potatoes** (2 in. wide), scrubbed

3 tablespoons **olive oil**

2 tablespoons chopped **fresh rosemary** leaves

**Salt** and **pepper**

1. Make cuts ⅛ inch apart across each potato, down to ¼ inch from bottom (see notes).

2. In a bowl or 9- by 13-inch baking pan, coat potatoes with oil and rosemary; sprinkle with salt and pepper. Place potatoes, cuts up, in pan or on rack beside beef.

3. Bake in a 425° oven until potatoes are tender when pierced, 40 to 50 minutes.

Per serving: 160 cal., 30% (48 cal.) from fat; 2.7 g protein; 5.3 g fat (0.7 g sat.); 26 g carbo (2.4 g fiber); 11 mg sodium; 0 mg chol.

## Lemony Green Beans

PREP AND COOK TIME: About 25 minutes

NOTES: Up to 1 day ahead, cook beans, drain, and immerse in ice water; when cold, drain and chill airtight. Reheat in boiling water 2 to 3 minutes.

MAKES: 8 servings

2 pounds **green beans**, ends trimmed

2 tablespoons **olive oil**

1 teaspoon finely shredded **lemon peel**

2 tablespoons **lemon juice**

2 tablespoons chopped **parsley**

---

## Countdown to a perfect holiday feast

☑ **Up to 2 months ahead:** *Bake* cake.

☑ **Up to 1 month ahead:** *Make* cranberry aperitif.

☑ **Up to 1 day ahead:** *Assemble* crab appetizers, *make* bisque, *prepare* salad ingredients, *cook* green beans, *soak* raisins in rum.

☑ **Up to 4 hours ahead:** *Assemble* roast.

☑ **Up to 1½ hours ahead:** *Cut* potatoes.

☑ **About 1 hour ahead:** *Cook* roast and potatoes.

☑ **About 10 minutes ahead:** *Reheat* bisque, *boil* water to reheat beans.

☑ **About 5 minutes ahead:** *Assemble* salad, *heat* and season beans, *set out* crab appetizers, *pour* aperitifs, *slice* beef.

☑ **Just before serving dessert:** *Slice* cake and *scoop* ice cream.

1 or 2 cloves **garlic**, pressed or minced

**Salt** and **pepper**

Thin **lemon** slices

1. In a 5- to 6-quart pan over high heat, bring about 3 quarts water to a boil. Add beans. Stir occasionally until tender-crisp to bite, 4 to 5 minutes. Drain.

2. In a large bowl, combine oil, lemon peel, lemon juice, parsley, and garlic. Add beans and mix to coat. Add salt and pepper to taste. Pour into a serving dish and garnish with lemon slices.

Per serving: 63 cal., 51% (32 cal.) from fat; 1.9 g protein; 3.5 g fat (0.5 g sat.); 7.6 g carbo (1.8 g fiber); 7.2 mg sodium; 0 mg chol.

## St. Nicholas Dried-Fruit Cake

PREP AND COOK TIME: About 4 hours

NOTES: Bake cake at least 1 day or up to 2 months ahead; cool and wrap in cheesecloth or a thin towel saturated with orange-flavor liqueur. Chill airtight, and about every 10 days, moisten cloth with more liqueur. Serve thin slices of cake plain, with vanilla ice cream topped with rum-plumped raisins, or with rum-raisin ice cream. Wrap and continue to age extra cake.

MAKES: 1 cake, about 25 servings

About 1 cup (½ lb.) **butter** or margarine, at room temperature

1 cup **sugar**

6 **large eggs**

¼ cup **molasses**

1¼ cups **all-purpose flour**

1½ teaspoons **ground cinnamon**

½ teaspoon **ground nutmeg**

½ teaspoon **ground cardamom**

DRIED APRICOTS, pineapple, and pecans adorn jam-glazed St. Nicholas Dried-Fruit Cake.

¼ teaspoon **ground cloves**

¼ teaspoon **ground allspice**

1 pound (2⅔ cups) **dried apricots**

½ pound (2 cups) **pecan halves**

½ pound **dried lightly sweetened pineapple**

½ pound (2 cups) **dried sweetened cranberries**

½ pound (2 cups) **dried cherries** or blueberries

½ cup **apricot jam**

2 tablespoons **orange-flavor liqueur**

1. Lightly butter a 5- by 9-inch loaf pan. Line with cooking parchment.

2. In a bowl with a mixer, beat 1 cup butter with sugar until fluffy.

3. Beat in eggs, 1 at a time, until well blended. Beat in molasses.

4. Mix flour, cinnamon, nutmeg, cardamom, cloves, and allspice. Add to egg mixture; beat just until blended.

5. Set aside 6 to 8 apricots, 10 to 12 pecan halves, and 1 pineapple ring.

6. Cut remaining pineapple into ¾-inch pieces and add to batter along with the remaining apricots and pecans and the cranberries and cherries. Stir until well mixed.

7. Scrape batter into parchment-lined pan, pressing firmly to eliminate air pockets; spread top level.

8. Bake in a 275° oven until cake is firm in center when touched, about 3 hours. If it browns too rapidly, drape with foil.

9. Cool in pan on rack at least 2½ hours. Lift out cake; peel off parchment.

10. Mix apricot jam with liqueur and brush over top of cake. Decoratively arrange reserved apricots, pecans, and pineapple in apricot glaze; brush more apricot jam mixture over fruit. Wrap airtight and chill at least 1 day.

Per 3 ounces: 351 cal., 38% (135 cal.) from fat; 3.6 g protein; 15 g fat (5.5 g sat.); 54 g carbo (2.8 g fiber); 105 mg sodium; 71 mg chol. ◆

# 101 best-loved holiday cookies

Sweet goodies—buttery cutouts, brownies, delicate lace cookies, biscotti, perfect chocolate chip, and more—make up this keepsake collection

BY ELAINE JOHNSON • PHOTOGRAPHS BY JAMES CARRIER

■ It's time for the annual holiday cookie-baking spree. And as a final salute to our Centennial, here is a cookie to commemorate each year—plus one for good luck. We hope you will find this mini-cookbook a treasured resource well into the next millennium.

To bring together these very special cookie recipes, we checked our records to see which ones had been requested most by *Sunset's* readers through the years. We also combed through thousands in our archives to find those we considered most memorable, some reflecting the ethnic evolution of the West, some just the best of their kind.

But this compendium isn't merely a recapitulation of old times. Curious dissimilarities among procedures popped up when we put favorite recipes side by side. So we tested extensively to determine which processes, ingredient combinations, techniques, and baking temperatures really work best for each cookie. The recipes also reflect advances in technology, such as nonstick baking sheets, nonstick pan liners, and silicone baking pads.

To make this Centennial collection easy to use and quick to peruse, we've divided the recipes into 10 basic types, from cutouts to brownies. For most of the cookies, you start with a master recipe, then add details from one of the individual recipes that follow. A few cookies that don't quite fit any mold are presented as separate recipes.

So dig in. Here are hand-held delights for gifts, for your own parties, for nibbling with a cup of coffee, for lunch boxes, for the freezer, and for enjoyable baking for years to come.

A DELECTABLE ASSORTMENT of cookies is always a welcome gift. Package them imaginatively, in a container that will remain useful long after the treats disappear. For holiday shimmer, put cookies in a metal baking mold, a polished jar, or a silver mug that can hold flowers later. Plastic wrap will keep the cookies fresh.

FOOD STYLING BY DIANA TORREY

# Cutout cookies

No holiday cookie collection is complete without cutouts. The fun is in the form, from stars to gingerbread people, and in the decorations, from a dusting of powdered sugar to artfully painted designs. We lead off with our Favorite Cutout Cookies. They're the synthesis of *Sunset's* best recipes for tender-crisp, golden butter cookies. This dough, remarkably versatile and easy to handle, is in turn the foundation for the four very different-looking and -tasting treats that follow. In this family of cookies, you'll also find filled choices.

## Master Recipe

1. Select recipe (choices follow). In a bowl with a mixer, beat butter with sugar and/or molasses and cream cheese, if specified, until very smooth. Then beat in any eggs, flavorings, and liquid.

2. In another bowl, combine flour mixture. Stir into butter mixture and beat until blended. Stir in any extra ingredients. If mixture is crumbly, squeeze into a smooth, compact ball.

3. Divide dough in half. Flatten each portion with your hands to make a 1-inch-thick round.

4. With a floured rolling pin on a board lightly coated with all-purpose flour, roll dough, a portion at a time.

5. With floured cookie cutters, cut dough into desired shapes (or shapes noted in recipe). If dough is too soft to handle, freeze briefly until firm.

6. Use 12- by 15-inch baking sheets. Butter pans if recipe specifies. With a wide spatula or your fingers, transfer cut dough to pans, spacing about 1 inch apart. Gather scraps, pat into a ball, and repeat rolling and cutting.

7. Bake in a 300° oven as directed in recipe; if using more than 1 pan in 1 oven, switch pan positions halfway through baking.

8. With a wide spatula, transfer cookies to racks to cool. Or, if hot cookies start to break, slide a thin spatula under them to release, let stand on pan to firm, about 5 minutes, then transfer to racks. Serve cookies, store airtight as recipe directs (if iced, put waxed paper between layers), or freeze to store longer.

## Favorite Cutout Cookies

PREP AND COOK TIME: About 1½ hours
Follow directions for **Cutout Cookies Master Recipe** (above). In step 1, beat 1 cup (½ lb.) **butter** or margarine (at room temperature) with ½ cup **granulated sugar**; then beat in 2 **large egg yolks** and 1 teaspoon **vanilla**. In step 2, use 2½ cups **all-purpose flour**.

Divide dough (step 3). Roll ⅛ inch thick (step 4). Cut (step 5) and put on baking sheets (step 6). If desired, sprinkle cutouts with **colored sugar** or candy decors, then bake (step 7) until golden, about 15 minutes. Let cookies cool (step 8). Leave plain, or decorate with **icing** (right). Serve, or store up to 3 days. MAKES: 45 (2¾-in.-wide rounds).

Per cookie: 74 cal., 54% (40 cal.) from fat; 0.9 g protein; 4.4 g fat (2.6 g sat.); 7.8 g carbo (0.2 g fiber); 42 mg sodium; 20 mg chol.

## Icing

PREP AND DRYING TIME: About 1¾ hours
*For spreading.* In a bowl, stir 3 cups **powdered sugar**, 1 teaspoon **vanilla**, and ¼ cup **water** until smooth. To tint, stir in **food coloring**, a few drops at a time. Icing should spread evenly, and after a second, settle to make a smooth surface. If too thick, mix in a few drops of water; if too thin, stir in powdered sugar, a little at a time. Spread icing onto cool cookies with a metal spatula. Let stand until icing is firm, about 1½ hours. MAKES: About 1 cup, enough to coat 1 recipe's worth of ⅛-inch-thick Favorite Cutout Cookies (left).
Per teaspoon: 29 cal., 0% (0 cal.) from fat; 0 g protein; 0 g fat; 7.5 g carbo (0 g fiber); 0.1 mg sodium; 0 mg chol.

*For piping.* In a bowl, stir 2 cups **powdered sugar**, ½ teaspoon **vanilla**, and 1½ tablespoons **water** until smooth. To tint, stir in **food coloring**, a few drops at a time. Icing needs to be stiff enough to hold a line when piped through a pastry bag fitted with an ⅛-inch tip. If too thick, add a little water; if too thin, add a little powdered sugar. Or

spoon icing into a heavy 1-quart plastic food bag, seal, and squeeze icing into a corner. Snip a very small opening at corner of bag and squeeze icing out. Let stand until icing is firm, about 5 minutes. MAKES: About ¾ cup, enough to decorate 1 recipe's worth of ⅛-inch-thick Favorite Cutout Cookies (left).
Per teaspoon: 26 cal., 0% (0 cal.) from fat; 0 g protein; 0 g fat; 6.6 g carbo (0 g fiber); 0.1 mg sodium; 0 mg chol.

## Apricot Sandwich Cookies

PREP AND COOK TIME: About 2 hours
Prepare dough for **Favorite Cutout Cookies** (far left). Following **Cutout Cookies Master Recipe** (above), divide dough (step 3). Roll ⅛ inch thick (step 4). Cut (step 5) into 1¼-inch-wide rounds, plain or fluted. Cut a ¾-inch round from center of half the cookies. Put on pans (step 6) and bake (step 7) until golden, 8 to 10 minutes. Cool (step 8). Then spread solid cookies with **apricot jam** (about 1¼ cups total) and top each with a ring cookie. Sift about 3 tablespoons **powdered sugar** over cookies. Serve, or store airtight up to 2 days. MAKES: 70 sandwich cookies.
Per cookie: 63 cal., 40% (25 cal.) from fat; 0.6 g protein; 2.8 g fat (1.7 g sat.); 9 g carbo (0.2 g fiber); 29 mg sodium; 13 mg chol.

## Chocolate Streaks

PREP AND COOK TIME: About 1½ hours
Make (in any shape desired), bake, and

CUTTING UP FOR FUN are Gingerbread People, Stained-Glass Cookies, Chocolate Streaks, Favorite Cutout Cookies, Cashew Stars, and Cookie Canvases.

cool **Favorite Cutout Cookies** (page 288). Cover baking sheets with waxed paper and arrange cookies in a single layer on top.

In a small pan over low heat, combine 1 ounce finely chopped **semi-sweet chocolate** and 1 tablespoon **butter** or margarine. Stir frequently until chocolate is smooth and melted.

Dip a fork into chocolate mixture and flick spatters from fork in thin streaks over cookies.

Chill until chocolate sets, about 10 minutes. Serve, or chill airtight up to 2 days. MAKES: 45 (2¾-in.-wide rounds).
Per cookie: 82 cal., 55% (45 cal.) from fat; 1 g protein; 5 g fat (3 g sat.); 8.6 g carbo (0.3 g fiber); 45 mg sodium; 21 mg chol.

## Cookie Canvases

PREP TIME: About 2½ hours
Prepare dough for **Favorite Cutout Cookies** (page 288). Following **Cutout Cookies Master Recipe** (page 288), divide dough (step 3). Roll ¼ inch thick (step 4). Cut with floured cutters (step 5), or use a sharp knife to make squares or rectangles. Put on pans (step 6). Bake (step 7) until cookies are golden, 15 to 18 minutes.

Cool cookies (step 8) until just warm to touch. Then coat each with plain white or palely tinted **icing for spreading** (page 288). Let icing dry until hard, about 4 hours.

***To paint cookies,*** put undiluted **food coloring** in small individual bowls; for less intense color, dilute with a little water. Use watercolor brushes to paint designs on iced cookies. Food coloring spreads, so leave a space between colors or allow each color to dry before painting with another. Freshly painted designs are well defined; after 24 hours, design edges soften. Serve, or store airtight up to 2 days. MAKES: 28 (2¾-in.-wide rounds).
Per cookie: 170 cal., 37% (63 cal.) from fat; 1.5 g protein; 7 g fat (4.2 g sat.); 25 g carbo (0.3 g fiber); 68 mg sodium; 33 mg chol.

## Stained-Glass Cookies

PREP TIME: About 2¼ hours
Prepare dough for **Favorite Cutout Cookies** (page 288). Following **Cutout Cookies Master Recipe** (page 288), divide dough (step 3). Roll ¼ inch thick (step 4). Cut (step 5). Because "stained glass" in cookies sticks, line pans (step 6) with nonstick pan liners, silicone baking pads, or cooking parchment. Put cookies on baking sheets. Then cut out and lift designs from center of each cookie (such as a small star from the center of a round or a larger star). Use

smaller, but at least ¾-inch-wide, floured cutters or a small, pointed knife and leave at least a ½-inch cookie border.

***To make stained glass:*** Chop **transparent, hard, colored candies,** such as lemon drops, cinnamon balls, or other flavors, into ¼-inch pieces to make about ¼ cup (or more, as needed). Fill cutout portions of dough just to the rim with candy; use 1 color of candy in each cutout.

Bake (step 7) until golden, 15 to 18 minutes. Let cookies cool on pans until candy is firm. Slide a thin spatula under cookies to release (step 8). Serve, or store up to 1 week. MAKES: 28 (2¾-in.-wide rounds).
Per cookie: 127 cal., 50% (63 cal.) from fat; 1.5 g protein; 7 g fat (4.2 g sat.); 15 g carbo (0.3 g fiber); 68 mg sodium; 33 mg chol.

## Almond Ravioli Cookies

PREP AND COOK TIME: About 3½ hours
Follow steps 1 and 2 for **Cutout Cookies Master Recipe** (page 288). In step 1, beat 1 cup (½ lb.) **butter** or margarine (at room temperature) with 1½ cups **powdered sugar;** then beat in 1 **large egg** and 1 teaspoon **vanilla.** In step 2, combine 2½ cups **all-purpose flour** and 1 teaspoon *each* **baking soda** and **cream of tartar.**

Cut 8 sheets of waxed paper, each 12 by 18 inches. Divide dough into 8 equal portions and flatten each into a 5-inch disk. Place a piece of dough in the center of a sheet of paper. Smoothly fold paper over to make an 8-inch square envelope with sharply creased sides. Turn packet over on a board. Roll dough into an even 8-inch square; lift paper to smooth any creases. Repeat with remaining dough and paper. Lay packets on a baking sheet and freeze until firm, 10 to 15 minutes. Meanwhile, cut 1 cup (8 oz.) **almond paste** into 100 equal pieces (each about ¼ teaspoon). Shape into balls and flatten slightly.

Fold back paper on 1 packet, lay flat. (If dough is too cold, it cracks; let stand briefly until warmer. If too warm, it's sticky; return briefly to freezer.) Evenly space 25 pieces of almond paste on dough, leaving rim bare. Peel paper from another packet and lay dough on first piece, aligning edges. Lightly press top sheet of dough onto bottom layer to adhere between almond pieces. With a knife, cut between pieces of almond paste to make square cookies. If needed, press edges to seal. Set cookies about 1 inch apart on 12- by 15-inch baking sheets. Push an **almond slice** (⅓ cup total) into the center of each. Repeat to

shape and fill remaining dough.

Bake in a 350° oven until golden, 10 to 12 minutes. With a wide spatula, transfer to racks to cool. Serve, store airtight up to 2 days, or freeze to store longer. MAKES: 100.
Per cookie: 44 cal., 52% (23 cal.) from fat; 0.6 g protein; 2.5 g fat (1.2 g sat.); 5 g carbo (0.1 g fiber); 32 mg sodium; 7.1 mg chol.

## Bizcochitos

PREP AND COOK TIME: About 2 hours
Follow directions for **Cutout Cookies Master Recipe** (page 288). In step 1, beat 1 cup (½ lb.) **butter** or margarine (at room temperature) with ¾ cup **granulated sugar;** then beat in 1 **large egg,** 1½ teaspoons **anise seed,** and 2 tablespoons **brandy.** In step 2, combine 3 cups **all-purpose flour** and 1 teaspoon **baking powder.**

Divide dough (step 3). Wrap each portion airtight; freeze until firm, about 30 minutes. Roll ⅛ inch thick (step 4). Cut (step 5) and put on pans (step 6).

Combine ¼ cup **sugar** and 1 teaspoon **ground cinnamon.** Sprinkle mixture over cutouts on pans.

Bake (step 7) until cookies are golden, about 15 minutes. Cool (step 8). Serve, or store up to 2 days. MAKES: 55 (2¾-in.-wide rounds).
Per cookie: 73 cal., 44% (32 cal.) from fat; 0.9 g protein; 3.5 g fat (2.1 g sat.); 9.1 g carbo (0.2 g fiber); 44 mg sodium; 13 mg chol.

## Brown Sugar Christmas Thins

PREP AND COOK TIME: About 1¼ hours
Follow directions for **Cutout Cookies Master Recipe** (page 288). In step 1, beat 2 cups (1 lb.) **butter** or margarine (at room temperature) with 2½ cups (1 lb.) firmly packed **brown sugar;** then add 1½ teaspoons **vanilla.** In step 2, use 4½ cups **all-purpose flour.**

For step 3, divide dough into 4 equal portions. Roll ⅛ inch thick (step 4). Cut (step 5). Put on pans (step 6) and bake (step 7) until slightly darker brown, about 15 minutes. Cool (step 8). If desired, decorate with **icing for piping** (page 288). Serve, or store up to 1 week. MAKES: 75 (2¾-in.-wide rounds).
Per cookie: 94 cal., 48% (45 cal.) from fat; 0.8 g protein; 5 g fat (3.1 g sat.); 12 g carbo (0.2 g fiber); 53 mg sodium; 13 mg chol.

## Cashew Stars

PREP AND COOK TIME: About 1¼ hours
Follow directions for **Cutout Cookies Master Recipe** (page 288). In step 1, beat 1 cup (½ lb.) **butter** or margarine (at room temperature) with ½ cup **powdered sugar** and ¼ teaspoon

**almond extract.** In step 2, combine 2 cups **all-purpose flour,** ½ teaspoon **baking powder,** ¼ teaspoon **salt,** and 1 cup minced **roasted, salted cashews.**

Divide dough (step 3). Wrap each portion airtight and freeze until firm, about 20 minutes. Roll ⅜ inch thick (step 4). Cut (step 5) with a 3-inch star cutter. Put on pans (step 6) and bake (step 7) until golden, 15 to 18 minutes. Cool (step 8). Dust with 2 tablespoons **powdered sugar.** Serve, or store up to 2 days. MAKES: 30.

Per cookie: 121 cal., 62% (75 cal.) from fat; 1.7 g protein; 8.3 g fat (4.2 g sat.); 10 g carbo (0.5 g fiber); 117 mg sodium; 17 mg chol.

## Mincemeat Cookies

PREP AND COOK TIME: About 1¼ hours Follow directions for **Cutout Cookies Master Recipe** (page 288). In step 1, beat 1 cup (½ lb.) **butter** or margarine (at room temperature) with 1 package (8 oz.) **cream cheese,** ½ cup **powdered sugar,** 1 teaspoon grated **lemon peel,** and ½ teaspoon **vanilla.** In step 2, use 2½ cups **all-purpose flour.**

Divide dough (step 3). Roll ⅛ inch thick (step 4). Cut (step 5) with 2½-inch round cutters. Put on pans (step 6).

Drop ½ teaspoon **canned mincemeat** (¾ cup total) in center of each round. Fold each round in half over filling and press edges to seal. Bake (step 7) until golden, 20 to 25 minutes.

Put ½ cup **powdered sugar** in a bowl. A few at a time, turn hot cookies in sugar, then set on racks to cool (step 8). Serve, or store up to 2 days. MAKES: 70.

Per cookie: 65 cal., 54% (35 cal.) from fat; 0.8 g protein; 3.9 g fat (2.3 g sat.); 6.9 g carbo (0.1 g fiber); 45 mg sodium; 11 mg chol.

## Walnut-Lemon Packets

PREP AND COOK TIME: About 2 hours Prepare dough for **Mincemeat Cookies** (above), but omit mincemeat.

In a food processor, finely grind 2½ cups **walnuts.** In a bowl with a mixer on high speed, whip 2 **large egg** whites and 2 teaspoons **lemon juice** until foamy. Gradually add 1 cup **granulated sugar,** beating until whites hold stiff peaks, 8 to 10 minutes. Stir in walnuts. In a small bowl, use a fork to blend 2 **large egg** yolks.

Following **Cutout Cookies Master Recipe** (page 288), step 3, divide dough into 4 equal portions. Roll (step 4) a portion at a time into a 10- by 12½-inch rectangle, turning dough over and flouring board occasionally to prevent sticking. Press edges to neaten. Cut (step 5) with a knife into 2½-inch squares. Place 1 teaspoon of the wal-

nut mixture in center of each square. Lift diagonally opposite corners of each square to the center over filling. Brush corners with beaten egg yolks and press together to secure.

Put on pans (step 6), and bake (step 7) until golden, 25 to 30 minutes. Transfer to racks (step 8). Sift ¼ cup **powdered sugar** over cookies, cool, then serve, or store up to 2 days. MAKES: 80.

Per cookie: 85 cal., 61% (52 cal.) from fat; 1.3 g protein; 5.8 g fat (2.3 g sat.); 7.5 g carbo (0.3 g fiber); 34 mg sodium; 15 mg chol.

## Dutch Spice Cookies

PREP AND COOK TIME: About 45 minutes Follow directions for **Cutout Cookies Master Recipe** (page 288). In step 1, beat ¾ cup (⅜ lb.) **butter** or margarine (at room temperature) with 1 cup firmly packed **brown sugar** and 2 tablespoons **milk.** In step 2, combine 1½ cups **all-purpose flour,** ½ teaspoon *each* **baking powder** and **ground nutmeg,** 1 teaspoon **ground cloves,** 2 teaspoons **ground cinnamon,** and ¼ cup ground **almonds** (grind in a food processor).

Divide dough (step 3). Roll ⅛ inch thick (step 4). Cut (step 5), put on pans (step 6), and bake (step 7) until slightly darker brown, about 15 minutes. Cool (step 8). Serve, or store up to 1 week. MAKES: 75 (2¾-in.-wide rounds).

Per cookie: 40 cal., 48% (19 cal.) from fat; 0.4 g protein; 2.1 g fat (1.2 g sat.); 5 g carbo (0.1 g fiber); 28 mg sodium; 5.1 mg chol.

## Gingerbread People

PREP AND COOK TIME: About 3 hours Follow directions for **Cutout Cookies Master Recipe** (page 288). In step 1, beat ¾ cup (⅜ lb.) **butter** or margarine (at room temperature) with ¾ cup *each* **granulated sugar** and **molasses.** In step 2, combine 3¼ cups **all-purpose flour,** 1 teaspoon **baking soda,** 2 teaspoons *each* **ground ginger** and **instant espresso coffee powder,** 1 teaspoon **ground cinnamon,** and ½ teaspoon **ground nutmeg.**

Divide dough (step 3). Wrap each portion airtight and freeze until firm, about 1 hour. Roll ¼ inch thick (step 4). Cut (step 5) with people-shaped cutters. Put on pans (step 6) and bake (step 7) until edges are brown, 15 to 20 minutes. Cool (step 8). Leave plain or decorate with **icing for piping** (page 288). Serve, or store up to 1 week. MAKES: 26 (3- by 4-in. shapes).

Per cookie: 156 cal., 32% (50 cal.) from fat; 1.8 g protein; 5.5 g fat (3.4 g sat.); 25 g carbo (0.4 g fiber); 107 mg sodium; 15 mg chol.

## Rye Rabbits

PREP AND COOK TIME: About 1¾ hours Follow directions for **Cutout Cookies Master Recipe** (page 288). In step 1, beat 1 cup (½ lb.) **butter** or margarine (at room temperature) with ½ cup *each* **granulated sugar** and **molasses;** then beat in 1 **large egg** yolk. In step 2, combine 2 cups **rye flour,** 1 cup **all-purpose flour,** 2 teaspoons *each* **ground cinnamon** and **ground cardamom,** 1 teaspoon **ground ginger,** and ½ teaspoon **ground nutmeg.**

Divide dough (step 3). Wrap each portion airtight and freeze until firm, about 15 minutes. Roll ⅛ inch thick (step 4). Cut (step 5) with a 2- by 3-inch cutter (rabbit or other shape). Put on pans (step 6) and bake (step 7) until firm to touch and slightly darker, 10 to 14 minutes. Cool (step 8), then serve, or store up to 4 days. MAKES: 100.

Per cookie: 38 cal., 45% (17 cal.) from fat; 0.4 g protein; 1.9 g fat (1.2 g sat.); 4.8 g carbo (0.3 g fiber); 20 mg sodium; 7.1 mg chol.

## Vanilla Sandwiches

PREP AND COOK TIME: About 1½ hours *Make dough:* In a food processor or in a bowl with your fingers, whirl or rub 2 cups **all-purpose flour** and 1 cup (½ lb.) **butter** or margarine (in chunks) until lumps are ¼ inch thick. Add ⅓ cup **whipping cream** and whirl or stir with a fork until dough holds together.

Pat into a ball and divide in half. Flatten each into a 5-inch-wide disk. Wrap airtight and freeze until firm, about 15 minutes.

Coat a board with about 6 tablespoons **granulated sugar.** Dust rolling pin with sugar. Roll dough on sugar, a portion at a time, to ⅛ inch thick, turning over frequently to prevent sticking. Cut dough with a 1-inch-wide round cutter.

Set rounds ½ inch apart on buttered, floured 12- by 15-inch baking sheets. Prick each round 3 or 4 times with a fork.

In a 300° oven, bake cookies until golden, about 20 minutes. With a wide spatula, quickly transfer to racks to cool.

In a bowl, beat 3 tablespoons **butter** or margarine (at room temperature) with 1¼ cups **powdered sugar** and 1 teaspoon **vanilla.** Stir in enough **milk,** 1½ to 2 tablespoons, to make a mixture that is smooth and thick enough to spread. Spread 1 side of half the cookies with vanilla-butter mixture. Top with remaining cookies. Serve, chill airtight up to 2 days, or freeze to store longer. MAKES: 65 sandwich cookies.

Per cookie: 63 cal., 56% (35 cal.) from fat; 0.5 g protein; 3.9 g fat (2.4 g sat.); 6.7 g carbo (0.1 g fiber); 36 mg sodium; 11 mg chol.

# Refrigerator cookies A 1929

*Sunset* cookie recipe instructs: "Form dough into rolls, wrap in waxed paper, and place in the ice-box to chill overnight. When wanted, slice thin and bake."

Ice boxes may be long gone, but not the convenience of refrigerated cookie dough that's ready to bake fresh when the mood strikes, or when unexpected guests drop in.

## Master Recipe

1. Select recipe (choices follow). In a bowl with a mixer, beat butter with sugar until smooth. As specified, add egg, vanilla, and other flavorings and beat to blend.

2. In another bowl, combine flour mixture. Add to butter mixture; stir, then beat until well mixed.

3. Divide dough into portions as recipe directs. Place each portion on a sheet of waxed paper or plastic wrap. Form portions into logs the size specified in each recipe. Roll paper smoothly and snugly around each log; wrap airtight. Freeze until firm enough to slice neatly as recipe directs (or chill at least 6 hours or up to 3 days in the refrigerator). To store longer, freeze up to 3 months; thaw just enough to cut neat slices.

4. Unwrap dough. Using a thin, sharp knife, cut logs crosswise into ⅛-inch-thick slices (or thickness recipe specifies). Lay slices 1 inch apart on nonstick or buttered 12- by 15-inch baking sheets; if cookies flattened when cut, reshape with fingers, if desired.

5. Bake as directed in recipe; if using more than 1 pan in 1 oven, switch pan positions halfway through baking.

6. With a wide spatula, transfer cookies to racks to cool. Serve, store airtight as recipe directs, or freeze to store longer.

## Chinese Pinwheels

NOTES: *To toast sesame seed*, shake often in an 8- to 10-inch frying pan over medium heat until golden, 5 to 7 minutes. Promptly remove from pan.
PREP AND COOK TIME: About 3 hours
In a 2- to 3-quart pan over medium heat, bring 2 cups chopped **pitted dates**, ¾ cup **granulated sugar**, and ¾ cup **water** to a boil. Simmer, stirring often, until mixture is as thick as jam, 15 to 20 minutes. Stir in ¾ cup toasted **sesame seed** (see notes). Let cool.

Follow directions for **Refrigerator Cookies Master Recipe** (above). In step 1, beat 1 cup (½ lb.) **butter** or margarine (at room temperature) with 2 cups firmly packed **brown sugar**; then beat in 2 **large eggs**. In step 2, combine 4 cups **all-purpose flour** and ½ teaspoon *each* **baking soda** and **salt**.

Divide dough (step 3) into 4 equal portions. Between sheets of waxed paper or cooking parchment, roll 1 portion at a time to form a neat 6- by 8-inch rectangle. Pull off top piece of paper and dot dough with ¼ of the date filling, then gently spread to evenly cover dough, leaving a ½-inch strip bare along an 8-inch side. Roll from opposite 8-inch side, pulling paper from dough. Freeze about 1¼ hours.

Cut (step 4), and lay slices on buttered, floured baking sheets. Bake (step 5) in a 350° oven until slightly darker brown, 10 to 12 minutes. Cool (step 6), then serve, or store up to 3 days. MAKES: 120.
Per cookie: 62 cal., 31% (19 cal.) from fat; 0.7 g protein; 2.1 g fat (1 g sat.); 10 g carbo (0.4 g fiber); 33 mg sodium; 7.7 mg chol.

## Cornmeal Wafers

PREP AND COOK TIME: About 3 hours
Follow directions for **Refrigerator Cookies Master Recipe** (above). In step 1, beat ½ cup (¼ lb.) **butter** or margarine (at room temperature) with ⅔ cup **granulated sugar**; then beat in 1 **large egg** and 1 teaspoon **vanilla**. In step 2, combine 1 cup *each* **all-purpose flour** and **cornmeal** and 1 teaspoon **baking powder.**

Divide dough (step 3) in half and form each portion into a 2-inch-thick log. Freeze about 2½ hours. Cut (step 4), and lay slices 3 inches apart on baking sheets. Bake (step 5) in a 350° oven until edges are slightly browned, 15 to 18 minutes. Cool (step 6), then serve, or store up to 3 days. MAKES: 40.
Per cookie: 60 cal., 38% (23 cal.) from fat; 0.8 g protein; 2.5 g fat (1.5 g sat.); 8.4 g carbo (0.3 g fiber); 37 mg sodium; 12 mg chol.

## Orange Refrigerator Cookies

PREP AND COOK TIME: About 2½ hours
Follow directions for **Refrigerator Cookies Master Recipe** (above). In step 1, beat 1 cup (½ lb.) **butter** or margarine (at room temperature) with ½ cup *each* **granulated sugar** and firmly packed **brown sugar**; then beat in 1 **large egg** and 2 teaspoons grated **orange** peel. In step 2, combine 3 cups **all-purpose flour**, ½ cup minced **walnuts**, and ½ teaspoon *each* **baking soda** and **salt**.

Divide dough (step 3) in half and form each portion into a 2½-inch-thick log. Freeze about 2 hours. Cut (step 4). Bake (step 5) in a 375° oven until edges are very lightly browned, about 12 minutes. Cool (step 6), then serve, or store up to 4 days. MAKES: 40.
Per cookie: 106 cal., 48% (51 cal.) from fat; 1.4 g protein; 5.7 g fat (3 g sat.); 13 g carbo (0.3 g fiber); 94 mg sodium; 18 mg chol.

## Sesame Butter Cookies

NOTES: *To toast sesame seed*, see notes for Chinese Pinwheels (far left).
PREP AND COOK TIME: About 3 hours
Follow directions for **Refrigerator Cookies Master Recipe** (above). In

CHILL AND SLICE for Orange Refrigerator Cookies (in box) and Two-Tone Cream Sandwiches (on box).

step 1, beat 1 cup (½ lb.) **butter** or margarine (at room temperature) with ½ cup **granulated sugar**. In step 2, combine 2 cups **all-purpose flour**, 3 tablespoons toasted **sesame seed** (see notes), and ½ teaspoon **ground cardamom**. Divide dough (step 3) in half and form each portion into a 1½-inch-thick log. Freeze about 2½ hours.

Cut (step 4) into ¼-inch-thick slices. Bake (step 5) in a 375° oven until edges are golden brown, about 15 minutes. Cool (step 6), then serve, or store up to 4 days. MAKES: 40.

Per cookie: 77 cal., 57% (44 cal.) from fat; 0.8 g protein; 4.9 g fat (2.9 g sat.); 7.4 g carbo (0.3 g fiber); 47 mg sodium; 12 mg chol.

## Two-Tone Cream Sandwiches

PREP AND COOK TIME: About 3¾ hours Follow directions for **Refrigerator Cookies Master Recipe** (page 291). In step 1, beat 1 cup (½ lb.) **butter** or margarine (at room temperature) with ½ cup **granulated sugar**; beat in 1 **large egg** yolk and 1 teaspoon **vanilla**. In step 2, use 2½ cups **all-purpose flour**.

Divide dough (step 3) in half. Mix 2 ounces melted **unsweetened chocolate** into 1 half. Divide each color of dough into 4 equal portions. Form each portion into a ¾-inch-thick log. Freeze about 20 minutes.

Cut (step 4) into ¼-inch-thick slices.

If chilled dough crumbles, let stand until it warms a little, then cut. Bake (step 5) in a 350° oven until plain cookies are lightly browned on the bottom and chocolate ones are slightly darker, 8 to 10 minutes. Cool (step 6).

Mix ½ cup (¼ lb.) **butter** or margarine, ¾ cup **powdered sugar,** and 1 teaspoon **vanilla**. Spread about ¼ teaspoon of the mixture onto each plain cookie, then top with a chocolate cookie. Serve, or store up to 2 days. MAKES: 150 (½-inch-wide sandwich cookies).

Per cookie: 31 cal., 61% (19 cal.) from fat; 0.3 g protein; 2.1 g fat (1.3 g sat.); 2.9 g carbo (0.1 g fiber); 19 mg sodium; 6.4 mg chol.

# Drop cookies
If drop cookies were your first baking project, you aren't alone. They're perfect for beginners. Just mix the ingredients, then drop the dough or batter from a spoon onto baking sheets. And there's no shortage of variations in flavor, texture, size, and shape. Drop cookies range from chocolate chip to macaroons. Some stay lumpy and thick, some spread thin; some are chewy, others are crisp; some are homespun, some are elegant. But all are easy.

## Master Recipe

1. Select recipe (choices follow). In a bowl with a mixer, beat butter with sugar and/or molasses until well blended. Then, as specified, beat in eggs, liquid, and vanilla.

2. In another bowl, combine flour mixture. Add to butter mixture. Stir, then beat until well mixed. Stir in any extra ingredients.

3. As recipe directs, drop dough onto buttered 12- by 15-inch baking sheets; measure the first few cookies precisely, then eyeball the rest.

4. Bake as directed in recipe; if using more than 1 pan in 1 oven, switch pan positions halfway through baking.

5. With a wide spatula, transfer cookies to racks to cool. If hot cookies start to break, slide a thin spatula under them to release, let stand on pan to firm, 2 to 5 minutes, then transfer to racks. Serve cookies, store airtight as recipe directs, or freeze to store longer.

## Bourbon Snaps

PREP AND COOK TIME: About 1 hour Follow directions for **Drop Cookies Master Recipe** (above). In step 1, beat ½ cup (¼ lb.) **butter** or margarine, melted and cooled, with ½ cup **granulated sugar,** ⅓ cup **molasses,** and 3 tablespoons **bourbon**. In step 2, combine 1 cup **all-purpose flour,** ¼ teaspoon **salt,** and 1 teaspoon **ground ginger**. Stir in ¼ cup chopped **almonds**.

Drop (step 3) 1-tablespoon portions 3 inches apart onto baking sheets. Bake (step 4) in a 300° oven until slightly darker brown, 20 to 25 minutes. Cool (step 5), then serve, or store up to 3 days. MAKES: 25.

Per cookie: 91 cal., 45% (41 cal.) from fat; 0.8 g protein; 4.5 g fat (2.4 g sat.); 11 g carbo (0.3 g fiber); 64 mg sodium; 10 mg chol.

DROP AND BAKE: Chocolate-dipped Coconut Macaroons, dark Gianduia Buttons, candy-dotted Peppermint Buttons, and crinkly Swiss Almond Macaroons.

## Brazil Nut Chews

PREP AND COOK TIME: About 1¾ hours

Follow directions for **Drop Cookies Master Recipe** (page 292). In step 1, beat ½ cup (¼ lb.) **butter** or margarine (at room temperature) with ¾ cup firmly packed **brown sugar**; beat in 1 **large egg** and ½ teaspoon **vanilla**. In step 2, combine 1¼ cups **all-purpose flour**, ½ teaspoon **baking powder**, ½ teaspoon **baking soda**, ½ teaspoon **ground cinnamon** and ¼ teaspoon **salt**. Stir in 2 cups coarsely chopped **Brazil nuts**, 1¼ cups chopped **pitted dates**, 1 cup *each* chopped **dried apricots** and chopped **pecans**, and ¾ cup chopped **dried pineapple**.

Drop dough (step 3) in 1½-teaspoon portions 1 inch apart onto baking sheets. Bake (step 4) in a 350° oven until lightly browned on bottom, about 7 minutes. Cool (step 5), then serve, or store up to 3 days. MAKES: 135.

Per cookie: 47 cal., 51% (24 cal.) from fat; 0.6 g protein; 2.7 g fat (0.9 g sat.); 5.5 g carbo (0.4 g fiber); 21 mg sodium; 3.6 mg chol.

## Caramelized-Sugar Cookies

PREP AND COOK TIME: About 1 hour

Butter a 12- by 14-inch piece of foil and set on a baking sheet. In an 8- to 10-inch frying pan over medium-high heat, melt ½ cup **granulated sugar**, frequently shaking and tilting pan. When mixture is a light caramel color, about 6 minutes, pour onto foil. Let stand until caramel is hard, about 5 minutes. Break into chunks, then finely crush (into ⅛- to ¼-in. pieces) in a food processor or in a heavy plastic food bag with a mallet.

Follow directions for **Drop Cookies Master Recipe** (page 292). In step 1, beat ¾ cup (⅜ lb.) **butter** or margarine (at room temperature) with ½ cup **granulated sugar**; then beat in ½ teaspoon **vanilla** and 2 tablespoons **water**. In step 2, combine 1¼ cups **all-purpose flour** and ½ teaspoon **baking powder**. Stir crushed caramelized sugar into the dough.

Drop dough (step 3) in 1½-teaspoon portions 2 inches apart onto buttered, floured baking sheets. Bake (step 4) in a 325° oven until edges are light brown, 12 to 15 minutes. Let stand on pans (step 5) until slightly firm, 1 to 2 minutes, then with a wide spatula, quickly transfer to racks to cool. Serve, or store up to 2 days. MAKES: 55.

Per cookie: 50 cal., 50% (25 cal.) from fat; 0.3 g protein; 2.8 g fat (1.7 g sat.); 6 g carbo (0.1 g fiber); 33 mg sodium; 7.4 mg chol.

## Chinese Five Spice Oatmeal Cookies

NOTES: *To toast almonds,* place in an 8- or 9-inch-wide pan and bake in a 350° oven, shaking often, until golden, about 15 minutes. Pour from pan.

PREP AND COOK TIME: About 55 minutes

Follow directions for **Drop Cookies Master Recipe** (page 292). In step 1, beat 1 cup (½ lb.) **butter** or margarine (at room temperature) with 1 cup **granulated sugar** and 1 cup firmly packed **brown sugar**; then beat in 2 **large eggs** and 2 teaspoons **vanilla**. In step 2, combine 1½ cups **all-purpose flour**, 1 teaspoon **baking powder**, ½ teaspoon **salt**, 1½ teaspoons **Chinese five spice**, and 1 teaspoon **ground cinnamon**. Stir in 2 cups **quick-cooking rolled oats** and 1 cup coarsely ground toasted **almonds** (see notes; grind in blender or food processor).

Drop dough (step 3) in 1⅓-tablespoon (4-teaspoon) portions 1½ inches apart onto baking sheets. Bake (step 4) in a 350° oven until golden, 12 to 15 minutes. Cool (step 5), then serve, or store up to 2 days. MAKES: 45.

Per cookie: 119 cal., 44% (52 cal.) from fat; 1.8 g protein; 5.8 g fat (2.8 g sat.); 15 g carbo (0.7 g fiber); 85 mg sodium; 21 mg chol.

## Gianduia Buttons

NOTES: *To brown butter* or margarine, place in an 8- to 10-inch frying pan over medium heat until lightly browned, 5 to 10 minutes. Pour into a bowl and cool. *To toast hazelnuts,* place whole nuts in an 8- or 9-inch-wide pan and bake in a 350° oven until golden brown under skins, 10 to 12 minutes. Pour nuts onto a towel and rub to remove loose skins.

PREP AND COOK TIME: About 1 hour

Follow directions for **Drop Cookies Master Recipe** (page 292). In step 1, beat ½ cup (¼ lb.) browned **butter** or margarine (see notes) with ¾ cup **granulated sugar**; then beat in 1 **large egg white** and 1 teaspoon **vanilla**. In step 2, combine ¾ cup **all-purpose flour**, ½ cup ground toasted **hazelnuts** (see notes; grind in a food processor or blender), 2 tablespoons **unsweetened cocoa**, 2 teaspoons **instant coffee powder**, and 1 teaspoon **baking soda**.

Drop dough (step 3) in ½-teaspoon portions 1 inch apart onto baking sheets. Bake (step 4) in a 350° oven until tops of cookies begin to look slightly cracked, 8 to 10 minutes. Cool (step 5), then serve, or store up to 3 days. MAKES: 105 (1 in. wide).

Per cookie: 20 cal., 55% (11 cal.) from fat; 0.2 g protein; 1.2 g fat (0.6 g sat.); 2.2 g carbo (0.1 g fiber); 21 mg sodium; 2.4 mg chol.

## Mint Sandies

PREP AND COOK TIME: About 45 minutes

Follow directions for **Drop Cookies Master Recipe** (page 292). In step 1, beat ½ cup (¼ lb.) **butter** or margarine (at room temperature) with 6 tablespoons *each* granulated sugar and firmly packed **brown sugar**; then beat in 1 **large egg** and ½ teaspoon **vanilla**. In step 2, combine 1¼ cups **all-purpose flour**, ½ teaspoon **baking soda**, and ¼ teaspoon **salt**. Coarsely chop 5 ounces **mint-flavor green-tinted candies** or thin chocolate-mint wafer candies; stir into dough.

Drop dough (step 3) in 2-teaspoon portions 2 inches apart onto baking sheets. Bake (step 4) in a 350° oven until lightly browned, 8 to 10 minutes. Cool (step 5), then serve, or store up to 3 days. MAKES: 50.

Per cookie: 61 cal., 48% (29 cal.) from fat; 0.7 g protein; 3.2 g fat (1.9 g sat.); 7.6 g carbo (0.1 g fiber); 49 mg sodium; 9.6 mg chol.

## Molasses Crunch Cookies

PREP AND COOK TIME: About 1 hour

Follow directions for **Drop Cookies Master Recipe** (page 292). In step 1, beat ½ cup (¼ lb.) **butter** or margarine (at room temperature) with 6 tablespoons *each* firmly packed **brown sugar** and **molasses**; then beat in 1 **large egg** and ½ teaspoon **vanilla**. In step 2, combine 1 cup **all-purpose flour**, ½ teaspoon **baking soda**, and ¼ teaspoon **salt**. Stir in ½ cup chopped **walnuts**.

Drop dough (step 3) in 1½-teaspoon portions 1½ inches apart onto baking sheets. Bake (step 4) in a 350° oven until slightly darker brown at edges, 8 to 10 minutes. Cool (step 5), then serve, or store up to 3 days. MAKES: 70.

Per cookie: 34 cal., 50% (17 cal.) from fat; 0.4 g protein; 1.9 g fat (0.9 g sat.); 3.9 g carbo (0.1 g fiber); 33 mg sodium; 6.6 mg chol.

## Peppermint Buttons

NOTES: *To brown butter* or margarine, see notes for Gianduia Buttons (left).

PREP AND COOK TIME: About 1 hour

Follow directions for **Drop Cookies Master Recipe** (page 292). In step 1, beat ½ cup (¼ lb.) browned **butter** or margarine (see notes) with ¾ cup **granulated sugar**; then beat in 1 **large egg white** and 1 teaspoon **vanilla**. In step 2, combine 1 cup **all-purpose flour** and 1 teaspoon **baking soda**. Stir in ½ cup coarsely crushed **hard peppermint candies.**

Drop dough (step 3) in ½-teaspoon portions 1 inch apart onto baking sheets. Bake (step 4) in a 350° oven until tops of cookies begin to look slightly cracked and are deep golden, 8 to 10 minutes. Cool (step 5), then serve, or store up to 1 week. MAKES: 120 (1 in. wide).

Per cookie: 19 cal., 38% (7.2 cal.) from fat; 0.1 g protein; 0.8 g fat (0.5 g sat.); 2.9 g carbo (0 g fiber); 19 mg sodium; 2.1 mg chol.

## Thick, Soft, and Chewy Chocolate Chip Cookies

PREP AND COOK TIME: About 40 minutes
Follow directions for **Drop Cookies Master Recipe** (page 292). In step 1, beat 1 cup (½ lb.) **butter** or margarine (at room temperature) with 1½ cups firmly packed **brown sugar;** then beat in 2 **large eggs** and 1 teaspoon **vanilla.** In step 2, combine 2½ cups **all-purpose flour,** 1 teaspoon **baking soda,** and ½ teaspoon **salt.** Stir in 2 cups (12 oz.) **semisweet chocolate chips** and 1 cup chopped **pecans** (optional).

Drop dough (step 3) in 2-tablespoon (⅛-cup) portions 2 inches apart onto baking sheets. Bake (step 4) in a 400° oven until cookies are lightly browned and no longer wet in center (break 1 open to check), 6 to 8 minutes. Cool (step 5), then serve, or store up to 1 day. MAKES: 28 (2½ in. wide).

Per cookie: 208 cal., 48% (99 cal.) from fat; 2.1 g protein; 11 g fat (6.3 g sat.); 28 g carbo (0.3 g fiber); 165 mg sodium; 34 mg chol.

## Thin, Crisp Chocolate Chip Cookies

PREP AND COOK TIME: About 35 minutes
Follow directions for **Drop Cookies Master Recipe** (page 292). In step 1, beat ½ cup (¼ lb.) cool melted **butter** or margarine with ⅓ cup **granulated sugar** and ½ cup firmly packed **brown sugar;** then beat in 3 tablespoons **water** and ½ teaspoon **vanilla.** In step 2, combine 1 cup **all-purpose flour,** ¾ teaspoon **baking soda,** and ¼ teaspoon **salt.** Stir in 1 cup (6 oz.) **semisweet chocolate chips** and ½ cup chopped **pecans** (optional).

Drop dough (step 3) in 1-tablespoon portions 2 inches apart onto baking sheets. Bake (step 4) in a 300° oven until cookies are lightly browned, 18 to 20 minutes. Cool (step 5), then serve, or store up to 2 days. MAKES: 32.

Per cookie: 88 cal., 47% (41 cal.) from fat; 0.6 g protein; 4.6 g fat (2.8 g sat.); 12 g carbo (0.1 g fiber); 81 mg sodium; 8.4 mg chol.

## White Chocolate Cranberry Rounds

PREP AND COOK TIME: About 55 minutes
Follow directions for **Drop Cookies Master Recipe** (page 292). In step 1, beat 1 cup (½ lb.) **butter** or margarine (at room temperature) with 1½ cups **granulated sugar;** then beat in 1 **large egg.** In step 2, combine 1½ cups **all-purpose flour** and 2 teaspoons **baking soda.** Stir in 1½ cups **quick-cooking rolled oats** and 1 cup (6 oz.) **white candy chips.**

Drop dough (step 3) in 1½-tablespoon (4-teaspoon) portions 2 inches apart onto baking sheets. Press 3 or 4 **fresh** or frozen **cranberries** (1½ cups total) into each cookie. Bake (step 4) in a 350° oven until light golden, 10 to 12 minutes. Cool (step 5), then serve, or chill up to 2 days. MAKES: 60.

Per cookie: 86 cal., 44% (38 cal.) from fat; 1 g protein; 4.2 g fat (2.7 g sat.); 11 g carbo (0.4 g fiber); 79 mg sodium; 12 mg chol.

## Chocolate-dipped Coconut Macaroons

PREP AND COOK TIME: About 1½ hours
In a bowl with a mixer, beat 4 **large egg** whites until frothy. Add 1½ teaspoons **vanilla,** ⅔ cup **granulated sugar,** and ¼ cup **all-purpose flour.** Beat until well mixed. Stir in 3½ cups lightly packed **sweetened flaked dried coconut.**

Drop dough in ¼-cup portions about 3 inches apart onto buttered, floured 12- by 15-inch baking sheets.

Bake in a 325° oven until macaroons are golden, about 25 minutes; if using more than 1 pan in 1 oven, switch pan positions halfway through baking. With a wide spatula, transfer macaroons to racks to cool.

In a 1- to 2-quart pan over low heat, stir 2 tablespoons **butter** or margarine and 4 ounces chopped **semisweet chocolate** until melted and smooth.

Hold 1 macaroon on 1 edge and dip opposite edge into melted chocolate to coat half of the cookie. Lift out, twisting your hand to break chocolate flow. Set macaroon, bottom down, on a waxed paper–lined baking sheet. Repeat to dip remaining cookies. Chill, uncovered, until chocolate is firm, about 30 minutes. Serve, chill airtight up to 1 week, or freeze to store longer. MAKES: 11 (2½ in. wide).

Per cookie: 285 cal., 47% (135 cal.) from fat; 3.1 g protein; 15 g fat (12 g sat.); 36 g carbo (2.7 g fiber); 124 mg sodium; 6.6 mg chol.

## Swiss Almond Macaroons

PREP AND COOK TIME: About 5 hours
Line 3 baking sheets, each 12 by 15 inches, with nonstick pan liners, silicone baking pads, or cooking parchment; or butter and flour nonstick pans.

In a small bowl, beat 3 **large egg** whites with a fork to froth slightly, then measure exactly ⅓ cup.

In a food processor or bowl with a mixer, whirl or beat 8 ounces (about 1 cup) **almond paste,** 1 cup **granulated sugar,** and 1 teaspoon grated **lemon** peel until fine crumbs form. Add ⅓ cup egg whites and whirl or beat on high speed until very smooth.

Spoon mixture into a pastry bag fitted with a plain ½-inch tip. Squeeze egg-almond mixture onto prepared baking sheets to form 1¼-inch-wide rounds spaced 2 inches apart. Or spoon in 1-teaspoon portions onto pans.

Sift ⅓ cup **powdered sugar** over mounds to coat evenly. Let unbaked cookies stand, uncovered, until they develop a slight crust, about 4 hours.

Pinch top of each round simultaneously with thumb and forefinger of both hands to crinkle cookies.

Bake in a 350° oven until macaroons are a rich golden brown, 8 to 12 minutes. Cool on pans. Slide a thin spatula under cookies to release. Serve, store airtight up to 3 days, or freeze to store longer. MAKES: 45.

Per cookie: 46 cal., 30% (14 cal.) from fat; 0.8 g protein; 1.5 g fat (0.2 g sat.); 7.5 g carbo (0 g fiber); 5.1 mg sodium; 0.5 mg chol.

## Low-fat Cornflake Chews

PREP AND COOK TIME: About 25 minutes
In a blender or food processor, finely grind 2½ cups **cornflake cereal.**

In a bowl with a mixer on high speed, beat 1 **large egg** white, ⅛ teaspoon **cream of tartar,** 1¼ cups **powdered sugar,** and 2 tablespoons **malted milk powder** until thick and smooth. Stir in ground cereal and another ½ cup **cornflake cereal.**

Drop dough in 1½-teaspoon mounds 2 inches apart onto buttered, floured 12- by 15-inch baking sheets.

Bake in a 375° oven until golden brown, 8 to 10 minutes; if using more than 1 pan in 1 oven, switch pan positions halfway through baking.

Let cookies firm on pans for 1 minute, then with a wide spatula, transfer to racks to cool. Serve, store airtight up to 3 days, or freeze to store longer. MAKES: 30.

Per cookie: 37 cal., 7.3% (2.7 cal.) from fat; 0.5 g protein; 0.3 g fat (0.2 g sat.); 8 g carbo (0 g fiber); 40 mg sodium; 0.9 mg chol.

# Shortbread cookies

Butter, flour, and sugar—in essence, shortbread is simple. Perfection comes from the balance of ingredients, which creates the dense, snappy texture, and from slow baking to bring out the buttery, toasted flavor. For subtle modifications, use cornstarch to enhance sandiness, masa flour to add earthiness, brown sugar for butterscotch-toffee overtones, ginger for pungency, or sesame seed for crunch.

## Master Recipe

1. Select recipe (choices follow). In a food processor, whirl butter, sugar, vanilla if specified, flour, and any additional ingredients until smooth. Or in a bowl with a mixer, beat butter, sugar, and vanilla until smooth, then stir in flour and any additional ingredients and press dough into a firm ball.

2. Evenly press dough into 2 cake pans (9 in. wide) with removable rims. Press edges of dough with fork tines to make a ridge pattern. Then, with fork tines, pierce dough all over in parallel lines 1 inch apart. Or shape dough as recipe directs.

3. Bake in a 300° oven as directed in recipe.

4. If baked in cake pans, remove rims from warm cookies. Cut each into 12 wedges. Cool on pan bottoms on racks, or as recipe directs.

5. Serve cookies, store them airtight as recipe directs, or freeze them to store longer.

## Brown Sugar Masa Shortbread

PREP AND COOK TIME: About 1¼ hours
In a food processor, finely grind (or mince with a knife) ½ cup **sweetened shredded dried coconut**. Follow directions for **Shortbread Master Recipe** (above). In step 1, whirl or beat the coconut, 1 cup (½ lb.) **butter** or margarine (at room temperature), 1 cup firmly packed **brown sugar**, 1 teaspoon **vanilla**, and 1 cup *each* **all-purpose flour** and **dehydrated masa flour** (corn tortilla flour).

Shape (step 2). Bake (step 3) until firm to touch and slightly darker brown, about 45 minutes. Mix ¼ cup **granulated sugar** and ¼ teaspoon **ground cinnamon**; sprinkle on hot cookies. Cut (step 4) and cool. Serve (step 5), or store up to 1 week. MAKES: 24.

Per cookie: 155 cal., 49% (76 cal.) from fat; 1.1 g protein; 8.4 g fat (5.2 g sat.); 19 g carbo (0.6 g fiber); 86 mg sodium; 21 mg chol.

## Brown Sugar Shortbread

PREP AND COOK TIME: About 1½ hours
Follow directions for **Shortbread Master Recipe** (above). In step 1, whirl or beat 1 cup (½ lb.) **butter** or margarine (at room temperature), ½ cup firmly packed **brown sugar,** and 2 cups **all-purpose flour.** Pat into a 1-inch-thick rectangle, wrap airtight, and freeze until firm, about 20 minutes.

To shape (step 2), unwrap dough and roll between sheets of waxed paper to make a 6- by 18-inch rectangle. Cut in half crosswise, through paper. Peel off top sheet of paper and invert each rectangle onto a baking sheet. Peel off remaining paper. With a long, sharp knife, cut dough into ¾- by 2-inch rectangles. Prick dough with a fork in parallel lines about ½ inch apart. Move rectangles about 1 inch apart.

Bake (step 3) until firm to touch and slightly darker brown, about 15 minutes. Cool (step 4). Serve (step 5), or store up to 1 week. MAKES: 72.

Per cookie: 41 cal., 56% (23 cal.) from fat; 0.4 g protein; 2.6 g fat (1.6 g sat.); 4.1 g carbo (0.1 g fiber); 27 mg sodium; 6.9 mg chol.

## Ginger Shortbread

PREP AND COOK TIME: About 1 hour
Follow directions for **Shortbread Master Recipe** (above). In step 1, whirl or beat 1 cup (½ lb.) **butter** or margarine (at room temperature), ½ cup **granulated sugar,** 2½ cups **all-purpose flour,** 2 tablespoons minced **crystallized ginger,** and ½ teaspoon **ground ginger.**

Shape (step 2). Bake (step 3) until firm to touch and golden at edges, 40 to 45 minutes. Sprinkle with 2 tablespoons **granulated sugar.**

Cut (step 4) and cool. Serve (step 5), or store up to 2 days. MAKES: 24.

Per cookie: 140 cal., 50% (70 cal.) from fat; 1.4 g protein; 7.8 g fat (4.8 g sat.); 16 g carbo (0.4 g fiber); 79 mg sodium; 21 mg chol.

## Scottish Shortbread

PREP AND COOK TIME: About 1 hour
Follow directions for **Shortbread Master Recipe** (above). In step 1, whirl or beat 1 cup (½ lb.) **butter** or margarine (at room temperature), ½ cup **granulated sugar,** 2½ cups **all-purpose flour,** and 6 tablespoons **cornstarch.** Shape (step 2). Bake (step 3) until firm to touch and golden at edges, about 45 minutes. Sprinkle hot cookies with 2 tablespoons **granulated sugar.** Cut (step 4) and cool. Serve (step 5), or store up to 1 week. MAKES: 24.

Per cookie: 143 cal., 49% (70 cal.) from fat; 1.4 g protein; 7.8 g fat (4.8 g sat.); 17 g carbo (0.4 g fiber); 79 mg sodium; 21 mg chol.

## Sesame Seed Shortbread

NOTES: *To toast sesame seed,* see notes for Chinese Pinwheels (page 291).
PREP AND COOK TIME: About 1 hour
Follow directions for **Shortbread Master Recipe** (above). In step 1, whirl or beat 1 cup (½ lb.) **butter** or margarine (at room temperature), 1 cup **granulated sugar,** 2 cups **all-purpose flour,** and ½ cup toasted **sesame seed** (see notes). Shape (step 2). Bake (step 3) until firm to touch and golden at edges, 40 to 45 minutes. Cut (step 4) and cool. Serve (step 5), or store up to 2 days. MAKES: 24.

Per cookie: 157 cal., 52% (82 cal.) from fat; 1.6 g protein; 9.1 g fat (5 g sat.); 18 g carbo (0.7 g fiber); 79 mg sodium; 21 mg chol.

SHORT AND SWEET: Scottish Shortbread triangles set the standard for toasted flavor in this cookie family. Subtle changes—such as brown instead of granulated sugar in Brown Sugar Shortbread—make big taste differences.

# Shaped cookies

Call it sculpture, or call it playing with food. Your hands work the magic on these cookies, pinching, pressing, and squeezing dough into balls, logs, strips, or free-form fantasies.

Shaped cookies include favorites such as thumbprints (ours are filled with jalapeño jelly), peanut butter mounds with chocolate kiss centers, snickerdoodles, and gingersnaps. More unusual recipes are provençal pine nut cookies and anise-jam ribbons.

## Master Recipe

1. Select recipe (choices follow). In a bowl with a mixer, beat butter or oil, peanut butter or almond paste, as specified, and sugar and/or molasses until very smooth. Then beat in eggs, liquid, and vanilla as directed.

2. In another bowl, combine flour mixture. Add to butter mixture and beat until well blended. Stir in any extra ingredients.

3. As recipe directs, shape dough and place on 12- by 15-inch baking sheets (butter pans if recipe specifies).

4. Bake as directed in recipe; if using more than 1 pan in 1 oven, switch pan positions halfway through baking.

5. Using a wide spatula, transfer the cookies to racks to cool. Serve the cookies, store airtight as recipe directs, or freeze them to store longer.

## Almond Butter Cookies

PREP AND COOK TIME: About 4 hours
Follow directions for **Shaped Cookies Master Recipe** (above). In step 1, beat ¾ cup (⅜ lb.) **butter** or margarine (at room temperature) with ⅔ cup **granulated sugar** and 8 ounces (about 1 cup) **almond paste**; then beat in 2 teaspoons **almond extract** and 2 **large eggs**. In step 2, combine 2½ cups **all-purpose flour,** 2½ teaspoons **baking powder,** and ¼ teaspoon **salt.**

Shape dough (step 3) into 1-inch balls. Roll balls in ¾ cup finely chopped **almonds**. Place 1 inch apart on buttered baking sheets. With a fork, flatten balls into 1¼-inch rounds. Bake (step 4) in a 350° oven until lightly browned, 10 to 12 minutes. Cool (step 5), then serve, or store up to 1 day. MAKES: 80.
Per cookie: 59 cal., 53% (31 cal.) from fat; 1.1 g protein; 3.4 g fat (1.3 g sat.); 6.2 g carbo (0.2 g fiber); 43 mg sodium; 10 mg chol.

## Almond Spoons

PREP AND COOK TIME: About 1¾ hours
Follow directions for **Shaped Cookies Master Recipe** (above). In step 1, beat 1 cup (½ lb.) **butter** or margarine (at room temperature) with ½ cup **granulated sugar;** then beat in 1 **large egg** yolk. In step 2, use 2¾ cups **all-purpose flour.**

Shape dough (step 3) into ¾-inch balls. Roll each ball to make a ¼-inch-thick log. Place logs 1 inch apart on baking sheets. Press an **almond** into dough at 1 end of each log to make an oval impression, then remove almond. Bake (step 4) in a 350° oven until golden on bottom, about 8 minutes. Quickly place a **semisweet chocolate chip** (6 tablespoons total) in each nut impression. Return to oven until chocolate softens, about 2 minutes. Press 1 **almond** (1 cup total) into chocolate on each cookie. Cool (step 5), then serve, or store up to 2 days. MAKES: **125.**
Per cookie: 35 cal., 57% (20 cal.) from fat; 0.5 g protein; 2.2 g fat (1.1 g sat.); 3.4 g carbo (0.2 g fiber); 15 mg sodium; 5.7 mg chol.

## Anise-Jam Ribbons

PREP AND COOK TIME: About 45 minutes
Follow directions for **Shaped Cookies Master Recipe** (above). In step 1, beat 1 cup (½ lb.) **butter** or margarine (at room temperature) with ½ cup **granulated sugar;** then beat in 1 **large egg** yolk. In step 2, combine 2½ cups **all-purpose flour** and 1 teaspoon crushed **anise seed**.

Divide dough (step 3) into 8 equal portions. Roll each portion into a ½-inch-thick rope. Evenly space 4 ropes on each baking sheet. With the side of

HANDMADE:
Cut Anise-Jam Ribbons into slices, push a chocolate drop onto Peanut Blossom Cookies, make an impression in Thumbprint Cookies with Chili Jelly, stud Black Pepper Cookies with peppercorns.

your little finger, press a $\frac{1}{4}$-inch-deep groove down the length of each rope.

Bake (step 4) in a 375° oven until cookies just begin to turn golden, about 10 minutes. Remove from oven and spoon **strawberry jam** ($\frac{1}{2}$ cup total) into grooves. Bake until dough is firm to touch and slightly darker, 5 to 10 minutes more. Cool on pans 5 minutes.

In a bowl, stir $\frac{1}{2}$ cup **powdered sugar** and 2 tablespoons **anise-flavor liqueur** until smooth. Drizzle mixture back and forth across cookie ropes. Cut ropes diagonally into 1-inch pieces. Cool (step 5), then serve, or store up to 3 days. MAKES: 75.

Per cookie: 52 cal., 44% (23 cal.) from fat; 0.5 g protein; 2.6 g fat (1.5 g sat.); 6.8 g carbo (0.1 g fiber); 26 mg sodium; 9.5 mg chol.

## Black Pepper Cookies

NOTES: *To brown butter,* see notes for Gianduia Buttons (page 293).
PREP AND COOK TIME: About 1 hour
Follow directions for **Shaped Cookies Master Recipe** (page 296). In step 1, beat $\frac{1}{2}$ cup ($\frac{1}{4}$ lb.) browned **butter** or margarine (see notes) with $\frac{3}{4}$ cup **granulated sugar.** In step 2, combine 1 cup **all-purpose flour,** 1 teaspoon **baking powder,** and 1 to $1\frac{1}{2}$ teaspoons coarsely crushed **black peppercorns.**

Shape (step 3) into 1-inch balls and set $\frac{1}{2}$ inch apart on baking sheets. Dip a flat-bottomed glass in **granulated sugar** (3 to 4 tablespoons total) and flatten balls to $\frac{1}{2}$ inch. Press a **black peppercorn** ($\frac{1}{2}$ teaspoon total) into each cookie center. Bake (step 4) in a 300° oven until lightly browned on the bottom, 25 to 30 minutes. Cool (step 5), then serve, or store up to 5 days. MAKES: 32.

Per cookie: 63 cal., 41% (26 cal.) from fat; 0.4 g protein; 2.9 g fat (1.8 g sat.); 8.9 g carbo (0.1 g fiber); 45 mg sodium; 7.8 mg chol.

## Brown Butter Sand Cookies

NOTES: *To brown butter,* see notes for Gianduia Buttons (page 293).
PREP AND COOK TIME: About $1\frac{1}{2}$ hours
Follow directions for **Shaped Cookies Master Recipe** (page 296). In step 1, beat 1 cup ($\frac{1}{2}$ lb.) browned **butter** or margarine (see notes) with $\frac{2}{3}$ cup **granulated sugar;** then beat in 1 **large egg** yolk. In step 2, combine 2 cups **all-purpose flour,** 1 teaspoon **ground cardamom,** and $\frac{1}{4}$ teaspoon **baking soda.**

Shape dough (step 3) into 1-inch balls. Place 1 inch apart on baking sheets. Bake (step 4) in a 325° oven until golden brown on bottoms, 16 to 18 minutes. Cool (step 5), then serve, or store up to 5 days. MAKES: 40.

Per cookie: 78 cal., 55% (43 cal.) from fat; 0.7 g protein; 4.8 g fat (2.9 g sat.); 8.1 g carbo (0.2 g fiber); 55 mg sodium; 18 mg chol.

## Christmas Gingersnaps

PREP AND COOK TIME: About 50 minutes
Follow directions for **Shaped Cookies Master Recipe** (page 296). In step 1, beat $\frac{3}{4}$ cup ($\frac{3}{8}$ lb.) **butter** or margarine (at room temperature) with 1 cup **granulated sugar** and $\frac{1}{2}$ cup **dark molasses;** then beat in 1 **large egg.** In step 2, combine $2\frac{1}{2}$ cups **all-purpose flour,** $1\frac{1}{2}$ teaspoons **baking soda,** 1 tablespoon **ground ginger,** 2 teaspoons **ground cinnamon,** and $\frac{1}{4}$ teaspoon *each* **ground allspice, ground cloves,** and **ground nutmeg.**

Shape dough (step 3) into 1-inch balls and set 2 inches apart on buttered baking sheets. With a flat-bottomed glass dipped in **granulated sugar** ($\frac{1}{4}$ cup total), flatten balls to $\frac{1}{4}$ inch.

Bake (step 4) in a 325° oven until cookies spring back when gently pressed in center, 10 to 12 minutes. Cool (step 5), then serve, or store up to 1 week. MAKES: 65.

Per cookie: 61 cal., 36% (22 cal.) from fat; 0.6 g protein; 2.4 g fat (1.4 g sat.); 9.3 g carbo (0.1 g fiber); 55 mg sodium; 9.4 mg chol.

## Crisp Oatmeal-Fruit Strips

PREP AND COOK TIME: About $1\frac{1}{2}$ hours
Follow directions for **Shaped Cookies Master Recipe** (page 296). In step 1, beat 1 cup ($\frac{1}{2}$ lb.) **butter** or margarine (at room temperature) with $1\frac{1}{2}$ cups **granulated sugar;** then beat in 1 **large egg.** In step 2, combine 2 cups **all-purpose flour** and 2 teaspoons **baking soda.** Stir in $1\frac{1}{4}$ cups **regular rolled oats** and 2 cups **raisins** or finely chopped pitted dates or prunes.

Divide dough (step 3) into 7 equal portions. Pinch each portion into a 12-inch rope and evenly space 2 or 3 ropes across each baking sheet. Flatten to make 2-inch-wide strips.

Bake (step 4) in a 350° oven until lightly browned, about 10 minutes. Let firm on pans about 2 minutes. Cut strips diagonally into 1-inch-wide pieces. Cool on pans (step 5), then serve, or store up to 3 days. MAKES: 65.

Per cookie: 77 cal., 35% (27 cal.) from fat; 0.9 g protein; 3 g fat (1.8 g sat.); 12 g carbo (0.5 g fiber); 69 mg sodium; 11 mg chol.

## Golden Almond Sculpture Cookies

NOTES: This dough is as malleable as potter's clay, and can be shaped with about as much freedom. Roll into coils to twist or braid; flatten into slabs to imprint or build upon; form into faces, fishes, feathers, angels, or alligators. Let the artist in you run free. To make impressions in dough, use a knife, fork tines, or other objects like screw heads and chopstick tips. For fine strands to make hair, beards, or manes, force dough through a garlic press. *Tips:* The thicker the cookie, the more it spreads and flattens as it bakes. Gently molded shapes hold better than sharp edges. Rounded shapes (noses, etc.) flatten slightly. Thinner areas brown more quickly. For even browning, keep the cookies the same thickness.
PREP AND COOK TIME: About $3\frac{3}{4}$ hours
Follow directions for **Shaped Cookies Master Recipe** (page 296). In step 1, beat 1 cup ($\frac{1}{2}$ lb.) **butter** or margarine (at room temperature) with $\frac{3}{4}$ cup **granulated sugar** and 7 ounces (about $\frac{3}{4}$ cup) **almond paste;** then beat in 1 **large egg.** In step 2, use 3 cups **all-purpose flour.**

To shape dough (step 3), work directly on baking sheets. Cookies no thicker than $\frac{3}{4}$ inch hold shapes best and bake most evenly; see notes for ways to sculpt dough. Space cookies 1 inch apart.

Bake (step 4) in a 300° oven until cookies are darker on bottom than on top and feel dry and firmer than the uncooked dough when lightly pressed (while hot, cookies are soft enough to hold an impression and are easily cut with a sharp knife). Allow 8 to 10 minutes for $\frac{1}{4}$-inch-thick cookies, about 15 minutes for $\frac{1}{2}$-inch, 20 to 25 minutes for $\frac{3}{4}$-inch. Cool (step 5) on pans, then serve, or store up to 3 days. MAKES: 1 pound, 14 ounces baked cookies; number depends on shapes.

Per ounce: 151 cal., 49% (74 cal.) from fat; 2.3 g protein; 8.2 g fat (4.1 g sat.); 17 g carbo (0.3 g fiber); 65 mg sodium; 24 mg chol.

## Macadamia Butter Cookies

PREP AND COOK TIME: About 50 minutes
Follow directions for **Shaped Cookies Master Recipe** (page 296). In step 1, beat 1 cup ($\frac{1}{2}$ lb.) **butter** or margarine (at room temperature) with 1 cup **granulated sugar.** Beat in 1 **large egg** and 1 teaspoon **vanilla.** In step 2, combine $2\frac{1}{2}$ cups **all-purpose flour** and 1 teaspoon **baking soda.** Stir in 1 cup chopped **salted roasted macadamia nuts.**

Shape dough (step 3) into 1-inch balls and set 1 inch apart on baking sheets. With a flat-bottomed glass dipped in **granulated sugar** ($\frac{1}{4}$ cup total), flatten balls to $\frac{1}{4}$ inch. Press a **whole** or piece of **salted roasted macadamia nut** ($\frac{1}{2}$ to $\frac{2}{3}$ cup total) into center of each cookie.

Bake (step 5) in a 350° oven until cookies are golden brown at edges, about 12 minutes. Cool (step 5), then serve, or store up to 1 week. MAKES: 70.
Per cookie: 75 cal., 59% (44 cal.) from fat; 0.8 g protein; 4.9 g fat (2 g sat.); 7.4 g carbo (0.1 g fiber); 58 mg sodium; 10 mg chol.

## Peanut Blossom Cookies

PREP AND COOK TIME: About 35 minutes
Follow directions for **Shaped Cookies Master Recipe** (page 296). In step 1, beat ½ cup (¼ lb.) **butter** or margarine (at room temperature) with ½ cup **granulated sugar**, ½ cup firmly packed **brown sugar**, and ¼ cup **peanut butter**; then beat in 1 **large egg** and 1 teaspoon **vanilla**. In step 2, combine 1¾ cups **all-purpose flour**, 1 teaspoon **baking soda**, and ½ teaspoon **salt**.

Shape dough (step 3) into 1-inch balls, then roll in **granulated sugar** (¼ cup total). Set balls 1½ inches apart on buttered baking sheets. Bake (step 4) in a 350° oven until slightly darker brown, 8 to 10 minutes.

Press 1 **chocolate candy kiss** (about 70 total; ¾ lb.) into center of each cookie; dough may crack. Continue to bake until chocolate is shiny and soft, about 3 more minutes. Cool (step 5), then serve, or store up to 2 days. MAKES: 70.
Per cookie: 70 cal., 46% (32 cal.) from fat; 1 g protein; 3.5 g fat (1.8 g sat.); 8.8 g carbo (0.1 g fiber); 59 mg sodium; 7.9 mg chol.

## Provençal Pine Nut Crescents

NOTES: Orange flower water is sold in liquor stores and with fancy foods in many supermarkets.
PREP AND COOK TIME: About 45 minutes
Follow directions for **Shaped Cookies Master Recipe** (page 296). In step 1, beat 1 cup (½ lb.) **butter** or margarine (at room temperature) with ⅔ cup firmly packed **brown sugar**; then beat in 3 **large egg** yolks, 1 teaspoon *each* **orange flower water** and grated **orange** peel, and ½ teaspoon **vanilla**. In step 2, use 2¾ cups **all-purpose flour**.

Shape dough (step 3) into 1½-inch balls. Roll each into a 2½-inch rope. Form each rope into a crescent on buttered baking sheets, spacing cookies 2 inches apart. Scatter **pine nuts** (½ cup total) over cookies and press nuts into dough to anchor. Liberally brush cookies with 3 tablespoons warm **honey**.

Bake (step 4) in a 350° oven until cookies are golden brown, 15 to 20 minutes. Cool (step 5), then serve, or store up to 2 days. MAKES: 45.
Per cookie: 94 cal., 53% (50 cal.) from fat;

1.4 g protein; 5.5 g fat (2.9 g sat.); 10 g carbo (0.4 g fiber); 45 mg sodium; 26 mg chol.

## Sally's Favorite Recipe

PREP AND COOK TIME: About 1¼ hours
Follow directions for **Shaped Cookies Master Recipe** (page 296). In step 1, beat 1 cup (½ lb.) **butter** or margarine (at room temperature); 1 cup *each* **salad oil**, **granulated sugar**, and firmly packed **brown sugar**; 1 **large egg**; and 1 teaspoon **vanilla**. In step 2, in a food processor (or a blender, a portion at a time), whirl 2½ cups **cornflake cereal**, 1 cup **regular rolled oats**, and ½ cup *each* **sweetened shredded dried coconut** and **pecans** or walnuts until finely chopped. Pour into a bowl and mix with 3½ cups **all-purpose flour** and 1 teaspoon **baking soda**.

Shape dough (step 3) into 1½-inch balls and set 2 inches apart on baking sheets. With a fork, press balls to flatten, making a crisscross pattern; dip fork in water as needed to prevent sticking. Press a **pecan** or walnut **half** (about 40 total) into the center of each cookie.

Bake (step 4) in a 350° oven until cookies are firm to touch, 12 to 16 minutes. Let firm on pans about 1 minute. Cool (step 5), then serve, or store up to 4 days. MAKES: 40.
Per cookie: 204 cal., 53% (108 cal.) from fat; 2 g protein; 12 g fat (4 g sat.); 22 g carbo (0.7 g fiber); 102 mg sodium; 18 mg chol.

## Snickerdoodles

PREP AND COOK TIME: About 30 minutes
Follow directions for **Shaped Cookies Master Recipe** (page 296). In step 1, beat 1 cup (½ lb.) **butter** or margarine (at room temperature); 1 cup *each* **salad oil**, **granulated sugar**, and **powdered sugar**; and 2 **large eggs**. In step 2, combine 4¼ cups **all-purpose flour**, 1 teaspoon *each* **baking soda** and **cream of tartar**, and ½ teaspoon **salt**.

In a bowl, mix ½ cup **granulated sugar** and 1 tablespoon **ground cinnamon**. Shape dough (step 3) into 1-inch balls, then roll each in cinnamon-sugar mixture. Place balls 3 to 4 inches apart on baking sheets. With a flat-bottomed glass dipped in cinnamon sugar, flatten each ball to about ¼ inch.

Bake (step 4) in a 375° oven until edges are lightly browned, 12 to 15 minutes. Cool (step 5), then serve, or store up to 5 days. MAKES: 110.
Per cookie: 66 cal., 52% (34 cal.) from fat; 0.6 g protein; 3.8 g fat (1.3 g sat.); 7.5 g carbo (0.1 g fiber); 40 mg sodium; 8.4 mg chol.

## Soft Ginger Cookies

PREP AND COOK TIME: About 1½ hours
Follow directions for **Shaped Cookies Master Recipe** (page 296). In step 1, beat 1 cup **salad oil**, 2½ cups firmly packed **brown sugar**, 2 **large eggs**, 1 teaspoon **vanilla**, and ½ cup **applesauce**. In step 2, combine 4½ cups **all-purpose flour**, 2½ tablespoons **ground ginger**, 1 tablespoon **baking soda**, 1½ teaspoons *each* **ground cinnamon** and **ground nutmeg**, and ½ teaspoon **salt**. Let mixture stand 30 minutes.

Shape dough (step 3) into ¼-cup balls and set 2½ inches apart on buttered baking sheets.

Bake (step 4) in a 350° oven just until cookies begin to brown, 8 to 10 minutes. Cool (step 5), then serve, or store up to 3 days. MAKES: 28.
Per cookie: 228 cal., 33% (76 cal.) from fat; 2.6 g protein; 8.4 g fat (1.2 g sat.); 36 g carbo (0.6 g fiber); 189 mg sodium; 15 mg chol.

## Sylvia's Danish Butter Cookies

PREP AND COOK TIME: About 1 hour
Follow directions for **Shaped Cookies Master Recipe** (page 296). In step 1, beat 1 cup (½ lb.) **butter** or margarine (at room temperature) with 1 cup **granulated sugar**. In step 2, use 2½ cups **all-purpose flour**. Stir in 1 cup **unsweetened shredded dried coconut**.

Cover baking sheets with waxed paper, nonstick pan liners, or silicone baking pads. On pans, shape (step 3) ½-cup dough portions into ¾-inch-thick logs, each about 13 inches long and 3 inches apart. Press fingers across each log to make ridges, flattening to ⅛ inch in thinnest parts.

Bake (step 4) in a 400° oven until edges are lightly browned, 8 to 10 minutes. Slide a thin spatula under cookies.

Mix ¾ cup **powdered sugar** with 2 tablespoons **rum** until smooth. Brush warm cookies with rum mixture, then immediately cut diagonally into 1-inch-wide strips. Cool (step 5) on pans, then serve, or store up to 3 days. MAKES: 80.
Per cookie: 55 cal., 45% (25 cal.) from fat; 0.5 g protein; 2.8 g fat (1.9 g sat.); 6.8 g carbo (0.2 g fiber); 24 mg sodium; 6.2 mg chol.

## Thumbprint Cookies with Chili Jelly

PREP AND COOK TIME: About 1¼ hours
Follow directions for **Shaped Cookies Master Recipe** (page 296). In step 1, beat ⅔ cup (⅓ lb.) **butter** or margarine (at room temperature) with ½ cup firmly packed **brown sugar**. Beat in 1 **large egg** and 1 teaspoon **vanilla**. In step 2, use 1½ cups **all-purpose flour**.

Beat 1 **large egg** white to blend.

Shape dough (step 3) into 1-inch balls. Dip into egg white, drain briefly, and roll in 1 cup finely chopped **salted roasted pistachios,** macadamia nuts, or pine nuts. Set balls 1 inch apart on baking sheets. With your thumb, press a well in center of each cookie.

Bake (step 4) in a 350° oven for 5 minutes. Remove from oven and press the handle end of a wooden spoon into each cookie impression. Quickly spoon ¼ teaspoon **red** or green **jalapeño jelly** (¼ cup total) into each hollow. Bake until nuts are golden brown, 10 to 12 minutes more. Cool (step 5), then serve, or store up to 3 days. MAKES: 40.

Per cookie: 62 cal., 47% (29 cal.) from fat; 0.7 g protein; 3.2 g fat (1.9 g sat.); 7.5 g carbo (0.1 g fiber); 36 mg sodium; 14 mg chol.

## Zinfandel Port Cookies

PREP TIME: About 15 minutes

In a food processor, combine 1 package (12 oz.) **vanilla wafer cookies,** ½ cup Dutch-process unsweetened cocoa, and 1 cup **pecans.** Whirl until fine crumbs form. Add ¼ cup **dark corn syrup** and ½ cup **Zinfandel port** or other port. Whirl or mix until blended.

Form into 1-inch balls. Roll balls in ½ cup **powdered sugar.** Serve, store airtight up to 1 month, or freeze to store longer. If stored, coat in more powdered sugar before serving. MAKES: 60.

Per cookie: 50 cal., 40% (20 cal.) from fat; 0.5 g protein; 2.2 g fat (0.4 g sat.); 7.1 g carbo (0.1 g fiber); 25 mg sodium; 0 mg chol.

# Biscotti

When *Sunset* published a recipe for biscotti in 1965, these cookies were a novelty. Now, biscotti are almost as familiar as doughnuts, and dunked as frequently in coffee.

## Master Recipe

NOTES: For longer cookies, cut loaves (step 5) on the diagonal.

1. Select recipe (choices follow). In a bowl with a mixer or spoon, beat butter or oil with sugar and/or molasses until well blended. Beat in vanilla and other flavorings, then beat in eggs.

2. In another bowl, combine flour mixture. Add to butter mixture and beat until well blended. Stir in any extra ingredients.

3. Spoon 1 cup dough in dollops down the length of 1 side of a buttered 12- by 15-inch baking sheet, 1 inch from pan edge. Spoon another 1 cup dough down the length of the other side of the pan. With floured fingers, pat each strip of dough into a flat 13-inch loaf, ½ inch thick and 2 inches wide. Repeat with remaining dough; you may need a total of 3 pans (dough can stand while some loaves bake). Shape any leftover dough into logs ½ inch thick and 2 inches wide.

4. Bake loaves in a 350° oven until golden or as recipe directs, 15 to 20 minutes; if using more than 1 pan in 1 oven, switch pan positions halfway through baking.

5. With a sharp or serrated knife, cut loaves crosswise into width specified in recipe. Gently tip slices onto a cut side; biscotti can touch.

6. Bake until toasted a slightly darker color and firm and dry to touch, 15 to 20 minutes more.

7. Gently slide biscotti onto racks to cool. Serve cookies, store airtight as recipe directs, or freeze to store longer.

## Anise Biscotti

PREP AND COOK TIME: About 1¼ hours

Follow directions for **Biscotti Master Recipe** (above). In step 1, beat ¾ cup (⅜ lb.) **butter** or margarine (at room temperature) with 1½ cups **granulated sugar;** then beat in 3 tablespoons *each* **anise seed** and **anise-flavor liqueur,** 2 tablespoons **bourbon** or whiskey, and 4 **large eggs.** In step 2, mix 4¼ cups **all-purpose flour** and 2 teaspoons **baking powder.** Stir in 1½ cups coarsely chopped **almonds.**

Shape dough (step 3) and bake (step 4). Cut cookies (step 5) ¾ inch wide. Complete baking (step 6). Cool (step 7), then serve, or store up to 3 days. MAKES: 90.

Per cookie: 47 cal., 57% (27 cal.) from fat; 0.8 g protein; 3 g fat (1.1 g sat.); 4.4 g carbo (0.2 g fiber); 30 mg sodium; 14 mg chol.

TWICE-BAKED TREASURES: Since biscotti have been recognized as ideal coffee companions, flavors have proliferated, from Chocolate-Hazelnut to golden Cornmeal.

## Chocolate-Hazelnut Biscotti

NOTES: *To toast hazelnuts,* see notes for Gianduia Buttons (page 293).

PREP AND COOK TIME: About 1½ hours
Follow directions for **Biscotti Master Recipe** (page 299). In step 1, beat ½ cup (¼ lb.) **butter** or margarine (at room temperature) with ¾ cup **granulated sugar**. Beat in 1 teaspoon **vanilla**, 1 tablespoon grated **orange** peel, and 3 **large eggs**. In step 2, combine 3 cups **all-purpose flour** and 1 tablespoon **baking powder**. Stir in 1 cup chopped toasted **hazelnuts** (see notes).

Shape dough (step 3); bake (step 4). Cut cookies (step 5) ¾ inch wide. Complete baking (step 6). Cool (step 7).

In a 1- to 1½-quart pan over low heat, stir 1¼ cups (8 oz.) **semisweet chocolate chips** until smooth.

Spread chocolate on 1 side of each biscotti. If chocolate gets too firm to spread, stir over low heat to soften.

Lay cookies in a single layer, icing up, on baking sheets and chill until chocolate is firm, about 20 minutes. Serve (step 7), or chill up to 3 days. MAKES: 60.

Per cookie: 81 cal., 46% (37 cal.) from fat; 1.4 g protein; 4.1 g fat (1.7 g sat.); 10 g carbo (0.3 g fiber); 44 mg sodium; 15 mg chol.

## Chocolate-Orange Biscotti

PREP AND COOK TIME: About 1½ hours
Follow directions for **Biscotti Master Recipe** (page 299). In step 1, beat ⅓ cup **olive oil** with ¾ cup **granulated sugar** and ½ cup firmly packed **brown sugar**; then beat in 1 teaspoon **vanilla**, 3 ounces melted **unsweetened chocolate**, 2 tablespoons *each* **orange juice** and **rum** (or more orange juice), 1 tablespoon grated **orange** peel, and 3 **large eggs**. In step 2, combine 3 cups **all-purpose flour**, 1 tablespoon **baking powder**, and ¾ teaspoon **salt**. Stir in 1 cup chopped **pecans** and 1 cup (6 oz.) **semisweet chocolate chips**.

Shape dough (step 3) and bake (step 4) until slightly darker. Cut cookies (step 5) ½ inch wide. Complete baking (step 6). Cool (step 7).

In a 1- to 1½-quart pan over low heat, stir 12 ounces chopped **white candy baking bar** (made with cocoa butter) and 1 tablespoon **butter** or margarine until smooth.

Dip 1 end of each biscotti about 1 inch into melted mixture. Lay in a single layer on baking sheets. Chill until icing is firm, about 15 minutes. Serve, or store up to 3 days. MAKES: 90.

Per cookie: 81 cal., 46% (37 cal.) from fat; 1.1 g protein; 4.1 g fat (1.6 g sat.); 10 g carbo (0.3 g fiber); 44 mg sodium; 7.5 mg chol.

## Cornmeal Biscotti

PREP AND COOK TIME: About 1 hour
Follow directions for **Biscotti Master Recipe** (page 299). In step 1, beat ½ cup (¼ lb.) **butter** or margarine (at room temperature) with ¾ cup **granulated sugar**; then beat in 1 teaspoon **vanilla**, 2 tablespoons **fennel seed**, 1 tablespoon **rum**, and 3 **large eggs**. In step 2, combine 1¾ cups **all-purpose flour**, 1 cup **cornmeal**, and 1½ teaspoons **baking powder**. Stir in 1 cup **pine nuts**.

Shape (step 3) and bake (step 4). Cut (step 5) ½ inch wide. Complete baking (step 6). Cool (step 7), then serve, or store up to 3 days. MAKES: 80.

Per cookie: 48 cal., 44% (21 cal.) from fat; 1.1 g protein; 2.3 g fat (0.9 g sat.); 5.7 g carbo (0.4 g fiber); 24 mg sodium; 11 mg chol.

## Gingerbread Biscotti

NOTES: *To toast almonds,* see notes for Chinese Five Spice Oatmeal Cookies (page 293).

PREP AND COOK TIME: About 1 hour.
Follow directions for **Biscotti Master Recipe** (page 299). In step 1, beat ½ cup (¼ lb.) **butter** or margarine (at room temperature) with ¾ cup **granulated sugar** and ½ cup **dark molasses**. Beat in ¼ cup minced **fresh ginger** and 3 **large eggs**. In step 2, combine 3 cups **all-purpose flour**, 1½ teaspoons **baking powder**, 1 tablespoon **ground cinnamon**, 1 teaspoon **ground nutmeg**, and ½ teaspoon *each* **ground allspice** and **ground cloves**. Stir in 1 cup coarsely chopped toasted **blanched almonds** (see notes). Shape (step 3) and bake (step 4) until slightly darker. Cut (step 5) ½ inch wide. Complete baking (step 6). Cool (step 7), then serve, or store up to 3 days. MAKES: 95.

Per cookie: 46 cal., 39% (18 cal.) from fat; 0.9 g protein; 2 g fat (0.7 g sat.); 6.1 g carbo (0.3 g fiber); 21 mg sodium; 9.4 mg chol.

## Hazelnut-Merlot Biscotti

NOTES: *To toast hazelnuts,* see notes for Gianduia Buttons (page 293).

PREP AND COOK TIME: About 1½ hours
Follow directions for **Biscotti Master Recipe** (page 299). In step 1, beat ½ cup (¼ lb.) **butter** or margarine (at room temperature) with ¾ cup **granulated sugar**; then beat in 1 teaspoon **vanilla**, 2 tablespoons **Merlot** or other dry red wine, and 2 **large eggs**. In step 2, combine 2 cups **all-purpose flour** and 1½ teaspoons **baking powder**. Stir in ¾ cup coarsely chopped toasted **hazelnuts** (see notes).

Shape (step 3) and bake (step 4). Cut (step 5) ½ inch wide. Complete baking

(step 6). Cool (step 7), then serve, or store up to 3 days. MAKES: 70.

Per cookie: 44 cal., 48% (21 cal.) from fat; 0.7 g protein; 2.3 g fat (0.9 g sat.); 5.2 g carbo (0.2 g fiber); 26 mg sodium; 9.8 mg chol.

## Lean Chocolate Biscotti

PREP AND COOK TIME: About 1¾ hours
Follow directions for **Biscotti Master Recipe** (page 299). In step 1, beat ¼ cup (⅛ lb.) **butter** or margarine (at room temperature) with ½ cup **granulated sugar**; then beat in 1 teaspoon **vanilla** and 4 **large egg** whites. In step 2, combine 2 cups **all-purpose flour**, ⅓ cup **unsweetened cocoa**, and 2 teaspoons **baking powder**.

Shape (step 3) and bake (step 4) until loaves spring back when lightly pressed. Cut (step 5) ½ inch thick. Complete baking (step 6). Cool (step 7).

In a bowl, stir ⅔ cup **powdered sugar** and 1 tablespoon **milk** until smooth. Drizzle decoratively over biscotti. Let stand until icing is dry, about 15 minutes. Serve, or store up to 2 days. MAKES: 60.

Per cookie: 38 cal., 24% (9 cal.) from fat; 0.8 g protein; 1 g fat (0.6 g sat.); 6.6 g carbo (0.3 g fiber); 29 mg sodium; 2.4 mg chol.

## Lemon-tipped Pistachio Biscotti

PREP AND COOK TIME: About 1 hour
Follow directions for **Biscotti Master Recipe** (page 299). In step 1, beat 5 tablespoons **butter** or margarine (at room temperature) with ½ cup **granulated sugar**. Beat in 1 teaspoon **vanilla**, 1½ teaspoons grated **lemon** peel, and 2 **large eggs**. In step 2, combine 2 cups **all-purpose flour** and 2 teaspoons **baking powder**. Stir in 1 cup chopped **salted roasted pistachios**.

Shape dough (step 3) and bake (step 4). Cut cookies (step 5) ½ inch wide. Complete baking (step 6). Cool (step 7).

In a bowl, stir 1 cup **powdered sugar**, 2 tablespoons **lemon juice**, and ½ teaspoon grated **lemon** peel until smooth. Spread lemon mixture onto 1 side of 1 end of each cookie. Let stand until icing is firm, about 20 minutes. Serve (step 7), or store up to 3 days. MAKES: 45.

Per cookie: 72 cal., 38% (27 cal.) from fat; 1.4 g protein; 3 g fat (1.1 g sat.); 10 g carbo (0.2 g fiber); 51 mg sodium; 13 mg chol.

## Tiered Biscotti Tree

NOTES: *To toast almonds,* see notes for Chinese Five Spice Oatmeal Cookies (page 293). If making biscotti ahead, store plain cookies airtight up to 3 days, or freeze to store longer. Assemble tree on the day it is to be served.

PREP AND COOK TIME: About 2¾ hours Follow steps 1 and 2 for **Biscotti Master Recipe** (page 299). In step 1, beat ¾ cup (⅜ lb.) **butter** or margarine (at room temperature) with 1 cup **granulated sugar**; then beat in 1 teaspoon **vanilla**, 1 tablespoon grated **orange peel**, and 4 **large eggs**. In step 2, combine 4½ cups **all-purpose flour**, 4½ teaspoons **baking powder**, 1 teaspoon **ground cinnamon**, ½ teaspoon *each* **ground coriander** and **ground nutmeg**, and ¼ teaspoon **ground cloves**. Stir in 1½ cups toasted **slivered almonds** (see notes).

Divide dough into 3 equal portions. Butter 3 baking sheets, each 12 by 15 inches. In the butter, use your fingertip to draw a triangle with its top cut off, 9 inches at the base, 12 inches on each side, and 2 inches across the top. Put a portion of dough in each triangle. Press dough level to fill the triangle; then, holding a ruler against each edge, make dough edges exactly match measurements.

Bake (step 4). Cut triangles crosswise into slices exactly ⅝ inch wide. Gently tip onto a cut side; biscotti can touch. Bake until deep golden, 10 to 15 minutes more. Cool on pans.

In a bowl, mix 4 cups **powdered sugar**, ¾ cup **orange marmalade**, and 1½ tablespoons **orange juice**.

***To assemble tree,*** lightly spread orange icing on 1 flat side of the 3 longest biscotti (1 from each pan). Lay cookies, icing down, on a flat platter, ends touching to form a triangle. Put remaining icing in a pastry bag with a ¼-inch plain tip. Squeeze a band of icing down the centers of biscotti on platter. Place the 3 next-longest biscotti on top of them, ends touching to form a second triangle, offset so the whole structure makes a 6-point star. Pipe icing on top of these cookies. Continue this pattern of icing and triangles, in order of decreasing size.

Thin remaining icing with 1 tablespoon **orange juice** and pipe onto tree to simulate snow. Lift off biscotti to eat. MAKES: 2 pounds, 10 ounces.

Per ounce: 196 cal., 31% (60 cal.) from fat; 3 g protein; 6.7 g fat (2.6 g sat.); 32 g carbo (0.6 g fiber); 99 mg sodium; 30 mg chol.

## Walnut Biscotti

NOTES: You can buy black walnut flavoring at a well-stocked food market or health food store. Or order it from Frontier Natural Products Co-op (800/669-3275); 2 ounces costs $3.25 plus shipping.

PREP AND COOK TIME: About 1½ hours Follow directions for **Biscotti Master Recipe** (page 299). In step 1, beat ¾ cup (⅜ lb.) **butter** or margarine (at room temperature) with 1½ cups **granulated sugar**. Beat in 2 teaspoons **vanilla**, 1 teaspoon *each* **anise extract** and **black walnut flavoring** (see notes), ½ teaspoon **almond extract**, and 4 **large eggs**. In step 2, combine 4¼ cups **all-purpose flour** and 4½ teaspoons **baking powder**. Stir in 1 cup coarsely chopped **walnuts**.

Shape (step 3) and bake (step 4). Cut (step 5) ¾ inch wide. Complete baking (step 6). Cool (step 7), then serve, or store up to 3 days. MAKES: 95.

Per cookie: 58 cal., 40% (23 cal.) from fat; 1 g protein; 2.6 g fat (1.1 g sat.); 7.8 g carbo (0.2 g fiber); 41 mg sodium; 13 mg chol.

BASIC METHOD

# Tea cakes
These rich, powdered sugar–coated cookies go by many names, including wedding cakes, but they all share one appealing characteristic: they practically dissolve on the tongue. This is why some are called "meltaways." In Mexico they're known as *polvorones;* in Greece as *kourabiedes;* in Austria as *kipferln.* It's the variation of spices, nuts, and flavorings, plus different shapes, that distinguishes one from another.

## Master Recipe

1. Select recipe (choices follow). In a food processor or with a mixer, blend basic ingredients specified until dough holds together. Stir in additional ingredients.
2. Shape dough into ¾-inch balls, or as individual recipe directs. Place cookies about 1 inch apart on 12- by 15-inch baking sheets (you'll need 2).
3. Bake in a 300° oven until cookies are pale golden brown, 15 to 20 minutes; if using more than 1 pan in 1 oven, switch pan positions halfway through baking. Cool on pans for 5 minutes.
4. Place 1½ cups **powdered sugar** in a bowl. A few at a time, gently turn warm cookies in sugar, then cool on racks. When cool, coat cookies again with sugar.
5. Serve, store airtight as recipe directs, or freeze to store longer.

## Chocolate Chip Peanut Meltaways

PREP AND COOK TIME: About 1¼ hours Follow directions for **Tea Cakes Master Recipe** (above). In step 1, blend the basic ingredients: 1 cup (½ lb.) **butter** or margarine (at room temperature), 1 teaspoon **vanilla**, ¼ teaspoon **almond extract**, ⅓ cup **powdered sugar**, and 2 cups **all-purpose flour**. Stir in ¾ cup chopped **salted roasted peanuts** and ½ cup minced **semisweet chocolate**.

MELT-IN-THE-MOUTH: Snowy with powdered sugar are Mexican Wedding Cakes, Pecan-Spice Tea Cakes, Greek Almond Tea Cakes, Florentine Wedding Cakes, and Viennese Vanilla Crescents.

Shape (step 2) and bake (step 3). To coat (step 4), add 2 tablespoons **unsweetened cocoa** to the powdered sugar. Serve (step 5), or store up to 1 week. MAKES: 120.

Per cookie: 37 cal., 54% (20 cal.) from fat; 0.5 g protein; 2.2 g fat (1.2 g sat.); 4.1 g carbo (0.2 g fiber); 23 mg sodium; 4.1 mg chol.

## Florentine Wedding Cakes

NOTES: *To toast hazelnuts,* see notes for Gianduia Buttons (page 293).

PREP AND COOK TIME: About 1¼ hours

Follow directions for **Tea Cakes Master Recipe** (page 301). In step 1, blend the basic ingredients: 1 cup (½ lb.) **butter** or margarine (at room temperature), 1 teaspoon **vanilla**, ⅓ cup **powdered sugar**, and 2 cups **all-purpose flour**. Stir in ¾ cup minced toasted **hazelnuts** (see notes).

Shape (step 2) and bake (step 3).

Coat with additional powdered sugar (step 4), then arrange cookies in a single layer and evenly sift 2 teaspoons **unsweetened cocoa** over them. Serve (step 5), or store up to 1 week. MAKES: 120.

Per cookie: 33 cal., 55% (18 cal.) from fat; 0.3 g protein; 2 g fat (1 g sat.); 3.5 g carbo (0.1 g fiber); 16 mg sodium; 4.1 mg chol.

## Greek Almond Tea Cakes

PREP AND COOK TIME: About 1½ hours

Follow directions for **Tea Cakes Master Recipe** (page 301). In step 1, blend the basic ingredients: 1 cup (½ lb.) **butter** or margarine (at room temperature), 1 **large egg** yolk, 1½ tablespoons **powdered sugar**, and 2 cups **all-purpose flour**. Stir in ⅓ cup minced **almonds.**

Shape dough (step 2) into 1¼-inch balls and roll each into a 2-inch rope. Set ropes on baking sheets. With fingers, pinch ends in opposite directions to make S shapes. Bake (step 3) until pale golden, 20 to 25 minutes. Coat (step 4). Serve (step 5), or store up to 3 days. MAKES: 40.

Per cookie: 90 cal., 53% (48 cal.) from fat; 1 g protein; 5.3 g fat (3 g sat.); 9.7 g carbo (0.3 g fiber); 47 mg sodium; 18 mg chol.

## Hazelnut Crescents

NOTES: *To toast hazelnuts,* see notes for Gianduia Buttons (page 293).

PREP AND COOK TIME: About 1¼ hours

Follow directions for **Tea Cakes Master Recipe** (page 301). In step 1, blend the basic ingredients: 1 cup (½ lb.) **butter** or margarine (at room temperature), 2 teaspoons **vanilla**, ½ teaspoon **ground cinnamon**, ½ teaspoon **baking powder**, ⅓ cup **powdered sugar**, and 1⅔ cups **all-purpose flour**. Stir in ¾ cup ground toasted **hazelnuts** (see notes; grind in a food processor or blender).

Shape dough (step 2) into ¾-inch balls and roll each ball to form a 1½-inch rope tapered to points at ends. On baking sheets, form each rope into a

crescent. Bake (step 3).

To coat (step 4), add 2 teaspoons **ground cinnamon** to the powdered sugar. Serve (step 5), or store up to 1 week. MAKES: 115.

Per cookie: 32 cal., 56% (18 cal.) from fat; 0.3 g protein; 2 g fat (1 g sat.); 3.4 g carbo (0.1 g fiber); 18 mg sodium; 4.3 mg chol.

## Mexican Wedding Cakes

PREP AND COOK TIME: About 1½ hours

Follow directions for **Tea Cakes Master Recipe** (page 301). In step 1, blend the basic ingredients: 1 cup (½ lb.) **butter** or margarine (at room temperature), 2 teaspoons **vanilla**, ⅓ cup **powdered sugar**, and 2 cups **all-purpose flour**. Stir in 1 cup minced **walnuts.**

Shape (step 2), bake (step 3), and coat (step 4). Serve (step 5), or store up to 1 week. MAKES: 120.

Per cookie: 35 cal., 57% (20 cal.) from fat; 0.4 g protein; 2.2 g fat (1 g sat.); 3.6 g carbo (0.1 g fiber); 16 mg sodium; 4.1 mg chol.

## Pecan-Spice Tea Cakes

PREP AND COOK TIME: About 1¼ hours

Follow directions for **Tea Cakes Master Recipe** (page 301). In step 1, blend the basic ingredients: 1 cup (½ lb.) **butter** or margarine (at room temperature), 1 teaspoon **vanilla**, ⅓ cup **powdered sugar**, and 2 cups **all-purpose flour**. Stir in ¾ cup minced **pecans.**

Shape dough (step 2) into 1¼-inch balls. Bake (step 3) until golden, 20 to 25 minutes.

To coat cookies (step 4), add ¾ teaspoon **ground cardamom** to the additional powdered sugar. Serve cookies (step 5), or store them up to 1 week. MAKES: 40

Per cookie: 99 cal., 55% (54 cal.) from fat; 0.8 g protein; 6 g fat (3 g sat.); 11 g carbo (0.3 g fiber); 47 mg sodium; 12 mg chol.

## Pine Nut Balls

PREP AND COOK TIME: About 1¼ hours

Follow directions for **Tea Cakes Master Recipe** (page 301). In step 1, blend the basic ingredients: 1 cup (½ lb.) **butter** or margarine (at room temperature), 1 teaspoon **vanilla**, 2 teaspoons **anise seed**, ⅓ cup **powdered sugar**, and 2 cups **all-purpose flour**. Stir in 1 cup **pine nuts.**

Shape the dough (step 2) into 1¼-inch balls. Bake (step 3) until golden, 20 to 25 minutes. Coat (step 4). Serve (step 5), or store cookies up to 1 week. MAKES: 40.

Per cookie: 104 cal., 57% (59 cal.) from fat; 1.6 g protein; 6.5 g fat (3.2 g sat.); 11 g carbo (0.6 g fiber); 47 mg sodium; 12 mg chol.

## Pine Nut Fingers

PREP AND COOK TIME: About 1½ hours

Follow directions for **Tea Cakes Master Recipe** (page 301). In step 1, blend the basic ingredients: 1 cup (½ lb.) **butter** or margarine (at room temperature), 1 teaspoon **vanilla**, ⅓ cup **powdered sugar**, and 2 cups **all-purpose flour**. Stir in 1 cup **pine nuts.**

Shape dough (step 2) on a lightly floured board into ½-inch-thick ropes. Cut into 2-inch lengths. Bake (step 3) and coat (step 4). Serve (step 5), or store up to 1 week. MAKES: 100.

Per cookie: 41 cal., 56% (23 cal.) from fat; 0.6 g protein; 2.6 g fat (1.3 g sat.); 4.3 g carbo (0.2 g fiber); 19 mg sodium; 5 mg chol.

## Sesame Moons

NOTES: *To toast sesame seed,* see notes for Chinese Pinwheels (page 293).

PREP AND COOK TIME: About 1¾ hours

Follow directions for **Tea Cakes Master Recipe** (page 301). In step 1, blend the basic ingredients: 1 cup (½ lb.) **butter** or margarine (at room temperature), 1 teaspoon **vanilla**, ⅓ cup **powdered sugar**, and 2 cups **all-purpose flour**. Stir in ¼ cup toasted **sesame seed** (see notes).

Shape dough (step 2) into 1-inch balls. Roll each ball into a 2½-inch rope tapered to points at the ends. On baking sheets, form each rope into a crescent.

Bake (step 3).

To coat (step 4), add 2 tablespoons toasted **sesame seed** to the powdered sugar. Serve (step 5), or store up to 1 week. MAKES: 80.

Per cookie: 46 cal., 52% (24 cal.) from fat; 0.4 g protein; 2.7 g fat (1.5 g sat.); 5.3 g carbo (0.2 g fiber); 24 mg sodium; 6.2 mg chol.

## Viennese Vanilla Crescents

PREP AND COOK TIME: About 1¾ hours

Follow directions for **Tea Cakes Master Recipe** (page 301). In step 1, blend the basic ingredients: 1 cup (½ lb.) **butter** or margarine (at room temperature), 2 teaspoons **vanilla**, ⅓ cup **powdered sugar**, and 2 cups **all-purpose flour**. Stir in 1 cup minced **almonds.**

Shape dough (step 2) into 1-inch balls. On a lightly floured board, roll each ball into a 3½-inch rope tapered to points at ends. On baking sheets, form each rope into a crescent. Bake (step 3) and coat (step 4). Serve (step 5), or store up to 1 week. MAKES: 80.

Per cookie: 53 cal., 55% (29 cal.) from fat; 0.7 g protein; 3.2 g fat (1.5 g sat.); 5.6 g carbo (0.3 g fiber); 24 mg sodium; 6.2 mg chol.

# Lace cookies

Warm from the oven, delicate lace cookies are so flexible you can fold or roll them like paper. But unless you're using nonstick pan liners or silicone baking pads—available in well-stocked cookware stores—the cookies must be removed from the baking sheets before they get rigid, a matter of minutes.

These thin, fragile cookies taste like brittle candy. One version is studded with nuts. Another, made with oats, looks like an amber snowflake. Classic Florentines are backed with chocolate, while toffee lace cookies are sandwiched with chocolate.

## Master Recipe

1. Select recipe (choices follow). In a 1- to 2-quart pan over low heat, melt butter. Add sugar and, as specified, corn syrup or whipping cream. Stir over high heat until boiling. Remove from heat and stir in flour and any extra ingredients.

2. For best results, line flat (not warped) 12- by 15-inch baking sheets with nonstick pan liners, silicone baking pads, or cooking parchment; or butter and flour-dust sheets, preferably nonstick. Drop batter on sheets as recipe specifies.

3. Bake 1 pan at a time in a 350° oven as recipe directs.

4. Let cookies cool on pan until firm enough to remove, about 2 minutes; to test, lift a corner of a cookie with your fingers, or slide a spatula under a corner. If too soft to hold its shape, wait a few seconds longer. If it's firm, lift off with fingers or spatula and shape if recipe directs. If cookies get rigid, return to oven for a few seconds to soften slightly. Place flat or shaped cookies on racks to cool.

5. Serve, or immediately package airtight (cookies soften quickly from moisture in the air) in rigid containers, putting waxed paper between layers. Store as recipe directs, or freeze to store longer.

## Brandied Toffee Lace Sandwiches

PREP AND COOK TIME: About 1¾ hours
Follow directions for Lace Cookies Master Recipe (above). In step 1, melt ½ cup (¼ lb.) butter or margarine, then add ½ cup firmly packed brown sugar and 2 tablespoons whipping cream. Stir in ⅓ cup all-purpose flour and 1 cup quick-cooking rolled oats.

Drop batter (step 2) in 1-teaspoon portions onto baking sheets, evenly spacing up to 6 portions on each sheet. Bake (step 3) until lightly browned, 4 to 5 minutes. Lift cookies from pans (step 4) and leave flat to cool.

In a 1- to 1½-quart pan over low heat, stir 3 tablespoons whipping cream, 1 cup (6 oz.) semisweet chocolate chips, and 2 tablespoons brandy until chocolate is melted. With a pastry brush, gently coat the back of 1 cookie with chocolate mixture. Press the back of another cookie against the chocolate coating. Cool on rack. Repeat to join remaining cookies.

Serve (step 5), or store up to 1 day.
MAKES: 28 sandwich cookies.
Per cookie: 99 cal., 54% (53 cal.) from fat; 0.9 g protein; 5.9 g fat (3.5 g sat.); 11 g carbo (0.3 g fiber); 36 mg sodium; 12 mg chol.

## Florentines

PREP AND COOK TIME: About 50 minutes
Follow directions for Lace Cookies Master Recipe (above). In step 1, melt ¼ cup (⅛ lb.) butter or margarine, then add ⅓ cup granulated sugar and ¼ cup whipping cream. Stir in 2 tablespoons all-purpose flour and ½ cup each finely chopped candied orange peel, ground almonds (grind in a food processor or blender), and sliced almonds.

Drop batter (step 2) in 1-tablespoon portions onto baking sheets, evenly spacing up to 6 portions on each sheet. With the back of a spoon, spread each portion into a 2-inch-wide round.

Bake (step 3) until edges are lightly browned (centers will still be bubbling), 10 to 12 minutes. Lift cookies from pans (step 4) and leave flat to cool.

In a 1- to 2-quart pan over low heat, frequently stir 4 ounces chopped semisweet chocolate until melted, 8 to 10 minutes. With a pastry brush, gently coat back of each cookie with chocolate. Lay coated cookies on racks, chocolate side up, and chill until chocolate is firm, about 10 minutes.

Serve (step 5), or store up to 2 days.
MAKES: 22.
Per cookie: 103 cal., 59% (61 cal.) from fat; 1.2 g protein; 6.8 g fat (3 g sat.); 11 g carbo (0.7 g fiber); 24 mg sodium; 8.9 mg chol.

## German Oatmeal Cookies

NOTES: Leave cookies flat or shape into cones. *To shape cones,* wrap warm cookies around cone pastry forms, available at cookware stores, or around 3-inch-long cones made from lightweight cardboard wrapped with foil. Or wrap around metal cannoli forms to make rolls.

PREP AND COOK TIME: About 1¼ hours
Follow directions for Lace Cookies Master Recipe (above). In step 1, melt ½ cup (¼ lb.) butter or margarine, then add ½ cup granulated sugar and 2 tablespoons whipping cream. Stir in ¼ teaspoon *each* salt, ground cloves, and ground ginger; ¼ cup all-purpose flour; and ⅔ cup quick-cooking rolled oats.

Drop batter (step 2) in 1-teaspoon portions onto baking sheets, evenly spacing 3 or 4 portions on each sheet. Bake cookies (step 3) until the edges are golden brown, 3 to 4 minutes. Lift the cookies from the pans (step 4) and cool flat or shape them (see notes). Serve cookies (step 5), or store up to 4 days. MAKES: 45.
Per cookie: 36 cal., 58% (21 cal.) from fat; 0.3 g protein; 2.3 g fat (1.4 g sat.); 3.6 g carbo (0.1 g fiber); 34 mg sodium; 6.3 mg chol.

AS FRAGILE as snowflakes—almost. Elegant, glossy Praline Cones and Brandied Toffee Lace Sandwiches require careful handling but are easily mastered.

## Nut Lace Cookies

PREP AND COOK TIME: About 45 minutes
Follow directions for **Lace Cookies Master Recipe** (page 303). In step 1, melt ¼ cup (⅛ lb.) **butter** or margarine, then add ¼ cup firmly packed **brown sugar** and ¼ cup **corn syrup**. Stir in ¼ cup **all-purpose flour** and 1 cup **plain** or salted roasted **mixed whole** or half **almonds, hazelnuts, macadamias, pecans, pine nuts, pistachios,** and/or **walnuts.**

Drop batter (step 2) in 2-tablespoon (⅛-cup) portions about 8 inches apart on baking sheets, evenly spacing 2 portions on each sheet. With your fingers, push nuts apart over surface of cookies.

Bake (step 3) until golden brown, about 10 minutes. Lift cookies from the pans (step 4) and cool flat. Serve (step 5), or store up to 5 days. MAKES: 7 (6 in. wide).

Per cookie: 249 cal., 61% (153 cal.) from fat; 4.2 g protein; 17 g fat (5.2 g sat.); 24 g carbo (2.2 g fiber); 89 mg sodium; 18 mg chol.

## Praline Flats or Cones

NOTES: *To shape,* see notes for German Oatmeal Cookies (page 303).
PREP AND COOK TIME: About 1 hour
Follow directions for **Lace Cookies Master Recipe** (page 303). In step 1, melt ¼ cup (⅛ lb.) **butter** or margarine, then add ¼ cup *each* firmly packed **brown sugar** and **corn syrup.** Stir in ¼ cup *each* **all-purpose flour** and **pine nuts.**

Drop batter (step 2) in 1-teaspoon portions about 3 inches apart onto baking sheets, evenly spacing 4 to 6 portions on each sheet.

Bake (step 3) until rich golden brown, 5 to 7 minutes. Lift warm cookies from pans (step 4). If desired, shape each around a cone form: hold cookie until rigid—almost at once. Slip from form and cool on racks. Serve (step 5), or store up to 5 days. MAKES: 26.

Per cookie: 45 cal., 51% (23 cal.) from fat; 0.5 g protein; 2.6 g fat (1.2 g sat.); 5.6 g carbo (0.2 g fiber); 23 mg sodium; 5 mg chol.

---

# Bar cookies

Bar cookies can be tender and cakelike, chewy, or firm and crisp. They can be plain or frosted, layered with a filling, or gilded in chocolate. This selection includes cookies of each persuasion, from simple to fancy.

## Master Recipe

1. Select recipe (choices follow). In a bowl with a mixer, beat butter or oil with sugar or honey until smoothly blended. As specified in individual recipe, beat in eggs, then beat in vanilla or other flavoring and any additional wet ingredients.

2. Add flour to butter mixture; or, if recipe directs, in another bowl, combine flour with dry ingredients, then add to butter mixture. Beat until well mixed. Stir in any extra ingredients.

3. As recipe directs, put cookie mixture into a pan, bake, and add additional toppings.

4. If recipe directs, cut while hot. Or cool in pan on a rack, then cut. With a sharp knife, make cuts straight down to divide into number of cookies specified. Use a small spatula to lift from pan.

5. Serve, store airtight as recipe directs, or freeze to store longer.

---

## Brandied Apricot Bars

PREP AND COOK TIME: About 1 hour
Follow directions for **Bar Cookies Master Recipe** (above). In step 1, beat 1 cup (½ lb.) **butter** or margarine (at room temperature) with ½ cup *each* **granulated sugar** and firmly packed

BAR NONE of this versatile gang: Clockwise from left, Nanaimo Bars, Chocolate-Caramel Pecan Cookies, Brandied Apricot Bars, and Nut Mosaic Triangles.

brown sugar; then beat in 4 **large eggs** and 1 tablespoon *each* **vanilla** and grated **orange** peel. In step 2, combine 1¼ cups **all-purpose flour,** 1 teaspoon **baking powder,** and ½ teaspoon *each* **baking soda** and **ground cinnamon.** Stir in 2 cups chopped **dried apricots** and 1 cup **golden raisins.**

Evenly spread batter (step 3) in a buttered, floured 10- by 15-inch pan. Bake in a 350° oven until center springs back when pressed and is no longer wet (cut to test), 20 to 25 minutes.

While cookie mixture bakes, in a 1- to 1½-quart pan, combine ½ cup **granulated sugar,** ¼ cup **apricot-flavor brandy** or liqueur (or orange juice), and 1 tablespoon **lemon juice.** Bring to a boil over high heat, then let stand. In a bowl, stir 4 teaspoons

lemon juice and ⅔ cup **powdered sugar** until smooth. Put lemon icing in a pastry bag with a ⅛-inch plain tip.

When cookie mixture is baked, evenly spoon syrup over it. Cool (step 4), then cut into 36 bars. Leave in pan. Squeeze icing over cookies, or drizzle from a spoon.

Serve (step 5), or store up to 3 days. MAKES: 36.

Per cookie: 148 cal., 35% (52 cal.) from fat; 1.6 g protein; 5.8 g fat (3.4 g sat.); 23 g carbo (0.9 g fiber); 94 mg sodium; 38 mg chol.

## Buttery Lemon Squares

PREP AND COOK TIME: About 1 hour and 20 minutes
Follow directions for **Bar Cookies Master Recipe** (above). In step 1, beat 1 cup (½ lb.) **butter** or margarine (at room temperature) with ½ cup **powdered sugar.** In step 2, add 2 cups **all-purpose flour.** Pat dough into a ball.

Press (step 3) evenly in a buttered, floured 9- by 13-inch pan. Bake in a 350° oven until golden, about 20 minutes.

While dough bakes, in a food processor or a bowl with a mixer, whirl or beat 2 cups **granulated sugar,** ⅓ cup **all-purpose flour,** 1 teaspoon **baking** powder, $1\frac{1}{2}$ teaspoons grated **lemon peel**, 6 tablespoons **lemon juice**, and 4 **large eggs** to blend. Pour onto hot crust.

Bake until lemon mixture is no longer runny in center (cut to test), 35 to 40 minutes. Remove from oven and dust with 2 tablespoons **powdered sugar.**

Cool (step 4), then cut into 24 squares. Serve (step 5), or chill airtight up to 2 days. MAKES: 24.

Per cookie: 205 cal., 39% (79 cal.) from fat; 2.4 g protein; 8.8 g fat (5.1 g sat.); 30 g carbo (0.3 g fiber); 112 mg sodium; 57 mg chol.

## Chocolate-Caramel Pecan Cookies

NOTES: You need an accurate candy thermometer to make caramel.

PREP AND COOK TIME: About 2 hours

Follow directions for **Bar Cookies Master Recipe** (page 304). In step 1, beat 1 cup ($\frac{1}{2}$ lb.) **butter** or margarine (at room temperature) with 1 cup firmly packed **brown sugar**; then beat in 1 **large egg** yolk and 2 teaspoons **vanilla.** In step 2, add 2 cups **all-purpose flour.** Stir in 2 cups chopped **pecans.** Squeeze dough into a compact ball.

Evenly press (step 3) over bottom and sides of a buttered, floured 10- by 15-inch pan. Bake in a 350° oven until golden brown, 15 to 20 minutes. While dough bakes, in a 2- to 3-quart pan over high heat, melt 6 tablespoons **butter** or margarine. Add $\frac{3}{4}$ cup *each* firmly packed **brown sugar** and **light corn syrup**; stir until caramel mixture reaches 240° on a thermometer, 5 to 8 minutes.

Pour caramel into crust and spread evenly. Sprinkle with 2 cups (12 oz.) **semisweet chocolate chips.** When chocolate is soft, about 5 minutes, spread evenly. If desired, sprinkle with 1 cup **sliced almonds.** Chill until filling and chocolate are firm, about 1 hour.

Cut (step 4) into 30 squares, then cut squares in half diagonally. Serve (step 5), or store up to 3 days. MAKES: 60.

Per cookie: 141 cal., 54% (76 cal.) from fat; 1 g protein; 8.4 g fat (3.8 g sat.); 17 g carbo (0.3 g fiber); 51 mg sodium; 15 mg chol.

## Cranberry-Prune Squares

PREP AND COOK TIME: About 1 hour and 10 minutes

Follow directions for **Bar Cookies Master Recipe** (page 304). In step 1, beat $\frac{1}{4}$ cup ($\frac{1}{8}$ lb.) **butter** or margarine, melted, with 1 cup **granulated sugar**; then beat in 2 **large eggs.** In step 2, combine 1 cup **all-purpose flour** and $\frac{1}{2}$ teaspoon *each* **baking powder**, **ground allspice**, **ground cinnamon**, and **ground cloves.** Stir in 1 cup *each*

chopped **almonds**, chopped **moist-packed prunes**, and **fresh** or frozen **cranberries.**

Evenly spread batter (step 3) in a buttered, floured 9-inch square pan. Bake in a 350° oven until edges begin to pull from pan, 45 to 50 minutes.

Cool (step 4), then cut into 16 squares. Serve (step 5), or store up to 2 days. MAKES: 16.

Per cookie: 192 cal., 39% (74 cal.) from fat; 3.6 g protein; 8.2 g fat (2.6 g sat.); 28 g carbo (2.1 g fiber); 58 mg sodium; 35 mg chol.

## English Toffee Cookies

PREP AND COOK TIME: About $1\frac{1}{4}$ hours

Follow directions for **Bar Cookies Master Recipe** (page 304). In step 1, beat 1 cup ($\frac{1}{2}$ lb.) **butter** or margarine (at room temperature) with 1 cup **granulated sugar**; then beat in 1 **large egg** yolk. In step 2, add 2 cups **all-purpose flour.**

Evenly press dough (step 3) into a buttered, floured 10- by 15-inch pan. In a bowl, with a fork, beat 1 **large egg white** to blend. Spread over dough with a pastry brush. Sprinkle 1 cup chopped **pecans** or walnuts over dough, then press them into it. Bake in a 275° oven until golden brown, about 45 minutes. Cut while hot (step 4) into $1\frac{1}{2}$-inch squares. Let cool.

Serve (step 5), or store up to 4 days. MAKES: 88.

Per cookie: 39 cal., 51% (20 cal.) from fat; 0.3 g protein; 2.2 g fat (1.3 g sat.); 4.5 g carbo (0.1 g fiber); 22 mg sodium; 8.2 mg chol.

## Honey-Sesame Bars

NOTES: ***To toast sesame seed***, see notes for Chinese Pinwheels (page 293). To observe Jewish tradition with these cookies, use margarine instead of butter in the syrup.

PREP AND COOK TIME: About 50 minutes

Follow directions for **Bar Cookies Master Recipe** (page 304). In step 1, beat $\frac{3}{4}$ cup **salad oil**, $\frac{1}{2}$ cup **granulated sugar**, $\frac{1}{3}$ cup **honey**, 2 **large eggs**, and $1\frac{1}{2}$ teaspoons grated **orange** peel. In step 2, combine 1 cup **all-purpose flour**, $\frac{1}{2}$ cup **whole-wheat flour**, $1\frac{1}{2}$ teaspoons **baking powder**, and $\frac{1}{4}$ teaspoon **salt.** Stir in $1\frac{1}{3}$ cups toasted **sesame seed** (see notes).

Evenly spread batter (step 3) in an oiled 9- by 13-inch pan. Bake in a 375° oven until center springs back when lightly touched and top is richly browned, 18 to 20 minutes.

While batter bakes, in a bowl mix $\frac{1}{2}$ cup **honey**, 3 tablespoons melted **butter** or margarine, and $1\frac{1}{2}$ teaspoons grated **orange** peel.

With a slender skewer, pierce warm baked cookie mixture at $\frac{1}{2}$-inch intervals. Evenly pour honey mixture over it. Cool (step 4) at least 10 minutes, then cut into 24 pieces. Serve (step 5), or store up to 2 days. MAKES: 24.

Per cookie: 201 cal., 54% (108 cal.) from fat; 2.6 g protein; 12 g fat (2.4 g sat.); 22 g carbo (1.6 g fiber); 78 mg sodium; 22 mg chol.

## Nanaimo Bars

PREP AND COOK TIME: About $2\frac{3}{4}$ hours

Follow directions for **Bar Cookies Master Recipe** (page 304). In step 1, beat 6 tablespoons cool melted **butter** or margarine with $\frac{1}{4}$ cup **powdered sugar**; then beat in 1 **large egg.** In step 2, stir in $1\frac{3}{4}$ cups **graham cracker crumbs**, 1 cup **sweetened flaked dried coconut**, $\frac{1}{2}$ cup finely chopped **pecans**, and $\frac{1}{4}$ cup **unsweetened cocoa.**

Evenly press dough (step 3) into a buttered, floured 8-inch square pan. Bake in a 350° oven until slightly darker, about 20 minutes. Cool (step 4).

While baked dough cools, in a bowl with a mixer, beat $\frac{1}{2}$ cup ($\frac{1}{4}$ lb.) **butter** or margarine (at room temperature), 2 cups **powdered sugar**, 2 tablespoons **milk**, and 1 tablespoon **vanilla** until smooth. Spread filling over cookie.

Also, in a 1- to 2-quart pan over low heat, stir 2 tablespoons **butter** and 3 ounces **unsweetened chocolate** until melted. Spread over filling.

Chill airtight until filling is firm enough to cut neatly, at least 2 hours. Cut (step 4) into 25 squares. Serve (step 5), or chill up to 3 days. MAKES: 25.

Per cookie: 196 cal., 60% (117 cal.) from fat; 1.7 g protein; 13 g fat (6.9 g sat.); 20 g carbo (1.4 g fiber); 138 mg sodium; 29 mg chol.

## Peanut Butter–Oat Bars

PREP AND COOK TIME: About 1 hour

Follow directions for **Bar Cookies Master Recipe** (page 304). In step 1, beat 1 cup ($\frac{1}{2}$ lb.) **butter** or margarine, melted, with $1\frac{1}{2}$ cups firmly packed **brown sugar.** In step 2, add 2 cups **all-purpose flour.** Stir in 2 cups **regular rolled oats** and $\frac{2}{3}$ cup *each* chopped **unsalted roasted peanuts** and **unsweetened shredded dried coconut.**

Evenly press dough (step 3) into a buttered, floured 10- by 15-inch pan. For chewy cookies, bake in a 350° oven until edges are lightly browned, about 20 minutes; for crisp cookies, bake until slightly darker brown, about 5 minutes more. Spread with $1\frac{1}{3}$ cups **peanut butter.** Let cool (step 4) about 15 minutes.

Seal $\frac{1}{2}$ cup **semisweet chocolate chips** in a heavy 1-quart plastic food bag. Heat in a microwave oven at 30%

power until chips are soft, about 2 minutes. Squeeze chocolate to 1 corner of bag, then snip a very small hole in corner. Squeeze chocolate from bag in thin lines over peanut butter. Chill until chocolate is firm, about 20 minutes. Cut into 20 squares. Serve (step 5), or chill up to 2 days. MAKES: 20.

Per cookie: 387 cal., 56% (216 cal.) from fat; 9.1 g protein; 24 g fat (9.6 sat.); 38 g carbo (2.7 g fiber); 184 mg sodium; 25 mg chol.

### Pumpkin–Cream Cheese Swirls

PREP AND COOK TIME: About 50 minutes
Follow directions for **Bar Cookies Master Recipe** (page 304). In step 1, beat 6 tablespoons cool melted **butter** or margarine, $1\frac{1}{2}$ cups **granulated sugar**, 2 **large eggs**, 1 cup **canned pumpkin**, and $\frac{1}{3}$ cup **water**. In step 2, combine $1\frac{3}{4}$ cups **all-purpose flour**, $1\frac{1}{2}$ teaspoons **ground cinnamon**, 1 teaspoon **baking soda**, and $\frac{1}{2}$ teaspoon *each*

**baking powder** and **ground nutmeg.** Evenly spread batter (step 3) in a buttered, floured 10- by 15-inch pan.

In a bowl with a mixer, beat 1 package (8 oz.) **cream cheese**, 1 **large egg**, and $\frac{1}{4}$ cup **granulated sugar** until smooth.

Drop cheese mixture in 24 evenly spaced 1-tablespoon portions over batter. Pull a knife tip through filling to swirl slightly into batter.

Bake in a 350° oven until center of cookie batter (not cheese) springs back when lightly touched, about 30 minutes.

Cool (step 4); cut into 24 pieces. Serve (step 5), or chill up to 3 days. MAKES: 24.

Per cookie: 164 cal., 38% (63 cal.) from fat; 2.6 g protein; 7 g fat (4.2 g sat.); 23 g carbo (0.4 g fiber); 130 mg sodium; 45 mg chol.

### Nut Mosaic Triangles

PREP AND COOK TIME: About 45 minutes
In a food processor or bowl, whirl or stir $1\frac{3}{4}$ cups **all-purpose flour,** $\frac{1}{2}$ cup **granulated sugar,** and 2 teaspoons

**baking powder.** Add $\frac{1}{2}$ cup ($\frac{1}{4}$ lb.) **butter** or margarine (at room temperature, cut into chunks); whirl or rub with fingers until fine crumbs form. Add 2 **large eggs**; whirl or stir until dough holds together. With floured fingers, press dough evenly into a buttered, floured 10- by 15-inch pan.

In a 1- to 2-quart pan over medium-high heat, stir $\frac{1}{2}$ cup ($\frac{1}{4}$ lb.) **butter** or margarine, $\frac{1}{4}$ cup **granulated sugar,** and 3 tablespoons **honey** until bubbling, about 3 minutes. Stir in 1 cup **sliced almonds,** $\frac{1}{2}$ cup **salted roasted pistachios,** and 1 teaspoon **almond extract.** Evenly spoon hot mixture over dough.

Bake in a 350° oven until topping is deep golden, 18 to 20 minutes. Let cool in pan. Cut into 18 squares, then cut squares in half diagonally. Serve, store airtight up to 5 days, or freeze to store longer. MAKES: 36.

Per cookie: 122 cal., 57% (69 cal.) from fat; 1.9 g protein; 7.7 g fat (3.5 g sat.); 12 g carbo (0.3 g fiber); 92 mg sodium; 26 mg chol.

---

# Brownies

For cookies in a hurry, brownies may be the answer: assemble ingredients, mix the batter, and bake. Brownies run the gamut from gooey and dark to cakelike and golden; we even include a low-fat, fudgy version. Enjoy them plain or frosted, warm or cool.

## Master Recipe

1. Select recipe (choices follow). In a 2- to 3-quart pan over low heat, frequently stir butter and chocolate (if specified) until melted. Remove from heat and stir in sugar, eggs, vanilla, flour, and any extra ingredients specified until smoothly blended.

2. Evenly spread batter in a buttered, floured 8-inch square pan, or in pan specified in recipe. Evenly scatter any toppings over batter.

3. Bake in a 350° oven until edges feel firm to touch and begin to turn a shade darker, 25 to 30 minutes; or bake as recipe directs.

4. Run a knife between pan rim and baked brownie. Leave plain, or if desired, spread with chocolate glaze (following). Cool in pan on a rack, about 1 hour. Cut into 9 or 16 squares, or number of pieces recipe specifies.

5. Serve, store airtight as recipe directs, or freeze to store longer.

*Chocolate glaze.* In a 1- to 2-quart pan over low heat, frequently stir $\frac{1}{3}$ cup *whipping cream* and 1 cup (6 oz.) *semisweet chocolate chips* until melted and smooth. Stir in 1 teaspoon *vanilla.* Use warm.

## Butterscotch Brownies

PREP AND COOK TIME: About 50 minutes
Follow directions for **Brownies Master Recipe** (above). In step 1, melt $\frac{1}{2}$ cup ($\frac{1}{4}$ lb.) **butter** or margarine. Stir in $1\frac{1}{3}$ cups firmly packed **brown sugar,** 2 **large eggs,** 1 teaspoon **vanilla,** and 1

cup **all-purpose flour.**

Put in pan (step 2) and sprinkle with $\frac{1}{2}$ cup **pecan halves.** Bake (step 3) and cool (step 4). Serve (step 5), or store up to 2 days. MAKES: 9 or 16.

Per small brownie: 185 cal., 44% (81 cal.) from fat; 2 g protein; 9 g fat (4.1 g sat.); 25 g carbo (0.4 g fiber); 76 mg sodium; 43 mg chol.

BROWNIES GALORE:
From top left: Fudgy Low-Fat, Peanut Butter, Dark Chocolate, another Peanut Butter, White & Dark, Rocky Road, Mocha Brownies in Silver Cups.

## Dark Chocolate Brownies

PREP AND COOK TIME: About 45 minutes
Follow directions for **Brownies Master Recipe** page 306). In step 1, melt ¹⁄₂ cup (¹⁄₄ lb.) **butter** or margarine and 3 ounces chopped **unsweetened chocolate.** Stir in 1¹⁄₃ cups **granulated sugar,** 2 **large eggs,** 1 teaspoon **vanilla,** ¹⁄₂ cup **all-purpose flour,** and ¹⁄₂ cup chopped **walnuts.** Put in pan (step 2), bake (step 3), and cool (step 4). Serve (step 5), or store up to 2 days. MAKES: 9 or 16.
Per small brownie: 195 cal., 55% (108 cal.) from fat; 2.4 g protein; 12 g fat (5.8 g sat.); 22 g carbo (1.1 g fiber); 70 mg sodium; 43 mg chol.

## Fudgy Low-Fat Brownies

PREP AND COOK TIME: About 35 minutes
Follow directions for **Brownies Master Recipe** (page 306). In step 1, melt 1 tablespoon **butter** or margarine and 2 ounces chopped **unsweetened chocolate.** Stir in 1 cup **granulated sugar,** 1 **large egg,** 1 **large egg** white, 6 tablespoons **applesauce,** 2 teaspoons **vanilla,** ¹⁄₂ cup **all-purpose flour,** 2 tablespoons **unsweetened cocoa,** and ¹⁄₄ teaspoon *each* **baking soda** and **salt.** Put in pan (step 2), bake (step 3), and cool (step 4). Serve (step 5), or store up to 2 days. MAKES: 9 or 16.
Per small brownie: 105 cal., 29% (30 cal.) from fat; 1.6 g protein; 3.3 g fat (1.9 g sat.); 18 g carbo (0.9 g fiber); 73 mg sodium; 16 mg chol.

## Malted Chocolate Brownies

PREP AND COOK TIME: About 1¹⁄₄ hours
Follow directions for **Brownies Master Recipe** (page 306). In step 1, melt ¹⁄₂ cup (¹⁄₄ lb.) **butter** or margarine and ¹⁄₂ cup (3 oz.) **semisweet chocolate chips.** Stir in ¹⁄₂ cup **granulated sugar,** 3 **large egg** yolks, 2 teaspoons **vanilla,** 1¹⁄₃ cups **all-purpose flour,** 1 teaspoon **baking powder,** and ³⁄₄ cup **malted milk powder.** Then stir in 1 cup (6 oz.) **semisweet chocolate chips.**

In a bowl with a mixer on high speed, beat 3 **large egg** whites until foamy. Gradually add ¹⁄₂ cup **granulated sugar,** beating until whites hold stiff, moist peaks, about 4 minutes. Add ¹⁄₃ of whites to chocolate mixture, stir to blend, then gently fold in remainder.

Put in a buttered, floured 9-inch pan (step 2). Bake (step 3) 40 to 45 minutes.

Spread with **chocolate glaze** (page 306). Cool (step 4). Cut into 20 pieces. Serve (step 5), or store up to 2 days. MAKES: 20.
Per brownie: 274 cal., 46% (126 cal.) from fat; 3.9 g protein; 14 g fat (7.9 g sat.); 37 g carbo (0.7 g fiber); 151 mg sodium; 51 mg chol.

## Mexican Chocolate Brownies

NOTES: *Piloncillo* (hard brown sugar) is available at Mexican markets. Crush with a mallet or grind into a powder in a food processor. Or instead, use ³⁄₄ cup firmly packed brown sugar. Mexican chocolate, flavored with cinnamon and sugar, is found in well-stocked supermarkets. *To toast pine nuts,* put in an 8- or 9-inch pan in a 350° oven and shake often until golden, 5 to 8 minutes. Pour from pan.
PREP AND COOK TIME: About 40 minutes
Follow directions for **Brownie Master Recipe** (page 306). In step 1, melt ¹⁄₂ cup (¹⁄₄ lb.) **butter** or margarine, 1 ounce chopped **unsweetened chocolate,** and 2 tablets (6¹⁄₂ oz. total) chopped **Mexican chocolate.** Stir in ³⁄₄ cup (about 6¹⁄₂ oz.) firmly packed crushed or ground **piloncillo** (see notes), 2 **large eggs,** ¹⁄₂ teaspoon **ground cinnamon,** 1 teaspoon **vanilla,** and ¹⁄₂ cup *each* **all-purpose flour** and toasted **pine nuts** (see notes).

Put in pan (step 2), bake (step 3), and cool (step 4). Serve (step 5), or store up to 2 days. MAKES: 9 or 16.
Per small brownie: 206 cal., 48% (99 cal.) from fat; 2.6 g protein; 11 g fat (5.1 g sat.); 24 g carbo (0.9 g fiber); 73 mg sodium; 43 mg chol.

## Mocha Brownies in Silver Cups

NOTES: Bake brownies in 1-inch silver foil (or paper) baking cups.
PREP AND COOK TIME: About 1 hour
Follow directions for **Brownies Master Recipe** (page 306). In step 1, melt ¹⁄₂ cup (¹⁄₄ lb.) **butter** or margarine, 2 ounces chopped **unsweetened chocolate,** and 1 cup **granulated sugar.** Stir in 2 **large eggs,** 1 teaspoon **vanilla,** 1 cup **all-purpose flour,** and 1 tablespoon **finely ground coffee.**

In step 2, fit 48 baking cups (see notes) snugly in a 9- by 13-inch pan. Fill cups and top each with a **coffee bean** (3 tablespoons total).

Bake (step 3) until centers spring back slightly when lightly pressed, 18 to 20 minutes. Cool (step 4). Serve (step 5), or store up to 2 days. MAKES: 48.
Per brownie: 52 cal., 48% (25 cal.) from fat; 0.7 g protein; 2.8 g fat (1.6 g sat.); 6.5 g carbo (0.3 g fiber); 22 mg sodium; 14 mg chol.

## Peanut Butter Brownies

PREP AND COOK TIME: About 40 minutes
Follow directions for **Brownies Master Recipe** (page 306). In step 1, melt 5 tablespoons **butter** or margarine. Stir in 1 cup **granulated sugar,** 2 **large eggs,** 1 teaspoon **vanilla,** ¹⁄₂ cup **all-purpose flour,** ³⁄₄ cup **peanut butter,** and ¹⁄₄ teaspoon **baking powder.**

Put in pan (step 2), bake (step 3), and cool (step 4). Serve (step 5), or store up to 2 days. MAKES: 9 or 16.
Per small brownie: 180 cal., 55% (99 cal.) from fat; 4.7 g protein; 11 g fat (3.6 g sat.);18 g carbo (0.8 g fiber); 111 mg sodium; 37 mg chol.

## Rocky Road Brownies

PREP AND COOK TIME: About 50 minutes
Follow directions for **Brownies Master Recipe** (page 306). In step 1, melt ¹⁄₂ cup (¹⁄₄ lb.) **butter** or margarine and 3 ounces chopped **unsweetened chocolate.** Stir in 1¹⁄₃ cups **granulated sugar,** 2 **large eggs,** 1 teaspoon **vanilla,** ¹⁄₂ cup **all-purpose flour,** and 1 cup **tiny marshmallows.** Put in pan (step 2); sprinkle with ¹⁄₂ cup chopped **walnuts.** Bake (step 3) until deep brown, 30 to 35 minutes. Cool (step 4). Serve (step 5), or store up to 2 days. MAKES: 9 or 16.
Per small brownie: 204 cal., 53% (108 cal.) from fat; 2.4 g protein; 12 g fat (5.8 g sat.); 25 g carbo (1.1 g fiber); 72 mg sodium; 43 mg chol.

## White Chocolate Brownies

PREP AND COOK TIME: About 50 minutes
Follow directions for **Brownies Master Recipe** (page 306). In step 1, melt 6 tablespoons **butter** or margarine and 1 cup (6 oz.) chopped **white candy baking bar.** Stir in 1¹⁄₂ teaspoons **vanilla,** ¹⁄₂ cup *each* **granulated sugar** and **all-purpose flour,** and 2 **large eggs.**

Put in pan (step 2); sprinkle with ¹⁄₃ cup *each* chopped **white candy baking bar** and **almond brickle chips.** Bake (step 3); cool (step 4). Serve (step 5), or store up to 2 days. MAKES: 9 or 16.
Per small brownie: 193 cal., 51% (99 cal.) from fat; 2.1 g protein; 11 g fat (6 g sat.); 21 g carbo (0.2 g fiber); 95 mg sodium; 40 mg chol.

## White & Dark Brownies

PREP AND COOK TIME: About 50 minutes
Follow directions for **Brownies Master Recipe** (page 306). In step 1, melt ¹⁄₃ cup (¹⁄₆ lb.) **butter** or margarine and 1 cup (6 oz.) **semisweet chocolate chips.** Stir in ¹⁄₄ teaspoon **baking soda,** 1 teaspoon **vanilla,** 2 tablespoons **water,** ³⁄₄ cup *each* **granulated sugar** and **all-purpose flour,** and 2 **large eggs.** Cool about 10 minutes, then stir in 1 cup (6 oz.) **white candy baking chips.**

Put in pan (step 2), bake (step 3), and cool (step 4). Serve (step 5), or store up to 2 days. MAKES: 9 or 16.
Per small brownie: 216 cal., 46% (99 cal.) from fat; 2.6 g protein; 11 g fat (7.1 g sat.); 28 g carbo (0.2 g fiber); 80 mg sodium; 38 mg chol. ◆

# Kitchen Cabinet

### READERS' RECIPES TESTED IN SUNSET'S KITCHENS

BY LINDA LAU ANUSASANANAN

TANGY GOAT CHEESE anchors marinated shrimp on crisp toast.

## Appetizers from California vintners

### Marinated Shrimp Bruschetta

Jill Murphy, Clos du Lac Cellars,
Ione, California

At the annual wine tasting at Clos du Lac Cellars, Jill Murphy, director of marketing and sales, serves shrimp toasts with Sauvignon Blanc or Viognier.

PREP AND COOK TIME: About 1 hour

MAKES: About 3 dozen appetizers

- 1 pound **shrimp** (36 to 42 per lb.), shelled and deveined
- 2 tablespoons **olive oil**
- 2 tablespoons **sherry vinegar** or white wine vinegar
- 1 clove **garlic**, pressed or minced
- 1 tablespoon drained **capers**, chopped
- 1 **baguette** (8 oz.)
- 1 **Roma tomato** (3 oz.)
- ¼ cup minced **green bell pepper**
- ¼ cup minced **green onion**
  **Salt**
- ¼ pound fresh **chèvre** (goat) **cheese**

**1.** In a 4- to 5-quart pan over high heat, bring about 2 quarts water to a boil. Add shrimp, cover, and cook just until opaque in thickest part (cut to test), about 2 minutes. Drain.

**2.** In a bowl, mix oil, vinegar, garlic, capers, and shrimp. Cover and chill, stirring occasionally, at least 30 minutes or up to 1 day.

**3.** Trim tips from ends of baguette and cut remaining bread crosswise into 36 equal slices. Set slices on racks on a 14-by 17-inch baking sheet.

**4.** Bake in a 425° oven until golden, 6 to 8 minutes. If making ahead, store cool slices airtight up to 4 hours.

**5.** Seed and finely chop tomato. Add tomato, bell pepper, and onion to shrimp mixture. Season with salt to taste.

**6.** Spread cheese on toast. Place vegetables and 1 shrimp on each piece.

Per piece: 47 cal., 38% (18 cal.) from fat; 3.3 g protein; 2 g fat (0.8 g sat.); 3.7 g carbo (0.2 g fiber); 81 mg sodium; 18 mg chol.

### Baked Spinach Parmesan Dip

Alice Chazen, Perry Creek Vineyards,
Somerset, California

This appetizer rates high for convenience and versatility with Alice Chazen, co-owner of Perry Creek Vineyards. You can mix the dip up to 2 days ahead, chill, then bake and serve. Vary the flavor by using cooked chopped artichoke hearts instead of spinach. Chazen serves a dry Chardonnay or fruity Riesling with this rich mixture.

PREP AND COOK TIME: About 40 minutes

MAKES: About 3 cups; 12 servings

- 1 package (10 oz.) **frozen chopped spinach**, thawed
- 1 cup **reduced-fat** or regular **mayonnaise**
- 1 package (3 oz.) **cream cheese**
- 1 **onion** (6 oz.), peeled and minced
- 1 clove **garlic**, pressed or minced
- 1 cup plus 2 tablespoons grated **parmesan cheese**
- ⅛ teaspoon **pepper**
- ½ teaspoon **paprika**
- 2 **baguettes** (8 oz. each), thinly sliced

**1.** Squeeze spinach to remove liquid. With a mixer, beat spinach with mayonnaise, cream cheese, onion, garlic, 1 cup parmesan cheese, and pepper.

**2.** Mound mixture in a 3- to 4-cup baking dish. Sprinkle evenly with 2 tablespoons parmesan cheese and paprika.

**3.** Bake in a 350° oven until hot in center and lightly browned on top, 25 to 30 minutes.

**4.** Serve hot to spread on baguette slices.

Per serving: 227 cal., 39% (89 cal.) from fat; 7.8 g protein; 9.9 g fat (3.9 g sat.); 26 g carbo (1.7 g fiber); 569 mg sodium; 14 mg chol.

### Green Herb Squares

Chatom Vineyards,
Douglas Flat, California

At wine-tasting events at Chatom Vineyards, medium-dry Sauvignon Blanc or Chardonnay is served with these moist and fresh-tasting herb squares. If making ahead, cover and chill up to 1 day.

PREP AND COOK TIME: About 1 hour

MAKES: About 64 appetizers

- 3 tablespoons **slivered almonds**
- 1⅓ cups coarsely chopped **Swiss chard** leaves
- 1 cup coarsely chopped **onion**
- 1 cup coarsely chopped **leeks** (white part only)
- ⅓ cup coarsely chopped **fresh sorrel** (or more Swiss chard)
- ¼ cup coarsely chopped **fresh mint** leaves
- 2 tablespoons chopped **parsley**
- 1 tablespoon chopped **fresh cilantro**
- 1 tablespoon chopped **fresh dill** or 1 teaspoon dried dill weed
- 1 tablespoon chopped **fresh tarragon** leaves or 1 teaspoon dried tarragon
- 4 **large eggs**
- 2 tablespoons **all-purpose flour**
- ½ teaspoon **salt**
- ¼ teaspoon **cayenne**
- ⅛ teaspoon **pepper**

**1.** In a blender or food processor, whirl almonds until very finely ground.

**2.** Add Swiss chard, onion, leeks, sorrel, mint, parsley, cilantro, dill, tarragon, eggs, flour, salt, cayenne, and pepper. Whirl until smoothly puréed. Pour into an oiled 8- or 9-inch square pan.

**3.** Bake in a 300° oven until center barely jiggles when gently shaken, about 30 minutes.

**4.** Cool and cut into ¾- to 1-inch squares. Lift out with a wide spatula.

Per piece: 10 cal., 45% (4.5 cal.) from fat; 0.6 g protein; 0.5 g fat (0.1 g sat.); 0.8 g carbo (0.1 g fiber); 25 mg sodium; 13 mg chol.

## Rice-filled Grape Leaves

Cynthia Gomes, Stevenot Winery, Murphys, California

Stevenot's retail marketing manager, Cynthia Gomes, finds dry and fruity Sauvignon Blanc a good match for stuffed grape leaves.

PREP AND COOK TIME: About 1¾ hours

MAKES: 2½ to 3 dozen appetizers

- 2 tablespoons **olive oil**

NEATLY ROLLED grape leaves surround well-seasoned rice.

- 1 cup chopped **onion**
- ¾ cup **long-grain white rice**
- 1 cup **dry white wine**
- ⅓ cup **tomato sauce**
- ¼ cup chopped **fresh mint** or cilantro
- ¼ cup **currants**
- 1 clove **garlic**, crushed or minced
- ½ teaspoon **Italian seasoning mix** or dried basil
- ¼ teaspoon **pepper**
- 1 jar (8 oz.) **grape leaves**
- 2 tablespoons **lemon juice**

**1.** In a 2- to 3-quart pan over medium-high heat, frequently stir oil and onion until onion is limp, 7 to 9 minutes. Add rice and stir 1 to 2 minutes more.

**2.** Add wine, ¼ cup water, tomato sauce, mint, currants, garlic, Italian seasoning, and pepper. Mix and bring to a boil. Cover and simmer over low heat, stirring occasionally, until rice is almost tender to bite, 12 to 15 minutes. Uncover and let cool at least 20 minutes.

**3.** Meanwhile, rinse grape leaves, drain, and pat dry. Line the bottom of a 9- by 13-inch baking dish with 5 or 6 leaves. Reserve 5 or 6 additional leaves.

**4.** With scissors, trim stems from remaining leaves. To fill each leaf, place underside of leaf up with stem end toward you. Shape 1 tablespoon seasoned rice filling into 2-inch log across stem end of leaf. Fold leaf sides over filling and roll snugly. Fit filled leaves, seams down, in a single layer in leaf-lined dish. Cover with reserved leaves. Mix 1 cup water and lemon juice. Pour over rolls. Cover dish with foil.

**5.** Bake in a 350° oven until liquid is absorbed, 30 to 45 minutes. Serve warm or cool. If making ahead, cover and chill up to 1 day.

Per roll: 33 cal., 22% (7.2 cal.) from fat; 0.4 g protein; 0.8 g fat (0.1 g sat.); 4.5 g carbo (0.2 g fiber); 270 mg sodium; 0 mg chol.

## Blue Cheese Spread with Spiced Walnuts

Pam Miller, Single Leaf Vineyards & Winery, Somerset, California

When her winery, Single Leaf Vineyards & Winery, participates in big festivals, owner Pam Miller uses this appetizer, which can be made ahead and easily multiplied. It goes well with Single Leaf's Chardonnay.

PREP AND COOK TIME: About 15 minutes

MAKES: About 1½ cups; 6 to 8 servings

- 1 package (8 oz.) **cream cheese**
- ¼ cup crumbled **blue cheese**
- ¼ cup fresh **chèvre** (goat) **cheese**
- 2 tablespoons **butter** or margarine, at room temperature
- 2 tablespoons **brandy** or milk
- 3 tablespoons thinly sliced **chives** or green onions
- ¼ teaspoon **salt**
- ¼ teaspoon **pepper**
- ⅛ teaspoon **ground cumin**
- ⅛ teaspoon **ground cinnamon**
- ⅛ teaspoon **ground cardamom**
- 2 teaspoons **chili oil**
- 2 teaspoons **olive oil**
- ½ cup coarsely chopped **walnuts**
- 2 teaspoons **sugar**
- 3 dozen **unsalted water crackers** or thin apple slices

**1.** Beat cream cheese, blue cheese, chèvre cheese, butter, and brandy until creamy. Stir in 2 tablespoons chives. Mound in a small, shallow dish. If making ahead, cover and chill up to 2 days.

**2.** In a small bowl, mix salt, pepper, cumin, cinnamon, and cardamom.

**3.** Pour both oils into a nonstick 8- to 10-inch frying pan over medium heat. Add walnuts. Stir often until toasted, 5 to 7 minutes. Add sugar and stir until it melts onto nuts, about 1 minute.

**4.** Pour hot nuts into bowl with spices and mix to coat. If making ahead, let cool and store airtight up to 2 days.

**5.** Sprinkle nuts and remaining 1 tablespoon chives over cheese. Spread mixture onto crackers.

Per serving: 299 cal., 69% (207 cal.) from fat; 6.9 g protein; 23 g fat (10 g sat.); 15 g carbo (0.8 g fiber); 356 mg sodium; 45 mg chol. ◆

# Articles Index

# Index of Recipe Titles

# Low-Fat Recipes

*(30 percent or less calories from fat)*

# General Index

Chilean seabass, oven-roasted 216

Chili. *See also* Chilies; Chipotle; Habanero
  -cumin chips, 143
  -glazed shrimp, 102
  -lime broth, 41
  loaf, 31
  -mango jam, 106
  -orange glaze, 254
  paste, Asian red, uses, 99
  relleno crêpes, 148
  ristras, by mail, 156
  salt, jicama with, 84
  strips, sautéed, 156
  turkey wraps, 150
  vegetable soup, red, 141

Chilies. *See also* Chili; Chipotle; Habanero
  with chorizo stuffing, 257
  with corn tamale filling, 198
  sticky red wings, 204
  stuffed with pomegranate salad, 203
  turkey mole, 199
  types and cooking tips, 68–73
  Windy Point Inn Spanish frittata, 228

Chinese pinwheels, 291
Chipotle honey–glazed lamb chops, 105
Chipotle sauce, 111
Chips, chili-cumin, 143

Chocolate. *See also* Brownies; White chocolate
  biscotti, lean, 300
  -caramel pecan cookies, 305
  dark velvet torte, 36
  -dipped coconut macaroons, 294
  favorites and sources, 37
  -hazelnut biscotti, 300
  leaves, gold-frosted, 276
  manufacture of, 37
  muffins, 40
  -orange biscotti, 300
  pots de crème, 35
  sauce, 36, 160, 265
  streaks, 288
  tofu frosting, 238
  truffle bites, 36

Chocolate chip cookies, 294
Chocolate chip peanut melt-aways, 301
Chocolate leaves, gold-frosted, 276
Christmas gingersnaps, 297
*Churrasco misto*, 56
Chutney, chicken, mango, 134
Chutney, quick apricot, 11
Cider chicken, 55
Citrus, avocado, jicama, and persimmon salad, 195
Citrus-cumin barbecued pork, 126
Citrus, segmenting, 10

Clam soup, for Tomoko, 32
Clams, pop-open barbecue, 85
Coconut
  -almond toffee bowl, 119
  hello Hawaii ice cream, 162
  macaroons, chocolate-dipped, 294
  milk, uses, 99
Coleslaw, classic, 32
Cookbooks. *See* Books
Cookies. *See also* Biscotti; Brownies; Shortbread
  almond butter, 296
  almond ravioli, 289
  almond spoons, 296
  anise-jam ribbons, 296
  apricot sandwich, 288
  bar, 304–306
  bizcochitos, 289
  black pepper, 297
  bourbon snaps, 292
  brandied apricot bars, 304
  bandied toffee lace sandwiches, 303
  Brazil nut chews, 293
  brown butter sand, 297
  brown sugar Christmas thins, 289
  buttery lemon squares, 304
  caramelized-sugar, 293
  cashew stars, 289
  Chinese five spice oatmeal, 293
  Chinese pinwheels, 291
  chocolate-caramel pecan, 305
  chocolate chip peanut melt-aways, 301
  chocolate-dipped coconut macaroons 294
  chocolate streaks, 288
  Christmas gingersnaps, 297
  cookie canvases, 289
  cornmeal wafers, 291
  cranberry crisp bars, 26
  cranberry-prune squares, 305
  crisp oatmeal-fruit strips, 297
  cutout, 288–290
  drop, 292–294
  Dutch spice, 290
  English toffee, 305
  favorite cutout, 288
  Florentines, 303
  Florentine wedding cakes, 302
  German oatmeal, 303
  gianduia buttons, 293
  gingerbread people, 290
  golden almond sculpture, 297
  Greek almond tea cakes, 302
  hazelnut crescents, 302
  holiday favorites, 286–307
    honey-sesame bars, 305
  icing for, 288
  lace, 303–304
  low-fat cornflake chews, 294
  macadamia butter, 297

Cookies (*cont'd.*)
  mega-ginger, 61
  Mexican wedding cakes, 302
  mincemeat, 290
  mint sandies, 293
  molasses crunch, 293
  nanaimo bars, 305
  nut lace, 304
  nut mosaic triangles, 306
  orange refrigerator, 291
  peanut blossom, 298
  peanut butter–oat bars, 305
  pecan-spice tea cakes, 302
  peppermint buttons, 293
  pine nut balls, 302
  pine nut fingers, 302
  praline flats or cones, 304
  Provençal pine nut crescents, 298
  pumpkin–cream cheese swirls, 306
  refrigerator, 291–292
  rye rabbits, 290
  Sally's favorite recipe, 298
  sesame butter, 291
  sesame moons, 302
  shaped, 296–299
  snickerdoodles, 298
  soft ginger, 298
  stained-glass, 289
  Swiss almond macaroons, 294
  Sylvia's Danish butter, 298
  tea cakes, 25
  thick, soft, and chewy chocolate chip, 294
  thin, crisp chocolate chip, 294
  thumbprint with chili jelly, 298
  two-tone cream sandwiches, 292
  vanilla sandwiches, 290
  Viennese vanilla crescents, 302
  walnut-lemon packets, 290
  white chocolate cranberry rounds, 294
  Zinfandel port, 299
Corn
  cakes, polenta, 111
  chayote soup, 140
  grilled, 174
  pudding, scorched, 260
  salad, 76
  tamale filling, chilies with, 198
  wheels and zucchini soup, 140
Cornbread, buttermilk, 22
Cornbread, Caribbean habanero, 72
Cornflake chews, low-fat, 294
Cornmeal biscotti, 300
Cornmeal piñon shortcakes with berries and lime cream, 192
Cornmeal wafers, 291

Crab(s)
  and artichoke salad, 85
  Belgian endive with, 283
  black pepper Dungeness, 200
  curried sweet potato soup with, 200
  lasagna rolls, 239
  Louis accents, 12
  paella, artichoke, 194
  pot, 26
  vermouth, 274
Cranberries, candied, with cheese and crisp crusts, 249
Cranberry
  crisp bars, 26
  linzer torte, 264
  –Meyer lemon relish, 258
  -prune squares, 305
  sauce, 226
  viva, 258
  white chocolate rounds, 294
  -wine aperitif, 283
Cream cheese–pumpkin swirls, 306
Cream sandwiches, two-tone, 292
Crema-grape parfaits, 147
Crème brûlée, lavender, 123
Crêpes
  chicken-mango, 148
  chili relleno, 148
  dosas, 66
  Durlacher Hof Austrian ricotta, 226
  ham-gouda, 149
  mushroom and arugula, 148
  turkey-pesto, 149
Crostini of chanterelles, 234
Cucumber, watermelon, and jicama salad, 142
Curry
  green curry duck and potatoes, 107
  leftover-lamb, 22
  paste, Thai, uses, 100, 107
  Roy's homestyle chicken, 102

Date shake supreme, 125
Desserts. *See also* Cakes; Cookies; Frozen yogurt; Ice cream; Pies; Sorbet; Tarts, Tortes
  chestnut tiramisu, 265
  chocolate pots de crème, 35
  chocolate truffle bites, 36
  coconut-almond toffee bowl, 119
  cornmeal piñon shortcakes with berries and lime cream, 192
  crema-grape parfait, 149
  lavender crème brûlée, 123
  marbled pumpkin cheesecake, 264
  Mexican sunrise, 147

Desserts (cont'd.)
   pineapple and papaya with
      tequila syrup, 146
   pineapple, blueberry, and
      kiwi fruit, 190
   pomegranate granita, 203
   quince-apple crisp, 217
   sangria fruit soup, 147
   spotted dog, 20
   strawberries with sour cream
      dip, 91
   strawberries with walnut
      puffs, 78
   toasted pound cake sandwich
      with ice cream, 164
Dosas, 66
Dressings, poultry
   artichoke-parmesan sour-
      dough, 256
   Italian chard, 256
   sausage and oyster cornbread,
      256
   wild rice and porcini mush-
      room, 257
Dressings, salad. *See* Salad
   dressings
Duck
   barbecued, 112
   confit with roasted cracklings,
      117
   pizza topping, Peking, 171
   and potatoes, green curry, 107
Dumpling soup, Asian, 38
Dutch spice cookies, 290

*E. coli*, the realities of, 201
Egg(s)
   baked, pilaf with, 269
   and golden onions on toast,
      77
   and Hungarian peppers, 185
   Japanese vegetable omelet, 21
   poached, salsa soup with, 77
   poaching, 44
   salad sandwich, 19
   Turkey Joe's special, 77
   window, for Easter, 64
   Windy Point Inn Spanish
      frittata, 228
Enchiladas
   chicken, with salsa verde, 72
   pork, 127
   stacked red chili, 19
English toffee cookies, 305
Espresso ice cream, 162

Falafel casserole, 30
Fennel, baked, with cambozola,
   260
Fennel-stuffed pork roast, 234
Fig and lemon tart, 118
Fig and prosciutto pizza, 121
Filo
   -crusted potpie, 97
   Hungarian ham strudel with
      watercress salad, 97

Filo (*cont'd.*)
   napoleons, 97
   spinach, cheese, and sausage
      packets, 97
Fish. *See also* specific fish
   cornmeal-crusted with tartar
      sauce, 20
Fisher, MFK, 92
Fish sauce, Asian, uses, 99
Florentines, 303
Florentine wedding cakes, 302
Foie gras, Fuyu persimmons
   with, 242
France, cooking in Provençal
   kitchen, 114–118
French toast for a queen, 25
Frittata, Windy Point Inn
   Spanish, 228
Frosting, chocolate tofu, 238
Frozen yogurt
   lemon cheesecake, 163
   peach, 163
   plum-cardamom, 163
Fruit. *See also* specific fruits
   and nut pilaf, Armenian, 270
   St. Nicholas dried-fruit cake,
      285
   salad, fall, 251
   salad, winter, 10
   salsa, 228
   sangria soup, 147
   tree-ripened stone, by mail,
      110
Fudgy low-fat brownies, 307

Garlic
   -cheese rolls, easy, 271
   mashed potatoes, 263
   oil, toasted, 74
   pistou, 280
Gazpacho, buttermilk, 213
Gazpacho, yellow tomato, with
   shrimp, 213
Gianduia buttons, 293
Giblet gravy, 254, 255
Ginger
   -caramel macadamia tart, 264
   cookies, mega-, 61
   cookies, soft, 298
   double-ginger dried cherry ice
      cream, 162
   fresh, uses, 100
   -pomegranate muffins, 204
   shortbread, 295
Gingerbread biscotti, 300
Gingerbread people, 290
Gingersnaps, Christmas, 297
Glaze for turkey, 254
Gold Country holiday traditions,
   276–285
Gold-frosted chocolate leaves,
   276
Grains, 269
   ancient grains salad, 144
   mixed grain pilaf, 88
Granita, pomegranate, 203

Grapefruit
   fall fruit salad, 253
   jicama salad, 138
   winter fruit salad, 12
Grape leaves, rice-filled, 309
Grape(s)
   -crema parfaits, 147
   sausages with shallots and,
      154
   sole with, 55
Gravy, giblet, 254, 255
Greek almond tea cakes, 302
Green bean(s)
   and jicama salad, 251
   in a mist, 260
   lemony, 285
   with mushroom duxelles, 260
Green curry paste, with duck
   and potatoes, 107
Green salsa, 12
Green wasabi potatoes, 244
Grilling instructions, 170
Grits, RiverSong giddy-up, 230
Guacamole, 176, 222
Guacamole, enlightened, 196
Guacasalsa, 103

Habanero
   cornbread Caribbean, 72
   ice cream, 161
   jelly, hasty, 218
   marmalade, 198
Halloween party, 220–223
Ham
   -gouda crêpes, 149
   strudel, Hungarian, with
      watercress salad, 97
Harvest celebrations, 205
Hazelnut(s)
   -chocolate biscotti, 300
   crescents, 302
   -Merlot biscotti, 300
   roasted sweet and white
      potatoes with, 262
   skinning, 244
   spiced 244
   truffle ice cream, 160
Herb squares, green, 308
Hibiscus tea, 139
High-altitude cooking, 231
Hoisin chicken, 237
Hoisin sauce, uses, 100
Hollandaise, 10-second, 89
Hominy, buttered, 261
Honey
   chipotle honey–glazed lamb
      chops, 105
   sauce, lamb in, 122
   -sesame bars, 305
   white truffle, 132
Honeydew sorbet, 164
Hot pots, Rick's pork and
   vegetable, 102
Huaraches, 144, 145
Huaraches, 4 toppings for, 145
Hummus, seeded, 129

Ice cream
   biscotti crunch espresso, 162
   double-ginger dried cherry,
      162
   espresso thyself, 162
   habanero, 161
   hazelnut truffle, 160
   hello Hawaii, 162
   lemon meringue, 162
   malted caramel, 160
   Mozambique spice, 162
   no-cook ultimate vanilla, 160
   orange-pistachio, 124
   ultimate vanilla, 159
   very berry, 162
Ice cream makers, 160–161, 162
Ice cream parlors and soda
   fountains, 165–167
Icing for cookies, 288
Indian relish, 85
Indian spiced potatoes, 30
Inns, bed and breakfast, for
   hikers, 224–230

Jam, mango-chili, 106
Jelly, hasty habanero, 218
Jicama
   antojitos tray, 249
   avocado, citrus, and
      persimmon salad, 195
   bleached bones, 222
   with chili salt, 84
   grapefruit salad, 138
   and green bean salad, 251
   slaw, 134
   watermelon, and cucumber
      salad, 142

Kitchen, *Sunset's* remodeled
   test, 206–209
Kiwi fruit
   miniature, 190
   pineapple, and blueberry
      dessert, 190
Kumquat(s)
   preserved, 275
   –red pepper relish, 275
   relish, spinach salad with, 275
   spinach salad, 78

Lamb
   with asparagus and tarragon,
      braised, 59
   chops, chipotle honey–glazed,
      105
   chops with mint risotto, 190
   curry, leftover-, 22
   grilled Merlot, 88
   in honey sauce, 122
   Lebanese meat loaf, 17
   sausage, and bean soup, 281
   soup, 269
Lasagna rolls, crab, 239
Lavender crème brûlée, 123
Lavender lemonade, Lynda
   Dowling's, 96